Editors

MARK A. NOLL
Professor of History
Wheaton College, Wheaton, Illinois

NATHAN O. HATCH
Director of Graduate Studies, Department of History
University of Notre Dame, Notre Dame, Indiana

GEORGE M. MARSDEN
Professor of History
Calvin College, Grand Rapids, Michigan

DAVID F. WELLS
Professor of Theology
Gordon-Conwell Theological Seminary, South Hamilton, Massachusetts

JOHN D. WOODBRIDGE
Professor of Church History and the History of Christian Thought
Trinity Evangelical Divinity School, Deerfield, Illinois

Christianity in America
A HANDBOOK

A LION BOOK

Copyright © 1983 William B. Eerdmans Publishing Company
255 Jefferson S.E., Grand Rapids, MI 49503

Published by
Lion Publishing plc
Icknield Way, Tring, Herts, England
ISBN 0 85648 700 7
Albatross Books
PO Box 320, Sutherland, NSW 2232, Australia
ISBN 0 86760 475 1

First edition 1983 William B. Eerdmans Publishing Company
First UK edition 1983

Contents

Preface   xii

Contributors   xiv

THE MANY FACES OF THE CHURCH   xvii

GOD AND THE COLONIES   1

Timeline   2

The European Roots of American Christianity   4
Reformation Europe   5
Roman Catholicism in North America   8
  Junípero Serra   15
  Jacques Marquette   16
  Contrasting Missionary Strategies   18
The Expansion of England   19
The English Reformation   19
Puritanism   21
  William Bradford   27
  History of Plymouth Plantation   28
  Puritans and Historians   31

Varieties of American Christianity Before the Great Awakening   33
Puritans in America   33
  John Winthrop   36
  John Winthrop's Sermon Aboard the Arbella   38
  Puritans and Sacred Places   39
The Half-Way Covenant   41
Declension?   43
New England Dissent and the Baptists   43
  Anne Hutchinson   45
  Roger Williams   47
  Obadiah Holmes and His Testimony   49
The Church of England   49
Catholics in Maryland   53
Reformed Dutch and Germans   54

Presbyterians   55
Quakers   56
  Primitive Christianity Revived   59

The Practice of Religion in Colonial America   61
The Bible in the Colonies   61
Puritan Piety   64
  Verses Upon the Burning of Our House July 10th, 1666 (Anne Bradstreet)   66
  "The Day of Doom" (Michael Sigglesworth)   66
  Edward Taylor   67
  The Salem Witch Trials   68
Varieties of Religion   71
  Pietism   74
Going to Church   74
  Psalm 23   81
Religion and the Family   83
Religion and the Underclasses   86
  Christianity and Slavery in the Colonial Period   91
  Quakers Oppose Slave Trade   93
  John Woolman   94

The Era of the Great Awakening   96
  Cotton Mather   99
The Great Awakening   101
  Jonathan Edwards   103
  George Whitefield   108
  Benjamin Franklin on George Whitefield   110
  Nathan Cole Goes to Hear Whitefield   112
What Caused the Revival   113
Effects   114
  A Hymn by Samuel Davies   115
Dissension   116
  Isaac Backus   117
  Shubal Stearns and Daniel Marshall   119
  The Danger of an Unconverted Ministry   120
  Jonathan Edwards on the Revival in New England   121
  Seasonable Thoughts on the State of Religion in New England   122
  The Sociology of Conversion in New England
    Through the Time of the Great Awakening   124
  The Transforming Effects of the Great Awakening   127

Christians and the Birth of the Republic   131
The Seeds of the Revolution   131
Christianity and Revolutionary Ideals   134
  The Religion of the Founding Fathers   135

"The Cause of America is the Cause of Christ"   137
"I will not raise my hand against my Sovereign"   140
"As a Christian I could not fight"   141
The War Itself   143
The War Brings Reform   145
Colonial Pluralism and Revolutionary Unity   147
  Were American Origins Christian?   150
For Further Reading   152

The Bible in America   154

CHRISTIANITY AND DEMOCRACY: FROM THE REVOLUTION TO THE CIVIL WAR

                                                                 159

Timeline   160

The Church in an Age of Revolution   162
The Church Under Fire   162
  National Religion: Ethan Allen's Thoughts on Prayer   164
Toward a Democratic Church   165
Toward a Voluntary Theology   166
Toward a New Order of the Ages   167
  The United States Elevated to Glory and Honor   168
  Timothy Dwight   171

The Swelling Tide of Revivalism   172
Revivalism as Religious Awakening   173
  Charles Grandison Finney and the Burned-over District   174
Revivalism as Technique   178
  Robert Baird on American Preaching   180
  Camp Meetings   181
  Revivalism as a Style of Christianity   184
  Peter Cartwright   185
  Gospel Hymns   186

An Age of Experiment and Reform   188
The Benevolent Empire: Arthur and Lewis Tappan   189
Foreign Missions: Adoniram and Ann Judson   191
  Indian Missions and Indian Removal   193
Radical Social Reform: Thomas and Mary Nichols   196
  Ellen G. White and the Gospel of Health   197

Joseph Smith and the Latter-day Saints   200
John Humphrey Noyes and the Oneida Community   203
New Harmony   205

The Triumph of the Voluntary Church   208
Religion on the Southern Frontier   209
Pragmatism   210
Primitivism   210
Women's Right and American Religion   213
Varieties of Quaker Experience   214
Slave Religion   215
Richard Allen   219

Theology and Religious Belief   221
The Evangelical Mainstream   223
The Founding of Church Colleges, 1820-1860   225
William Ellery Channing Defines the Essence of Christianity   228
Challenges to Revivalism   228
The Pilgrimage of Ralph W. Emerson   230
Hodge, Taylor, and Bushnell   232

The Immigrant Church   234
Cultural Conflicts   235
Lyman Beecher's Fear of Roman Catholicism   236
Protestants and the Parochial School   238
The Perils and Promise of Ethnicity   240
Cincinnati's Religious Mosaic   243
Trusteeism   245
Archbishop John Carroll   246
Edward Frederick Sorin and the Founding of Notre Dame   248
Mother Elizabeth Ann Seton   252
Catholic Revivalism   255

The Church and the Impending Crisis   257
Slavery and Southern Nationalism   257
Frederick Douglass on the Religion of Slaveholders   259
The Revolution in the North   261
The Splintering Churches   261
Brown, Turner, and Lincoln   263
The Religion of Abraham Lincoln   266
For Further Reading   269

Separation of Church and State   271

Christianity and American Literature   274

THE ERA OF CRISIS:
FROM CHRISTENDOM
TO PLURALISM   277

Timeline   278

Did Success Spoil American Protestantism?   280
The "Gilded Age"   280
   The Corrupt Senator Dilsworthy Addresses a Sunday School   282
The Evangelical Empire   283
Urbanization and Secularization   285

The Stars   289
Henry Ward Beecher   290
Phillips Brooks   291
   The Law of Growth   291
Josiah Strong   291
   The American Dream   292
Dwight L. Moody   293
   The Student Volunteer Movement   295

The Era of Crusades (1890-1917)   296
Missions   296
   Foreign Missions, 1865-1930   299
   John R. Mott   302
Women's Causes   303
   Frances Willard   305
   Roles of Women in the Church, 1860-1920   308
Social Involvement and Retraction   311
   The Social Creed of the Churches   314
   Social Service and the Churches, 1865-1930   315
   The Social Gospel   318

New Departures and Conservative Responses (1865-1917)   321
Liberalism and Modernism   321
   The Fatherhood of God and the Brotherhood of Man   323
   The Crisis in Authority of the Bible   327
   Dispensationalism   327
   Conservative Innovations   331
   The Holiness Movement   332
   The Pentecostal Movement   336
   Christian Science   339
   Jehovah's Witnesses   341

Beyond the Walls of Anglo-Saxon Zion   343

Christianity Among Blacks   343
    The Black Church Grows   347
    Education, Publication, and Foreign Missions in the Black Church   349
    The Double Crisis of Black Christianity   351
God is a Negro   353
American Catholicism   354
    Polish-American Catholics   359
    Italian-American Catholics   360
    Cardinal Gibbons and Americanism   362
The Papal Condemnation of Modernism   365
Protestant Immigration   365
The Eastern Orthodox Churches   367

End of an Era: World War I and the 1920s   368
Responses to the War   368
    Billy Sunday   371
    "The Premillennial Menace" to the War Effort   373
The Aftermath   373
    The Bare Knee Instead of the Bended Knee   375
    The Prohibition Movement   376
Fundamentalists Versus Modernists   378
    Modernism as Evangelical Christianity   379
    Protestant Modernism   383
    Fundamentalism   384
    The Scopes Trial   385

For Further Reading   387

Christianity and American Higher Education   388

American Worship: Contrasting Styles   390

**CHRISTIANITY IN A SECULAR AGE:
FROM THE
DEPRESSION TO THE PRESENT**   393

    Timeline   394

Looking Back on Fifty Years (1930-1980)   396
One Nation...?   397
Under God?   399
The Church and Minorities   399
    American Christianity and the New Pluralism   402

From the Great Depression to the War   404
The Torn Social Fabric   404
How the Churches Survived   407
    The Aftermath of Protestant Controversy   409
    New Churches of the 1920s and 1930s   411
    Catholics and the American Nation   413
Patterns of Belief   416
    The Church Must Go Beyond Modernism   419
    Karl Barth Speaks   420
    The Niebuhrs   421

World War II and Postwar Revival   423
From Pearl Harbor to Hiroshima   423
    The Churches and War   426
    The Ecumenical Movement   428
Revival and Civil Religion   430
    Civil Religion   434
    Billy Graham   435
    The Psychology of a Frustrated Soul   437
Americanization   439
    The Orthodox Churches   442
    Prodigals, Come Home!   444
    Martin Luther King, Jr.   445
    The Black Revolution and the Churches   447

An Unruly Time (1960-1980)   449
Public Turmoil and Its Aftermath   450
    The Urban Church   452
Church and Society   453
Theology at Bay   458
    Liberation   462
The Relevance of Denominations?   463
    Foundations of the Evangelical Resurgence   465
    The Christian Counterculture   469
    The Bible Belt   474
    Renewal Movements in the Mainline Denominations   476
    The Electronic Church   478
    The Second Vatican Council on Religious Freedom   480
    The Charismatic Movement   482
    Change in American Catholicism   485
The Bible Boom   488

On the Brink of the Future   491
For Further Reading   492

    Indexes   495
    Acknowledgments   507

Preface

As Americans we do not have a consuming interest in our past. Only on a few scattered occasions in the year is our national memory stirred, and then it usually subsides as rapidly as it was kindled. Much of the past seems to us like a harmless irrelevance. Those who want to busy themselves recording it are therefore forewarned that they should expect to suffer from some benign neglect. When, however, the past is equated with what is dated, obsolete, and superseded, then our attitude toward it is less benign. Then our past begins to look like a tiresome ball and chain from which we are convinced we must liberate ourselves at all costs if we are to progress. And progress we must, for we are a future-oriented society that is utterly unforgiving of all that is "behind the times." New histories, then, do not start their lives in very fertile soil!

Our future-orientation and the almost sacramental significance we attach to what is new, we need to say, has led to success in some ways. It is this outlook, this need, which provides the dynamism, for example, which drives our incredibly virile capitalistic enterprise. Our society is abundantly provided for with new products all the time. If a need does not seem to exist for a product, Madison Avenue will create the need ex nihilo. If the consumer becomes bored, the ad people will ply the theme of novelty, tease the curiosity, entice the unwary buyer into thinking that the new product really is newer than the new product for which it is an infinitely superior substitute. Without this itch for novelty, this desire for what is the latest and best, it is difficult to see how business could flourish as it now does.

So it is, too, in the extraordinary technological breakthroughs of our time. The fact that we have not rested content with old theories and techniques but have continued to press back the frontiers of our knowledge now means that we can cure more, do more, control more, make more, and kill more than any previous generation. And we have done all of this without reading a single history book!

As soon as we ask, however, whether there is a difference between brilliance and wisdom, what role conscience should have in the exercise of power, and how we find meaning in the secular process, we discover ourselves to be in a field of discourse where inventive genius and technological competence are often peculiarly incompetent to answer. Extraordinary achievements in one field of endeavor seldom transfer automatically to another.

This is not something that we find easy to understand. Our whole culture is dominated by our pragmatic, future-oriented technology with its constant quest for innovation and its underlying impatience with all that is traditional. This conditions the way we think about everything. Thus we have come to idealize our youth, whose freshness and vitality is a symbolic reminder that there are always new beginnings. And thus we have come to fear the tokens of our own aging process. Wrinkles and gray hair are the forewarnings of that wretched state of life into which we finally sink, one that is "sans teeth, sans eyes, sans taste, sans everything," as Shakespeare put it. And perhaps worst of all, it is a state that is sans all new possibilities. We do not welcome this, and seldom understand it. In a future-oriented society this is an enigma. We are conquering everything except that which is human.

In those cultures which are oriented to the past, the situation is the opposite of what we have come to think is the norm. In most African countries, for example, wrinkles and gray hair are seen as the symbols of wisdom. The aged are respected; they are approached almost with awe. Often they are spoken to in honorific forms of address. Children are treated as children. African cultures, in no hurry to project themselves into the future, are not driven by our obsession with time and punctuality. It is usually enough if one knows the hour or even the approximate part of the day in which a meeting is to take place! There is profound respect for the tradition that links past and present, and there is an equally profound suspicion about innovation.

It is not, of course, possible for us to have our cake and eat it, too. If we want a way of life that is all chrome, gadgets, and plastic, the price we must pay is to live at the tempo and in the manner prescribed by our industrial machine. We cannot, at one and and the same time, have a "premodern" psychology, blissfully ignorant of the time of day, and a home computer plugged into the local supermarket. But in the midst of this sophisticated technology it is all the more necessary to talk about meaning and values because we are gaining the whole world but losing our own souls. History is an entrée to this discussion.

History is therefore not just a "great dust-heap," as Augustine Birrell supposed. It may be, on its darker side, a chronicle of "the crimes, follies and misfortunes of mankind," as Edward Gibbon said, but it is also in part "philosophy derived from examples," to use Dionysius of Halicarnassus' words. It is about individual people, strong and dominant people, who leave the imprint of their will on their times and lead historians to ask why they did it and how they were able to do it. It is about those on the fringes of society, the powerless, whose presence always raises the question of the meaning and proper functioning of the social order. And it is about countless men and women who were by most standards ordinary, whose individual dreams were seldom recorded, whose hopes were probably seldom realized, whose lives may have passed unnoticed but who, nevertheless, have been the actors in a vastly meaningful drama. History asks why the chronicle of the past is as it is, and in answering this it gives us a vantage point from which to view our own times.

It is possible to write the story of the past — in this case, it is the story of the Christian past — from a particular angle of vision. There are intellectual histories, ecclesiastical histories, doctrinal histories, and biographical histories. We have tried to avoid doing this. This book is about Christian faith in what we now know as the United States of America. It tells the story of individual leaders, but it also looks beyond them. It is an account of the organized church, and it also looks at popular movements as well as the organizations which grew up to service them. It is about Christians as behavers and Christians as believers. It speaks of their faith and also of the culture with which it was sometimes confused. It considers the society in which they were reared and, on the periphery of its vision, the nation to which they belonged. It is written in the conviction that next to the Word of God this history is our richest depository of wisdom as we prepare for the difficult and uncertain years which lie ahead.

The similarity in format and style between this volume and *Eerdmans' Handbook to the History of Christianity* is not accidental. The coverage given to Christianity in the United States in the first *Handbook* was rather brief. It was therefore felt that American readers who had responded so enthusiastically to the first *Handbook* would welcome this second volume, which continues the tradition and is written with the same purposes but provides a full account of the planting, growth, and development of Christian belief on the American side of the Atlantic.

Sectional editors were responsible for writing the narrative section ("God and the Colonies," Mark Noll; "Christianity and Democracy," Nathan Hatch; "The Era of Crisis," George Marsden), soliciting the help of specialists in producing essays that would shed more light on selected topics, and searching for appropriate illustrative material. In the final section ("Christianity in a Secular Age"), however, the preliminary work on the narrative was done by Mark Noll and John Woodbridge. David Wells completed the narrative and was responsible for the essay and graphic material. He also coordinated the sections and served as general editor for the whole volume.

July 4, 1982   D.F.W.

Contributors

Sydney E. Ahlstrom, Professor of American History and Modern Church History, Yale University, New Haven, Connecticut. *Civil Religion.*

Thomas A. Askew, Professor of History, Gordon College, Wenham, Massachusetts. *The Founding of Church Colleges, 1820-1860; Foundations of the Evangelical Resurgence.*

Raymond J. Bakke, Professor of Ministry, Northern Baptist Theological Seminary, Lombard, Illinois. *The Urban Church.*

Hugh Barbour, Professor of Religion, Earlham College, Richmond, Indiana. *John Woolman.*

James E. Barcus, Professor of English, Baylor University, Waco, Texas. *Edward Taylor.*

Stephen E. Berk, Associate Professor of History, California State University, Long Beach. *Timothy Dwight.*

John B. Boles, Professor of History, Tulane University, New Orleans, Louisiana. *Camp Meetings; Slave Religion.*

Henry Warner Bowden, Professor of Religion, Rutgers University, New Brunswick, New Jersey. *Junipero Serra; Jacques Marquette; Indian Missions and Indian Removal.*

John Briggs, Associate Professor, Education and History, Syracuse University, New York. *Italian-American Catholics.*

Robert M. Calhoon, Professor of History, University of North Carolina at Greensboro. *Separation of Church and State.*

Patrick Carey, Assistant Professor of Theology, Marquette University, Milwaukee, Wisconsin. *Trusteeism.*

Joel Carpenter, Assistant Professor of History, Trinity College, Deerfield, Illinois. *Billy Sunday; The Scopes Trial; The Aftermath of Protestant Controversy.*

Kevin Cragg, Associate Professor of Church History, Bethel College, St. Paul, Minnesota. *The Churches and War.*

Jay P. Dolan, Associate Professor of History, Marquette University, Milwaukee, Wisconsin. *Catholic Revivalism.*

John Tracy Ellis, Professorial Lecturer in Church History, Catholic University of America, Washington, D.C. *Cardinal Gibbons and Americanism.*

Ronald M. Enroth, Professor of Sociology, Westmont College, Santa Barbara, California. *The Christian Counterculture.*

Joseph H. Fichter, Professor of Sociology, Loyola University of New Orleans, Louisiana. *Change in American Catholicism.*

Lawrence Foster, Assistant Professor of Social Science, Georgia Institute of Technology, Atlanta. *Joseph Smith and the Latter-day Saints.*

Edwin S. Gaustad, Professor of History, University of California, Riverside. *Anne Hutchinson; Roger Williams.*

William E. Graddy, Associate Professor of English, Trinity College, Deerfield, Illinois. *The Pilgrimage of Ralph W. Emerson.*

Stanley S. Harakas, Protopresbyter and Dean, Holy Cross Greek Orthodox School of Theology, Brookline, Massachusetts. *The Orthodox Churches.*

David Edwin Harrell, Distinguished Professor of History, University of Arkansas, Fayetteville. *Billy Graham; The Bible Belt.*

Anthony A. Hoekema, Professor of Systematic Theology, Emeritus, Calvin Theological Seminary, Grand Rapids, Michigan. *Christian Science; Jehovah's Witnesses.*

Susan B. Hoekema, Historian, Northfield, Minnesota. *Frances Willard; Roles of Women in the Church, 1860-1920.*

William R. Hutchison, Charles Warren Professor of the History of Religion in America, Divinity School, Harvard University, Cambridge, Massachusetts. *Protestant Modernism.*

James E. Johnson, Professor of History, Bethel College, St. Paul, Minnesota. *Charles Grandison Finney and the Burned-over District.*

C. Norman Kraus, Adjunct Professor of Religion, Goshen College, Indiana; on assignment with Mennonite Board of Missions in Japan. *Dispensationalism.*

Anthony J. Kuzniewski, S.J., Assistant Professor of History, College of the Holy Cross, Worcester, Massachusetts. *Polish-American Catholics.*

Richard Lovelace, Professor of Church History, Gordon-Conwell Theological Seminary, South Hamilton, Massachusetts. *The Salem Witch Trials; Cotton Mather; Renewal Movements in the Mainline Denominations.*

Rockne McCarthy, Professor of History, Dordt College, Sioux Center, Iowa. *Protestants and the Parochial School.*

Norris Magnuson, Professor of Church History and Director of the Resource Center, Bethel Theological Seminary, St. Paul, Minnesota. *Social Service and the Churches, 1865-1930.*

Robert P. Markham, Professor and Coordinator of Archives/Micrographics, University of Northern Colorado, Greeley. *The Bible in America.*

George M. Marsden, Professor of History, Calvin College, Grand Rapids, Michigan. *Were American Origins "Christian"?; Fundamentalism.*

Martin E. Marty, Fairfax M. Cone Distinguished Service Professor, University of Chicago, Illinois. *The Electronic Church.*

J. Gordon Melton, Director, Institute for the Study of American Religion, Evanston, Illinois. *American Christianity and the New Pluralism; New Churches of the 1920s and 1930s.*

Gerald F. Moran, Professor of History, University of Michigan at Dearborn. *The Sociology of Conversion in New England Through the Time of the Great Awakening.*

John Thomas Nichol, Vice President and Dean, Bentley College, Waltham, Massachusetts. *The Charismatic Movement.*

Mark A. Noll, Professor of History, Wheaton College, Illinois. *Puritans and Historians; The Prohibition Movement; Christianity and American Higher Education.*

Ronald L. Numbers, Professor of the History of Medicine, University of Wisconsin, Madison. *Ellen G. White and the Gospel of Health.*

David J. O'Brien, Professor of History, College of the Holy Cross, Worcester, Massachusetts. *Catholics and the American Nation.*

Donald E. Pitzer, Professor of History, Indiana State University, Evansville. *John Humphrey Noyes and the Oneida Community; New Harmony.*

Malcolm A. Reid, Professor of Philosophy, Gordon College, Wenham, Massachusetts. *The Niebuhrs.*

Ronald D. Rietveld, Professor of History, California State University, Fullerton. *The Religion of Abraham Lincoln.*

Michael J. Roach, Visiting Professor of Ecclesiastical History, Mount St. Mary's Seminary, Emmitsburg, Maryland. *Archbishop John Carroll; Mother Elizabeth Ann Seton.*

Wesley A. Roberts, Assistant Dean for Academic Programs and Associate Professor of Church History, Gordon-Conwell Theological Seminary, South Hamilton, Massachusetts. *Richard Allen; Martin Luther King, Jr.; The Black Revolution and the Churches.*

Lester B. Scherer, Professor of History, Eastern Michigan University, Ypsilanti. *Christianity and Slavery in the Colonial Period.*

Thomas J. Schlereth, Professor of American Studies, University of Notre Dame, Indiana. *Edward Frederick Sorin and the Founding of Notre Dame.*

Bruce L. Shelley, Professor of Church History, Denver Conservative Baptist Seminary, Colorado. *Isaac Backus; Shubal Stearns and Daniel Marshall.*

Harold P. Simonson, Professor of English, University of Washington, Seattle. *Jonathan Edwards.*

Sandra S. Sizer, Assistant Professor of Religious Studies, San Diego State University, California. *Gospel Hymns.*

James W. Skillen, Executive Director, Association for Public Justice, Washington, D.C. *The Religion of the Founding Fathers.*

Howard A. Snyder, Author; Pastoral Coordinator, Irving Park Free Methodist Church, Chicago. *Peter Cartwright.*

Keith L. Sprunger, Oswald H. Wedel Professor of History, Bethel College, North Newton, Kansas. *William Bradford; John Winthrop.*

F. Ernest Stoeffler, Professor of Religion, Emeritus, Temple University, Philadelphia, Pennsylvania. *Pietism.*

Harry S. Stout, Professor of History, University of Connecticut, Storrs. *George Whitefield; The Transforming Effects of the Great Awakening.*

Donald Tinder, Associate Professor of Church History, New College Berkeley, California. *The Student Volunteer Movement; Foreign Missions, 1865-1930; John R. Mott; The Church and Minorities.*

Robert G. Torbet, Former Assistant General Secretary for Ecumenical Relations, American Baptist Churches, U.S.A., Philadelphia, Pennsylvania. *The Ecumenical Movement.*

Grant Wacker, Assistant Professor of Religion, University of North Carolina at Chapel Hill. *The Social Gospel; The Holiness Movement; The Pentecostal Movement.*

James P. Walsh, Professor of History, Central Connecticut State College, New Britain. *Puritans and Sacred Places.*

David F. Wells, Professor of Theology, Gordon-Conwell Theological Seminary, South Hamilton, Massachusetts. *Hodge, Taylor, and Bushnell.*

Ronald A. Wells, Professor of History, Calvin College, Grand Rapids, Michigan. *Turner, Brown, and Lincoln: Christian Morality and Slavery.*

Thomas Werge, Professor of English, University of Notre Dame, Indiana. *Christianity and American Literature; American Worship: Contrasting Styles.*

Joseph M. White, Faculty Fellow, Cushwa Center for the Study of American Catholicism, University of Notre Dame, Indiana. *Cincinnati's Religious Mosaic.*

David W. Wills, Associate Professor of Religion, Amherst College, Massachusetts. *The Black Church Grows; Education, Publication, and Foreign Missions in the Black Church; The Double Crisis of Black Christianity.*

Richard E. Wood, Assistant Professor of History, Bethany Nazarene College, Oklahoma. *Varieties of Quaker Experience.*

The Many Faces
of the Church

*Of all the means of estimating
American character...the pursuit of
religious history is the most
complete.*

FRANKLIN JAMESON,
1907

The Church is not a gallery for the exhibition of eminent Christians, but a school for the education of imperfect ones.

HENRY WARD BEECHER

How shall we labour with any effect to build up the Church, if we have no thorough knowledge of her history, or fail to apprehend it from the proper point of observation? History is, and must ever continue to be, next to God's word, the richest foundation of wisdom, and the surest guide to all successful practical activity.

PHILIP SCHAFF,
What is Church History? A Vindication of the Idea of Historical Development, 1846

CHURCH
OF THE
NAZARENE

No such thing exists on the face of the earth as Christianity in the abstract....Every man you see is either an Episcopalian or a Methodist, a Presbyterian or an Independent, an Arminian or a Calvanist. No one is a Christian in general.

CHARLES HODGE,
1836

One Lord · One Mission

Father Abraham, whom have you in heaven? Any Episcopalians? No! Any Presbyterians? No! Any Independents or Methodists? No, no, no! Whom have you there? We don't know those names here. All who are here are Christians....Oh, is this the case? Then God help us to forget party names and to become Christians in deed and truth.

GEORGE WHITEFIELD, preaching from the courthouse balcony, Philadelphia, 1740

Pilgrim Church

We came hither because we would have our posterity settled under pure and full dispensation of the gospel, defended by rulers that should be ourselves.

COTTON MATHER,
election sermon, early 1690s

Every member must work or quit.
No honorary members.
CHARLES GRANDISON FINNEY

Going to church don't make a man a
Christian any more than going to a
stable makes a man a horse.

WILLIAM A. (BILLY) SUNDAY

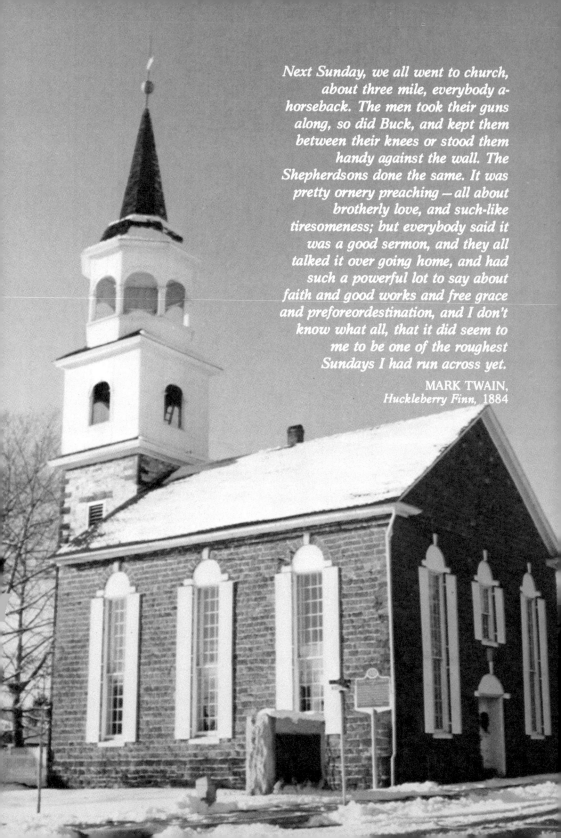

Next Sunday, we all went to church, about three mile, everybody a-horseback. The men took their guns along, so did Buck, and kept them between their knees or stood them handy against the wall. The Shepherdsons done the same. It was pretty ornery preaching — all about brotherly love, and such-like tiresomeness; but everybody said it was a good sermon, and they all talked it over going home, and had such a powerful lot to say about faith and good works and free grace and preforeordestination, and I don't know what all, that it did seem to me to be one of the roughest Sundays I had run across yet.

MARK TWAIN,
Huckleberry Finn, 1884

Present-day Christianity…has lower standards for church membership than those for getting on a bus.

HARRY R. RUDIN,
"Has the Church a Message of
Salvation," 1952

THEATRE

NOW SH

WHOLLY

DRIV

DRIVE IN CHURCH S

WOODLAND
DRIVE-IN
CHURCH
EVERY SUNDAY 11AM

WOODLAND
DRIVE IN

WING

IOSES

IN

11 AM YEAR ROUND

We must not sit still and look for miracles; up and be doing, and the Lord will be with thee. Prayer and pains, through faith in Christ Jesus, will do anything.

JOHN ELIOT (1604–1690),
"Apostle to the Indians"

*It required a martyr's fortitude
to go to church anymore. Banners, singing, balloons, endless
haranguing of the congregation
by usurpative laypeople: stand,
sit, sing, breathe. It was like
camp. Boot camp. Rogerson
found it a parody of his Protestant youth. He preferred the
Polish parish downtown, where
one could count on orthodoxy
and speed. Nonetheless, he
drove to the campus and the
Newman Club and an hour's
assault on his faith.*

RALPH McINERNY,
Rogerson at Bay, 1976

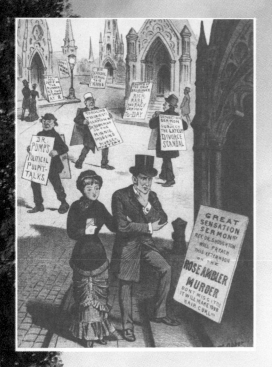

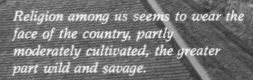

Religion among us seems to wear the face of the country, partly moderately cultivated, the greater part wild and savage.

THOMAS BACON

Without new measures it is impossible that the church should succeed in gaining the attention of the world to religion. There are so many exciting subjects constantly brought before the public mind...that the church cannot maintain her ground, cannot command attention, without very exciting preaching, and sufficient novelty in measures, to get the public ear.

CHARLES GRANDISON FINNEY

Welcome to MARTIN LUTHER KI

MARTIN LUTHER KING
BAPTIST CHURCH
REV. ALVIN HILLS

A...basic fact that characterizes nonviolence is that it does not seek to defeat or humiliate the opponent, but to win his friendship and understanding.

MARTIN LUTHER KING, JR.

R. BAPTIST CHURCH · Rev. Alv

For a long time the Negro Church was the one place in the life of a people which was comparatively free from interference by the white community.

HOWARD THURMAN,

The crisis of the church...is not the crisis of the church in the world, but of the world in the church.

H. RICHARD NIEBUHR,

The Church cannot be content to live
in its stained-glass house and
throw stones through the picture
window of modern culture.
ROBERT McAFEE BROWN,

There is no country in the world
where the Christian religion retains a
greater influence over the souls of
men than in America.

ALEXIS DE TOCQUEVILLE,
1831

God and
the Colonies

BY MARK A. NOLL

Colonial Roots

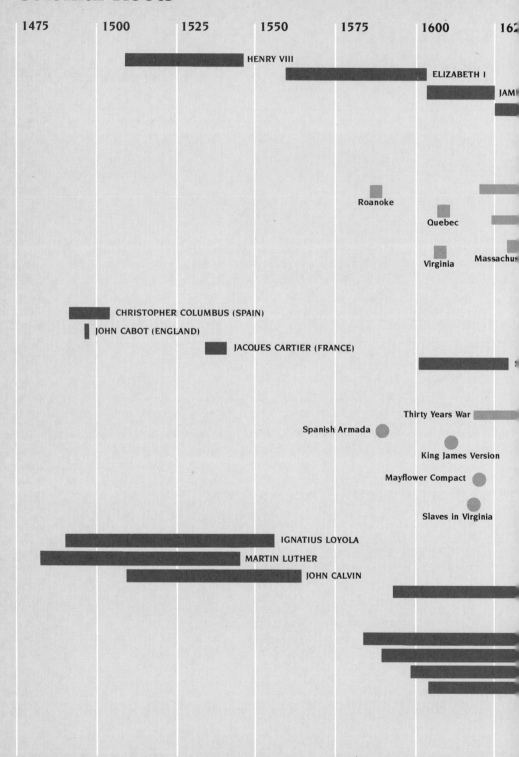

1475   1500   1525   1550   1575   1600   162

HENRY VIII

ELIZABETH I

JAM

Roanoke

Quebec

Massachus

Virginia

CHRISTOPHER COLUMBUS (SPAIN)

JOHN CABOT (ENGLAND)

JACQUES CARTIER (FRANCE)

Thirty Years War

Spanish Armada

King James Version

Mayflower Compact

Slaves in Virginia

IGNATIUS LOYOLA

MARTIN LUTHER

JOHN CALVIN

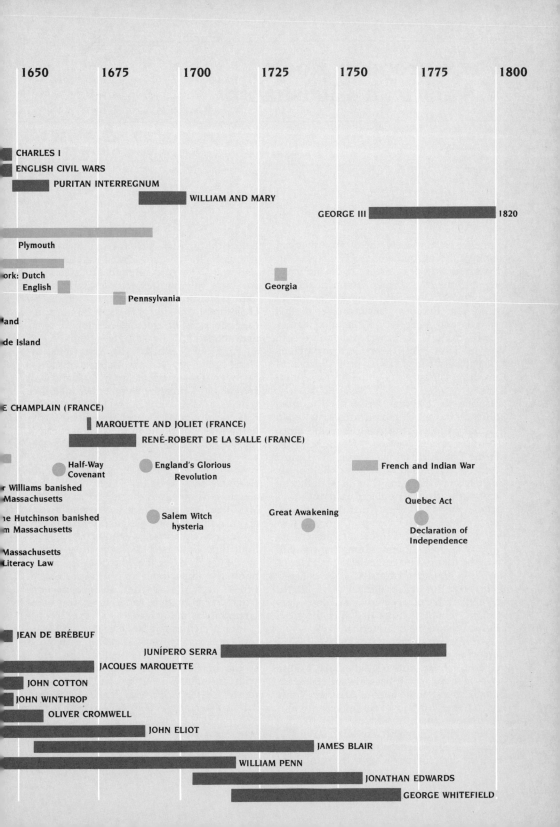

1650　　　1675　　　1700　　　1725　　　1750　　　1775　　　1800

CHARLES I

ENGLISH CIVIL WARS

PURITAN INTERREGNUM

WILLIAM AND MARY

GEORGE III　　1820

Plymouth

ork: Dutch

English

Pennsylvania

Georgia

land

de Island

E CHAMPLAIN (FRANCE)

MARQUETTE AND JOLIET (FRANCE)

RENÉ-ROBERT DE LA SALLE (FRANCE)

Half-Way
Covenant

England's Glorious
Revolution

French and Indian War

r Williams banished
Massachusetts

Quebec Act

he Hutchinson banished
m Massachusetts

Salem Witch
hysteria

Great Awakening

Declaration of
Independence

Massachusetts
Literacy Law

JEAN DE BRÉBEUF

JUNÍPERO SERRA

JACQUES MARQUETTE

JOHN COTTON

JOHN WINTHROP

OLIVER CROMWELL

JOHN ELIOT

JAMES BLAIR

WILLIAM PENN

JONATHAN EDWARDS

GEORGE WHITEFIELD

The European Roots of American Christianity

For better and for worse, the North American continent first encountered the Christian faith in western European dress. It did not take long until the American environment and the creativity of American believers began to modify that European heritage. Yet to this day it is only necessary to mention names like Britain's C. S. Lewis, Poland's Carol Wojtyla (John Paul II), or Germany's Hans Küng to recall how strong the influence of European Christianity remains for Americans.

During the colonial period the European influence was much more concentrated than it is today. Catholic missionaries from France and Spain ranged over all of North America, but the settlements from which the United States would come were overwhelmingly English and Protestant. The great influx of immigration from central and eastern Europe and the religious diversity that this immigration would bring (Orthodox, Catholic, Jewish, establishment Protestant, dissenting Protestant—in a rainbow of tongues) was still far in the future. The evangelization of blacks, unwilling immigrants from Africa, was barely under way. But that project, which mingled stupendous hypocrisy and miraculous conversions, would one day also alter the western European tone of American faith.

As different as colonial Christianity was from what it would become in the nineteenth and twentieth centuries, it did exhibit a number of features which have always characterized the course of the faith in America. While it is true that Puritanism dominated religious life in the northern English colonies and that the Church of England was the established church in the southern, it is also true that seeds of diversity were sown from the first.

Before the English Puritans arrived in Massachusetts in 1630, the Dutch Reformed had settled in New York. Before 1700 German-speaking Mennonites were established in Pennsylvania and Swedish Lutherans in Delaware. Even among the speakers of English, the story of colonial religion is more than the story of Puritan New England and an Anglican South, for that story must include Catholics, Quakers, Baptists of several varieties, Presbyterians from Scotland and Ireland, and smaller numbers from other groups.

If the diversity of later American Christianity was embryonic in the colonial period, the characteristically American tension between Christianity and cultural values arrived full grown. Early immigrants were both *European* and *Christian*. Sometimes this had a neutral effect—as in the transfer to the New World of European forms of ecclesiastical organization (Congregational, Presbyterian, Protestant Episcopal, Catholic Episcopal). Sometimes it would have a positive impact on the faith—as in the European insistence upon the importance of scripture. Sometimes, particularly when Europeans confronted the Native Americans, the combination was disastrous.

Indian civilization could indeed be barbarous by almost anyone's standard, with blood feuds of explosive viciousness and widespread immorality. But so could European, with interminable warfare and callous disregard for the powerless. Evaluated from a modern perspective—informed by a better understanding of both scripture and so-called primitive cultures—European attitudes to the Indians were frequently inexcusable, whether those of the Catholic Louis Hennepin for whom the Indians were "brutish in all their Inclinations," or the Puritan Cotton Mather, who styled them "the veriest *Ruines of Mankind*." In the grip of such ethnocentricism, European practice toward the Indians often became genocidal.

Yet the settlers of America were Christians as well as Europeans. They also exhibited the triumph of Christian universalism over cultural particularism. Some missionaries to the Indians did exhibit the worst features of cultural imperialism. Others, like the Catholic Jean de Brébeuf in French Canada and the Puritan John Eliot in Massachusetts, displayed a wholehearted willingness to become all things even to the Indians in order to win them for the gospel. Positive aspects of the faith surfaced even more often in daily life than in evangelism. When most of the West-

The English Parliament under Oliver Cromwell resolved in 1649 to support the godly commonwealth established by fellow Puritans in New England.
BILLY GRAHAM CENTER

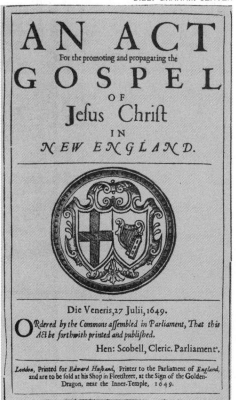

ern world was beset by tumults of one sort or another during the second half of the seventeenth century, the Puritans of Massachusetts—who had labored most consistently to ground their society on biblical principles—experienced extraordinary peace, stability, and social cohesion. And volumes have, with justice, been written to praise the charity, Christian devotion, and sweet spirits of the Pilgrim William Bradford, the Puritan John Winthrop, the Puritan dissenter Roger Williams, the Anglican James Blair, the Quaker William Penn, the Catholic missionary Junípero Serra, and many more colonial Christians.

The pages that follow tell the histories of these and other notable Christians, and the groups to which they belonged. It is well to remember that such histories can never escape the tension that American believers have always encountered: pulled in one direction to view all of life as a gift of God, pulled in the other to let standards of particular cultures restrict the universal appeal of the gospel.

Reformation Europe

The European discovery of America and the Reformation appeared together as harbingers of the modern world. Martin Luther was nearly ten years old when Columbus first arrived in the Western Hemisphere. John Calvin was seeing the first edition of his *Institutes of the Christian Religion* through the press while Jacques Cartier claimed Canada for France. And Hernando de Soto was exploring Florida and the lower Mississippi Valley for Spain at the very time Ignatius Loyola received papal approval for the Society of Jesus. It was, thus, only to be expected that the Protestant Reformation and its Catholic counterpart would greatly affect the European settlement of America.

Yet the age of Reformation was much more than a time of religious renewal. It was also a time of social and intellectual ferment, national self-assertion, and economic expansion. And these aspects of European life would also influence the way in which the Old World colonized the New.

The nations of Europe entered the sixteenth century stronger and more aggressive than at any time in their history. In Spain, Ferdinand and Isabella solidified their rule

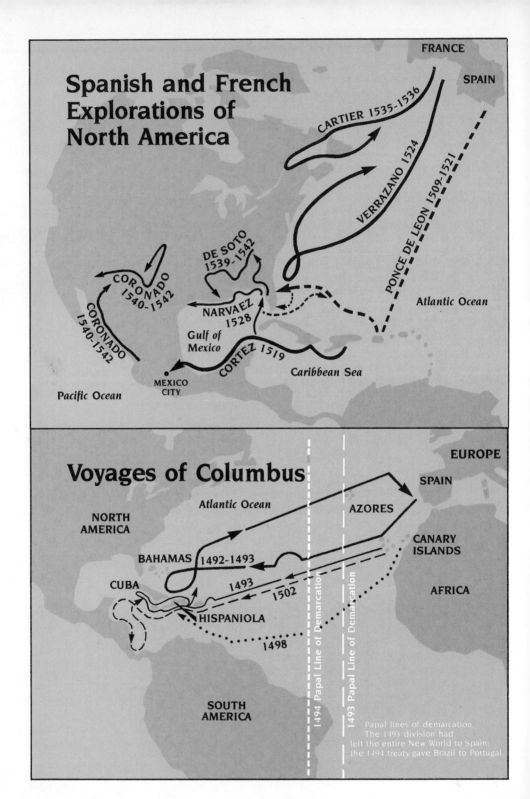

Spanish and French Explorations of North America

FRANCE

SPAIN

CARTIER 1535-1536

VERRAZANO 1524

PONCE DE LEON 1509-1521

Atlantic Ocean

DE SOTO 1539-1542

CORONADO 1540-1542

CORONADO 1540-1542

NARVAEZ 1528

Gulf of Mexico

CORTEZ 1519

Caribbean Sea

MEXICO CITY

Pacific Ocean

Voyages of Columbus

EUROPE

SPAIN

Atlantic Ocean

AZORES

NORTH AMERICA

CANARY ISLANDS

BAHAMAS 1492-1493

CUBA

1493

1502

AFRICA

HISPANIOLA

1498

SOUTH AMERICA

1494 Papal Line of Demarcation

1493 Papal Line of Demarcation

Papal lines of demarcation.
The 1493 division had
left the entire New World to Spain;
the 1494 treaty gave Brazil to Portugal

in 1492—the very year of Columbus' first voyage—by ousting the last of the Muslims who had occupied parts of their country for more than seven hundred years. In England the disruptive War of the Roses came to an end in 1485 when Henry Tudor assumed the throne and set his nation on a course of aggressive independence. His son, Henry VIII, and granddaughter, Elizabeth I, would carry that beginning to great heights. Europe's other major power, France, did not experience such an epochal event, but the long process by which its kings consolidated their power continued into the sixteenth century. The great nations of Europe were eager to test their mettle against each other at home, and they wished to see their influence expand abroad.

Each of the European powers thought it could steal a march on its competitors by exploiting the economic potential of the New World. In this effort only Spain succeeded, and only for a short while. The Spanish conquistadors subdued, then enslaved the Indians of Central and South America and set them to work—mining the fabulous silver deposits of Mexico and Peru, farming the great haciendas of Spanish colonial lords. The French who looked for gold in Canada and the English who arrived late on the scene never reaped much profit from America. But this did not keep either country away.

One of the most important reasons why Europeans sought to exploit and eventually colonize the American continent was their desire for trade. This had also been a major motive behind Columbus' effort to find a speedier pathway to the Far East. By the sixteenth century the demand for goods from the Orient—spices and textiles, for instance—was high and becoming higher. In Europe, breakthroughs in agricultural methods and industrial technology released more energy for trading and more time for enjoying the fruits of trade. They also created growing pools of capital which the rising middle class was eager to put to use. This desire for trade and for investment would likewise stimulate the settlement of America.

Sixteenth-century Europe was also heir to the Renaissance. The legacy of that intellectual movement went well beyond the poems of a Petrarch or the statues of a Michelangelo. In its broadest manifestations this new

Statue of Martin Luther (1483–1546) on the grounds of Concordia Theological Seminary, Springfield, Illinois RELIGIOUS NEWS SERVICE PHOTO

spirit encouraged Europeans to place more confidence in their own abilities and less in the collective wisdom of the community. It scorned the traditions passed down from the Middle Ages and called for a recovery of classical virtues, whether of ancient Greece and Rome or the Christian purity of the New Testament. It made many uneasy with the status quo and encouraged intellectual experimentation. In so doing, the Renaissance paralleled in influence the Reformation, and its spirit encouraged the Age of Discovery.

The Protestant Reformation occurred after kings had begun to consolidate their power, merchants to cast their eyes afield for trade, and intellectuals to call into question the immediate past. Yet it, too, was a source of fundamental change in sixteenth-century Europe. It was first and foremost a theological, biblical, and ecclesiastical movement, but it became also a movement whose effects went far beyond the narrow religious sphere. Martin Luther wanted to restore the purity of justification by faith and to make that doctrine preeminent in the church. The times—changing, questioning, innovating, the issue—touching the heart of the Christian message, and the man—trenchant, bombastic, sublime—combined for success. Soon other forceful leaders—Ulrich Zwingli, John Calvin, Martin Bucer, Thomas Cranmer, Conrad Grebel—proposed modifications to or advancements beyond Luther's message. Together they signaled the emergence of a dynamic religious force. Many Europeans turned to this Protestant faith because they believed it, others because it offered a convenient means to escape the power of the Catholic church.

As Catholics denounced the Protestant interpretations of scripture and drew their cloak of traditional authority ever more tightly about themselves, the Reformers insisted that the Bible alone must be the ultimate spiritual authority. And these reformers found in the New Testament a view of the church in which, whatever gradations might remain for the sake of expediency, the essential reality was the priesthood of all believers. Luther certainly had never met a person who had been in America and Calvin probably had not, but their convictions—especially on

Ignatius Loyola (1441–1556), founder of the Society of Jesus LIBRARY OF CONGRESS

scripture and the church—would flourish in North America as nowhere else in the world.

Parallel to the reform which resulted in Protestantism was a reform which renewed Catholicism. Ignatius Loyola and the Jesuits as well as participants at the Council of Trent shared much of the Protestant discontent with Catholic practice in the late Middle Ages. They felt, however, that the solution was to purify the church's traditional ideals rather than abandon them. They dedicated themselves to making the inherited system work—restoring the papacy to spiritual concerns, clarifying the responsibilities of both God and man in salvation, and removing the church and its sacraments from the marketplace. The church, they held, needed priests fulfilling their responsibilities honorably more than it needed the priesthood of all believers. It needed a careful reassertion of the hierarchy's role in interpreting the Bible more than *scriptura sola*. It needed a proper appreciation of the natural capacities which God gives to all people and the special gifts he bestows upon the church more than it needed a radical notion of belief. By the end of the sixteenth century, Catholics joined Protestants in a faith that was far more energetic, far more profound, and far more dedicated than it had been a century before.

The emergence of great nations, the new importance of trade, the intellectual creativity of the Renaissance, and the religious fervor of the Reformation joined and acted on one another in every possible combination, setting the stage for the first act of the European settlement of America. The story of Christianity in the colonies would eventually be linked most closely with the Protestant Reformation. It begins, however, with forces released and individuals inspired by the movement for Catholic reform.

Roman Catholicism in North America

Fascination with the Puritans and a general Protestant bias have encouraged most Americans, including some very good historians, to forget that the first Christians in the New World held worship in Latin, said the Mass, and encouraged devotion to the Virgin Mary. Before the English settled permanently at Jamestown in 1607, a Catholic university and two theological seminaries were well estab-

San Xavier Mission, Tucson, Arizona   KEYSTONE-MAST COLLECTION, UNIVERSITY OF CALIFORNIA, RIVERSIDE

lished in Mexico City, and thousands of Indians had become at least nominal Catholics in the New Mexico territories. Decades before John Eliot began to translate the Bible for the Algonquian-speaking Indians of Massachusetts, Franciscans had prepared Catholic literature in Rimucuan for the Indians of Florida. While the Father of Waters, the Mississippi River, was still an unverified rumor for English colonists, its banks were the scene of active evangelism by French missionaries. Too often Americans lose sight of the reasons why towns in the southern part of the United States bear names like St. Augustine, San Antonio, or Los Angeles, and in the Midwest Vincennes, Dubuque, or Louisville. More often than not, it was because some intrepid Jesuit or Franciscan had

come to such localities in an effort to spread the gospel.

The Spanish presence in North America lasted from 1520 to 1840. Even earlier, in 1494, Pope Alexander VI had settled a territorial dispute between Spain and Portugal that would leave Brazil to speak Portuguese and the rest of Latin America Spanish. The French, whose explorers reached the continent nearly as soon as the Spanish, did not arrive in force in the New World until the early 1600s because of the Wars of Religion between Catholic and Protestant (1562-1594) which so distracted French energy at home. Still, the Christian history of New Spain—a great arc from Florida through Texas and New Mexico into California—and that of New France—encompassing Canada and the

Mississippi Valley—share many features. In both cases dedicated missionaries accompanied or preceded civil and military officials seeking territorial and economic gain for the mother country. In both cases the tight bond between American church and European state created some opportunities, but led to even greater frustration. In both cases priests and lay brothers left a martyr's trail of blood, along with congregations of converts, to mark their progress. And in both cases the absence of a significant number of lay Christian families to support the work of the clerics undermined their long-term impact. Protestants who think only of New England when considering the early Christian history of North America would do well to look also to New Spain and New France.

From the outset Christian concerns permeated the Spanish interest in America. Christopher Columbus recorded them in the very first entry of the diary which chronicled the entrance of Spain into the New World. One of his goals was the establishment of contact with native peoples in order to dis-

cover "the manner in which may be undertaken their conversion to our Holy Faith." This concern remained with Spanish leaders, including the Spanish king and Holy Roman Emperor Charles V, who in 1523 described the conversion of Florida's Indians as "the chief motive" for the expedition thence. Unfortunately for the Indians whom such expeditions encountered, Spanish generals in the field often paid little heed to the Christian aspirations of their rulers at home. Such great conquistadors as Cortez in Mexico or Pizarro in Peru regularly took priests along, but their hearts burned much more for treasure on earth than for treasure in heaven. As a result, Spanish settlement in the New World led to a brutal oppression and exploitation of the native population, which was decimated by the twin scourges of European disease and European greed.

Yet everywhere that Spain went, priests and friars went too. Their early protests about the conquistadors' use of the Indians—some considered them *bruta animalia* and treated them accordingly—led Pope Paul III to is-

"Landing of Columbus," painting by John Vanderlyn in the rotunda of the U.S. Capitol   ARCHITECT OF THE CAPITOL

Artist's conception of Columbus and his companions attending the first Christian religious ceremonies in the New World LIBRARY OF CONGRESS

sue in 1537 a formal declaration (*Sublimis Deus*) that the Indians were people indeed and able to become Christians. In 1542 the Franciscan Father Juan de Padilla, in the company of Vasquez Coronado, became the first of many Catholic missionaries who would pay with their lives in the effort to convert the Indians, when he was struck down in what is now Kansas.

By the seventeenth century considerable progress had been made in the difficult task of converting the Indians. In the New Mexico region as many as 35,000 Christian Indians were gathered around twenty-five mission stations in the year 1630. Over the next two centuries dedicated missionary ac-

tivity continued in the American Southwest and California. Franciscans, like the intelligent Junípero Serra, took the lead in establishing a Christian presence in California. From 1769 to 1845, 146 Franciscans participated in the California work. Together they baptized nearly 100,000 Indians.

The two great difficulties for Spanish missionary work were the heavy hand of Spanish colonial rule and the intractability of the Indians. While friars sought converts, viceroys sought submissive native workers. While priests labored for eternal life, military commanders displayed ruthless disregard for physical life. The situation was gravely complicated by the fact that the popes had granted

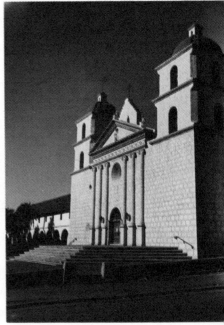

California Spanish missions. Clockwise from left: San Luis Rey, Santa Barbara, San Miguel COURTESY FRANCISCAN FATHERS

blanket authority over New World ecclesiastical matters to the Spanish government. Civil officials collected tithes and appointed church leaders. Priest and brother, try as they might, could not escape the Spanish colonial system. Also, try as they might, they were never entirely successful in evangelizing the Indians. The cultural gap was immense. The exploitation of Indian laborers worked against the development of viable Christian converts. Despite many baptisms and many conversions, the Indian churches which remained after the departure of Spanish colonial rule were weak and very far between. In this, however, the Spanish experience was little different than the French or the English.

From the founding of Quebec by Samuel de Champlain in 1608 until their defeat by the British outside that same city in 1759, the French dominated Canada and the American Midwest. French explorers and traders roamed widely in these vast areas. Wherever they went in search of glory for France or profit from furs, Christian missionaries also came in search of souls for God. The Jesuit Jacques Marquette accompanied Louis Jolliet in the pioneering exploration of the Upper Mississippi in 1673. The Franciscan Louis Hennepin traveled in modern-day Minnesota with René-Robert de La Salle, who eventually claimed Louisiana and the mouth of the Mississippi for the mother country in 1682. By that time mission work in Canada had been under way for more than sixty years.

The great bulk of Canadian missionary activity was carried on by the Jesuits. On the shores of the Great Lakes and into the wilderness beyond, Jesuits like Jean de Brébeuf displayed a remarkable toleration for Indian ways and a signal devotion to Christ and the church. They suffered privation and disease. Many of them—like Brébeuf, who was caught in the warfare of Huron and Iroquois—paid with their lives. And results were meager. An occasional convert, like Catharine Tegahkouita, brightened their labors. This young woman from upper New York was converted in 1676 under the ministry of the Jesuit Jacques de Lamberville, suffered sharp rebuke from her family, and died in 1680 full of faith; her tomb became the object of pilgrimages where miracles were said to occur. But such triumphs were rare. More frequently, missionary efforts were sacrificed to the needs of civil rulers laboring to gain imperial advantage over the English or to the warfare which plagued the northern Indians.

The enemy of the human race . . . inspired his satellites . . . to publish abroad that the Indians of the West and the South, and other people of whom We have recent knowledge should be treated as dumb brutes created for our service, pretending that they are incapable of receiving the Catholic Faith.

We . . . consider, however, that the Indians are truly men and that they are not only capable of understanding the Catholic Faith but, according to our information, they desire exceedingly to receive it. . . . they may and should, freely and legitimately, enjoy their liberty and the possession of their property; nor should they be in any way enslaved.

POPE PAUL III,
from the bull *Sublimis Deus,*
June 2, 1537

On his Desire to Reach the Indians

[I want] to seek toward the south sea [Gulf of Mexico] nations new and unknown to us, in order to make them know our great God of whom they have been up to now ignorant.

JACQUES MARQUETTE

A composite depiction of the martyrdom suffered by Jesuit missionaries in New France NEW YORK PUBLIC LIBRARY

French colonial officials were neither as callous to the Indians as the Spanish nor as oppressive in their oversight of the church. Jesuit authorities and eventually a full hierarchy took a jealous regard for matters of the faith. Particularly when Francis Xavier de Montmorency Laval arrived in Quebec as apostolic vicar in 1659 (he became Quebec's first bishop in 1674), the church asserted its authority very distinctly. Laval ruled his diocese tightly, he opposed the liquor traffic with the Indians, and he founded a seminary. He set Quebec, which had been more successful in attracting French settlers than most outposts, on the religious course which it has never entirely abandoned.

The record of Jesuit missions in Canada and the Upper Midwest remains a stirring tale. The greatest long-lasting result of French settlement in the New World, however, was the erection of a French-Catholic enclave in Canada. It remained firmly in place even after the Jesuits fell from official favor in Canada, and the entire Catholic world, during the 1760s. For the rest of American history, Quebec would offer a sharp contrast to English and Protestant settlements that were taking shape so rapidly to its south.

Our clear duty is to conform ourselves in all things to the Will of God, and to prepare to die as well. That is what counts: nothing else matters. If this is secured, it matters little if we lose all the rest: without this all else is useless.

JUNÍPERO SERRA,
as he left Majorca, August 20, 1749

Junípero Serra

HENRY WARNER BOWDEN

Miguel José Serra was born on November 24, 1713 at Petra, Majorca, a Spanish island in the Mediterranean. When he was sixteen he joined the Franciscan order and changed his name to Junípero after a companion of the monastic founder, Francis of Assisi. He proved so adept at his studies that Franciscan authorities made him professor of philosophy from 1743 to 1749 at their most distinguished university on Majorca. Though deservedly renowned for sound doctrinal lectures and brilliant debating abilities, he abandoned academic pursuits in 1750 for mission work in the New World. Serra then divided his time between teaching at San Fernando College in Mexico City and evangelical work in the Sierra Gorda

Statue of Junípero Serra in the U.S. Capitol
ARCHITECT OF THE CAPITOL

mountains to the northeast. While preaching to the Pames Indians, he suffered an insect bite on his left leg which grew infected and plagued him with swelling and festering sores the rest of his life. Despite that personal hardship and the burden of collegiate administrative duties, Serra persevered in various Mexican gospel enterprises. For two years he supervised missions in Baja California, assuming responsibility for a series of stations when papal action forced Jesuits to leave the area. Then he undertook a new apostolate in 1769.

The Viceroy authorized an expedition under Capt. Gaspar de Portolá to explore and colonize Alta California as a preventive against Russian encroachment down the Pacific coast. Serra led the missionary contingent to plant the gospel in new fields. This small, frail, yet strong-willed individual founded nine missions with the occasional help, and often against the opposition, of crown officials. His work ranged from San Diego, and efforts to convert the Chumash natives, to San Francisco, and similar efforts among the Costanoans. As he won thousands of new Christians, Serra taught them to adopt settled agricultural habits and develop greater material prosperity as well as spiritual consolation. Always a meticulous administrator, the Father President supervised ascetic discipline among his fellow monks and encouraged elementary religious growth among new believers. He was a zealous humanitarian as well, and protested vigorously whenever soldiers or colonists abused Indian rights. Twenty-one California missions eventually flourished as part of Serra's early plan. After serving his order for fifty-four years the gray-robed pioneer died on August 28, 1784 in San Carlos mission near Carmel.

Jacques Marquette

HENRY WARNER BOWDEN

Born on June 1, 1637 at Laon in the Champagne province of France, Jacques Marquette enjoyed a normal childhood. His family sent him to Jesuit schools at Rheims in 1646, and eight years later he decided to enter the Society of Jesus. Beginning his novitiate at Nancy, young Marquette proceeded through the usual *ratio studiorum* and taught introductory classes himself before volunteering for mission work. He received ordination in March 1666 before completing his theological studies and sailed that summer for New France. During the next two years he studied Algonquian dialects at Sillery, one of the first intertribal towns of Christian Indians established near Montreal. His chief

Father Jacques Marquette (1637–1675)
MARQUETTE UNIVERSITY

mentor, Gabriel Druillettes, used his missionary experiences in Maine and Ontario to help Marquette appreciate native customs as well as understand their language and thought patterns.

By 1668 Jesuit superiors considered the young blackrobe ready for evangelical work and assigned him to a western outpost. Marquette joined Claude Allouez at a mission named Sainte Marie du Sault, located where Lake Superior flows into Lake Huron. That site 1,500 miles west of Montreal was an important trading center for surrounding tribes whose annual fairs allowed French priests an opportunity to preach the gospel. Marquette performed admirably and was soon allowed to conduct a mission alone. Between 1669 and 1671 he managed another station, Saint-Esprit, located on Chequamegon Bay five hundred miles west of the Lake Superior rapids. There he tended a small flock of scattered Hurons and the Kiskakon branch of the Ottawa nation. Unstable relations with the Sioux made that mission untenable, however, and Marquette persuaded his charges to move closer to Sault Sainte Marie. Settling briefly on Mackinac Island, by 1672 he founded St. Ignace mission on the northern tip of the Michigan peninsula.

Père Marquette had often heard of the Illinois, a powerful and civilized confederacy to the south. He longed to explore territory in that direction, and in 1673 seized an opportunity to accompany Louis Jolliet on a voyage that could expand Jesuit missionary endeavors. Jolliet and five other companions ventured for trade and the glory of France; Marquette went for souls and the glory of God. Probably the first Europeans to explore the great Mississippi River, they charted its course as far south as its confluence with the Arkansas. On their return trip Marquette met friendly Kaskaskia Indians, a branch of the Illinois, and promised to establish a mission at their central village (near present-day Utica). But he began to suffer from fever and other disorders in 1674, postponing his new mission despite a strong desire to reach new converts. A winter trip proved disastrous, and he reached Kaskaskia in April so weak he could hardly celebrate Easter Mass. Naming the new mission after the Immaculate Conception, he vowed to return if his waning health permitted. The zealous priest died on May 18, 1675, two weeks short of his thirty-eighth birthday, while attempting to reach St. Ignace. Fellow Jesuits noted that his lonely grave somewhere on the eastern shore of Lake Michigan signified the martyr's end each of them sought.

Marquette and Jolliet entering the Upper Mississippi River   LIBRARY OF CONGRESS

Contrasting Missionary Strategies

You must have sincere affection for the Savages — looking upon them as ransomed by the blood of the son of God, and as our brethren with whom we are to pass the rest of our lives. To conciliate the Savages, you must be careful never to make them wait for you in embarking. You should try to eat their sagamité or salmagundi in the way they prepare it, although it may be dirty, half-cooked, and very tasteless. As to the other numerous things which may be unpleasant, they must be endured for the love of God, without saying anything or appearing to notice them. You must so conduct yourself as not to be at all troublesome to even one of these Barbarians.

Leaving a highly civilized community, you fall into the hands of barbarous people who care little for your Philosophy or your Theology. All the fine qualities which might make you loved and respected in France are like pearls trampled under the feet of swine, or rather of mules, which utterly despise you when they see that you are not as good pack animals as they are. If you go naked, and carry the load of a horse upon your back, as they do, then you would be wise according to their doctrine, and would be recognized as a great man, otherwise not. Jesus Christ is our true greatness; it is He alone and His cross that should be sought in running after these people, for, if you strive for anything else, you will find naught but bodily and spiritual affliction. But having found Jesus Christ in His Cross, you have found the roses in the thorns, sweetness in bitterness, all in nothing.

JESUIT JEAN DE BRÉBEUF,
*"Instructions for the Fathers of Our Society
Who Shall be Sent to the Hurons,"* 1637

Our ancient Missionary Recollects of *Canada*, and those that succeeded them in that work, have always given it for their opinion, and I now own 'tis mine, that the way to succeed in converting the Barbarians, is to endeavour to make them men before we go about to make them Christians. Now in order to civilize them, 'tis necessary that the *Europeans* should mix with them, and that they should dwell together, which can never be done for certain till the Colonies are augmented. ... Yet before this be done, there's no way to convert these Unbelievers. Thus the covetousness of those who are for getting a great deal in a short time, has mightily retarded the establishment of the Gospel among the Savages.

Hence 'tis manifest, that the office of a Missionary is very troublesome and laborious amongst these numerous Nations, and it must be granted that 'tis necessary to spend many Years, and undergo a great deal of pains to civilize People so extremely stupid and barbarous.

So that Christianity is not like to gain much ground among the Savages, till the Colonies are strengthened by a great Number of Inhabitants, Artisans and Workmen, and then the Treaty betwixt the Barbarians and us should be freer, and extended to all *Europeans*: But chiefly it should be endeavour'd to fix the Barbarians to a certain dwelling Place, and introduce our Customs and Laws amongst them, further'd by the Assistance of zealous People in *Europe*, Colleges might be founded to breed up the young Savages in the Christian Faith, which might in time contribute very much to the Conversion of their Country-men. This is a very proper Method without doubt, to strengthen the Temporal and Spiritual Interests of the Colonies; but the generality of Mankind are bent upon Gain and Traffick, and are little concern'd to procure God's Blessing upon them, and endeavour the advancement of his Glory.

FRANCISCAN LOUIS HENNEPIN,
on difficulties of Indian Missions, 1697

The Expansion of England

The first permanent English settlements in the New World did not appear until the seventeenth century. Yet they were outgrowths of a period of national renewal stretching back into the fifteenth century. Henry VII (1485-1509) began the ascent. Henry VIII (1509-1547) carried it further. After the uncertain reigns of Henry's first two heirs, Edward VI (1547-1553) and Mary (1553-1558), his third, Elizabeth (1558-1603), brought the renewal to great heights. The Elizabethan Age—the age of William Shakespeare and Sir Francis Drake—was a time when all England hummed with economic, political, and social vigor. It was, not coincidentally, also the age of England's Reformation.

For Henry VIII, reformation of the Church of England was strategic for personal, political, and economic goals. He wanted male heirs, which his wife, Catherine of Aragon, had not provided, and he hankered after Anne Boleyn. To obtain a divorce from Catherine, which was accomplished in 1534, Henry had to break loose from the authority of the pope, a step he was not at all reluctant to take in a general effort to free England from foreign influence. Once the breach with Rome occurred, Henry turned rapidly to England's church lands, particularly its monasteries, to finance his own expanding government. When Henry had himself proclaimed "the only supreme head in earth of the Church of England" by the Act of Supremacy (1534) and when he had begun his assault upon the monastic lands (1539), he may have felt the Reformation in England was at an end. In fact it had just begun.

Henry was participating in a much more significant drama than even he, with his vast ego, could comprehend. The stability and strength which he had given to England would expand after his death to move the country into the very first ranks of Europe's great nations. His differences with Spain, exacerbated by the divorce from Catherine (aunt of Spain's Charles V), would overshadow England's overseas development until his daughter's navy and a bad storm smashed Spain's Armada in 1588. The harvest of new money, reaped from the dissolution of the monasteries, enriched first the crown and then a much wider circle. This windfall only accelerated the economic transformation of England which over the course of the sixteenth century provided more usable wealth for a wider population than anywhere else in Europe.

It is little wonder that the tremendous energy of Tudor England found an outlet in lands beyond the seas. Explorers Martin Frobisher and Humphrey Gilbert sought a pathway to the lucrative China trade through Canada during the 1570s and 1580s. They also thought it might be possible to establish permanent colonies to exploit the land and service the ships which were sailing by. Gilbert and another of England's great adventurers, Sir Walter Raleigh, actually followed through in an effort to found the colonies. But their efforts, in Newfoundland and Roanoke Island respectively, came to naught.

These ventures lacked one advantage that several later efforts at English colonization enjoyed: the stimulus of Christian motivation. The great Tudor age of Henry VIII and Elizabeth was, it is true, an era of intellectual, social, literary, and financial awakening. It was also, however, an age of spiritual renewal. The story of Christianity in British North America, as well as the story of the first permanent English settlements themselves, cannot be told without describing that renewal.

The English Reformation

It is all too easy, with the attention accorded Henry VIII, his six wives, and his aggressive politics, to overlook the vibrant spiritual quality of the English Reformation. Yet even before Henry ascended the throne currents of spiritual renewal were flowing in England. Among the elite, scholars like John Colet (1467-1519) and statesmen like Sir Thomas More (1478-1535) railed against abuses in the Catholic church and looked for a more ennobling faith. Among the humble, the effects of Lollardy—the biblically based, anticlerical movement arising from the reform of John Wycliffe in the fourteenth century—never entirely ceased. When news of Luther's reform arrived in England, it fell on fertile soil. Some Englishmen, like More and the reforming bishop John Fisher (1469-1535), maintained the ideal of a purified Catholicism and repudiated Luther. Others, like the

English reformers and Marian martyrs, Archbishop Thomas Cranmer (left, 1489–1556) and Bishop Nicholas Ridley (1500?–1555) BILLY GRAHAM CENTER

Cambridge scholar and preacher Robert Barnes (1495-1540), accepted his message without reservation. The most influential reformers, however, adapted the general substance of Luther's message to the exigencies of the English situation.

The main body of English reformers made their peace with Henry's desire to be the head of the church. Not until well into the 1600s would a significant number of Protestants challenge the right of the monarch to oversee the church. But within that framework reformers like the Archbishop of Canterbury, Thomas Cranmer (1489-1556), and Henry VIII's right-hand man, Thomas Cromwell (1485-1540), set England on a distinctly Protestant course. Cranmer, one of the master liturgists in the entire history of the church, prepared forms and prayers for regular worship (eventually to become the Book of Common Prayer), wrote evangelical homilies for use in the churches, and supported the work of such colleagues as Nicholas Ridley (*ca.* 1500-1555) and Hugh Latimer (1485-1555). Cromwell saw to the welfare of Protestant preachers and officials, and worked

with Cranmer to make the Bible available in English translation. The course which these early reformers set—conservative in churchmanship, satisfied with the state church, Reformed and evangelical in theology—defined the path for most English Protestants until the Civil Wars of the 1640s, and for many beyond that turbulent era.

The pace of reform spurted during the brief reign of Edward VI (1547-1553), who had both Protestant counselors and Protestant convictions. The reforming interest mourned his premature death as the passing of Josiah and braced itself for his half-sister Mary, who was a dedicated Roman Catholic. Her reign (1553-1558) administered a sharp rebuke to the Protestant cause. During her rule, 288 Protestants endured the flames for their faith, including Cranmer, Ridley, and Latimer. Many more were forced to flee England for the continent. But that removal proved vital for the later history of Protestantism in England. Refugees found Lutheran lands, preoccupied by both political and theological turmoil, uncongenial. By contrast, the Reformed cities of Switzerland and South Ger-

John Knox (1505–1572) *denouncing his monarch Mary, Queen of Scots* BILLY GRAHAM CENTER

many opened their doors wide to the refugees and provided them with warm fellowship and support. When the reign of Mary came to an end, they streamed back to England from Geneva, Zurich, Strasbourg, and Frankfurt with a renewed appreciation for the Re-

Elizabeth I (1533–1603), *whose "settlement" of religious diversity served only to fuel the fires of Puritanism* FROM THE ART COLLECTION OF THE FOLGER SHAKESPEARE LIBRARY

formed faith and its cultural expressions. John Knox, the Scottish reformer who had lived many years in England, exaggerated only slightly the impression made on many refugees by their experience on the continent when he called Calvin's Geneva "the most perfect school of Christ since the days of the Apostles."

During the reign of Elizabeth, Protestantism was firmly established as the religion of the realm. But as much as Good Queen Bess prized religious uniformity, she was forced to deal with a diverse mixture of Protestant allegiances. A few read the Book of Common Prayer and the Thirty-Nine Articles as a natural development from the Catholic Middle Ages. Many more found these standards for worship and doctrine, along with the settlement between state and church, entirely satisfactory. But others called for more reform. Those who wished to see a further purification of the English church eventually became known as Puritans. Although they arose in England, they would exert their greatest impact in America.

Puritanism

Much ink has flowed in the effort to define Puritanism. Historians have pointed out, correctly, that Puritanism was strong among those who supported the prerogatives of Parliament and among those who were rising economically in town and countryside. But neither political nor economic concerns ever became more important for the whole Puritan movement than religious matters. Puritans thought too much corruption from the Catholic past remained in the church. They felt that ministers should preach a purer and more energetic gospel throughout the land. In the flow of events these convictions broadened and deepened so that Puritanism soon came to signal an effort also to purify the self and to purify all of English society.

Like its even vaguer counterpart, "Anglicanism," Puritanism included many strands. Thomas Cartwright (1535-1603), a Cambridge scholar and preacher, argued as early as 1570 that the reformed Church of England still fell short of the standards set forth in the second chapter of Acts. Other divines over the next two generations echoed Cartwright in appealing for further reform. Some, like the Cambridge scholar William Perkins (1558-1602), stressed the need for practical spirituality in the pulpits and pews of the churches. Others, like the expatriate William Ames (1576-1633) who was eventually forced to settle in Holland, carefully set out theological principles to govern all of life. Still others urged that the system of governing the church by bishops (Episcopalianism) should be reformed in favor of a system in which elders and a graduated series of participatory courts ruled (Presbyterianism), or one in which the various local assemblies governed themselves (Congregationalism). But Puritanism extended well beyond the studies of the scholars. It eventually drew into its orbit a large number of parish ministers, some of whom like John Cotton (1584-1652) and Thomas Hooker (1586-1647) eventually left England for the New World. It also included many prominent laymen, like future leaders of Massachusetts Bay John Winthrop and Thomas Dudley, who had legal training, official position in the counties, or inherited wealth. And it included many of the "middling sort" whose names are not remembered, but whose participation transformed Puritanism from an intellectual exercise into a dynamic movement.

The reach of Puritanism was broad. Defined in its widest sense as a Reformed protest against the ecclesiastical status quo, it is possible to see Puritan tendencies in Edmund Grindal, Archbishop of Canterbury 1575-1583, who was Calvinistic in theology, who encouraged clergymen to meet in "prophesyings" for Bible study and mutual edification, and who was not afraid to rebuke the Queen when she asked him to stop such meetings. It appears also in Robert Browne (ca. 1553-1633), who became disillusioned with the entire episcopal structure and who organized congregational churches entirely separated from the state's control. His goal, as one of his books put it, was *Reformation without Tarrying for Anie*. In between Grindal and Browne lay most of the Puritans— very uneasy with the Catholic traces remaining in the state church (such as the ceremonial garment, the surplice), willing to experiment with new forms of ecclesiastical authority, eager to emphasize the New Birth, but reluctant to break entirely with the English church that God, to their thinking, had

so miraculously revived in the days of the Tudors.

Most of the Puritans shared basically common beliefs about the Christian faith and its outworking in the world. Almost all were Reformed in theology. But they believed with Luther, as well as with Calvin, that people were spiritually debilitated by original sin. All people were unwilling, and therefore unable, to meet the demands of God or enjoy his fellowship unless God himself changed their hearts of stone into flesh. They believed as well that God's gift of grace led to living faith in Christ. The distinctive contribution of the Puritans on the subject of human salvation was their emphasis on conversion. For them, becoming a genuine believer would normally entail an intense period of introspection and repentance, followed by the experience of liberating faith.

With all the Protestant reformers, the Puritans also believed in the supreme authority of scripture. Such a representative Anglican as Richard Hooker (*ca.* 1554-1600) could agree in his monumental *Laws of Ecclesiastical Polity*—but only up to a point. Unlike the Puritans, Hooker held that ecclesiastical traditions, local customs, and a judicious use of reason could act as valid religious authorities under the umbrella of scripture. Puritans, more and more, came to affirm that the Bible and only the Bible deserved to be followed. Anglicans would say that Christians should not do what the Bible prohibited, but could use reason and tradition to set practices within that boundary. Puritans argued, with a subtle but profound difference, that Christians should do only what the Bible commanded. Unfortunately for the Puritans, when they came to power in England, and to a lesser extent when some had migrated to America, they could never agree among themselves exactly what scripture mandated for a wide variety of practical matters, including the basic question of church government—whether a reformed episcopacy, congregationalism, presbyterianism, or even liberty of conscience.

For all their reforming zeal, the Puritans clung tightly to one conviction handed on from the Middle Ages and the early days of the Reformation. This conviction, which greatly influenced their course in America, concerned the solidarity of society under God, the unity of life. Puritans were not modern individualists. They held, rather, that a single, coordinated set of authorities should govern both public and private life. The result was that Puritans wanted nothing less than to make all England Puritan, or failing that, to establish a thoroughly biblical commonwealth in the New World. Modern ideas of tolerance only appeared during the rule of Oliver Cromwell in the 1650s, and then only briefly. They had little influence on most Englishmen, whether Puritan or Anglican, whether they lived in England or America.

Puritanism Abroad: Virginia and Plymouth

It is customary to regard the colonization of Virginia as a thoroughly secular affair. Whatever the settlers at Jamestown might have shared with the Puritans of Massachusetts as seventeenth-century Englishmen, it was certainly not religion. There is at least a grain of truth to this conventional wisdom. The Virginia Company of London, which sponsored the colony founded at Jamestown in 1607, was much more interested in profit than in Puritanism. And the colony in Virginia never did partake of the religious fervor or Christian purpose that motivated many New Englanders. Still, more than an occasional religious note attended the settlement of Virginia. In some respects the early Virginians even bore a striking resemblance to the later colonists to the north.

As soon as the first settlers arrived on Virginia soil in May 1607, they joined the Rev. Robert Hunt ("an honest, religious, and couragious Divine," according to Capt. John Smith) in a service of communion. Such religious observances were common during the critical moments of the colony's early history. When Lord de La Warr, the new governor, arrived in 1610, as the colony teetered on the brink of collapse, his first action was to organize a worship service in order to issue a biblical call for sacrifice and industry. Later

John White's map illustrating "The Arrival of the Englishmen in Virginia"   LIBRARY OF CONGRESS

Baptism of Pocahontas

the military officials sent by the Virginia Company in a desperate effort to salvage a profit insisted that "the Almighty God be duly and daily served." Virginia's earliest legal code also made attendance at Sunday services compulsory and contained harsh reprisals against violations of the sabbath, adultery, extravagant dress, and other moral lapses. The missionary motive, so prominent in Spanish and French colonization, was present also in Virginia. James I had included instructions in the Virginia Company's charter for propagating the "Christian religion to such people, as yet live in darkness and miserable ignorance of true knowledge and worship of God." John Rolfe married the legendary Pocahontas as much for the sake of her soul as for the sake of his love. "I will never cease," Rolfe wrote of his desire to see Pocahontas become a Christian, "untill I have accomplished, & brought to perfection so holy a worke, in which I will daily pray God to blesse me, to mine, and her eternall happiness." Alexander Whitaker, the outstanding minister in Virginia's early history, never lost his desire to convert the Indians, even as he maintained a regular and effective spiritual work among the English.

From the beginning, the Church of England was established by law as the official church of Virginia. When Civil War broke out in England during the 1640s, Virginia sided with the King and Episcopacy against Parliament and the Puritans. Still, in the early years of the century the faith which the first settlers brought to Virginia was not as different in belief or practice from that of the Puritans as it would later become.

Church within the walls of the restored fort at Jamestown, Virginia

The Pilgrims in art: above, embarkation from Holland aboard the Speedwell; below, going to church
ABOVE: LIBRARY OF CONGRESS   BELOW: BILLY GRAHAM CENTER

Above: Plimoth Plantation, a restoration of seventeenth-century Plymouth; below: "The First Thanksgiving"
ABOVE: PLIMOTH PLANTATION BELOW: COURTESY OF THE PILGRIM SOCIETY, PLYMOUTH, MASSACHUSETTS

Such Puritanism as the first settlers in Virginia displayed existed securely within the framework of the established church. The Puritanism of the next permanent settlement had gone well beyond it. The Pilgrims of Plymouth Colony—to set aside the myths and the glow of Thanksgiving legends—were in reality Puritans who had somewhat less patience with the Church of England, somewhat less confidence in the future of reform, and somewhat less money than the Puritans who would later come to Massachusetts Bay.

When James I assumed the English throne in 1603, some Puritans had already despaired of a further reform of the national church and had removed themselves from its jurisdiction. These Separatists were creating a growing number of local congregations, in spite of official disapproval. One of them, founded in 1606 in Scrooby, Nottinghamshire, was particularly uneasy with the situation in England, and determined to seek relief in the more tolerant atmosphere of the Netherlands. Under its pastor, John Robinson (*ca.* 1575-1625), the congregation removed to Leiden, Holland, in 1609. There the Separatists found the freedom they desired but not the satisfaction. Worthwhile work was scarce, the children were growing up Dutch, and several members of the community broke away to join other bodies that had also found refuge in Holland. As a result, the Scrooby congregation began to look further afield and eventually cast their eyes on America. After securing sponsorship from London merchants, and after complicated and frustrating efforts in England to find provisions for the voyage, the group set sail—102 passengers

William Bradford

KEITH L. SPRUNGER

William Bradford (1590-1657) was a Pilgrim Father, governor of Plymouth Colony, and America's first historian. Born at Austerfield, Yorkshire in England, he early fell under radical Puritan influence. As a youth he withdrew from the parish church and joined a Separatist congregation at Scrooby (other members were Richard Clyfton, John Robinson, and William Brewster). Although he had only a modest elementary education, he eventually taught himself Greek, Latin, Hebrew, and other languages. In 1608 the Scrooby Separatists decided to emigrate to the Netherlands in search of religious freedom. They settled in the Dutch city of Leiden, where Bradford lived from 1609 to 1620 and where he earned his living in a textile workshop.

In 1620 Bradford joined the exodus to America on the Mayflower. These Pilgrim Fathers founded the colony of Plymouth. Bradford very soon was chosen governor of the colony, and was re-elected governor nearly every year until his death. He is respected for his skillful administration of Plymouth and also for his religious piety. The Separatist religion of the Plymouth settlers eventually merged with some other non-Separatist Puritans into the Congregationalist church.

Bradford is most remembered for his work as historian. His history, *Of Plymouth Plantation*, is a classic of seventeenth-century Puritan literature. It tells clearly the story of the founding of Plymouth, and it is the first history to refer to the Plymouth settlers as "pilgrims." Bradford enthusiastically described the events of his people in terms of the mighty sovereignty of God, and he relates many stories in which God intervened to bless the Pilgrims. The "marvelous providence of God" protected them. His providential view of early American history helped to give later Americans a confidence that they rested in God's all-wise hands.

and a crew of twenty-five—aboard the *May-flower* on September 6, 1620. Their destination was Virginia. But when they arrived instead off Cape Cod in early November, they decided to stay. Before they embarked, the male passengers put their names to a covenant, or compact, which pledged them to uphold the solidarity of the group and to forsake any thought of self-seeking license.

The first winter was brutal for the poorly prepared settlers. Although they did obtain corn from the Wampanoag Indians, relations with the Native Americans were uneasy. Half of the Pilgrims died. Unremitting toil, their sturdy faith in God, and inspiring leadership from Capt. Miles Standish, Elder William Brewster, and soon-to-be-governor William Bradford pulled them through to spring. Soon the Pilgrims adapted themselves to their new home, mastered the agricultural skills necessary for survival, and conscientiously repaid the debt owed to their English backers. The quiet, reserved life was under way which Plymouth maintained for the rest of its history until it was absorbed into Massachusetts in 1691. The colony did not grow rapidly. It numbered only three hundred in 1630 after

a decade in the New World. But it had shown that a migration motivated by faith could survive in "the howling wilderness."

We . . . Do . . . solemnly and mutually in the Presence of God and one another, covenant and combine ourselves together into a civil Body Politick, for our better Ordering and Preservation, and Furtherance of the Ends aforesaid; And by Virtue hereof do enact, constitute, and frame, such just and equal Laws, Ordinances, Acts, Constitutions, and Offices, from time to time, as shall be thought most meet and convenient for the general Good of the Colony; unto which we promise all due Submission and Obedience.

Mayflower Compact, 1620

History of Plymouth Plantation

On leaving Leiden:
So they left the goodly and pleasant city which had been their resting place near twelve years; but they knew they were pilgrims and looked not much on those things but lifted their eyes to the heavens, their dearest country, and quieted their spirits.

On arriving in New England:
Being thus passed the vast ocean, they had now no friends to welcome them, no inns to entertain or refresh their weather-beaten bodies, no houses or much less towns to repair to, to seek for succour. . . . And for the

season it was winter, and they that know the winters of that country know them to be sharp and violent and subject to cruel and fierce storms dangerous to travel to known places and more so to search an unknown coast. Besides what could they see but a hideous and desolate wilderness full of wild beasts and wild men.

On the first winter:
In two or three months half of their company died, especially in January and February, being the depth of winter, and wanting houses and other comforts, being affected with the scurvy and other diseases which this

Puritanism at Home

In England, meanwhile, the Puritan struggle went on, but under ever greater duress. James I was in many ways a poor figure of a king. He was pretentious about his modest intelligence, overbearing in person, and morally suspect. His son, Charles I, who succeeded to rule in 1625, led a much more admirable private life. To James' credit, however, he did possess a bit of his predecessor Elizabeth I's ability to conciliate and unify her subjects. This quality was conspicuous by its absence in his son. Charles I wished to be a monarch in the European grand style—ruling by divine right, reaching out to regulate the kingdom in its length and breadth.

If Charles had tried, he could not have taken actions and adopted policies more offensive to the Puritans. For example, in the very year he ascended the throne he married a Catholic, Henrietta Maria of France, and in so doing stirred the antipapal emotions which were always so strong among the Puritans. He also made William Laud (1573-1645) the dominant force in the church to the threefold displeasure of the Puritans.

Laud was an Arminian, a ritualist who reintroduced Catholic-appearing practices in worship, and a meddler who stuck his nose into the nooks and crannies where Puritans had placed their own. Charles, further, had little use for Parliament, particularly when it insisted upon defining its own privileges before considering the monarch's requests for money. Charles rapidly ran through three Parliaments (1625, 1626, 1628-1629), calling them into session when his funds were low, dismissing them when they overstepped what he considered their bounds. Finally, exasperated with "that noise," as Laud called Parliament, Charles determined to rule England by himself. To the chagrin of the Parliamentarians and their Puritan allies, he succeeded fairly well throughout the 1630s. Only his own misguided policy toward Scotland forced him to recall Parliament in 1640. And that action led eventually to Civil War and the rule of the Puritan Oliver Cromwell.

Given the state of affairs in the late 1620s, many Puritans began to think seriously about emigration. England seemed to be repudiating the Reformation. It seemed to be turning its back on the special role to which God had

long voyage and lack of accommodation had brought upon them, so as there died some two or three a day in the aforesaid time; that of one hundred and odd persons scarce fifty remained. And of these in the time of most distress there were but six or seven sound persons who to their great commendation be it spoken spared no pains night nor day but with abundance of toil and hazard of their own health, fetched them wood, made them fires, dressed them meat, made their beds, washed their loathsome clothes, clothed and unclothed them; in a word did all the homely and necessary offices for them which dainty and queasy stomachs cannot endure to hear named, and all this willingly and cheerfully without any grudging in the least.

On the entire enterprise:
Thus out of small beginnings greater things have been produced by His hand that made all things of nothing, and gives being to all things that are; and as one small candle may light a thousand, so the light here kindled hath shone to many, yea in some sort to our whole nation; let the glorious name of Jehovah have all the praise.

WILLIAM BRADFORD

The death warrant (1649) of King Charles I, signed by Cromwell (on the left, third from the top)
BILLY GRAHAM CENTER

called it. What would be the result? A gradual wasting away into sin and insignificance, or a cataclysmic outpouring of God's judgment? Perhaps the lofty goals of Puritan reform—for the church, for the individual, for society—could be achieved if only the weight of England could be left behind. Puritans knew about the dangers and hardship of colonization, but they also knew by the 1620s that colonization was not a pipe dream.

Oliver Cromwell (1559–1658)
BILLY GRAHAM CENTER

Some Puritans resisted all thought of emigration as abandoning the country in its hour of greatest need. Others, like Oliver Cromwell, seriously considered moving to the New World and only reluctantly decided to see the struggle in England through to the end. A substantial minority, however, finally concluded that migration to America was the best course. Such a move would preserve a godly remnant and perhaps even provide an example of fully realized reform for those who remained behind.

And so the migration began. In 1628 a group of congregationally inclined Puritans purchased a controlling interest in the New England Company; in 1629 the company reorganized to emphasize colonization and deemphasize commerce, and it obtained a new charter from the King; in 1630 more than 1,000 settlers embarked for Massachusetts Bay, including Governor John Winthrop and a dozen of the company's directors. In the next ten years some 20,000 more would make the same journey.

A few who joined the Puritan migration did so simply to make a new start—whether personal or economic—in the New World. Many others went because their friends or family were going. Even for these, however, religious motives were not absent. And such religious motives dominated the purposes of many, including the venture's most important leaders. With the Puritan migration, not only American church history but American history itself entered a new era.

Puritans and Historians

MARK A. NOLL

Only in the last century has "Puritan" become a synonym for joyless, repressive, and often hypocritical fanaticism. This interpretation arose during the Progressive Era of American history when so many intellectuals felt so confident about understanding the real roots of human behavior, which they deemed to be largely economic and psychological, and when they were hailing so surely the march of civilization from superstitious darkness to democratic light. The carnage of World War I, the moral crisis of the 1920s, and the economic collapse of the 1930s disabused most scholars of the idea that they were living in a new Golden Age. These shocks also created a climate in which the Puritans, who had understood something of human evil, the complexity of human existence, and the deeply engrained human longing for the divine, could be studied more objectively. Yet the popular image of Puritanism created by the Progressives lingers on. It is still possible to hear its echo, yet no one today has any good reason to be satisfied with H. L. Mencken's clever but woefully inadequate definition of a Puritan as "a person in constant dread that someone somewhere might be happy."

Early historians of America, like Thomas Hutchinson who wrote in the mid-eighteenth century, honored the Puritans as courageous pioneers who had labored to construct a freer world in a difficult environment. Although Hutchinson as the last royal governor of Massachusetts did not share the view, many in his day praised the Puritans for working toward the same kind of freedom from English tyranny that the patriots sought in the Revolutionary period. During the nineteenth century, American historians generally, and mistakenly, thought of the Puritans as early defenders of the liberty which loomed as such an important ideal in that century. The great George Bancroft noted Puritan intolerance of deviance but thought it inessential. In its essence, rather, "Puritanism was Religion struggling for the People. ... The fanatic for Calvinism was a fanatic for liberty."

Opinion turned against the Puritans in the late nineteenth century when America itself became more secular,

---

It is not easy to describe these people truthfully, yet with meaning to moderns. For the men of learning and women of gentle nurture who led a few thousand plain folk to plant a new England on ungrateful soil were moved by purposes utterly foreign to the present America. Their object was not to establish prosperity or prohibition, liberty or democracy, or indeed anything of currently recognized value. Their ideals were comprehended vaguely in the term puritanism, which nowadays has acquired various secondary and degenerate meanings. . . . My attitude toward seventeenth-century puritanism has passed through scorn and boredom to a warm interest and respect. The ways of the puritans are not my ways, and their faith is not my faith; nevertheless they appear to me a courageous, humane, brave, and significant people.

SAMUEL ELIOT MORISON
on the Puritans, 1930

less concerned about religion, and more enamored with the concept of moral progress. Brooks Adams could write in 1887 of The Emancipation of Massachusetts as the time when New England shucked off its Puritan heritage. Charles Francis Adams called the Puritan period an era of "utter intellectual aridity" (1896). And V. L. Parrington drew a telling contrast between earlier English Congregation-

---

Certainly many amenities of social life have increased in New England and in America, in direct proportion as Puritanism has receded. But while we congratulate ourselves upon these ameliorations, we cannot resist a slight fear that much of what has taken the place of Puritanism in our philosophies is just so much failure of nerve.

I assume that Puritanism was one of the major expressions of the Western intellect, that it achieved an organized synthesis of concepts which are fundamental to our culture, and that therefore it calls for the most serious examination.

PERRY MILLER
on the Puritans, 1938-1939

alism, "the robust and rebellious child of a great age," and later New England Puritanism, "the stunted offspring of a petty environment" (1927).

All this began to change in the late 1920s when a small group of scholars, mostly at Harvard, began out of curiosity to take another look at the Puritans. Their curiosity soon turned to respect. Samuel Eliot Morison described The Builders of the Bay Colony in 1930 as serious-minded religious individuals worthy of rewarding study. Kenneth Murdock performed the same service for the reputation of Increase Mather, once a symbol of Puritan narrowness. And, in a series of brilliant works, Perry Miller described Puritan theology as sophisticated, tough-minded, and durable.

In the wake of this new outlook, an avalanche of serious scholarship ensued until the best of the modern scholars, Edmund S. Morgan, foresaw the day when there would be more good books about the Puritans than there had been Puritans. Since the time of Morison, Murdock, and Miller, scholars have not neglected the weighty consequences of Puritan religion even as they study Puritans as economic, social, psychological, and political beings. Only the most uninformed would now repeat the error of the Progressives and think of the Puritans as insubstantial or contemptible.

Varieties of
American Christianity
Before the Great Awakening

By 1700, Quakers, Baptists, Presbyterians, and Catholics from England; Reformed Protestants from Germany and Holland; and smaller numbers from other continental religious groups had joined Puritans and Anglicans in the English colonies. A fact which we know, but they of course did not—that the diverse groups in the different colonies would one day form a single country—has often led historians of the United States to see greater similarities among the various Christian groups in colonial America than actually existed. There were common themes, but these had more to do with common origins in Europe than with common aspirations or practices in the New World. On at least one point, however, the traditional picture is correct. The Puritans were, in fact, the most dynamic Christian force in the colonies.

Puritans in America

Early New England included four Puritan colonies: quiet Plymouth and energetic Massachusetts Bay, which would merge in 1691; agrarian Connecticut and commercial New Haven, which Connecticut's new charter of 1662 joined into a single unit. New England also included a colony which accepted what the Puritans would not, the renegade Rhode Island. This last colony became a refuge for Roger Williams, Anne Hutchinson, and other Puritan outcasts, as well as for Quakers, Baptists, Jews, and many more. It was, depending upon one's point of view, a haven of liberty or a hotbed of lawlessness.

The Puritans wished to fulfill their original aspirations for England in the American colonies. They wanted to see a purified gospel applied to the lives of individuals. They wanted a complete reformation of the church.

They wanted society in all its expressions to glorify God. The American history of Puritanism is the story of how these goals—personal, church, social—complemented each other at first and then began to conflict.

In technical terms, Puritans saw their New World efforts as manifestations of covenant. As one of them summarized the essential elements, "The Covenant of Grace is cloathed with Church-covenant in a Political visible Church-way." In Puritan thinking, the basis for individual salvation was God's promise (i.e., covenant) that he would redeem those who placed faith in Christ. Puritans explained that promise as the outworking of a covenant within the Godhead whereby the Father chose those who would be saved, the Son accomplished their redemption, and the Spirit made it effective. They felt, furthermore, that the basis for a truly reformed church was the commitment of its members to God and to each other. In New England this commitment was expressed in the formal acceptance ("owning") of a written church covenant. Puritans also held that the basis for health in society was the promises which God had made to his covenanted people as a whole. Even before the Puritans arrived in America, Governor John Winthrop had explained the meaning of this social covenant in a memorable sermon on board ship, "A Model of Christian Charity."

Puritan spokesmen and many of the inhabitants in each colony saw life in these covenantal terms. Massachusetts, as the largest and most diverse colony, as well as the one with the greatest sustained contact with the Old World, felt the strains between different aspects of the covenant most sharply. Plymouth, particularly after the death of Bradford and others of the first generation, took its cues from Massachusetts. Connecticut, established in 1636 along the Connecticut River by emigrants from the Massachusetts towns of Newton, Watertown, and Dorchester, was from the first a "land of steady habits." Its early leaders, like the powerful minister Thomas Hooker (1586-1647), needed fewer explicit rules to maintain more of the Puritan ideal than the relatively more cosmopolitan Massachusetts.

The colony of New Haven arose from the efforts of the Rev. John Davenport and Theophilus Eaton, Esq., leaders of a group of Puritans from St. Stephen's Church, London, who came to the New World in 1637. The next year these St. Stephen's Puritans began settling Long Island Sound, first at the site of modern New Haven, and then at several other locations on both the Connecticut and New York sides of the Sound. New Haven was commercially aggressive, but under Davenport's ministry and Eaton's governorship, it was also the most self-consciously Puritan of all the colonies, where the "worde of God" was "the onely rule to be attended unto in ordering the affayres of government."

In each of the New England colonies except Rhode Island, leaders pursued the Puritan goals systematically. Ministers like Davenport, Hooker, and John Cotton (1584-1652) of Massachusetts proclaimed week-in and week-out a Reformed message of salvation and a biblical appeal to godliness. From the outset, Puritan churches were "gathered," as individuals pledged themselves to each other and to the demands of scripture. And governmental leaders worked

---

We Covenant with the Lord and one with an other; and doe bynd our selves in the presence of God, to walke together in all his waies, according as he is pleased to reveale himself unto us in his Blessed word of truth.

A Very Early Church Covenant, Salem, Massachusetts, 1629

to transform these outposts in the wilderness into genuine Bible Commonwealths.

American Puritans displayed their organizational genius in the way they combined their concerns for personal belief, ecclesiastical purity, and a godly social order. In the first years of settlement ministers and magistrates agreed on a somewhat more visible standard of conversion than had prevailed in England, where a willingness to tangle with the established church and the crown provided proof enough for a Puritan's spiritual state. In the New World, where such external religious enemies were scarce, a new stress was placed on internal spiritual realities as a criterion for church membership. Prospective members were asked not only to accept Puritan doctrines and to lead lives free from scandal—the regular requirements for church membership in the Old World even for Separatists like the Scrooby congregation—but also to testify before the assembled body that they had experienced a saving revelation of God's grace. Such a profession entitled the men to become freemen (or voters) as well as members of the church. Women, who regularly made up a majority of church members, did not vote in New England or anywhere else in the world during the seventeenth century. By this procedure—worked out most fully in Massachusetts and New Haven, but with only slight variations in Connecticut and Plymouth—Puritan leaders made the crucial covenants interlocking. The covenant of grace qualified a person for church membership and (for males) a voting role in the colony's public life. This public life fulfilled the social covenant with God, since freemen selected rulers and accepted laws that honored God's written word. And the church covenant linked converted individuals and the social enterprise without interposing the burdensome church-state machinery which Archbishop Laud and his colleagues had employed in England to the Puritans' great displeasure.

New England was not, thus, a theocracy. Its ministers did not rule. However often they were consulted on policy matters, it was extraordinarily rare for a minister to have any official position in government. New England was, rather, the scene of a singular social and ecclesiastical experiment which historians have called Nonseparating Congregationalism. New England was Congregational; its leaders established the form of church government in which local assemblies selected their own officers and governed their own affairs. Yet New England was also Nonseparating. The local congregations were not to go their own way, but were to unite together through their elected magistrates to promote good order and godliness throughout the colony. It was only natural for the magistrates to regulate external religious behavior and to mediate religious controversies.

Under this general system the first generation of New England Puritans achieved considerable success. In Massachusetts, Governor Winthrop and other investors in the Massachusetts Bay Company voluntarily reinterpreted the terms of the charter in 1630 in order to make male church members eligible to vote for colonial officers (thus, freemen). Winthrop was not entirely pleased when the freemen demanded representation for their own towns (1634) and when they insisted upon a separate legislative chamber (1644) to balance the governor and the more aristocratic executive council, whom freemen also elected. Still, he presided over a government which was, by the standards of its day, marked by a high degree of popular support. Estimates on the proportion of eligible males actually participating range from one-fourth to one-half, in all events considerably higher than the England of the seventeenth century. Much more importantly to the Puritans, this government continued to implement biblical standards in its regulation of society and promotion of the churches.

New England leaders seized upon the uncertainties of the 1640s in the mother country to clarify the nature of their church order. When Presbyterianism seemed to be gaining the upper hand among English Puritans during the early days of their country's Civil War, and when dissatisfied New Englanders appealed to Parliament for freedom from the rule of the Bible Commonwealth, New World Puritans responded by spelling out the New England Way in detail. The Cambridge Platform of 1648, which endorsed the doctrinal parts of the English Westminster Confession of 1646, supplied a full rationale for the Congregationalism of New England.

The New England Puritans, with matters in church and in state settled pretty much as they desired, turned swiftly to the reconstruc-

tion of culture on a biblical model. The concern for education, which English Puritans had cultivated so actively, took root immediately in America. In 1636 the Massachusetts General Court (legislature) voted to establish a college. In 1638 when a recently arrived single minister died of tuberculosis and bequeathed half his estate and his four hundred-volume library to the fledgling venture, it actually got under way. The minister's name was John Harvard, and the college eventually became one of the world's great universities.

The things which are requisite to be found in all church members, are, Repentance *from sin, &* faith *in Jesus Christ. And therfore these are the things wherof men are to be examined, at their admission into the church & which then they must profess & hold forth in such sort, as may satisfie* rationall charity *that the things are there indeed. . . .*

Magistrates, have powr to call a Synod, by calling to the Churches to send forth their Elders & other messengers, to counsel & assist them in matters of religion: but yett the constituting of a Synod, is a church act, & may be transacted by the churches, even when civil magistrates may be enemyes to churches and to church assemblyes.

Church-government stands in no opposition to civil government of common-welths, . . . wheras the contrary is most true, that they may both stand together & flourish the one being helpfull unto the other, in their distinct & due administrations. . . .

Cambridge Platform,
1648

Massachusetts leaders did not neglect lower levels of education either. In 1642 the General Court mandated fines for local authorities who failed to insure that children could "read & understand the principles of religion & the capitall lawes of this country." In 1647 it noted that "yᵉ ould deluder, Satan," discouraged learning in order "to keepe men from the knowledge of yᵉ Scriptures," and ordered each town of fifty households or more to appoint a teacher for its children. Puritan communities did not always follow through in beginning such schools, but in general they made startling progress in educating the populace. By the mid-eighteenth century, New England as a whole was one of the most literate regions in the whole world.

The Puritans soon set up a printing press as well. In 1640 the first volume came from the press which, like the college, was established in Cambridge, Massachusetts: *THE WHOLE BOOKE OF PSALMES Faithfully TRANSLATED into ENGLISH Metre, Whereunto is prefixed a discourse declaring not only the lawfullnes, but also the necessity of the heavenly Ordinance of singing Scripture Psalmes in the Churches of God*. This "Bay Psalm Book" was the firstfruits of the learning that would distinguish New England for much of its history.

The first generation of American Puritans achieved remarkable success. They had foiled their enemies in England, they had accomplished many of their goals in New England, they had begun to establish godly Commonwealths. The one enemy they could not defeat was time.

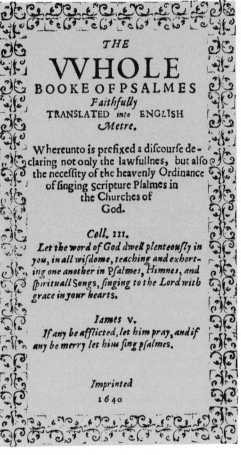

The Bay Psalm Book was the first book published in America NEW YORK PUBLIC LIBRARY

John Winthrop

KEITH L. SPRUNGER

John Winthrop (1588-1649), born in Suffolk, England, was the first governor of Massachusetts Bay Colony and one of the leading citizens of early New England. In England he attended Cambridge University briefly, studied law at Gray's Inn, London, and became an attorney before returning home as lord of the family manor at Groton. The Winthrops were Puritans, and as King Charles I and Archbishop Laud thrust ceremonial Anglicanism upon the country, John Winthrop nearly despaired about the future of religion. He greatly feared that "God will bring some heavy affliction upon this land, and that speedily." Like many other Puritans, Winthrop weighed the pros and cons of immigration to America.

He decided to go, and joined the Massachusetts Bay Company, which began colonization in 1629. While in London, Winthrop was elected the first governor of the company and sailed to America on the ship Arbella in 1630. He settled at Boston; until his death nineteen years later, he served nearly every year as governor or deputy governor of Massachusetts Colony.

Under Winthrop's direction, the Puritan migration to America exhibited a spirit of deep Christian mission. Although some of the settlers undoubtedly operated from material motives, Winthrop kept alive the vision that the founding of America was part of God's plan for his kingdom. While sailing over on the Arbella, Governor Winthrop preached a lay sermon, "A Modell of Christian Charity" (1630), which outlined a Puritan religious and political program. It was one of the first, and perhaps the best, statements about America's moral mission in the world.

Transforming the vision into fact was not easily done. Church and state were intricately connected in Massachusetts Bay, and Governor Winthrop felt a responsibility to see both firmly established. In Winthrop's view of politics, both church and state were founded upon the consent of the people. The Massachusetts Puritans were Congregationalists, and they based the church upon the voluntary consent of Christians joining together by a church covenant. Every town established its own church. The Massachusetts Congregationalists drew upon the inspiration of non-Separatist English Puritan theologians like William Ames, Henry Jacob, and William Bradshaw. Winthrop sought religious advice from Ames on behalf of the Massachusetts Bay Company and invited him to come to America with

John Winthrop (1588–1649) AMERICAN ANTIQUARIAN SOCIETY

them. Ames declined to immigrate. The American Congregationalists, although drawing off by themselves into purified congregations, declared that they were not officially separating from the Church of England. They claimed not to be Separatists.

Government, like the church, was also dependent on the consent of the people, Winthrop believed. Government worked in cooperation with the church for the people's "mutual safety and welfare." Nevertheless, Winthrop was no democrat. Under the Massachusetts system of government, only Congregational church members could be freemen or voters and the elected magistrates, people like Winthrop, were to have a final authority. In this way, Winthrop hoped to balance the two goals of liberty and authority. When troublesome dissenters, like Roger Williams and Anne Hutchinson, upset that balance, Winthrop supported their expulsion from the colonies. To the day of his death he gave himself to the building of a truly Puritan commonwealth in the New World.

John Winthrop's Sermon Aboard the Arbella

For the persons, we are a Company professing ourselves fellow members of Christ. . . .

For the work we have in hand, it is by a mutual consent through a special overruling providence, and a more than an ordinary approbation of the Churches of Christ to seek out a place of Cohabitation and Consortship under a due form of Government both civil and ecclesiastical. . . .

The end is to improve our lives to do more service to the Lord, the comfort and increase of the body of Christ whereof we are members, that ourselves and posterity may be the better preserved from the Common corruptions of this evil world to serve the Lord and work out our Salvation under the power and purity of his holy Ordinances. . . .

Thus stands the cause between God and us, we are entered into Covenant with him for this work, we have taken out a Commission, the Lord hath given us leave to draw our own Articles, we have professed to enterprise these Actions upon these and these ends, we have hereupon besought him of favour and blessing. Now if the Lord shall please to hear us, and bring us in peace to the place we desire, then hath he ratified this Covenant and sealed our Commission, and will expect a strict performance of the Articles contained in it, but if we shall neglect the observation of these Articles, which are the ends we have propounded, and dissembling with our God, shall . . . embrace this present world and prosecute our carnal intentions, seeking great things for ourselves and our posterity, the Lord will surely break out in wrath against us, be revenged of such a perjured people, and make us know the price of the breach of such a Covenant.

Now the only way to avoid this shipwracke and to provide for our posterity is to follow the Counsel of Micah, to do Justly, to love mercy, to walk humbly with our God. For this end, we must be knit together in this work as one man, . . . we must be willing to abridge ourselves of our superfluities, for the supply of others' necessities, . . . we must delight in each other, make others Conditions our own, rejoice together, mourn together, labour, and suffer together, allways having before our eyes our Commission and Community in the work, our Community as members of the same body, so shall we keep the unity of the Spirit in the bond of peace, the Lord will be our God and delight to dwell among us, as his own people and will command a blessing upon us in all our ways, so that we shall see more of his wisdom, power, goodness, and truth than formerly we have been acquainted with, we shall find that the God of Israel is among us, when ten of us shall be able to resist a thousand of our enemies, when he shall make us a praise and glory, that men shall say of succeeding plantations: the Lord make it like that of New England: for we must Consider that we shall be as a City upon a Hill, the eyes of all people are upon us; so that if we shall deal falsely with our God in this work we have undertaken and so cause him to withdraw his present help from us, we shall be made a story and a byword through the world, we shall open the mouths of enemies to speak evil of the ways of God's worthy servants, and cause their prayers to be turned into Curses upon us till we be consumed out of the good land whither we are going. . . . Beloved, there is now set before us life and good, death and evil, in that we are Commanded this day to love the Lord our God, and to love one another, to walk in his ways, and to keep his Commandments and his Ordinance, and his laws, and the Articles of our Covenant with him that we may live and be multiplied, and that the Lord our God may bless us in the land whither we go to possess it. But if our hearts shall turn away so that we will not obey, but shall be seduced and worship other Gods, our pleasures, and profits, and serve them; it is propounded unto us this day, we shall surely perish out of the good Land whither we pass over this vast Sea to possess it.

Therefore, let us choose life, that we, and our Seed, may live; by obeying his voice, and cleaving to him for he is our life, and our prosperity.

"A *Modell of Christian Charity*," 1630

Puritans and Sacred Places

JAMES P. WALSH

Mircea Eliade, historian of religion, characterizes the religious person as one for whom space is never homogeneous, for whom some places must be holier than others. The New England Puritans shared this characteristic, but they shared too an allegiance with Reformed Protestantism, which rejected the possibility that certain places could be holier than others.

Reacting against the Catholic and Anglican custom of distinguishing between sacred and profane space, the Puritans argued that "under the New Testament all places ... are equally holy." The Puritans frequently translated this belief into practice. They built meetinghouses, for example, according to the "Protestant Plain Style" of architecture. Within the meetinghouse, the Puritans avoided a central sacred space such as the altar occupied in traditional churches. Early meetinghouses did without a permanently placed communion table, and the Puritans further diffused the spatial focus of the Lord's Supper by having communicants consume the bread and wine in their pews. The Puritans also frustrated attempts by other, more traditional Englishmen to create consecrated space in New England. When the settlers at Merry-

mount raised a maypole as part of a ritual designed to transform Indian soil to Christian, the Puritans hewed down the pole and renamed its site Mount Dagon (after the idol of the Old Testament Philistines).

But even as the Puritans attempted to create a space of homogeneous sanctity in New England, they accepted certain areas as holier than others. Puritans sought out private places of worship where, they assumed, prayer was more effective than elsewhere. Cotton Mather prayed so intensely in his study that it became for him an "axis mundi," an opening between Heaven and Earth. Not only did Mather receive an angelic visit in the study and hear there the voice of God, he also learned from a possessed girl that although her devils could go freely in the house, they dared not enter his study.

In similar fashion, the Puritans sanctified the space within which they worshipped together. They could accept only one site as appropriate for a meetinghouse and that was at the "center" of settlement. The Puritans actually tried to create perfectly square or circular towns in New England so that the meetinghouse would stand "at the center of the wholl cir-

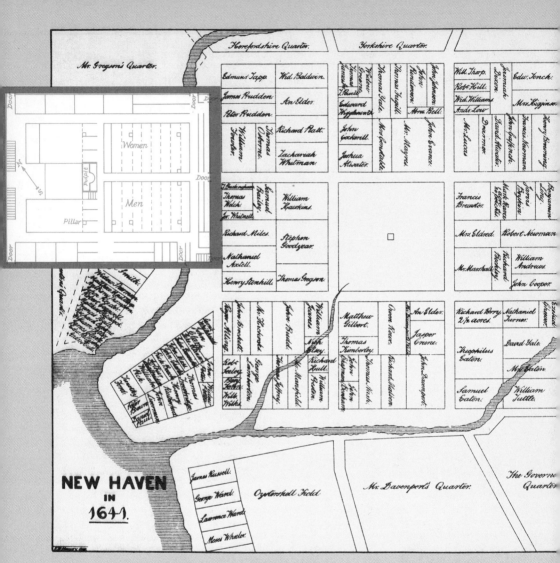

The town plan of New Haven in 1644 shows the meetinghouse in the center of the community. The inset shows the interior plan of the original New Haven meetinghouse. NEW YORK PUBLIC LIBRARY INSET: YALE UNIVERSITY LIBRARY

cumferance." Most towns, however, were so misshapen and their residential patterns so irregular that the Puritans could never have calculated the point most accessible to all, nor did they even try. The Puritans did not determine the center of settlement by considerations of convenience, but by forces of personal and collective influence. In Milford, Connecticut, for example, the meetinghouse was erected in the midst of a group from Hertfordshire, England, who had remained bound together as neighbors despite having thrice emigrated from place to place. Other Milford residents, equal to the Hertfordshire group in wealth and incidence of church membership, found themselves more than eight hundred yards from the meetinghouse but consented to its location. In Boston, the first meetinghouse was located next to Gov. John Winthrop's home because Winthrop's combination of social, political, and even religious authority made his residence the "center" of town.

Indeed, the Puritans described New England as a sacred place of refuge, an image that English Puritans considered blasphemous. This Puritan tendency to mark off certain space as especially holy must be reconciled with the Puritan commitment to Reformed theology. It must be assumed that if the Puritans themselves felt no contradiction, there was none. The Puritans held together what now seem to be opposing concepts of space because they apprehended space on two distinct levels. The Puritans shaped a space of homogeneous sanctity on the level of ideology, which certainly influenced Puritan life to a considerable degree. But it did not do so totally. The Puritans also apprehended space as an "everyday reality," to borrow a phrase from sociologist Peter Berger, and on this level the Puritans sanctified space unequally. Because the special sanctity of certain places presented itself to the Puritans as a "natural" phenomenon, it needed no analysis. The Puritans, therefore, could remain consistently Reformed even while they believed and behaved in ways that marked them as even more religious than they realized.

The Half-Way Covenant

The principal difficulty of the New England Way occurred among the children. Increasingly, sons and daughters of first-generation settlers failed to experience the marks of conversion, as that first generation had defined the experience. Consequently, fewer and fewer of the second generation presented themselves for church membership. This was bad enough. Leaders foresaw a shrinking pool of church members, a declining number of freemen, and the gradual drying up of the Puritan enterprise. Even worse were prospects for the third generation. If a husband and wife of the second generation did not present themselves for church membership on the basis of conversion, they at least were under the keeping of the church and commonwealth. By virtue of their baptism, they had been taken into a covenant relationship with the Puritan institutions. But what of their children? Were third-generation youngsters to remain unbaptized? Were they no different in fact from pagan Indians and the minority of the English who spurned all religion?

In the face of this crisis, which affected every aspect of the New England Way—personal faith, church membership, the Puritan society—leaders proposed an ingenious expedient. They decided, as Perry Miller put it, "Damned or saved, the children had to be made subject to the watch and ward of the church, or the Bible commonwealth was ruined." Meeting as a Synod in 1662, New England ministers proposed what later historians have called the Half-Way Covenant. Under this plan, baptized individuals of good behavior could present their own children for baptism, but neither they nor their children

---

The children of Church-members are members of the Church as well as their parents, and do not cease to be members by becoming adult, but do still continue in the Church, untill in some way of God they be cast out; and . . . they are subject to Church-discipline, even as other members, and may have their children baptized before themselves be received to the Lords Supper; and yet that in this way there is no tendency to the corrupting of the Church by unworthy members, or of the Ordinances by unworthy partakers.

Half-Way Covenant, 1662

could take the Lord's Supper unless they made a personal profession of faith. The framers of the Half-Way Covenant wished to preserve both the integrity of the local churches as the gatherings of the elect and the participation of as many people as possible in the Puritan system.

The new adjustment had mixed success. Many laypeople and a few ministers rejected it as a dilution of the faith. Other ministers, especially along the Connecticut River in western Massachusetts and central Connecticut, wished to go further toward a parish system in which all inhabitants could receive baptism, and even take the Lord's Supper. Solomon Stoddard (1643-1729), Jonathan Edwards' grandfather who pastored the Congregational church at Northampton, Massachusetts, for fifty-seven years, advocated this position under the conviction that the Lord's Supper was a "converting ordinance" which could help the sincere seeker find true faith. Still others employed the Half-Way system to maintain the balance between the first generation's heart-felt faith and the later generations' desire to preserve a unified society.

Contemporaries and historians alike have differed greatly in their evaluation of this sys-

A *romanticized nineteenth-century view of a stalwart Puritan couple on their way to church*
BILLY GRAHAM CENTER

tem. Some took it to be a step to religious formalism, others a step toward society-wide renewal. Some thought it weakened Puritan theology, by emphasizing the rights of the unregenerate to baptism; some thought it strengthened that theology, by scrupulously preserving the lofty standard of regeneration for the Lord's Supper. However one judges these matters, it is probably safe to conclude that Puritans were victims of their own history. Traumatic experiences in England had fostered heightened standards of spirituality which Puritan emigrants carried to the New World. There, however, dangers came more from a harsh environment than from evil bishops or a scheming ruler. Members of the second and third generations may in fact have been devout, but their steady-state religious experiences were no match for the dramatic crises of the founders. Later New Englanders may have been as thoroughly converted as their forebears, but the circumstances of such conversions were certainly different. These differences, as well as a possible loss of religious zeal, were the final causes of the Half-Way system.

The call to church in colonial New England
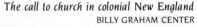
BILLY GRAHAM CENTER

Declension?

Debate over the Half-Way Covenant was only one indication of a general feeling that the Puritan New England of the last third of the seventeenth century had fallen off from the vigorous Puritanism of the preceding thirty years. A Puritan of 1700 looking back over the previous three decades could indeed have noted many marks of a frowning providence. In 1675 and 1676 a vicious war with Indians under the Wampanoag chief King Philip left several thousand colonists dead and more than half the towns of Plymouth and Massachusetts destroyed or damaged. In 1676 and 1679 great fires ravaged Boston. In 1685 all New England colonies, as well as New York and New Jersey, lost their representative assemblies, and suffered until 1689 in the Dominion of New England, a short-lived effort by the short-reigned James II to corral his colonies. When William and Mary replaced James in 1688 through England's Glorious Revolution, they gave back only part of New England's traditional rights: Massachusetts' new charter of 1691 provided for a royally appointed governor and made voting a function of property rather than church membership. In 1692 the Massachusetts village of Salem experienced a shattering wave of hysteria over witchcraft which left remorse and confusion in its wake. In 1699 leading Boston merchants established a new church on Brattle Street which consciously emphasized its differences with Puritan traditions. By 1700 as well, more Baptists and Quakers had made New England home, more wealthy women seemed to be swarming for London fashions, and many stalwarts of society seemed more concerned about wealth than worship.

Some of the Puritan ministers certainly felt that decay had set in. In 1679 Massachusetts ministers met in a Reforming Synod to note "that God hath a controversy with his New-England People." They detailed the spiritual causes of God's displeasure (e.g., "a great and visible decay of the power of Godliness among many Professors in these Churches," "much Sabbath-breaking," "Sinful Heats and Hatreds"). And they called on magistrates, ministers, and laypeople for "a thorough and heart Reformation," and prayed for God to "pour down his Spirit from on High."

But was there real declension? At the same time that ministers called for repentance only the barest handful of New Englanders questioned traditional Puritan convictions. Towns, except during the Indian War or when beset by natural disasters, were remarkably peaceful and stable. The New England governments were unusually responsive to the needs of the people. And while great wealth was rare, New England enjoyed considerable sufficiency.

Certainly Puritanism was changing as it entered the eighteenth century. New England was not as compact, either geographically or ideologically, as it had been during the founders' generation. Both the Half-Way Covenant and changes in government had weakened the links among personal Christianity, church membership, and a godly society. The fervor of the founders was also increasingly rare. Yet the Puritans may have been too harsh on themselves. They were not the same in 1700 as they had been in 1630, and the achievements of Winthrop, Cotton, Hooker, and Davenport could not be repeated. Yet the New England of 1700 was a stable land where many indeed could still be found who honored the same God as the forebears, in much the same way, with at least some of the same zeal.

New England Dissent and the Baptists

Puritanism dominated New England for its first century, but not without opposition. From the first, a few early settlers such as Thomas Morton, who insisted on setting up a maypole and pursuing other frivolities at Mt. Wollaston near Plymouth, wanted nothing to do with Puritanism whatsoever. More potent disagreement came from within the Puritans' own ranks or from groups that shared their spiritual heritage. In the first decade of settlement, two of the most capable of the Puritans' own members arose to question the foundations of the Bible Commonwealth. Anne Hutchinson's complaint touched the heart of Puritan theology, Roger Williams' the effort to apply that theology in the world. When the first Quakers arrived in 1656, Massachusetts would have to deal with another systematic affront to Puritan rule. Well before then, however, a Baptist challenge was securely lodged in New England.

ILL
NEWES
FROM
NEW-ENGLAND:
OR
A Narative of *New-Englands*
PERSECUTION.
WHERIN IS DECLARED

That while old *England* is becoming new,
New-England is become Old.

Alſo four Propoſals to the Honoured Parliament and Councel of State, touching the way to *Propagate the Goſpel of Chriſt* (with ſmall charge and great ſafety) both in Old *England* and New.

Alſo four concluſions touching the faith and order of the Goſpel of Chriſt out of his laſt Will and Teſtiment, confirmed and juſtified

By JOHN CLARK Phyſician of Rode Iſland in *America*.

> *Revel.* 2. 25. *Hold faſt till I come.*
> 3. 11. *Behod I come quickly.*
> 22. 20. *Amen, even ſo come Lord Jeſus.*

LONDON,

Printed by *Henry Hills* living in *Fleet-Yard* next door to the *Roſe* and *Crown,* in the year 1 6 5 2.

John Clark's account of New England Puritan intolerance was published in Cromwell's Puritan commonwealth.

The Baptists were themselves offshoots of English Puritanism. The Separatist John Smyth (died 1612) had emigrated to Holland at about the same time as the Scrooby Pilgrims. There he came to accept the practice of Dutch Mennonites who baptized adults upon their own confession of faith. Some of Smyth's followers established the first Baptist congregation in England near London in 1612.

In America, Baptists appeared soon after the founding of Massachusetts. Roger Williams helped organize immigrant English and Welsh into America's first Baptist church in 1639, although he himself remained a Baptist for only a few months. 1639 was also the year in which John Clarke, the most important Baptist in early America, arrived in Rhode Island to establish the town of Newport near Williams' Providence. Clarke and his like-minded associates quickly carried Baptist ideas into Plymouth and then Massachusetts itself. Although the Baptists shared common roots with the Puritans, they also differed in several significant ways, differences which Puritans perceived as subverting their entire effort. Baptists refused to let the state play any role in the church. They held that believers should maintain their own churches voluntarily and not rely on the state or any other external support. And they be-

Having bought truth dear, we must not sell it cheap — not the least grain of it for the whole world.

ROGER WILLIAMS,
The Bloody Tenent of Persecution, 1644

lieved that baptism should be reserved for those who could make a self-conscious confession of faith.

Baptists gained a significant convert in 1654 when the president of Harvard College, Henry Dunster (1609-1659), refused to have his fourth child baptized and publicly criticized the baptism of infants. About the same time Clarke gained a hearing in England when he published a tract detailing the Baptists' difficulties in the New World, *Ill Newes from New-England; Or A Narrative of New-Englands Persecution* (1652). Except in Rhode Island, Baptists would suffer official disabilities of one sort or another throughout New England until the American Revolution. And then it would not be until 1833 that the Massachusetts legislature would do away with the last vestiges of the established church, a goal which Baptist dissenters had pursued for nearly two centuries.

Anne Hutchinson

EDWIN S. GAUSTAD

Mother of some fifteen children, wife of a successful businessman, midwife and nurse, and yet Anne Hutchinson survives in American history for none of these reasons. She survives because of her brilliant intellect, her bold spirit, and her steady courage. Those qualities aroused so much fear and opposition in Massachusetts as to force the expulsion of an English woman from an English colony.

Born in Lincolnshire, England in 1591, young Anne moved with her family to London in 1605. Upon her marriage to William Hutchinson in 1612, she returned to her birthplace where she began to raise her large family and where she matured theologically under the ministrations of the leading Puritan preacher in Lincolnshire, John Cotton. When England's mounting pressures against Puritanism

Anne Hutchinson (1591–1642)
BROWN BROTHERS

tence in the business of saving poor, weak, sinful men and women. Salvation was by grace and not by works: all were agreed on that point. And yet, were works totally irrelevant to this cosmic act of redemption? Could one not (at least) help prepare him- or herself for the arrival of that saving grace? And if saved, did not one inevitably "show forth good works" as evidence to all of his or her salvation?

Puritanism survived for so long by holding so much in tension, by following fundamental premises thus far, not too far. Also, Puritanism survived by moving swiftly against those determined to pursue the extremes. As Hutchinson gathered dozens, then scores, of eager or perplexed listeners to her home for "explication" of John Cotton's sermons, she unfolded too much. Yes, salvation is of God and not of man: thus, altogether of God and not at all of man. Men and women can do nothing to prepare for it; men and women can do nothing to demonstrate that they have it. Works were filthy rags.

All this proved most unsettling to a colony hardly begun, to a colony set upon a grand errand but also set upon by enemies at home and abroad. If the elect were no more moral than the nonelect, if religion were not (in some way) tied to morality, then whence stability or even survival for that city supposedly set upon a hill? Christians must be exemplars of God's moral law, not skeptics or (God forbid) even opponents — antinomians — of that law.

Anne Hutchinson stood firm in her convictions or remained stubborn in her perversities, depending upon one's point of view. In 1637 she was summoned before the colony's General Court for encouraging erroneous opinions, conducting unauthorized meetings, and insulting the clergy. The trial stumbled between absurdity and farce, saved at last only by the defendant's incriminating volubility. Hutchinson spoke at length of her "immediate revelations" from God.

forced Cotton to leave for the New World, Anne Hutchinson persuaded her husband that they should sail as well. Within a year, they too had become part of the Great Migration.

In Boston, Anne Hutchinson soon affiliated with the church now led by Cotton, assisted women in their illnesses and the delivery of children, and reveled in Cotton's emphasis upon God's initiative and omnipo-

Bad enough to be an antinomian, but now an enthusiast too. Persons who claimed that God spoke directly to them, not only via scripture, were fanatics potentially beyond the control of all authority, deluded subversives beyond the endurance of all reasonable men.

Banished by the court, Hutchinson a few months later was excommunicated from the church whose doctrines she thought to elaborate and defend. Along with her family and a large number of supporters, she made her way in 1638 to the island of Aquid-neck in Rhode Island — a colony recently formed because of another expulsion for religious opinions, those of Roger Williams. Four years later, following the death of her husband in 1642, Anne Hutchinson and six younger children moved into the Dutch colony of New Netherlands (into what is now Westchester County). A year later she and all but one of her children were slain by Indians. Nearby a river and a parkway bear her name, a token at least of a spirit which would not surrender.

Roger Williams
EDWIN S. GAUSTAD

A native of England, a graduate of Cambridge University, a minister of the Church of England, Roger Williams (1603?-1683) arrived in the New World in 1631. Williams was warmly welcomed in Boston, for "godly ministers" were few in the young Bay Colony. He was promptly invited to occupy the pulpit of Boston's only church, but he declined because of his growing uneasiness over the relationship between the local churches in New England and the National Church of Old England. Was Boston's church part of or separate from that official established Church which the Puritans had left behind? Some thought yes, some no, and still others clung to a middle position between complete separation and complete identification.

Williams answered that there was no such middle ground. One had to make a clear choice between establishment on the one hand and separation on the other. "This middle walking is no less than halting," he wrote, adding the query: How can a man "walk with an even foot between two extremes?" Everything which Puritanism stood for, Williams argued, demanded "a separation of holy from unholy, penitent from impenitent, godly from ungodly." Trying to stand on some hypothetical middle ground was, he argued, like trying to build a square house on the keel of a ship; the resulting structure will never be a "soul-saving true ark or church of Christ Jesus."

Other elements of the Massachusetts Bay Colony also troubled Williams. He discovered that his fellow Christians had simply taken over land belonging to the Indians: they had neither bought it nor traded for it — they simply took it. Massachusetts elders responded that they had the land by charter rights bestowed by King Charles I. And who, replied Williams, had given the land to Charles? Since no one had done so, the land clearly still belonged to the Indians and would continue to belong to them until the settlers — no, trespassers — properly paid for it.

One further anxiety, and in the long

run the most fundamental of all, disturbed Williams' ever restless soul.
The civil order in New England (as in
Old) exercised authority over the
ecclesiastical order. Yet, in Williams'
view, the former had no authority
whatever over the latter. The state can
preserve law and order, but it
cannot — it must not — interfere with
religious beliefs or opinions. In the
whole history of mankind, most of the
bloody chapters have been written
by nations using force in matters
of religion. Nothing is more absurd,

Williams wrote, than "the setting up of
civil power and officers to judge the
conviction of men's souls." The
absurdity is especially evident when
the state demands this particular
religious opinion today, then tomorrow or the next year or the next
century it demands with equal force
an altogether different doctrine. "It
has been England's sinful shame
to fashion and change [her] garments
and religions with wondrous ease, as a
higher power or a stronger sword has
prevailed."

For the Massachusetts authorities,
the limits of endurance had been
reached. Williams had accused their
churches of being impure, their title to
land invalid, and their enforced religious conformity bloody and absurd.
Clearly this zealot could be tolerated
no longer. In a formal trial, Roger
Williams was found guilty of spreading
"diverse new and dangerous
opinions." When Williams refused to
recant or change his mind, he was
ordered "to depart out of this
jurisdiction."

Thus exiled from Massachusetts,
Williams, leaving behind a wife and
small child, walked southward "in the
bitter winter season" (January 1636)
through an Indian-dominated wilderness. For fourteen weeks he wandered
"sorely tossed, not knowing what
bread or bed did mean." Finally, he
came to the headwaters of Narragan-
sett Bay where he purchased some
land from the Indians. And his new
settlement was named Providence, "in
a sense of God's merciful providence
to me in my distress." Thus the colony
of Rhode Island and Providence Plantations came into being.

Roger Williams lived in Rhode
Island the remainder of his life, fighting for a secure charter for the colony,
writing treatises on the Indians, on
theology, and on religious liberty, and
above all continuing to wrestle within
himself over basic spiritual questions.
He died in 1683, in retirement and
in poverty, the exact day of his death,
like that of his birth, unknown.

Statue of *Roger Williams* (1603?–1683) *in* U.S. *Capitol*
BAPTIST JOINT COMMITTEE ON PUBLIC AFFAIRS

Obadiah Holmes and His Testimony

Obadiah Holmes (*ca.* 1607-1682) migrated from England to Massachusetts in 1638. He became a Baptist in 1649 and moved to Rhode Island in 1651. That same year he returned to Massachusetts to console an elderly Baptist and to speak of his faith. For his pains he was haled before the Boston court, convicted of promoting Anabaptism, and whipped in public. As an old man, Holmes wrote a testimony of his faith (1675). It is a unique record from an ordinary person of the convictions which, while similar in many respects to the Puritans', led some beyond all forms of established church life to the Baptist faith.

I believe there is no salvation but by Him alone, no other Name under heaven by which man can be saved. . . .

I believe none has power to choose salvation or to believe in Christ, for life is the gift only of God. . . .

I believe that the true baptism of the Gospel is a visible believer with his own consent being baptized in common water by dipping, or, as it were, drowned to hold forth death, burial, resurrection, by a messenger of Jesus into the name of the Father, Son and Holy Spirit. . . .

For this faith and profession I stand and have sealed the same with my blood at Boston in New England, and hope through the strength of my Lord to be able to witness the same to death.

The Church of England

The story of Anglicanism in colonial America is really two stories: the progress of the established Church of England in Virginia from earliest settlement, and a much more freewheeling competition with Puritan Congregationalists, Presbyterians, and other denominations to the north from the late seventeenth century.

In Virginia

It has been traditional to paint the picture of Anglicanism in colonial Virginia with dark colors, "the dissolute dregs of the English clergy" in "unregulated colonial parishes," as one historian exaggerates for effect. Historians have not always liked the New England Puritans, but they have acknowledged their industry, zeal, and seriousness. By contrast, they have been slow to say anything good about the Church of England in Virginia.

It is indeed true that the Church of England experienced unique difficulties in Virginia. Anglicanism was the established church in that colony, informally under the early charters of the Virginia Company, formally under the Royal Charter of 1624. And it became the established church in the Carolinas and Georgia when these colonies were founded, in Maryland after 1691, and in parts of New York City after 1693. Yet the American establishment was as much a burden as a blessing. It had the debits of the English establishment (a tendency to formalism, a susceptibility to governmental domination, and a marked talent for offending Nonconformists) without the credits (episcopal oversight, a sense of cohesion, and parish-wide popular participation). American Anglicans never did have a resident bishop during the colonial period. This lack forced ministerial candidates to sail to England for ordination, prevented proper confirmations, and weakened the church's stance against other centers of power.

The Church of England had more than organizational problems, however, for Virginia culture was, at best, a sore trial to organized religion. Settlement of the colony in

Above: "The Plantation," ca. 1825, artist unknown; below: two series of drawings illustrating methods of transporting and curing tobacco ABOVE: THE METROPOLITAN MUSEUM OF ART, GIFT OF EDGAR WILLIAM AND BERNICE CHRYSLER GARBISCH, 1963 BELOW: ARENTS COLLECTION, NEW YORK PUBLIC LIBRARY

plantations along the rivers which penetrated the Tidewater dispersed the population and created huge parishes (averaging 550 sq. mi. in 1724) with little natural sense of community. The cultivation of tobacco, the early turn to black slaves for labor, and a passion for exploiting natural resources all worked to create a value system that made "looking out for number one" a way of life. The historian who applied this modern phrase to colonial Virginia, T. H. Breen, has summarized well that colony's cultural values: "Virginians transformed an extreme form of individualism, a value system suited to soldiers and adventurers, into a set of regional virtues, a love of independence, an insistence upon personal liberty, a cult of manhood, and an uncompromising loyalty to family." In such a setting the Church of England labored against long odds.

From the first as well, governmental officials at all levels were reluctant to allow the church very much freedom. In 1643 the House of Burgesses (the legislature) gave local vestries (lay trustees) control over the parish churches. And until the Church of England was disestablished after the Revolution, strife prevailed between the church and various governmental officials over naming ministers to parishes and paying their salaries. The lack of a resident bishop contributed greatly to the church's weakness vis-à-vis the local authorities.

It has also been a commonplace to perceive the Virginia clergy, in the words of an early planter, as "black-cotted raskolls." Anglican clergymen, so the story goes, came to America because they could not make it in England, and once here, spent their lives in dissolution and drink. This picture, however, owes much more to the wounded social feelings of Virginia aristocrats than to reality. Recent studies have established the fact that Anglican clergymen performed honorably in the midst of a very difficult religious climate. Actual malfeasance on the part of Anglican clergymen was rare. And in the person of ministers such as James Blair, Anglican fidelity rose to honorable heights.

Blair (1655-1743) was born in Scotland and was ordained there into the Church of England. He came to Virginia in 1685. In 1689 the Bishop of London, who supervised religious matters in the colonies, appointed Blair

James Blair (1655–1743), first president of the College of William and Mary THE COLLEGE OF WILLIAM AND MARY IN VIRGINIA

commissary (i.e., administrator) of the Virginia church. His powers as commissary were slight, but Blair made the most of them. He called the colony's clergy together for mutual edification and support. The first such gathering in 1690 proposed a college for Virginia, a proposal which Blair nursed painstakingly until it became a reality in 1693 as the College of William and Mary. Blair served this struggling institution as president until his death. He preached constantly and learnedly

The Wren Building of the College of William and Mary in Williamsburg, Virginia. Built in 1695–98 from plans said to have been prepared by Christopher Wren, it is the oldest academic building standing in the United States COLONIAL WILLIAMSBURG

(one of his works was a five-volume exposition of the Sermon on the Mount). He battled governors and vestrymen who ran roughshod over the churches. He was, in sum, an admirable figure in nearly every way. Yet it must be admitted that the labors of clergymen like Blair and his less prominent colleagues were never able to create as vibrant a Christian witness in colonial Virginia as the Puritans did in New England, or even as other Anglicans did in other colonies.

Outside Virginia

Beyond Virginia, the Church of England owed much of its success to two organizations founded by Thomas Bray (1656-1730). Bray served as commissary of Maryland's Church of England for only a few years, 1696-1700, but he transformed personal concerns for education and missions into the Society for Promoting Christian Knowledge (SPCK) and the Society for the Propagation of the Gospel in Foreign Parts (SPG). The first subsidized theological libraries, and over

Eighteenth-century SPG *bookplate*

forty were eventually founded in colonial America. The second sent out Anglican missionaries. Soon SPG missionaries were advancing the cause of the gospel, and of the Church of England, on many fronts in America. In New York they promoted Indian missions and aided the work of Trinity parish in New York City. (This church was founded in 1693; it eventually became the wealthiest congregation in America because of the rising value of its endowment, a grant of land in lower Manhattan that was originally a farm but became valuable commercial real estate shortly thereafter.) The SPG supported Anglican work among frontier populations in New Jersey and Pennsylvania, where some of the strongest Anglican parishes eventually grew up. It also pioneered in setting up Anglican churches in New England. Puritans, of course, balked at seeing themselves as fit candidates for proselytizing. But under forthright ministers like Boston's Timothy Cutler, rector of Old North church from 1723 to 1765, and Connecticut's Samuel Johnson, who eventually became president of King's College (later Columbia University), Anglicans made inroads even in the Bible Commonwealths. And SPG efforts contributed to the philanthropic vision which led to the founding of Georgia in the early 1730s.

It would be wrong to forget that well-known British Anglicans also made contact with American religious history in the colonial period. The idealistic philosopher, George Berkeley, resided in Newport, Rhode Island, from 1729 to 1731, while waiting—in vain— to found a missionary school in the colonies. John and Charles Wesley endured a fruitless missionary venture to Georgia, 1735-1738. Their friend and Anglican colleague, George Whitefield, later achieved much greater success in the colonial Great Awakening.

None of the colonies possessed a truly strong Anglican church by the mid-eighteenth century. But where ministers like James Blair had been active in Virginia, and where strong leaders had brought Anglican churches into existence elsewhere in the colonies, the Church of England was a force to be reckoned with. And so long as the colonies remained under King and Parliament, the Church of England continued to loom large, either as a threat or as a haven, for many believers in America.

Cecilius Calvert, Second Lord Baltimore (1605–1675) FROM THE COLLECTIONS OF THE ENOCH PRATT FREE LIBRARY, BALTIMORE   BY PERMISSION

Catholics in Maryland

English Catholics, a despised and feared minority in the mother country, secured a foothold in the English colonies through the dedicated patronage of a noble family. George Calvert, first Lord Baltimore, who had nourished a long-standing interest in colonization, was a favorite of James I. He was also a Catholic. His religion made him suspect to the Virginia Company, but his loyalty to James I, and then Charles I, earned him his own grant, ten million acres surrounding the Chesapeake Bay. Calvert died in 1632, and his son, Cecilius, also Lord Baltimore, carried out the actual settlement. The Calvert family wished to establish a feudal barony in their colony, and they wished to create a haven for their coreligionists. In Maryland, named for Charles' wife, they succeeded fairly well on both accounts.

The first settlers, about twenty mostly noble Catholics and two hundred others who were mostly humble, arrived in early 1634. Their number included two Jesuit priests, Andrew White (1579-1656) and John Altham. White, known as "the Apostle to Maryland," was an Englishman educated at continental Catholic universities who became an active and effective missionary in the New World. He succeeded in converting many of the non-Catholic English to his faith, and he also achieved some success among the Indians. For this latter effort, White reduced the Piscataway Indian language to writing—probably the first English person to do this for an Indian language—and produced a grammar and a catechism. Soon, however, the Jesuits' very success led to problems, and at the highest level. Lord Baltimore was afraid that the acquisition of land by Jesuits would jeopardize his economic interests and that their aggressive proselytizing would anger English Protestants on both sides of the Atlantic. So in 1641 Baltimore began

We have not ceased in an active manner to exert our endeavors for our neighbors; and although it is not yet permitted us by the rulers of the province to live among the barbarians . . . nevertheless, we hope in a short time that we will obtain one station of our own among the barbarians. In the interim we are more earnestly intent on the English, and since there are protestants as well as catholics in the colony, we have labored with both, and God has blessed our labors. For of the protestants who came from England this year, 1638, almost all have been converted to the faith, besides many others, with four servants that we bought for necessary use in Virginia.

FATHER ANDREW WHITE,
1638

to rein in Jesuit activities and soon even got Rome to agree that Franciscans and secular priests should replace the Jesuits in ministering to Maryland's Catholics. White himself was forced to leave Maryland in 1644.

From the first, Lord Baltimore had encouraged a great deal of toleration in Maryland. He needed Protestants to make the colonizing effort successful. He knew that England would not accept an exclusively Catholic colony in America, but he also seems to have believed sincerely in the principle itself. He instructed the first Catholic settlers

---

... And whereas the inforceing of the conscience in matters of Religion hath frequently fallen out to be of dangerous Consequence in those commonwealthes where it hath been practised, And for the more quiett and peaceable governement of this Province, and the better to preserve mutuall Love and amity amongst the Inhabitants thereof. Be it Therefore ... enacted ... that noe person or persons whatsoever within this Province, or the Islands, Ports, Harbors, Creekes, or havens thereunto belonging professing to believe in Jesus Christ, shall from henceforth bee any waies troubled, Molested or discountenanced for or in respect of his or her religion nor in the free exercise thereof within this Province or the Islands thereunto belonging nor any way compelled to the beleife or exercise of any other Religion against his or her consent, soe as they be not unfaithful to the Lord Proprietary, or molest or conspire against the civill Government established or to bee in this Province under him or his heires.
Maryland Toleration Act of 1649

privately to go out of their way to avoid offending Protestants. During the 1640s Maryland made its stand for toleration official. Suspicious Protestants in England accused their rival, Charles I, of harboring a secret Catholic enclave in the New World. Some Virginians, who were offended both by Baltimore's religion and by his ownership of so much land, looked hungrily at the Chesapeake region. Baltimore responded by naming a Protestant as resident lieutenant governor. And in 1649 the Maryland legislature itself promulgated a toleration act, whose spirit was far ahead of its times.

Baltimore's measures were not entirely successful in preserving Maryland's independence. During Cromwell's rule, Maryland Protestants temporarily seized the colony, plundered Catholic lands, and repealed the Toleration Act. Later in the century Anglicans gained control of Maryland and passed legislation making the Church of England Maryland's established faith. Still, the legacy of Lord Baltimore prevailed and Catholics maintained a secure foothold in Maryland.

Catholic Maryland testifies to the "roominess" of American religious life in the Protestant colonial period. The number of Roman Catholics in British North America remained quite small (numbering only 25,000 out of four million in 1785), but a vanguard was in place for the great Catholic immigrations of the nineteenth century. More importantly, Maryland's experience shows that although Catholics were often hated, always distrusted, and occasionally outlawed in colonial America, coastal lands along the Atlantic were spacious enough for them too.

Reformed Dutch and Germans

The Dutch settlement of New Netherlands (New York) cannot compare favorably with any of the major English colonies. Its proprietor, the Dutch West India Company, wanted profits from furs and cared about little else. In 1609 Henry Hudson explored for the Netherlands the river that would bear his name; in 1613 a few trading outposts appeared on Manhattan Island; in 1624 the Company sent more than thirty families to foster settlements on the Hudson and Delaware Rivers, but not until 1628 did a Dutch Reformed minister arrive in New Amsterdam

NIEUW AMSTERDAM ofte NUE NIEUW IORX opt TEYLANT MAN

A view of New Amsterdam as it appeared in 1650   MUSEUM OF THE CITY OF NEW YORK

(New York City). Dutch administrators like Peter Stuyvesant were cantankerous and incompetent, the village on Manhattan never acquired a communal identity, and the grandiose plan to develop vast estates along the Hudson never materialized. Midst this confusion a trickle of Dutch Reformed clergymen brought the steady Calvinism and the "classical" (from "classes," the Dutch equivalent of a presbytery) church order which gave Holland such a vigorous church life in the seventeenth century. In 1664 the English under Charles II's brother, the Duke of York (later James II), took New York. There were then six Dutch Reformed ministers working with more than twice that many small congregations.

The end of Dutch rule coincided ironically with genuine growth among the Dutch Reformed churches. Steady immigration from Holland to New York, New Jersey, and other colonies led to a total of twenty-six churches by 1700 and triple that number forty years later. By that time also, many immigrants from southern Germany who also shared the Reformed faith had come to the New World. Forced from the Palatinate and other German principalities by civil war, French invasion, and persecution, these Germans constituted the substantial population from which more than fifty German Reformed congregations, concentrated in Pennsylvania, would be established by 1740.

Presbyterians

The Presbyterians arose in England and, especially, Scotland during the sixteenth century as a Calvinistic group which favored church rule by elders and representative church courts. By 1800 they became the most influential denomination in the middle states of New York, New Jersey, and Pennsylvania. But they did not have great strength until Scots and Scotch-Irish began to migrate to America at the end of the seventeenth century. From that point the denomination grew rapidly in size and even more rapidly in influence.

Francis Makemie (1658-1708) more than any other person was responsible for founding American Presbyterianism. He was born in Ireland, educated in Scotland, and commissioned in Northern Ireland to serve as a missionary in America (1681). Makemie evangelized throughout the English-speaking New World (New England, New York, Virginia, North Carolina, the Barbados) and established the first Presbyterian congregation in America at Snow Hill, Maryland, in 1684. The Mathers of New England spoke highly of his work, and Congregationalists in general wished him well. In 1706 he succeeded in bringing together Presbyterians of different backgrounds (English, Welsh, Scottish, Scotch-Irish, and from New England) into the Presbytery of Philadelphia. Its purpose was "to meet yearly and oftener, if necessary, to consult the most proper measure for advancing religion and propagating Christianity in our various stations." These Presbyterians agreed that the Westminster Confession should be their doctrinal basis, even if they did not see eye to eye on what "subscription" to such a standard meant in practice.

In 1707 Makemie was arrested by New York's governor, Lord Cornbury, for preaching without a license in a private home on Long Island. Cornbury scorned Makemie as a "Jack of all Trades, a Preacher, a Doctor of Physick, a Merchant, an Attorney, or Counsellor at Law, and which is worst of all, a Disturber of Governments." But Makemie defended himself by appealing to the English Toleration Act of 1689, which granted substantial toleration to non-Anglicans in the mother country. He was acquitted, but did have to pay the high costs of his trial. In the long run this event solidified the image of Presbyterians as defenders of freedom and won new respect for the denomination in America.

Quakers

In New England

When the first Quakers, Mary Fisher and Ann Austin, arrived in Boston on board ship in July 1656, the Puritan authorities were ready. They immediately put the two women in prison, confiscated their books, and soon expelled them from the colony. But two days after Fisher and Austin left, eight more Quakers arrived. A struggle which led to martyrdom had begun.

Quakers arose as one of the radical groups in England's Puritan Revolution. Inspired by George Fox (1624-1691), Friends, as they wished to be known, stressed the internal, subjective, and spiritual side of Christianity at the expense of the external, objective, and legal. They also were remarkably egalitarian in the belief that the Inner Light of Christ could enlighten anyone. Yet under Fox and other early leaders Friends also developed great internal discipline, a cohesive if informal organization, a capacity to preserve many traditional Protestant doctrines, and a driving missionary zeal. Quakers were tolerated in Cromwell's England, but all who placed a premium on order, hierarchy, and external rule—as the New England Puritans did—feared them greatly.

When the Massachusetts Puritans rebuffed the first Quakers who came by sea, the next attempts were made by land. Rhode Island's Roger Williams denounced them sharply, but his colony had long tolerated virtually all comers, and Quakers found a refuge there. Friends quickly won many converts in Plymouth and other Puritan regions adjacent to Rhode Island. And they persisted in their as-

---

So after a little time that I had been there [Rhode Island] . . . the Word of the Lord came unto me, saying, "Go to Boston with thy brother William Robinson." And at his command I was obedient and gave up myself to do his will, . . . And for yielding obedience to and obeying the voice and command of the Everliving God, which created heaven and earth, and the fountains of waters, do I with my dear brother suffer outward bonds near unto death.

MARMADUKE STEPHENSON,
shortly before his execution, 1659

A *Quaker exhorter in New England* COURTESY ESSEX INSTITUTE, SALEM, MASS.

In Pennsylvania

William Penn (1644-1718) was the founder of Pennsylvania and one of the most engaging religious figures of his age. He was born in London, raised there and in Ireland, and given all the privileges befitting his station as the eldest son of Admiral William Penn, who had captured Jamaica from the Dutch in 1655. By 1661, however, a very worldly William Penn had begun to fall under the sway of the Friends' teaching, and by 1666 he had become a Quaker. A prolific writer throughout his life, Penn ran afoul of the law in 1668 with a tract attacking the doctrines of the Church of England. While in prison in 1669 he wrote the devotional classic, *No Cross, No Crown*, an exposition concerning Christian suffering. After his release from prison he grew steadily disillusioned about the prospects for Quakers in England.

Penn took his first steps toward finding a refuge for Friends in the New World by backing a Quaker expedition to New Jersey in 1677 and 1678. In 1681 he acquired a huge tract of land from King Charles II to settle a large debt owed to his father. Pennsylvania ("Penn's Woods") thereafter became the most secure home for religious toleration in the world. In 1682 the city of Philadelphia was

William Penn (1644–1718) NEW YORK PUBLIC LIBRARY

sault upon Boston. The clash between immovable object (Puritan order) and irresistible force (Quaker zeal) soon led to tragedy. In the last disorderly days of Puritan rule in England, Puritans in New England were left on their own to deal with their dissenters. After a series of lesser deterrents (fines, banishment, whipping) failed to check the Quakers, Massachusetts made the repeated preaching of the Friends' faith a capital offense. As a result, four Quakers—Mary Dyer, William Leddra, William Robinson, and Marmaduke Stephenson—met the hangman in the years 1659-1661. Charles II, who loved the Puritans even less than he did the pesky Quakers, saw that the executions ceased. In 1672 George Fox himself visited the colonies, where he sparked a violent literary duel with Roger Williams. Quakers formed "Meetings" in Rhode Island and elsewhere in the northern colonies. But the expansion of the Friends in America did not take place until a talented young aristocrat in England accepted their faith.

"Penn's Treaty with the Indians" by Benjamin West   PENNSYLVANIA ACADEMY OF FINE ARTS

laid out and, of certainly equal importance, Pennsylvania's "Frame of Government" was published. This constitution set out the terms of what Penn called a "Holy Experiment." It allowed unprecedented freedom of religion to any who believed in one God; it was also a politically liberal document for its times. Although Penn realized little profit from his colony, Pennsylvania flourished from the start. One of the reasons for this was Penn's vigorous promotion of the colony on the European continent. Another was the colony's reputation for toleration. The European home of many early settlers was memorialized in the name chosen for a town founded in 1683 near Philadelphia—Germantown, a grant from Penn to a group of German Mennonites and Dutch Quakers. One of the most appealing features of the Penn administration was its fair and just treatment of the Indians.

Penn himself experienced serious personal difficulties for the rest of his life. He was able to remain in his colony for only two brief periods (1682-1684, 1699-1701). He lost control of Pennsylvania from 1692 to 1694 because of his friendship with the deposed English king, James II. And his financial reverses landed him briefly in debtors' prison. Through it all he continued to write, publishing more than one hundred tracts, pamphlets, and books on a wide variety of subjects. Modern historians have written correctly in calling Penn a "compassionate humanitarian, mystic, theologian, and profound political theorist"—or more simply, "the Renaissance Quaker."

Pennsylvania generally and Philadelphia specifically continued to be the stronghold of Quaker influence in early America long after Penn's death. Pennsylvania Quakers had to deal with dissent themselves in the early 1690s when the bombastic George Keith (1639-1716) led away a group of Friends who agreed with him that New World Quakerism had become formalized and lax. Quakers became a smaller and smaller minority in their own colony as first Scotch-Irish and then German immigrants poured into Pennsylvania's interior. The Quakers' very commercial success, in great measure a result of their serious religious approach to life, threatened the world-denying character of the earlier faith. Yet it was not until the 1750s and the French and Indian War that Quakers found themselves unable to balance their own principles (in this case, pacifism) and their political control of the colony. Until that time they had succeeded in promoting the Inner Light while governing public life. Afterward, their development was much more like that of their English brethren. The bands that had once been radical and missionary-minded became ingrown and exerted only an occasional impact on society, as when their pacifist principles came into conflict with American militarism.

Primitive Christianity Revived

That which the People call'd Quakers lay down, as a Main Fundamental in Religion, is this, That God, through Christ, hath placed a Principle in every Man, to inform him of his Duty, and to enable him to do it; and that those that Live up to this Principle, are the People of God, and those that Live in Disobedience to it, are not God's People, whatever Name they may bear, or Profession they may make of Religion. This is their Ancient, First, and Standing Testimony: With this they began, and this they bore, and do bear to the World. . . .

They call it, The Light of Christ within Man, or, Light Within, which is their Ancient, and most General and Familiar Phrase. . . .

In short, there is no becoming Virtuous, Holy and Good, without this Principle; no Acceptance with God, nor Peace of Soul, but through it. But on the contrary, that the Reason of so much Irreligion among Christians, so much Superstition, instead of Devotion, and so much Profession without Enjoyment, and so little Heart-Reformation, is, because People in Religion, Overlook this Principle, and leave it behind them. . . .

We also believe, that War ought to cease, among the Followers of the Lamb Christ Jesus, who taught his Disciples to forgive and love their Enemies, and not to war against them, and kill them; and that therefore the Weapons of his true Followers are not Carnal but Spiritual; yea mighty, through God, to cut down Sin and Wickedness, and dethrone him that is the Author thereof. And as this is the most Christian, so the most rational Way; Love and Perswasion having more Force than Weapons of War. Nor would the worst of Men easily be brought to hurt those that they

Eighteenth-century Quaker meeting QUAKER COLLECTION, HAVERFORD COLLEGE LIBRARY, HAVERFORD, PA.

The leopard with the harmless kid laid down
And not one savage beast was seen to frown

The wolf did with the Lambkin dwell in peace
His grim carnivorous nature there did cease

The lion with the fatling on did move
A little child was leading them in love;

When the great PENN his famous treaty made
With indian chiefs beneath the Elm-tree's shade.

"*The Peaceable Kingdom*" *by Edward Hicks*   PHILADELPHIA MUSEUM OF ART: BEQUEST OF CHARLES C. WILLIS

really think love them. 'Tis that Love and Patience must in the End have the Victory. . . .

For the same Reason we have returned to the first Plainness of Speech, viz. Thou and Thee, to a single Person, which though Men give no other to God, they will hardly endure it from us. It has been a great Test upon Pride, and shewn the Blind and weak Insides of many. This also is out of pure Conscience, whatever People may think or say of us for it. We may be despised, and have been so often, yea, very evilly entreated, but we are now better known, and People better informed. In short, 'tis also both Scripture and Grammar, and we have Propriety of Speech for it, as well as Peace in it.

WILLIAM PENN,
*The Faith and Practice of
The People Called Quakers,* 1696

The Practice of Religion in Colonial America

Most colonial Christians were not overly concerned with the large-scale issues involved in founding denominations in the wilderness, or with the actions of famous preachers in colonial capitols and the even higher and mightier religious elite in England. They were interested, rather, in how their faith touched the day-to-day realities of their lives. While the minister and a few educated laymen in any locality might have been interested in technical theological discussion, a substantial majority of all colonial Americans—South as well as New England—would have attended church with some regularity. Many colonials led their families (which often included servants) in Bible reading and prayer. Many regarded family responsibilities, especially the raising of children, as spiritual duties. Christian aspirations and vocabulary also affected relationships with their peers and with the underclasses in America society, blacks and Indians. It is a shame that records for day-to-day religion are not as readily available as for denominational concerns, but historians have nonetheless been able to reconstruct at least its general outline.

What they have shown is that several different styles of practical Christianity prevailed in colonial America. A recent student of child-rearing practices, Philip Greven, speaks, for example, of three forms of Protestant "temperament"—evangelical, moderate, and genteel. And a historian of spirituality itself, Richard Lovelace, talks of Puritan and pietistic strands growing together into the evangelicalism of the nineteenth century. It is possible to see America as a place to which English and Continental forms of piety migrated, but also where environmental conditions changed these imported forms into something distinctively American. In the effort to describe colonial religious life, these and other categories help sort out the complex but deeply human nature of Christian life in colonial America.

The Bible in the Colonies

A central feature of colonial religious life was the Bible. Almost all Christians in the colonies would have agreed with the English Puritan William Bradshaw, who wrote in 1605 that "the word of God contained in the writings of the Prophets and Apostles, is of absolute perfection, given by Christ the head of the Churche, to bee unto the same, the sole Canon and rule of all matters of Religion, and the worship and service of God whatsoever." And almost all colonial ministers expended great effort in bringing biblical messages to their flocks. Puritan ministers always grounded their two weekly sermons on passages of scripture, but so did Anglicans in their somewhat less frequent sermons, and the ministers of other denominations.

But did the laity also study the Bible? Inventories of colonial wills attest that if common people possessed any books at all, the Bible was sure to be among them. Records left by wealthy Virginians show a common familiarity with scripture. William Byrd II (1674-1744), the master of stately Westover, for example, normally read a biblical passage—in Greek or Hebrew—at the start of each day. Where schools existed in the colonies, the Bible was regularly used as a text

1.Cor.11.8.

*Or, Mannes, because she com-eth of man:for in Ebr Ish, is man, and Ishah the woman.

Mat.19.5.
mar.10,7.
1 cor.6,16.
ephes.5,31.
p So that ma-riage requi-reth a greater ductie of vs towarde our wiues, the other-wise we are bounde to shewe to our pa-rents.

23 Then the man said, * This now is bone of my bones, and flesh of my flesh . She shalbe called "woman, because she was ta-ken out of man.

24 * Therefore shal man leaue p his father and his mother, and shal cleaue to his wife, and they shalbe one flesh.

25 And they were bothe naked, the man & his wife, and were not q ashamed.

q For before sinne entred, all things we-re honest and comely.

THE SITVACION OF THE GARDEN OF EDEN.

La grand Ar-menie
"Or, Armenia the great.

Terre de Hani-lah:
"Or, land of Hauilah.

Li cheine d Euphrates
"Or, the fall o. Euphrates.
La cheute de Tygris.
Or, the fall of Tigris.
Le golf de la mer Persique.
Or, the golfe of the Persian sea.

Because mencion is made in the tenth verse of this seconde chapter of the riuer that watered the garden, we muste note that Euphrates and Tygris called in Ebrewe, Perath and Hiddekel, were called but one riuer where they ioyned together, als they had sure heades:that is, two at their springs, & two where they fel into the Persian sea. In this cuntrey an imoste plentiful land Adam dwelt, and this was called Paradise:that is, a garden of pleasure, because of the frutefulnes and abundance thereof. And whereas it is said that Pishon compasseth the land of Hauilah, it is meant of Tygris, which is some place as it passed by diuers pla-tes, was called by sundry names, as some time Diglito, in other places Pasitygris, & some Phasin or Ti-sion. Likewise Euphrates towarde the countrey of Cush or Ethiopia, or Arabia was called Gihon. So that Tygris and Euphrates which were but two riuers and some time when they ioyned together, were called after one name) were according to diuers places called by these foure names so that they might seme to haue bene foure diuers riuers.

2 Cor.11.3.
d This is Sa-tans chiefest subtiltie, to cause vs not to feare Gods threatnings: & although he shulde say, God doeth not forbid you to eat of the frute:saue that he knoweth that if you shulde eat thereof, you shalde be like to him.

Ecclef 25.33.
1.tim.2,14.
f Not so mu-che to please his wife, as moued by am-bition at her persuasion.

g They began to fele their miserie, but they soght not to God for re-medie.
"But, things to gird about the to hide their priuities.

CHAP. III.

1 The woman seduced by the serpet. 6 Entiseth her hus-bad t sinne. 14 They thre are punished. 15 Christ is promised. 19 Man is dust. 22 Man is cast out of paradise.

Wisde. 2.25
a A. Satan can change him selfe into an Angel of light, so did he ab-use the wisdo-me of the ser-pent to deceaue man.
b God suffe-red Satan to make the ser-pent his instru-ment and to speake in him.
c In douting of Gods threa-tning, she yel-ded to Satan.

1 NOw *the serpent was more a subtil then anie beast of the field, which y Lord God had made:and he b said to the woman, Yea, hathe God in dede said, Ye shal not eat of euerie tre of the garden?

2 And the woman said vnto the serpet, We eat of the frute of the trees of the garden,

3 But of the frute of the tre, which is in the middes of the garden, God hathe said, Ye shal not eat of it, nether shal ye touche it, c lest ye dye.

4 Then *the serpent said to the woman, Ye shal not d dye at all,

5 But God doth knowe, that when ye shal eat thereof, your eyes shaibe opened, & ye shalbe as gods, e knowing good and euil.

6 So the woman (seing that the tre was good for meat, and that it was pleasant to the eyes, & a tre to be desired to get know-ledge) toke of the frute thereof , and did * eat, and gaue also to her housband with her, and he f did eat.

7 Then the eyes of them bothe were ope-ned, & they knewe that they were naked, and they sewed figtre leaues together, and made them selues "breeches.

8 ¶ Afterwarde they heard the voyce of

a.ii.

Watonsſeongaſh Christ　　　Chap. 1.　　　*wunneetuonk Jeſus Chriſt*

WUNAUNCHEMOOKAONK NASHPE

MATTHEVV.

CHAP. I.

Ppometuongane *a* book Jeſus Chriſt, wunnaumonuh David, wunnaumonuh Abraham.

2 *b* Abranam wunnaumonieu Iſaakoh, kah *c* Iſaak wunnaumonieu Jakobuh, kah *d* Jakob wunnaumonieu Judaſoh, kah weematoh.

3 Kah *e* Judas wunnaumonieu Pharcſoh kah Zarahoh wutch Tamarhut, kah *f* Phares wunnaumonieu Ezromoh, kah Ezrom wunnaumonieu Aramoh.

4 Kah Aram wunnaumonieu Aminadaboh, kah Aminadab wunnaumonieu Naaſonoh, kah Naaſſon wunnaumonieu Salmonoh.

5 Kah Salmon wunnaumonieu Boazoh *c* achab, kah Boaz wunnaumonieu ... h Ruth, kah Obed wunnar...

kah Eleazar wunnaumonieu Matthanoh, kah Matthan wunnaumonieu Jakoboh.

16 Kah Jakob wunnaumonieu Joſephoh, weſukeh Mary noh mo wachegit Jeſus uttiyeuoh ahennit Chriſt.

17 Nemehkuh wame pometeongaſh wutch Abrahamut onk yean Davidut, nabo yauwudt pometeongaſh; neit wu ch Davidut onk yean umniniinohkonauh ut Babylon, nabo yauwudt pometeongaſh: neit wutch ummiſſinohkonaoh ut Babylon nô pajeh uppeyonat Jeſus Chriſt, nabo yauwudt pometeongaſh.

18 Kah Jeſus Curiſt *m* wunneetuonk yeu mo, nagum okaſoh Maryhoh kah Joſeph quoſhodhettit (aſquam naneeinhettekup) miikauau wutchéketeauonat naſhpe Nathauanittcoh.

...it weſukeh Joſephuh wunno... atta mo wuttenantamcor Tidewautut, ur ant...

a Luke 3.23.
b Gen. 21.3.
c Gen. 25.26.
d Gen. 29.35.
e Gen. 38.27.
f 1 Chr. 2.5.
Ruth 4.19.

m Luke 1.27.

Title page (right) and opening of the Gospel of Matthew (above) in Algonquin, from John Eliot's Indian Bible of 1663 NEW YORK PUBLIC LIBRARY

to teach reading. In New England it was not uncommon for individuals to meet in private homes for Bible reading, particularly when bad weather or long distances made it difficult to attend services. One well-known laywoman who led such a Bible study, Anne Hutchinson, was able to quote lengthy portions of scripture at her trial before the Massachusetts magistrates in 1637. Although the evidence is not conclusive, it is probable that many laypeople in the colonies knew the Bible nearly as well as their ministers.

Anne Hutchinson's knowledge of the Bible points up a tension over the use of different translations in early New England. The Bible for the early English Puritans was the Geneva Bible, a translation made by exiles in Calvin's Geneva in 1560, during the reign of the Catholic Queen Mary. It was, in the words

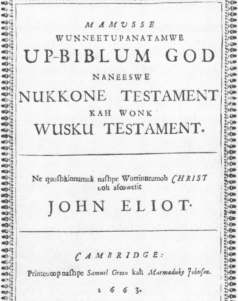

MAMUSSE
WUNNEETUPANATAMWE

UP-BIBLUM GOD

NANEESWE

NUKKONE TESTAMENT

KAH WONK

WUSKU TESTAMENT.

Ne quoſhkinnumuk naſhpe Wuttinneumoh *CHRIST* noh aſoowelit

JOHN ELIOT.

CAMBRIDGE:

Printeuoop naſhpe *Samuel Green* kah *Marmaduke Johnſon.*

1 6 6 3.

of a modern historian, "rich in the common idiom of the day," and it contained nearly 300,000 words in notes and prefaces providing a Calvinistic interpretation of scripture. The notes of this translation, however, did not include a discussion of national covenant—the foundation of social organization so important for New England's founders—but rather stressed the individual covenant of grace between Christ and the believer. By 1620, many Puritans, including most New England leaders, had come to prefer the Authorized (or King James) Version, published in 1611. (James I had promoted this translation in part because he was so infuriated with the Geneva Bible's notes, like that for Exodus 1:17 which praised the Hebrew midwives for disobeying the Egyptian king!) The Authorized Version, without notes and with a somewhat more classical and elite vocabulary, was better suited to the construction of a social theory that emphasized community responsibilities as well as personal salvation. Significantly, however, Hutchinson and most of those who felt with her that the communal emphasis in New England was undermining the individual covenant of grace, used the Geneva Bible. The removal of Hutchinson from Massachusetts Bay was, thus, also an occasion for those who preferred the Authorized Version to secure the acceptance of that translation. This may have played only a small part, but the King James Version did indeed become virtually the only translation used by speakers of English in colonial America.

It was quite late in the day, however, before English-language Bibles were actually printed in America. A crown monopoly restricted publication of the King James Version to the king's printer in England. As a result, colonists had to import their Bibles from the Old World. The first Bible actually printed in America was John Eliot's Algonquian translation of the New Testament in 1661, followed two years later by the entire Bible. The first European-language Bible appeared in 1743, when Christopher Sauer (a member of the pietistic Church of the Brethren) published in Pennsylvania an edition of Luther's German Bible (with Apocrypha) on type carried from Frankfurt. Throughout the colonial period portions of scripture were published in English, particularly as part of prayer books, and also in Indian languages. There

is also some evidence that around 1750 two Boston firms—Rogers & Fowle and Kneeland & Green—"pirated," respectively, a King James Version New Testament and entire Bible by putting the proper London imprint on books that they themselves produced. The Continental Congress authorized the first regular printing of the Authorized Version in 1777 when it granted Robert Aitken, printer to Congress, permission to publish the New Testament. It was not until 1807, however, that the bad feeling caused by the American Revolution passed and American printers began to include once again the traditional dedication to King James. From that time to this, the printing of the Authorized Version, and many other translations, has been a major American enterprise indeed.

Puritan Piety

Puritan piety rose higher and plunged lower than other forms of Christian devotion in the colonies. Its very strength became the source of its weakness, an irony that appears most clearly in the Puritans' spiritual earnestness and in their conviction that they were a singular people of God.

Puritans committed enough crimes against humanity in the name of God to keep alive the old slander that they were people who loved God with all their souls and hated their neighbors with all their hearts. So firmly did Puritans believe that they had grasped the essence of Christianity that they could only regard those who disagreed as willfully perverse. John Cotton, defending Massachusetts Bay against the attacks of Roger Williams, charged that Williams sinned not so much in holding wrong ideas as in stubbornly clinging to those ideas after the authorities had demonstrated their error. The same sort of reasoning made it possible for Massachusetts to hang the four Quakers in 1659-1661. Sin against their own consciences compounded their sins against society and truth.

Puritan zeal led to other tragedies as well. Puritans knew that they wrestled not with flesh and blood but with the satanic principalities of this age. Usually they matched that conviction with a comparable attention to the problems involved in living in the mundane world. But on occasion, most disastrously during the Salem witch trials in the early

1690s, Puritan preoccupation with the supernatural burst normal bounds.

The other side of Puritan spiritual earnestness reveals a different picture altogether. The Puritans' faith allowed them to meet personal crises with balance and confidence. Thomas Shepard (1605-1649), the minister at Cambridge from 1634 and one of the great preachers in early New England, left this testimony in his diary after his wife died in 1646:

> But the Lord hath not bin woont to let me live long without some affliction or other, & yet ever mixt with some mercy, & therefore . . . as he gave me another son, John, so he tooke away my most deare precious meeke & loving wife, in childbed. . . . This affliction was very heavy to me, for in it the Lord seemed to withdraw his tender care for me & mine, which he graciously manifested by my deare wife; also refused to heare prayer, when I did thinke he would have hearkened & let me see his bewty in the land of the living, in restoring of her to health agayne . . . but I am the Lords, & he may doe with me what he will, he did teach me to prize a little grace gained by a crosse as a sufficient recompense for all outward losses; but this losse was very great.

This devotion to righteousness also offered a means for Puritans to check their own pride and to repent in frank confession of failure. The diary of Judge Samuel Sewall (1652-1730) records such an example. Several years after the Salem witch trials, in which he had played a major role, Sewall stood in church to make public confession of his sin:

> Jan. 14, 1697. Copy of the Bill I put up on the Fast day; giving it to Mr. Willard [the minister] as he pass'd by, and standing up at the reading of it, and bowing when finished; in the Afternoon.
>
> Samuel Sewall, sensible of the reiterated strokes of God upon himself and family; and being sensible, that as to the Guilt contracted upon the opening of the late commission of Oyer and Terminer at Salem . . . he is, upon many accounts, more concerned than any that he knows of, Desires to take the Blame and shame of it, Asking

pardon of men, And especially desiring prayers that God, who has an Unlimited Authority, would pardon that sin and all other his sins; personal and Relative: And according to his infinite Benignity, and Sovereignty, Not Visit the sin of him, or of any other, upon himself or any of his, nor upon the Land: But that He would powerfully defend him against all Temptations to Sin, for the future; and vouchsafe him the efficacious, saving Conduct of his Word and Spirit.

Puritans matched their general spiritual zeal with the specific conviction that God had called them in a special way. Edward Johnson (1598-1672), the First Citizen of Woburn, Massachusetts, published an account of New England's early history in 1654, *Wonder-Working Providence of Zion's Saviour in New England*, which expressed this conviction forthrightly. "This is the place," he wrote of New England, "where the Lord will create a new Heaven, and a new Earth in, new Churches, and a new Commonwealth together." The Reforming Synod of 1679 expressed a widespread opinion when it likened New England to the Lord's Old Testament nation: "The Wayes of God towards this his People, have in many respects been like unto his dealings with Israel of old."

The belief that God had elected the New England nation, that it was like "Israel of old," constituted a powerful ideology. It encouraged harmony in social relationships, a willingness to forego private good for the public welfare, and a contentment with one's own position in the body politic. Although these characteristics received clearest expression from ministers and the important civil authorities, they seem to have reached other levels of society also. The humble Thomas Gibbes family of seventeenth-century Sandwich, Massachusetts, provides one example of their operation among the common people. Gibbes had promised all of his small amount of land to his oldest son, John, but died before making a will. The court, following the intestate statute, gave John a double portion of the land and his brothers, Thomas and Samuel, a single share. But the two younger sons asked the court to follow "our fathers desire" and give all the land to John because "wee All desire peace and union amongst us." To be sure, Puritans were not entirely successful, even in their own eyes, at making the reality of New England life fulfill the high ideals of this spiritual vision. Yet it is also true that nowhere in the West during the seventeenth century did a more cohesive or stable Christian society exist on as large a scale as in New England.

The worm in the apple of Puritan righteousness was the highhandedness which their belief in national election fostered in relationships with non-Puritans. It was bad enough for Englishmen who dissented from the New England Way. It was much worse for the Native Americans. Puritan actions toward the Indians were, in reality, little different from, and perhaps little better than, those of other colonists. What made them reprehensible was the hypocrisy which allowed Puritans to ravage the natives under the cant of biblical righteousness. The same Thomas Shepard who regarded the death of his wife as an inducement to piety saw the death of Pequot Indians, during the War of 1637, as only their just due for having harassed God's people. After one battle Shepard could write of the Indians' "divine slaughter by the hand of the English" and say that "the Lord had utterly consumed the whole company" of Native Americans.

Puritan piety has never seen its like in later American history. Modern Christians and secularists, for very different reasons, have both been glad of that.

Piety was one of the factors that produced a number of poets in New England before poetry was written elsewhere in the colonies. The relatively high level of education in New England and the presence of printing facilities there also contributed to the presence of verse in the Bible Commonwealths. But the intensity of Puritan devotion played the major role in bringing a poetic voice to the public. Poets like Anne Bradstreet (the wife of a Massachusetts governor who published the first important book of poems by an American in 1650) and Michael Wigglesworth (whose "The Day of Doom," a poem about the Last Judgment, appeared in 1662 and was reprinted frequently in the colonial period) enjoyed popular acceptance and remain interesting historically. Yet New England's poetry, with one exception, was not particularly remarkable. The Puritan immersion in scriptural language did yield a lively feeling for allegory, but the Puritan commitment to explicit edification also led to a heavy-handed didacticism. The one exception to the middling character of Puritan verse was the poetry of Edward Taylor, who wrote some of the finest poems ever to appear in America.

VERSES UPON THE BURNING OF OUR HOUSE, JULY 10TH, 1666

Thou hast an house on high erect,
Fram'd by that mighty Architect,
With glory richly furnished,
Stands permanent though this bee fled.
It's purchased, and paid for too
By him who hath enough to doe.

A Prise so vast as is unknown,
Yet, by his Gift, is made thine own.
Ther's wealth enough, I need no more;
Farewell my Pelf, farewell my Store.
The world no longer let me Love,
My hope and Treasure lyes Above.

Anne Bradstreet

"THE DAY OF DOOM"

Before his face the Heav'ns gave place, and Skies are rent asunder,
With mighty voice, and hideous noise, more terrible than Thunder.
His brightness damps heav'ns glorious lamps and makes them hide their heads,
As if afraid and quite dismay'd, they quit their wonted steads.

Ye sons of men that durst contemn the Threatnings of Gods Word.
How cheer you now? your hearts, I trow, are thrill'd as with a sword.
Now Atheist blind, whose brutish mind a God could never see,
Dost thou perceive, dost now believe that Christ thy Judge shall be?

Michael Wigglesworth, 1662

Edward Taylor

JAMES E. BARCUS

Paradox characterizes Edward Taylor's character and life, as well as his poetic themes and style. Born in Coventry, England in 1642, he died in the village of Westfield, Massachusetts in 1729. His Puritan sympathies probably drove him to the colonies, where he seems to have entered Harvard College with advanced standing, graduating in 1671. Following a call to the ministry, Taylor served the rural and frontier settlement of Westfield, where he gained a considerable reputation for his sincerity and integrity. Yet, after his death, he was plunged into several centuries of obscurity until his papers were uncovered in Yale University library in 1939. And not until 1960 were his complete poems published, earning Taylor a firm place in American literature, despite his desire that his poems never see the light of day. A preacher now known for poetic exercises in spiritual devotion, Taylor was a frontiersman as well as the owner of a cosmopolitan library. He wrote private devotional poetry which tells little about either his personal life or frontier living, but his work demonstrates both a commitment to Puritanism and extensive reading in seventeenth-century English meditative verse.

Taylor's intellectual commitment to Puritan thought and theology permeates both his meditations preparatory to Holy Communion and the long dramatic poem, "God's Determinations." In the latter poem, Justice and Mercy debate the disposition of the human soul, God elects whom he wills, Satan rages, and Christ responds:

> Peace, Peace, my Hony, do not Cry,
> My Little Darling, wipe thine eye,
>   Oh Cheer, Cheer up, come see.
> Is anything to deare, my Dove,
> Is anything too good, my Love
>   To get or give for thee?

In the two series of "Preparatory Meditations," poems written to prepare Taylor for the preaching of Communion sermons, the poet dramatizes a sinner redeemed by unmerited favor.

> My Sin! my Sin, My God, these
>   Cursed Dregs,
>   Green, yellow, Blew streakt Poy-
>   son hellish, ranck,
> Bubs hatcht in natures nest on
>   Serpents Eggs,
>   Yelp, Cherp and Cry; they set my
>   Soule a Cramp.

But sin is not triumphant.

> Nails made of heavenly Steel, more
>   Choice than gold
> Drove home, Well Clencht, eternally
>   will hold.

Even in these meditations, however, Taylor's accounts are not personal revelations. Following the Puritan tradition, his emphasis is not personal experience so much as the significance of a universal condition.

If Taylor is Puritan in thought and in his approach to art, he was not, however, ignorant of the great English religious meditation tradition. A contemporary of John Dryden, he looked back to the earlier generation of English metaphysical poets, especially John Donne and George Herbert. Although he was familiar with Herbert's themes and style, Taylor was not a mere imitator. Whatever he borrowed, he assimilated and transformed into a peculiarly American style. In "God's Determinations" he employs the metaphysical love of paradox, but he amplifies his premise with homely, functional images.

> Infinity, when all things it beheld
> In Nothing, and of Nothing all did build,
> Upon what Base was fixt the Lath, wherein
> He turn'd this Globe, and rigalld it so trim?
> Who blew the Bellows of his Furnace Vast?

* * *

Who in this Bowling Alley
  bowld the Sun?
Who made it always when it rises set
To go at once both down,
  and up to get?

For Taylor, the Communion bread is
"Food too fine for Angelles," yet God
invites man "Eate thy fill. Its heavens
Sugar Cake." In the Incarnation,

Gods only Son doth hug Humanity,
Into his very person. By which Union
His Humane Veans its
  golden gutters ly.

In order to save man, "These Golden
Pipes, to give my drink, did burst."

Thus the poet anticipates the
Communion wine:

Lord, make thy Butlar draw, and fill
  with speed
My Beaker full; for this is drink
  indeed.

Homely, but cosmopolitan; intellectually a Puritan but deeply read in
the Christian meditative tradition,
Taylor forged a unique poetic voice.
Paradoxically, his desire to preserve
poetic anonymity, to pass through the
self to the essence of religious experience guaranteed him a permanent
place in American literature.

The Salem Witch Trials
RICHARD LOVELACE

Until the Enlightenment, most of the
civilized West took for granted the
existence and powers of sorcerers. In
the fifteenth century the Roman Catholic Inquisition intensified its attack
on witchcraft, and trials and executions of witches continued to increase
in both Catholic and Protestant territories through the seventeenth
century. The Salem Witch Trials of
1692 played a decisive role in halting
this pattern.

New England Puritanism was not
extraordinarily susceptible to fear of
witchcraft. While theologians like Perkins and Bernard believed that black
magic could do real harm, and was
therefore a crime punishable by death
according to scripture and the common practice of Western governments,
they sought to refine the methods of
detecting and trying witches to avoid
superstition and conviction of the'
innocent. While five thousand witches
had been burned in Alsace in the
1600s, and five hundred in the city of
Bamberg alone, only a dozen were
executed in New England before 1692.

In that year, however, the shift in the
colony's charter, the attendant loss
of Puritan control, and the battles with
Native Americans and the French on
the frontier may have created a sense
of spiritual siege in New England
which exacerbated the witchcraft crisis.

The trials in Salem originated in a
group of adolescent girls associated
with the parish church in Salem Village (now Danvers), including a
daughter and niece of the minister,
Samuel Parris, and the daughter of
Thomas Putnam, the parish clerk. The
girls had experimented with divination
of the future through the use of
eggwhite in a glass, and may also
have been influenced by West Indian
magic through Tituba, Parris' slavegirl
from Barbados. In February 1692 they
became subject to severe convulsive
fits. Asked about the cause of these,
they claimed to be bewitched by
Tituba as well as two old women with
doubtful reputations, Sarah Good
and Sarah Osburn. When these were
arraigned and examined, the girls
again suffered convulsions and

claimed to be tormented by apparitions emanating from the women. Tituba confessed that she was indeed a witch, that she had made a pact with Satan, and that there were seven other witches known to her besides the three already accused.

From this point onward a repetitive pattern developed: the girls accused other women and men whose apparitions visited and tormented them; the malign power of these was confirmed by the girls' convulsions in their presence; and the suspects were convicted on the basis of the girls' accusation and behavior. By the summer of 1692 the jails were full of the accused, and about fifty had confessed to witchcraft. The Salem authorities were more lenient than common European practice; they released those who confessed and were presumed repentant. But in May a Special Court of Oyer and Terminer under Lieutenant Governor William Stoughton began to execute the unrepentant "guilty," and by September 22 nineteen persons had been hanged, and one pressed to death because he would not testify.

The phenomena associated with the afflicted girls and the accused fit readily into four categories. The bodily contortions and the occasional presence of alternate personalities in the afflicted indicate hysteria and other psychopathic conditions. These are also classic symptoms of demonic possession, according to the literature of exorcism. Paranormal abilities encountered at Salem include clairvoyance, telepathy, and levitation, and

"Trial of George Jacobs of Salem for Witchcraft"

Original Salem witchcraft documents. Above: depositions of Mrs. Ann Putnam and daughter Ann against Rebecca Nurse before magistrates Hathorne and Corwin. Below: indictment against Abigail Hobbs, who "a Covenant with the Evil Spirritt the Devill did make." COURTESY ESSEX INSTITUTE, SALEM, MASS.

there were poltergeist phenomena associated with some of the afflicted. Occult elements included sympathetic magic with the use of images, divination, casting of spells, and palmistry.

Those who confessed claimed to be witches, and some may have been in earnest. It may be that some of those earlier accused and executed harbored the same belief. But the girls' accusations gradually implicated persons whose character and testimony were unimpeachable. This and the rapid expansion of the number of the accused began to erode confidence in the trials, although the magistrates and a majority of the public were reluctant to discredit what seemed to be the evidence of their own eyes. The clergy had consistently urged caution, beginning with Deodat Lawson, Samuel Parris' predecessor at Salem Village, who had warned against the use of "spectral evidence" which could be counterfeited by Satan acting as an accuser of the innocent. Cotton Mather had repeated this warning, and had recommended prayer and pastoral care as a cure for the afflicted, and mercy toward the accused. After the first execution the Boston clergy drew up a document which gave nominal support to the magistrates but warned at length against superstition and inadequate evidence. Finally Increase Mather directly challenged the court with the publication of a tract against spectral evidence, although his son argued that there had been real witchcraft at Salem and that the Puritan establishment had not been wholly misled.

By 1697 Massachusetts was ready to confess its guilt in the shedding of innocent blood by observing a public fast day. The common opinion by that time was that the Devil had indeed been active in Salem, but not so much in the suspected witches as in their accusers, who had been both tormented and used as instruments to slander the innocent. Anticlerical witnesses like Robert Calef, however, would twist the evidence against the clergy and use the incident to discredit the existence of witches and devils and the intelligence of Christians. It is ironic that just when theologians were using witchcraft as an indirect proof of the reality of the supernatural and the divine, the stream of witchcraft and demonry was about to go underground, not to emerge again to public view until the late twentieth century.

Varieties of Religion

Convenient as it is to lump all New Englanders together in talking about "Puritan piety," such an action oversimplifies unjustly what is a much more complicated situation. In fact, wide differences were present within New England in actual religious goals and practices. Boston merchants who prized peace and good order as an expression of God's blessing expressed different religious attitudes than ministers in the Connecticut River Valley, like Solomon Stoddard, who looked for conversions as the crucial sign of God's presence. And there was always a substantial element in New England which, if it shared Puritan religious exercises, did not share the Puritan's faith.

If this kind of variety existed in relatively homogeneous New England, it is not surprising that a much broader spectrum of religiosity prevailed in other colonial regions. By 1730 immigrants from centers of European Pietism had begun to exert a strong influence in the colonies. Increasing numbers of Lutherans, Mennonites, Moravians, Brethren, German Baptists, and Schwenkfelders were entering America and bringing with them the practices of Pietism. Pietists

In 1731, all Lutherans were expelled from Salzburg, Austria. The SPCK helped the Salzburg emigrants relocate in Georgia. Literally, the poem reads: "Nothing but the gospel forces us into exile. Should we leave the Fatherland, we are still in God's hand." LIBRARY OF CONGRESS

were similar in several ways to the Puritans—for example, in their devotion to scripture and their belief in the New Birth—yet they also contributed an experiential, outward-looking element largely lacking before that time in the colonies.

The middle colonies generally, and Pennsylvania particularly, welcomed the greatest number of Pietists. This region also received Puritan influences filtering down from New England and the Presbyterian ethos associated with Scottish and Scotch-Irish immigration. As a result, the middle colonies possessed a striking variety, not only of denominations and ethnic groups, but also of religious styles. To the extent that the United States became a pluralistic culture encompassing many spiritual varieties, its prototype was Pennsylvania and the other middle colonies.

In the South the aristocratic spirituality of the planter class gravitated in the direction of Anglican latitudinarianism during the eighteenth century. It concentrated upon the benevolence and reasonableness of God, the creator of an orderly universe. Such a faith, however, was usually less influential in shaping upperclass Virginia values than the aggressive and independent spirit which planters

had nourished since Virginia's earliest days.

An entirely different approach to religion also appeared in the South during the eighteenth century. Particularly in the backcountry, where churches were scarce and the population thinly scattered, some individuals gave up the pretense of organized religion to meet informally for reading the Bible and published sermons and for encouraging each other in times of trial. Those who practiced this kind of piety constituted a fertile field for the seeds of revival that Presbyterians, Baptists, and Methodists would sow after midcentury.

Throughout the colonies many people lived out their lives without the benefit of formal Christianity. First-time visitors to America as well as travelers in the backcountry frequently commented upon this fact. A New Jersey official remarked in 1702 that his still very young colony had "public worship of any sort" in only two or three communities, and that in general the "people live very mean like Indians." On August 16, 1768, a missionary for the SPG, Charles Woodmason, preached at Flat Creek in the South Carolina upcountry to a group of people who had never before heard a minister. "After the Service," the disgruntled itinerant recorded in his journal, "they went out to Revelling, Drinking, Singing, Dancing and Whoring, and most of the Company were drunk before I quitted the Spott."

For such people as Woodmason encountered, who lived beyond the pale of regular church life—as also for many in settled regions who attended church regularly—another form of religion (using the term broadly) was quite important. This was the occult. Recent studies have shown that particularly in the period before the Great Awakening and the Enlightenment exerted their influence in the colonies (before, that is, 1720 or so), many colonists cultivated astrology, divination, and witchcraft. The English practice of looking to local "cunning men" or "wise women" for supernatural aid in finding cures for bodily ills seems to have taken root in some American regions. We know much about the Salem witch trials, but not about the many other individuals and accusations involving witchcraft that continued into the eighteenth century; the last American executions for witchcraft were, however, at Salem.

The presence of such practices in colonial America points up the fact that almost all Europeans and Americans in the seventeenth and eighteenth centuries had a sharper sense

Right: title page of Increase Mather's treatise on witchcraft. Below: eighteenth-century baptism in Pennsylvania RIGHT: LIBRARY OF CONGRESS BELOW: BILLY GRAHAM CENTER

Cases of Conscience
Concerning evil
SPIRITS

Personating Men, Witchcrafts, infallible Proofs of Guilt in such as are accused with that Crime.

All Considered according to the Scriptures, History, Experience, and the Judgment of many Learned men.

By Increase Mather, President of Harvard College at Cambridge, and Teacher of a Church at BOSTON in New-England.

Prov. 22. 21. —— *That thou mightest Answer the words of Truth, to them that send unto thee.*

Efficiunt Dæmones, ut quæ non sunt, sic tamen, quasi sint, conspicienda hominibus exhibeant. Lactantius Lib. 2. Instit. Cap. 15. *Diabolus Consulitur, cum ijs medijs utimur aliquid Cognoscendi, quæ a Diabolo sunt introducta.* Ames. Cas. Consc. L. 4. Cap. 23.

BOSTON Printed, and Sold by *Benjamin Harris* at the London Coffee-House. 1693.

SCHUYLKILL

of the supernatural than is common, even among Christians, today. Thus we find common people in Chester County, Pennsylvania, during the 1690s consulting Robert and Philip Roman with "questions Concerning Loss and gain," and receiving answers after the Romans had read the stars or their petitioners' palms. Almanacs sold very widely in colonial America (with far greater sales than Bibles), in part because their astronomical data enabled people to cast their own horoscopes. But the traffic in the paranormal was not restricted to the humble folk. John Winthrop's son brought with him to America a very large library on alchemy. And in his diary Cotton Mather recorded visits from angels on three different occasions.

In sum, a lively sense of the supernatural, several strands of traditional Christian piety, and wide varieties of non-Christian religious practices all existed in colonial America, sometimes tightly interwoven with each other. To understand colonial religious life, therefore, it is necessary to avoid stereotypes about the early settlers' spiritual condition and to look further afield than the usual experiences of regular church life.

Going to Church

At the same time, however, colonial church life (more narrowly conceived) presents an interesting picture to modern Americans. The residents of the colonies went to different kinds of church buildings, sang different sorts of hymns, and heard a different style of

Pietism

F. ERNEST STOEFFLER

Pietism is a discernible historical phenomenon which arose within Continental Protestantism during the latter half of the seventeenth century. Among Lutherans it has been customary to date its beginnings from the publication of Philip Jacob Spener's *Pia desideria* in the fall of 1675, a tract which called for a thoroughgoing reform of church and society through religiously renewed individuals. In point of fact, however, its emphases were anticipated within the Reformed communion and shared by many so-called "radicals" whose association with established Christendom was very tenuous.

In reaction against the general religious climate of the day Pietists were profoundly convinced of the individual's need for religious renewal (new birth), which would then have to be evidenced by a life of piety. They accepted a more or less literal, commonsense interpretation of the Bible as their unfailing guide for faith and life. Their deep commitment to Christian fellowship was often fostered by

small group meetings to strengthen their devotional life. It was symbolized, furthermore, by the fact that they referred to one another as "brother" or "sister," a brother or sister being anyone who adhered to the Pietist perspective irrespective of church affiliation. Their sense of distinctiveness was expressed by their lifestyle which was fashioned in conscious opposition to the more or less shallow folk religion of the religious establishment. Pietism was thus interested primarily in ethical living rather than religious polemics, in social engagement rather than mere theological consent, in the present and the future as much as in the past, and in brotherhood rather than ecclesiastical or socio-cultural affiliations.

The influence of Pietism upon the Protestant churches would be difficult to overestimate. The sermons and hymns it produced reshaped much of Christian worship, while its emphasis on pastoral concern helped to alter the perception of the Christian ministry. It gave the laity its rightful place

preaching than churchgoers do today. But before examining these aspects of colonial religious life, it would be well to address the knotty question of how many people actually went to church.

To obtain an answer to this question it is necessary to avoid two extremes—the mythological view which sees all colonial Americans in church every Sunday of the year and the historical myopia which considers statistics for church membership as a reliable guide to the numbers of those actually in church. These statistics do reveal a low proportion of church membership in colonial America— never more than one-third of New England's adults, and as low as five percent of southern adults. (By contrast, more than sixty percent of American adults are now church mem-

bers.) What these figures fail to note, however, is that church attendance was always much higher than church membership. In New England the scrupulousness with which residents looked upon conversion (not to speak of the fear which some souls felt at testifying before a full congregation) made joining the church a major step indeed. In the South the absence of bishops prevented proper confirmations, and in the middle colonies a more rapidly shifting population kept formal membership low. But in every region a large number of people attended church who were not actually members. The most recent studies of this subject do show a decline in church attendance throughout the eighteenth century, but argue that in 1700 about four-fifths of the colonial population

in the life of the churches, lifted Protestantism's sights to its missionary obligations, introduced the devotional study of the Bible and other materials to the home, set up a network of charitable as well as educational institutions, stimulated church attendance, and introduced the first glimmers of ecumenical concern.

In colonial America Pietism, like Puritanism, was one of the most pervasive influences. Among Lutherans it was especially promoted by Henry Melchior Muhlenberg, a loyal disciple of August Hermann Francke who had been the founder and guiding genius of the Halle institutions.

Theodore J. Frelinghuysen, whose religious maturation took place in the Reformed Pietist centers of the lower Rhine, introduced the first revival among his Dutch constituency of the Raritan Valley in New Jersey. Among the German Reformed people of the middle colonies Michael Schlatter and Philip William Otterbein gave the greatest Pietist impulse. The latter also became one of the founders of

the United Brethren. The Renewed Moravian Church grew out of a visit to America by Count Nikolaus Ludwig von Zinzendorf, who had also imbibed the religious stance of Francke. Pietism influenced the German Baptist Brethren as well as the Mennonites. Through the Wesleys it had an impact on Methodism, and through Isaac Backus and others on the Baptist churches. The effect it had on the Congregationalists, the Presbyterians, the Episcopalians, as well as various revivalist movements and later evangelicalism, is not yet fully understood, though the lines of development are beginning to emerge.

Whether it is Puritanism or Pietism which dominantly shaped Protestantism in colonial America, as well as its impact on American institutions, is impossible to say at this time. There can be little doubt, however, that the Pietist understanding of life contributed heavily both to the excellencies and shortcomings of American culture during its early history.

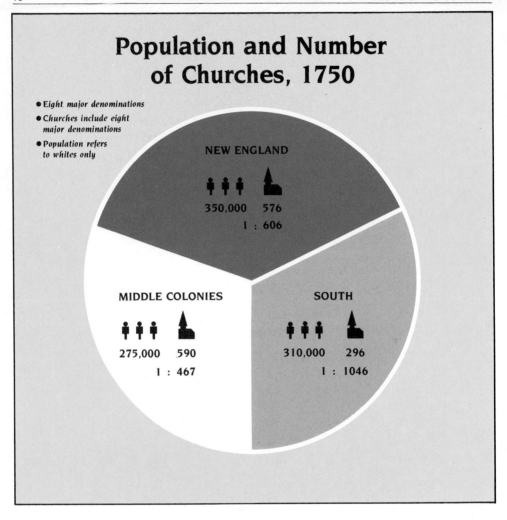

Population and Number
of Churches, 1750

- Eight major denominations
- Churches include eight major denominations
- Population refers to whites only

NEW ENGLAND

350,000   576

1 : 606

MIDDLE COLONIES

275,000   590

1 : 467

SOUTH

310,000   296

1 : 1046

attended church regularly (at least two out of three Sundays) and in 1780 about three-fifths. Attendance was lower in the South where distances between churches were greater and where even regular members went less frequently. (George Washington was a vestryman, yet he attended his Truro Parish church only about ten times a year in the decade before the start of the Revolutionary War.) But even in that region a surprisingly large number of inhabitants attended church frequently. Throughout the colonies, bad weather—particularly the snow of winter and rains with swollen creeks of spring—reduced attendance. In general, however, a substan-

tial number, certainly never less than a majority, of early Americans were in church most Sundays. And what were their places of worship like?

In New England the spire or steeple was a late addition because of the fear of imitating "popish" churches. The early "meetinghouse" (sometimes called "the Lord's Barn" but not until much later a "church") was quite small, as tiny as 350 square feet and only occasionally as much as 1500-2000 square feet. The classical New England church beloved by painters and calendar-makers—with white clapboard, elongated windows, and a graceful steeple—began to appear only in the

Above: first meetinghouse in Hartford, Connecticut
(1638); right: eighteenth-century colonial spire;
below: Lutheran Church, Fifth Street, Philadelphia
ABOVE: THE GRANGER COLLECTION   RIGHT: BILLY
GRAHAM CENTER   BELOW: LIBRARY OF CONGRESS

eighteenth century. In New England as well as in other colonies, any old structure was used at first for Sunday worship. It was as likely to look like—and be—a fort, a granary, or a barn as a modern church. When permanent buildings were constructed, they tended to be made of wood in New England, of stone in the middle colonies, and of brick in the South.

A "Typical" Sunday in Seventeenth-Century New England

The Puritan sabbath began, as it had for Old Testament Israel, the night before. Sundown Saturday commenced the Puritan day of worship, when in pious households fathers read the scriptures to their families and led them in prayer. The next morning a drum or cannon (later a bell) would call them to worship.

The meetinghouse was usually centrally located in the village and only a modest distance from the homes of most residents. This building anticipated the multipurpose community centers of the twentieth century by serving also as a town hall, public works building, and, in the days of Indian warfare, fortified refuge. In the first meetinghouses colonists sat on narrow wooden benches without back supports. By the mid-seventeenth century Puritans had begun to "seat the meeting," whereby an appropriate committee assigned pews or boxes according to social position, and the families paid to have them constructed for themselves. It was also an early practice to reserve seating in the front for the elderly and hard of hearing. Meetinghouses were not fancy. Stoves did not appear regularly until the nineteenth century; daubing or plastering was also a late addition. The first meetinghouse usually had only one window, located behind the pulpit. The result was that in winter particularly, it took much fortitude to attend services in the cold and gloom. It was not infrequent for ministers, who preached in greatcoat and gloves from November to April, to ask their numbed congregations to stamp their feet more quietly during the sermon. After a few years, a number of communities added galleries, or balconies, to their meetinghouses where servants and other marginal residents sat. The only ornamental feature in the early meetinghouses was a cushion with corner tassels for the pulpit Bible, which local ladies con-

Nineteenth-century version of Puritan preaching, entitled "The Long Sermon"   COURTESY ESSEX INSTITUTE, SALEM, MASS.

structed from as much as four yards of velvet and ten of silk.

Most Puritan churches held two services on Sunday, one before noon and one about an hour after the end of the first. Between services in the winter the people who lived nearby returned to their homes for warmth and cold cuts (no cooking fires were to be started on the sabbath), while those who came from a distance gathered at the "nooning house," where there was a stove. The interval between services was also put to use in teaching children their catechism.

Sermons and prayers were more serious matters then than now. Prayers could last up to an hour, and sermons under an hour would have been rare as late as the Revolution. Seventeenth-century meetinghouses usually had an hourglass beside the pulpit, and it was far from uncommon for ministers to "preach the glass around" two or even three times. Not surprisingly, parishioners sometimes fell asleep, whereupon specially deputed tithingmen might awaken the ladies with a caress from a hare's foot and the men with a tap on the head from a knobbed stick. In the early meetinghouses men and women (often with small children) sat on different sides of the building, a situation which changed after the construction of family pews.

The Puritan sermon was at once simple and profound. It began with a text of scripture which the minister resolved into a one-sentence "Doctrine," or proposition, which itself was resolved into several subsidiary "doctrines." These were expounded in a "plain style" which used illustrations and stories sparingly, but which was rich in the imagery of the people—metaphors and conceits from the agricultural round and the life of common artisans. It closed with a series of "Uses," or applications, that spoke more directly to the condition of the congregation.

The sermon was the central intellectual event for many, if not most, New Englanders well into the eighteenth century. It set out a powerful picture of reality as a cosmic struggle between God and his agents, on one side, and Satan and his, on the other. It then drew in the congregation as participants in that great battle. As individuals they learned how they could be joined through Christ with the Lord of righteousness and commit their lives to faithfully fulfilling his covenant. As a corporate body, they also received instruction on how God dealt with peoples generally, and with his covenanted people particularly. The sermon, in short, was the principal means by which the Puritan vision was communicated to the Puritan folk. No one has yet assessed satisfactorily its vast impact on the consciousness of early New England generations.

A "Typical" Sunday in Eighteenth-Century Virginia

The Sunday of Virginia Anglicans differed in many respects from the Sunday of New England Puritans. But a number of elements were the same. The Anglicans, like the Congregationalists, usually had two services, one in the morning and, after a break, one in the early afternoon. Anglicans as well as Puritans performed baptisms as part of their regular Sunday worship. (Anglicans also performed weddings during the church services, but Puritans, who wished to remove the taint of "popery" that had made marriage

a sacrament, performed their weddings before civil authorities.) And both kinds of service were affected more directly by disturbing elements—stray dogs, late arrivals, blustery weather—than is the case today. (The rail surrounding the Anglican altar, or communion table, was in fact first erected during the seventeenth century to keep wandering dogs away from the expensive hangings with which it was decked.)

The great differences between southern and New England worship stemmed from Anglican use of the Book of Common Prayer. Anglican church buildings reflected the emphases of the prayer book, with the font (for baptism), the pulpit (for preaching), and the table (for communion) providing the liturgical focus. The communion table was regularly at the east end of the building, with the font in the west, and the pulpit somewhere in the middle, usually along a wall but sometimes (as in Puritan churches) in the middle. Pulpits were double- or triple-deckers, with a reading desk for a lay clerk at the lowest level, a second-level desk for the minister to read scripture, and sometimes a third deck from which the sermon was preached. Seating was considerably more flexible than it

Bruton Parish Church, the court church of eighteenth-century Virginia in its capital, Williamsburg LIBRARY OF CONGRESS

later became, and parishioners were able to turn their stools or chairs to the altar or pulpit as the service moved from one part to another. Children, who sat on stools in the pew boxes or sometimes on the stairs to the balcony, had a good view of the minister raised in the high pulpit—and he, presumably, of them!

The church service itself followed the Prayer Book fully, which provided a rich liturgical experience considerably longer than Anglican or Episcopalian services today. A Sunday without communion would normally include the singing of a metrical psalm, Opening Sentences that called to repentance, the General Confession, the Absolution, the Lord's Prayer, other liturgical prayers, scripture lessons from the Psalms, the Old Testament, and the New, a service of baptism (if this was required), another song, the Apostles' Creed, the Kyrie Eleison, the Collect (or fixed prayer) for that Sunday, the Litany (a lengthy formal prayer), a sermon, further prayers, and the final Blessing. On communion Sundays (perhaps three or four a year, compared to the monthly communions in most Puritan churches) there would be further scripture, offerings, Confession, Absolution, perhaps a song, and the actual

Trinity Episcopal Church, Newport, Rhode Island (1724), showing its "triple-decker" pulpit
TRINITY EPISCOPAL CHURCH

celebration of the Eucharist. The large flagons of the day attest the fact that communicants were expected to do more than sip daintily the communion wine (ministers sometimes figured a quarter of a pint of wine for each communicant). Depending on the minister, the sermon would be short and perfunctory, or intense and nearly as long as the Puritans'.

Sundays were social days in the South as well as in New England, but in Virginia the values of the aristocrats sometimes worked at cross purposes with the values of the church. By the time of the Revolution, "gentlemen" had begun to use Sunday worship as an occasion to solidify their own ranks and to accentuate their differences with the common people. One contemporary Virginian reported that it was "a general custom on Sundays here, with Gentlemen to invite one another home to dine, after church; and to consult about, determine their common business, either before or after Service" when they discussed "the price of Tobacco, Grain, etc. and setting either the lineage, Age, or qualities of favourite Horses." The same observer also noted that it was "not the Custom for Gentlemen to go into Church til Service is beginning, when they enter in a Body, in the same manner as they come out."

The Music

From the start both Puritans and Anglicans raised their voices in song during church services. During the seventeenth century both types of Protestants sang metrical psalms without accompaniment. A deacon (in New England) or the parish clerk (in Virginia) would announce the tune to be used (about forty popular ones were commonly in use) and then "line out" the psalm for the congregation. This procedure called for the leader to read or sing one or several lines of the psalm and then for the congregation to sing them back. Lyrics came from collections like the Bay Psalm Book or, for Anglicans, Tate and Brady's 1696 Psalter, whose "Supplement" contained hymns that are still in use, such as "Jesus Christ is Risen Today" and "While Shepherds Watched Their Flocks."

Historian Ola Winslow, quoting critics who came to decry this method, provides a description of what such singing was like in New England:

> To sing the Old Way, or as its adherents chose to call it, "the Usual Way", was to sing without regard to the time and pitch of anyone else. One merely "took the Run of the Tune", as the saying was, and then added "little Flourishes" of one's own according to one's own vocal talents and the inspiration of the moment, clipping some notes or hanging on to them, singing some "too *high*, others too *low*, and most too *long*", performing "little Slidings and Purrings, raisings and lowerings" as the heart inclined. Thereby was the singing made individual and thereby was the Lord pleased. Naturally, on such a course no one came out at the same time as anyone else. While the singer in one pew was continuing to intone line three, possibly taking two breaths to one note, his neighbor in the next pew was halfway through line four and charging along to the finish. "Indecent jargon" resulted.

Anglican churches were less reluctant to use a choir, either to aid in congregational singing or to offer an occasional anthem, or to employ a barrel organ. Such musical embellishments were, however, rare in Anglican services because of expense and the difficulty in organizing choirs. Puritans resisted them as remnants of Roman Catholic formalism.

In the eighteenth century rising standards of taste, declining fear of Rome, and growing financial resources combined to alter the nature of singing in New England churches. Robert Tufts, a young Harvard graduate, published in 1715 a small guide to singing by the note, *An Introduction to the Singing of Psalm Tunes, in a Plain & Easy Method, With a Collection of Tunes in Three Parts*. Other manuals soon followed, and a "Singing Quarrel" ensued. Older laypeople saw regular, unified, and more musical singing as a return to "popery," but most ministers and younger laypeople favored the "New Way." Soon singing in parts and specially trained choirs were the order of the day. Organs, which came into use increasingly in Anglican churches during the eighteenth century, followed in Congregational churches in the next century.

The eighteenth-century interest in singing created dissatisfaction with the older metrical psalms. English-speaking Protestants began to import newer hymns and their tunes from the mother country, and a few Americans began to write their own. The best of these composers was William Billings (1746-1800) who published *The New Eng-*

PSALM 23

The Lord to mee a shepheard is, want therefore shall not I.
Hee in the folds of tender-grasse, doth cause mee downe to lie:
To waters calme me gently leads
Restore my soule doth hee: he doth in paths of righteousness:
    for his names sake leade mee.
Yea though in valley of deaths shade I walk, none ill I'le feare:
    because thou art with mee, thy rod, and staffe my comfort are.
For mee a table thou hast spread, in presence of my foes:
    thou dost annoynt my head with oyle, my cup it over-flowes.
Goodnes & mercy surely shall all my dayes follow mee:
    and in the Lords house I shall dwell so long as dayes shall bee.

The Bay Psalm Book

Frontispiece of William Billings's The New England Psalm Singer (1770), *engraved by* Paul Revere
THE WILLIAM CLEMENTS LIBRARY, UNIVERSITY OF MICHIGAN

land Psalm-Singer in 1770, the first book of hymns or of any totally American music published on American soil. Billings brought out several other anthem collections, all of which contained hymns of genuine quality that may still be heard today (for example, "Methinks I See a Heavenly Light," "I Am the Rose of Sharon"). Billings was the best musician in colonial America, yet he was never able to earn his living at music, but was forced to serve the city of Boston as hogreeve (who kept swine off the streets) and streetcleaner, among other posts.

The most notable church music in colonial America, however, came not from the Puritans or the Anglicans, but from the Moravians. These European Pietists, who

traced their origins back to the Bohemian Brethren and the Czech martyr John Hus of the early fifteenth century, were part of the revitalization movement of Count Nikolaus Ludwig von Zinzendorf (1700-1760). Under Zinzendorf's leadership the Moravians became active missionaries, with the first group arriving in America during the 1730s. Soon there were Moravian communities in North Carolina (Salem) and Pennsylvania (Bethlehem, Nazareth). Moravians brought with them much of the rich heritage of Lutheran music and a great love of music in general. From the first they accompanied their singing with flutes and trumpets, violins and horns. As they became more established, they added organs and orchestras. Some Moravian

Moravian community store, Salem, North Carolina
OLD SALEM, INC.

churches eventually had separate choirs for young boys, young girls, adolescent males, adolescent females, single women, married couples, widows, and widowers. Moravians helped introduce Bach and Handel to America, although they performed the music of Johann Christian Bach before that of his father Johann Sebastian. They also wrote a great deal of fine music themselves. The best of the Moravian hymn writers in colonial America was Johann Friedrich Peter (1746-1813), who came to Pennsylvania in 1770 and lived to produce a series of outstanding anthems. Moravians had none of the Puritan fear of formal music and possessed more musical expertise than the Anglicans. Their music remains not only a testimony of praise to God (as they meant it), but also a testimony to the broadening importance of continental ecclesiastical practices for American religious life.

Religion and the Family

Everyone knows that the most fundamental human values are bound up with the home, but only recently have historians examined the relationship between family and religion in colonial America. As with most aspects of colonial religious history, the great bulk of the work in this area has focused on the Puritans, both because of the abundance of records from New England and because of the fascination which this group has exercised for later Americans.

Puritans regularly used domestic images to describe relationships between God and his people. John Cotton, for example, interpreted the "marriage bed" in the Song of Solomon as "the publick worship of God in the Congregation of the Church." He went on, "the publick Worship of God is the bed of lovers: where, 1. Christ embraceth the souls of his people, and casteth into their hearts the immortal seed of his Word, and Spirit, *Gal.* 4:19. 2. The Church conceiveth and bringeth forth fruits to Christ." As this quotation suggests, Puritans were not overly squeamish about sex. They spoke more frankly than Victorians though less salaciously than moderns about sexual matters. Unlike Roman Catholics, they considered companionship an even more important goal than procreation in sexual relations between husband and wife. Puritans did deal harshly with adultery and fornication, but they did so much more because they valued sex within marriage in accordance with traditional biblical guidelines than because they were opposed to sexual pleasure. Many Puritans enjoyed marriages that, by the standards of any age, were triumphs of warmth and stability. As an example, the letters which John Winthrop and his wife Margaret exchanged while they were separated during the first year of colonization are filled with tender feelings and concern for each other's welfare.

The covenantal emphasis also played an important role in Puritan domestic relations. Husbands and wives, parents and children, masters and servants—all were expected to offer each other their just due. In a well-ordered marriage, husbands and wives offered each other exclusive cohabitation, husbands directed the family and mediated contact with the outside world, and wives managed the hearth and labored as much as possible in the fields or workshop. By the standards of the seventeenth and eighteenth centuries, colonial women enjoyed considerable freedom, including recourse at law for bringing an erring husband to book and for retaining at least some control over her own property.

and in Teſtimony of our Deſires, and Aſſurance to be heard, we ſay, AMEN.

Bleſſed are they that do his Commandments, that they may have Right to the Tree of life, and may enter in through the Gates into the City. Rev.22 14.

SPIRITUAL MILK
FOR
AMERICAN BABES.

Drawn out of the Breaſts of both *Teſtaments*, for their Souls Nouriſhment,

By JOHN COTTON.

Queſt. WHAT hath God done for you ? *Anſ* God hath made me, he keepeth me, and he can ſave me.

Q. *What is God ?*
A. God is a Spirit of himſelf and for himſe'f.
Q. *How many Gods be there ?*
A. There is but one God in three Perſons, the Father, the Son, and the Holy Ghoſt.
Q. *How did God make you ?*
A. In my firſt Parents Holy and Righteous.

Q. *Are you then born Holy and Righteous ?*
A. No, my fiſt Father ſinned and I in him.
Q. *Are you then born a Sinner ?*
A. I was conceived in Sin,&born in Iniquity.
Q. *What is your Birth Sin ?*
A. Adam's Sin imputed to me, and a corrupt Nature dwelling in me.
Q. *What is your corrupt Nature ?*
A. My corrupt Nature is empty ofGrace bent unto Sin, only unto Sin and that continually.
Q. *What is Sin ?*
A. Sin is a Tranſgreſſion of the Law.
Q. *How many Commandments of the law be there ?* A Ten.
Q. *What is the firſt Commandment ?*
A. Thou ſhalt have no other Gods before me.
Q. *What is the meaning of this Commandment ?*
A. That we ſhould worſhip the only true God, and no other beſides him.
Q. *What is the ſecond Commandment ?*
A Thou ſhalt not make to thyſelf any graven Image, &c.
Q. *What is the meaning of this Commandment ?*
A. That we ſhould worſhip the only true GOD, with true worſhip, ſuch as he hath ordained not ſuch as Man hath invented.
Q. *What is the third Commandment ?*

John Cotton's catechism (above) helped parents instruct their children in the Bible, while the New England Primer (right) taught both the alphabet and orthodox doctrine. LIBRARY OF CONGRESS

As early as 1600, when efforts at reforming English public life were not immediately successful, Puritans turned to the home as the one domain where their vision of godliness could prevail. American Puritans also took seriously the business of raising children for God. Fathers and mothers were expected to equip the children for reading the Bible and to catechize them faithfully. Fines were provided, though haphazardly enforced, for failure to instruct the children in Christian doctrine. Colonial parents had a great number of catechisms to choose from to perform that task, all of which attempted to instill the rudiments of the faith through direct questions and answers. Puritans also strove to see their children "well-settled" in the world. To that end parents provided suitable apprenticeships, arranged for marriage partners from families of similar backgrounds (prospective spouses retained veto power), bestowed land, money, or tools as marriage gifts, and also took great pains at spiritual instruction.

The family religion of the Puritans had a definite impact on the churches. Although Puritan ministers talked of free grace, an unusually high proportion of church members came from the sons and daughters of previous church members. In Milford, Connecticut, for example, three-fourths of the people who entered the church during the seventeenth century were descendants of the first group of church members, and families accounting for less than sixty percent of the population contributed nearly eighty percent of the church members. This situation has led some historians to speak of a "Puritan tribalism," in which Puritans came to be so obsessed with the salvation of their own children that they neglected the spiritual needs of everyone else. There is considerable truth to this charge, even if other historians have observed that such "tribalism" has been a regular feature of most religious groups throughout history.

Puritans did place high demands upon their children, at least after the first year of life

A

In *Adam's* Fall
We Sinned all.

B

Thy Life to Mend
This *Book* Attend.

C

The *Cat* doth play
And after flay.

D

A *Dog* will bite
A Thief at night.

E

An *Eagles* flight
Is out of fight.

F

The Idle *Fool*
Is whipt at School.

when babies were held frequently, nursed often, and kept thoroughly warm. Others in the colonies, as historian Philip Greven has pointed out, had more relaxed standards for their children. Greven has identified a "moderate" style of child-rearing which retained many of the "evangelical" (or Puritan) religious expectations, but which allowed more freedom for children in youth and adolescence. "Genteel" households, generally the wealthy families of the South and to a lesser extent the rest of the colonies, indulged children much more freely than did either "evangelicals" or "moderates." The borderlines between psychological temperament, religious convictions, and child-rearing practices are imprecise enough in modern times, and they continue to be so for students of colonial America. It is, nonetheless, important to realize that not all colonists raised their children as Puritans nor did all Puritans raise their children "puritanically," at least as that term is a synonym for a loveless severity.

Children's portraiture: right, Eleanor Darnell (Maryland); below, Sarah Northey King and daughter Sarah (New England) RIGHT: MARYLAND HISTORICAL SOCIETY BELOW: COURTESY ESSEX INSTITUTE, SALEM, MASS.

Religion and the Underclasses

The story of relations between English colonists and non-Europeans (blacks and Indians) is not a pretty one. It brightens only slightly when missionary efforts enter the picture. Twenty blacks arrived in Virginia in 1619 and were immediately sold into servitude, although some of these later secured their freedom. Racial suspicion of blacks prevailed from the start, but it was not until later in the seventeenth century that economic conditions and social tension among whites led to the full-blown slavery that prevailed in the South until the Civil War. As reformers of "the peculiar institution" would eventually point out, some very upstanding Puritan merchants joined southern planters in establishing racial slavery in America.

Eventually, and against great odds, the Christian faith took deep root among American blacks. The same cannot be said for the

Indians who greeted the European immigrants. In spite of persistent, if not too extensive, missionary efforts, only a few Indians became Christians. And, sad to say, the colonial Christians' own biblical convictions concerning divine justice, the equality of all people before God, and freely given grace in Christ did little to bridge the gap between their own culture and that of the Indians.

The Puritan Indian Mission

In spite of pious wishes in many colonial charters, only two groups worked consistently to convert Native Americans, the Puritans of New England during the middle third of the seventeenth century and the Moravians of Pennsylvania one hundred years later. The charter itself of Massachusetts Bay expressed the desire to evangelize the Indians. Its seal bore the image of an Indian and the words of the Macedonian to the Apostle Paul, "Come Over and Help Us." Yet missions did not begin immediately. Preoccupation with establishing a foothold in the New World, unfortunate conflict with one tribe (the Pequots of Connecticut), and an inability to fathom the nature of Indian culture retarded early efforts. Active missions only began when commentators in England asked pointedly about Indian converts and when the dedicated ministers John Eliot (1604-1690) and Thomas Mayhew, Jr. (1621-1657), put missionary programs into practice.

Eliot, minister of the Roxbury, Massachusetts church, preached successfully for the first time to an Indian audience on October 28, 1646. By 1651 he had gained enough converts to establish a "praying town" at Natick, a village laid out in imitation of the Puritans' own settlements where Indians were to escape the corruptions of their fellows and prepare for full Christian (and European) life. Eliot wrote constitutions for this and thirteen other praying towns in the next twenty years. To do this he relied heavily on Old Testament models—under the general supervision of a Massachusetts official, Indians elected leaders of ten, fifty, and one hundred on the pattern of Exodus 18. After years of work, and with the assistance of capable Indian helpers, Eliot published a translation of the Bible in the Massachuset dialect of Algonquian in 1661 (New Testament) and 1663

I now come to lay before you the duties you owe to your masters *and* mistresses *here upon earth. And for this, you have one general rule that you ought always to carry in your minds; — and that is, —* to do all service for them, as if you did it for God himself. . . . *Your* masters *and* mistresses *are God's* overseers, —*and . . . if you are faulty towards them, God himself will punish you severely for it in the next world.*

THOMAS BACON,
Two Sermons Preached to a Congregation of
Black Slaves, 1749

John Eliot (1604–1690) BILLY GRAHAM CENTER

John Eliot, the "Apostle to the Indians"

(the entire Bible). By the time of King Philip's War (1675), some 2,500 Indians (perhaps twenty percent of the Indian population of New England) had become at least nominally Christian. It was, however, an on-going problem to establish regular churches in the praying towns since Indian knowledge of doctrine and their ability to recount conversion experiences never met Puritan standards.

The other leader of Puritan missions, Thomas Mayhew, Jr., began his labors on Martha's Vineyard in 1647. Mayhew died within a decade after the beginning of the work, but his father, Thomas Mayhew, Sr., took up the task. By 1659 an Indian church was in place. Almost all of the Indians on Martha's Vineyard and the neighboring islands of Nantucket and Chappaquiddick had become nominally Christian by 1675. Descendants of the Mayhew family continued to work with the Indians on these Massachusetts islands well into the eighteenth century. Their work achieved the most long-lasting results of any colonial efforts to convert Native Americans.

In spite of efforts by Eliot and the Mayhews, however, Puritan missions were ultimately a failure. In the first place, even the most dedicated missionaries remained, by modern standards, incurably ethnocentric. They simply could not see how an Indian could become a Christian and not repudiate every aspect of Indian culture in favor of the European. Indians must, Eliot wrote, "have visible civility before they can rightly enjoy visible sanctities in ecclesiastical communion." Cotton Mather put it even more sharply in his biography of Eliot: Indians "must be *civilized* e'er they could be Christianized." The "praying towns" existed to liberate Indians from their own people as much as to bring them the gospel. In addition, Puritans uniformly regarded Indian culture as systematically infused with witchcraft and demon worship. Given these circumstances, Indian converts had little opportunity to internalize the faith in ways that were meaningful within their own culture. Puritans, at least for the first two generations, were not racists—they called upon whites to repent as strenuously as they did Indians, and whites who raped, murdered, or abused Indians felt the force of the law. But they were culturally blinkered and never conceived the possibility that an Indian Christianity could parallel their European faith without being identical to it. This attitude brought to naught several efforts to aid Indians in gaining spiritual maturity, including educational ventures. Eliot and the Mayhews worked diligently at writing grammars and establishing primary schools, and Harvard even built a special structure as an Indian college in 1659. But Indians who went to school often died from exposure to European diseases, and Puritans could not reproduce their love of learning among the converts.

Besides, many Puritans did not possess the benevolent intentions of Eliot and the Mayhews. New Englanders desired Indian land, and some—even the professedly godly— would do anything to get it. Particularly at times of crisis, efforts to evangelize the Indians gave way before outbursts of hostility. King Philip's War in the mid-1670s dealt a particularly damaging blow to white-Indian relations. The sachem Metacom (King Philip), convinced that English settlements were strangling Indian life, organized a powerful attack on white towns which took many lives and destroyed much property. Immediately, all Indians, and their friends like John Eliot, became suspect. Colonists assaulted some praying Indians. They rounded up all of the converts and hustled them to desolate Deer Island in Boston Harbor, where the Indians lived for the duration of the conflict with slim provisions and inadequate shelter. Although friendly Indian scouts eventually contributed greatly to the ultimate triumph over King Philip, white-Indian relations were irremediably damaged. From that time mission work among the Indians declined, efforts to bridge the cultural gap nearly ceased, and the systematic destruction of Indian culture went on unimpeded.

The Moravian Indian Mission
Moravian missions suffered less from their own cultural biases and more from the un-

friendliness of white settlers than did the Puritan. Moravians established mission work among the Indians almost as soon as they arrived in the colonies—Pennsylvania in 1734; Georgia, 1735; South Carolina, 1738; North Carolina, 1752. Count Zinzendorf himself went on three preaching tours in Indian areas during his brief stay in the colonies in 1742. The problems Moravians would have in mission efforts surfaced in their first work, at Shekomeko (now Pine Plains), Dutchess County, New York. Christian Henry Rauch preached among Mohicans beginning in 1740, soon gained converts, and established a church. By 1743 Shekomeko had sixty-three baptized converts, and the mission had spread to neighboring Indian communities. Then opposition commenced. White liquor sellers complained of lost business. Civil officials were uneasy with these foreigners who spoke only broken English. Some colonists even accused the Moravians of being Catholics or agents of French Canada. In addition, Moravians followed literally the New Testament injunction not to swear by anything in heaven or on earth, and thus refused to take the oath of allegiance to the English king. (They were prepared to "affirm" their loyalty, however.) As a result, the missionaries were imprisoned, and the mission had to be abandoned.

The major Moravian effort then shifted to the Indians of the Six Nations in Pennsylvania. There Moravians had similar successes but also met similar hostility. Pressure from unfriendly whites and Indians made it necessary to establish a special compound for converts near Bethlehem which the Moravians called Gnadenhütten ("sheltered by grace"). By 1748, five hundred Christian Indians had gathered at this mission station. The French and Indian Wars that began in the 1750s, however, destroyed the Moravian mission much as King Philip's War had the Puritan. In 1755 Indian allies of the French attacked Gnadenhütten, killed ten missionaries, and burned the Indian compound to the ground. Most of the Christian Indians escaped to Bethlehem, but they could not escape the suspicion of white settlers. In 1763 Scotch-Irish residents near Harrisburg, angered at the Pennsylvania government's inability to protect them from Indian attack, resolved to rid the land of Indians entirely.

Moravians baptizing Indian converts in Pennsylvania

These "Paxton Boys" slaughtered a small band of peaceful Conestoga Indians in Lancaster County. They next set out after the Moravian converts. The Indians fled first toward New York, but being repulsed there, they finally found refuge in Philadelphia. After hostilities ceased, the Christian Indians were shunted to northeastern Pennsylvania, then into the Ohio Territory. Settlers in Ohio eventually pushed them toward Detroit where, during the War of 1812, American forces under General Hull wiped them out almost completely.

Indian work did revive briefly in connection with the Great Awakening. Evangelists Samuel Davies in Virginia, David Brainerd in Pennsylvania, Eleazar Wheelock in Connecticut and New Hampshire, Jonathan Edwards in Massachusetts, and other proponents of revival went out of their way to preach to the Indians. Yet the cultural bias remained, and there were few long-term results of the

increased activity. Christian colonists, who conquered so much in securing the gospel for themselves, could not in the last analysis conquer themselves to secure the gospel for the Indians.

The Reverend Samson Occom (1723–1792), Mohegan Indian and a graduate of Eleazer Wheelock's Indian school in Lebanon, Connecticut, was ordained a Presbyterian clergyman in 1759.
NATIONAL PORTRAIT GALLERY, SMITHSONIAN INSTITUTION, WASHINGTON, D.C.

Christianity and Slavery in the Colonial Period
LESTER B. SCHERER

African slaves were first used in the British colonies early in the seventeenth century. When the Declaration of Independence was signed 150 years later, one of every five residents of the new nation was African or African-descended, and slavery existed in all thirteen states.

Clergy and laypeople of all the colonial churches — Catholics, Anglicans, Congregationalists, Presbyterians, Baptists, Friends, Methodists, Lutherans, and various national Reformed bodies — were slaveholders and slave traders; Mennonites, Amish, and other "communitarian" sects were the only exceptions. Some parishes were supported by slave labor and were involved in enforcing slave codes. Devout Christians were among those who rode patrol, served as constables, and administered public and private punishment to slaves.

Most colonial Christians found no reason to oppose slavery because no segment of the Christian church had ever done so consistently. Beginning in New Testament times, the church embraced both slaveholders and slaves. Biblical advice to both parties was elaborated by patristic and medieval authorities. Later on, both Protestants and Catholics shared the traditional acceptance of slavery, so that colonists in North America could draw on a strong tradition for defending slavery, while looking in vain for a Christian tradition to oppose it. (1) Africans could be enslaved, because they were under Noah's curse upon his son Ham. (2) God's people Israel had held slaves. (3) Christ did not prohibit slavery. (4) Slavery was merely the lowest grade in a divinely approved social order. (5) Enslavement of Africans actually improved their lives, particularly in giving them access to the gospel.

"The thin edge of anti-slavery" emerged late in the seventeenth century, largely within the Society of Friends (Quakers). Quaker protest was directed originally to the slaveholding Friends, who were numerous in the seventeenth and early eighteenth centuries. Several protesters were expelled from the Society before Quaker opinion shifted (partly owing to the work of John Woolman), and the Friends gradually abolished slaveholding from their own fellowship. They were the only religious body that reversed its position on slaveholding in the colonial period. An increasing number of non-Quaker antislavery Christians appeared in the 1770s, most notably Samuel Hopkins, the Congregationalist minister.

Antislavery colonists used religious arguments that Christians had never advanced before. (1) No one wants to be a slave, therefore no one should enslave another (Golden Rule). (2) Africans are united with all humanity in descent from Adam. (3) Noah's curse applied only to the Canaanites and not to the Cushites (Africans). (4) Mosaic law has been (implicitly) abrogated, so that the example of ancient Israel does not apply. (5) "Man-stealing" was a crime punishable by death in biblical times (Exod. 21:16). (6) Although Christ did not expressly prohibit slavery, it is "repugnant to the very genius and spirit of Christianity."

The religious life of North American Africans in the colonial period was characterized by growing acquaintance with Christianity. The black population in that period spoke many languages and represented many religions. Arriving in this land, a few Africans were nominal Roman Catholics, a few were Muslims, and most represented the various African traditional religions.

Early evangelistic efforts depended largely upon the zeal of individual ministers. The Society for the Propagation of the Gospel (Anglican) directed the only organized effort to convert slaves. Up to the middle of the eighteenth century these approaches were not very successful. Not only were the efforts weak and sporadic, but most slaveholders felt that conversion might subvert their mastery in various ways. Furthermore, Africans resisted, partly because the Christian message to slaves was tailored to the requirements of the slave system, suppressing ideas of freedom and emphasizing wholehearted service to one's master and mistress. Heaven was promised as a reward for such service.

The situation changed gradually after midcentury. More slaveholders were persuaded that Christianity made blacks into better slaves. Linguistic developments allowed African-

Phillis Wheatley (1753?–1784), a freed slave and America's most famous black poet of the eighteenth century
UNIVERSITY OF NORTH CAROLINA PRESS

descended people to understand each other better and to understand whites better. Furthermore, the Southern Awakening, following the Great Awakening proper, reached a larger number of blacks than had its northern counterpart. Some of the features of revivalistic religion attracted Africans by reminding them of the religions of their homeland. Then, too, there were antiauthoritarian implications (political as well as religious) in the revivalism of that early period. Some blacks were quick to see the value of "true" Christianity (not the slaveholder's version) as a basis for physical and psychic resistance to slavery. For these reasons Christian religion began converging and overlapping within the black community. Some blacks "converted," but in varying degrees of approximation to white ideals. At one end of the spectrum some were thoroughly acculturated to the white model; at the other end some merely added a Christian item or two to a thoroughly African religious system. All told, only one or two percent of American blacks were professing Christians in 1776.

Even though one could not have predicted in 1776 that Protestant Christianity would become a major part of Afro-American life, there were hints even then of certain durable features of black religion. One was the prominence of the black preachers, just then beginning to appear in the record. Another was the degree of contempt and physical abuse directed by whites at black church people. This sort of behavior led to the formation of separate black churches in the early national period. Third was the remarkable range of ritual expression, from calm dignity to frenzied ecstasy. Finally there was the conviction that slavery was ungodly and that Christ was on the side of the slaves in their struggle against slaveholders. This conviction stirred the flame of rebellion in some and consummate patience in others.

Quakers Oppose Slave Trade

These are the reasons why we are against the traffic of men-body ... How fearful and faint-hearted are many at sea, when they see a strange vessel, being afraid it should be a Turk, and they should be taken, and sold for slaves into Turkey. Now, what is this better done, than Turks do? Yea, rather it is worse for them, which say they are Christians; for we hear that the most part of such negers are brought hither against their will and consent, and that many of them are stolen. Now, though they are black, we cannot conceive there is more liberty to have them slaves, as it is to have other white ones. There is a saying, that we should do to all men like as we will be done ourselves; making no difference to what generation, descent, or colour they are. And those who steal or rob men, and those who buy or purchase them, are they not all alike? ... Ah! do consider well this thing, you who do it, if you would be done at this manner — and if it is done according to Christianity! ... This makes an ill report in all those coun-tries of Europe, where they hear of [it], that the Quakers do here handel men as they handel there the cattle. ... Pray, what thing in the world can be done worse towards us, than if men should rob or steal us away, and sell us for slaves to strange countries; separating husbands from their wives and children. ... And we who profess that it is not lawful to steal, must, likewise, avoid to purchase such things as are stolen, but rather help to stop this robbing and stealing, if pos-sible. And such men ought to be delivered out of the hands of the rob-bers, and set free as in Europe. ... Have these poor negers not as much right to fight for their freedom, as you have to keep them slaves?

Quakers, with Mennonite influence, protest slavery, Germantown, Pennsylvania, February 18, 1688

Benjamin Lay was among the most outspoken Quaker opponents to slavery in the eighteenth century. NATIONAL PORTRAIT GALLERY, SMITHSONIAN INSTITUTION, WASHINGTON, D.C., GIFT OF THE JAMES SMITHSON FOUNDATION

John Woolman

HUGH BARBOUR

John Woolman's (1720-1772) lifelong concern to obey truth, the "pure leading" of God undistorted by human self-interest, made him the clearest voice against slave-owning and war in colonial America. His grandfather had been in 1678 one of the original settlers in Quaker West Jersey, four years before Pennsylvania began across the Delaware. In 1741, young Woolman moved from the family farm up Rancocas Creek to become a tailor

Title page of the second section of Woolman's famous treatise

CONSIDERATIONS

ON KEEPING

NEGROES;

Recommended to the PROFESSORS of CHRISTIANITY, of every *Denomination.*

PART SECOND.

By *JOHN WOOLMAN.*

Ye shall not respect Persons in Judgment; but you shall hear the Small as well as the Great: You shall not be afraid of the Face of Man; for the Judgment is GOD's. Deut. i. 17.

PHILADELPHIA:

Printed by B. FRANKLIN, and D. HALL. 1762.

in Mt. Holly and for a while shop owner, until he simplified his life in 1756 to allow time and inner freedom for religious service.

Before he was twenty-three, Woolman had felt moved to speak in a silent Quaker meeting. He was anguished over having said more than his "leading," and learned to present simply what he was shown within, finally being "recorded as a minister" among Friends. He was for thirty-seven years the "clerk" or chairman of the "Quarterly Meeting for business" of Friends in Burlington County, and began to travel to visit other Quaker communities: thirty-nine trips in twenty-five years, averaging a month a year away from his wife and daughter, usually on horseback with another Friend, but later alone and on foot.

Beginning in Virginia and Carolina in 1746, Woolman showed his slave-owning hosts the perversion of their own lives as well as those of slaves, whom he often felt obliged to pay for their help, while their guest. Though slavery had been condemned by Pastorius' Mennonite congregation resettled in Germantown, and by Benjamin Lay and other Friends, Woolman's stand began when as a young clerk he handled a will and a bill of sale for slaves. In 1754 and 1762 he wrote the two sections of *Considerations on the Keeping of Negroes.* Hoping never to lose the friendship and respect of people whose consciences he prodded, Woolman felt special anxiety on two four-month trips to New England, where Rhode Island Quakers included shipowners deeply involved in the African slave trade. Yet he persuaded the New England Friends to listen, eventually to act, and to bring pressure upon the Rhode Island legislature.

In Pennsylvania, the Assembly retained a Quaker majority through the votes of German settlers, though Friends were by 1750 much outnumbered. They had resisted, stalled, and often finally compromised when pressed by the English Crown and non-Quaker governors to raise war taxes and a militia, through each of the wars England had fought against France under William III, Anne, and George I. Friends had kept peace with the Indians, and in 1763 Woolman himself would visit the Christianized Delawares on the upper Susquehanna, just as Pontiac's War was beginning. But in 1756, Braddock's disaster, feuds of Indians with Scotch-Irish settlers, and Governor Morris' declaration of war against the French and Indians forced Friends to choose between forgetting their "Peace Testimony" and losing control of Pennsylvania, their "holy experiment." Pressure from English Friends, but still more from Woolman and John Churchman, led most Quaker assemblymen to resign. Woolman drafted a Yearly Meeting Epistle warning Friends against war involvements, and a letter by twenty-one Quaker leaders pledged to refuse war taxes, and he struggled over the billeting of soldiers and conscription for the militia.

Feeling the war as divine judgment upon the greed for land, wealth, and comfort of all Pennsylvanians, Woolman's greatest achievement was to persuade the Philadelphia Yearly Meeting to a collective decision against owning slaves. Most Pennsylvania Friends were "clear" or else were "disowned" by 1775. Meanwhile Woolman had gone further, rejecting slave-grown food and dyed clothing and a trip to the West Indies in a slave-produce ship. His simple life and his *Plea for the Poor* intensified Penn's warning that the luxuries of the rich could provide for the needs of the hungry. The *Journal* summarizing his experiences and inner visions was left in two manuscript versions when Woolman sailed in 1772 for a visit to Friends in England. There he died at York of smallpox, having earlier refused inoculation, to leave his life in God's hands.

The Era of
the Great Awakening

The religious picture in America was noticeably different in 1740 than it had been a century or so before. Changes in colonial conditions contributed to the differences, and time had also not stood still within the churches themselves. By the mid-eighteenth century the American population was much larger and much more widely spread than in the mid-seventeenth. From 1660 to 1760 the number of colonists rose over twenty-fold, from 75,000 to nearly 1,600,000. And that population had pushed deep into the interior—west to the Blue Ridge Mountains in Virginia and to Fort Pitt in Pennsylvania, north along the Connecticut and Merrimack Rivers into New Hampshire. The number of non-English migrants was also growing rapidly—from German-speaking Switzerland, the lands of Germany itself, Scotland, Ireland, the Netherlands, and (through the coercion of slavery) Africa. Trade along the coast, with Europe, and to Africa stimulated the growth of cities. Compared to great European metropolises like London, colonial cities were insignificant, yet by the time of the Revolution five would exceed 10,000 in population (Philadelphia, New York, Boston, Charleston, and Newport), and another fifteen had grown to more than 3,000. The mingling of peoples which has always characterized American history was also well under way, a situation which amazed foreign visitors even as it promoted social fluidity.

All of these changes affected the churches in one way or another. The spread of population made it more difficult for groups clustered on the coast to preserve tight control over far-flung congregations. Trade and the growth of cities made it possible for wealthier and larger churches to flourish, but it also concentrated the unchurched populations in a much more obvious way. Some ministers worried openly about the effect of city living on godliness. They noted that traditional Christian practices, like strict sabbath observance, seemed to break down most easily in towns. They saw merchants sacrifice traditional Christian ethics to the gods of influence and wealth. They saw traditional deference to religious figures eroding. One of the first examples of that erosion came from the pen of sixteen-year-old Benjamin Franklin, who published in 1722 a series of satirical letters in his brother's newspaper, *The New-England Courant*, critical of the establishment, including its churches, its colleges, and its ministers.

Benjamin Franklin on
"The Temple of Theology"

The Business of those who were employ'd in this Temple being laborious and painful, I wonder'd exceedingly to see so many go towards it; but while I was pondering this Matter in my Mind, I spy'd Pecunia [*i.e., Money*] *behind a Curtain, beckoning to them with her Hand, which Sight immediately satisfied me for whose Sake it was, that a great Part of them (I will not say all) travel'd that Road.*
Silence Dogood Letters, May 14, 1722

Number of Churches — Eight Major Colonial Denominations

TOTAL NUMBER OF CHURCHES:

1660: 154
1700: 373
1740: 1176
1780: 2731

ANGLICAN

BAPTIST

CONGREGATIONAL

DUTCH REFORMED

GERMAN REFORMED

LUTHERAN

PRESBYTERIAN

ROMAN CATHOLIC

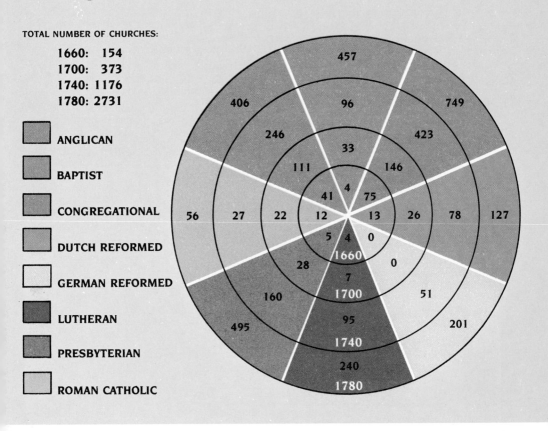

457

406   96   749

246   423

33

111   146

41   4   75

56   27   22   12   13   26   78   127

5   4   0

1660

28   0

1700   51

160

495   95   201

1740

240

1780

The most important change in American church life, however, was probably the lessening domination of the Puritan and Anglican establishments. The bare statistics tell part of the story. While the numbers of Anglican and Congregational churches had risen sharply in the century before 1740, they were not rising as fast as the total number of American churches. In 1660 Congregational and Anglican churches had made up seventy-five percent of all churches from the eight largest colonial denominations (including also Baptists, Dutch Reformed, German Reformed, Lutherans, Presbyterians, Roman Catholics). By 1740 the proportion had dropped to fifty-seven percent, a decline that accelerated after the Great Awakening. More Baptists and Quakers had arrived from Eng-land, and these groups attracted others who were dissatisfied with churches in America. Migration from Scotland and Ireland brought Presbyterians. From Switzerland came Mennonites. From the German principalities arrived Lutherans, German Reformed, Moravians, Brethren, and others. Holland added its Dutch Reformed. By the Revolution there were even five synagogues to serve the thousand or so Jews who had come to America. The results of this growing pluralism showed up first in the middle colonies. Pennsylvania became a fertile field for a wide. variety of religious groups, both traditional and esoteric. One of the latter was the Ephrata Community, founded by the German immigrant Conrad Beissel (1691-1768), which flourished for nearly forty years as a communal and quasimonastic closed society. New York City, because of its early cosmopolitan character, also witnessed the growth of different traditions. In 1742 it had nine churches from eight denominations. The increasing diversity of churches meant that American religion in general was less distinctly Puritan than it once had been.

By 1740 even the Puritans were less puri-

tan than they once had been. Transitional leaders in the early years of the century, such as Cotton Mather, did strive to revive the spirit of the founders, but they also drew upon pietistic resources to reinvigorate New England's faith. Puritan theology had begun to place somewhat greater emphasis upon human capabilities and responsibilities before God than upon God's sovereign prerogatives.

New York City in 1742, including drawings of its nine churches   COURTESY OF THE NEW YORK HISTORICAL SOCIETY, NEW YORK CITY

By the early eighteenth century as well, Puritan ministers had begun to take a more "professional" attitude to their ministry. Whether because of strife between minister and congregation (which did seem to be growing) or the increasing influence of royal governors and their official formalism, Congregational ministers had begun to look upon themselves more as an elite spiritual fellowship and less as leaders of individual congregations. The changes within New England, America's most traditional region, were usually not dramatic, but they were taking place. As time wore on, even the Congregational churches of the early eighteenth century resembled less and less those of the earliest Puritan years.

It has been a frequent Thing with mee, to redeem the silent, and otherwise, thoughtless, Minutes of my Time, in shaping Thousands of ejaculatory Prayers for my Neighbours. And by reciting a Few of them, the Way of my shaping the Rest, may bee conjectured. . . . In passing along the Street, I have sett myself to bless thousands of persons, who never knew that I did it; with secret Wishes, after this manner sent unto Heaven for them.
COTTON MATHER, *Diary*

Cotton Mather
RICHARD LOVELACE

Cotton Mather (1663-1727) was the third member of colonial New England's most important dynasty of ministerial leaders, descended from Richard and Increase Mather. He was also a grandson of John Cotton. During his lifetime New England changed from the status of a colony, in which the Congregational Way exercised virtual control, to that of a province with a number of Christian denominations. During the same period Puritan orthodoxy was beginning to feel the pressure of the European Enlightenment. Cotton Mather's response to these challenges, and especially his extensive writing ministry, make him perhaps the most significant American intellectual before Jonathan Edwards.

Mather entered Harvard College in 1675 at the age of eleven, already reading the Greek and Latin classics and studying Hebrew grammar. After gaining bachelor's and master's degrees in 1678 and 1681, he became pastor of the North Church in Boston in 1683, remaining in this post until his death. Mather was married three times: to Abigail Phillips (1686); upon her death, to the widow Elizabeth Hubbard (1703); and again to the widow Lydia George upon Elizabeth's death in 1713. He was the father of fifteen children, of whom nine died in infancy. By the late 1680s he had begun to publish the series of sermons, tracts, and larger works which made him one of the most prolific American authors, with a bibliography of more than four hundred works. Mather's most signficant writings include the *Magnalia Christi Americana* (1702), *Manductio ad Ministerium* (1726), *Bonifacius* (1710), and the unpublished *Biblia Americana* and *Tri-Paradisus*. Mather assisted his father in the latter's important diplomatic ministry at the time of the changing of the charter in the early 1690s, and the two men worked together also in attempting to moderate the witchcraft hysteria at this time. From this point until his death Mather sought to promote a progressive form of Puritan orthodoxy, while resisting the drift toward liberal and rationalist thought at Harvard College and in the rest of New England society.

Mather has been characterized as a main villain in the Salem witchcraft scandal, as a reactionary defender of the old Puritan establishment, and even as a prototype of liberal eighteenth-century rationalism. Actually he is best understood as a protoevangelical, a transitional figure in the movement of the American church from its earlier theocratic strategy toward the leavening activism of nineteenth-century Revivalism. Like his father, he was strongly influenced by the English Puritan Richard Baxter to promote freedom of religious expression in New England during the late 1680s and 1690s. He also displayed a fervent ecumenical spirit deriving both from Baxter and from the German Pietist August Hermann Francke, with whom he corresponded. While he acted charitably toward any who manifested *aliquid Christi* ("anything of Christ") his theology was

Cotton Mather (1663–1727)   BILLY GRAHAM CENTER

thoroughly Calvinistic, rooted in the Reformation and opposing the Enlightenment. Like the European Pietists, however, he sought to distill the essence of biblical faith out of the expanded intellectual systems of Protestant orthodoxy. He was also a wide-ranging scholar who appreciated other traditions of mystical and experimental Christianity, including Patristic, Medieval, and Counter-Reformation Catholicism, although he vigorously opposed the Roman Catholic system.

One very influential component of Mather's theology was his premillennial eschatology, inherited from his father, which by 1696 had led him to begin praying for, and expecting, spiritual awakening in Western Christendom. Mather was convinced that Christ's imminent return would be preceded both by the extensive spiritual decline which he saw in New England and European Protestantism, and by extraordinary outpourings of the Holy Spirit producing bright spots of revival and world missions, and especially the ingathering of Jewish converts. Mather believed that evangelical Christians in all denominations — those holding to the list of fundamental tenets he called "the Maxims of the Gospel" — should unite in an informal network of prayer and fellowship to anticipate the millennial reign of Christ by evangelizing and also by Christianizing society. *Bonifacius*, subtitled *Essays to Do Good*, set forth Mather's program for transforming American culture by nontheocratic means, including voluntary societies for the reformation of manners and the promotion of the gospel, Christian influence in lay vocations, and other strategies adopted by nineteenth-century evangelicals. Mather's hope for widespread spiritual awakening persisted almost until his death in 1727, flagging just as winds of renewal were beginning to blow in Germany, at Zinzendorf's Herrnhut, and in the middle colonies of America.

The Great Awakening

No one knows where these gradual changes would have taken the American churches, for they were not destined to continue unimpeded. Instead, a series of revivals broke out during the 1730s and 1740s which had an effect on almost every aspect of colonial religious life. The evolution of the American churches continued. They still reflected social and demographic changes, and they still had their own internal development. But the Great Awakening exerted a force which left the churches altered forever.

A modern historian, Richard Bushman, has said of the colonial revival that it was "like the civil rights demonstrations, the campus disturbances, and the urban riots of the 1960s combined. All together these may approach, though certainly not surpass, the Awakening in their impact on national life." The Great Awakening remains intriguing because it was so obviously important for both the spiritual and secular sides of colonial life. It did mark a revival of Christianity. But it also marked dramatic changes in social organization, political allegiance, and communication strategies.

The Awakening was "Great" because it touched so many regions, as well as so many aspects, of colonial life. Although the reputation of Massachusetts' Jonathan Edwards and the sensational New England tours of George Whitefield have sometimes led historians to treat the revival as a northeastern affair, it probably exerted as great an impact in the middle and southern colonies. The Awakening renewed and divided the churches of New England, but it also quickened Presbyterians and Reformed in New York and New Jersey, it troubled Anglicans in the South and elsewhere, it prepared the backcountry for the great expansion of the Baptists and Methodists, and it pulled foreign language groups closer to the mainstream of American religion. What Edwin Scott Gaustad said of the Awakening in New England also applies quite well to the rest of the colonies: "The religious turmoil . . . was in fact 'great and general,' . . . it knew no boundaries, social or geographical, . . . it was both urban and rural, and . . . it reached both lower and upper classes."

Firstfruits

The first spark of revival appeared not among English-speaking Puritans but among Dutch-speaking residents of New Jersey. In 1720 Theodore Jacob Frelinghuysen (1691-1748), a German-born, Dutch-educated clergyman, arrived to minister among the Dutch settlers in the Raritan River Valley. Frelinghuysen brought with him the conviction that the Christian life required profound, not perfunctory, commitment. Although not under the direct influence of German Pietism, Frelinghuysen's experiential Calvinism—nurtured by a reading of English Puritan literature—resembled the Pietists' subjective, active faith. Immediately upon his arrival, he began to warn his parishioners about the dangers of religious formalism and to speak bluntly about their need for conversion. Within a few years the Dutch Reformed churches were experiencing a revival, marked by growing numbers and deepening piety.

Frelinghuysen's most influential "convert," however, came from outside his own church. In 1726 a member of America's most

Gilbert Tennent (1703–1764)
BILLY GRAHAM CENTER

remarkable family of colonial Presbyterians, Gilbert Tennent (1703-1764), became the minister of the church in New Brunswick. This brought him into contact with Freling-huysen, who became a fast friend and min-isterial model. Soon Tennent was proclaiming the same warnings about flaccid spirituality, preaching with the same intensity about heartfelt faith, and achieving the same ex-cited results. Tennent was joined in these exertions by his brothers, John and William, Jr. The father of this brood of evangelists, William Tennent, Sr. (1673-1746), saw his long-standing concern for active faith blos-som under the ministry of his sons. The elder Tennent, an Irish-born Scot, had emigrated to America in 1716, held Presbyterian pas-torates in Bedford, New York, and Nesham-iny, Pennsylvania, and pioneered in educating young men for the ministry. His "log col-lege" at Neshaminy—so called because of its very modest physical accommodations—trained his three sons and several other young men who became Presbyterian leaders. It also served as a model for the more formal college which Presbyterians helped establish at Princeton in the 1740s. The Tennent family did not labor alone in seeking to revive reli-gion among the Presbyterians. They counted as allies particularly those Presbyterians who had migrated southward from Puritan New England with some of Cotton Mather's con-cern for spiritual quickening. Most notable among these was the capable Jonathan Dick-inson (1698-1747), who gladly joined the Tennents in promoting revival.

A third harbinger of the Great Awakening was Jonathan Edwards, who, unlike Dick-inson, remained in his native New England.

Edwards' grandfather and pastoral predeces-sor at Northampton, Solomon Stoddard, had experienced five "harvests" (periods of reli-gious conviction and increased accessions to the church) throughout his sixty-year min-istry. It was, thus, only one further instance in a series of local awakenings when Ed-wards' activities occasioned a similar revival in the early 1730s. Edwards was concerned about the "licentiousness" of Northampton's young people, and he was troubled about the spread of spiritual self-reliance (i.e., "Armin-ianism"). He addressed the first problem by visiting the youth in their homes; he attacked the second with a series of sermons in 1734 on justification by faith alone. The result was electric. In the winter of that year and throughout the next, a great concern for god-liness swept over Northampton as individu-als clamored to be sure of salvation, and the church was thronged. "The town," Edwards wrote later, "seemed to be full of the presence of God. It never was so full of love, nor so full of joy, and yet as full of distress, as it was then. There were remarkable tokens of God's presence in almost every house." Although this revival faded quickly, it had reverbera-tions throughout the English-speaking world. Edwards published an account in 1737, *A Faithful Narrative of the Surprising Work of God in the Conversion of Many Hundred Souls in Northampton*, which stimulated other ministers to look for similar revivals in their congregations. Indeed, a number of local churches did experience revival in western Massachusetts and Connecticut in the late 1730s. But the great and general revival of religion had to await the arrival in America of the "Grand Itinerant," George Whitefield.

Jonathan Edwards

HAROLD P. SIMONSON

Born October 5, 1703, at East Windsor, Connecticut, Jonathan Edwards entered Yale College in 1716 at the early age of thirteen. After graduation in 1720 he stayed two additional years to study theology, then went as a minister to a Presbyterian church in New York City. In 1724 he returned to Yale as a tutor but resigned two years later because of illness. In 1726 he became a colleague of his grandfather, the Rev. Solomon Stoddard, at Northampton, Massachusetts; married Sarah Pierrepont the following year; and assumed full ministerial duties when Stoddard died in 1729. Edwards remained in Northampton until 1750. The next year he settled with his family in Stockbridge, Massachusetts, where he served as teacher and missionary to the Indians. In January 1758 he took up duties as third president of the College of New Jersey (now Princeton) but died of smallpox three months later (March 22) in Princeton where he was buried.

These facts say little of Edwards' brilliance as the leading theologian of his day. It is not too much to claim him one of America's greatest theological thinkers. Embroiled in controversy throughout his career, he made clear his position in three early published sermons.

The first was "God Glorified in Man's Dependence," delivered by invitation to a Boston audience in 1731. He attacked head-on the liberal argument that sin was merely a condition of ignorance or moral desuetude, and salvation only a life lived in reasonable accord with Christ's ethical teachings. Edwards insisted that human sin was inherent enmity against God, and that salvation meant a radical conversion of the heart. Such salvation depended totally upon the absolute sovereignty of God. Not since the first-generation Puritans a hundred years earlier had Boston heard such outspoken avowal of Calvinist doctrine.

The second sermon, delivered two years later, was "A Divine and Supernatural Light," in which Edwards described religious knowledge as "a true sense of the divine excellency of the things revealed in the word of God." Edwards' all-important distinction is between a "sense" of divine truth and an "understanding" of it. The first concerns the innermost will (the heart), whereas the second applies to rational speculation (the head). Edwards stressed that unless the heart is affected through regenerative grace, religion is nothing more than what unregenerate man can know through natural reason.

The third sermon, "Justification by Faith Alone" (preached 1734), enunciated the doctrinal bulwark of the

Jonathan Edwards (1703–1758) LIBRARY OF CONGRESS

Reformation, namely, that justification (divine acceptance, freedom from the guilt of sin, and the righteousness that unites all believers) comes not through good works but through faith (*sola fide*). Edwards defined faith in Pauline terms of total response to Christ, of one's being in Christ: "Our being in him is the ground of our being accepted [justified]."

Throughout his writings Edwards' central theme was that of religious experience or what he called a "sense of the heart." Although "sense" suggests indebtedness to Lockean psychology, which accounted for ideas

---

Jonathan Edwards Writes of Sarah Pierrepont

They say there is a young lady in [New Haven] who is beloved of that Great Being, who made and rules the world, and that there are certain seasons in which this Great Being, in some way or other invisible, comes to her and fills her mind with exceeding sweet delight, and that she hardly cares for any thing, except to meditate on him. . . . She is of a wonderful sweetness, calmness and universal benevolence of mind; especially after this Great God has manifested himself to her mind. She will sometimes go about from place to place, singing sweetly; and seems to be always full of joy and pleasure; and no one knows for what. She loves to be alone, walking in the fields and groves, and seems to have some one invisible always conversing with her.

Edwards wrote these words in 1723 when he was twenty and Sarah was thirteen. Four years later they became husband and wife.

in terms of prior sense experience, Edwards never regarded religious experience as having a natural cause. Furthermore, Lockean empiricism in its scientific neutrality and detachment represented the antithesis of Edwards' religion of the heart. For Edwards, religion was the total experiential response to God's revealed truth. Edwards linked religious experience and will, and believed that religion directs mankind's deepest wellsprings of action away from the natural tendencies of self-love and, instead, toward the divine and supernatural glory of God.

Edwards recounted his own religious experiences in his *Diary*, started on December 18, 1722, and finished some four years later; and in *Resolutions*, all written before he was twenty. By far the most important account is his *Personal Narrative*, written sometime after 1739. For its beauty of language and religious intensity no spiritual autobiography in America surpasses it.

Religious experience on a large scale describes New England's Great Awakening, which by 1735 involved not only Northampton but towns situated up and down the Connecticut Valley. In a letter entitled "A Narrative of Surprising Conversions," sent in 1736 to the Rev. Benjamin Colman in Boston, Edwards interpreted the religious revival as evidence of God's redemptive work in New England. The following year the letter was published in enlarged form as A *Faithful Narrative of the Surprising Work of God*. It was widely read in America and abroad.

Notwithstanding the fervent sermons of the Rev. George Whitefield, the English evangelist who visited Northampton in 1740, the most famous sermon preached during the Great Awakening if not in all American history was Edwards' "Sinners in the Hands of an Angry God" in 1741, an eloquent exposition of Deuteronomy 32:35.

In order to make religious revivalism theologically understandable,

Edwards wrote *The Distinguishing Marks of a Work of the Spirit of God* and *Some Thoughts Concerning the Present Revival*, published respectively in 1741 and 1743. The latter treatise is a major work. In both, he defended the revival as authentic religious experience. Yet he felt compelled on the one hand to temper the Enthusiasts who allowed religious feelings to become aberrant, and, on the other hand, to answer the Arminian critics whose disparagement of emotional fervor Edwards denounced as a sign of their own lukewarm spirituality.

Edwards believed that God performs saving works, sometimes in extraordinary ways; but he also affirmed that vital piety, consisting of holy affections seated in the heart, requires constant self-scrutiny. His analysis of religious experience culminated in A *Treatise Concerning Religious Affections*, published in 1746 when the Great Awakening already had subsided. Not even William James' *The Varieties of Religious Experience*, which appeared more than 150 years later, surpasses Edwards' treatment of religious phenomenology. Of the treatise's three major sections, the first affirms the heart as the locus of religious experience; the second treats manifestations that are not true signs of a prior religious event; and the third describes the true signs originating from religious conversion.

The real subject of this treatise is the transformed heart and Christian practice — i.e., the integration of the heart and visible acts. The troublesome aspect came in the idea of visibility: "false" signs and "true" signs. In 1742 Edwards drew up a covenant for his congregation to sign, binding them to live their faith visibly. He also required verbal profession of faith as a necessary qualification for partaking of the Lord's Supper. Furthermore, in 1747 he boldly envisioned all American congregations as joining in prayer at common times with Scottish congregations. The title of his treatise proposing and defending the plan bore the self-explanatory designation, *An Humble Attempt to Promote Explicit Agreement and Visible Union of God's People*. By 1749, controversy in his own congregation over the issue of visibility required another defense. In *An Humble Inquiry* he set forth explicit qualifications for "complete standing and full communion in the visible Christian church." In striving for a faith made visible in Christian practice, he envisioned boldly and expected much of his congregation. By overwhelming vote he was dismissed from his pulpit the next year, the occasion for his justly famous "Farewell Sermon" of July 1, 1750.

Edwards' subsequent Stockbridge years proved to be among his most productive. Relentlessly concerned

---

Indeed I am far from thinking that it is of absolute necessity that persons should understand, and be agreed upon, all the distinctions needful particularly to explain and defend this doctrine against all cavils and objections (though all Christians should strive after an increase of knowledge, and none should content themselves without some clear and distinct understanding in this point): but that we should believe in the general, according to the clear and abundant revelations of God's word, that it is none of our own excellency, virtue, or righteousness, that is the ground of our being received from a state of condemnation into a state of acceptance in God's sight, but only Jesus Christ, and his righteousness, and worthiness, received by faith.

JONATHAN EDWARDS,
"Justification by Faith Alone," published 1738

with the nature of will, he made what he called A *Careful and Strict Inquiry into ... Freedom of the Will*, published in 1754. In this important work he argued that prior to will, by which the mind voluntarily chooses either one thing or another, there is a more fundamental cause identified as motive. By this term he meant "the *whole* of that which moves, excites or invites the mind to volition." According to Edwards, freedom of the will is exercised in subsequent actions, but the willing itself is determined by a prior motive or propensity of the heart. This motive necessarily directs the regenerate will in the direction of the greatest good or, theologically speaking, toward irresistible grace.

But Edwards made clear in another major work of these years — *The Great Christian Doctrine of Original Sin* published in 1758 — that in Adam's fall people are not governed (motivated) by the principle of divine benevolence but instead are given over to self-love. In this a person declares himself ontologically independent. It is both his grand illusion and his awesome depravity. Self-love is the failure to relish divine things, to consent to Being, to "close" with Christ. Unless the heart is redirected toward God, people live in a state of spiritual death, which Edwards saw as equivalent to self-love. The subject is carried over into Edwards' shorter works, *The Nature of True Virtue* and *Treatise on Grace*, published posthumously in 1765 and 1865 respectively.

Edwards' vision went beyond personal salvation to include a millennial design of history, explained in a series of sermons preached in 1739 and published as A *History of the Work of Redemption* in 1774. His death in 1758 prevented him from completing this work which he intended to be his *chef d'oeuvre*. Before he died he succeeded in writing a work embracing his fullest soteriological vision. In A *Dissertation Concerning the End for Which God Created the World*, published posthumously in 1765, he held that God's ultimate purpose in creation is not only the personal salvation of man and the redemption of the world but the revelation of his own glory. The essence of Christian experience is to participate in the revelation.

Although his theological writings demonstrate intellectual discipline, finely honed logic, and reasoned argument of the highest order, their central theme concerns religious knowledge as held not in the head but in the heart, where life's antipodes are known and reconciled.

Full Flowering

Whitefield, an ordained minister of the Church of England, was a colleague of John and Charles Wesley who had showed the way to the Wesleys in both preaching out-of-doors and traveling wherever he could to air the message of salvation. He had visited Georgia briefly in 1738 in connection with the establishment of an orphanage. He returned in 1739, when his dramatic and effective preaching soon made him a sensation in the colonies. His preaching tour of New England in the fall of 1740, when Whitefield addressed crowds of up to 8,000 nearly every day for over a month, was probably the most sensational event in the whole history of American religion. Wherever he went in those early years—New England, New York, Ben Franklin's Philadelphia, Charleston, Savannah—he left a lively interest in religion. There were hundreds for whom the sole important question had become, "What must I do to be saved?" and he left not a few who wondered what awakened religion would do to the social fabric. Whitefield was, in short, a phenomenon.

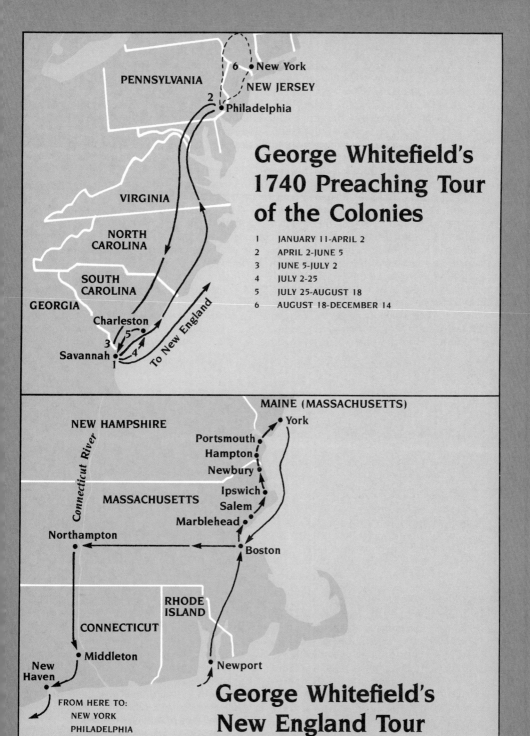

George Whitefield's 1740 Preaching Tour of the Colonies

1	JANUARY 11-APRIL 2
2	APRIL 2-JUNE 5
3	JUNE 5-JULY 2
4	JULY 2-25
5	JULY 25-AUGUST 18
6	AUGUST 18-DECEMBER 14

PENNSYLVANIA

New York
NEW JERSEY
Philadelphia

VIRGINIA

NORTH CAROLINA

SOUTH CAROLINA

GEORGIA

Charleston

Savannah

To New England

George Whitefield's New England Tour
August 18-December 14, 1740

MAINE (MASSACHUSETTS)

NEW HAMPSHIRE

York
Portsmouth
Hampton
Newbury
Ipswich
Salem
Marblehead

Connecticut River

MASSACHUSETTS

Northampton

Boston

RHODE ISLAND

CONNECTICUT

Middleton

New Haven

Newport

FROM HERE TO:
NEW YORK
PHILADELPHIA
CHARLESTON
SAVANNAH

In his wake came other itinerants. Some, like Gilbert Tennent, traveled widely—New England and Virginia as well as his own New Jersey—and nearly matched the great Whitefield in effect. Others, like Jonathan Edwards, ventured from their own pulpits only occasionally; it was on one of those visits to Enfield, Connecticut, for the evening lecture on July 8, 1741, that Edwards preached his famous "Sinners in the Hands of an Angry God." Still others, like the unstable James Davenport (1716-1757) of Southold, Long Island, ranted their way across the country-side, and in so doing brought discredit on the revival as a whole. The religious excitement remained at a high pitch in New England for only a couple of years. In the mid-1740s Yale and Harvard, which had welcomed White-field and other itinerants at first, issued stern warnings to their students about the dangers of "enthusiasm." Opponents of the revival were coming into the open. And even the Awakening's defenders were having second thoughts about some of its manifestations.

Still, the effects of the revival survived. Jonathan Edwards bent his great mind to plumb the spiritual, psychological, and philosophical meaning of what had gone on and produced the finest series of theological works ever written by an American. The revival fires, though damped in New England, continued to spread in the middle colonies. In the South, dynamic preachers like the Presbyterian Samuel Davies (1723-1761) evangelized energetically among backcountry whites, Indians, and blacks. And the message of the revival was carried ever farther south by expatriate New Englanders who pushed into North and South Carolina. By 1750 the Awakening had receded from public prominence. But it continued to have profound effects on American church life and serious consequences for American culture as a whole.

George Whitefield
HARRY S. STOUT

Religious revivals conducted by local pastors in their particular churches were an integral part of colonial life from the very earliest settlements. But these were largely isolated affairs that seldom transcended local boundaries to speak to the country as a whole. Then, in 1739, a preacher appeared on the American scene whose spiritual zeal was so great and whose exhortatory abilities so sharply honed that he altered the conventions of preaching and religious association forever after. It was George Whitefield (1714-1770), a mere novice of twenty-five years old, who began a preaching tour of America that evoked a mass religious response of dimensions never before witnessed in the colonies. Contemporaries from Georgia to Maine could only understand White-field's revival as a special outpouring of divine grace that constituted nothing less than a "Great Awakening."

The causes of Whitefield's staggering success have intrigued historians for two centuries. Certainly the raw power of his delivery cannot be ignored in accounting for his appeal. The colonial sage, Benjamin Franklin, himself no convert to evangelical Christianity, nevertheless remained a careful student of Whitefield's career and a close personal associate. He was part of the crowd at Whitefield's first stop in Philadelphia and noted with wonder how the itinerant could be heard easily from the furthest reaches of a crowd numbering in excess of twenty thousand people. To his dynamic appeal and commanding pulpit presence must be added his tremendous speaking endurance. Itinerancy was generally a young man's profession, and travelling preachers seldom lasted for more than one tour. Yet from the time he began preaching at age twenty-three until his death thirty-three years later, Whitefield preached several times weekly to mass audiences. In all, he made seven preaching tours of the colonies, each of which lasted for more than a year in duration. By his own estimation, he preached more than fifteen thousand sermons in his thirty-year career.

At the same time that Whitefield brought a wealth of talent and dedication to the pulpit he also altered the setting in which the gospel was proclaimed. Early in his career he discovered what political speakers would learn a generation later, namely that in mass public address the speaker cannot speak "down" to his audience, but instead must aim his discourse directly to their hearts and sentiments. As a preacher who was unattached to local churches Whitefield was free to cast his message in the language of the common man, and did not hesitate to publicly criticize any and all leaders who opposed his ministry as overly crude or "vulgar" in delivery. Even as he won the hearts of the American populace, he encountered bitter hostility from many authorities, especially those in his native Anglican church and the leaders at the colonial colleges, Harvard and Yale.

Whitefield's greatest triumphs in the New World were reserved for New England, which had long been recognized as the spiritual and intellectual center of the New World. Following moderate successes in South Carolina, Whitefield arrived in New England in September 1740 and conducted a whirlwind six-week tour that left the region in a spiritual uproar. Unprecedented crowds numbering in the thousands and tens of thousands appeared from nowhere to hear the simple but dramatic message of spiritual rebirth and justification by faith alone.

In Newport, Rhode Island, on October 15, 1770, Whitefield died suddenly as he always hoped he would, in the midst of a preaching tour. His influence would not cease with his death, but would continue to inspire generations of American revivalists attuned to the message of the New Birth. His simple dramatic presentations can still be read with profit. Both in style and tone his sermons stand the test of time and read with remarkable clarity and contemporaneity. Until George Washington, no colonial figure enjoyed greater popularity among the American populace. It was entirely fitting that, of the scores of elegies composed at his death, the one enjoying the greatest circulation was composed by a seventeen-year-old Negro servant girl named Phillis:

Hail happy saint on thy immortal
  throne!
  To thee complaints of grievance
  are unknown:
We hear no more the music of thy
  tongue,
Thy wonted auditories cease to
  throng.
Thy lessons in unequal'd accents
  flow'd!
While emulation in each bosom
  glow'd;
Thou didst, in strains of eloquence
  refin'd
Inflame the soul, and captivate the
  mind.
Unhappy we, the setting Sun
  deplore:
Which once was spendid, but it
  shines no more;
He leaves this earth for Heaven's
  unmeasur'd height:
And worlds unknown, receive him
  from our sight;
There WHITEFIELD wings, with
  rapid course his way,
And sails to Zion, through vast seas
  of day.

Benjamin Franklin on George Whitefield

In 1739 arrived among us from England the Rev. Mr. Whitfield, who had made himself remarkable there as an itinerant preacher. He was at first permitted to preach in some of our churches; but the clergy, taking a dislike to him, soon refused him their pulpits, and he was obliged to preach in the fields. The multitudes of all sects and denominations that attended his sermons were enormous, and it was matter of speculation to me, who was one of the number, to observe the extraordinary influence of his oratory on his hearers and how much they admired and respected him, notwithstanding his common abuse of them, by assuring them they were naturally "half beasts and half devils." It was wonderful to see the change soon made in the manners of

George Whitefield (1714–1770) NATIONAL PORTRAIT GALLERY, SMITHSONIAN INSTITUTION, WASHINGTON, D.C.

our inhabitants; from being thoughtless or indifferent about religion, it seemed as if all the world were growing religious, so that one could not walk through the town in an evening without hearing psalms sung in different families of every street. . . .

Mr. Whitfield, in leaving us, went preaching all the way through the colonies to Georgia. . . . [where there were] many helpless children unprovided for. The sight of their miserable situation inspired the benevolent heart of Mr. Whitfield with the idea of building an orphan house there. . . . Returning northward he preached up this charity and made large collections; for his eloquence had a wonderful power over the hearts and purses of his hearers, of which I myself was an instance. . . . I happened soon after to attend one of his sermons, in the course of which I perceived he intended to finish with a collection, and I silently resolved he should get nothing from me. I had in my pocket a handful of copper money, three or four silver dollars, and five pistoles in gold. As he proceeded, I began to soften and concluded to give the coppers. Another stroke of his oratory made me ashamed of that and determined me to give the silver; and he finished so admirably that I emptied my pocket wholly into the collector's dish, gold and all. At this sermon there was also one of our club, who being of my sentiments respecting the building in Georgia and suspecting a collection might be intended, had by precaution emptied his pockets before he came from home; toward the conclusion of the discourse, however, he felt a strong desire to give and applied to a neighbor who stood near him to borrow some money for the purpose. The application was unfortunately made to perhaps the only man in the company who had the firmness not to be affected by the preacher. His answer was, "At any other time, Friend Hopkinson, I would lend to thee freely, but not now; for thee seems to be out of thy right senses."

Some of Mr. Whitfield's enemies affected to suppose that he would apply these collections to his own private emolument, but I who was intimately acquainted with him (being employed in printing his sermons and journals, etc.) never had the least suspicion of his integrity, but am to this day decidedly of opinion that he was in all his conduct a perfectly honest man. And methinks my testimony in his favor ought to have the more weight as we had no religious connection. He used, indeed, sometimes to pray for my conversion but never had the satisfaction of believing that his prayers were heard. Ours was a mere civil friendship, sincere on both sides, and lasted to his death.

The following instance will show something of the terms on which we stood. Upon one of his arrivals from England at Boston, he wrote to me that he should come soon to Philadelphia but knew not where he could lodge when there, as he understood his old, kind host, Mr. Benezet, was removed to Germantown. My answer was, "You know my house; if you can make shift with its scanty accommodations, you will be most heartily welcome." He replied that if I made that kind offer for Christ's sake, I should not miss of a reward. And I returned, "Don't let me be mistaken; it was not for Christ's sake but for your sake." . . .

He had a loud and clear voice, and articulated his words and sentences so perfectly that he might be heard and understood at a great distance, especially as his auditories, however numerous, observed the most exact silence. He preached one evening from the top of the courthouse steps, which are in the middle of Market Street and on the west side of Second Street, which crosses it at right angles. Both streets were filled with his hearers to a considerable distance. Being among the hindmost in Market Street, I had the curiosity to learn how far he could be heard by retiring backwards down the street toward the river, and I found his voice distinct till I came near Front Street, when some noise in that street obscured it. Imagining then a semicircle, of which my distance should be the radius, and that it were filled with auditors, to each of whom I allowed two square feet, I computed that he might well be heard by more than thirty thousand. This reconciled me to the newspaper accounts of his having preached to twenty-five thousand people in the fields, and to the ancient histories of generals haranguing whole armies, of which I had sometimes doubted.

By hearing him often I came to distinguish easily between sermons newly composed and those which he had often preached in the course of his travels. His delivery of the latter was so improved by frequent repetitions that every accent, every emphasis, every modulation of voice was so perfectly well turned and well placed that, without being interested in the subject, one could not help being pleased with the discourse, a pleasure of much the same kind with that received from an excellent piece of music. This is an advantage itinerant preachers have over those who are stationary, as the latter cannot well improve their delivery of a sermon by so many rehearsals.

1740

Nathan Cole Goes to Hear Whitefield

Then on a Sudden, in the morning about eight or nine of the Clock there came a messenger and said Mr. Whitfield preached at Hartford and Weathersfield yesterday and is to preach at Middletown this morning at ten of the Clock. I was in my field at Work, I dropt my tool that I had in my hand and ran home to my wife telling her to make ready quickly to go and hear Mr. Whitfield preach at Middletown, then run to my pasture for my horse with all my might; fearing that I should be too late; having my horse I with my wife soon mounted the horse and went forward as fast as I thought the horse could bear, and when my horse got much out of breath I would get down and put my wife on the Saddle and bid her ride as fast as she could and not Stop or Slack for me except I bad her and so I would run untill I was much out of breath; and then mount my horse again, and so I did several times to favour my horse; we improved every moment to get along as if we were fleeing for our lives; all the while fearing we should be too late to hear the Sermon, for we had twelve miles to ride double in little more than an hour and we went round by the upper housen parish.

And when we came within about half a mile or a mile of the Road that comes down from Hartford weathersfield and Stepney to Middletown; on high land I saw before me a Cloud or fogg rising; I first thought it came from the great River, but as I came nearer the Road, I heard a noise something like a low rumbling thunder and presently found it was the noise of Horses feet coming down the Road and this Cloud was a Cloud of dust made by the Horses feet; it arose some Rods into the air over the tops of Hills and trees and when I came within about twenty rods of the Road,

I could see men and horses Sliping along in the Cloud like shadows and as I drew nearer it seemed like a steady Stream of horses and their riders, scarcely a horse more than his length behind another, all of a Lather and foam with sweat, their breath rolling out of their nostrils every Jump; every horse seemed to go with all his might to carry his rider to hear news from heaven for the saving of Souls, it made me tremble to see the Sight, how the world was in a Struggle; I found a Vacance between two horses to Slip in mine and my Wife said law our Cloaths will be all spoiled see how they look, for they were so Covered with dust, that they looked almost all of a Colour Coats, hats, Shirts, and horses.

We went down in the Stream but heard no man speak a word all the way for three miles but every one pressing forward in great haste and when we got to Middletown old meeting house there was a great Multitude it was said to be three or four thousand of people Assembled together; we dismounted and shook off our Dust; and the ministers were then Coming to the meeting house. I turned and looked towards the Great River and saw the ferry boats Running swift backward and forward bringing over loads of people and the Oars Rowed nimble and quick; everything men horses and boats seemed to be Struggling for life; The land and banks over the river looked black with people and horses all along the twelve miles I saw no man at work in his field, but all seemed to be gone.

When I saw Mr. Whitfield come upon the Scaffold he Lookt almost angelical; a young, Slim, slender, youth before some thousands of people with a bold undaunted Countenance, and my hearing how

God was with him every where as he came along it Solemnized my mind; and put me into a trembling fear before he began to preach; for he looked as if he was Cloathed with authority from the Great God; and a sweet sollome solemnity sat upon his brow And my hearing him preach, gave me a heart wound; by Gods blessing: my old Foundation was broken up, and I saw that my righteousness would not save me; then I was convinced of the doctrine of Election: and went right to quarrelling with God about it; because that all I could do would not save me; and he had decreed from Eternity who should be saved and who not.

October 23, 1740

What Caused the Revival?

It is much easier to chart the course of the Awakening, to sketch the activities of its prominent leaders, to note the attacks of such opponents as Boston's Charles Chauncy (1705-1787), and to record the reactions of laypeople like Benjamin Franklin and Nathan Cole than it is to say exactly why it all took place. Most Christians, during the Awakening and after, have wished to regard it as a special outpouring of the Holy Spirit, for conversions did manifestly occur and godly living did ensue for many who were touched by the revival. At the same time, many believers—not least Jonathan Edwards—have recognized that other causes affected the course of revival. Historians, whether Christian or not, have tended to focus their attention on the evidence for these other causes. In so doing, they have in fact uncovered interesting connections between spiritual and nonspiritual worlds.

Jonathan Edwards's account of the Great Awakening, first published in 1737

A

FAITHFUL NARRATIVE

OF THE

SURPRISING WORK OF GOD,

IN THE

CONVERSION OF MANY HUNDRED SOULS,

IN NORTHAMPTON,

AND THE

NEIGHBOURING TOWNS AND VILLAGES OF NEW HAMPSHIRE,

IN NEW ENGLAND;

IN A

LETTER TO THE REV. DR. COLMAN, OF BOSTON.

SOME THOUGHTS

CONCERNING

THE PRESENT REVIVAL OF RELIGION

IN NEW ENGLAND,

AND THE

WAY IN WHICH IT OUGHT TO BE ACKNOWLEDGED AND PROMOTED;

HUMBLY OFFERED TO THE PUBLIC,

IN A TREATISE ON THAT SUBJECT.

Isa. xl. 3.—Prepare ye the way of the Lord, make straight in the desert a high-way for our God.

Edwards was quick to provide an analysis of the Awakening, as he did in this treatise in 1742 (excerpt on p. 121).

In a few towns the rapid spread of revival followed closely upon the heels of serious illness, especially the "throat distemper" (diphtheria) which carried away large numbers of New Englanders in the 1730s. In other awakened localities, economic problems had been a troubling source of tensions. Some merchants worried about the effects of conflict following Britain's declaration of war on Spain in 1739. Many others joined the merchants in concern about the absence of an adequate currency. Some historians have speculated that the shift from rural and agricultural to urban and commercial styles of life may have engendered guilt in those leaving "the old ways" behind. Others have suggested that tensions between generations over the inheritance of diminishing amounts of land may have created similar feelings. All of these observations lead toward the conclusion that environmental factors prepared the colonial population to embrace a spiritual message which, even if it could not deal directly with such problems, brought inner peace and an escape from guilt.

Debate over the causes of the Great Awakening should be informed by history, but will probably be resolved ultimately by belief. Christians should learn from secularists.

They should recognize that nonspiritual factors came into play; such factors need not explain the whole story, especially since Christians believe that the gospel is intended precisely to answer humanity's deepest needs in times of distress. But secularists also should learn from Christians. They should recognize that similar environmental "preconditions" had existed at other times when revival did not occur and that no exact correlation can be established between the outbreak of revival and any set of social conditions. The final evaluation, as in most such historical questions, will depend less upon the evidence of history than upon the convictions of historians.

Effects

The number of Americans actually converted during the Awakening is hard to ascertain. Early estimates ranged from several thousand to half a million, although the latter figure is quite high given a total colonial population around one million in 1740. In New England, where again records are best, the years of revival witnessed a marked increase in the number of people joining the church (often the only reliable guide to measure conversions). The Connecticut churches, for example, admitted on the average about eight people each per year in 1739 and 1740, but then about thirty-three per year in 1741 and 1742. Similar gains took place in Massachusetts. The picture changes somewhat, however, if long-term trends are analyzed. Very soon after the revival the average number of admissions dropped considerably below where they had been in the 1730s. While it is true that these figures do not fully reflect the formation of new "Separate" and Baptist churches, they do seem to suggest that revival did not drastically increase the total number of people actually joining the church with a profession of faith over the entire period, 1730-1750. It seems rather to have concentrated church admissions in the years of its great impact. The one imponderable with these figures is the question whether conversions and admissions to church would have continued at their old rate without a revival. It is possible that the Awakening, while not increasing the rate of conversion when calculated over the long run, did keep that rate at its former level when it otherwise might have fallen.

For the other colonies it is very difficult to obtain accurate figures for the revival's effect. In the middle colonies, the Presbyterians who favored revival did grow much more rapidly than those who did not. In 1741 there were about twenty-five prorevival Presbyterian ministers and an equal number opposed. By 1758 the number of prorevivalists (and churches) had risen to seventy-three, the antirevivalists had fallen to twenty-three. And in the South, evangelists by 1760 had made inroads into the backcountry population which had less and less use for the formalities of the Church of England, and more and more interest in the informal piety of the Baptists.

Apart from the individuals actually converted, a number of other things were also revived during the Great Awakening. In the first place, the prominence of Whitefield and Edwards encouraged a resurgence of Calvinism. Whitefield eventually broke with the more Arminian Wesleys over his belief that God sovereignly called the elect by his grace alone. Edwards' devotion to the greatness of God's power and his conclusion that sinners

do not wish to act contrary to their own sinful natures led him to restate Calvinistic conceptions of salvation in powerful and influential books.

The Great Awakening also revived experiential piety. It encouraged people to devote their practical, daily exertions to loving God and serving their neighbors. A new desire to see the churches purified of all but the elect was an ecclesiastical reflection of this more intense piety. Led by Edwards, many Congregational and Presbyterian churches repudiated the Half-Way Covenant. The fellowship of the faithful on earth, so this reasoning ran, should reflect the purity of God's grace as closely as possible.

The Great Awakening also stimulated a concern for higher education. In 1740, Harvard, William and Mary, and Yale (founded 1701) were the only colonial colleges. Leaders elsewhere in the colonies had long expressed an interest in founding colleges, and the revival added to that interest. The Awak-

---

A HYMN BY SAMUEL DAVIES

Great God of wonders! all thy ways
Are worthy of thyself divine;
And the bright glories of thy grace
Among thine other wonders shine:
Who is a pard'ning God like thee?
Or who has grace so rich and free?

Pardon from an offended God!
Pardon for sins of deepest dye!
Pardon bestowed through Jesus' blood!
Pardon that brings the rebel nigh!
Who is a pard'ning God like thee?
Or who has grace so rich and free?

O may this glorious, matchless love,
This God-like miracle of grace,
Teach mortal tongues, like those above,
To raise this song of lofty praise:
Who is a pard'ning God like thee?
Or who has grace so rich and free?
                                            Amen

The founding of Dartmouth by Eleazar Wheelock,
1769 BILLY GRAHAM CENTER

ening led more young men to pursue the
ministry, and it encouraged greater boldness
on the part of laypeople in appropriating the
faith for themselves. A combination of ecclesiastical and other motives, thus, led to the
rapid founding of several more colleges: the
College of New Jersey at Princeton by Presbyterians in 1746, Rhode Island College (later
Brown University) by Baptists in 1764,
Queen's College (later Rutgers) by Dutch
Reformed in 1766, Dartmouth by the Congregationalist Eleazar Wheelock in 1769 (an
institution which had begun in 1754 as an
Indian mission school).

Dissension

The revival of individuals, theology, piety,
and education did not proceed without opposition. In fact, the Great Awakening did
nearly as much to promote controversy as it
did to stimulate revival. In the middle colonies, Presbyterians divided over the revival
and its effects. Most of the recent Scotch-
Irish immigrants, the "Old Side," favored a
tightly organized church with traditional educational standards for ministers and great
emphasis on the Westminster Confession.
Presbyterians from New England and the
Tennent group, the "New Side," did not turn
away from these traditional Presbyterian emphases, but they did want to promote revival
and vital piety even if it meant relaxing traditional standards. A similar set of differences divided the Dutch Reformed in 1755
between a prorevival "Coetus" (following the
path first established by Theodore Frelinghuysen) and a traditionalist "Conferentie"
(which sought direction from Amsterdam).
Eventually, Presbyterians (1758) and Dutch
Reformed (1771) reunited. In both groups the
prorevival perspective became dominant. Still,
questions raised by the Great Awakening
concerning church order and the nature of
popular religion remained to trouble Presbyterians and Reformed into the nineteenth
and even twentieth centuries.

In New England, the Great Awakening
sounded the death knell for the comprehensive Puritan conception of the world. Its immediate impact was to divide the Puritan
churches into four more or less distinct
groups. Proponents of revival were known as
"New Lights," but this broad designation
covered at least two distinct groups. Jonathan
Edwards represented the moderate New
Lights who wished to remain within established Congregationalism, but who did not
mute their evangelistic zeal, their renewed
Calvinism, and their belief in pure churches.
To the left of these Edwardseans was a more
radical camp. Many who had been quickened
by revival found the established church sterile and oppressive. Such people often broke
away to form "Separate" churches. Historian
C. C. Goen has painstakingly identified 321
separations of one kind or another by these
New Lights. Some of these splits were healed
rapidly. Others led to the continuation of

Baptists in Philadelphia performing immersion during a storm THE METROPOLITAN MUSEUM OF ART, ROGERS FUND, 1942

"Separate Congregational" churches. But most eventually became Baptist congregations. Baptists like Isaac Backus often appreciated Edwards and his theology. But they grew convinced that the state had no business in the church and that the baptism of adult believers was the proper way to testify to God's saving work.

The Baptists were in fact the greatest beneficiaries of the Great Awakening. The number of Baptist churches throughout the colonies rose dramatically in the generation after the revival (from 96 in 1740 to 457 in 1780, a number in the latter year which exceeded the total of Anglican churches). And the renewal of the Baptists in New England eventually had great impact throughout the land. Baptist emigrants from New England moved as far south as the Carolinas during the 1750s to begin what would become a tremendous expansion of Baptist churches in that region.

Isaac Backus

BRUCE L. SHELLEY

Isaac Backus, a Baptist pastor in Middleborough, Massachusetts, was a champion of religious liberty in the American colonies. He carried his fight for freedom all the way to the First Continental Congress, gathered in Philadelphia in 1774.

Isaac's early years were far from revolutionary. He was born into the ruling elite of Puritan Connecticut. His father, a well-to-do farmer in Norwich, served several terms in the General Assembly; and one of his uncles entered the Congregational ministry and married Jonathan Edwards' sister.

As a New England farm boy, Isaac learned that religious training and the laws of the state provided for the good order of society. Taxes paid to the state helped to support the established Congregational churches.

The crumbling of these social foundations came in the 1740s with the shock of revival called the Great Awakening. Seventeen-year-old Isaac was "born again" without the usual emotion. He was mowing alone in the field, but he confessed that he was "enabled by divine light" to trust the righteousness of Christ for his salvation.

Although young Backus joined the Congregational church in Norwich, he was not happy. He craved a church where spiritual conversion was preached as essential to Christian living. Some time later a conviction seized him that God had called him to proclaim the gospel.

Backus began traveling by horseback through southern New England, preaching at every opportunity. In time a Separate (revivalistic) Congregational church in Middleborough, Massachusetts, called him as its pastor. There he remained for more than fifty years.

Slowly he came to accept Baptist beliefs. For two years he struggled with whether or not the Bible taught infant baptism. Finally, on August 22, 1751, he and six members of the church entered the waters to be baptized. Five years later this nucleus formed the Middleborough Baptist Church.

Backus' revivalistic and Baptist views drew him into the struggle with the Congregational establishment in New England over the rights of conscience and freedom of belief.

Aroused by subtle forms of oppression from the established churches, a group of Baptist churches formed

Isaac Backus (1724–1806)
LIBRARY OF CONGRESS

the Warren Association and appointed Backus as their official agent in their fight for full religious liberty. As spokesman for the Warren group, Backus wrote tracts, visited churches, and rode thousands of miles to present petitions in support of religious liberty. In addition to the First Continental Congress he attended the first Provincial Congress meeting at Cambridge, Massachusetts, on December 9, 1774, and at the Colonial Assembly at Watertown, Massachusetts, in July 1775.

These labors for liberty explain why Anson Phelps Stokes, the scholar of church and state relations in the United States, puts Backus in a "small band of farsighted men living in the Revolutionary Period to whom we owe our religious freedom."

Shubal Stearns and Daniel Marshall

BRUCE L. SHELLEY

Shubal Stearns (1706-1771) and his brother-in-law Daniel Marshall (1706-1784) were revivalists who transplanted the Great Awakening in New England to the southern backcountry in the generation before the American Revolution.

When the fiery George Whitefield ignited the New England Awakening in 1740 many Congregational churches felt the shock waves. Prorevivalists called New Lights (or Separates) arose and antirevivalists called Old Lights tried to restrain them. During the strife many Separates joined Baptist ranks, inspiring Whitefield's remark, "My chickens have turned to ducks." Stearns and Marshall were ducks.

Born in Boston, Stearns moved to Tolland, Connecticut, in his youth and joined the Congregational church. During Whitefield's second tour of New England in 1745, he was soundly converted.

Daniel Marshall's commitment came at the same time. He had come from a pious home and had served as a deacon for twenty years in the Windsor, Connecticut church. But like Stearns his decision in 1745 made him a public New Light believer.

Following the death of his first wife, Marshall married Martha Stearns, Shubal's sister. Thus, after the wedding in 1747, the two men were linked by kinship as well as faith. Both were radical Separates and soon leaders of small revivalistic groups in Connecticut.

In 1751, after a thorough study of the scriptures, Stearns became a Baptist and persuaded enough of his Separate church members to withdraw from Congregationalism to form a Baptist church in Tolland. Stearns was ordained as pastor in May and served the church for three years.

During this time Marshall had taken up a ministry among the Mohawk Indians and after eighteen months had moved to Opekon (now Winchester, West Virginia) where he found the Mill Creek Baptist Church and he too was baptized.

Stearns soon joined Marshall in Virginia, seeking God's special place to preach the gospel. Both sensed the call of God when they received word about the spiritual hunger of people in the Piedmont section of North Carolina.

Late in 1755 Stearns led a company of fifteen, including the Marshalls, to Sandy Creek in Guilford (now Randolph) County, North Carolina. The region was expanding rapidly and Stearns' choice proved unusually wise.

Within three years the Sandy Creek church, started by the New Englanders, had planted two sister churches and formed the Sandy Creek Association. It proved to be a mere beginning.

The key to the growth of these Separate Baptists in the South was the itinerating ministries of Stearns and Marshall. Although Stearns lacked formal preparation for the ministry, he was a man of vision, action, and administrative skills. His preaching, however, was his supreme attribute. Baptist historian Morgan Edwards reports that his voice was "musical and strong" and he could use it "to make soft impressions on the heart" or "to throw the animal system into tumults."

Marshall was no match for Stearns in preaching. Edwards called him "a stammerer." But what Marshall lacked in eloquence he recouped in zeal and courage.

Stearns died in 1771, completing his sixteen-year mission to the South. The next year his associates counted forty-two churches and 125 ministers who had sprung from the Sandy Creek church. Marshall continued in the expanding work for another thirteen years, setting the pace for southern Baptists to come.

Opposed to both the moderate and radical New Lights stood a group uneasy about the supernaturalism, the emotionalism, and the radicalism of the revival. Charles Chauncy of Boston's First Church was the spokesman for this group. It had a higher view of human capabilities than the strict Calvinists, it feared for social chaos if "enthusiasm" should prevail, and it emphasized the natural evidences of God's power over the supernatural. These "Old Lights" were, in modern terms, more theologically liberal and more socially conservative than the New Lights.

Members of a final group, the "Old Calvinists," were caught in the middle. With Old Lights they shared an uneasiness about the socially disruptive effects of the Awakening; with the New Lights they held to a generally evangelical theology. Ezra Stiles (1727-1795), who eventually became president of Yale College in 1778, was representative of this point of view. He was a broad-minded and tolerant man by the standards of his day who did not like the dogmatism of New Light theology, the disorder of unruly revivalism, or the division of the churches. Yet Stiles also did not appreciate the Old Light drift to rationalism and Unitarianism. These Old Cal-

vinists found themselves faced with hard choices as the century wore on. Some chose to tolerate revivalism in order to retain a more traditional theology, others chose to modify that theology in order to support social and ecclesiastical stability.

In the face of this ecclesiastical fragmentation, the older Puritanism had no chance. The New Lights, Edwardseans and Separates, urged *individuals* to turn in repentance to Christ. They urged those who heeded their message to purge the churches of all who were not converted. Old Lights, on the other hand, feared for the safety of *society*. They wanted the churches, through the Half-Way Covenant, to remain open to most citizens, and in so doing to exert a stabilizing effect on society. The parts of the Puritan synthesis were going different directions. New Lights stressed the individual covenant of grace, Old Lights the social covenant. Arguments over the church covenant divided the two main groups and rent also Baptists from New Light Congregationalists. However great an impact elements of Puritanism would retain in American life, the Puritan synthesis was no more.

The fragmentation of Puritanism in New

The Danger of an Unconverted Ministry

Such who are contented under a dead Ministry, have not in them the Temper of that Saviour they profess. It's an awful Sign, that they are as blind as Moles, and as dead as Stones, without any spiritual Taste and Relish. And alas! isn't this the Case of Multitudes? If they can get one, that has the Name of a Minister, with a Band, and a black Coat or Gown to carry on a Sabbathdays among them, although never so coldly, and insuccessfully; if he is free from gross Crimes in Practice, and takes good care to keep at a due Distance from their Consciences, and is never troubled about his Insuccessfulness; O! think the poor Fools, that is a fine Man indeed; our Minister is a prudent charitable Man, he is not

always harping upon Terror, and sounding Damnation in our Ears, like some rash-headed Preachers, who by their uncharitable Methods, are ready to put poor People out of their Wits, or to fun them into Despair; O! how terrible a Thing is that Dispair! Ay, our Minister, honest Man, gives us good Caution against it. Poor silly Souls consider seriously these Passages, of the Prophet, Jeremiah 5. 30, 31. . . .

And let those who live under the Ministry of dead Men, whether they have got the Form of Religion or not, repair to the Living, where they may be edified.

GILBERT TENNENT, 1741

England and the growth of dissent in the South provided more elbow room for other Christian bodies. While the Church of England suffered in the South from the first onslaughts of Baptists and Presbyterians, it grew in the North as a haven for colonials upset with the emotions of revival. Only after the Great Awakening did the Anglicans become in the North the church of the elite that it had always been in the South. Other denominations also were able to take indirect advantage of the revival. The subjective elements of the Awakening, for example, paralleled and strengthened emphases of the Pietists. In all, the Awakening made the American ecclesiastical situation much more fluid than it had been before.

The Great Awakening also had a profound impact on American society. Some of the hierarchism and authoritarianism common to all Western societies of the period gave way before the revival's theology and its practice. The renewed Calvinistic emphasis on divine predestination, free grace, and the inability of position to insure salvation had social implications. Gilbert Tennent, who in 1741 preached a famous sermon on "The Danger of an Unconverted Ministry," showed how corrosive such a theology could be. If conversion was the only condition for standing in the church, then ecclesiastical office and social prominence must not be as important as once thought. And what was true in church might also be true in society. Charles Chauncy was worried about the theology of the Awakening, but he was appalled by its effects on traditional social order. He once complained that the lay "exhorters" which the Awakening spawned were "babes in age as well as understanding. They are chiefly, indeed, young persons, sometimes lads, or rather boys; nay, women and girls, yea, Negroes, have taken upon them to do the business of preachers." Revivalists were not primarily concerned about the rights of laypeople, women, blacks, and youth. It is nonetheless the case that their concern to promote the glory of God also promoted the democratization of America.

The Great Awakening, then, retains great fascination for the historical imagination. It offers dramatic action and a complex web of causation. It presents dynamic and brilliant leaders. It left a direct and powerful impact on American religion, and a subtle but no less telling impact on America itself.

Jonathan Edwards on the Revival in New England

Some make philosophy, instead of the Holy Scriptures, their rule of judging of this work.... And though they acknowledge that a good use may be made of the affections in religion, yet they suppose that the substantial part of religion does not consist in them, but that they are rather to be looked upon as something adventitious and accidental in Christianity.

But I cannot but think that these gentlemen labor under great mistakes. ... It is true, distinction must be made in affections or passions. There is a great deal of difference in high and raised affections, which must be distinguished by the skill of the observer. Some are much more solid than others. There are many exercises of the affections that are very flashy, and little to be depended on; and oftentimes there is a great deal that appertains to them, or rather that is the effect of them, that has its seat in animal nature, and is very much owing to the constitution and frame of the body; and that which sometimes more especially obtains the name of passion, is nothing solid or substantial. But it is false philosophy to suppose this to be the case with all exercises of affection in the soul, or with all great and high affections; and false divinity to suppose that religious affections do not appertain to the substance and essence of Christianity: on the contrary, it seems to me that the very life and soul of all true religion consists in them. . . .

If we take the Scriptures for our rule then, the greater and higher are the exercises of love to God, delight and complacence in God, desires and longings after God, delight in the children of God, love to mankind, brokenness of heart, abhorrence of sin, and self-abhorrence for sin; and the peace of God, which passeth all understanding, and joy in the Holy Ghost, joy unspeakable and full of glory; admiring thoughts of God, exulting and glorifying in God; so much the higher is Christ's religion, or that virtue which he and his apostles taught, raised in the soul. . . .

It is not unlikely that this work of God's spirit, that is so extraordinary and wonderful, is the dawning, or at least, a prelude of that glorious work of God, so often foretold in Scripture, which in the progress and issue of it shall renew the world of mankind. . . .

And if these things are so, it gives more abundant reason to hope that what is now seen in America, and especially in New England, may prove the dawn of that glorious day: and

the very uncommon and wonderful circumstances and events of this work, seem to me strongly to argue that God intends it as the beginning or forerunner of something vastly great. . . .

This work, that has lately been carried on in the land, is the work of God, and not the work of man. Its beginning has not been of man's power or device, and its being carried on, depends not on our strength or wisdom; but yet God expects of all, that they should use their utmost endeavors to promote it, and that the hearts of all should be greatly engaged in this affair, and that we should improve our utmost strength in it, however vain human strength is without the power of God; and so he no less requires that we should improve our utmost care, wisdom and prudence, though human wisdom of itself be as vain as human strength. . . . The work that is now begun in New England, is, as I have shown, eminently glorious, and if it should go on and prevail, would make New England a kind of heaven upon earth: is it not therefore a thousand pities, that it should be overthrown, through wrong and improper management, that we are led into by our subtle adversary in our endeavors to promote it?

Some Thoughts Concerning the Present Revival of Religion in New England, 1742

Seasonable Thoughts on the State of Religion in New- England

The true Account to be given of the many and great Mistakes of the present Day, about the SPIRIT's Influence, is not the Newness of the Thing, the not having felt it before; but a notorious Error generally prevailing, as to the Way and Manner of judging in this Matter. People, in order to know,

whether the Influences they are under, are from the Spirit, don't carefully examine them by the Word of GOD, and view the Change they produce in the moral State of their Minds and of their Lives, but hastily conclude such and such internal Motions to be divine Impressions, meerly from the

Charles Chauncey (1705–1787), Boston clergyman and staunch opponent of the Great Awakening BILLY GRAHAM CENTER

A meer passionate Religion, 'tis true, has always led to this, and always will; but not that, which enlightens the Understanding, renews the Will, and makes the Heart good and honest. — How far 'tis a Truth, that this People have scarce heard of such a Thing as the Outpouring of the Spirit of GOD, or had no Notion of it, may admit of Dispute; but that the Out-pouring of the Spirit should introduce such a State of Things, as that those upon whom he has been poured out, should not know how to behave, will, I think, admit of no good Plea in its Defence. 'Tis a plain Case, one of the main Ends of the Out-pouring of the Spirit, is to dispose and enable People to behave as Christians, in their various Stations, Relations and Conditions of Life; ...

Nay, what Engine has the Devil himself ever made Use of, to more fatal Purposes, in all Ages, than the Passions of the Vulgar heightened to such a Degree, as to put them upon acting without Thought and Understanding? The plain Truth is, an enlightened Mind, and not raised affections, ought always to be the Guide of those who call themselves Men; and this, in the Affairs of Religion, as well as other Things: And it will be so, where GOD really works on their Hearts, by his Spirit. ...

And can any good End be answered in endeavouring, upon Evidence absolutely precarious, to instill into the Minds of People a Notion of the millennium State, as what is now going to be introduced; yea, and of America, as that Part of the World, which is pointed out in the Revelations of GOD for the Place, where this glorious Scene of Things, "will, probably, first begin?" How often, at other Times, and in other Places, has the Conceit been propagated among People, as if the Prophecies touching the Kingdom of Christ, in the latter Days, were now to receive their Accomplishment? And what has been the Effect, but their running wild?

CHARLES CHAUNCY, 1743

Perception they have of them. They are ready, at once, if this is unusual, or strong, to take it for some Influence from above, to speak of it as such, and to act accordingly. This is the Error of the present Day; and 'tis indeed the *proton Pseudos*, the first and grand Delusion: And where this prevails, we need not be at a loss to know the true Spring of other Errors. ... 'Tis a great Mistake to think, that the new Nature, or those Influences that produce it, however extraordinary, are apt to put Men upon making wrong and strange Judgments, either of Persons or Things: They have a contrary Tendency: and 'tis a Reproach to them both, to suppose otherwise.

The Sociology of Conversion in New England Through the Time of the Great Awakening

GERALD F. MORAN

English Puritans considered themselves reborn Christians whose hearts had been touched by God's saving grace, and when they settled New England during the 1630s they made rebirth the centerpiece of their religious system, erecting churches based upon the experience of religious conversion. By demanding purity of heart from church members, the settlers were breaking new ground, for before the "Great Migration" to New England the few existing Puritan churches had not required a conversion experience from members, just belief, understanding of doctrine, and good behavior. But in the New World people had room to experiment. And the settlers, zealous for purity, committed to advancing the Reformation, and sensing the approach of the Kingdom of God, added to previous practice a call for conversion. By 1648, New England ministers, meeting in synod at Cambridge, Massachusetts, could say in unison that "The matter of a visible church are *Saints* by calling."

In New England conversion thus took on important social overtones. It became not only the cornerstone of a new institution, the established Congregational church, but also the source of a new religious drama, the trial of admission. Anyone desiring membership had to appear before the brethren and convince them that he had experienced a true and lasting conversion. He had to tell how God had awakened him to sin, had turned his heart to him, and had implanted faith in his soul. To such testimony the brethren listened intently, and in the course of it asked questions aimed at tapping the source of the candidate's assurance. How had he been convinced of his conversion? Did he understand doctrine on regeneration?

Was he familiar with the elements of piety? The brethren also examined the candidate's everyday life, his past behavior as neighbor, villager, and citizen. During the trial, or before it, people could come forward with supporting or damaging evidence on the prospective member's sanctity, and this could be introduced during the testimony. Had he conformed to local mores? Had he acted according to the dictates of the law? At admission, the whole person was held up to public scrutiny, his righteousness as well as his piety.

Once admitted into membership, people could obtain baptism for their children, vote on church matters, help admit new saints and admonish or excommunicate wayward ones, and receive religious edification from fellow members. They also could participate in the sacramental center of the Puritan religion, the Lord's Supper. Through this sacrament and the other rewards of membership an individual attained not only a sense of religious belonging but also a new cultural identity. Church membership placed him at the heart of the culture, at the source of New England's ideals. Membership put him into covenant with people whose forbears had been part of the founding myth, the Puritan exodus from England to New England. It also placed him with people who were committed through covenant to promoting the highest values of society, love, brotherhood, and charity. And it put him with people who shared the goals of the exodus, the completion of the Reformation. In these and other ways membership also contributed to a person's sense of self worth.

Urged on by the rewards of membership, numerous New England men and women surmounted the obstacles to admission and became church members. Actually, admissions moved in cycles, as church records show. At the time of settlement the pure church touched many households and in some communities membership eventually embraced almost all adults. But during the late 1640s and the 1650s admissions declined abruptly, leading some ministers to bewail the impiety and waywardness of New Englanders. A religious crisis began brewing, because as churches aged and more and more members died off without being replaced, the insularity of saints to inhabitants became increasingly pronounced. Conceivably, the churches could wither and die. But just as the future looked darkest, the rising generation began taking an active interest in the church, and through the late 1660s and into the 1670s admissions shot upward. Again churches reached out to their communities, although not to the earlier extent. In time, however, the second generation spent its piety, causing admissions to plummet. And so it went from one generation to the next until the early 1740s, when the Great Awakening erupted and thousands poured into the churches. Not since the days of the founders had people witnessed such a dramatic increase in admissions. But once enthusiasm for the revival waned, new membership dwindled, and continued low for the remainder of the colonial period.

Before the Awakening abrupt increases in admissions came at prolonged intervals, after pauses of some twenty-five to thirty years, in part because of the delayed timing of personal conversions. Unlike today, people in early New England did not experience conversion in their teenage or adolescent years, but rather much later in life, during their mid-twenties and beyond. Typically, according to church and town records, men tended to undergo conversion and join the church in their late twenties and early thirties, while women did so in their early and middle twen-

ties. Just as New England women married at earlier ages than men, so they entered the church at earlier ages. But such sexual differences in experience fade when other vital events are considered. At admission men and women alike tended to be married, and on occasion became members with their spouses. Moreover, they tended to be three or four years beyond marriage, and the parents of one or two children whom they wished to see baptized. No matter what congregation one looks at, conversion and admission punctuated the same stage of the life cycle, that time of life when men and women begin producing a new generation and start assuming responsibility for its guidance.

When Increase Mather said that "God hath seen meet to cast the line of Election ... through the loyns of godly parents," he was speaking from his many years of experience as a second-generation pastor to a New England church. In many parishes, including Mather's Boston Second, one generation of church members produced the next, as new members usually came from families with one parent in communion and often from families with both parents in membership. In the aftermath of settlement New England villages sprouted Puritan tribes, networks of families who persisted as church members over generations, often intermarried, and participated frequently in the major institutions of the town, including appointive and elective offices. Whenever churches did admit new blood, it usually belonged to women who had entered the community to marry. Otherwise, from one decade to the next the tribal blood flowing through the congregations of New England remained unmixed.

While in 1630-1740 many of the circumstances accompanying admission remained constant, the gender of new members changed significantly. At the beginning of settlement men and women became members in equal numbers, but from the 1650s

onward proportionately more and
more women started entering the
church. So striking did their preponderance at admission become, that by
the last decade of the century they
made up as much as seventy-five percent of new membership in such Massachusetts churches as Boston First
and Salem First. In other parishes
they comprised as much as fifty-five
to seventy percent of admissions.

As this trend continued into the
eighteenth century, some ministers
like Cotton Mather searched for explanations. Perhaps, he concluded,
feminine piety derived from such
sources as "the *Curse* in the *Difficulties*
. . . of *Child bearing*," "the *Pains*," threat
of death, and concern for salvation
arising therefrom, the availability of
"*Time* to Employ in the more Immediate Service" of the soul. Moreover,
in the course of the trend some ministers began singling women out for
special praise, noting their deep
piety, virtue, and pervasive religiosity.
Well into the eighteenth century these
praises rang out from Puritan pulpits,
and by exciting women to emulation,
added further to their preponderance
at admission.

With the outbreak of the Great
Awakening came several important
changes in the traditional pattern of
religious experience. In many New
England towns scores of both women
and men flocked into the churches,
thus tipping the sexual balance of
membership toward males. At the
same time, married adults with children no longer predominated at
admission. Rather, the typical new
member was now young, unmarried,
and in his teenage years or early
twenties. Also, the Awakening convert,
unlike his predecessor, lacked the
land and the house that signified
autonomy in New England. No longer
"generativity" but something akin to
today's adolescence had become the
normative timing for conversion, and
for the first time in Puritan America
admission was a predominantly youthful experience.

But all these changes took place
along a continuum supplied by Puritan tribes. To the message of the
revivalists responded young men and
women who had fed on Puritan piety,
while the evangelists touched emotions made sensitive by the family
nurture especially of pious mothers.
Like communicants before them, people admitted during the revival came
from church families whose lines
stretched back to the origins of congregation and town, and who, like
previous generations, had demonstrated a remarkable ability to
revitalize religious commitments over
time. The great revival, then, took root
in ground made fertile by generations
of church families, and in this sense
was a parochial, home-grown
movement.

But in the long run the Awakening
rent the union of Established church
and Puritan tribes. In their zeal for
purity and reformation, many young
men and women criticized their
churches for being corrupt, split apart
from them, and formed their own
churches, with their own preachers
and rituals. In many areas the descendants of the saints became the
founders of Baptist churches.

In a way Awakening separatism was
an unintended consequence of actions
undertaken by the established ministry. During the 1720s and 1730s they
had prayed, preached, and exhorted
for revivals, and had developed an
evangelical strategy aimed especially
at young people. Instead of ignoring
youth's potential for piety, like their
predecessors, many clergymen had
worked hard at promoting youthful
conversions. With revivals in mind,
they had invited the youthful George
Whitefield to New England, and he
in turn had done much to generate
the youthful enthusiasm for religion.
But they had unwittingly called forth a
force whose power they could not
contain. In their clerically inspired zeal
for religion, many tribal youths sought
to revivify the church, but by so doing
broke its hold over New England.

The Transforming Effects of the Great Awakening

HARRY S. STOUT

The spiritual renewal of American churches in the era of the Great Awakening (1740-1743) is a well-known story. Under the evangelical ministrations of itinerant preachers like George Whitefield church congregations swelled to record numbers and conversions became daily occurrences. Considered as a religious event, the Great Awakening was the most momentous occasion in the spiritual life of colonial America. Less well known, but equally important to the history of American society, were the social and political repercussions of the revivals. If the message of repentance and spiritual rebirth was familiar to colonial ears, the electrifying manner of its presentation and the open-air setting of its address were novel and rife with social and political implications. The prospect of huge audiences meeting without the direction of local pastors was a matter of deep concern to both friends and foes of the revival. Nothing comparable had ever occurred in the American setting and neither side could be certain of the effects of mass revival and unprecedented popular assembly on traditional conceptions of social order and political authority.

Considered as a social event, the issues of the revivals hung particularly on questions of free speech related to the novel practice of clerical itinerancy, lay exhorting, and lay ordination. All of these activities involved a new role of leadership and assertion for common people who hitherto had

The Great Awakening was the forerunner of gatherings like this early nineteenth-century Methodist camp meeting. BILLY GRAHAM CENTER

been content to sit under the ministry of local clergymen supported by public taxes. The new wave of popular speakers born in the revivals issued not only in spiritual "enthusiasm," but in a social enthusiasm as well. The Great Awakening transformed traditional conceptions of public address and social authority and paved the way for emerging democratic ideals which would triumph in the American Revolution. The innovations in organization and rhetoric that Whitefield and his allies first perfected would experience their own "new birth"; they would become familiar and popular institutions during the creation of the American Republic a generation later.

To modern observers accustomed to two centuries of religious revival, campfire meetings, lay testimonials and preaching, and the separation of church and state, the novelty of the Great Awakening is hard to understand. It is as if these principles of voluntary organization and popular assertiveness were always accepted truths in the Christian tradition as far back as the simple fishermen of the gospels. Yet nothing could be further from the actual setting of colonial religious affairs where inflexible rules governed who could speak in public settings, where, when, and to what extent. Like their Old World contemporaries, most American churchmen believed traditionally with the New England Puritan preacher Samuel Willard that God did "ordain orders of Superiority and Inferiority among men." In this hierarchical world view rules of public speech were rigidly circumscribed and limited to an elite, college-educated "speaking aristocracy" who would brook no interference from the lower orders. Public preaching and prayer remained the sole province of the established, tax-supported clergymen who had been set apart for their work by years of classical learning and study in the ancient tongues of the scriptures. The machinery of the civil state lay at their disposal to enforce orderly worship that stayed within the prescribed bounds. Voices from the lower orders — no matter how sincere and pious — were ruthlessly suppressed as usurpers who spoke out of "place" or "station" and, in so doing, threatened to "turn the world upside down." The well-known suppression and banishment of Anne Hutchinson and Roger Williams in Massachusetts Bay illustrates how seriously these rules of public address were taken.

In a society where everyone had his place and where public preaching was limited exclusively to the local pastor there was no room for itinerant preachers unattached to particular congregations. As the Rev. Increase Mather, President of Harvard College and pastor to one of the largest congregations in the New World pointed out, "to say that a Wandering Levite who has no flock is a Pastor, is as good sense as to say, that he that has no Children is a Father." That ministers be "settled" was no idle proposition but rather an insistence carrying with it responsibility for the whole social order. An institution as critically important as the church could deny the forms of social hierarchy and deference only at the peril of undermining the entire organization of social authority.

These traditional conceptions would be exploded by the first evangelistic tour of the youthful English itinerant, George Whitefield. His celebrated journeys in the colonies stimulated an innovative style of communications that redefined the social context in which public address took place by encouraging the people to take direct control of their religious lives. In place of local congregations presided over by settled ministers, huge audiences suddenly materialized out of nowhere to hear the words of salvation articulated by travelling strangers whose only credential for public speech was their stated intention to proclaim the gospel. The sheer size and heterogeneity of the audiences exceeded anything in the annals of colonial

A century after the Great Awakening, meetings like this one at Duck Creek, near Cincinnati, were an American institution. BILLY GRAHAM CENTER

popular assembly and, in a dramatic departure from existing modes of worship established by civil authority, were purely voluntary in origin. The established leaders had no special place in the revivals. If they attended at all, they participated in an extra-institutional meeting that granted them no particular status or standing. Indeed, it was not uncommon to find Whitefield and his native-born disciples like Gilbert Tennent of Pennsylvania, James Davenport of New York, or Eleazar Wheelock of Connecticut actually attack opposing ministers and label them "unconverted formalists" lacking in any "experimental piety." They could get away with such seditious speech only by virtue of their huge public following. And that popular following, in turn, discovered a power in their collective association that they never before knew existed. In a New World environment lacking the coercive controls of a monarchy, aristocracy, or

powerful standing army, they found that they could defy existing institutional arrangements and there was nothing the authorities could do to stop them. It was a lesson that would not be forgotten.

To organize the mass meetings of the revival, both speaker and audience altered the roles and language they customarily adopted in public worship. The itinerant speakers' preference for "extemporaneous" address rather than written, erudite essays read from the pulpit attests to their desire to create a new sound in pulpit oratory that would speak to common people in their own idiom. And if everyday language could be sacralized, everyman could speak it. In the revival the right to speak was a gift of the Spirit dispensed without regard to college training, social position, sex, or age: anyone was a potential public speaker.

Insofar as preaching represented the dominant medium of public communications in the colonies, a fundamental change in preaching style and public assembly revealed, in a way it never could do today, an altered setting in which ideas were dispensed. For the first time in American society a rhetoric appeared whose object was to persuade or communicate on a large, impersonal level, detached from any one church or community. The very technique of itinerant preaching and lay exhorting created new concepts of authority and order by leaving existing institutional channels behind and creating alternative settings based solely on the consent of the audience. The frenzy raised by the itinerants was not born of madness as opponents would have it, but was derived from the self-initiated associations of the people meeting outside of regularly constituted religious or political meetings and, in so doing, creating new models of organization and authority premised on the sovereignty of the people.

In terms of social and political effects, the rhetorical transformations wrought in the Great Awakening signified an emerging popular culture asserting itself against a paternalistic social ethic. Of course, this was not the conscious intent of the revivalists, whose primary concern was the saving of souls. Nevertheless, in the course of organizing their revivals they unleashed democratic forces that would spill over into a broad range of political contexts in the course of wars with France and England. Changes wrought in pulpit style would be applied to political oratory, and the lessons learned in the revivals would be applied to the task of popular mobilization for revolt. Considered as a social event, the Great Awakening signified nothing less than the first stage of the American Revolution.

Christians and the Birth of the Republic

If the most important colonial event during the first half of the eighteenth century was a religious one, the Great Awakening, the events that mattered most in the century's second half were political. From the French and Indian War, which began in 1754, to the first session of the United States Congress in 1789, a series of momentous political events occupied the consciousness of Americans. Amid the political tumults, religious events did not loom as large as they had either during the Great Awakening or during the seventeenth century. But vigorous life went on in many of the churches. Religious problems and Christian individuals played important roles in many phases of the political drama as well.

The Seeds of the Revolution

The American Revolution was the result of both an imperial crisis and an ideological struggle. How would England rule its Empire and how could Americans preserve virtue with freedom? England's efforts to rule its American colonies created increasing difficulties, particularly after the French and Indian War ended in 1763 and the cooperation between mother country and colonies which had been so evident in that war collapsed. In 1764 Parliament passed a Stamp Act to tax certain colonial transactions as a way of having the colonies help pay off a part of the war debt. The colonists saw this as a tax without representation, or tyranny, and they protested vociferously. In 1773 Parliament tried to aid the struggling East India Company by giving it exclusive rights to sell tea in America. The action angered colonists, who were already chafing under an ar-

bitrary tax on the beverage, and the Boston Tea Party ensued. When Britain sent troops to restore order in Massachusetts the colonists saw this as a virtual invasion. Lexington and Concord (April 1775), the Battle of Bunker Hill (June 1775), and the Declaration of Independence (July 1776) followed in short order.

The imperial crisis would never have led to Revolution if most colonials had not believed in a certain political ideology, a particular way of perceiving and interpreting public events. Eighteenth-century theorists and later historians have called this "Whig" ideology, or "Real Whig" thought (to distinguish it from the Whig coalition which dominated the British Parliament during that century). It held that power was the key to the political process, that unchecked power corrupted the one who held it, and that such unchecked power also destroyed liberty and all natural rights. The only antidote to the rise of tyranny was a vigilant defense of traditional liberties and a careful employment of checks and balances to restrain the centers of power. Because they believed in these general principles, many Americans regarded Parliamentary actions after 1763 not simply as careless blundering, but as a vile conspiracy to undercut colonial freedom and virtue.

And given the highly charged morality of Real Whig thought, it is not surprising that many colonists linked it with Christian values. Although religious concerns were not paramount in the outbreak of hostilities, they did constitute an important background. It is well to make clear, however, that by no means did all colonial Christians accept Whig theories, or feel that they necessarily justified division from Great Britain. Many colonial

Paul Revere's engraving of the Boston Massacre, 1770 THE METROPOLITAN MUSEUM OF ART, GIFT OF MRS.
RUSSELL SAGE, 1909

believers were not overly concerned with politics, many condemned all military and political conflict, and many found the existing
relationship with Great Britain entirely satisfactory. Still, it is true that religious issues
interacted regularly and profoundly with political ones, so that in the coming of war
Christian concerns were never far away.

For a number of well-known ministers, a
connection between political and religious
liberty was a lively concern for some years
before the actual hostilities. Jonathan Mayhew (1720-1766), Congregationalist pastor of
Boston's West Church and a descendant of
the Indian missionaries on Martha's Vineyard, stood in the forefront of this group. In

1750 Mayhew expressed his views in a sermon on the anniversary of the execution of
Charles I (who died in 1649 at the hands of
the Puritans). He proclaimed that all mon-
archs should rule for the good of their people
or fear the fate which came to Charles. Mayhew spoke as he did partly to counter the
growing Anglican power in Boston itself and
partly to express his own growing commitment to eighteenth-century Real Whig ideas.
His *Discourse, Concerning Unlimited Submission and Non-Resistance to the Higher
Powers* did not mince words, nor attempt to
hide its irreducible Protestantism: "the he-
reditary, indefeasible, divine right of kings,
and the doctrine of non-resistance, which is

*Jonathan Mayhew (1720–1766) preached in favor
of liberty twenty-five years before the Revolution.*
NATIONAL PORTRAIT GALLERY, SMITHSONIAN
INSTITUTION, WASHINGTON, D.C.

built upon the supposition of such a right,
are altogether as fabulous and chimerical, as
transubstantiation." Mayhew later engaged
in sharp controversy with a representative of
the SPG, the Rev. East Apthorp, who had
tried to take Boston by storm, and in 1765
during the Stamp Act crisis he preached an
inflammatory sermon on Galatians 5:12-13
("brethren, ye have been called unto liberty")
which incited a riot against Crown officials.

Mayhew's public concerns illustrate how
large the Church of England loomed in the
minds of colonists, who feared for their freedom. The particular bone of contention was
a question of a bishop for the colonies. Anglican clergymen, and laypeople outside of
the South, wanted one desperately. A bishop
in America would indeed have strengthened
the Crown's political position in the colonies. Most Anglicans, however, were much
more concerned about narrower spiritual and
ecclesiastical matters—better order in the
church, firmer leadership, greater convenience for ordinations and confirmations.

Other colonists—particularly Congregationalists and Presbyterians—saw the prospect of an Anglican bishop very differently.
They thought it would be the first step to the
loss of rights for non-Anglicans. The SPG
was a flashpoint in the controversy. Congregationalists in Boston no less than Presbyterians in Philadelphia wondered why so
many SPG "missionaries" ended up in their
cities where strong Protestant groups already
existed. To them, these "missionaries" were
nothing but the vanguard of religious imperialism.

During the 1760s the Presbyterians and
Congregationalists joined their efforts more
formally in the attempt to keep Anglican
bishops out of America. They were led in the
effort by Ezra Stiles, then a pastor in Newport, Rhode Island. In 1761 Stiles published
a *Discourse on the Christian Union*, which
called for an intercolonial fellowship of Calvinist churches. With the aid of others, like
the Philadelphia Presbyterian Francis Alison, Stiles' vision became a reality when
Congregationalists and Presbyterians met in
1766. Soon "A Plan of Union" was in place,
and representatives from the two denominations were meeting annually. In a 1766 letter
to Stiles, Alison summed up his conception
of the Union: "The grand points to be kept
in view, are the promoting religion and the
good of the Societies [i.e., Congregationalists
and Presbyterians], and a firm union against
Episcopal Encroachments. . . . What we dread
is their political power, and their courts, of
which Americans can have no notion adequate to the mischiefs that they introduce."

While Presbyterian and Congregational
ministers had a long-standing fear that tyranny could creep into America via the church,
other colonists came to the same conclusion
because of the Quebec Act of 1774. This piece
of Parliamentary legislation dealt with the
Catholic Church in French-speaking Canada, an area that had come under English
rule as a result of the French and Indian War.
The Act gave Catholics in Quebec the right
to "the free exercise of the religion of the
Church of Rome subject to the King's Supremacy," and it authorized the church to
collect its "accustomed dues and rights" (i.e.,
taxes). British authorities regarded the Act as
merely an effort to clarify the general rights

"The Mitred Minuet" satirized the Quebec Act of 1774, pointedly suggesting that Parliament could attempt to establish the Anglican Church in the colonies. NEW YORK PUBLIC LIBRARY

of French Canadians. American patriots, on the other hand, saw it as a sign of the future. If England could "establish" the Roman Catholic church in Canada—and Protestant Americans regularly spoke of the pope as the great example of religious tyranny—what would stop her from establishing the Church of England in the other colonies. Perhaps, these same colonists thought, no difference existed between the religious tyranny of Rome and the political tyranny of Parliament. In any event, the fear of religious oppression was one of the strands that went into the general distrust of British rule.

Christianity and Revolutionary Ideals

It is occasionally said that the United States was founded on "Christian principles." While that is not true in any specific political sense, it is true that certain themes from the Puritan past contributed to Revolutionary thought. In particular the Puritan idea of covenant lent force to some Real Whig ideas. Puritans had believed that settlers in the New World sustained a special relationship with God. This conviction gave a moral overtone to all of life. To the extent that colonists in 1776 still believed in the divine mission of British

North America, they were ready to interpret Parliament's administrative errors as assaults upon God and his people. In addition, the idea of "mutual obligation" which covenant thought entailed could easily be turned into an indictment of Parliament. If this body broke trust with the colonists by attempting to enslave them, then certainly the colonists no longer owed it allegiance.

These Puritan ideas added moral force to patriotic arguments, even though patriotic leaders made very little effort to justify their political actions by appealing to religious traditions or specific biblical sanctions. It was, rather, the Real Whig picture of power and corruption which drove the patriots toward independence.

To be sure, the wide support of Whig thought may have had something to do with America's religious heritage, for a number of Real Whig themes resembled cherished Puritan themes, at least in form. First, Puritans and Whigs shared a pessimistic view of human nature. Puritans believed that natural depravity predisposed individuals to sin; Whigs held that political power brought out the worst in leaders. Both emphasized that freedom meant liberation from something. For Puritans it was freedom from sin; for

Whigs it was freedom from political oppression. Both also linked freedom and virtue. Puritans held that sinful behavior led to spiritual and other forms of tyranny; Whigs felt that tyrannical behavior grew from corruption and, in turn, nourished it. Finally, Puritans and Whigs both regarded history in similar terms. It was the struggle of evil against good, dark against light, whether for the Puritan (Antichrist versus Christ) or the Whig (tyranny versus freedom). This similarity in form between Whig political ideas and the traditional theology of some Americans made it easier for many to blur the distinction between a political struggle for rights and a spiritual conflict for the kingdom.

Again, however, it must be emphasized that the combination of patriotism and Christianity did not characterize all colonial Christians. Substantial numbers of believers remained loyal to England, and substantial numbers refused to fight for either side. Since the patriots eventually won, the record of Christian patriotism is better known than that of either Christian loyalism or Christian pacifism. As will be seen, however, history has recorded the convictions of Loyalists and Pacifists as well as Patriots about the momentous decisions which the War of Independence demanded from all Americans.

The Religion of the Founding Fathers

JAMES W. SKILLEN

The founders of the American Republic, though generally Protestant, were a diverse lot, religiously speaking. Some of them were quite orthodox Christians of Presbyterian, Episcopalian, Congregationalist, or Baptist persuasion. Others such as Thomas Jefferson were notably unorthodox if judged by basic standards of Christian faith. Jefferson, for example, did not believe in the deity of Jesus Christ. Roman Catholic, Jewish, and other religious convictions were insignificant influences in early America.

But whatever might be said about the traditional religious convictions and connections of the Founding Fathers, there was an additional spirit that brought most of them together in the cause of building the Republic. That spirit arose from the renaissance of humanism beginning before the time of the Protestant Reformation — a spirit which gave birth to seventeenth-century rationalism and to the eighteenth-century Enlightenment. It was a religious spirit, without doubt, and the religion it inspired was a human-centered moral philosophy more than a God-centered life of dependence upon God through his revelation. Most of the Founding Fathers gave evidence of the struggle between these two spirits in their lives.

On the one hand, orthodox (and even some unorthodox) Christians expressed a traditional private piety that included prayer, church attendance, Bible reading, and testimony of personal faith in God. On the other hand, the quest for political order on the part of these same people was directed by the conviction that a common moral philosophy rooted simply in human reason could supply the foundation for public community. The religion of the Founding Fathers was a synthesis of these two faiths. Benjamin Franklin, for instance, valued the influence of Christian churches, but had no use for a Philadelphia minister whose aim was "to make men good Presbyterians rather than good citizens." And for all of his moral seriousness, George Washington referred to God with language drawn more from nature and reason than from the Bible. His names for God include Supreme Being, Providence, Grand Architect, Higher Cause, Great Ruler of Events, Great Creator, Supreme Ruler, and Director of Human Events.

This duality can perhaps best be illustrated by pointing to Thomas Jefferson. Although Jefferson's personal piety was not the rule among early Americans, and though many evangelical believers rejected his unorthodox opinions, nevertheless his public philosophy (his religion) became the majority conviction that shaped the structure of public life in America. God functioned in Jefferson's moral philosophy not as the historical God of Abraham, Isaac, and Jacob, not as the Father of Jesus Christ, Head of the church, and Lord of the world, but as the benevolent Creator who pre-

serves people in this life and judges them according to their moral worth and good deeds.

Jefferson advised his nephew, Peter Carr, for example, to read the Bible critically to see if it could pass the rational and moral test for truth. "Do not be frightened from this inquiry," advised Jefferson in a letter of August 10, 1787. "If it ends in a belief that there is no God, you will find incitements to virtue in the comfort and pleasantness you feel" in the exercise of virtue and in "the love of others which it will procure you." If, on the other hand, you find reason to believe that there is a God, then that faith will give you additional comfort and motivation.

Clearly, for Jefferson, the existence and identity of God were only of secondary importance. The primary

"The First Prayer in Congress" illustrates the traditional understanding of the piety of the Founding Fathers.
BILLY GRAHAM CENTER

concern was for a person to find "incitements to virtue," to feel "comfort and pleasantness" in doing good deeds. God's existence and the divinity of Jesus were important for Jefferson only if they were useful for human virtue.

The moral philosophy which functioned as the integrating religion for many of the Founding Fathers, therefore, was not preoccupied with private morality, but was much more a public moral philosophy oriented toward the good of society. Life was duty for them, and the moral duty was to serve society. This attitude was rooted in the classical Roman philosophy of Stoicism, particularly as expressed by Cicero.

Furthermore, in Jefferson's view, people are able to be upright, moral servants of society because all have been granted a common moral sense, a conscience, that guides them to know what is good, even if their religious opinions differ in other respects. For Jefferson, a common moral conscience among all people meant that only the truths common to all religions were important. In a letter to Thomas Fishback (September 27, 1809) Jefferson commented: "Reading, reflection and time have convinced me that the interests of society require the observation of those moral precepts only in which all religions agree ... and that we should not intermeddle with the particular dogmas in which all religions differ, and which are totally unconnected with morality. ... The practice of morality being necessary for the well-being of society, he [the Creator] has taken care to impress its precepts so indelibly on our hearts that they shall not be effaced by the subtleties of our brain."

Probably the most important consequence of this religion of public morality was its victorious power over orthodox, evangelical Christianity in the public arena. It led to the establishing of a civil religion in the United States as both America and the public faith matured. Evangelical Christians held on dearly to their doctrines and churches as matters of private faith. At the same time, however, they came to accept a great deal of Jefferson's "public philosophy," believing that it was simply a good secular basis for a common public life. What the more orthodox Christians did not seem to recognize was that the new public philosophy was an all-embracing religion — a religion that continues in many ways to dominate the Republic, even among Christians. As Sidney Mead describes it, America is a "nation with the soul of a church."

"The Cause of America is the Cause of Christ"

Christian support for the Revolutionary War was concentrated among Congregationalists and Presbyterians. But believers from other communions also lent their support to the struggle for independence. The literature which testified to that support came in many forms, including passionate appeals, reasoned argumentation, and forceful pleading.

ROBERT SMITH
(Presbyterian; Pennsylvania; sermon, "The Obligations of the Confederate States of North America to Praise God," 1781)
You have been addressed by the politicians of the day, as citizens; I now address you upon the same topics, as Christians and professors of the religion of Jesus Christ. The cause of America is the cause of Christ.

CHARLES CARROLL

(*Catholic layman; Carrollton, Maryland, 1773*)

What my speculative notions on religion may be, this is neither the place nor time to declare; my political principles ought only to be questioned on the present occasion; surely they are constitutional, and have met, I hope, with the approbation of my countrymen. ... [My opponent] asks, who is this Citizen? A man ... of an independent fortune, one deeply interested in the prosperity of his country: a friend to liberty, a settled enemy to lawless prerogative.

Charles Carroll (1737–1832)   LIBRARY OF
CONGRESS

GENERAL ASSOCIATION OF CONGREGATIONAL MINISTERS

(*Connecticut; address to their churches, 1776*)

[The colonists face] the sad Necessity of defending by Force and Arms those precious Privileges which our Fathers fled into this Wilderness quietly to enjoy. ... A large Army of Foreign Mercenaries, hired at a most extravagant Price, [has been] employed to dragoon us into Obedience, or rather abject Submission to Tyranny. ...
Our Children, our Friends, our dearest Connections [have been] called from our Bosoms to the Field of Battle; and some of them captivated and enslaved by our cruel and insulting Foes: Detestible Parricides [are] interspersed among us, aiming to give a fatal stab to the Country which gave them birth, and hath hitherto fostered them in her indulgent Bosom.

ABRAHAM KETELTAS

(*Presbyterian; Newburyport, Massachusetts; sermon, "God Arising and Pleading His People's Cause," 1777*)

The most precious remains of civil liberty the world can now boast of, are lodged in our hands. ... [This war is] the cause of truth, against error and falsehood, ... the cause of pure and undefiled religion, against bigotry, superstition, and human inventions. ... In short, it is the cause of heaven against hell — of the kind Parent of the universe against the prince of darkness, and the destroyer of the human race.

JOHN WITHERSPOON

(*Presbyterian; New Jersey; signer of the Declaration of Independence; sermon from Psalm 76:10; 1776*)

You shall not, my brethren, hear from me in the pulpit, what you have never heard from me in conversation, I mean railing at the king personally, or even his ministers and the parliament, and people of Britain, as so

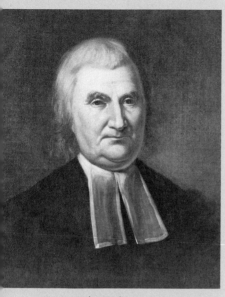

John Witherspoon (1723–1794)
INDEPENDENCE NATIONAL HISTORICAL PARK
COLLECTION

many barbarous savages. Many of their actions have probably been worse than their intentions. That they should desire unlimited dominion if they can obtain or preserve it, is neither new nor wonderful. I do not refuse submission to their unjust claims, because they are corrupt or profligate, although probably many of them are so, but because they are men, and therefore liable to all the selfish bias inseparable from human nature. I call this claim unjust of making laws to bind us in all cases whatsoever, because they are separated from us, independent of us, and have an interest in opposing us. Would any man who could prevent it, give up his estate, person and family, to the disposal of his neighbour, although he had liberty to chuse the wisest and the best master? Surely not. This is the true and proper hinge of the controversy between Great-Britain and America. It is however to be added, that such is their distance from us, that a wise and prudent

administration of our affairs is as impossible as the claim of authority is unjust. Such is and must be their ignorance of the state of things here, so much time must elapse before an error can be seen and remedied, and so much injustice and partiality must be expected from the arts and misrepresentation of interested persons, that for these colonies to depend wholly upon the legislature of Great-Britain, would be like many other oppressive connexions, injury to the master, and ruin to the slave.

NATHANIEL WHITAKER

(*Presbyterian; Salem, Massachusetts; sermon, "An Antidote against Toryism," 1777*)

Curse ye Meroz, said the angel of the Lord, curse ye bitterly the inhabitants thereof, because they came not to the help of the Lord against the mighty. Judges, V. 23.

... This discourse also shows us how we ought to treat those who do not join in the cause of freedom we have espoused.

JOHN DEVOTION

(*Congregationalist; Connecticut; new hymn concluding his election sermon, 1777*)

Lo! the angel Gabriel comes.
From him that sits upon the
    throne;
All nations hear the great
    Jehovah's will;
America, henceforth separate,
Sit as Queen among the nations.

* * *

Live, Live, Live
Beloved of the Lord, until he
    comes.
Whose right it is to reign:
Call her Free and Independent
    STATES of AMERICA!
Hallelujah, Praise the Lord. Amen.

"I will not raise my hand against my Sovereign"

Christians loyal to Great Britain came, as could be expected, mostly from the Church of England. Yet others — Baptists weary of oppression from Massachusetts' Congregationalists, a few Presbyterians opposed to political revolution, a few Catholics who appreciated the liberty which England had given to Catholics in Quebec, and a surprising number of Congregationalists who had become friends of English government or individual representatives of the Crown — also repudiated Independence. The writings of the Loyalists reflected biblical convictions about "The powers that be," an abiding commitment to British rule, and a general distrust of new American forms of government.

THOMAS BRADBURY CHANDLER
(*Anglican; Elizabethtown, New Jersey, 1774*)

The principles of submission and all lawful authority are as inseparable from a sound, genuine member of the Church of England, as any religious principle whatever. The Church has always been famed and respected for its loyalty, and its regard to order and government.

MILES COOPER
(*Anglican; New York City*)

When once they ["the People"] conceive the governed to be superior to the Governors and that they may set up their pretended Natural Rights in Opposition to the positive law of the state, they will naturally proceed to despise dominion and speak evil of dignities and to open a door for Anarchy, confusion, and every evil work to enter.

HENRY CANER
(*Anglican; Boston; regarding the Boston Tea Party, 1773*)

Such are the Effects of popular Government, Sedition, Anarchy, and Violence, and all this flame kindled and kept alive by about 1/2 dozen men of bad principles and morals.

ISAAC WILKENS
(*Anglican layman; New York; member of the colonial legislature; left America rather than fight England, 1775*)

It has been my constant maxim through life to do my duty conscientiously and to trust the issue of my actions to the Almighty. . . . I leave America and every endearing connection because I will not raise my hand against my Sovereign, nor will I draw my sword against my Country.

ELI FORBES
(*Congregationalist; Brookfield, Massachusetts, 1773; later forced to abandon his pastorate*)

[The good Christian] will form no party schemes, or [enlist] under dividing names. . . . All such party attachments discover a carnal mind, and the want of the true spirit of Christianity.

JOHN SMALLEY
(*Congregationalist; New Britain, Connecticut, 1775*)

[Massachusetts is] guilty of downright rebellion against Majesty itself. . . . What! Will you fight against your King?

JONATHAN ODELL

(Anglican; Burlington, New Jersey; satirizing John Witherspoon, the leading Presbyterian Patriot of New Jersey, 1779)

Member of Congress we must hail
    him next:
Come out of Babylon, was now his
    text.
Fierce as the fiercest, foremost of
    the first,
He'd rail at Kings, with venom well-
    nigh burst:
Not uniformly grand — for some bye
    end

To dirtiest acts of treason he'd
    descend.
I've known him seek the dungeon
    dark as night,
Imprison'd Tories to convert or
    fright;
Whilst to myself I've humm'd, in
    dismal tune,
I'd rather be a dog than
    Witherspoon.
Be patient, reader — for the issue
    trust,
His day will come — remember,
    Heav'n is just.

"As a Christian . . . I could not fight"

A Christian protest against all warfare arose during the Revolutionary years from the traditional pacifist groups, Quakers (Friends), Mennonites, Moravians, Church of the Brethren. A few other believers from Baptist, Congregational, Lutheran, and Methodist groups echoed the themes of the traditional Pacifists, who often had to face the fury of both Patriots and Loyalists for their stand. During the conflict they wrote to encourage themselves and to make their convictions known in the wider world.

NORTH CAROLINA YEARLY MEETING
(1777)

And although we do Charitably hope & firmly believe that the Intentions and Desires of Many of those Ingaged in the Present Disputes with England are Honest and Upright both towards King and Government, yet being apprehensive that a Conformity to their Resolves and Requests will be a Contradiction to our Principles and a Snare to us, we do Earnestly advise and Caution all Friends to be Strictly carefull to Put the Good advice and Cautions, in Practice that hath been Given to us by the yearly Meetings of Friends in London and Philadelphia, and our Last yearly Meeting, not to Interfere Meddle or Concur in those Party affairs.

PHILADELPHIA YEARLY MEETING
(affirmation of the traditional Quaker stand on war, 1776)

It is our judgment that such who make religious profession with us, and do either openly or by connivance, pay any fine, penalty, or tax, in lieu of their personal services for carrying on war; or who do consent to, and allow their children, apprentices, or servants to act therein do thereby violate our Christian testimony, and by so doing manifest that they are not in religious fellowship with us.

BENJAMIN HERSHEY
(Mennonite; Pennsylvania; thanking the
Pennsylvania Patriot Assembly for granting
Mennonites and German Baptists exemption
from military duty, 1775)

The advice to those who do not find
freedom of conscience to take up
arms, that they ought to be helpful to
those who are in need and in distressed circumstances, we receive with
cheerfulness towards all men of what
station they may be — it being our
principle to feed the hungry and give
the thirsty drink. We have dedicated
ourselves to serve all men in everything that can be helpful to the
preservation of men's lives, but we
find no freedom in giving, or doing, or
assisting in any thing by which men's
lives are destroyed or hurt. We beg
the patience of all those who believe
we err in this point.

We are always ready, according to
Christ's command to Peter, to pay the
tribute, that we may offend no man;
and so we are willing to pay taxes,
"and to render unto Caesar those
things that are Caesar's, and to God
those things that are God's."

JESSE LEE
(Methodist; North Carolina)

I weighed the matter over and over
again, but my mind was settled; as a
Christian and as a preacher of the
gospel, I could not fight. I could not
reconcile it to myself to bear arms, or
to kill one of my fellow creatures;
however, I determined to go, and to
trust in the Lord, and accordingly
prepared for my journey. ... I told [my
officer] that I could not kill a man
with a good conscience, but I was a
friend to my country, and was willing
to do anything I could, while I continued in the army, except that of
fighting. He then asked me if I would
be willing to drive their baggage
wagon? I told him I would, though I
had never driven a wagon before.

JOSEPH HOAG
(Quaker; New York, 1780)

As I commenced all fear departed,
words flowed rapidly, and I was
enabled to ... open to him our principles, give him our reasons for them,
and to prove them by many Scripture
passages; and finally, to show him it
was impossible for a true Quaker,
to be either whig or tory, for they
implied opposite parties, and both
believed in war, but Friends did not.

JOHN ETTWEIN
(Moravian; Pennsylvania)

If we now endure some suffering for
the sake of our principles and freedom we shall approve ourselves in
the sight of God and man; if we permit ourselves to be frightened and
unmanned by threats, we must continue a shameful existence; and our
adversaries will be encouraged to
force us to renounce our faith and
place ourselves on the level of this
world. ... I would rather permit myself
to be hacked to pieces than go to
war, butcher people, rob people of
their property or burn it down, swear
that I owe no obedience to K[ing]
G[eorge], that I desire to help maintain the independence of
Pennsylvania, until and before time
and circumstances make it clear and
incontestable that God has severed
America from England.

WORCESTER COUNTY QUAKERS
(Massachusetts; petition to the Patriot legislature to release three of their number who
have been drafted, 1776)

That they Profess themselves Friends
& Cannot in Conscience take arms
on Either Side in the Unnatural War
Subsisting Between Great Britton and
the American Colonies or in any other

Warrs Whatever Because they think it is Contrary to the Precepts of Christ as Sett forth in many Places in the New Testament and in no ways Lawful to Such as will Be the Disciples of Christ — first Christ['s] Command that we should Love Our Enemies ... But warr on the Contrary teacheth us to Hate & Destroy them — The apostle Saith ... that we Warr not after the Flesh & that we fight not with flesh & Blood: But Outward warr is according to the flesh and against flesh & Blood for the shedding of the One & destroying of the other. ...

The apostle Saith ... that the Weapons of Our Warfare are not Carnal But Spiritual But the Weapons of Outward Warr fare are Carnal Such as Cannon, musketts Spears, Swords & of which there is no mention in the Armour Described By Paul.

Because that James Testafied that Warrs & Strifes Came from the Lust which was in the members of Carnal men But Christians those that are Truly Saints have Crucified the Flesh with the affection of Lusts therefore they Cannot Indulge them By Waging Warr.

Christ says ... that his Kingdom is not of this world and therefore that his Servants Shall not fight Therefore Those that fight are not his Disciples nor Servants and many other Passages which are omitted.

The War Itself

The Revolutionary War abounded with incidents involving Christians and their convictions. Many clergymen took an active role, both as chaplains and as actual participants. One of the most dramatic among the combatants was John Peter Gabriel Muhlenberg (1746-1801), son of the "father" of American Lutheranism, Henry Melchior Muhlenberg. The elder Muhlenberg (1711-1787) was educated by Lutheran Pietists in Germany before coming to America in 1742. Soon he had coordinated the work of struggling German Lutheran congregations and provided a sturdy foundation for his denomination's later growth. During the Revolution, he was so disgusted with the rowdy, unprincipled behavior of both Loyalists and Patriots that he remained effectively neutral. His son, however, felt quite differently. Peter Muhlenberg was ministering in Woodstock, Virginia, when war broke out. At the close of a Sunday sermon shortly after the Battle of Bunker Hill (June 1775), Muhlenberg proclaimed to his congregation, "The Bible tells us 'there is a time for all things,' and there is a time to preach, and a time to pray, but the time for me to preach has passed away; and there is a time to fight, and that time has now come."

He then stepped into the vestry room, swiftly changed into the uniform of an American officer, and proceeded to enlist most of the men of his congregation in the Continental militia. Muhlenberg eventually became a general and played important roles in several of the crucial battles of the war.

Most ministers who contributed to the war effort did so less spectacularly. From the very

In this somewhat more dramatized version of the Peter Muhlenberg story, he removes his clerical robes in the pulpit, revealing his colonel's uniform underneath. NEW YORK PUBLIC LIBRARY

outbreak of hostilities ministers were present with the troops as chaplains. Many pastors served for brief periods without pay to provide regular preaching and special care for the sick and wounded. In August 1775, George Washington reported that fifteen chaplains were ministering to his army, which was laying siege to the British in Boston. In December of that same year Washington urged the Continental Congress to raise the pay of regular chaplains. "I need not point out," he wrote, "the great utility of gentlemen, whose lives and conversation are unexceptionable, being employed in that service [chaplaincy] in this way." More than one hundred ministers served as chaplains for the American forces during the war, and several Anglican ministers performed similar service for the British. One of the most interesting stories involving a chaplain features the Presbyterian James Caldwell (1734-1781). Although the accuracy of the report cannot be verified, it is told that Caldwell was in attendance upon American troops near his Springfield, New Jersey, home when a skirmish with the British ensued on June 23, 1780. When the American troops began to run out of wadding paper to ram powder and ball into their muskets, Caldwell dashed to his church, gathered up the hymnals of Isaac Watts, and charged back to the soldiers with the cry, "Now put Watts into them, boys!"

The war witnessed many acts of Christian charity, some performed at great personal sacrifice. Members of the peace churches often suffered for nonmilitary actions which Patriots or Loyalists interpreted as aid to the enemy. Moravians and Mennonites in the Philadelphia area who provisioned either British or American troops, which alternated their control of the city, often received reprisals from the other side for their pains. The Pennsylvania Pacifists also fell afoul of authorities in their efforts to do good to those in need. This was especially true when Mennonite farmers provided shelter and food for British prisoners of war escaping from the Patriots. Mennonites saw their service as a cup of water in Christ's name. Patriots regarded it as aiding and abetting the enemy. Christians, both ministers and laypeople, also went out of their way to care for the wounded. Quakers in North Carolina provided one of the most sterling examples of such service when they treated casualties on both sides after the battle of Guilford Courthouse, March 15, 1781.

The revolutionary impact which war can have on traditional convictions shows up clearly in attitudes toward Roman Catholics. It had long been the practice for Englishmen to celebrate November 5, Guy Fawkes Day, in commemoration of the failure of a Catholic-connected plot to blow up Parliament in 1605. These celebrations, which also took place in many American cities, regularly included the burning of the pope in effigy. Some places even called the celebration "Pope's Day." In the first months of the war in 1775 George Washington issued an order forbidding his troops to commemorate Guy Fawkes Day. Washington called the ceremony a "ridiculous and childish custom," and he also pointed out how offensive such actions were to the French Canadians whom the Continental Congress was then wooing to join the rebellion. Even more importantly, some of the new state constitutions—especially

The pulpit was used as an effective rallying point for the cause of the Revolution. BILLY GRAHAM CENTER

Pennsylvania and Maryland, both from 1776—established broad principles of religious toleration. And the new constitutions of other states—like New York (1777) and Massachusetts (1780)—which still contained either prejudicial statements against Catholics or provisions singling out Protestants for special support, nonetheless brought Catholics closer to full religious freedom than had been the case under less tolerant colonial charters.

The War Brings Reform

The upsetting circumstances and charged ideology of the war became an occasion for some Christians to promote reform in American society. Although most Americans who thought about public affairs during the Revolution did so in terms of the British-American clash or the effort to frame new American governments, a few believers attempted to inject specifically Christian considerations into public life. And although most Americans seemed to have been mostly concerned about the evils of Parliament and the British, a few Christians used the war to attack evils at home. The areas of greatest concern for these reformers were traditional ties between church and state and the slavery of blacks.

Baptists spoke out most forthrightly on the question of church and state. Isaac Backus, leading spokesman for New England's Baptists, represented many in his denomination when he pointed out inconsistencies in the struggle against British tyranny. The Baptists had long felt that the establishment of religion was itself tyrannical—whether the Church of England in the mother country, Virginia, or elsewhere, or Congregationalism in Massachusetts and Connecticut. To force citizens to pay taxes to support an established church or to expect coercion of any sort to promote true faith was both absurd and un-Christian. For a state to meddle in the internal affairs of churches was to subvert the liberty which God had given to his children. The gospel itself demanded that churches be free.

Such sentiments had created friction between Baptists and the Congregational state churches in New England as far back as the age of Roger Williams. The growth of the Baptists after the Great Awakening increased the strife, and the Revolution stimulated further acrimony. In the early 1770s Baptists and Massachusetts authorities had in fact clashed several more times over Baptist failures to heed the Congregational establishment. Authorities had disrupted Baptist meetings, taken the property of Baptists who refused to pay taxes for constructing Congregational churches, and made it difficult to obtain the licenses which Baptist congregations needed.

The war, with its cries of "No taxation without representation" and its talk of Parliamentary "slavery," naturally encouraged the Baptists to ask embarrassing questions of New England governments. In 1773 Backus wrote, "A very great grievance which our country has justly complained of is that by some late proceedings [of Parliament] a man's house or locks cannot secure either his person or his property from oppressive officers. Pray then consider what our brethren have suffered." In sum, Baptists were asking New England's governments to treat them as they themselves wished to be treated by Parliament.

Others, including the Separate Congregationalists, echoed the arguments of the Baptists. A Connecticut Separate, Israel Holley, preached a sermon after the Boston Tea Party in which he accused the colonies of acting just like Parliament in their treatment of religious dissent: "Is not New-England, the government and authority of some of the colonies in New-England, guilty of exercising the same arbitrary power, to abridge many of [the dissenters'] natural and constitutional liberty and privileges?"

After the war, statesmen like Thomas Jefferson and James Madison would join Baptists and Separates in calling for division of church and state, although their arguments were much more political than religious. The end to established religion and complex debates over matters of church and state would constitute major developments in later American church history. The Revolutionary turmoil had made it possible for the advocates of separation to gain a political hearing for their religious convictions.

Samuel Hopkins (1721–1803)   LIBRARY OF
                            CONGRESS

Other Christians attacked an even more persistent evil during the Revolutionary crisis. While Quakers, Mennonites, and a few others had protested against slavery earlier, the war years provided an opportunity for even more pointed criticism. Samuel Hopkins (1721-1803) of Newport, Rhode Island, was the most active critic of slavery during the war, outside of Quaker circles. Hopkins, a student and friend of Jonathan Edwards, was a New Light who delighted in the harder and more obscure doctrines of Calvinism. He was also a skillful polemicist against slavery. With his Congregationalist colleague in Newport, Ezra Stiles, Hopkins promoted a plan to raise money to free slaves and return them as missionaries to Africa. He also gave his views to the public.

In 1776 Hopkins dedicated his *Dialogue Concerning the Slavery of the Africans* to the Continental Congress. This sharp attack contended that slavery was "very inconsistent . . . with worshipping God thro' Christ." Hopkins conceded that it was common to treat blacks as if they were "not . . . our brethren, or in any degree on a level with us, but as quite another species of animals, made only to serve us and our children." But such an attitude violated "that benevolence, which loves our neighbors as ourselves, and is agreeable to truth and righteousness." The patriotic Whig ideology lent great force to Hopkins' essentially religious case against slavery. He pointed out "the inconsistence of promoting the slavery of the Africans, at the same time we are asserting our own civil liberty, at the risque of our fortunes and lives." He asked what slaves must think about the patriotic argument against Britain, when "they see the slavery the *Americans* dread as worse than death, is lighter than a feather, compared to their heavy doom; and may be called liberty and happiness, when contrasted with the most abject slavery and unutterable wretchedness to which they are subjected." He concluded in language worthy of a revivalist: "Oh, the shocking, the intolerable inconsistence! And this gross, barefaced, practiced inconsistence, is an open, practical condemnation of holding these our brethren in slavery; and in these circumstances the crime of persisting in it becomes unspeakably greater and more provoking in God's sight."

A few other Congregational and Presbyterian Calvinists joined Hopkins in protesting against slavery from religious and political standpoints. One of these, the New Jersey Presbyterian Jacob Green (1722-1790), added a perceptive prophecy to his denunciation of slavery in 1776:

> What a dreadful absurdity! What a shocking consideration, that people who are so strenuously contending for liberty, should at the same time encourage and promote slavery! . . . However we may be free from British oppression, I venture to say, we shall have inward convulsions, contentions, oppressions, and various calamities, so that our liberty will be uncomfortable, till we wash our hands from the guilt of negro slavery.

Unfortunately, such protests were not successful. It would take nearly another century, ferocious strife in the churches and society as a whole, and a great civil war until slavery was abolished. Yet during the Revolution at least a few Christians had redeemed the times by protesting against the slave system.

Colonial Pluralism and Revolutionary Unity

The Revolution was a momentous event for American churches, just as it was a momentous event for the country as a whole. It reaffirmed the belief of many that God had taken a special providential interest in America and that he had special designs for its future. It also enshrined a heady concept of freedom, which would have many ramifications for the churches. It hastened the separation of church and state. And, perhaps most importantly, it opened vast areas west of the Appalachians to settlement, areas where virtually no churches existed and few traditional religious standards applied. These consequences of the Revolution had a great impact upon the future of Christianity in America. But the Revolution was also an important religious event for the way it changed conditions in its own times.

By 1776 America was well on the way to becoming a pluralistic Protestant country. The small, but significant numbers of Catholics, Jews, and "free thinkers" who also lived in the country on the eve of Independence had even begun to erode that Protestant hegemony. Although many believers had not come to terms with this pluralistic situation, it was a fact. In 1776 Presbyterians and Baptists together outnumbered Anglicans in Virginia, and each outnumbered Anglicans in North and South Carolina. A rich diversity of Protestants inhabited Pennsylvania, New Jersey, New York, and Delaware. Baptists, Anglicans, and Quakers made up growing minorities in New England. And this was at a time when such denominational differences often meant a great deal. In the 1770s, we must recall, Baptists lost property in New England for being Baptists, Presbyterians and Baptists in Virginia felt the literal touch of the lash from aristocratic planters for meeting as Presbyterians and Baptists, and Mennonites and Quakers suffered imprisonment, fines, and rougher treatment for holding to their traditional pacifistic views. In addition, the colonies were not nearly as English as they once had been. In 1776 one-fifth of the population was of African descent, nearly another fifth was Scotch or Scotch-Irish, and a tenth was German or Dutch.

The great impact of the Revolution on religion was to mask this pluralism. The war made patriotism more important for many Protestant groups than the historical or doctrinal differences which had separated them. In New England, Baptists, Separate Congregationalists, New Lights, Old Calvinists, and Old Lights—all of whom had battled each other for more than a generation—rallied around the flag. In Virginia, backcountry evangelical dirt farmers and Tidewater Anglican aristocrats with virtually nothing else in common found it possible to unite for common political purposes. The new country itself gave a common cause to diverse Christian groups. Loyalty to that country became a greater unifier of religious groups than were ethnic, doctrinal, and historical similarities. Thus the Revolution, in the first place, hid American religious pluralism by providing a symbol (the country) and an ideology (the Whig idea of freedom) that drew many of the different groups together.

In the second place, the Revolution obscured that pluralism by cutting off nonpatriot groups from the mainstream of American life. Anglicans, who would eventually form the Protestant Episcopal Church in the United States, had little influence in the early days of the new country until they adapted the forms of their communion to republican standards and joined in the general affirmation of the United States. Quakers, Mennonites, and other Pacifists (who diverged from the patriotic consensus for doctrinal reasons), Lutherans and other immigrant groups (who diverged for ethnic reasons), and black Christians (who diverged because of their bondage) often seemed to drop out of public view.

The result was that the Revolution did more to unite religious groups in the United States than any other factor in colonial America. American religion after the Revolutionary War was generally Protestant and largely evangelical. But because of the Revolution it was also self-consciously American. Religious points of view which strayed from that nationalistic center would have to wait until the twentieth century to be recognized as significant factors in the culture of American religion.

Religious Congregations 1775–1776

(After Paullin and Wright)

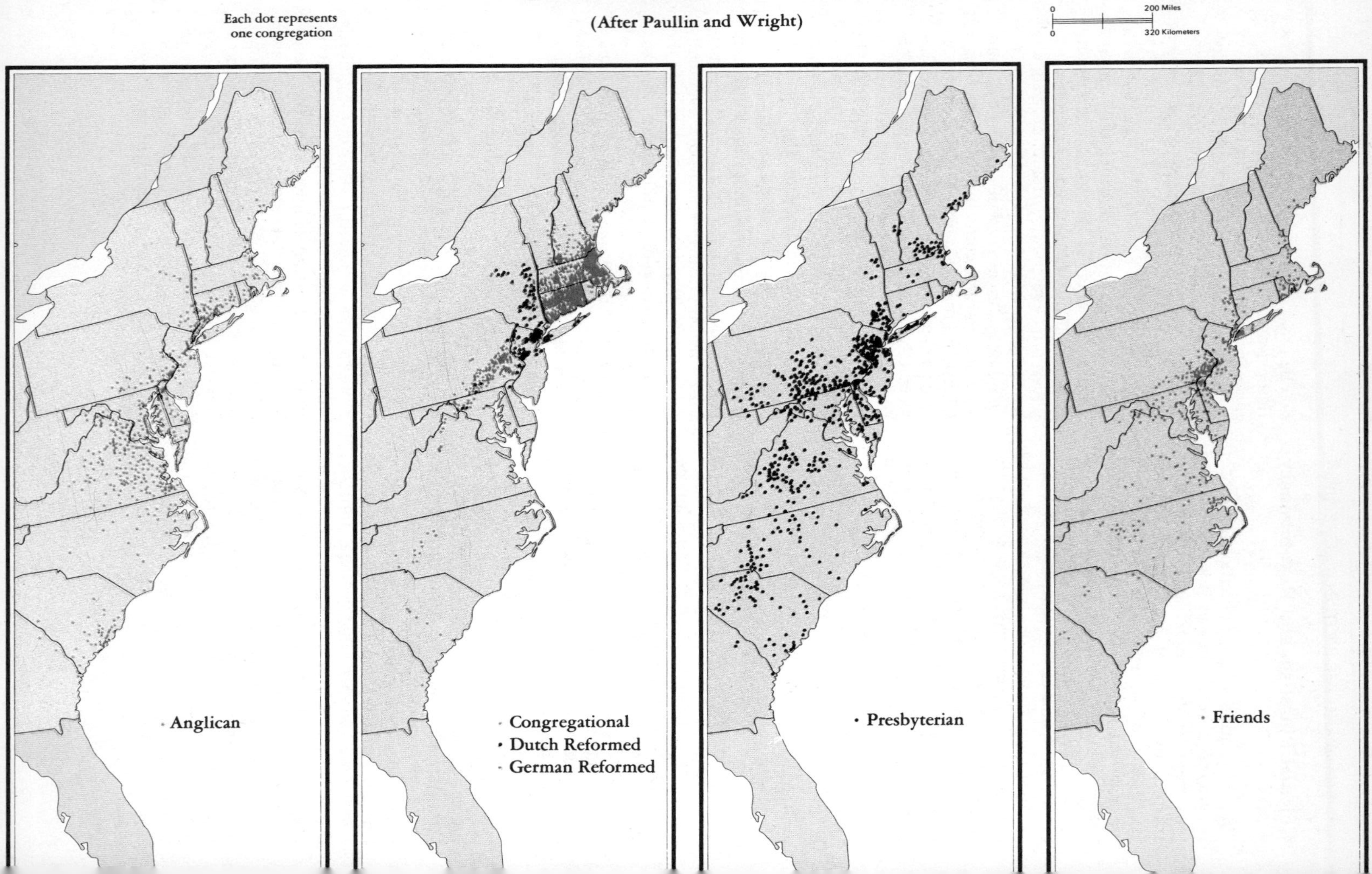

Each dot represents
one congregation

200 Miles

320 Kilometers

· Friends

· Presbyterian

· Congregational
· Dutch Reformed
- German Reformed

· Anglican

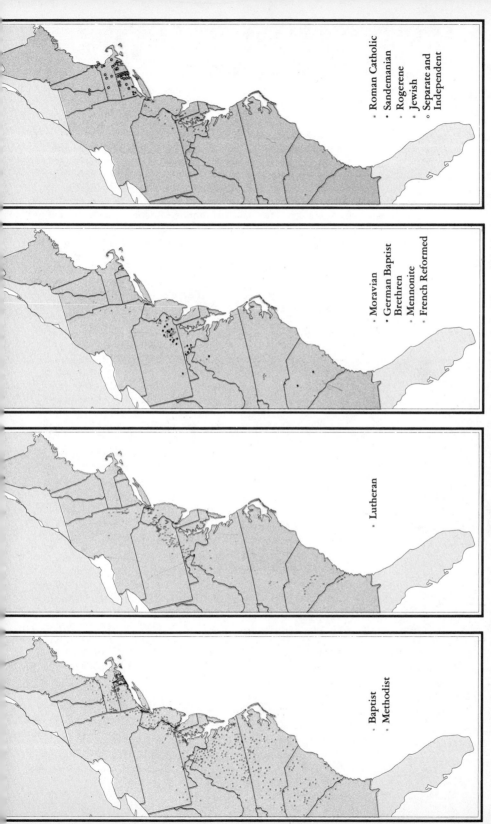

Baptist
Methodist

Lutheran

Moravian
German Baptist Brethren
Mennonite
French Reformed

Roman Catholic
Sandemanian
Rogerene
Jewish
Separate and Independent

From Lester J. Cappon et al., *Atlas of Early American History: The Revolutionary Era, 1760–1790*. Copyright © 1976 by Princeton University Press. Reprinted by permission of Princeton University Press.

Were American Origins "Christian"?

GEORGE M. MARSDEN

Americans frequently have claimed that the origins of their nation were uniquely "Christian." Often Christians suggest that Americans should return to the ideals of the now-lost Christian age. So the question of America's Christian origins remains both interesting and practical.

Certainly America's origins were Christian in the sense that the earliest white settlers were by-and-large professing Christians from nations that called themselves Christian. Early America was an extension of the

Thomas Jefferson (1743–1826) BAPTIST JOINT COMMITTEE ON PUBLIC AFFAIRS

WE HOLD THESE TRUTHS TO BE SELF-EVIDENT. THAT ALL MEN ARE CREATED EQUAL. THAT THEY ARE ENDOWED BY THEIR CREATOR WITH CERTAIN INALIENABLE RIGHTS, AMONG THESE ARE LIFE, LIBERTY AND THE PURSUIT OF HAPPINESS. THAT TO SECURE THESE RIGHTS GOVERNMENTS ARE INSTITUTED AMONG MEN. WE··· SOLEMNLY PUBLISH AND DECLARE, THAT THESE COLONIES ARE AND OF RIGHT OUGHT TO BE FREE AND INDEPENDENT STATES···AND FOR THE SUPPORT OF THIS DECLARATION, WITH A FIRM RELIANCE ON THE PROTECTION OF DIVINE PROVIDENCE. WE MUTUALLY PLEDGE OUR LIVES, OUR FORTUNES AND OUR SACRED HONOUR.

bounds of "Christendom." The important question, however, is whether these Christian origins were more than matters of name and formal observance. Were the British colonies indeed Christian in the sense of demonstrating Christian ideals that ought to be models for future generations?

The view that the colonies were significantly Christian has a good bit to recommend it. Two of the most influential settlements, New England and Pennsylvania, were founded explicitly on Christian principles. Each was a remarkable attempt to establish a holy commonwealth. Each manifested many admirable efforts to incorporate Christian principles into the fabric of society. On the other hand, these two examples must be viewed in the context of the other British North American settlements that have to be described as more nominally Christian. For every settler who was an active participant in a holy experiment there were many others (even within New England and Pennsylvania) who lived in a world that seemed far from Christian influences. Much of colonial America was a seventeenth- or eighteenth-century version of the wild west. As Nathaniel Hawthorne long ago pointed out in a famous story, when the Puritans arrived in Massachusetts, they were met by the libertine Thomas Morton of Merrymont. In the colonies as a whole, the Thomas Mortons probably were always more numerous than the strict Christians. They are just as legitimately part of the American heritage.

Another qualification is in order if American origins are to be regarded as Christian. How purely Christian can any society be? Take the case of Puritan Massachusetts, which was probably as intense an effort as any in history to construct a model Christian society. In many respects the Puritans succeeded. Their colony was notable for a sense of mutual responsibility of the members of the community for each other. The poor were well cared for, ostentation and profiteering were outlawed, education was promoted, strong family structures were encouraged. God's name was widely reverenced and his will constantly sought. Seventeenth-century Puritan towns were in many respects idyllic models of peaceful Christian communities. They seem models worth imitating.

On the other hand, even this outstanding example of a model Christian society had some serious shortcomings. Paradoxically, perhaps the most serious were related to the very idea under discussion — that they thought of themselves as an uniquely Christian society. The Puritans supposed that they stood in the same relation to God as had Old Testament Israel. They thought that God had chosen them to play a special role in the history of the New World, to be a new Israel. They even put some of the Old Testament legislation into their law books. So it is not unfair to claim, as Puritan opponents always were quick to do, that their society had a proud and legalistic tinge about it. Furthermore, the Puritans, as the new Israel, thought that their special destiny in history gave them special rights. They strictly banned all teaching of non-Puritan forms of Christianity from their communities. Although they were following practices common at the time, the Puritans' treatment of outsiders and dissenters was nonetheless far from charitable. Most especially, their record toward the Native Americans was marred by their own sense of being a Christian people. Fancying themselves the new Israel, they claimed the land as though the Indians were the Canaanites. Their sincere missionary efforts, therefore, were undercut by such imperialism draped with biblical rationales.

Pennsylvania and Rhode Island were far better in relationships to outsiders and dissenters; but then their policies of tolerance meant that they were less thoroughgoing in their efforts to establish a Christian society. Roger Williams in fact thought such an ideal impossible. He recognized what may be the truth of the matter: there are very definite limits as to how Christian any society can be. To enforce strictly Christian principles, freedom and tolerance must be limited accordingly. Moreover, as Williams recognized, there are great dangers of overestimation of a nation's virtue when it regards itself as an extension of God's kingdom.

Still other qualifications should be added. Certainly practices such as the rule of law even over kings, equality before the law, and representative government had strong support from a heritage of Christian ideals. But none of these ideals was purely Christian in any strict sense. The Christian origins of these practices were mixed with Greek, Roman, Anglo-Saxon, Renaissance, and Enlightenment roots. So men like Thomas Jefferson or Benjamin Franklin had more directly to do with the shaping of American political ideals than did the more strictly Christian leaders. Nonetheless, the heritage of Western Civilization out of which leaders like Jefferson and Franklin grew was permeated with Christian ideals, and such men reflected those ideals in their political thinking. Yet, as in every other case, the point must be repeated — America's Christian origins were mixed with many traditions that were not strictly Christian.

So, indeed, some commendable examples of Christian principles and practices can be found in America's origins. But since such principles and practices seldom appeared in anything like pure forms, claims about America's Christian origins should be carefully qualified. If the colonial or revolutionary past is to be used as a model, it must be done selectively.

For Further Reading

Excellent general texts with full sections on the colonial period are Sydney E. Ahlstrom, *A Religious History of the American People* (1972), and Winthrop S. Hudson, *Religion in America,* 3rd ed. (1981). Hilrie S. Smith, Robert T. Handy, and Lefferts Loetscher, *American Christianity: An Historical Interpretation with Representative Documents,* 2 vols. (1960), John Tracy Ellis, ed., *Documents of American Catholic History,* 2nd ed. (1962), Perry Miller and Thomas H. Johnson, eds., *The Puritans,* 2 vols. (1963), and Alan Heimert and Perry Miller, *The Great Awakening* (1967), provide useful collections of primary sources. Henry Warner Bowden, *American Indians and Christian Missions* (1981), Albert J. Raboteau, *Slave Religion: The "Invisible Institution" in the Antebellum South* (1978), and Lester B. Scherer, *Slavery and the Churches in Early America 1619-1819* (1975), are expert surveys of once neglected topics.

Study of Christianity in early America is dominated by interest in New England Puritanism, and study of the New England Puritans stands in the long shadow of Perry Miller. Miller's works, which are among the great books of the twentieth century, include a collection of essays, *Errand into the Wilderness* (1956), and two superb volumes on *The New England Mind* (1939, 1953; repr. 1961). Those who approach Miller in the depth of their own probings into the Puritan mind include Sacvan Bercovitch, *The Puritan Origins of the American Self* (1975), Norman Fiering, *Moral Philosophy at Seventeenth-Century Harvard* (1981), and especially Edmund S. Morgan, whose work on the early Puritans includes studies on *The Puritan Family,* rev. ed. (1966; repr. 1980) and on the Puritans' idea of the church, *Visible Saints* (1963).

Several Puritan studies from earlier in the century are still valuable, such as Samuel Eliot Morison, *Harvard College in the Seventeenth Century,* 2 vols. (1936), and Ola Winslow, *Meetinghouse Hill 1630-1783* (1952; repr. 1972). But most of the best work on religious aspects of the Puritan experience is the result of intense labors since the mid-1960s. As outstanding examples from a vast number of good books, see Norman Pettit, *The Heart Prepared: Grace and Conversion in Puritan Spiritual Life* (1966), Robert G. Pope, *The Half-Way Covenant: Church Membership in Puritan New England* (1969), Stephen Foster, *Their Solitary Way: The Puritan Social Ethic in the First Century of Settlement in New England* (1971), Robert Middelkauff, *The Mathers: Three Generations of Puritan Intellectuals, 1596-1728* (1971), David D. Hall, *The Faithful Shepherd: A History of the New England Ministry in the Seventeenth Century* (1972), and E. Brooks Holifield, *The Covenant Sealed: The Development of Puritan Sacramental Theology in Old and New England, 1570-1720* (1974). Books which emphasize New England social relationships have also illuminated the place of religion among the Puritans. As examples see John Demos, *A Little Commonwealth: Family Life in Plymouth Colony* (1970), T. H. Breen, *Puritans and Adventurers: Change and Persistence in Early America* (1980), and Philip Greven, *The Protestant Temperament: Patterns of Child-rearing, Religious Experience, and the Self in Early America* (1977). For a convenient overview, Francis J. Bremer, *The Puritan Experiment* (1976), is useful.

The colonial revivals have been the focus of excellent history since Joseph Tracy published his still useful work, *The Great Awakening,* in 1842 (repr. 1976; rev. ed. 1945, repr. 1969). Edwin Scott Gaustad, *The Great Awakening in New England* (1957), and J. M. Bumsted and John E. Van de Wetering, *What Must I Do To Be Saved? A Great Awakening in Colonial America* (1976), are solid surveys. C. C. Goen, *Revivalism and Separatism in New England 1740-1800: Strict Congregationalists and Separate Baptists in the Great Awakening* (1962; repr. 1969), and Richard L. Bushman, *From Puritan to Yankee: Character and the Social Order in Connecticut, 1690-1765* (1970), are among the best specialized studies of the event and the period.

Publication of a definitive edition of Jonathan Edwards' works by John E. Smith began in 1957. Biographies of Edwards' external life by Ola Winslow (1972) and his internal life by Perry Miller (1949) are still the places to begin study of this theological giant. Specialized studies also abound, including C. Conrad Cherry, *The Theology of Jonathan Edwards* (1966), Edward H. Davidson, *Jonathan Edwards: The Narrative of a Puritan Mind* (1966), and Harold P. Simonson, *Jonathan Edwards: Theologian of the Heart* (1974). Edwards' theological legacy is the subject of Joseph Haroutunian, *Piety Versus Moralism: The Passing of the New England Theology* (1932), and Frank Hugh Foster, *A Genetic History of the New England Theology* (1907). Haroutunian did not appreciate the changes after Edwards; Foster did. An especially lucid work by Henry F. May, *The Enlightenment in America* (1976), sheds light on the general intellectual history of Edwards' age.

The best studies of Christians in the Revolutionary period are Alan E. Heimert, *Religion and the American Mind: From the Great Awakening to the Revolution* (1966), who argues that the revival gave shape to the new nation, and Nathan O. Hatch, *The Sacred Cause of Liberty: Republican Thought and the Millennium in Revolutionary New England* (1977), who is concerned to show how patriotic ideas shaped the church. Among other useful books on the subject are John F. Berens, *Providence and Patriotism in Early America, 1640-1815* (1978), and Mark A. Noll, *Christians in the American Revolution* (1977).

Not all the good books on colonial American religion deal with New England Puritans. Fine studies exist of the Baptists by William G. McLoughlin, *New England Dissent, 1630-1833: The Baptists and the Separation of Church and State*, 2 vols. (1971), of the Unitarians by Conrad Wright, *The Beginnings of Unitarianism in America* (1955; repr. 1976), and of colonial Anglicans by Carl Bridenbaugh, *Mitre and Sceptre: Transatlantic Faiths, Ideas, Personalities, and Politics, 1688-1775* (1967). A solid collection of essays, edited by F. Ernest Stoeffler, *Continental Pietism and Early American Christianity* (1976), contains useful summaries on the Dutch Reformed, Mennonites, Moravians, Methodists, and the Church of the Brethren. Other examples of valuable work on the non-Puritan denominations include Leonard J. Trinterud, *The Forming of an American Tradition: A Re-examination of Colonial Presbyterianism* (1949; repr. 1978), John Tracy Ellis, *Catholics in Colonial America* (1965), Frank Baker, *From Wesley to Asbury: Studies in Early American Methodism* (1976), and Richard K. MacMaster et al., *Conscience in Crisis: Mennonites and Other Peace Churches in America, 1739-1789* (1979). Pathbreaking studies on religion and society beyond New England are Jon Butler, *Power, Authority, and the Origins of American Denominational Order: The English Churches in the Delaware Valley, 1680-1730* (1978), and Rhys Isaac, *The Transformation of Virginia, 1740-1790* (1982).

Journal articles that were useful in preparing this section demonstrate the wealth of such material for the colonial period: Jon Butler, "Magic, Astrology, and the Early American Religious Heritage, 1600-1760," *American Historical Review* 84 (1979): 317-346; Marion J. Hatchett, "A Sunday Service in 1776," *Historical Magazine of the Protestant Episcopal Church* 45 (1976): 369-385; Gerald F. Moran and Maris A. Vinovskis, "The Puritan Family and Religion," *William and Mary Quarterly* 39 (1982): 29-63; Harry S. Stout, "Religion, Communications, and the Ideological Origins of the American Revolution," *William and Mary Quarterly* 34 (1977): 519-541; James P. Walsh, "'Black-Cotted Raskolls': Anti-Anglican Criticism in Colonial Virginia," *Virginia Magazine of History and Biography* 88 (1980): 21-36.

Among biographies or edited primary sources that deserve special mention are those for John Winthrop (Edmund S. Morgan, 1958), Thomas Hooker (Frank Shuffleton, 1977; and George H. Williams et al., 1975), Thomas Shepard (Michael McGiffert and Winfred E. Bernhard, eds., 1972), John Cotton (Larzer Ziff, 1962), Edward Taylor (Donald E. Stanford, ed., 1960), Cotton Mather (David Levin, 1978; Richard Lovelace, 1979), Roger Williams (Perry Miller, 1953; repr. 1962; Edmund S. Morgan, 1967; and W. Clark Gilpin, 1979), Anne Hutchinson (Emery Battis, 1962; David D. Hall, ed., 1968), William Penn (Melvin B. Endy, Jr., 1973), John Woolman (ed. Phillips Moulton, 1971), George Whitefield (Stuart Clark Henry, 1957; Arnold Dallimore, 2 vols., 1970, 1980), Charles Chauncy (Edward M. Griffin, 1980), Jonathan Mayhew (Charles W. Akers, 1964), Ezra Stiles (Edmund S. Morgan, 1962), Isaac Backus (William G. McLoughlin, 1967), Samuel Seabury (Bruce E. Steiner, 1971), Samuel Johnson (Joseph Ellis, 1973), Samuel Hopkins (Joseph A. Conforti, 1981), and William Billings (David P. McKay and Richard Crawford, 1975).

The Bible in America

ROBERT P. MARKHAM

The story of the Bible in America began with the arrival of the pilgrims who were carrying their most treasured possession, *The Geneva Bible* (published in 1560). For two hundred years most of the Bibles used in America were purchased from England because only the king's designated printers were permitted to print them. The most notable exception was the Bible translated into the language of the Massachusetts Indians (1663) by John Eliot using an alphabet which he himself had devised. The Revolutionary War brought about a radical change in Bible publication.

America's First Bibles

Because Bibles could no longer be brought from England, Robert Aitken, printer to Congress, printed the first English New Testament in America, an edition of the Authorized (King James) Version (1777) and later the complete Bible (1882). After the war, however, America continued to be indebted to England for many Bibles. The famous London Polyglot in eight languages (1824) was distributed in America primarily only in English though still called the Polyglot Bible. The chief possession of many of the pioneers was "a polyglot Bible, a tin reflector, and a wooden clock." The Authorized Version, undoubtedly, was the most widely used, and great care was taken to produce accurate editions. Isaiah Thomas (1791), S. Payson (1815), the American Bible Society (1828, 1856, 1966), the American Bible Union (1862-1863), Oxford University Press (1911), among others, made special efforts to ensure the accuracy of their editions of the Authorized Version. Publishers adopted a wide variety of helps for readers,

such as pictorial engravings (1796), Greek and English interleaved pages (1805), notes and comments (1813), and a significant new departure, text paragraphs instead of verse paragraphs.

The first completely new translation of the Bible into English in America was the translation of the entire Greek Bible, except the Apocrypha, by Charles Thompson, secretary of the Continental Congress. It was published in 1808 and was reprinted as recently as 1954.

The Bible Speaks to the Common Person

In 1833 Noah Webster, of dictionary fame, completed a revision of the Authorized Version. He pointed out that some 150 words had signficantly changed meaning and in most printings there were grammatical and translation errors. But his efforts were met by an indifferent public. As recently as 1966, nevertheless, the American Bible Society published its *English Reference Bible* edition of the AV with an extensive list of English biblical words which have changed meaning through the centuries.

Another attempt to make the Bible more readable was the effort to use phonetic spelling. Andrew Comstock designed a "purfekt alfabet" in which he had the New Testament printed in "Filadelphia" (1848). The Longley brothers (Lonli Bruderz) devised their own "Fonetik Spelin" and printed New Testaments in "Sinsinati" (1855, 1864). Neither of these attempts had any lasting results.

The most long-lasting impact upon ordinary readers was the use of modern language in contrast to Elizabethan English.

It is important to note that the English Revised Version (1881-1885) produced in England, its counterpart, the American Standard Version (1901) containing some alterations from the ERV, and the even more widely popular Revised Standard Version (1946-1952) were deliberate attempts to revise and retain as much as possible of the language of the 1611 Authorized Version. Modern speech translators, on the other hand, have tried to make the Bible speak as clearly in contemporary English as it had to its original audience. J. W. Hanson (1884-1885) produced the first American modern speech translation directly from the newly edited Greek New Testament of Westcott and Hort. Other popular translations are: Twentieth Century (1901), F. S. Ballentine (1889-1901), E. J. Goodspeed (1923), W. G. Ballentine (1923), Helen B. Montgomery (1924), C. B. Williams (1937), G. Verkuyl (1945-1959), Kenneth Taylor (1970), and Clarence Jordan (1969-1973). Probably the most successful of all of them is *Today's English Version* (The Good News Bible, 1966-1976). Its simplicity, clarity, and accuracy have made an impact on Bible translators in many parts of the world.

Bible Societies Distribute Scriptures

Historic Philadelphia was the site of the first Bible society organized in America (1809). Other states, counties, and regions soon followed so that by 1816, when many of the local societies joined in establishing the American Bible Society, there were some thirty separate Bible societies in twenty-four states and forty foreign countries. By 1900 there were 1,500 auxiliaries which helped to raise funds for distributing the scriptures.

From the early years the American Bible Society observed these basic principles: distribute the scriptures without note or comment, circulate the version in common use, serve the churches at home and abroad, assist in the translation and revision of the Bible, and provide editions at the lowest possible cost. Special groups have long received its attention. Braille editions, talking books, and tapes are provided to the blind below cost. Service personnel from the Confederate States and both world wars have been given Bibles. The migrants who built America and continue to come to its shores needed Bibles in Danish, Dutch, French, German, Irish, Italian, Polish, Portuguese, Russian, Spanish, Swedish, Welsh, and southeast Asian languages. Furthermore, early Bible Society reports expressed concern about the needs of "the brethren of the woods" and "the language of the forest," i.e., the American Indians. Although only the Massachusetts Indians ever received the entire Bible, numerous tribes did get a complete Testament in due time: Apache, Cherokee, Cheyenne, Choctoaw, Dakota, Hopi, Inupiat, Kuskokwim, Muskogee, Navajo, and Ojibwa.

The Bible and World Missions

During the great missionary era of the late nineteenth and early twentieth centuries the national Bible societies faced increasing needs of supplying "their missionaries" with assistance. Problems of translation, revision, publication, distribution, and administration were seen as transcending national boundaries, and this led to the concept of shared responsibility for the work. The British and Foreign Bible Society, the National Bible Society of Scotland, the Netherlands Bible Society, the American Bible Society, and others, established the United Bible Societies (1946). By May 1980 the UBS reported that as of December 1979 at least one book of the Bible had been translated into 1,685 languages, twenty-seven of them published in 1979 alone. Worldwide distribution amounted to more than 9 million Bibles, 12 million New Testaments, 28 million portions (Gospels, Letters, or other books), 38 million selections for new readers, and 394 million other types of selections. The societies were engaged in providing translation assistance in more than 750 languages spoken by eighty-five percent of the world's population. The American Bible Society alone provided more than half of the required financial assistance.

Since 1946 a number of other organizations have also begun to play an increasing role in Bible translation, publication, and distribution. The Gideons, although founded in 1898, have begun Bible distribution in foreign languages outside the United States in recent years. The World Home Bible League, the New York Bible Society (recently changed to the New York International Bible Society), and especially the Wycliffe Bible Translators now translate and publish in many languages. In 1980 WBT and its counterpart, the Summer Institute of Linguistics, estimated that they had completed translations in 146 languages, with five hundred more in progress. Linguists estimate that some 3,000 languages still have no part of the Bible; on the other hand, it might be observed that the great majority of these are very small languages which involve some two percent of the world's peoples. WBT/SIL is perhaps unique in its goal of trying to translate some part of the scripture for every tribe or language. They usually view themselves as linguists who make analysis of tribal languages, conduct literacy work, carry out anthropological studies, assist community development, and prepare Bible translations. Their efforts are not to transplant churches but to encourage indigenous Christianity.

American Biblical Scholarship

While it has been notable in the field of biblical archaeology, American biblical scholarship has been somewhat less productive in scholarly editions of biblical texts. James Murdock prepared an edition of the Peshito Syriac (1851), and George Lamsa translated the entire Bible from the Syriac (1957). Isaac Leeser translated the Old Testament from Hebrew into English for American Judaism (1853), as did the Jewish Publication Society (1917); a new translation was begun in 1967. While there have been several printings of Hebrew Bibles, all were first published in Europe.

The Greek New Testament was translated in America many times but not critically edited until 1966. That year was the 150th anniversary of the American Bible Society, and it was their sponsorship which led to the publication of *The Greek New Testament*. The editorial team was made up of two Americans, a Scot, a German, and later an Italian. The text was composed by a Jewish firm in Philadelphia, printed by a Bible society in Germany, copyrighted by the United Bible Societies in London, and made available to scholars and translators around the world. It was, in fact, the first critical edition of the Greek or Hebrew scriptures produced in America.

There have been many other English translations [see Table], and there have also been a number of significant Bible commentaries produced in America with either a traditional version or an entirely new translation of the text. Alden Bradford, descendant of historic Governor William Bradford and John Alden, produced the first American commentary on the New Testament (1813). Some of the major multivolume sets including English translations are: J. Benson (5 vols., 1822-1824), W. Jenks (5 or 6 vols., 1834-1838), D. D. Whedon (5 vols., 1860-1880), Lyman Abbott (5 vols., 1875-1888), American Bible Union (2 vols., 1862-1863), A. Hovey (1881-1939), C. F. Kent (6 vols., 1904-1927), S. Matthews (14 vols., 1908-1922), J. Bewer (15 parts, 1949-1956), G. A. Buttrick (12 vols., 1951-1957), the New International Commentary, the Old Testament Library, Hermeneia, and, perhaps most comprehensive of all, the Anchor Bible (begun 1964).

The task of Bible translation and distribution is never-ending, ever-changing, increasingly cooperative, and always challenging. Even when the task seems to be done, and it never really is, the task of understanding and applying the scriptures to life remains. In that respect at least, the Bible is yet to be realized in American life.

AMERICAN SCRIPTURE TRANSLATIONS IN THE ENGLISH LANGUAGE

BIBLES		NEW TESTAMENTS	
C. Thompson, Septuagint trans.	1808	A. Kneeland	1823
G. R. Noyes	1827-1869	J. G. Palfrey, AV revised	1828
N. Webster, AV corrected	1833	R. Dickinson, AV corrected	1833
F. B. Kenrick	1849-1862	J. Morgan	1848
L. A. Sawyer	1858-1889	N. N. Whiting, AV corrected	1849
Julia Smith	1876	S. H. Cone and W. A. Wyckoff	1851
F. W. Grant, AV revised	1891-1931	A. Norton	1855
American Standard Version	1901	L. Thorn	1861
American Bible Union	1912	H. T. Anderson	1864
A. E. Knock	1919-1926	B. Wilson	1865
J. M. P. Smith and E. J. Goodspeed	1931	Joseph Smith	1867
Edition with Apocrypha	1939	N. S. Folsom	1869
W. W. Martin	1928, 1937	C. Jackson	1883
Revised Standard Version	1946-1952	J. W. Hanson	1884-1885
Catholic edition	1966	W. D. Dillard	1885
Ecumenical edition	1977	R. D. Weeks	1897
G. Lamsa	1957	F. A. Spencer	1898, 1937
G. Verkuyl, also called the		F. S. Ballentine	1899
Berkeley Version	1945-1959	Twentieth Century	1901
New World, also called		W. B. Godbey	1902
Watchtower Society	1950-1960	A. S. Worrell	1904
F. E. Siewert, Amplified Version,		I. Panin	1914
Lockman Foundation	1965	W. G. Ballentine	1923
American Bible Society, AV revised	1966	Helen B. Montgomery	1924
C. I. Scofield, AV revised	1967	A. E. Overbury	1925
New Scofield Reference Bible		G. Le Fevre	1928
Joseph Smith	1970	R. C. H. Lenski	1931-1946
Revision of 1867 edition	1970	C. C. Torrey, Four Gospels	1933
K. Taylor, Living Bible	1970	J. Greber	1937
New American Bible	1970	C. B. Williams	1937
S. T. Byington	1972	E. L. Clementson	1938
W. F. Beck	1976	E. E. Stringfellow	1943-1945
A. Edington	1976	G. Swann	1947
Today's English Version		Brotherhood Authentic Version	1951
Good News Bible	1966-1976	O. M. Norlie	1951
Edition with Apocrypha	1979	J. A. Kleist and J. Lilly	1954
New American Standard Bible	1976	G. A. Moore	1954
New International Version	1978	K. S. Wuest	1959
J. P. Green, Interlinear Bible,		F. S. Nolie	1961
Old Testament vols. 1-3	1979	C. Jordan, Cottonpatch Version	1969-1973
		J. E. Adams, Counselor's Edition	1977
		English Version for the Deaf	1978
		New King James Version, AV revised	1979

*Based on Margaret Hills, *The English Bible in America* ...1777-1957
(New York: American Bible Society and New York Public Library,
1962)

Christianity and Democracy: From the Revolution to the Civil War

BY NATHAN O. HATCH

From the Revolution to the Civil War

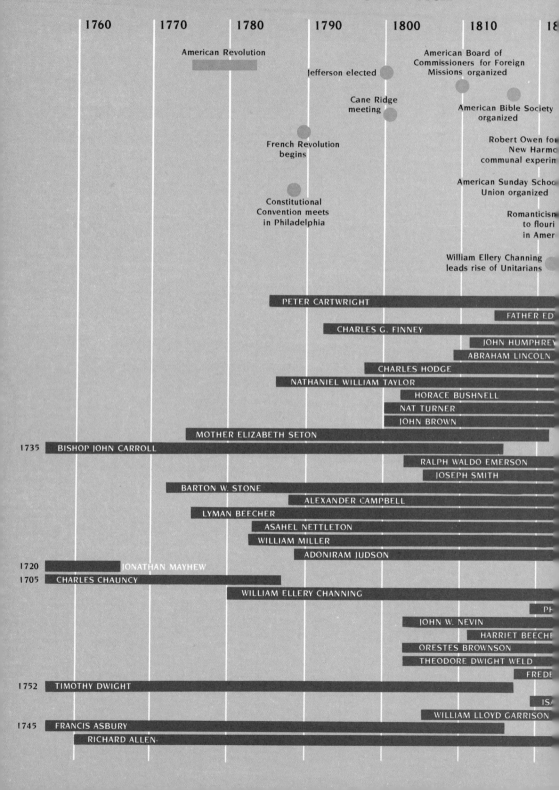

1760 1770 1780 1790 1800 1810 18

American Revolution

Jefferson elected

American Board of
Commissioners for Foreign
Missions organized

Cane Ridge
meeting

American Bible Society
organized

French Revolution
begins

Robert Owen fo
New Harmo
communal experim

Constitutional
Convention meets
in Philadelphia

American Sunday Schoo
Union organized

Romanticism
to flouri
in Amer

William Ellery Channing
leads rise of Unitarians

PETER CARTWRIGHT

FATHER ED

CHARLES G. FINNEY

JOHN HUMPHRE\

ABRAHAM LINCOLN

CHARLES HODGE

NATHANIEL WILLIAM TAYLOR

HORACE BUSHNELL

NAT TURNER

JOHN BROWN

MOTHER ELIZABETH SETON

1735 BISHOP JOHN CARROLL

RALPH WALDO EMERSON

JOSEPH SMITH

BARTON W. STONE

ALEXANDER CAMPBELL

LYMAN BEECHER

ASAHEL NETTLETON

WILLIAM MILLER

ADONIRAM JUDSON

1720 JONATHAN MAYHEW

1705 CHARLES CHAUNCY

WILLIAM ELLERY CHANNING

PH

JOHN W. NEVIN

HARRIET BEECHE

ORESTES BROWNSON

THEODORE DWIGHT WELD

FREDE

1752 TIMOTHY DWIGHT

IS\

WILLIAM LLOYD GARRISON

1745 FRANCIS ASBURY

RICHARD ALLEN

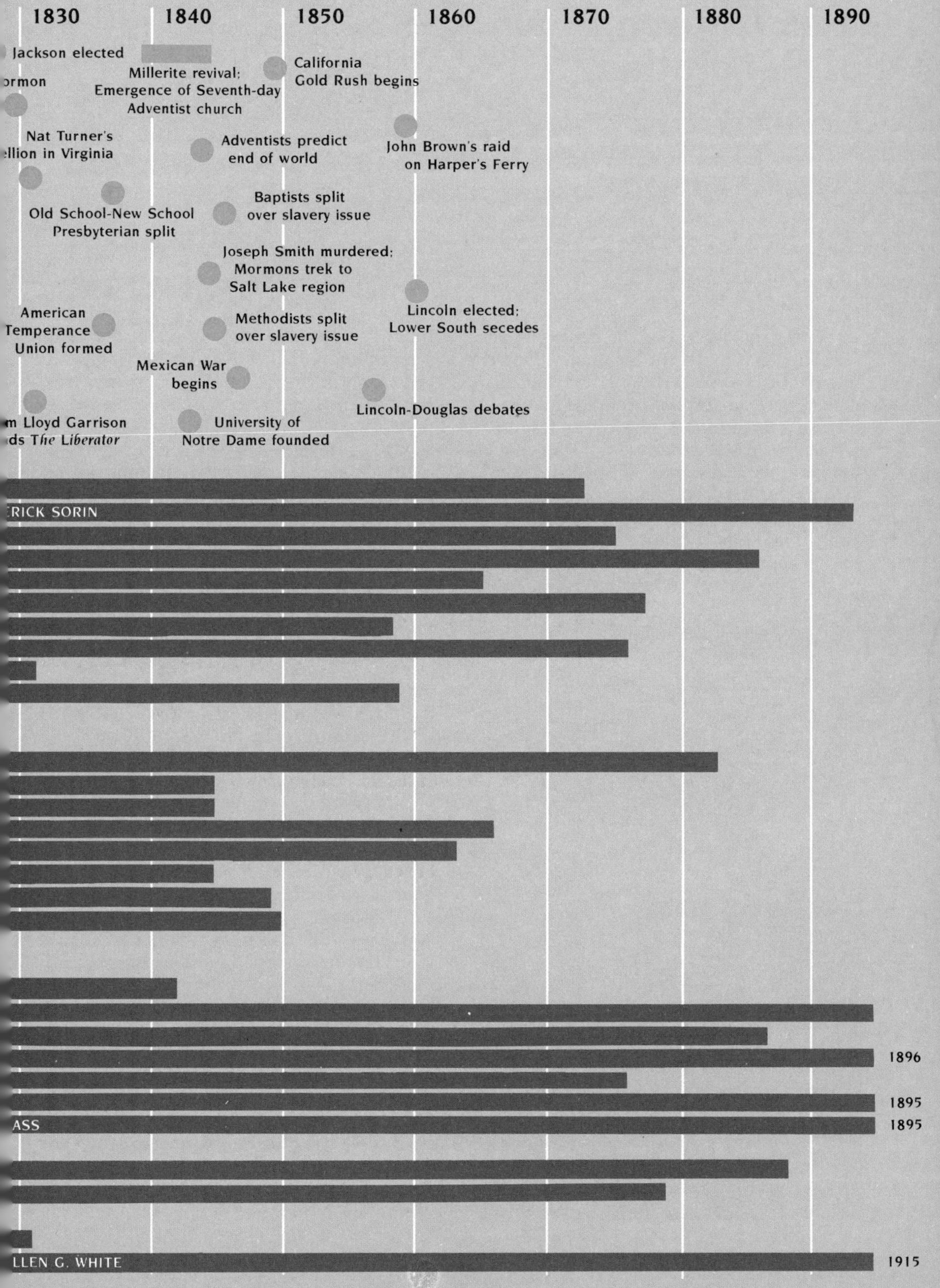

1830
1840
1850
1860
1870
1880
1890
Jackson elected
Millerite revival; Emergence of Seventh-day Adventist church
California Gold Rush begins
ormon
Nat Turner's
ellion in Virginia
Adventists predict end of world
John Brown's raid on Harper's Ferry
Old School-New School Presbyterian split
Baptists split over slavery issue
Joseph Smith murdered; Mormons trek to Salt Lake region
American Temperance Union formed
Methodists split over slavery issue
Lincoln elected; Lower South secedes
Mexican War begins
Lincoln-Douglas debates
m Lloyd Garrison
ds *The Liberator*
University of Notre Dame founded
ERICK SORIN
1896
1895
ASS
1895
LLEN G. WHITE
1915

The Church in an Age of Revolution

In many ways the era of the American Revolution stands as the hinge upon which the history of Christianity in America really turns. The birth of the Republic laid the foundation for the separation of church and state. It worked to instill democratic values into religious organizations; it deepened the conviction that God had chosen America for a special purpose; and it rewarded churches attuned to needs of common people and willing to appeal to them with a personal, voluntary, "go-getter" style. The experience of

The Liberty Bell in Independence Hall, Philadelphia, is among the nation's most venerated relics of the Revolution. LIBRARY OF CONGRESS

fighting for liberty and building from scratch a republic altered, for better or worse, the center of gravity of American Christianity. It was no accident that in a republican environment Baptists and Methodists quickly outstripped the churches which had dominated religious life in the colonies, the more formal and structured Presbyterians, Congregationalists, and Anglicans.

The Church Under Fire

At the close of the War of Independence, one of New England's most respected young ministers, Timothy Dwight, complained bitterly that "seven years of war had unhinged the principles, the morality, and the religion of the country more than could have been done by a peace of forty years." For Dwight and other clergymen the hope that the Revolution would serve to strengthen and purify American churches gave way to the realization that the war probably had the opposite effect. The turmoil of war left many congregations without ministers and strained relationships between ministers and their churches—due, among other things, to a staggering rate of inflation. What seemed even more damaging than declining church membership was the wave of apathy toward matters religious among the nation's young people. The war had wrenched many out of safe and familiar environments and exposed them to a broader world often unfriendly to Christian virtues. To those who had sacrificed their lives for liberty and equality, the demands of traditional religion could easily come to seem irrelevant. The following incident of a New Hampshire veteran refusing

Commonwealth of Maſſachuſetts.

In the Year of our LORD, *one thouſand ſeven hundred and ninety eight.*

An Act to prevent profane Curſing and Swearing.

WHEREAS the horrible practice of profane Curſing and Swearing is inconſiſtent with the dignity and rational cultivation of the human mind, with a due reverence of the Supreme Being and his Providence, and hath a natural tendency to weaken the ſolemnity and obligation of oaths lawfully taken in the adminiſtration of juſtice ; to promote falſehood, perjuries, blaſphemies and diſſoluteneſs of manners, and to looſen the bonds of civil ſociety :

SECT. 1. *Be it therefore enacted by the Senate and Houſe of Repreſentatives, in General Court aſſembled, and by the authority of the ſame,* That if any perſon, who has arrived at diſcretion, ſhall profanely curſe or ſwear, and ſhall be thereof convicted, ſuch perſon ſo offending, ſhall forfeit and pay a ſum not exceeding *two dollars,* nor leſs than *one dollar,* according to the aggravation of the offence, and the quality and circumſtances of the offender, in the judgment of the Court or Juſtice of the Peace before whom the conviction may be ; and in caſe the ſame perſon ſhall after one conviction as aforeſaid, offend a ſecond time, ſuch offender ſhall forfeit and pay upon ſuch ſecond conviction, double the ſum forfeited on the firſt conviction ; and in caſe the ſame perſon ſhall after two convictions as aforeſaid, again offend, ſuch offender ſhall forfeit and pay upon each and every ſubſequent conviction, treble the ſum forfeited on the firſt conviction ; and if, on any trial and conviction, proof ſhall be made that more than one profane oath or curſe were ſworn or uttered, by the ſame perſon at the ſame time, and in the preſence or hearing of the ſame witneſs or witneſſes, the perſon ſo offending, for every profane oath or curſe, after the firſt, ſhall forfeit and pay a ſum not exceeding *fifty cents,* nor leſs than *twenty-five cents,* in addition to the ſum forfeited as firſt above ſpecified : One moiety of the ſeveral forfeitures, aforeſaid, to be to the uſe of the poor of the town in which the offence ſhall have been committed, and the other moiety thereof to the uſe of the perſon or perſons who ſhall make complaint thereof, or proſecute for the ſame. And in caſe any perſon convicted of profane Curſing or Swearing, ſhall not immediately pay the ſum or ſums ſo forfeited, ſuch perſon ſhall be committed to the common gaol or houſe of correction, there to remain, not leſs than one day, nor more than five days. *Provided nevertheleſs,* That when any perſon ſhall have been convicted of profane Curſing or Swearing before any Juſtice of the Peace, and having appeared before ſuch Juſtice, and pleaded the general iſſue, or demurred to the charges in the complaint againſt him, it ſhall be lawful for ſuch Defendant to appeal from the ſentence of ſuch Juſtice to the Juſtices of the next Court of General Seſſions of the Peace, to be holden in and for the county wherein the offence was committed, who ſhall hear and finally determine the ſame ; the appellant claiming ſuch appeal at the time of declaring ſuch ſentence by ſaid Juſtice, and then and there recognizing with ſufficient ſurety or ſureties in a reaſonable ſum, not exceeding *twenty dollars,* to proſecute his ſaid appeal with effect, and to perform the order of ſaid Court therein.

SECT. 2. *And be it further enacted,* That if any perſon ſhall profanely Curſe or Swear in the hearing of any Sheriff, Deputy Sheriff, Coroner, Conſtable, Grand Juror or Tythingman, it ſhall be the duty of ſuch Officers, reſpectively, forthwith to give information thereof to ſome Juſtice of the Peace of the county wherein the offence was committed, in order that the offender may be taken, convicted and puniſhed for the ſame ; Which conviction ſhall be drawn up in the form following, ———— ſſ. Be it remembered, That on the ——day of ———, in the year of our Lord ————, A. B. was convicted before me, one of the Juſtices of the Peace for the County of ————, of Swearing one (or more) profane oath (or oaths) or of uttering one (or more) profane curſe [or curſe] as the caſe ſhall be. Given under my hand the day and year aforeſaid. *Provided always, and it is hereby further enacted,* That no perſon ſhall be convicted or troubled for the offence of profane curſing or ſwearing, unleſs the proſecution, for ſuch offence, ſhall be commenced within twenty days next after the offence ſhall be committed.

SECT. 3. *And be it further enacted,* That the Clerks of the ſeveral towns, diſtricts and plantations in this Commonwealth ſhall cauſe this Act to be publickly read at the opening of their reſpective annual meetings in the month of March or April ; and if the Clerk of any town, diſtrict or plantation ſhall neglect ſo to do, he ſhall forfeit and pay the ſum of *ten dollars* for each neglect, to be recovered by an action of debt in any Court proper to try the ſame ; one moiety thereof to the uſe of the perſon or perſons ſuing therefor, and the other moiety thereof to the uſe of this Commonwealth.

SECT. 4. *And be it further enacted,* That the Secretary ſhall cauſe to be tranſmitted a printed copy of this Act to each of the public teachers of Religion within this Commonwealth, to whom it is hereby recommended to read, or cauſe the ſame to be publickly read to their ſeveral congregations annually, on the day of the Public Faſt.

SECT. 5. *And be it further enacted,* That all Laws heretofore made for preventing profane Curſing and Swearing, be, and hereby are repealed.

In the Houſe of Repreſentatives, June 28, 1798.

This Bill having had three ſeveral readings, paſſed to be enacted.

EDWARD H. ROBBINS, *Speaker.*

In Senate, June 28, 1798.

This Bill having had two ſeveral readings, paſſed to be enacted.

SAMUEL PHILLIPS, *Preſident.*

June 29, 1798.—By the Governor approved.

INCREASE SUMNER.

True Copy—*Atteſt,*

JOHN AVERY, *Secretary.*

Massachusetts made this attempt in 1798 to legislate at least one of the Christian virtues. BILLY GRAHAM CENTER

to pay his ministerial tax—supplying wood for the minister—suggests the corrosive impact that the Revolution could have upon traditional religious values:

I have attended church these fifty years; I have fought the British seven years; I have slept in a tent on the frozen ground with nothing but a blanket to cover me; and I have trod the snow path with bleeding feet nearly naked ... and if Mr. Merrill [the clergyman] needs a fire, let him go to the place where they keep one year round.

If the war seemed particularly unfriendly to the church, it also accelerated Enlighten-ment values, natural theology, and secularized thought. Revolutionary heroes like Ethan Allen (*Reason the Only Oracle of Man*, 1784) and Thomas Paine (*Age of Reason*, 1794-1796) launched savage attacks upon orthodox Christianity and advocated Deism, a system of thought that dispensed with revelation, ridiculed the Incarnation—a Creator meddling with the laws of the universe—and exalted human reason and ethical endeavors. The first three elected Presidents of the United States—Washington, Adams, and Jefferson—all advocated a form of reasonable religion that drained the supernatural from religion and valued piety primarily for its civic

Natural Religion:
Ethan Allen's Thoughts on Prayer

Before we conclude our discourse upon miracles, it will be requisite that we consider those supposed miraculous alterations of nature, or of divine providence, which by some are thought to have taken place in the world, merely in conformity to the prayer of Man. The arguments, which have been already advanced against miracles, are in substance equally applicable, to such as may be supposed to be effectuated by prayers, remonstrances or supplications of finite beings. That God should countermand his order of nature, which is the same thing as to alter his providence, merely in dictatorial conformity to the prayers or praises of his creatures, or that he should alter it merely from motives from himself are not essentially different. In as much as the consequence of a supposed alteration from either of the causes before mentioned would equally and necessarily imply mutability in wisdom, in the one case, as in the other; for in both cases the arguments terminate against any supposed miraculous alterations of nature or providence, merely from the consideration of the immutable perfection of the divine nature. For a departure from, or alteration of the eternal order, or government of things would be equally derogatory from the absolute perfection of God, whether those alterations are supposed to take place merely in conformity to the prayers or remonstrances of his creatures, or from reasons, which may be supposed to have originated merely from the divine mind itself. There is no thing, which can be mentioned, that would more manifestly argue mutability in God, than that he should alter his order of nature or providence to comply with the prayers of his mutable creatures; or to do that in conformity thereto, which the eternal regulation and government of nature would not have effectuated or accomplished independent of them. For if the eternal laws of nature were absolutely perfect, which must be admitted, a deviation from, or countermanding of them, must unavoidably imply mutability and imperfection, be it from what cause it will.

Reason the Only Oracle of Man, 1784

utility. Although this form of enlightened religion never came to command the allegiance of most common people, it did enjoy great popularity among educated Americans and was quite the intellectual rage among college students in the last two decades of the eighteenth century. At Princeton in 1782 only two students professed Christianity, and Bishop Meade wrote that the College of William and Mary had become a hotbed of French skepticism. In assessing what it meant that only five Yale students belonged to the college church in New Haven in 1800, Lyman Beecher lamented: "That was the day of the infidelity of the Tom Paine school. Boys that dressed flax in the barn, as I used to, read him and believed him."

Toward a Democratic Church

The War of Independence also raised troubling organizational questions for American Christians. While churches such as the Congregational, Baptist, and Presbyterian had to think of establishing national organizations, those with ecclesiastical links abroad such as the Methodist and Anglican had to fashion wholly new organizations.

The Anglican church suffered a devastating blow as a result of the Revolution. Not only did American independence make a church governed by the English king and his appointed bishops suspect in an independent republic, it also brought an exodus of those clergymen and leading laymen who chose to remain loyal to Great Britain. At the war's end, two-thirds of Virginia's rectors left their parishes, and the states of New Jersey, Massachusetts, New Hampshire, and Rhode Island each could count their Episcopal clergymen on the fingers of a single hand.

Conflicting ideas of how to restructure the Episcopal church made the situation even more desperate. The first American bishop, Connecticut's Samuel Seabury (1729-1796), had been an outspoken Loyalist during the Revolution. He struggled to make the American church as much like the Anglican as possible. Dr. William White of Philadelphia and Samuel Provost of New York City, the other American bishops, sought to build a church less elitist and more in tune with American notions of representative govern-

ment. At a convention in 1789 these parties worked out their differences, and the Protestant Episcopal church came into existence. The church adopted a republican-type ecclesiastical constitution which permitted laymen an equal voice in selecting bishops and which transferred to local clergymen many powers, such as the right of ordination, that English bishops had wielded in local affairs.

Yet despite these concessions to republican norms, the Protestant Episcopal church had little drawing power in the early years of the United States. At the time of the Revolution, they had rivaled the Baptists and Presbyterians for being the second largest communion in America (behind the Congregationalists); by 1820, Episcopalians were outstripped by Baptists, Methodists, Presbyterians, and Lutherans. A decade later Episcopalian membership nationally numbered only thirty thousand, only one-sixth that of Presbyterians, one-tenth that of Baptists, and one-eighteenth that of Methodists. Episcopalian reliance upon historical continuity, formal liturgy, and ecclesiastical authority cut against the grain of popular values that had formed in the early Republic, a culture that exalted the right of the common person to think for himself.

Francis Asbury (1745–1816), ordained in 1784 as the first Methodist bishop in America BILLY GRAHAM CENTER

The separation of the United States from England also posed a serious threat to American Methodists, a movement which had only taken hold in America in the 1760s, which still depended upon English clergy, and which remained formally a part of the Anglican church. John Wesley's open denunciation of American independence in 1775 sent all of his American missionaries packing save Francis Asbury; it left American Methodism stranded and endangered. Yet the War of Independence did not arrest the growth of the Methodists. On the contrary, Methodists began to grow at an astonishing rate. Numbering no more than three thousand in 1775, the Methodists claimed almost ten thousand by 1780. By 1790, their numbers swelled to about sixty thousand—a sevenfold increase in a decade. Baffled by this phenomenal growth, the geographer Jedidiah Morse exclaimed in 1792: "Their numbers are so various in different places, at different times, that it would be a matter of no small difficulty to find out the exact amount." How does one explain the phenomenal success of the Methodists?

Unlike the Episcopalians, the Methodists demonstrated that they understood the dynamics of a democratic society. Most importantly, they continued the distinction of their founder by not being respecters of persons but proclaiming the gospel to common folk, preferably those who remained outside the influence of any church. The *Form of Discipline* written at the Baltimore "Christmas Conference" of 1784 instructed Methodist itinerants: "Do not affect the gentleman. A preacher of the gospel is the servant of all."

This commitment to an antielitist form of ministry steeled the Methodist circuit rider to serve at all costs the widely scattered and highly mobile population of the United States in its early years. A second dynamic of early American Methodism was a message simple to understand and straightforward in asserting that people were free to accept or reject God's grace. Streamlining what they proclaimed, thereby avoiding theological and ecclesiastical wrangling, Methodist preachers attempted to fulfill their instructions that they had "nothing to do but save souls." This message they proclaimed indoors and out, for seven days a week, and in no one place for any longer than was strictly necessary.

Toward a Voluntary Theology

In the years after the American Revolution, the new republic witnessed a revolt of substantial proportions against Calvinism. "This is an age of freedom," declared one Presbyterian minister, "and men will be free." Abner Jones, a New England itinerant preacher who refused denominational affiliation, made plain the unsettling effect that popular notions of equality could have upon Calvinist orthodoxy. In his memoir, written in 1807, he began:

> In giving the reader an account of my birth and parentage I shall not (like the celebrated Franklin and others) strive to prove that I arose from a family of eminence; believing that all men are born equal, and that every man shall die for his own inequity.

Equality for Jones exploded the notion of original sin, that people were not morally free to choose for themselves.

In this period one finds evidence of a similar revolt against each of the so-called five points of Calvinism. Just as notions of "total depravity" did not stand up well to the belief that individuals were capable of shaping their own destiny, so "unconditional election" seemed to deny that people were fully capable of determining the course of their own lives. The antidemocratic tendency of the doctrine of election emerged even more clearly in the idea of a "limited atonement"—that the design of Christ's death was restricted to those whom God elected to sal-

---

Let us be republicans indeed. Many are republicans as to government, and yet are but half republicans, being in matters of religion still bound to a catechism, creed, covenant or a superstitious priest. Venture to be as independent in things of religion, as those which respect the government in which you live.

ELIAS SMITH, 1809

HERALD OF GOSPEL LIBERTY.

BY ELIAS SMITH.

NO. 1.]   THURSDAY EVENING, SEPTEMBER 1, 1808.   [VOL. 1.

" I FROM REALMS FAR DISTANT, AND FROM CLIMES UNKNOWN ; WE MAKE THE KNOWLEDGE OF OUR KING YOUR OWN."

ADDRESS TO THE PUBLIC.

To the Subscribers for this paper, and to all who may hereafter read its contents.

BRETHREN AND FELLOW CITIZENS,

THE age in which we live may be distinguished

the United States. A member of Congress said to me not long ago (while speaking upon the state of the people in this country, as it respects Religious Liberty) two amount, "the people in this country are in general free, as ... ters ; but in things of religion, ... em are apparently ignorant ...

The utility of such a paper has been suggested to me, from the great use other papers are to to the community at large. In this way almost the whole state of the world is presented to ... short and cheap way, a g... ur affairs is diffused ... looking into

Elias Smith launched America's first religious newspaper in 1808 to sound the call of religious "liberty."
AMERICAN ANTIQUARIAN SOCIETY

vation. Similarly, the concept of "irresistible grace" seemed to make God a tyrant of uncontrollable power, just that from which Americans had fought to free themselves. Finally, the focus on volitional commitment as the primary human obligation made the idea of the "perseverance of the saints"—that Christians are sustained by the choice of another and preserved in grace to the end of their days—irrelevant, if not contradictory.

Given this potential for a revolt against Calvinism premised on certain self-evident principles of democracy, what is striking is the number of Calvinists in this period undergoing a serious crisis of conscience, a deconversion from Calvinism. Barton W. Stone, the founder of the "Christians" in Kentucky and Illinois in the wake of the Second Great Awakening, began as a Presbyterian but after great intellectual turmoil came to harmonize his theology with social experience. Stone confessed that as a Calvinist he had been "embarrassed with many obtrusive doctrines. . . . Scores of objections would continually roll across my mind." What he called the "Labyrinth of Calvinism" left him "distressed," "perplexed," and "bewildered." He concluded that "Calvinism is amongst the most discouraging hindrances to sinners seeking the Kingdom of God." He was relieved from this dissonance of values only when he jettisoned Presbyterianism for what he called "the rich pastures of gospel liberty."

The Freewill Baptist minister William Smyth Babcock, similarly, found Calvinism antithetical to common sense. He spoke of its "senseless jargon of election and repro-

bation" and concluded that it had covered salvation "with a mist of absurdities." "Its doctrine is denied in the Practice of every converted soul in the first exercises of the mind after receiving liberty." Babcock, an itinerant preacher in rural New England, included in his diary the poem of a nine-year-old girl from one of his congregations. The sentiments of this child capture Babcock's conception of the gospel revolving around the issues of liberty and bondage:

Know then that every soul is free
To choose his life and what he'll be
For this eternal truth is given
That God will force no man to heaven

He'll draw, persuade, direct him right
Bless him with wisdom, love, and light
In nameless ways be good and kind
But never force the human mind.

Toward a New Order of the Ages

Times of political turmoil and social unrest have often rekindled an interest in biblical prophecy and led Christians to link the fulfillment of prophecy to perplexing current events of their own day. The revolutions in America and in France late in the eighteenth century created in America a profound sense that events of truly apocalyptic significance were unfolding before people's eyes. Judged by the number of sermons and books addressing prophetic themes, the first generation of United States citizens may have lived in the shadow of Christ's second coming more intensely than any generation since. What is most striking about the numerous attempts

The United States Elevated to Glory and Honor

EZRA STILES

This great American revolution, this recent political phenomenon of a new sovereignty arising among the sovereign powers of the earth, will be attended to and contemplated by all nations. Navigation will carry the American flag around the globe itself and display the Thirteen Stripes and New Constellation at Bengal and Canton on the Indus and Ganges, on the Whang-ho and the Yang-tse-kiang; and with commerce will import the wisdom and literature of the east. That prophecy of Daniel is now literally fulfilling — there shall be an universal travelling "too and fro, and knowledge shall be increased." This knowledge will be brought home and treasured up in America: and being here digested and carried to the highest perfection, may reblaze back from America to Europe, Asia and Africa, and illumine the world with TRUTH and LIBERTY.

---

to interpret their own day as the end times is the almost universal conclusion that the United States had a unique role in bringing on the millennial kingdom: "And may we not view it, at least as probable," confessed the Congregationalist John Mellen in 1797, "that the expansion of republican forms of government will accompany that spreading of the gospel, in its power and purity, which the scripture prophecies represent as constituting the glory of the latter days?"

What fired apocalyptic imagination far more than the mere fact that battles had been won and constitutions written was the realization that the very structures of society were undergoing a drastic democratic winnowing. The atheism of revolutionary France—an "apocalyptic earthquake," said one minister—the crumbling of European monarchies, the separation of church and state, the domination of the papacy by civil authority all took on a more awesome moment as the cement of an ordered and hierarchical society seemed to be dissolving. In face-to-face ways, people confronted new kinds of issues: common folk not respecting their betters, organized factions speaking and writing against civil authority, sharp attacks against elite professions, the growth of new and strange religious groups such as Shakers, Universalists, Freewill Baptists, "Christians." The Rev. Joseph Vail, a Congregationalist from Had-

lyme, Connecticut, expressed his concern in March 1803:

I cannot approve of the method in which some Christian people conduct their religious meetings, in giving license for everybody to speak and to exhort. Though I think it proper for Christians, who are persons of knowledge and experience, at suitable times to give a word of exhortation, yet to encourage all to speak and exhort, and to tell what they think, and how they feel, and to exhibit their feelings as a rule to others, opens the door for the ignorant and inexperienced, who in such cases are commonly the most forward exhorters, and many of them appear to discover a spirit of pride and great self-importance.

The most dramatic example of American clergymen identifying current events with the convulsions of the end times came in 1798 when scores of Congregational and Presbyterian clergy accepted as true the tale that an international plot led by "Bavarian Illuminati" threatened to destroy American society. On the morning of May 9, 1798, Rev. Jedidiah Morse (father of the telegraph's inventor) unveiled to the New North Church in Boston a shocking plot. Supposedly he had documents in his possession to prove that a secret association of anarchists had successfully plotted the French Revolution and was

The Shakers were among the most rigorous of the millennial communities. Music and dance, depicted here, were central elements in their worship. LIBRARY OF CONGRESS

now extending its influence to America. Influential Presbyterians such as Ashbel Green, David Ramsey, and Charles Nisbet also found the revelations of Morse believable. In a sermon, "Political Instructions from the Prophecies of God's Word," the influential pastor of Hartford's First Church, Nathan Strong, gave the common explanation of these events. Using the biblical text from Revelation, "Come out of her, my people, that ye be not partakers of her sin, and that ye receive not her plagues," Strong built a case that the kind of levelling which had issued from the French Revolution represented "the last stage of anti-Christian apostacy"—the dying breath of Daniel's beast. A year later, the Congregational clergy of Massachusetts, assembled in annual convention, applied the same text to the threat of radical democracy.

Many Christians, however, interpreted divine providence differently, especially those who had not known the formal education and social standing that most Congregationalists and Presbyterians enjoyed. To them, a potent dose of liberty, equality, and fraternity seemed just the needed tonic for church and society. Championing Christianity as a religion of liberty, many of these dissenters saw the election of Jefferson in 1800, not as a sign of approaching doom, but a herald of a coming age of freedom. Elias Smith, founder of the "Christian Connection" in New England, viewed Jefferson's election as the most momentous event since the Incarnation. "The time will come," he said, "when there will not be a crowned head on earth.... Every small piece, or plan, of Monarchy which is a part of the *image* [of Antichrist] will be wholly dissolved, when *the people* are resolved to 'live free or die.' " In the highly charged political atmosphere around 1800 one finds some Christians identifying democracy with Antichrist, others with the coming kingdom. For all their differences, what both groups did share was the common conviction that the American Republic had been chosen to point the way to the approaching millennium. To a conservative like Timothy Dwight, it was a heritage of religious virtue that safeguarded America's identity as a city

Yale College, New Haven, in Dwight's era

on a hill. To a reformer like Alexander Campbell, however, America had come to embody a new order of the ages because here men would be delivered from the dead hand of the past—"the melancholy Thraldom of relentless systems." These differences notwithstanding, both those who recoiled from democratic revolutions and those who endorsed them joined in bestowing upon America a powerful legacy: that the civil and religious liberty embodied in the Republic would henceforth serve as a powerful herald of Christ's kingdom, a force before whom none of the gates of tyranny could stand. As the nineteenth century dawned, American Christians had little cause to be timid. "We Americans are the peculiar chosen people— the Israel of our time," the writer Herman Melville confessed. "We bear the ark of the liberties of the world."

Timothy Dwight

STEPHEN E. BERK

Timothy Dwight (1752-1817), theologian and educator, was president of Yale College from 1795 until his death. Like his grandfather, Jonathan Edwards, he was a pivotal figure in establishing the direction of the New England theology. He diverged from the Edwardsean orthodoxy of his time in deemphasizing the ethereal metaphysics of high Calvinism. A practical, energetic man and active defender of Connecticut's Congregational establishment against democratizing trends, he geared his theology to concrete issues. He agreed that humanity is depraved and in need of divine revelation and spiritual conversion. But for Dwight repentance came as the regular product of humanly administered religious ordinances — preaching, parental nurture, religious education. Edwardsean "Consistent Calvinists" saw conversion as a virtually miraculous divine intervention in the lives of helpless sinners.

Dwight preached his theology in sermon form to successive classes of Yale students. He interspersed his utilitarian disquisitions on doctrine and ethics with emotional calls to repentance which produced more than one revival of religion on the Yale campus. When he succeeded Ezra Stiles in the Yale presidency, his first purpose was to counter "infidel philosophy," deism and skepticism, fashionable among students as in elite intellectual circles during the Revolutionary epoch. His sermons on the subject stress the fact that denial of Christian revelation did only harm in the countries where it had become a prevailing trend. As a conservative Federalist, Dwight saw revolutionary France as exemplar of the social catastrophe which follows in the wake of such apostasy. To this chaos of passion, he counterposed the pastoral virtue of Congregational Connecticut, where a pure Protestant gospel animated the people's hearts and institutions.

While Dwight successfully promoted revivals at Yale, he was not ready to abandon church establishments as the means of insuring the gospel's support. It took his students Lyman Beecher and Nathaniel W. Taylor to complete American evangelicalism's transition from coercive European statism to revivalistic persuasion and private, voluntary support of religion.

Timothy Dwight (1752–1817)
BILLY GRAHAM CENTER

The Swelling Tide of Revivalism

"Revivals of Religion have been gradually multiplying," the American Calvin Colton informed a British audience in 1832, "until they have become the grand absorbing theme and aim of the American religious world." Between 1800 and the Civil War, revivals became in America a distinct national ritual. American Christians, confronted by a mushrooming population—from five to thirty million during these years—and a rush across the Appalachians to settle what is now the Midwest, championed revivalism as the primary means for the young nation to maintain its Christian moorings. The success of this evangelistic fervor was striking. By 1840 the Frenchman Alexis de Tocqueville noted that "no country in the whole world existed in which the Christian religion retains a greater influence over the souls of men than in America." Church statistics bear out these impressions, membership roles swelling tenfold in fifty years, bringing membership from one in fifteen Americans to one in seven. And by 1850 seventy percent of Protestant church members found their names on Baptist and Methodist rolls, churches whose names had become synonymous with revivalism. The dominant theme in America from 1800 to 1860, Perry Miller concluded, was "the invincible persistence of the revival technique." But in what ways might the term "revival" be used?

The "Central Circle" of a camp meeting at Round Lake, New York   BILLY GRAHAM CENTER

It was not long before accusations of hucksterism were directed at the camp meetings, as this contemporary cartoon illustrates. BILLY GRAHAM CENTER

Revivalism as Religious Awakening

Since the days of the Great Awakening in the 1740s, American Christians had continued to pray and work for similar periods of renewal and expansion. On a small scale, such revivals were common in the South in the 1760s and 1770s and in New England in the following two decades. But these were merely the foretaste of the extensive revivals after 1800 that Americans would come to call "the Second Great Awakening." The most dramatic outbreak of revival came from the frontier of Kentucky in 1801 when rawboned preachers such as James McGready (1758?-1817) and Barton W. Stone (1772-1844) organized large camp meetings first at Gasper River and then at Cane Ridge. This second gathering lasted a full week and drew crowds estimated between ten and twenty-five thousand—at a time when the city of Lexington could only boast a population of two thousand. Reports of the Cane Ridge Revival spread like wildfire and put to rest notions that vital religion could not survive conditions of the frontier. What happened at

Cane Ridge became a sort of litany of revivalism in antebellum America, more extreme to be sure, but exhibiting unmistakable characteristics: simple, lively, and persuasive preaching; common folk turning to evangelical faith often with untamed emotion; cooperation between a variety of denominations; and controversy between opponents and supporters of the revival.

At the turn of the century revivalism also rippled through New England, but in far more sedate form. "God, in a remarkable manner, was pouring out his Spirit on the Churches of New England," the well-known clergyman Bennet Tyler concluded. "Within the period of five or six years ... not less than one hundred and fifty churches in New England, were visited with times of refreshing from the presence of the Lord." In 1800 the *Connecticut Evangelical Magazine* was founded to report and encourage a movement heartily endorsed by leaders such as Yale's president Timothy Dwight (1752-1817), Asahel Nettleton (1783-1844)—the most effective Congregationalist evangelist—and Lyman Beecher (1775-1863), the influential leader of the next generation, "baptized in the revival spirit" under Dwight at Yale College. The Second Great Awakening in New England, as these men knew it, was staid, churchly, socially conservative. In the words of one observer, it was characterized by a "respectful silence."

Yankee evangelicals of this stripe could not be expected to endorse the kind of emotional excess and hostility to institutions that the West had spawned. Many would even have agreed with David Rice, the most influential Presbyterian minister in Kentucky, who speculated that the kind of religious anarchy that came out of Cane Ridge must have had at least some connection with the French Revolution.

By the 1820s, however, a form of revivalism closer to home came to trouble staid Yankee evangelicals: the phenomenal success in New York of Charles G. Finney and his "New Measures." From 1825 to 1830, Finney gained national attention by a spectacular series of revival meetings in cities along the Erie Canal—Rome, Utica, Troy, Rochester. Finney's success, later seen throughout the country—even to the portals of Boston—made the issues which he raised unavoidable. What made him most controversial was the introduction of novel techniques to promote revivals: protracted nightly meetings, exhortations by women, "the anxious bench" to which seekers were invited for counsel and prayer, and forthright publicity. These meetings were characterized by speech that was tough, direct, popular, and inescapably premised on the free will of the individual. Finney was an enormously successful practitioner, if not the inventor, of modern high-pressure revivalism.

Finney was also instrumental in the rise of urban evangelism during the 1850s, a fourth distinct kind of revivalism that flourished in antebellum America and what some historians have called the "Third Great Awakening." This period of renewed religious interest was not brought on so much by the preaching of lively evangelists as by lay businessmen who sponsored, among other activities, noontime prayer services. By the spring of 1858 twenty such meetings were being held daily in New York City and more than two thousand people jammed Chicago's daily service at the Metropolitan Theatre. The newly formed Young Men's Christian Association helped to organize many union prayer services and revival meetings.

By the time of the Civil War, then, Americans had become accustomed to seasons of spiritual renewal, revivals that had come in widely differing forms—urban and rural, spontaneous and planned, sober and emotional, clerical and lay.

Charles Grandison Finney and the Burned-over District
JAMES E. JOHNSON

The Burned-over District was located in upper New York State with the Catskills as the eastern boundary and the Adirondacks as the northern perimeter. Many New England settlers moved there in the early nineteenth century. Following a "psychic highway" into the region, these settlers brought with them an experimental approach to new ideas in religion and reform. This "ultraism," described by critics as heretical, provided the wellspring for many of the reforms of the Jacksonian era.

Charles Grandison Finney referred to it as a "burnt district," so named because of the frequent revivals which occurred within the area. "There had been," said Finney, "a few years previously, a wild excitement passing through ... which they called a revival of religion, but which turned out to be spurious." The outcome, said the evangelist, was to leave "a reaction so extensive and profound, as to leave the impression on many minds that religion was a mere delusion." Indeed, the path from New England carried the germ of such movements as Mormonism, Shakerism, Spiritualism, abolitionism, perfectionism, and the sexual communism of the Oneida community.

Born in Connecticut in 1792, Charles G. Finney migrated with his parents along the "psychic highway," settling in upper New York State. After a rather conventional youth and adolescence, he went through an unusual conversion experience in the fall of 1821. His pastor, the Rev. George W. Gale, offered to tutor him after he announced his intention to enter into the ministry, and he soon was retained as a missionary to Jefferson County by the Female Missionary Society of the Western District of New York State. Subsequently, the St. Lawrence Presbytery, in session at the Evans Mills Church, ordained Finney to the ministry on July 1, 1824.

Finney's own unusual conversion influenced his later views as he began to construct a theology that he felt was suitable in the context of the Jacksonian era. He rejected Old School Calvinism at the outset, con-

Charles Grandison Finney (1792–1875) *with his wife* BILLY GRAHAM CENTER

fessing at his ordination that he had not even read the Westminster Confession of Faith of the Presbyterian Church. Eventually deciding that Calvinism was too restrictive for his method of conducting revivals, he modified Calvinism and introduced some innovative ideas called "New Measures," thus paving the way for New School Presbyterianism and the inevitable controversies that accompanied the movement. Finney and his friends, a group sometimes referred to as the "Holy Band," spread the New School theology throughout the Burned-over District. Their ideas were published in the *New York Evangelist*, *Western Recorder*, the *Rochester Observer*, and in a multitude of pamphlets.

Finney began his revivalistic career in such small upper New York villages as Evans Mills, Antwerp, Perch River, Brownville, LeRayville, Rutland, Gouverneur, and Dekalb. From the very beginning, his methods, preaching style, and theology created controversy. His approach was direct, his language was blunt, and his attitude at times appeared to be almost arrogant.

"When Charles Grandison Finney left his law office in 1821 to devote his life to saving souls," states William McLoughlin, "he inaugurated a new era in American revivalism. He not only developed new techniques for promoting conversions and a new style for pulpit oratory, but he transformed the whole philosophy and process of evangelism." Finney used these new techniques most successfully in the years 1825-1832 and rose to national fame as a result. He conducted spectacular revivals in the towns of Western, Rome, Utica, Auburn, and Troy. Eastern newspapers began to carry reprints from New York State papers, and Finney soon became known far and wide. He and his wife were on their way home from a Utica Synod meeting in October 1825 when they stayed overnight at the home of George W. Gale, his former pastor, now at the town of

Western. At the request of Gale, they stayed, and Finney began preaching every night at the church. They continued on through the winter, and reports stated that interest in religion was almost universal. Finney referred to these meetings and the subsequent ones as the "great Western revivals." He then preached in Rome with similar results, and on March 12, 1826, 184 persons were accepted as members of the First Congregational Church as one of the "fruits of the 'Great Revival' which occurred in connection with the labors of the Rev. Charles G. Finney." He held similar meetings in Utica and obtained perhaps his most famous convert in the person of Theodore Dwight Weld.

Opposition to Finney, his methods, and his imitators arose in several quarters. The Unitarians and Universalists launched a veritable barrage of pamphlets exposing what they thought to be the crudities and inconsistencies in Finney's approach. The two ministers who came forward to confront Finney were Asahel Nettleton, a representative from New England of Old School orthodoxy, and Lyman Beecher, father of the famous son, Henry Ward, and daughter, Harriet. The most troubling aspect of Finney at that time was his use of the so-called "New Measures": the practice of praying for people by name, females praying in public meetings, the invasion of towns without an invitation from the local pastor, overfamiliarity with Deity in public prayer, protracted meetings, the use of an anxious seat, inquiry meetings, and the immediate admission of converts into the churches. The opposition succeeded in convening a conference at New Lebanon, New York, in July 1827 for the purpose of discussing the advisability of the continued use of Finney's New Measures. The line-up of forces represented the Finney supporters from the Burned-over District and Eastern men supporting the views of Beecher and Nettleton. The issues

were not resolved, although they did agree that certain measures could be used in promoting revivals as long as caution would be observed at all times. Finney emerged from the New Lebanon Conference more than ever a national figure with new worlds to conquer outside the Burned-over District. He also began to moderate some of his views, and he did eventually achieve a reconciliation with Lyman Beecher.

Rochester was the zenith of Finney's career as an itinerant. It was also his last stand in the Burned-over District, since he went from there in 1831 eventually to a settled pastorate in New York City and then spent the last forty years of his life at Oberlin College. The rough edges of the earlier years were gone. The Holy Band and their alleged excesses were conspicuously absent. Finney provided a dignified appearance, and made temperance reform a leading issue in the meetings. "It did not sound like preaching," said an eyewitness, "but like a lawyer arguing a case before a court and jury. ..." Finney somewhat smugly recalled years later that the audience was made up of lawyers, merchants, physicians, and "all the

Oberlin College with a revival tent on Tappan Square and Finney's house in the rear of the scene to the right
BILLY GRAHAM CENTER

PRAYERS & EXHORTATIONS
Not to exceed 5 minutes,
in order to give all an opportunity.

NOT MORE *than* 2 CONSECUTIVE
PRAYERS OR EXHORTATIONS.

NO CONTROVERTED POINTS
— DISCUSSED.—

Finney also helped spark the urban revival of 1858; this was the notice posted at the Noon-Day Prayer Meeting in New York's North Dutch Church in 1858.
COURTESY EDWIN S. GAUSTAD

most intelligent people. . . ." Various figures were cited regarding the influence of the Rochester revival. Probably about 350 new members were added to Rochester's three Presbyterian churches, and there were numerous revivals in the Burned-over District as a result. Finney later claimed that 100,000 persons had been added to the churches nationwide as a result of the revival started in Rochester. The numbers are not as important as the fact that the Second Great Awakening was in full swing and Finney's revival was the high-water mark. Scores of calls for his services came from pastors and others across the eastern United States. He was a force to be reckoned with and, according to a leading writer on the subject, was the "creator of modern revivalism."

The historian Whitney Cross saw revivalism as a folk movement of the Jacksonian era which contested clerical conservatism. That being so, Finney was the folk hero of the movement. "Finney did not deliberately attempt to make Presbyterianism palatable to the rising common folk," said Cross, but his conclusions "did just that." The people of the Jacksonian era were attracted to the liberalized Calvinism offered by Finney which made them participants in the religious drama.

Anyone who was willing to repent, said Finney, could obtain assurance of salvation immediately. This message blended with the leveling aspect of the age and fitted frontier individualism. Further, his espousal of ultraism unleashed forces that pointed toward perfectionism. Although Finney disavowed any connection with John Humphrey Noyes and the Oneida community, their ideas were rather similar. His preaching on disinterested benevolence was the main highway to abolitionism. His postmillennialism was in harmony with the optimistic spirit of the Jacksonians, including the Transcendentalists. His New Divinity and New Measures blended faith and reason, thus anticipating pragmatism. His preaching that the right use of means could produce a revival provided a scientific rationale for what the Old School Presbyterians insisted was a divine mystery. Finney blazed a path in the Burned-over District which was followed at a later date by Dwight L. Moody, Billy Sunday, and others to the present day. He would marvel at the well-oiled machinery which prepares for a Billy Graham crusade, but he would recognize the elements as the right use of means discussed in his *Lectures on Revivals of Religion*.

The Burned-over District revivals were but an episode in the career of Charles G. Finney. His influence grew in later years with the publication of several books, as editor of the *Oberlin Evangelist*, as professor of theology and later president of Oberlin College, as a leader in perfectionist thought, as an advocate of abolitionism, and in his two trips to Great Britain for the purpose of conducting revival meetings. In spite of this varied career, however, he maintained throughout his life that the conducting of revival meetings was the most important task for the church here on earth. He never wavered from that belief, a belief that had been launched in the Burned-over District revivals.

The Young Men's Christian Association was instrumental in promoting revivalism; pictured here is the New York City YMCA in the 1860s.
BILLY GRAHAM CENTER

Revivalism as Technique

The activity of Charles G. Finney clearly came to symbolize revivalism in the Age of Jackson as the efforts of Jonathan Edwards had a century before. In the interval between 1740 and 1840, however, Americans came to see revivals in strikingly different ways. Typical for his day, Edwards had seen spiritual awakenings as a "surprising work of God," the inexplicable outpouring of God's spirit. Edwards explained the revival in his own church in 1735 as "a very extraordinary dispensation of Providence; God has in many respects gone out of, and much beyond, his usual and *ordinary way*." A nineteenth-century observer of such attitudes toward revivals commented: "Men stood still as God's conquering chariot rolled along." But a century later this theological explanation of revivals had given way to what might be called a "Newtonian" or cause-and-effect model. "A revival is not a miracle, or dependent on a miracle in any sense," affirmed Charles G. Finney. "It is a purely philosophic [i.e., scientific] result of the right use of the constituted means." Another supporter of revivals, Calvin Colton, made the same point when he wrote in 1832: "They are made matters of human calculation by the arithmetic of faith in God's engagement."

These widely shared convictions confirmed that an activist style of religious lead-

ership would come to the fore in American Christianity. No longer would revivalists be father figures but, rather, agents of popular will. Men without formal training like Barton Stone the Christian, William Miller the Adventist, Joseph Smith the Latter-day Saint, Peter Cartwright the Methodist, and Charles Finney the Presbyterian, went outside the normal denomination frameworks to develop huge followings by the democratic art of persuasion. They drummed up support for their cause with an appeal to popular sentiment. Of Joseph Smith it was said that he had "his own original eloquence, peculiar to himself, not polished, not studied, not smoothed and softened by education and refined by art." A New England Congregationalist, baffled by these sectarians, put it this way: "They measure the progress of religion by the numbers

Already in 1803 the religious presses were producing such items as this bookplate. COURTESY ESSEX INSTITUTE, SALEM, MASS.

who flock to their standards, not by the prevalence of faith and piety, justice and charity and the public virtues in society in general." This new style of gospel minister, radically dependent upon popular will and thus remarkably attuned to it, is what Alexis de Tocqueville found when he came to America in 1840. "Where I expect to find a priest," he said, "I find a politician."

A central feature of this democratic style was that clergy learned to employ the latest communication techniques. Elias Smith, the New England religious reformer, founded the first religious newspaper in the country in 1807 with the explicit goal of keeping common people attached to his cause. By the 1820s evangelical sects were masters at using the printing press to campaign for their point of view. They cranked out a veritable tidal wave of popular newspapers, journals, magazines, tracts, and pamphlets.

The best example of this clever use of public relations was the Adventist William Miller. His publicity agent, Joshua V. Himes, turned the name of this obscure New York preacher into a household word. Himes had been one of Elias Smith's preachers in New England

and had undoubtedly mastered the techniques of popular persuasion. Upon meeting Miller in 1839, he adopted his view that the second coming of Christ would occur in 1843 and turned his restless energy to the crusade of preparing people for this event. In 1840 he began publishing a newspaper in Boston, *The Sign of the Times*; by 1842 New Yorkers could read the same message in their paper *The Midnight Cry*. Within two years journals were flourishing in Philadelphia, Rochester, Cincinnati, and elsewhere. Under Himes' directions tracts, pamphlets, and books streamed from the press and were shipped literally to the ends of the earth. It was Joshua V. Himes, far more than William Miller, who made the Adventist cause a national phenomenon.

Nineteenth-century Christianity was replete with democratic authority figures, men and women attuned to the latest communication techniques. Such measures buttressed the only authority democratic preachers have ever been able to muster, the good will of their audience. It is no wonder that revivalists, as masters of the democratic art of persuasion, came to play such a major role in American Christianity.

Open air preaching, early nineteenth century   BILLY GRAHAM CENTER

Robert Baird on American Preaching

Some of the tourists from abroad that have visited the United States have affected to despise our "uneducated" and "ignorant" ministers, and have thought what they call the "ranting" of such men a fit subject of diversion for themselves and their readers. Such authors know little of the real worth and valuable labours of these humble, and in comparison with such as have studied at colleges and universities, unlettered men. Their plain preaching, in fact, is often far more likely to benefit their usual hearers, than would that of a learned doctor of divinity issuing from some great university. Their language, though not refined, is intelligible to those to whom it is addressed. Their illustrations may not be classical, but they will probably

Camp meeting preaching demonstrated the accuracy of Baird's description of American "plain preaching."
BILLY GRAHAM CENTER

be drawn either from the Bible or from the scenes amid which their hearers move, and the events with which they are familiar; nor would the critical knowledge of a Porson, or the general acquirements of a Parr, be likely to make them more successful in their work. I have often heard most solemn and edifying discourses from such men. I have met with them in all parts of the United States, and though some, doubtless, bring discredit upon the ministry, by their ignorance, their eccentricities, or their incapacity, and do more harm than good to the cause of religion, yet, taken as a whole, they are a great blessing to the country. A European who should denounce the United States as uncivilized, and the inhabitants as wretched, because he does not everywhere find the luxuries and refinements of London and Paris, would display no more ignorance of the world and want of common sense, than were he to despise the plain preaching of a man who enters the pulpit with a mind replete with scriptural knowledge, obtained by frequent perusal of the Bible, and the assistance of valuable commentaries, besides being generally well informed, and with a heart full of love to God and concern for men's souls, even although he may never have frequented the groves of an academy, or studied the nicer graces of oratory. To the labours of such men more than 10,000 neighbourhoods in the United States are indebted for their general good order, tranquility, and happiness, as well as for the humble but sincere piety that reigns in many a heart, and around many a fire-side.
Religion in America, 1844

Camp Meetings

JOHN B. BOLES

Since before the memory of man there have been outdoor religious services, but what became popularly known as the camp meeting evolved in the first years of the nineteenth century in the American South. Beginning with the Presbyterians in the 1740s, the Baptists in the 1750s, and the Methodists in the 1760s, evangelical Protestantism had spread across the South, establishing a thin network of churches and a folk belief in the providence of God. In the decade on either side of the Revolution there had been revivals, some even with outdoor preaching in the evening, but the services were narrowly denominational and the participants had returned to their homes at the conclusion of the evening services. On several occasions emotional displays of conversion had occurred, though nothing of real novelty distinguished these revivals. Such was not to be the

case for a series of revivals that erupted like wildfire across the South after June 1800.

Before 1800 a number of factors — population shifts, economic and political turmoil, religious dissension — had limited the growth of a vigorous religious establishment in the South. In many sections during the 1790s there was an absolute loss in church membership. This religious decline was primarily institutional, but churchmen interpreted the decline more broadly as a punishment by God for public sins. A religious malaise enveloped the region as ministers commiserated among themselves over what they saw as the hopeless state of religion. Yet as they sought in sermons and ministerial letters to understand the region's plight, they slowly developed a belief that since God was chastising the region for its preoccupation with, among other things, politics and speculation, once the people of the South recognized their faults, were contrite, and asked God for forgiveness, he would forgive

Camp meeting at Sing Sing, New York, in 1838

them and send blessings showering down upon them. By the end of the eighteenth century clergy in the South had transformed their religious depression into a season of hope. Prayer societies and fasting throughout the region were taken as evidence the wayward churchgoers had learned their lesson, and ministers by 1800 were expecting God to announce in some awesome fashion that the "religious declension" was over.

It was in this cultural context that Presbyterian James McGready in June 1800 held a joint communion service for his three small churches in south-central Kentucky. McGready had shared in the prevalent interpretation of the religious decline as a chastisement by God, and had organized his congregations into prayer societies wherein the people prayed for a revival and were told repeatedly that at any time God could be expected to answer their prayers. At the June meeting, after three long days of fervent preaching by McGready and two cooperating ministers, the congregations were exhausted and expectant. On the fourth day two traveling ministers, one a Methodist, helped officiate. Suddenly at the close of the services, with the people at a fever pitch, the two visiting preachers began an emotional exhortation, their zeal spread to the crowd, and many practically collapsed with what was labeled conviction of sin. The startled ministers, particularly McGready, became convinced they had just witnessed a visitation of the Holy Spirit akin to that described at Pentecost.

As word spread of this novel behavior, tremendous interest arose for McGready's next services. McGready saw the opportunity, and suggested that all should come prepared to stay at his Gasper River church until the Spirit descended again. As rumors of the religious happenings spread, so did a desire to attend the July communion services. Beginning on the last weekend of July 1800, many hundreds were in the crowd, from all denomina-

tions, prepared to camp out in wagons, tents, or temporary shelters until another "miracle" occurred. This was the first camp meeting—interdenominational, participants staying on the site of the religious services for several days. Expectation of great things was so strong it could be felt, and the huge crowds, the fervent preaching from several makeshift pulpits, and the sense that this was a special occasion all combined in a maelstrom of emotions to produce widespread religious conversion. Ministers and laymen alike instantly interpreted the event as the long-hoped-for answer from God, and the more unusual the conversion symptoms—swoonings, religious ecstasy, and so on—the more proof it seemed that God was at work. Persons desiring certainty of their conversions unconsciously saw the more extreme manifestations of "revival exercises" as proof of their conviction; as hundreds of people sought this mark of salvation, such symptoms as fainting and uncontrollable shaking ("the jerks") spread like a contagion. And as expectant laymen and ministers elsewhere heard of the events at Gasper River, they believed the moment of deliverance had arrived, and revivals erupted. Everywhere huge crowds came, camped out for days, teams of ministers preached, and the camp meeting revival swept through Kentucky and Tennessee, then east to the seaboard southern states. The South's Great Revival had begun.

The most famous camp meeting was held at Cane Ridge, Kentucky, in August 1801, and contemporaries estimated the crowd as high as twenty-five thousand, probably about double the number actually in attendance. It was not until sometime in 1802 that the term "camp meeting" came into use, but its descriptive quality led it to be widely employed. For several years Presbyterians, Methodists, and Baptists all participated in the camp meeting revival and shared in its results, but by 1805 Presbyterians and

Emotional invocations of God's power often were carried on in several tents simultaneously, as at this camp meeting at Eastham, Massachusetts. BILLY GRAHAM CENTER

Baptists began withdrawing their support for a variety of reasons, primarily because they judged the camp meetings too emotional. Thereafter the camp meetings were considered a Methodist institution, and, gradually calmed down and held according to handbook rules, the camp meetings became an accepted part of American religious life in the nineteenth century. They spread throughout the South, up the Atlantic seaboard, and across the Midwest. Usually regularly scheduled, with announcements in the newspapers, and held at permanent locations with wooden stands and cabins, the camp meeting became a part of folk religious culture. In the growing urban areas their purpose was fulfilled by protracted meetings, for the camp meeting was essentially a rural phenomenon.

At first camp meetings were a novel revival technique whereby thousands were converted to evangelical Protestantism, including in the South many slaves. As the institution became formalized it also served each year to reclaim backsliders and invigorate the faith of believers. It was accepted as a ceremonial device authenticating the faith of thousands of rural Christians, and was a social occasion looked forward to for months. Camp meetings are still held today throughout the nation, but they are only a gentle reminder of the once controversial frontier revival.

Revivalism as a Style of Christianity

Amidst all the diversity within American Christianity before the Civil War, the common theme of revivalism seemed everywhere—even among Lutherans, Episcopalians, and certain Unitarians. Not even Roman Catholics entirely avoided an evangelistic ethos.

A Christianity colored by revivalism has in at least two respects made certain themes dominant at the expense of others. First, religious experience came to emphasize the individual's right and ability to choose; second, it was assumed the convert understood the conversion process.

Notions of conversion in a democratic culture, as they evolved, increasingly made the process tame and predictable, stripped of mystery and wonder. The subtle but profound change in descriptions of conversion after the American Revolution attests to this shift.

Accounts of eighteenth-century conversion experiences were, by and large, expressed in the passive voice. Down to the Revolution what is remarkable is that, despite fervent appeals for people to repent and believe, the process seems to be understood as out of human hands. A person under conviction of sin waited—quite literally—to be converted. No simple mental gymnastics offered an easy way out. George Whitefield, for instance, spent weeks in agony before his conversion and by his own testimony had no real control over when that moment of release would come: "After having undergone innumerable buffetings of Satan, and many months in inexpressible trials by night and day under the spirit of bondage, God was pleased at length to remove the heavy load."

The same process of waiting for God to turn a heart of stone into flesh is evident in the spiritual diary of the unschooled Connecticut farmer Nathan Cole, who fell under conviction during Whitefield's tour of 1741 but did not experience the light of conversion for another two years. The same pattern is true for fifty-three conversion narratives written down by the Rev. John Cleaveland when revival came to his parish in Ipswich, Massachusetts, in 1763. Careful use of the passive voice—God comforting people mindful that they had no power to do it themselves— expresses the extent to which this process was a mystery to people. It was always beyond their manipulation.

In the early republic, religious conversion takes on a whole new vocabulary. The Disciples of Christ were most explicit about this as they commonly referred to conversion as "finding liberty" or "coming into liberty." Barton W. Stone attributed the success of the Great Revival in Kentucky shortly after 1800 to the fact that people were told that they were free to choose their spiritual destiny: "When we began first to preach these things, the people appeared as just awakened from the sleep of ages—they seemed to see for the first time that they were responsible beings." The resulting tendency was to reduce conversion to a simple matter of individual choice. Walter Scott, a forceful lieutenant of Alexander Campbell, patterned a five-finger exercise to make plain the process to common folk. If people would (1) have faith, (2) repent, (3) be baptized for remission of sins, (4) they would be forgiven and (5) receive the gift of the Holy Spirit and salvation. The process was neat and rationally predictable.

Americans in an age of democracy excelled at bringing religious experience to the level of the people; they were less successful at teaching people to bow in awe and wonder, admitting that a person's destiny does, in fact, lie outside one's own hands.

Peter Cartwright

HOWARD A. SNYDER

Colorful apostle of frontier American Methodism during its great westward surge, Peter Cartwright (1785-1872) was in many ways the successor to Francis Asbury as pioneer evangelist and church planter.

Born in Virginia, Cartwright moved with his family to the Kentucky wilderness frontier as a child. In the wake of the Cane Ridge revival he was converted in a combined Presbyterian-Methodist camp meeting after weeks of spiritual struggle. He soon joined the Methodists, to the joy of his devout Methodist mother.

In 1802 Cartwright, then sixteen, was licensed to exhort and some months later, when he and his family moved further west, was shocked to learn he had been commissioned to carve out a new frontier Methodist circuit. The next year Cartwright began his life-long career as circuit rider, traveling over large, thinly populated circuits in Tennessee, Kentucky, and surrounding areas. He was ordained deacon by Asbury in 1806 and received full ordination as elder in 1808. Asbury appointed him presiding elder (superintendent) in 1812.

Cartwright moved to the Illinois frontier in 1824, largely to escape the evils of slavery. The slavery question soon embroiled him in politics, and he was twice elected to the Illinois General Assembly. In 1846 he was defeated by Abraham Lincoln in a bid for U. S. Congress. Though an ardent foe of slavery he disdained abolitionism, arguing that moral suasion would end slavery without dividing the church.

For sixty-five years Cartwright served frontier circuits from the Appalachians to the Mississippi, traveling, preaching, organizing, and watching over the preachers under his charge. Rough-hewn, quick-witted, and resourceful, Cartwright preached a

This Harper's Weekly *depiction of the circuit rider was inspired by the sort of figure cut by* Peter Cartwright.

BILLY GRAHAM CENTER

muscular frontier Christianity whose success contributed largely to Methodism's growth from 120,000 members in 1804 to more than one million by midcentury.

Much like John Wesley in his stamina, boldness, discipline, and evangelizing skill, he contrasts with Wesley in his rough backwoods style and his readiness to enforce words with muscle.

Gospel Hymns

SANDRA S. SIZER

One of the remarkable developments in middle and late nineteenth-century evangelicalism was the emergence of a popular American hymnody. Puritans before the Great Awakening had chanted psalms from the Bible but disapproved of the use of hymns in church services. After the revivals of Edwards and Whitefield, New Light Presbyterians and Baptists used some hymns, mostly those of the British hymnist Isaac Watts. Methodists coming to America brought Wesleyan hymns with them. But at the turn of the nineteenth century most evangelicals were still singing either psalms or hymns by British composers.

The camp-meeting revivals on the western frontiers sparked the composition or adoption of more popular tunes and easily learned words. Some elements came from English sources, while others — especially the pattern of verse-and-refrain — were borrowed from black folk music. Still, however, the more conservative church leaders, especially among Presbyterians and Congregationalists, tried to keep such songs out of regular services, reserving them only for seasons of revival. Not until after the Finney revival era, 1825-1835, did the proscriptions on popular religious song fall away. During the same period, the teaching and learning of music, especially singing in choruses, was becoming a popular pastime. The music teacher became a familiar figure in the West and the music institute in the East, bringing songbooks and the skills of reading musical notation to the populace at large. These developments opened the way for the genre of popular religious song called the "gospel hymn."

The gospel hymn, with a simple melody and chorus, and lyrics proclaiming the love of Jesus, was soon to become a prominent feature of the American evangelical scene. Ordinary clergy and laypeople, including large numbers of women, wrote the lyrics themselves, modeling their poetry on Wesleyan-style verses such as "Jesus, Lover of My Soul." By the time of the 1857-1858 prayer-meeting revival, songbooks were in great demand. Hymns like "Just As I Am" and "What a Friend We Have in Jesus" were favorites. Over the next few decades, devotional poetry that had appeared in religious magazines and lyrics from Sunday-school songs were collected together with the writings of professional hymnists. Fanny Crosby, the famous blind hymnist, became known across the country for the thousands of hymns she wrote ("Rescue the Perishing," "Pass Me Not, O Gentle Saviour"). P. P. Bliss, whose career was cut short by his death in a train accident in 1876, was one of the most prolific, writing both words and music to such songs as "Let the Lower Lights Be Burning" and "Hold the Fort." After Bliss's death, Ira D. Sankey, the partner of Dwight L. Moody, became the best-known of revival singers and musicians. Together with other musical evangelicals, he compiled a series, *Gospel Hymns*, which was the most popular set of hymnals in the late nineteenth century. This movement transformed the appearance of urban revivalism. By the time of Moody the singers were as popular as the preachers; and for decades to come no great revivalist would be without his companion, a professional singing evangelist, to provide a counter-point to prayer and sermon.

The popularity of the gospel hymn is closely tied to the emerging forms of nineteenth-century white urban revivalism and to the social conditions of the period. Middleclass Protestants in postindustrial America were increasingly literate, producing and devouring newspapers, magazines, histories, novels, and poetry in enormous quantities. At the same time, male and female roles were being redefined, and many men spent their energies in the business and politics of an expanding society. Those were arenas from which both women and ministers, by custom and/or law, were excluded. Religion itself was becoming a separate sphere, no longer directly linked to government and public affairs, and ministers had lost the prestige their forefathers had as scholars and advisers to magistrates. Together with their most faithful followers, middleclass women, they created a realm of intense religious experience, separate from the larger society, and gave it expression in poetry and hymnody.

Revivals in urban America were no longer occasions for the church to renew itself as a community, but meetings of individuals who did not know one another to share their religious feelings. The revivals created a community of feeling among people who had no other communal bonds. Further, as the minister and his sermon declined, personal prayer and testimony came to the fore. Correlatively, the hymn lyrics usually either bore witness to a generalized personal experience, as in "I Love to Tell the Story," or made personal pleas: "I Need Thee Every Hour." With personal experience as the ultimate authority, they could disregard the ordinary world — so the hymns portrayed the world as a stormy sea, full of turmoil and strife, and looked forward to personal transformation and the hope of heaven after death.

The gospel hymns thus became an important medium of expression for the emotions and yearnings of Protestants — first, the clergy and women who ruled the religious sphere, and later evangelicals generally, as the churches attempted to defend themselves against the challenges of American religious pluralism. The hymns represented a burst of creativity from the people themselves, a rich, intensely devotional experience by which one could rise above the ordinary world. The danger, however, was that the inward-turning quality of the hymns and their sentimental melodies would reinforce the retreat from social issues which by 1875 was visible throughout Protestant evangelicalism. The power of poetry and music, sweeping revival crowds along on "billows and tides of heavenly emotion," as a nineteenth-century writer put it, could become a mere mass movement, without the discipline of intellect and organized action that Protestantism needed to meet the challenges of the era.

Manuscript copy of Fanny Crosby's "My Soul Shall Trust in Thee"   BILLY GRAHAM CENTER

An Age of Experiment and Reform

"We are all a little wild here with numberless projects of social reform," Ralph Waldo Emerson confessed to Thomas Carlyle in 1840. "Not a reading man but [he] has a draft of a new community in his waistcoat pocket." Emerson was attempting to convey the extent to which Americans were rejecting conventional social arrangements and joining missionarylike crusades to regenerate the social order. Possessing a heady confidence that much could be done to transform human character, Americans organized scores of reform societies in fields such as antislavery, temperance, peace, women's rights, missions, and educational and penal reform. More than one hundred communitarian experiments emerged from these endeavors. Radical experimentation with alternate marriage and sexual patterns occurred among Mormons, Shakers, and in the Oneida communities. Americans experienced what would have been unthinkable in the eighteenth cen-

This pair of Currier and Ives prints (below and opposite page) presents a cautionary parable on a subject that perennially attracted the reformers' interest.   BILLY GRAHAM CENTER

tury, the widespread adoption of a confidence in human perfectibility, even among many Presbyterians and Congregationalists.

The Benevolent Empire: Arthur and Lewis Tappan

In the early nineteenth century, it was England that pioneered in the formation of specialized agencies of Christian reform. The British and Foreign Bible Society, founded in 1804, became the model for hundreds of societies. Among these were organizations to promote Christianity among the Jews, to keep the sabbath, to suppress immorality, to aid the indigent blind, to help the industrious poor, and even to encourage and aid "the Poor Infirm Aged Widows and Single Women of Good Character, Who Have Seen Better Days." British Evangelicals, led by William Wilberforce—who was himself a member of sixty-nine benevolent societies—were effective in abolishing the African slave trade in 1807. This effort became a model for American endeavors.

Many organizers of America's "Benevolent Empire" were young graduates of Andover Theological Seminary in Massachusetts, a seminary which had been founded by conservative Congregationalists in 1807 to counter the Unitarian drift of Harvard. Andover men were restless organizers. Adoniram Judson helped establish the first mission society, the American Board of Commissioners for Foreign Missions (1810). Samuel J. Mills, also active in foreign missions, helped launch the American Bible Society (1816) and the American Colonization Society (1817). Justin Edwards, also of Andover, helped organize the New England Tract Society (1814) and later the American Tract Society (1825), an agency which in a decade had sold more than a million pieces of literature. He also was involved in the American Society for the Promotion of Temperance (1826), a group claiming 1.25 million members in the 1830s. Another son of Andover, Louis Dwight, traveled first as an agent of the American Bible Society and later turned his energies to penal reform.

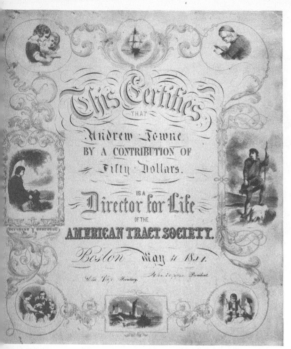

Certificate of a contribution to the American Tract Society, organized by Justin Edwards in 1825
BILLY GRAHAM CENTER

This Benevolent Empire was clearly the emporium of Congregationalists and Presbyterians, groups who often seemed indistinguishable after the 1801 Plan of Union linked their forces for westward expansion. For the most part these activists were anything but social radicals. The world to which they appealed was a traditional and homogenous one, considerably out of step with an America that was increasingly pluralistic. The Benevolent Empire never enjoyed the success of its English counterparts, in part because slavery in America would not vanish through moral suasion and in part because the sprawling democracy of America refused, as David B. Davis has said, "to be homogenized, especially under Yankee direction."

Of all the Yankees and ex-Yankees involved in this kind of moral reform, none is more interesting or illuminating than the two Tappan brothers, Arthur (1786-1865) and Lewis (1788-1873). The Tappans were wealthy New York merchants and influential supporters of a wide range of reform activi-

ties. They made fortunes in New York as silk merchants and later in founding the first commercial credit-rating agency (later to become Dun and Bradstreet). With this wealth they became principal financial supporters of the evangelism of Charles G. Finney and of a host of social reforms. They kept Oberlin College afloat financially after it became a hotbed of Abolitionist activity in the 1830s and endured great personal risk for their open support of other Abolitionist activities. In addition, the Tappans supported a host of other causes, including the American Sunday School Union, the American Bible Society, and the American Education Society; they also joined crusades for temperance, sabbath observance, and the banning of tobacco.

The lives of these archetypical evangelical reformers are equally revealing of certain deep changes in evangelical outlook. The Tappans had been raised in Northampton, Massachusetts, of all places, by a mother who remained a stalwart follower of Jonathan Edwards. As a young man Lewis Tappan rejected Calvinism in favor of the Unitarians,

Arthur Tappan (1786–1865) BILLY GRAHAM CENTER

Lewis Tappan (1788–1873) BILLY GRAHAM CENTER

man's relationship to God into guilt about man's relationship to man. In the end, their restless consciences drove them from one reform to another. Although both came to espouse a belief in Christian perfection, theology as such was never really their concern. Their lives are remembered today, as they would have wished, not as stalwarts of divinity but as models of Christian humanitarianism.

Foreign Missions: Adoniram and Ann Judson

One of the most enduring legacies of the Benevolent Empire was the modern movement for foreign missions. The interest in missions at Andover Seminary, originally kindled at Williams College around 1806, bore fruit in the founding of the American Board of Commissioners for Foreign Missions

The Missionary Herald *was the periodical that published accounts of the activities of the ABCFM.*
BILLY GRAHAM CENTER

but returned to evangelical orthodoxy in the 1820s. The most striking thing about this return, however, according to his biographer Bertram Wyatt-Brown, is how far his evangelical faith came to differ from that of his parents. His return manifested,

> not so much his rededication of orthodoxy as the gulf separating him from his mother's theocentric faith. His arguments did not treat in any depth the innate sinfulness of man, the concept of regeneration, or even the majesty and mercy of God. The doctrine of election was dismissed as "a merely speculative subject. . . ." Almost totally absent was any heartfelt sense of contrition or appreciation of the beauty and majesty of God. For Tappan, as for [Lyman] Beecher and Nathaniel Taylor, the Calvinist deity had died, to be replaced by one concerned with the happiness of mankind, the growth of the visible Church, the extinction of heresy, and the establishment of a moral order which reflected the ethics but not the theology of Calvinism.

Lewis and Arthur Tappan were, in a sense, no less God-intoxicated than their parents' generation but had transferred guilt about

THE

MISSIONARY HERALD.

| VOL. XVII. | JANUARY, 1821. | No. 1. |

VIEW OF THE MISSIONS, FUNDS, EXPENDITURES, AND PROSPECTS OF THE AMERICAN BOARD OF COMMISSIONERS FOR FOREIGN MISSIONS.

The Board was instituted in June, 1810, and incorporated June 20, 1812.

The Rev. SAMUEL WORCESTER, D.D. of *Salem, Mass. is the Corresponding Secretary and Clerk of the Prudential Committee.*

JEREMIAH EVARTS, *No. 22, Pinckney Street, Boston, Treasurer.*

I. MISSION AT BOMBAY, 1814 *

Rev. Gordon Hall,	1814
Mrs. Hall,	1816
Rev. Samuel Newell,	1814
Mrs. Philomela Newell,	1818
Rev. Horatio Bardwell,	1816
Mrs. Rachel Bardwell,	
Rev. Allen Graves,	1818
Mrs. Mary Graves,	
Rev. John Nichols,	
Mrs. Elisabeth Nichols.	

II. MISSION IN CEYLON, 1816.

Rev. James Richards,	1816
Mrs. Sarah Richards,	
Rev. Benjamin C. Meigs,	
Mrs. Meigs,	
Rev. Daniel Poor,	
Mrs. Susan Poor,	
Rev. Levi Spaulding,	1819
Mrs. Mary Spaulding,	
Rev. Miron Winslow,	
Mrs. Harriet L. Winslow,	
Rev. Henry Woodward,	
Mrs. Woodward,	
Dr. John Scudder,	
Mrs. Maria Scudder,	

| Mr. James Garrett, *Printer*.† | 1820 |

III. MISSION AMONG THE CHEROKEES.

Rev. Ard Hoyt,	1818
Mrs. Hoyt,	
Rev. Daniel S. Butrick,	
Rev. William Chamberlain,	
Mrs. Flora Chamberlain,	
Rev. William Potter,*	1820
Mrs. Potter.	

Mr. Moody Hall, *Teacher*,	1817
Mrs. Hall,	
Miss Sarah Hoyt, *Teacher*,	1818
Miss Anne Hoyt, *Helper*,	
Mr. Milo Hoyt, *Teacher*,	
Mr. Abijah Conger, *Farmer and Mechanic*,	1819
Mrs. Conger,	
Mr. John Vail, *Farmer*,	
Mrs. Vail,	
George Halsey, *Mechanic*,	
Dr. Elizur Butler,	1820
Mrs. Butler,	
Mrs. Ann Paine, *Teacher*.	

IV. MISSION AMONG THE CHOCTAWS.

Rev Cyrus Kingsbury,	1818
Mrs. Sarah B. V. Kingsbury,	1819
Rev. Alfred Wright,	1820

Mr. Loring S. Williams, *Teacher*,	
Mrs. Matilda Williams,	
Mrs Judith C. Williams,	1819
Mr. Moses Jewell, *Mechanic*,	
Mrs. Jewell,	
Dr. William W. Pride,	1819
Mr. Anson Dyer, *Teacher & Farmer*,	1820
Mr. Zech. Howes, *Teach. & Farm.*	
Mr. Joel Wood, *Teacher & Farmer*,	
Mrs. Wood,	
Mr. John Smith, *Farmer*,†	
Mrs. Smith,	

* The missionaries arrived at Bombay, Feb. 11, 1813; but did not consider themselves as settled in the mission, till the beginning of 1814. The dates, in this summary, refer to the time, when the respective missions were established, and the time when the missiona-

Adoniram Judson (1788–1850)
BILLY GRAHAM CENTER

(1810). Patterned after British missionary societies and inspired by their most famous son, the Baptist missionary to India William Carey, the ABCFM first sent missionaries abroad in 1812, when five Andover students sailed for India. Two of them, Adoniram Judson (1788-1850) and Luther Rice (1783-1846), became persuaded of Baptist convictions abroad ship and were influential in the formation of a Baptist missionary society in 1814. Out of this initial attempt came the two most prominent features of American foreign missions before the Civil War: the larger-than-life reputation of Adoniram and Ann Hasseltine Judson and the continued activity of the ABCFM.

"For more than thirty years his name has been a household word," wrote Hannah Conant after Adoniram Judson's death. "A whole generation has grown up, familiar with the story of his labors and sufferings, [yet] not one of them had ever seen his face." Judson's thirty-eight years as a missionary in Burma, which included pathbreaking translation work, made him the foremost exemplar of the foreign mission movement. In Conant's words he was "a sort of Christian Paladin, who had experienced wonderful fortunes, and achieved wonderful exploits of philanthropy, in that far off almost mystical land of heathenism." Biographies of Judson's four successive wives, particularly the sainted Ann Hasseltine (1789-1826) and Sarah Hall (1803-1845), enshrined them as models for female religious behavior. When Judson returned to the United States, after almost thirty-four years in Burma, he was accorded a triumphant reception wherever he went—in New York, Providence, Albany, Philadelphia, and Washington. His fame transcended denominational barriers. When the president of Brown, Francis Wayland, published the authorized biography of Judson in 1853, it sold 26,000 copies within a year despite a market glutted with other biographies. The most popular biography of Ann Judson, of which new editions appeared almost annually from 1830 until 1856, was described by the Unitarian Lydia Maria Child "as a book so universally known that it scarcely need be mentioned."

The lionization of the Judson family indicates the extent that evangelical America was becoming caught up in "the great moral enterprise" of foreign missions. Actually, America came to send large numbers of foreign missionaries only after the Civil War, with the five major boards which existed in 1860 multiplying into ninety-four sending and forty-three supporting agencies by 1900. But it was pioneers like Judson who captured the imagination of American evangelicals and etched the burden of foreign missions deep within their collective conscience.

Before the Civil War denominations such as the Baptists, Methodists, and Episcopalians did have footholds in India, Africa, Brazil, Greece, and China, but none of these agencies employed more than a score of missionaries at any one time. It was the ABCFM, representing Congregationalists and Presbyterians, with primary fields in the Orient and the Pacific islands, that alone mobilized large numbers of missionaries, sending out almost one thousand persons in its first fifty years. Before 1860, interestingly enough, very few single women were sent as missionaries. This trend was dramatically reversed after the Civil War, which served to overturn social patterns and draw women into positions of responsibility.

Indian Missions and Indian Removal

HENRY WARNER BOWDEN

The War of 1812 ended British influence among Native Americans who opposed white encroachment onto tribal lands. When that support collapsed, Indian resistance to federal policies faded too, and the young nation spread westward more confidently. Planners in Washington recognized that Indians still posed a problem, but throughout the early national period they were ambivalent about solutions. Some advocated using treaties to remove Indians from any place pioneering whites wanted to settle. They did not acknowledge native independence as separate groups and argued that all of them should be removed beyond the Mississippi River, by force if necessary.

Others held that Indians could be assimilated into American patterns. They urged Congress to provide the means for transforming natives into yeoman farmers, thus qualifying them for citizenship in the new nation. Between the Revolution and the Civil War these conflicting attitudes split American opinion, each side maintaining that the alternative viewpoint was unrealistic. Hapless Indians were caught in the middle.

Congress took many steps to aid Indian acculturation and by 1819 had regularized those activities with an annual appropriation. The "civilization fund," created in that year, provided money for schools and model agricultural stations to help Indians acquire

The Reverend Abel Bingham, missionary to the Indians, with two of his teachers and a group of their converts BILLY GRAHAM CENTER

the fundamentals of acceptable behavior. Most Americans assumed that an enlightened and self-sufficient electorate was essential to democracy. If tribesmen were to avoid expulsion from the Republic, then nonliterate peoples would have to learn to read, and nomadic hunters accept sedentary habits. Protestant churches added Christianity as a third requisite to citizenship and utilized government funds to accomplish their purpose. They nominated their own missionaries to serve as schoolteachers and farmers in tribal territories. Federal support of these evangelists shows how church and state cooperated to affect both religious and cultural aspects of native lifestyles and to mold Indians into potential Americans.

Sustained antebellum missionary activity was most effective in the southeastern United States. There Baptist, Methodist, Presbyterian, and Moravian missionaries contacted some of the most accomplished of Native American groups. Powerful tribes such as the Choctaws and Creeks had flourished in that region for centuries, but the Cherokees excelled all of them in material and intellectual sophistication. Cherokees occupied land in western North Carolina, eastern Tennessee, and northern Georgia. Their substantial houses, bountiful gardens, and strong kinship alliances gave native life cohesiveness and permanency. Their religious ceremonies and rich mythology bestowed a sense of meaning and purpose which its adherents often preferred to Christian alternatives. But despite precontact accomplishments, many Cherokees accepted gospel teachings and blended them with aspects of their earlier lifestyle. Several of them were ordained as Baptist or Methodist ministers in the 1820s. In addition to having developed impressive cultural achievements before whites arrived in their region, Cherokees also proved to be the ones capable of adapting best to new standards. That adaptability was crucial to the survival of native patterns and the perpetuation of Christianity within them.

Besides government seed money, the agency conspicuous for supporting evangelical efforts in Cherokee territory was the American Board of Commissioners for Foreign Missions. The ABCFM usually sent Presbyterian or Congregationalist ministers into the field, and in the 1820s their notable Indian missionaries featured Cyrus Kingsbury and Samuel Worcester, each of whom began his career in northern Georgia. Within a few years these evangelists succeeded in winning converts to the new faith and modified lifestyle. Under ABCFM guidance and that of other denominational spokesmen, Cherokees built many churches and adapted to other white cultural patterns. As a nation they adopted a republican government and drafted laws copied from the United States Constitution. They augmented an agricultural economy, owned large herds of livestock, built grist mills, bridges, and toll roads.

The brilliant Sequoyah (1770?–1843) produced the Cherokee alphabet that enabled Samuel Worcester to translate part of the Bible into that language. NATIONAL PORTRAIT GALLERY, SMITHSONIAN INSTITUTION, WASHINGTON, D.C.

Young Indian converts entered the ministry, one of them with the adopted name of Elias Boudinot traveling north to finish his education at Andover Theological Seminary. By 1828 Worcester and Boudinot succeeded in importing a printing press that issued the *Cherokee Phoenix*, the first native American newspaper utilizing a written Indian language.

But two events in 1828 signaled a decade of suffering for Cherokees: Andrew Jackson was elected president, and gold was discovered in northern Georgia. The state quickly laid claim to Cherokee lands, and the new president, never one to recognize Indian sovereignty, backed Georgia's action. In 1830 he won a larger victory, pushing through Congress the Indian Removal Bill that required all southeastern Indians to relocate west of the Mississippi. Most tribes soon acquiesced: Choctaws in 1830, Chickasaws, Creeks, and Seminoles in 1832. But the Cherokees resisted displacement and received the support of ABCFM missionaries in their stand. In 1831 several white ministers were arrested for opposing state laws. Most accepted a pardon, but Worcester and another missionary, Elizur Butler, preferred jail to abandoning their natives' cause. By 1832 the issue reached the U. S. Supreme Court where Chief Justice John Marshall decided in favor of the Indians. He declared in *Worcester* v. *Georgia* that no state had the right to extend its authority over Indian lands existing legally as a separate nation. President Jackson and Georgia officials refused to enforce that ruling and acted with opposite intentions. They used force to make Cherokees either subject to state laws or dependent on federal authority for resettlement far away from white territorial claims.

The Cherokees tried for years to avoid both options of Jackson's draconian ultimatum. But by 1833 Worcester finally accepted clemency and, once released from prison, began urging native Christians to recognize the harsh realities of white dominance. Most Cherokees could not understand why they had to leave. Many were Christian; most were literate and substantially prosperous. They fulfilled general expectations for American acceptance, yet federal and state officials were bent on expelling them from ancestral lands. In retrospect it seems that the basic factor preventing racial harmony was a deep-seated American suspicion and hostility against Indians per se. Probably no degree of similar cultural values and behavior patterns would have caused whites to accept Indians as equal partners in collective action. Not even a shared Christian faith and a common Bible made much difference to American agents who were determined to rid their country of "aliens." By 1835 they pressured several local Indian spokesmen into signing a treaty that forfeited all native claims in the area. Elias Boudinot was one of the Cherokees who sanctioned that capitulation, called the Treaty of New Echota.

Some Cherokee recognized that the end was near and began moving west to Oklahoma, then known as Indian Territory. Many others vowed to stay and lobbied among unsympathetic bureaucrats in Washington. By 1838 further delay was impossible, and U. S. troops forced reluctant Cherokees to leave at bayonet point. The great migration west constituted a "Trail of Tears" for Cherokees because of losses behind, uncertainty ahead, and intense suffering along the way. Shortly after reaching their new homes, some embittered refugees assassinated Rev. Boudinot and other Cherokees who had signed the treaty. But Worcester remained with his people, the churches survived, and some younger natives responded to ministerial callings. Cherokee churches of different Protestant affiliations exist today, living testimony to the staying power of both Native American lifestyles and the gospel once it permeates human hearts.

Radical Social Reform: Thomas and Mary Nichols

"The whole world seems to be looking for a revolution," John Humphrey Noyes confessed in 1847. "Some expect an orthodox millennium; others a golden age of phrenology [a popular science that claimed to assess character by precise measurements of the form and shape of the head]; others still physiological regeneration of the human race; and not a few are awaiting, in anxious or hopeful suspense, the trump of the Second Advent and the day of judgment." Like no generation before or since, antebellum Americans rejected conventional social arrangements as artificial and oppressive and dreamed of a thousand different ways to perfect the individual and society. The ex-Calvinist turned radical abolitionist and anarchist Henry Clarke Wright articulated the kind of assumption behind many of the one hundred or so communitarian experiments of these years: "I regard all Human Governments as usurpation of God's power over Man."

A world of confusing and fluid expectations spawned schemes which seemed as imminently plausible a century and a half ago as they seem bizarre today: the attempt of Sylvester Graham (inventor of the graham cracker) to perfect body and soul through radical dietary reform, Samuel Thompson's plan of health through herbal medicines, Orson Fowler's system of self-improvement through phrenology, and dozens of reformers employing hydropathy (water cure) and spiritualism (communicating with the dead). In this climate, it was no accident that the 1830s saw the genesis of the Mormons and the Millerites.

The reformers Thomas and Mary Nichols represent a fascinating example of such impulses. They were Yankees who, by the time they were married in 1848, had dabbled in practically every reform and intellectual fad then current, from vegetarianism, hydropathy, phrenology, mesmerism, Swedenborgianism, to spiritualism, women's rights, and free love. After moving from New York to Cincinnati in 1855, they planned to open in Yellow Springs, Ohio—site of well-known mineral springs—an institute called Memnonia. Just as the fabled statue of Memnon on the banks of the Nile broke into song with the rise of the sun, so, they claimed, the "Social Harmony" of Memnonia would herald "the dawn of a New Era of Humanity." What the Nichols advocated was an unsystematic amalgam of socialism, spiritualism, free love, phrenology, hydropathy, and other health and dietary notions. The premise upon which their system rested was the staggeringly optimistic assumption that human affairs could be perfected.

In Yellow Springs, the Nichols were resoundingly opposed by Horace Mann, the great educational reformer, who had moved west to take charge of the newly opened Antioch College. He was adamantly opposed to his students' imbibing the heady intellectual mix that the Nichols had brought to town.

Before these tensions came to a head, the story of the Nichols took an unexpected twist: Thomas and Mary Nichols converted to Roman Catholicism. By their own account, the Nichols began to consider Catholicism after the spirit of a Jesuit priest reportedly appeared to Mary. She wrote to Archbishop John B. Purcell of Cincinnati who, despite serious reservations about the Nichols' spiritualist practices, provided pastoral counsel and welcomed them into the Catholic church in March 1857. After spending a few weeks at a convent school in southern Ohio, the Nichols began writing apologetic articles on behalf of Catholicism and undertook a series of lecture tours through the Midwest. Given their penchant for the extreme, the Nichols' outlook remained surprisingly orthodox, as when they lectured at the University of Notre Dame in 1858 and compared the failure of utopian communes with the success of the school founded by the French priest Edward Sorin.

For all its eccentricity, the story of the Nichols points up the absence of limits, the boundless potentiality, which many nineteenth-century Americans experienced. This was partly a response to the great democratic changes that had taken place in America since the Revolution. As old authorities and hierarchies fell away, common people found themselves groping for stable moorings. The Nichols were two pilgrims whose quest to realize what they called "the Newness" eventually led them back to the most ancient of Christian havens.

Ellen and James White and their two sons in the early 1860s   BILLY GRAHAM CENTER

Ellen G. White and the Gospel of Health
RONALD L. NUMBERS

On the evening of June 5, 1863, Ellen G. White, thirty-five-year-old spiritual leader of the fledging Seventh-day Adventist church, joined friends in rural Michigan for vespers. For years she had suffered ill health, the result of a disfiguring rock-throwing incident in childhood; and now her husband, James, appeared to be on the verge of a physical and mental breakdown. While praying, she went into a hypnotic-like trance, as she had often done since the age of seventeen, and began receiving instructions from heaven on the preservation and restoration of health. God's people, she learned, were to give up eating meat and other stimulating foods, shun alcohol and tobacco, and avoid drug-dispensing doctors. When sick, they were to rely solely on Nature's remedies: fresh air, sunshine, rest, exercise, proper diet, and — above

all — water. Adventists sisters were to abandon their fashionable, floor-length dresses for "short" skirts and pantaloons similar to the Bloomer costume, and all believers were to curb their "animal passions." The horrible consequences of self-abuse or masturbation especially caught her attention. "Everywhere I looked," the prophetess later recalled, "I saw imbecility, dwarfed forms, crippled limbs, misshapen heads, and deformity of every description."

Although White professed surprise at what she saw, the content of her vision had been circulating in the United States for three decades. Since the early 1830s the Presbyterian evangelist and temperance lecturer Sylvester Graham (remembered today for his crackers) had been warning Americans of the dire consequences of flesh foods, drugs, corsets, stimulants, and frequent sex. In 1837 he united with other health reformers, including the physician William A. Alcott, to form the American Physiological Society. This educational organization taught "That the millennium ... can never reasonably be expected to arrive, until those laws which God has implanted in the *physical* nature of man are, equally with his moral laws, universally known and obeyed."

Unlike the postmillennialists in the American Physiological Society, Seventh-day Adventists believed in the imminent second coming of Christ. Many of them, including the prophetess herself, were former Millerites, who had vainly waited for Christ to appear in 1843 and 1844. In one of Ellen's early visions an angel had explained that Christ could not return to earth until the elect obeyed the Ten Commandments, particularly the fourth, which decreed the observance of the seventh-day sabbath. By teaching that "It is as truly a sin to violate the laws of our being as it is to break the Ten Commandments," she elevated health reform from a physiological to a theological obligation, essential to salvation.

From 1863 until her death in 1915 Ellen White, with varying degrees of success and zeal, proclaimed the gospel of health. As a result many Adventists adopted a twice-a-day diet of fruits, vegetables, grains, and nuts and gave up tea, coffee, meat, butter, eggs, cheese, rich desserts, and "all exciting substances." Such dietary articles, White argued, not only caused disease but stimulated unholy sexual desires.

Although she at first reported great progress in changing the eating habits of Adventists, there soon appeared signs of "a universal backsliding on health reform." Fish and flesh reappeared on Adventist tables, and even among ministers vegetarianism became the exception rather than the rule. By the mid-1870s White herself was indulging her appetite for flesh

foods, to the chagrin of the few who remained true to the health-reform message. It was not until the 1890s that she finally gained a permanent victory over meat and began leading her church back into the vegetarian fold.

Dress reform proved equally frustrating. Immediately after her 1863 vision White damned "the so-called reform dress" — only to change her mind within two years and begin advocating a skirt-and-pants costume she claimed to have seen in the trance. She further confused her followers by first saying that God wanted skirts to clear the ground by "an inch or two," then declaring that they should reach "somewhat below the top of the boot," and finally settling on nine inches from the floor. White's dress, called a "woman-disfigurer" by her own niece, never caught on. In 1873 the prophetess complained that it was "treated by some with great indifference, and by others with contempt." Two years later God mercifully allowed her to discard her pantaloons and end her divisive dress-reform campaign.

During her seminal 1863 vision White, who had long held physicians in low esteem, learned that she was to direct the world "to God's great medicine, water." Since the 1840s, water enthusiasts, called hydropaths, had been curing the sick with an arsenal of baths, packs, and douches; and water-cure establishments had sprung up across the nation. In 1864 and again in 1865 Ellen and James White visited one of the most successful of these operations, in Dansville, New York, and returned home determined to start an Adventist water cure in Battle Creek, Michigan. Their Western Health Reform Institute experienced a rocky first decade. Then a young protégé of theirs, Dr. John Harvey Kellogg, took over and turned the ailing institute into a world-famous sanitarium. In his spare time he invented corn flakes and other health foods, from which his brother W. K. made a fortune.

Over the years Ellen White wrote hundreds, perhaps thousands, of pages on health-related subjects. Although she repeatedly stressed the divine origin of her "testimonies" and denied acquaintance with earthly sources — "My views were written independent of books or of the opinion of others" — a comparison of her writings with those of other health reformers reveals close parallels in both content and language. But if not the most original health reformer, she certainly was among the most influential. When she died at age eighty-seven, she left behind a string of thirty-three sanitariums and countless treatment rooms on six continents, a medical school in Loma Linda, California, and 136,000 disciples to preach the gospel of health in the twentieth century.

Ellen White's pamphlet on dress reform

BILLY GRAHAM CENTER

THE DRESS REFORM.

AN APPEAL TO THE PEOPLE IN ITS BEHALF.

WE are not Spiritualists. We are Christian women, believing all that the Scriptures say concerning man's creation, his fall, his sufferings and woes on account of continued transgression, of his hope of redemption thro' Christ, and of his duty to glorify God in his body and spirit which are his, in order to be saved. We do not wear the style of dress here represented to be odd,—that we may attract notice. We do not differ from the common style of woman's dress for any

Joseph Smith and the Latter-day Saints

LAWRENCE FOSTER

The Church of Jesus Christ of Latter-day Saints, or Mormon Church as it is popularly known, is the largest and one of the most controversial of the religious groups native to the United States. Originating during the turbulent Jacksonian years when so many institutions and beliefs were being called into question, the Mormon movement both reflected and challenged American values of its time. Joseph Smith, the Mormon prophet, grew up and founded his church in western New York State, an area of rapid economic and social change that was repeatedly "burned over" by the fires of religious revivalism and crusades to transform society. Although he was poor and lacked formal education, Smith was a precocious and

Joseph Smith (1805–1844) NATIONAL PORTRAIT GALLERY, SMITHSONIAN INSTITUTION, WASHINGTON, D.C.

sensitive young man who was deeply disturbed by the cacophony of ideas and causes that surrounded him. How was he or anyone else to know what was really true, he asked.

After a series of visionary experiences beginning in the early 1820s, Smith concluded that all existing religions were wrong; God had specially called him to set up a new religious and social synthesis. Smith began by engaging in what he described as a "translation ... by the gift and power of God" of inscriptions on golden plates that he claimed to have found buried in a large hill near his home. The Book of Mormon, which Smith dictated from those alleged records and published in 1830 (the same year he founded his church), purported to be an ancient religious history. It focused primarily on two peoples of Hebrew extraction who were said to have migrated to the American continent about 600 B.C. and had experienced many conflicts and apostasies. These struggles supposedly culminated about A.D. 400 in the destruction of the lighter-skinned Nephites by the darker-skinned Lamanites, ancestors of the American Indians.

Heated debates have raged during the past century and a half over the origin of the Book of Mormon — whether the golden plates ever existed, whether Smith could have translated them if they did, and what evidence, if any, might corroborate or disprove the account. The primary significance of the Book of Mormon, however, lies not so much in its origin as in its content. The book is a highly complex work of the religious imagination which addressed and provided answers for most of the religious questions that had been troubling people in areas of the Northeast such as the one in which Smith grew up.

This epic story of two great cultures in conflict and of a direct biblical linkage between Old World and New had immense appeal in an early nineteenth-century America seeking a sense of its historical roots and a uniquely American identity.

The revelations that Joseph Smith began receiving in the 1820s and 1830s were second in importance only to the Book of Mormon in the growth of his new church. Later collected in the Doctrine and Covenants (which along with the Bible, the Book of Mormon, and the Pearl of Great Price now form the four parts of Utah Mormon scripture), these revelations gradually unfolded a distinctive set of beliefs that Smith described as a restoration of the faith of early Christianity and a synthesis of all previously valid human truth. God's direct intervention in human affairs had not ceased with the apostolic age; revelation was continuing to be expressed through Smith as God's prophet and through the one true church which he was attempting to establish on earth once again. Smith declared that the new faith would ultimately usher in a millennium of peace and harmony — the kingdom of God on earth.

These extraordinary beliefs and the tightly knit religious organization that Smith developed to spread them resulted in repeated conflicts between the Mormons and their non-Mormon neighbors. Many antebellum Americans hoped to see the faith of early Christianity restored and the millennium commence, but few were prepared to accept the Mormons and their prophet Joseph Smith as the sole interpreter of that faith. The Mormons made exclusive claims to being both the heirs of early Christianity and a New Israel. Their view of themselves as a chosen people with an almost tribal loyalty to the group frightened Americans who believed in religious and social pluralism. The result was intense and repeated persecution that led the Mormons to

move over and over again — from New York, to Ohio, to Missouri, to Illinois, and eventually, after Smith was murdered in 1844, to Utah.

Persecution did not stop the Mormon movement from growing rapidly and achieving considerable worldly success. In just five years after migrating to Illinois in 1839, for example, Smith and the Latter-day Saints transformed an unhealthy and almost uninhabited swampland along the Mississippi River into the boom town of Nauvoo. With more than ten thousand inhabitants, Nauvoo briefly became one of the largest urban centers in Illinois and appeared to hold the balance of political power in the state. Also in Nauvoo, Smith secretly began an attempt to introduce a form of polygamy among his closest followers and, with equal secrecy, to set up a form of government giving him exceptional powers going far beyond his religious role as spokesman for the

An *early photograph of Nauvoo, Illinois, in* 1846 CHURCH ARCHIVES, THE CHURCH OF JESUS CHRIST OF LATTER-DAY SAINTS

church. Hostile outsiders were unaware of the full scope of these activities, but within the upper echelons of the church, many became convinced that Smith was arrogating excessive authority to himself and must be stopped. A combination of internal dissatisfaction and external hostility led to Smith's incarceration and murder in Carthage, Illinois, in 1844.

After the brief but disruptive struggle for succession which followed Smith's death, Brigham Young emerged as the leader of the main body of the Mormons, who continued to suffer persecution in Nauvoo. In addition, a smaller number of Saints from splinter groups which rejected Young, polygamy, and extreme separatism would eventually, under the leadership of Joseph Smith's eldest son, form the Reorganized Church of Jesus Christ of Latter Day Saints. Most Mormons, however, under the leadership of Young and the Council of the Twelve Apostles, which he headed, made the difficult migration to the valley of the Great Salt Lake, where the first settlers began arriving in 1847. In that arid, inhospitable, and initially isolated land, Young commenced the arduous task of setting up a cohesive, self-sufficient theocracy. A cooperative irrigation system which eventually helped the desert to

"bloom as the rose," and a new marriage and family system based on polygamy as the ideal were among the most distinctive features of the new Mormon lifestyle. By his death in 1877, Young had directed the establishment of more than 350 settlements, comprising more than 100,000 Mormons, not only in Utah but also in adjacent areas of the Intermountain West upon which the hardworking Latter-day Saints placed their indelible social and cultural imprint.

The last decades of the nineteenth century saw great changes in Mormon life. Intense federal pressure led the Mormons to begin to give up their controversial practice of polygamy in 1890, and at the same time the church also began to reduce its direct intervention in Utah politics. New church programs were introduced in an attempt to maintain Mormon distinctiveness and cohesiveness while also reaching a more realistic accommodation with the larger society. Since World War II, the Latter-day Saints have increasingly reached out beyond their base in the Intermountain West to the rest of the United States and the world in an attempt to create a truly universal church. This complex and rapidly growing group, now numbering over five million members worldwide, has received increasing attention from those interested in the origin, development, and transformation of religious movements.

Salt Lake City in 1868 CHURCH ARCHIVES, THE CHURCH OF JESUS CHRIST OF LATTER-DAY SAINTS

John Humphrey Noyes and the Oneida Community

DONALD E. PITZER

John Humphrey Noyes (1811-1886) was one of the most innovative religious thinkers and radical social reformers in nineteenth-century America. Born to well-to-do parents in Brattleboro, Vermont, he graduated youngest in his Dartmouth class at age nineteen, but failed in a brief attempt at law because of extreme shyness and anxiety. After an emotional conversion to Christianity in 1831, he decided upon the ministry. At Andover Theological Seminary and Yale Divinity School he began a life-long identification of his life with that of St. Paul and an assemblage of elements for his unique, perfectionist theology. From Matthew 24 he developed the idea that Christ's Second Advent occurred in A.D. 70 as Jerusalem and Judaism fell and the Christian church became spiritualized. He inferred from Romans 7 that all sin is cleansed at conversion, leading the individual to perfection. When he declared himself filled with the Holy Spirit and therefore sinless in 1834, he was expelled from Calvinistic Yale, relieved of his preaching license, alienated from

friends and professors, and rejected by his first love, Abigail Merwin. A vain attempt to gain control of the emerging Perfectionist movement nearly shattered his fragile psyche and forced him to continue his efforts outside established institutions.

Since further public abuse greeted his increasingly antinomian doctrines when published in his *Witness* and *Perfectionist* journals, Noyes turned to communitarianism as a potential shield from the sanctions of religious and social convention. On the family homestead in Putney, Vermont, in 1841 he organized his first converts, family and friends, into the Society of Inquiry, which was always a group carefully selected for commitment, skill, and wealth and which grew to more than 250 at Oneida, New York, between 1848 and 1881. Putney, Oneida, and five smaller offshoots in New York, New Jersey, Connecticut, and Vermont offered the charismatic reformer social microcosms in which his total domination could alleviate his own emotional insecurity and facilitate the introduction of the king-

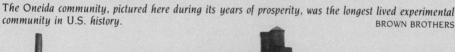

The Oneida community, pictured here during its years of prosperity, was the longest lived experimental community in U.S. history.
BROWN BROTHERS

dom of God on earth by implementing biblical communism, mutual criticism, divine healing, male continence, complex marriage, eugenic experimentation, and theocratic democracy. The Putney Perfectionists announced in 1847 that the millennial kingdom had come in their community as evidenced by divine healings and their attainment of an unselfish spiritual state which permitted them to abandon private property in material goods and in mates. The complex marriage which set them apart from all contemporary religious groups was justified on the grounds that Christ intended his saints on earth to transcend worldly monogamy and marriage and to enjoy the affection and ecstasy of the heterosexual relations freely engaged in by the angels in heaven (Mark 12:25). This practice rested on Noyes' earlier discovery of male continence (*coitus reservatus*) as a birth control method. This permitted amative relations without propagation. Although such sexual activity brought the charges of adultery which forced Noyes to move his community to Oneida in 1848 and to escape into Canada in 1879, the practices were so regulated and efficient that less than two children were born per year dur-

ing Oneida's first twenty. Then, in 1869, fifty-three women and thirty-eight men formally committed their bodies to Noyes for his unprecedented experiment in human breeding to produce a superior spiritual generation. This stirpiculture endeavor not only produced fifty-eight children, nine of them Noyes', who were studiously nurtured and educated, but also intensified outside pressure sufficiently to cause Oneida's communal dissolution in 1881.

In the meantime, Oneida had become the longest-lived and most radical native American commune, had become affluent on a well-managed economy based on the manufacture of cruel animal traps and travel bags, and had developed a secular, socialistic air that was influenced by Brook Farm's *Harbinger*. The expansive Victorian Gothic Mansion House complex, which still survives, replete with classrooms, library, auditorium, turkish bath, chemical laboratory, and photographic studio, had become the scene of stage performances open to the public. Noyes' own survey of American communal societies, which was researched by journalist A. J. Macdonald, was titled *History of American Socialisms* (1870).

New Harmony

DONALD E. PITZER

New Harmony on the Wabash River in southwest Indiana was the site of the religious utopian community of the Harmonists (1814-1824) and the secular one of the Owenites (1825-1827). The town was founded by eight hundred communitarian Separatists from the German province of Württemberg, disciples of Johann Georg Rapp and members of his Harmony Society. ("Father") Rapp (1757-1847) separated from the Evangelical (Lutheran) church at Iptingen in 1785 and attracted thousands to his pietistic, premillennial, perfectionist teachings. He and his followers drew inspiration and unity from biblical prophecy regarding Christ's second appearing, adventist interpretations of current events, Johann Herder's view of history moving inexorably toward cosmic harmony, Jakob Boehme's conception of man's God-like sinless, sexless condition in the Garden of Eden and in the future kingdom of God on earth, and Johann Valentin Andreae's literary vision of the ideal communitarian republic of Christianopolis. Rapp summarized his own ideas in his only book, *Gedanken über die Bestimmung des Menschen* (*Thoughts on the Destiny of Man*), published in German and English at New Harmony in 1824.

Rapp led some twelve hundred dissenters from Germany to the American wilderness after 1803 to await Christ's return as the Sunwoman of Revelation 12:6. Later, he conceived his faithful to be a modern manifestation of the church of Philadelphia

A view of New Harmony during the brief tenure of the Owenites between 1825 and 1827
THE GRANGER COLLECTION

THE CRISIS,

OR THE CHANGE FROM ERROR AND MISERY, TO TRUTH AND HAPPINESS.

1832.

IF WE CANNOT YET   RECONCILE ALL OPINIONS,

LET US ENDEAVOUR   TO UNITE ALL HEARTS.

IT IS OF ALL TRUTHS THE MOST IMPORTANT, THAT THE CHARACTER OF MAN IS FORMED FOR—NOT BY HIMSELF.

Design of a Community of 2,000 Persons, founded upon a principle, commended by Plato, Lord Bacon, Sir T. More, & R. Owen.

EDITED BY
ROBERT OWEN AND ROBERT DALE OWEN.

London:

PRINTED AND PUBLISHED BY J. EAMONSON, 15, CHICHESTER PLACE, GRAY'S INN ROAD.

STRANGE, PATERNOSTER ROW. PURKISS, OLD COMPTON STREET, AND MAY BE HAD OF ALL BOOKSELLERS.

1833.

destined to participate actively in the millennial kingdom. While building their first village at Harmonie, Pennsylvania, Rapp's disciples organized their communal Harmony Society in 1805 in imitation of the first-century Christian church (Acts 2:44-45; 4:34-35), and elected Rapp president and his adopted son Frederick (Reichert) a trustee and business manager. During a perfectionist revival in 1807, they adopted the celibacy which contributed to a schism by 175 members in 1832 and the Society's gradual demise.

The Harmonists migrated to the Indiana frontier in 1814 in search of land for new arrivals, a navigable river, and a mild climate for vineyards. They planned New Harmony's efficient rectilinear design, built 180 structures including a brick cruciform church, cultivated three thousand of their twenty thousand acres, and manufactured woolen cloth and other goods that they marketed to twenty-two states and ten foreign countries. New Harmony became a Harmonist religious, ethnic, and cultural sanctuary with a school for both sexes, an extensive library, and encouragement to compose and perform vocal and instrumental music, to sketch flowers and wildlife, and to write prose and poetry for public readings and for printing on their own press. The united political voice of the town, strong and sometimes resented, effected a clause in the first Indiana constitution permitting payment in lieu of military service. In 1824, Rapp moved his entire community back to Pennsylvania because of internal restlessness over the long-delayed

millennium and the unstable economy of the west. The Harmony Society erected its third town, called Economy, north of Pittsburgh, where it endured until 1916.

New Harmony was sold to Robert Owen, wealthy cotton manufacturer and social reformer from New Lanark, Scotland, for his model Community of Equality that was to produce human happiness and usher in the New Moral World through replication around the globe. A Benthamite Utilitarian and environmentalist who believed that "the character of man is formed FOR — not BY — himself," Owen projected a community to free people from ignorance, superstition, economic insecurity, violence, and discrimination by race, sex, or nationality. Freedom of thought, communally oriented education from kindergarten through adulthood, communitarian ownership and enterprise, democratic institutions, and universal good will were to effect these results. Despite inadequate leadership, heterogeneous membership, and frequent dissension that produced a dozen constitutions, Owen's New Harmony experiment drew eight hundred utopians including feminist Frances Wright and a boatload of distinguished Pestalozzian educators and natural scientists whose work gave the town an international reputation decades after Owen's community dissolved in 1827. The Workingmen's Institute, endowed by Owen's associate William Maclure, remains as a research facility along with restored historic buildings and cultural programs reflecting New Harmony's utopian past.

The Triumph
of the Voluntary Church

The establishment of religious freedom in the United States created a historical situation genuinely unique. For the first time a predominantly Christian nation unfettered the church from state control and allowed different and competing manifestations of the church to operate freely. The result was that no church could rely any longer on imposed authority but had to work for the voluntary response of the people.

What developed were not churches in the traditional sense, primarily confessional and territorial; nor sects, exclusive groups that set themselves over against an establishment. Instead, America witnessed the development of denominations which were purposive in character, what historian Sidney E. Mead has described as "a voluntary association of like-hearted and like-minded individuals, who are united on the basis of common beliefs for the purpose of accomplishing tangible and de-

fined objectives." Even a Yankee Congregationalist like Lyman Beecher, who had much to fear from the end of state support for the church, came to believe that it was "the best thing that ever happened to the State of Connecticut." The churches, he said, thrown "on their own resources and on God," had increased dramatically their influence "by voluntary efforts, societies, missions, and revivals."

This kind of voluntarism, of course, made antebellum Christianity anything but monolithic. The colonial legacy of pluralism, compounded now by a certain propensity to divide old denominations and organize fresh ones, left many wondering how to cope with fragmentation as a central feature of church life. The German Reformed minister John W. Nevin, who valued churchly traditions, found little consolation in the multiplication of denominations. Commenting after reading a

An idealized notion of a single Christian Church remained alive even in the midst of antebellum religious pluralism, as this 1845 engraving entitled "Christian Union" illustrates. BILLY GRAHAM CENTER

The Americans demanded that they were free, masterless individuals; they sought absolute independence and equality of status. They imagine that their whole destiny is in their own hands. . . . They acquire the habit of always considering themselves as standing alone.

ALEXIS DE TOCQUEVILLE,
Democracy in America, 1835

Religion on the Southern Frontier

The rapid increase of the population in some of the new villages and towns of the west, when favourably situated for trade, is astonishing, and strikes one particularly in its early stages. Thus, when in the State of Alabama, in February, 1831, I visited the town of Montgomery, in company with a worthy Baptist minister, in the course of an extensive tour through the western States, in behalf of one of our benevolent societies. It was then hardly more than a large village, and on the night of the second of the two days we spent in it, we preached in a large school-house, which, if I remember rightly, was the only place for holding religious meetings existing there at the time. We had a good congregation, though a circus was held hard by. Just three years after, when repeating the same tour, I spent a Sabbath and one or two days more at the same spot, but under amazingly different circumstances. In the morning I preached in a Presbyterian church built of frames and covered with boards, and every way comfortable, to at least 600 persons. The church, which reckoned 100 members, had got a young man as pastor, to whom they gave a yearly stipend of 1000 dollars. At night I preached in a Baptist church, built of brick, but not quite finished, which could hold 300 persons at least. Besides these, there were one Methodist Episcopal and one Protestant Methodist church, each, in so far as I can recollect, as large as the Baptist church. Then there was an Episcopal church, not less in size, though probably with a smaller congregation, than the Baptist Church. And withal there was a Roman Catholic church, though not a large one, I believe. All this after an interval of only three years! Eventful years they had been. A revival of religion, which took place during one of them, had brought many souls to the knowledge of salvation.

ROBERT BAIRD,
Religion in America, 1844

---

compendium of the beliefs of fifty-three American denominations, he asked:

> But what are we to think of it when we find such a motley mass of protesting systems, all laying claim so vigorously here to one and the same watchword. If the Bible be at once so clear ... how does it come to pass that when men are left most free to use it in this way ... they are flung assunder so perpetually in their religious faith, instead of being brought together by its influence.

Some Americans found that the multiplication of denominations actually bred skepticism. Joseph Smith, the founder of the Mormons, began to explore the possibility of direct revelation after competing Protestant claims seemed to cancel out each other. More often, however, denominationalism came to be seen in a positive light. "Each denomination," said a leading evangelical, "is working out some problem in the Christian life, developing some portion of truth. Each has its part to perform, its particular work to do for the Kingdom of Christ, which it, in the present condition of things, is better equipped to do than any other." A Baptist editor put it this way: "However we may *wish* all men to become Baptists, we *will* all become evangelical Christians." It was this evangelical core that maintained in America a surprisingly unified Christian culture, as Robert Baird noted in his *Religion in America*, first published in 1844. Baird divided denominations into the "Evangelicals" and the "Unevangelicals"—the former to include all the major Protestant denominations, the latter Roman Catholics and certain smaller religious groups such as Unitarians, Universalists, Swedenborgians, Jews, and Deists. What kind of common characteristics defined the denominations that comprised this evangelical mainstream? Apart from a dominant strain of revivalism and a certain penchant for separatism, issues which have already received ample treatment, two other traits stand out.

Pragmatism

The voluntary principle that was the mainspring of American denominations had the virtue of bringing Christian faith to the common person. The arcane and abstract gave way to practical insights that could be understood by all. The Presbyterian church, for instance, gladly welcomed into its ranks the young revivalist Charles G. Finney, a man without theological education and without, it turned out, any real knowledge of the Westminster Confession. Given the undeniable power of his revivalism, however, theological objections would have come across as scholastic nit-picking.

An active and success-oriented Christianity perfectly suited the new American republic—an age inspired by myths of "the self-made man" and made prosperous by the efforts of aspiring entrepreneurs. To this kind of pragmatism one can certainly attribute the considerable vitality of the American church. But one can also detect a tendency in this age for problems to become oversimplified, leaving complex issues reduced to a bare

---

I am a Christian . . . calling no man father or master; holding as abominable in the sight of God, everything highly esteemed among men, such as calvinism, arminianism, freewillism, universalism, reverend, parsons, chaplains, doctors of divinity, clergy, bands, surplices, notes, creeds, covenants, platforms.

ELIAS SMITH,
founder of the Christian Connection, *ca.* 1810

The Presbyterians, and other Calvinistic branches of the Protestant Church, used to contend from educated ministry, for pews, for instrumental music, for a congregational or stated salaried ministry. The Methodists universally, opposed these ideas; and the illiterate Methodist preachers actually set the world on fire, (the American world at least,) while they were lighting their matches!

PETER CARTWRIGHT,
Methodist circuit rider, *ca.* 1830

---

choice between contrasting alternatives. The Second Great Awakening in America, like the revivals of Finney, produced no theologian of great stature. It may, in fact, also have given many the impression that serious intellectual activity could be counterproductive of genuine piety. "There is an impression somewhat general," an observer confessed, "that a vigorous and highly cultivated intellect is not consistent with distinguished holiness; and that those who live in the clearest sunshine of communication with God must withdraw from the bleak atmosphere of human science . . . , that an intellectual clergyman is deficient in piety, and that an eminently pious minister is deficient in intellect."

Primitivism

American denominations in this era also made little use of the accumulated wisdom of the centuries. Inspired by the hope of a pure and normative beginning to which return was possible—"the New Testament church," Americans typically viewed the intervening eighteen hundred years as a story of aberration and corruption which was better ignored. This ahistorical approach flourished in a republic which took pride in an ability to put aside the decaying traditions of Europe.

Such attitudes, however, brought into question the traditional function and significance of the institutional church. Institutional reordering became the norm after 1800, the most striking example being the formation of the "Christians" by Barton W. Stone (1772-1844) and the "Disciples" by Alexander Campbell (1788-1866). Stone and five colleagues not only left the Presbyterian church in Kentucky in the wake of the Cane Ridge revival but went on to issue a manifesto, "The Last Will and Testament of Springfield Presbytary," which denied the validity of any church organization whatsoever. Campbell, rejecting the idea that the Disciples were a "church" or "denomination," said he did not even want to hear the term "church government": "We have no system of our own, or of others, to substitute in lieu of the reigning systems. We aim only at substituting the New Testament."

The hope that a New Testament polity could emerge naturally had an unsettling effect within a variety of denominational structures. Out of such ferment were born the Cumberland Presbyterian church, the Landmark Baptists, and the Church of God, a splinter group from the German Reformed led by John Winebrenner. Methodism, whose discipline and hierarchy never pretended to be democratic, was particularly beset with defections on issues of polity: James O'Kelly's Republican Methodists and William Hammett's Primitive Methodists, both organized in the 1790s; Pliny Brett's Reformed Methodist church formed in New England in 1814; and the New York Stillwellites begun in 1820. The Methodist Protestant church (1830), the only of these groups to gain widespread support, sprang from concerns common to all these movements: "the recovery of mutual rights of ministers and

Alexander Campbell (1788–1866) late in his life, with his second wife LIBRARY OF CONGRESS

members of the Church from the usurpation and tyranny of hierarchies." The ideal of primitivism, which democracy had accelerated, made fragile any ecclesiastical polity that did not spring from the uncoerced will of the individual.

Open the New Testament as if mortal man had never seen it before.
ALEXANDER CAMPBELL

Abolitionist and feminist Sojourner Truth (1797?–1883) spoke throughout the North on behalf of all persons' rights, including those of blacks and women. BILLY GRAHAM CENTER

Women's Rights and American Religion

Groton [Mass.] 8th Month 12. [1837]
My Dear Brother
No doubt thou hast heard by this time of all the fuss that is now making in this region about our stepping so far out of the bounds of female propriety as to lecture to promiscuous assemblies. My auditors literally sit some times with "mouths agape and eyes astare", so that I cannot help smiling in the midst of "rhetorical flourishes" to witness their perfect amazement at hearing a woman speak in the churches. I wish thou couldst see Brother Phelp's letter to us on this subject and sisters admirable reply. I suppose he will soon come out with a conscientious protest against us. I am waiting in some anxiety to see what the Executive Committee mean to do in these troublous times, whether to renounce us or not. But seriously speaking, we are placed very unexpectedly in a very trying situation, in the forefront of an entirely new contest — a contest for the *rights of woman* as a moral, intelligent and responsible being. Harriet Martineau says "God and man know that the time has not come for women to make their injuries even heard of": but it seems as tho' it had come *now* and that the exigency must be met with the firmness and faith of woman in by gone ages. I cannot help feeling some regret that this sh'ld have come up *before* the Anti Slavery question was settled, so fearful am I that it may injure that blessed cause, and then again I think this must be the Lord's time and therefore the *best* time, for it seems to have been brought about by a concatenation of circumstances over which we had no control. The fact is it involves the interests of every minister in our land and therefore they will stand almost in a solid phalanx against woman's rights and I am afraid the discussion of this question will divide in Jacob and scatter in Israel; it will also touch every man's interests at home, in the tenderest relation of life; it will go down into the very depths of his soul and cause great searchings of heart. I am glad H. Winslow of Boston has come out so boldly and told us just what I believe is in the hearts of thousands of men in our land. I must confess my womanhood is insulted, my moral feelings outraged when I reflect on these things, and I am sure I *know just* how the free colored people feel towards the whites when they pay them more than common attention, it is *not paid as a* RIGHT, but *given as a* BOUNTY on a *little* more than *ordinary* sense. There is not one man in 500 who really understand what kind of attention is alone acceptable to a woman of pure and exalted moral and intellectual worth. Hast thou read Sisters letters in the Spectator? I want thee to read them and let us know what thou thinkest of them. That a wife is *not* to be subject to her husband in any other sense than I am to her or she to me, seems to be strange and *alarming* doctrine indeed, but how can it be otherwise unless *she surrenders her moral responsibility*, which *no woman has a right* to do! ... WHO will stand by woman in the great struggle? As to our being Quakers being an *excuse* for our speaking in public, we do *not* stand on this ground at all, we ask *no* favors for ourselves, but *claim* rights for our *sex*. If it is wrong for woman to lecture or preach then let the Quakers give up their false views, and let other sects refuse to hear their women, but if it is *right* then let *all* women who have gifts, "mind their calling" and enjoy "the liberty wherewith Christ hath made them free", in that declaration of Paul, "In Christ Jesus there is neither male nor female." O! if in our intercourse with each other we realized this great truth, how delightful, enobling and dignified it would be, but as I told the Moral Reform Society of Boston in my address, *this* reformation *must begin with ourselves*.

ANGELINA GRIMKÉ

Varieties of Quaker Experience

RICHARD E. WOOD

American Quakers in 1776, except a few schismatic militant Patriots, stood united in recommitment to their distinctive practices and ideals. Known for pacifism, humanitarianism, and, as of 1776, the exclusion of slaveholders from membership, Friends also expelled many other disciplinary offenders.

Nevertheless, the denomination split in 1827 as a combination of mysticism with implicit biblical orthodoxy crumbled. Apologists before 1700 had insisted that the Inward Light of Christ never contradicts scripture. But afterwards, leaders had promoted subjective experience and ethics, not belief. When doctrinal orthodoxy received increasing emphasis after 1800, especially from visiting English Quaker ministers, certain American mystics, notably the aging Elias Hicks of rural Long Island, reacted with shrill antievangelicalism. In turn, Hicks's claim that the Inward Light made Christ's historic atonement unnecessary alarmed "orthodox" leaders. They then devised tests to weed out sympathizers with Hicks. In consequence, the Orthodox alienated some who merely disliked their tactics.

"Hicksite" (liberal) Quakers outnumbered their Orthodox counterparts from New York to Virginia, but not nationally. Tending toward theological liberalism and emphasizing benevolence, they remained moderately conservative in practice. They even disowned a few "Progressive Friends" during the 1840s for dissent from Quaker traditions and radical views on social reform. Effects of the Great Separation, westward migration, and an aversion to evangelism contributed to nineteenth-century membership attrition; but Hicksite (now Genéral Conference) Friends gained dedicated adherents after 1900, especially in urban and university communities.

In 1827-1828 most Quakers chose the Orthodox side, which enjoyed British support. Two further schisms before 1860 did further damage, however. First, the majority temporarily expelled antislavery zealots in Ohio and Indiana, including Levi Coffin. A larger split resulted in 1845-1854 when conservatives, who controlled the Orthodox Ohio and Philadelphia Yearly Meetings, denounced the evangelicalism of Joseph John Gurney. Nationally, nevertheless, "Gurneyite" Friends predominated. Conservatives continued to stress sectarian distinctives, including plainness, Inner Light mysticism, and rigid discipline, while holding orthodox views of scripture and the atonement. Membership losses accompanied this traditionalism.

From the 1820s till 1846, Gurney, prominent English banker and Quaker minister, had effectively spread evangelical views both in Britain and America. Though loyal to such traditions as plainness and worship arising from silence, he stressed what he believed Friends shared with other Christians, identifying the Inner Light as the Holy Spirit. He expounded on the atonement and promoted Bible study and evangelism. Furthermore, his warm spirituality, moderate antislavery views, and worldly success especially appealed to members who sought a more active faith and prosperity in commerce or western land.

Indiana Quakers led in endorsing Gurney's evangelicalism before 1860. Presiding clerk Elijah Coffin, a banker, cautiously encouraged Sunday schools in the 1830s, but opposed radical antislavery in the 1840s. After 1850 he promoted evangelism through tract and Bible distribution. In 1858, Charles F. Coffin, his son and successor, initiated home devotional gatherings, inspired by reports of contemporary ecumenical lay-led revivals. Then followed a massive testimony service during the Indiana Yearly Meeting in 1860, which further weakened traditionalism and led to widespread revivals among Gurneyite Friends by 1867. Revivalism brought many practices of other denominations, notably singing and paid pastors, into most of this largest branch of Quakerism. Thus, while Hicksite (liberal-traditional) and Conservative Friends maintained unique sectarian identities and suffered membership losses, evangelical Quakers (now Evanglical Friends Alliance and most of the Friends United Meeting) grew in numbers and enthusiasm while declining in distinctiveness.

Quaker philanthropy survived the era of schisms, despite some intramural criticism of reformers. Gurneyites emphasized both social concerns and evangelism, with priorities shifting toward the latter and foreign missions after the 1870s. Following 1861 most Friends focused on assistance to freed blacks, temperance reform, and paternalistic programs for American Indians.

Slave Religion

JOHN B. BOLES

The first Africans arrived in Virginia in 1619, but their status was uncertain. Clearly in the beginning not all blacks were slaves for life, and some were freed after a period of servitude. Others were freed because they could prove Christian baptism (either in the West Indies or Europe) before coming to Virginia. As long as his Christianity could jeopardize a black's slave status, slaveowners were reluctant to allow missionary activity among their bondsmen. In 1667 the Virginia assembly made clear by law "that the conferring of baptism doth not alter the condition of the person as to his bondage or freedom. . . ." Subsequently occasional slaves were converted, but the feebleness of the religious establishment and the growing prejudice toward Africans meant that slave Christianity in terms of numbers was inconsequential for the initial century after 1619.

The slave population began to reach sizable proportions in the first third of the eighteenth century, augmented by substantial African imports but increasing primarily because of a high birth rate. By about 1720 the number of slaves being born in the mainland colonies outnumbered those imported. These American-born, or creole, slaves began slowly, unconsciously, almost imperceptibly creating a creolized culture, part African but predominantly American. Unlike in the West Indies or Brazil, the slaves in the mainland colonies were hugely outnumbered by the whites, scattered in small groups across the rural landscape, and increasingly American-born. A constantly reinvigorated African cultural heritage was largely absent in the mainland colonies. The emerging Afro-American culture was more influenced by the surrounding white culture in the United States than anywhere else in the Americas.

At the very moment the demography of the mainland slave community was allowing the initial creation of an Afro-American culture, in the mid-eighteenth century, the foundations of evangelical Protestantism were being established in the South. By the 1750s Samuel Davies had hundreds of slave worshippers in his Virginia churches, and the burgeoning Baptist and later Methodist movements welcomed converts of any color or status in life. Still most planters were skeptical of the effect of preaching to their slaves, but evangelical ministers assured the owners that devout Christian slaves would be more honest, more obedient, simply better slaves. The ministers, especially the Methodists and Baptists before 1800, were often foes of slavery, but when they realized that such a stance would close off opportunities to preach among the blacks, they convinced themselves that their duty to spread the gospel required them to moderate their abolitionist sentiments. As the Methodist bishop Francis Asbury wrote in his diary in 1809, "What is the personal liberty of the African which he may abuse, to the salvation of his soul; how may it be compared?"

Afro-American Christianity began to develop then by the mid-eighteenth century as the creolized slaves adapted the surrounding evangelical culture to the remnants of their African culture. Little if no specifically African rituals persisted outside limited regions of high black concentration like the sea islands of

A *post-Civil War camp meeting among freed slaves in the South* BILLY GRAHAM CENTER

South Carolina and Georgia. The heritage from West African traditional religions of one omnipotent god and intermediary ancestral gods, however, did bear a transferable resemblance to the evangelicals' Jehovah and Jesus. Moreover, the evangelicals' emphasis on religion as the center of life and their emotional commitment to their faith struck responsive chords of memory within many Africans. When ministers presented Christianity as a meaning for life and a reward after death, many slaves became devout Christians, particularly after the Great Revival of 1800-1805 via camp meetings spread an emotional, conversion-oriented evangelical Protestantism across the South with slaves welcome converts. Before the Great Revival the South had been a region with a weak Episcopal church, much indifference, and a smattering of deism. The Great Revival was a watershed, and with surging church growth and hundreds of men feeling called to the ministry, a trinity of evangelical churches — the Baptists, Methodists, and Presbyterians — came to dominate the region, with the Baptists gaining the numerical majority and the Presbyterians garnering most prestige and influence. All three welcomed black worshippers, especially the Baptists and Methodists. By the 1820s thousands of slaves and free blacks swelled the membership rolls of the so-called white churches. In Baptist churches even in the Deep South blacks often constituted more than one-third of the membership, and occasionally more than one-half. Blacks sat in the same buildings (usually in reserved pews at the rear or in a balcony), heard the same sermons, took communion with the whites, were buried in the same cemeteries, and shared in a religious culture remarkably biracial. In Baptist churches, for example, blacks and whites alike were called brother and sister, letters of dismissal and transferal were equally sought for blacks and whites, and in church disciplinary sessions blacks testified against whites and vice versa. Both races were held accountable to the same moral code. In church the races met each other more equally than anywhere else in southern life. On many occasions whites heard black preachers, and attended integrated Sunday schools.

In a number of instances when congregational growth necessitated a new church, the blacks were given the old structure and were organized as an adjunct to the parent white church (because slaves could not legally own property). Such adjunct black churches elected their own deacons, chose their minister, and shaped their own religious life with a minimum of white supervision. In southern cities there were numerous independent black churches, often dominated by free blacks and often the largest church in the city. Whether in integrated churches, adjunct churches, or independent ones, blacks not only found a comforting faith but gained experience in organization, leadership, and self-expression. They participated willingly in church discipline, grasping a chance to take responsibility for their moral life. Such participation broadened the psychological living space of bondsmen, giving a sense of purpose and self-worth and providing avenues for personal and spiritual growth.

Especially after the 1840s, when the dominant three churches had effectively broken institutional ties with the northern churches, no longer could planters associate missionary activities with abolitionism. Moreover, southern denominational leaders wanted to step up their efforts toward converting the slaves in order to refute a prevalent northern charge that slaves were kept in a state of heathenism. Many also had a sincere commitment to mission work, and the last two decades of the antebellum period saw the development of a vigorous missionary program directed toward the slaves. Thousands of new slave converts were made, and ministers like the Rev. C. C. Jones wrote handbooks for converting slaves and prepared special slave catechisms. On the eve of the Civil War many southern church-leaders took real pride in their mission to the slaves, considering them a vital part of southern Christendom.

Black religious experience was not exhausted by affiliation with formal churches. Many slaves were dissatisfied with that portion of the white ministers' sermons directed specifically at them. While in the whole sermon slaves heard the full gospel, in that section addressed to them they heard a paternalistic message of control: slaves, obey your master. Often bondsmen hungered for more self-expression, more spiritual growth. Seizing hidden hours at night or on Sunday afternoons, and secreted in isolated "brush arbors" in the woods, they created a separate slave religion. This "invisible institution" — unknown to most whites — allowed free vent to emotion, African-style clapping and movement, and spirited hymn-singing that resulted in the spirituals. The belief system of this underground religion was mostly orthodox Christian, expressed — especially in the spirituals — in a fashion more African-like than the white churches permitted. Nevertheless, black religion in the Old South was far less African than was slave religion in the West Indies and Brazil, where constant and sizable infusions of African imports kept Old World memories fresh, and where the numbers of supervising whites were so few as to have little cultural impress.

Religion meant different things to different bondsmen. Some interpreted the gospel as a radical call for rebellion, and most slave insurrections from Gabriel's in 1800 to Nat Turner's in 1831 had religious overtones. For some slaves spirituals were a code language of rebellion and calls to escape, but for most slaves religion offered a different kind of solace, spiritual not earthly. Certain biblical

A plantation preacher exhorts the slaves.

themes were particularly prominent in slave Christianity, especially the concept of a chosen people who after bondage were redeemed, and the idea of Jesus, the suffering servant, who was a personal friend, helpmate, and savior. In their self-identification with the epic of the Hebrew people the slaves discovered self-respect and a feeling of moral superiority. Here was the sustenance that enabled the black personality to prevail despite two centuries of slavery. Life was to be accepted, not rebelled against in self-destructive rage. Forgiveness through Christ meant being able to accept oneself while outwardly acquiescing to the institution of slavery. Forgiveness and a sense of moral worth provided the strength of character to endure slavery without being enslaved psychologically. Here was a type of submission that because of its religious nature paradoxically made the slave the spiritual victor over his master. Here was a profound spiritual rebellion that, while it subdued hate and feelings of personal worthlessness, spared the rebel from the almost certain death physical insurrection would bring. Through their Christian faith many bondsmen found the inner strength to survive chattel slavery and keep their personalities remarkably intact. Their belief held them together as a people, gave joy and hope to a world filled with sorrow and sadness, and offered a subtle and devastating critique of slavery without requiring genocidal rebellion. In part through their religion, black people prevailed in the midst of an institution that otherwise might have destroyed them.

Richard Allen

WESLEY A. ROBERTS

Richard Allen, the first bishop of the African Methodist Episcopal church, was born a slave in Philadelphia, February 14, 1760. Eight years later his parents and their four children were sold to Mr. Stokeley, near Dover, Delaware.

At about the age of seventeen Richard and his brother came under the preaching of a Methodist circuit rider and were converted. Their changed lives had a powerful effect on their master, who also became a convert. Convinced that Christianity and slavery were incompatible, Stokeley gave his young slaves the opportunity to purchase their freedom. Richard for the next five years did odd jobs until he earned enough money to purchase his freedom in 1783. During this time he also became an itinerant preacher and traveled the circuit with some of the most popular Methodist preachers of the day.

In response to a preaching invitation by the Methodist elder in Philadelphia, Richard Allen returned to the city of his birth in February 1786, intending to spend no more than two weeks, but ended up staying permanently. He became a member of St. George's Methodist Episcopal Church where he taught classes for adults and conducted prayer meetings. Seeing that the majority of free blacks attended no church, Allen conceived the idea of creating a separate African Methodist church to reach them. His idea received very little support, but as an alternative he and a few friends organized the Free African Society, a nonsectarian benevolent association, in 1787.

With an increase in the number of black worshippers at St. George's Church, a pattern of segregation in seating developed. This convinced Allen that a separate church for blacks was now a necessity. One Sunday morning, in protest of the humiliating treatment of black worshippers, Richard Allen, Absolom Jones, and a group of blacks walked out of St. George's Church resolving never to return.

On July 29, 1794, Bethel, the first Methodist church for blacks, was dedicated by Bishop Francis Asbury. In 1799 he ordained Richard Allen a Deacon, and Allen assumed the role of pastor of Bethel Church.

Following nearly twenty years of conflict with the white Methodist elders over jurisdiction, Allen and two other black Methodist preachers invited other black Methodist churches to meet in Philadelphia on April 9, 1816. At the meeting the delegates voted to organize the African Methodist Episcopal church. Richard Allen was elected and consecrated as the Church's founding bishop and the first black bishop in America. He continued to serve as pastor of Bethel A.M.E. Church while overseeing the expansion of the new denomination.

Richard Allen (1760–1831)   BILLY GRAHAM CENTER

Richard Allen was a man of many interests. In addition to his unsalaried pastoral duties, he was a successful businessman. He operated a boot and shoe store, a hauling business, and served as a labor contractor for black chimney sweeps. He was also a respected member of the Philadelphia community and was involved in every cause affecting the welfare of the city. Completely dedicated to the betterment of his people, Allen preached against the vices of drunkenness and dishonesty and encouraged moral reform, education, and self-help. He sponsored the First National Negro Convention which met in Philadelphia under his presidency in 1830. This was the first national meeting of free blacks in America designated to further the welfare of blacks. Seeing clearly the relationship between spiritual liberation and physical liberation, he was not only a strong critic of slavery but worked untiringly for the emancipation of the slaves. His home in Philadelphia was a refuge for fugitive slaves.

The establishment of the African Methodist Episcopal church under Bishop Allen's leadership had a profound influence on the development of black self-reliance, black self-respect, and black dignity. When he died on March 26, 1831, he left a flourishing church and a denomination that had increased more than sevenfold since its inception.

A free blacks' prayer meeting in the pre-Civil War North.   BILLY GRAHAM CENTER

PRAYER MEETING

Theology and Religious Belief

Historian Henry Steele Commager once noted that during the nineteenth century religion in America prospered while theology went slowly bankrupt. While this judgment might seem unduly severe, there is less question about Kenneth Scott Latourette's admission that "no theologian or theology of the first rank issued from the nineteenth-century Christianity of the United States." Ralph Waldo Emerson, it is true, has been lauded as an authentic genius. Yet Emerson's pilgrimage passed well beyond the pale, not only of Christian orthodoxy, but of any recognizable expression of Christianity. More typical of American theologians was Nathaniel William Taylor, the influential architect of the "New Haven Theology" about whom Sydney E. Ahlstrom concludes: "In the revivalistic churches of antebellum America, Taylorism proved itself eminently satisfactory, even though it ignored almost a century's development in Western philosophy and scholarship as well as many profoundly new currents of thought and feeling."

Why did theology in America lose its cutting edge? First, the advent of a democratic culture undercut the authority of classically trained elites. Popular leaders of the masses such as Andrew Jackson (whom the Englishman Lord Bryce once called an intellectual pigmy) replaced leaders such as Adams, Jefferson, and Madison, all political theorists of the first order. That this democratization of leadership advanced so easily within the church raises a second issue. Most nineteenth-century Protestants were buoyantly optimistic about the direction American culture had assumed and were quick to embrace the ideals of equality and freedom of thought. But having made peace with a pragmatic age, they could not expect the quality of theology to remain untouched. As a matter of fact, few

thought through the theological implications of democracy in the rush to applaud a shift from theoretical to applied divinity.

Third, there was a widespread reaction against existing theological ground rules. Some, like the Disciples of Christ, were convinced that a new form of biblical Christianity could replace one that had become encrusted with human theological traditions.

A pair of Currier and Ives prints (below and p. 223) illustrate the conventional judgment that an orthodox Christianity is vital to the personal- and social-wellbeing of the nation. BILLY GRAHAM CENTER

DANIEL'S VISIONS,

"NOTED IN THE SCRIPTURES OF TRUTH," "FOR OUR LEARNING."

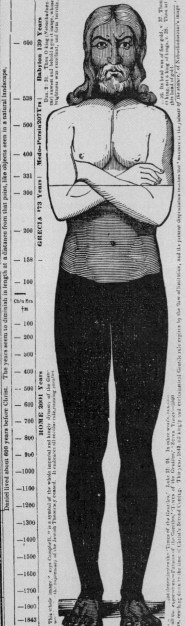

This whole image," says Campbell, "is a symbol of the whole imperial and kingly dynasty of the Gentile world, determinate the "Times of the Gentiles," Luke 21. 24. In other words, the supremacy of the Gentile world, reaching down to the time of Christ's Second Coming. The year 1843, all kingly and ecclesiastical Gentile rule expires by the law of limitation, and the present dispensation reaches the "measure in the places of the statue, of Nebuchadnezzar's image."

Daniel lived about 600 years before Christ. The years seem to diminish in length at a distance from that point, like objects seen in a natural landscape.

— 600	Babylon 139 Years
— 538	Medo-Persia 207 Yrs
— 500	
— 400	GRECIA 173 Years
— 331	
— 300	
— 200	
— 158	
— 100	
Ch'n Era †æ	ROME 2001 Years
— 100	
— 200	
— 300	
— 400	
— 500	
— 600	
— 700	
— 800	
— 900	
—1000	
—1100	
—1200	
—1300	
—1400	
—1500	
—1600	
—1700	
—1800	
—1843	

Dan. 2: 31. Thou O king (Nebuchadnezzar) whose image, whose brightness was excellent, and form terrible.

v. 32. Its head was of fine gold. v 37. Thou O king, art a king v. 38. Thou art this head of gold.

BABYLONIAN EMPIRE, B. C. 677. Dan. 7: 4.

In its glory, it was like a lion, soaring with wings as the eagle. But in Belshazzar's time, it had lost its wings and its lion-hear, becoming feeble and faint.

MEDO-PERSIA, B. C. 538. Dan. 7: 5.

The two arms meeting in one breast,—the bear raising up one side, or dominion,—and the ram with two horns, are all appropriate emblems of Med-Persia. "The Syrian bear, in strength and ferocity scarcely yields to the lion," says Paxton. "Ancient historians stigmatize the Medes and Persians as the greatest robbers and spoilers that ever oppressed the nations." The bear represents the nature of the monarchy, but the ram with two horns was its well-known national emblem.

GRECIA, B. C. 331. Dan. 7: 6.

This was founded by Alexander. It was like the leopard, active, crafty and cruel. The lion had 2 wings, but the leopard had 4,—Grecia being more rapid in its conquests than Babylon. But the goat was the known emblem of Greece. It came against the ram with incredible swiftness, making up in speed what it lacked in size. Alexander conquered Persia with a very small army.

ROMAN EMPIRE, B. C. 158. Dan. 7: 7.

"Behold, a fourth beast, dreadful and terrible, and strong exceedingly, which was diverse from all the others, exceeding dreadful, whose teeth were of IRON, and his nails of brass; it devoured, and brake in pieces, and STAMPED the residue with the feet of it. It had ten horns."

THE TEN HORNS.

1	A.D 356	Huns
2	" 377	Ostrogoths
3	" 378	Visigoths
4	" 407	Franks
5	" 407	Vandals
6	" 407	Sueves
7	" 407	Burg'nd'ns
8	" 476	Saxons
9	" 476	Heruli
10	" 483	Lombards

"I considered the horns, and behold there came up among them another little horn, before whom there were three of the first horns plucked up by the roots;—that horn had eyes, and a mouth that spake very great things, whose look was more stout [or who was more mighty, as Luther's German Bible reads] than his fellows." Dan. 7: 8.

Papacy.

PAPACY, the horn that had eyes (as an overseer) arose among the 10, and 3 fell before it. The Heruli in Italy were conquered in 493, the Vandals in 534, & the Ostrogoths were driven from Rome in March, 538.

"I beheld, even till the beast was slain, and his body destroyed, and given to the burning flame."

VISION OF THE RAM AND HE GOAT. Dan. 8.

Daniel saw the vision of the ram, he-goat, and exceeding great horn, two years after he saw the representations of the four beasts. According to Lightfoot, Townsend, and other eminent chronologers, it was *after* the fall of Babylon; hence he was "in Shushan," the capital of Persia. Babylon being then a subject of history, had no place in this prophecy.

"Behold, a ram which had two horns, and the two horns were high, but the higher came up last." The ram which came from the east, with its two horns, was Media and Persia; and the rough goat which darted upon him from the west, was Grecia—so said the angel. The Grecian empire was at first united, as is represented by the single horn of the goat. It was afterwards divided into four parts, represented by the four horns, of which the angel said—"Four KINGDOMS shall stand up out of the nation" Here we are taught, in the plainest manner, that a horn in this vision means a kingdom.

MEDO-PERSIA.

GRECIA.

Enlarged View of the Four Horns.

After the death of Alexander, Grecia was divided into four parts, toward the four WINDS of heaven. v. 8. And out of one of them, came forth a little horn, which waxed EXCEEDING great, (v. 9.) even to the host of heaven. v.10.

In chapter 2, Rome is represented by the feet and legs of the image. In chapter 7, it is represented by the fourth Beast having ten horns. But in the 8th chapter it is symbolized by an EXCEEDING great horn.

That this exceeding great horn represents Rome, is evident from the following and many other reasons.

1. It rises "In the latter part of their kingdom," that is, of the four kingdoms. So did Rome, as far as its place in the prophecy is concerned. Its connection with the Jews commenced 158 years before Christ.

2. It was "of fierce countenance." So was Rome.—See Deut. 28: 49, 50.

3. It was "little" at first. So was Rome.

4. It waxed "exceeding great," towards the east and towards the south." So did Rome.

"From this horn increasing towards the *south* and *east*, particularly Sir Isaac Newton sagaciously infers, that it arose in the northwest corner of the Goat's dominion, i. e. in Italy,—which points directly to the Romans."

4. It cast down some of the host and of the stars to the ground. So did Rome;—persecuting Christians, Apostles and ministers of Jesus, as no other power ever did.

6. "He magnified himself even to the Prince of the host." So did Rome, when the Pope became the "head of all the churches." But the margin reads more properly, "He magnified himself AGAINST the PRINCE of the host," and in the interpretation the angel says: "He shall stand up against the PRINCE of princes." *Thus did Rome,* when both Herod and Pontius Pilate conspired against the holy Jesus.

7. "He shall destroy wonderfully, and shall destroy the mighty and holy people." Thus did Rome.

The Disciples, accordingly, refused to use theological abstractions not found in scripture, such as the Trinity, foreordination, and original sin. "We are not personally acquainted with the writings of John Calvin," wrote two associates of Barton W. Stone, "nor are we certain how nearly we agree with his views of divine truth; neither do we care." Others found the study of divinity, as traditionally practiced, simply incapable of addressing the needs of the largely unchurched populations of the West. "I do not wish to undervalue education," affirmed the Methodist Peter Cartwright, "but ... I have seen so many of these educated preachers who forcibly reminded me of lettuce growing under the shade of a peach tree, or like a gosling that had got the straddles by wading in the dew." Charles G. Finney, similarly, refused the offer of a Princeton education because he found their graduates "wrongly educated."

The fact that theology in America became less intellectual certainly does not imply that it was any less abundant. On the contrary, as theology lost its elitist image it became the hobby of any person with Bible in hand. The central appeal of the Adventist William Miller, for instance, was not an emotional harangue that the Second Coming in 1843 would catch people unawares; rather, it was an appeal that rational people should resist deferring to clergymen and should learn to study biblical prophecies on their own. Miller attacked all denominations for not acknowledging "the right of the people to *interpret* the Bible for themselves." The "divinity" taught in our school, he protested,

is always founded on some sectarian creed. It may do to take a blank mind and impress it with this kind, but it will always end in bigotry. A free mind will never be satisfied with the views of others. Were I a teacher of youth in divinity, I would first learn their capacity, and mind. If these were good, I would make them study bible for themselves, and send them out free to do the world good. But if they had no mind I would stamp them with another's mind, write bigot on their forehead, and send them out as slaves.

In this climate, it is no wonder that American clergymen were given to restructuring theology for popular consumption.

The Evangelical Mainstream

Evangelical theology, Calvinist and Wesleyan, moved in a similar direction in antebellum America. The two issues that commanded the greatest attention were perennial ones: the process by which salvation is achieved (justification) and the means by which the Christian life is lived (sanctification). It was the Presbyterians and Congregationalists, interestingly enough, who did most of the theological shifting during this era. These modifications led many Calvinists to a point not far removed from where Wesleyans had been for a century.

Nathaniel William Taylor (1786-1858) devoted most of his theological labors to wrestling with practical dimensions of the doctrine of justification. How could one reconcile the tenets of Calvinism with effective evangelistic methods? An effective revival preacher himself, Taylor became professor of didactic theology at the newly formed Yale Divinity

BILLY GRAHAM CENTER

Nathaniel W. Taylor (1786–1858)
BILLY GRAHAM CENTER

School in 1822. Growing out of his more than three decades at Yale, his "New Haven Theology" became the most serious intellectual grounding for moderate Presbyterians—the "New School." Taylor was most concerned about the issues of guilt and human freedom. On the former issue, he came to relax the stern Calvinist insistence on original sin, teaching that "Sin is the sinning" and hence original only in the sense that it has come to contaminate all by acts of individual choice. Instead of being totally depraved, people stood as free moral agents. "There can be no sin in choosing evil," he argued, "unless there be power to choose good." Traditional Calvinism, in his view, had paralyzed revival preaching and seemed absurd to the common person. This last issue weighed heavily upon Taylor, who at one point speculated on the "sneer of contempt" that average persons must have felt toward, for instance, the imputation of Adam's sin. Theologies that would not square with common sense did not sit well with Nathaniel William Taylor.

The evangelist Charles G. Finney had similar convictions about truth standing be-

fore the bar of public opinion; he also liked Taylor's emphasis upon the reality of free choice and of evil as voluntary acts. Where he went beyond Taylor was in declaring that people were free to attain a new level of sanctification. Apart from Methodist influence apparently, he reached the conclusion "that an altogether higher and more stable form of Christian life was attainable and was the privilege of all Christians." Later, Finney did read John Wesley's *Plain Account of Christian Perfection*, which confirmed his own views about "entire sanctification." This teaching became a trademark of Oberlin College, where Finney came to teach. At Oberlin a vocabulary of the Christian life that still prevails came into existence with references to "holiness," "Christian perfection," and "the baptism of the Holy Spirit." The first president of Oberlin, Presbyterian Asa Mahan, did much for this theology of the Christian life. Not all New School Presbyterians endorsed these views of sanctification, by any means; but what happened at Oberlin does point up the powerful quest for perfection that gripped many Protestants at midcentury.

The Yale Divinity School, founded in 1822 in Taylor's era, as it appears today
COURTESY EDWIN S. GAUSTAD

The Founding of Church Colleges, 1820-1860

THOMAS A. ASKEW

The peopling of the Transappalachian West created a direct challenge to the energies and commitment of American Protestantism in the decades separating the close of hostilities with England in 1815 and the opening of the War between the States in 1861. Every denomination entered the fray to save the frontier from ignorance, barbarism, and irreligion. Not only were missionaries dispatched to spread the gospel, but approximately 150 colleges were founded to provide an educated ministry and to propagate intellectual culture in those remote regions. It can accurately be asserted that these small religious liberal arts colleges, along with their eastern forebears, constituted the backbone of American higher education throughout most of the nineteenth century.

Several characteristics of these scattered institutions fitted them to meet the needs of an expanding society marked by social and geographic mobility. Building on the precedent of Harvard in the 1630s, the great majority were organized as private nonprofit corporations. Legally defined as a corporation with a state-granted charter and a board of directors (or trustees), the schools were given wide freedom of action. Considerable experimentation took place, including various work-study plans and the admission of female students. Usually a preparatory academy was attached. Some campuses became training centers for evangelical social reform efforts, especially for the northern abolitionist movement.

The corporate structure ensured close ties between the college and the sponsoring constituency, which often supplied both money and students. In this regard, the colleges

Daguerrotype of the Emerson School, a "female academy"
THE METROPOLITAN MUSEUM OF ART, GIFT OF I. N. PHELPS STOKES, EDWARD S. HAWES, ALICE MARY HAWES, MARION AUGUSTA HAWES, 1937

were not primarily controlled by independent scholar-faculties, as were contemporary European universities, but by the denominational and geographic communities from which they sprung. Thus, the religious purposes of the institutions were largely preserved until overwhelmed by the secularizing trends of the twentieth century.

The leadership capacity of the president frequently determined the effectiveness and prosperity of his college. Appointed by the trustees, and typically a clergyman, he had to obtain funds, disciple students, befriend parents, recruit faculty, woo the public, and administer the entire enterprise; often the college became an extension of his personality. While somewhat diminished in power in the twentieth century, the college presidency continues to be pivotal in American higher education.

The proliferation of colleges accommodated the aspirations of a booster

REGULATIONS

OF THE

THE Principal expects of the young Ladies attending his Seminary,

1. That they will attend at the Academy, regularly and punctually, at the hours appointed by the Principal.

2.—That all noise and disorder in the house, before the Principal arrives, and after the exercises are closed, will be carefully avoided.

3.—That, during the hours of instruction, they will give constant and diligent attention to the exercises prescribed, avoiding every thing which would be an interruption to the teacher or pupils.

4.—That, during the recitations, all the members of a class will close their books, except the nature of the recitation requires their being open.

5.—That the young Ladies will constantly attend public worship on the Sabbath.

6.—That they will always board in those families, which have the approbation of the Principal.

7.—That they will not attend balls, assemblies, or other parties for the indulgence of frivolous mirth.

8.—That the social visits of the young Ladies, among the families of the village, will be arranged by the Principal, whenever invitations are extended.

9.—That they will avoid walking or riding, with persons of the other sex, at unseasonable hours.

10.—That they will not leave town, without permission from the Principal.

11.—That they will be subject in all respects to the superintendence and direction of the Principal, while belonging to his school.

TUITION, for each term. Arithmetic, Grammar, or Geography, $3,50.—— Rhetoric, History, or Latin, $4,50.——Geometry, Natural Philosophy, Chemistry, Algebra, Euclid, Logic, Intellectual Philosophy, or Moral Philosophy, $5.00.——French, Music, and Painting will probably be taught the ensuing spring.

Sept. 1825.

E. AND G. MERRIAM, PRINTERS, BROOKFIELD.

Regulations of the "female seminary" at Brookfield, Massachusetts, 1825   AMERICAN ANTIQUARIAN SOCIETY

age. Practically every community planted in the wilderness hoped to launch a college. At the same time, the denominational leaders in each state rallied their congregations to found an institution for training preachers and teaching denominational youth. While inordinate duplication of effort and lack of quality control allowed many weak schools to subsist, the overall result was accessibility to a bachelor's degree for thousands of students who otherwise would have been denied the opportunity. In short, the decentralized, localized character of American higher learning before 1860 aided democratization by fostering learning in remote locations and bringing collegiate instruction to youth from every social quarter.

The curriculum of these "old time colleges" provided a unifying force to American culture in general and higher education in particular. For the common course of study distilled the truths and values deemed worthy of preservation over the generations. Following the pattern of the English university tradition and the older eastern colleges, the curriculum sought to blend the moral absolutes of biblical theism with the heritage of

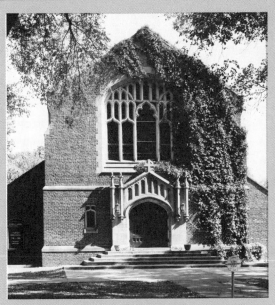

The chapel of Grinnell College, founded in Iowa in 1847 by Congregationalist Josiah Bushnell Grinnell, to whom Horace Greeley addressed his famous "Go west, young man"
GRINNELL COLLEGE INFORMATION SERVICE

Old Middle College (1847) of Beloit College. Founded by Yale alumni on the Wisconsin frontier in 1847, Beloit was one of the few independent, nonsectarian old-style colleges.
COURTESY EDWIN S. GAUSTAD

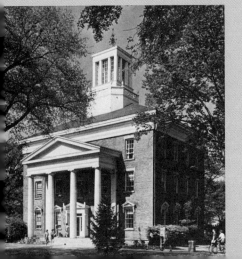

Western learning, especially emphasizing the classical languages of Greece and Rome. Mathematics and limited science were also included, as was a capstone, integrating course called "Moral philosophy," which purposed to explicate a Christian American world view.

Such a curriculum suited the triple objectives of imparting knowledge, training young minds, and preparing responsible leaders for a burgeoning society. The last decades of the nineteenth century would witness the rise of the new research-oriented, diversified, and secularizing forces of the university, which would overshadow the unitary Christian learning of the churchly colleges. Nevertheless, the old-style colleges were founded as avowedly Christian institutions and nurtured the ideal of mental and moral education for the whole person. As such, they contributed stability to a society in flux and perpetuated a noble tradition.

William Ellery Channing
Defines the Essence of Christianity

I believe that Christianity has ONE GREAT PRINCIPLE, which is *central*, around which all its truths gather, and which constitutes it the Glorious Gospel of the Blessed God. I believe that no truth is so worthy of acceptance and so quickening as this. In proportion as we penetrate into it, and are penetrated by it, we comprehend our religion, and attain to a living faith. This great principle can be briefly expressed. It is the doctrine, that "God purposes, in His unbounded fatherly love, to PERFECT THE HUMAN SOUL, to purify it from all sin, to create it after His own image, to fill it with His own spirit, to unfold it for ever; to raise it to life and immortality in heaven: — that is, to communicate to it from Himself a life of celestial power, virtue and joy." The elevation of men above the imperfections, temptations, sins, sufferings, of the present state, to a diviner being, — that is the great purpose of God, revealed and accomplished by Jesus Christ; this it is that constitutes the religion of Jesus Christ — glad tidings to all people: for it is a religion suited to fulfil the wants of every human being.

In the New Testament I learn that God regards the human soul with unutterable interest and love; that in an important sense it bears the impress of His own infinity, its powers being germs, which may expand without limit or end; that He loves it, even when fallen, and desires its restoration; that He has sent His Son to redeem and cleanse it from all iniquity; that He forever seeks to communicate to it a divine virtue which shall spring up, by perennial bloom and fruitfulness, into everlasting life. In the New Testament I learn that what God wills is our PERFECTION, by which I understand the freest exercise and perpetual development of our highest powers — strength and brightness of intellect, unconquerable energy of moral principle, pure and fervent desire for truth, unbounded love of goodness and greatness, benevolence free from every selfish taint, the perpetual consciousness of God and of His immediate presence, co-operation and friendship with all enlightened and disinterested spirits, and radiant glory of benign will and beneficent influence, of which we have an emblem — a faint emblem only — in the sun that illuminates and warms so many worlds. Christianity reveals to me this moral perfection of man, as the great purpose of God.

The Perfect Life, 1873

Challenges to Revivalism

Unitarianism was the full flowering of a tradition of liberal theology in New England that dated back at least to the 1740s. A firm opposition to revivalism and the whole pietist emphasis had always been settled in the convictions of forerunners of this movement such as Jonathan Mayhew (1720-1766) and Charles Chauncy (1705-1787). They placed high priority upon reason, natural theology, human ability, and Enlightenment ideas of progress. The influential Chauncy made the first real break with orthodoxy when he published his belief in universalism in the 1780s. By 1805, when this liberal party assumed clear control of Harvard, it had nudged ever closer to views of Christ and the atonement that English Unitarians had espoused for a generation. William Ellery Channing (1780-1842), for almost forty years the minister of Boston's Federal Street Church, became the clear patriarch of the movement; it was his sermon "Unitarian Christianity" in

1819 that became the manifesto of the denomination that would emerge in the 1820s, when Unitarians and those more orthodox in belief struggled for control of congregations throughout eastern Massachusetts. Although it would be unfair to take seriously the old quip that Unitarian beliefs were limited to "the Fatherhood of God, the brotherhood of man, and the neighborhood of Boston," the movement did have only limited appeal and one that seemed to decline with time. Yet its humanitarian efforts were sizable, as was its role in nourishing the intellectual life of antebellum New England. One finds a substantial legacy to American culture in the person of Channing himself; Ralph Waldo Emerson, William Cullen Bryant, and Henry Wadsworth Longfellow all expressed their indebtedness to him.

While the Unitarians largely ignored revivalism, the Presbyterian theologians at Princeton spared no ink in warning of its fatal consequences. In 1833 Samuel Miller, professor at Princeton Seminary, gave this typical indictment of both revivalism and the theologies which supported it:

> When this exciting system of calling to "anxious seats,"—calling out into the aisles to be "prayed for," &c, is connected, as, to my certain knowledge, it often has been,

with erroneous doctrines:—for example, with the declaration that nothing is *easier*, than conversion:—that the power of the Holy Spirit is not necessary to enable impenitent sinners to repent and believe;—that if they only resolve to be for God—resolve to be Christians—*that* itself is regeneration—the work is already done:—I say, where the system of "anxious seats," &c, is connected with such doctrinal statements as these, it appears to be adapted to destroy souls wholesale!

Charles Hodge (1797-1878), Princeton's leading theologian, taught some three thousand students in nearly fifty years at the seminary. In theological matters, Hodge was resolutely opposed to the spirit of his own age and drew upon Reformed classics such as the Westminster Confession of Faith (1643-1646) and the works of François Turretin (1623-1687) to shore up orthodox Calvinism. In this conservative endeavor, the Princeton theologians appealed, with impressive erudition, to the principles of unquestioned biblical authority and strict confessionalism. It was not intellectual rigor mortis but a keen sense of being out of step with his own times that occasioned Hodge's oft-quoted statement, "There has never been a new idea at Princeton."

The chapel of Princeton Theological Seminary in the 1830s; Charles Hodge's home is at the far right.
BILLY GRAHAM CENTER

Equally dismayed by American revivalism were Philip Schaff (1819-1893) and John W. Nevin (1803-1886), both professors at the Mercersburg (Pennsylvania) Seminary of the American German Reformed church. A Scotch-Irish Presbyterian trained at Princeton, Nevin came to Mercersburg in 1840. He was joined a year later by Schaff, who left a promising career at the University of Berlin to come to America. These two theologians wrought a theological perspective at odds with the evangelical mainstream on at least three issues. The "Mercersburg Theology," as it came to be known, above all was historical and called for a catholic evangelicalism that would partake of the full riches of Christian history—a case Schaff made explicit in *The Principle of Protestantism* and implicit in *Creeds of Christendom* and his seven-volume *History of the Christian Church*. Schaff and Nevin, secondly, called for a God-centered faith, focused more on the objective work of Christ and less on subjective experience. Nevin's sharp tract of 1843, *The Anxious Bench*, claimed that the techniques of revivalism actually diverted the penitent from placing full confidence for salvation in God alone. Finally, these men were real churchmen, taking seriously the church's sacramental life and its organic development. They inveighed against those who treated ecclesiastical bodies as if they were merely utilitarian agencies of the like-minded. And they attacked individualistic biblical interpretation as well as the separatism to which it often led. Despite the shrewd insights of the Mercersburg theology, it is little wonder that few Americans ever stopped long enough to examine its claims. An attempt to be both Catholic and Reformed found little support during a time that had become, theologically considered, the golden age of American Methodism.

The Pilgrimage of Ralph W. Emerson
WILLIAM E. GRADDY

Historian Sydney Ahlstrom calls Ralph Waldo Emerson (1803-1882), essayist, poet, sometime Unitarian minister, the first of America's "death of God" theologians. Emerson himself would have been appalled at the label. Many of his most vigorous writings challenge what he termed the "corpse-cold Unitarianism" of his day. "Men have come to speak of the revelation as somewhat long ago given and done," he said in disgust to Harvard's 1837 senior divinity class, "as if God were dead." Nevertheless, Ahlstrom's claim is valid in an important sense. For the God whose being and potency Emerson hymned, not just in the divinity school address but in all his mature writings, was an impersonal deity, one which, although forever active in nature and endlessly productive of order, goodness, beauty, and love, was itself beyond propositional description, and knowable only through an individual's intuitive responses to nature and human culture.

To arrive at such a position, Emerson had to move a considerable distance from the theistic tradition in which he was nurtured, both at home — Aunt Mary Moody Emerson, whom he acknowledged as a very influential guide, was an ardent Trinitarian — and at Harvard. Quite a dramatic public break with this tradition came in 1832, when Emerson resigned the pastorate of Boston's Second Church because he could no longer administer the Lord's Supper in good conscience. But private documents, particularly the voluminous journals Emerson kept for more than fifty-five years, record even more

Ralph Waldo Emerson (1803–1882)
LIBRARY OF CONGRESS

fundamental changes of thought and conviction. As late as 1825, according to biographer Ralph L. Rusk, Emerson responded quite defensively to reports about higher criticism from his elder brother William, who had gone to Germany for theological study. In two letters to Aunt Mary summarized by Rusk, Emerson observes that such criticism posed a radical threat to Christianity, and then resolves to defend that religion and its "august Founder" from such attacks. Yet by 1836, by which time Emerson was progressing rapidly in his study of the German language, he calmly testifies that he has "no curiosity respecting

historical Christianity; respecting persons and miracles." "I take the phenomenon as I find it," he continues, "careless whether it is a poem or a chronicle."

Simply to present Emerson as the foremost exponent of American Transcendentalism or as another nineteenth-century intellectual who exchanged a comparatively orthodox faith for a mildly pantheistic religion of nature would be to misrepresent him. Worse, it would leave totally out of account the perennially arresting freshness of his expression and the power of his thought. Two closely related sources of this power are Emerson's unceasingly moral and his radically holistic view of human experience. "Every animal function from the sponge up to Hercules shall ... echo the Ten Commandments," he wrote in his first important published essay, and he passionately resisted any attempt to separate beauty from utility in nature, or knowledge from character in man.

His idealism was sorely tried by personal sorrows (three of the persons he loved most dearly—a wife, a son, and a brother—died prematurely) and by the increasing materialism and skepticism of his era. Visiting West Point during the bleak days of the Civil War, he wrote, "I saw a civilization built on powder." And in his 1844 essay, "Experience," he admits that he finds it impossible to see "if one be caught in this trap of the so-called sciences, any escape for man from ... the chain of physical necessity." Perhaps both his greatest strength and his greatest weakness are revealed in Perry Miller's shrewd comment that Emerson was a Jonathan Edwards "in whom the concept of original sin has evaporated."

Hodge, Taylor, and Bushnell

DAVID F. WELLS

It was the misfortune of Charles Hodge (1797-1878), Nathaniel William Taylor (1786-1858), and Horace Bushnell (1802-1876) to be contemporaries for more than fifty years. In another age, each one might have been the dominant theological figure; as it was, they had to contend fiercely with each other for the church's mind, and in the process the church was wounded.

In 1801 Congregationalists and Presbyterians joined together. It was a marriage more of convenience than of convinction, brought about by the need to develop westward where both were numerically weak. The union, however, brought into proximity ecclesiastical and theological traditions that were at odds with each other, and these differences were articulated by Taylor, a Congregationalist, and Hodge, a Presbyterian, both of whom were appointed professors in 1822. Congregationalists tended to be "New School," holding ideas that were theologically fluid, and looked to Yale Divinity School for their ministers and to Taylor for leadership. Presbyterians were more often "Old School," holding tighter Calvinistic views, and thus were serviced by Princeton Seminary and revered Hodge. The controversy between Hodge and Taylor was really the controversy of these traditions, and it produced the undoing of the Congregational-Presbyterian union in 1837.

Taylor's controversial talents were first sharpened in the acrimonious debate which ensued when Henry Ware, a Unitarian, was appointed to the Hollis Chair of Theology at Harvard in 1805. Taylor attacked both the Unitarians and their Calvinistic opponents. He felt that the Calvinists were wrong in propounding original sin. We are culpable before God, he contended, not because we were ever "in" Adam, but because we choose to

sin. Sin is in the sinning. We sin inevitably but not necessarily, and that, said Taylor, was also Calvin's view.

Although Taylor also claimed to be articulating Jonathan Edwards' theology, he was, in fact, subverting it. Against Edwards, he claimed that sinful motives which produce a person's actions can be "suspended" and that regeneration occurs when a person thus negates his or her sinfulness. Later, especially in his *Lectures on the Moral Government of God* (1859), he argued that the cross was necessary to show that God still cared about justice. Jesus was punished to demonstrate this. He did not bear anyone's sins in particular nor was the wrath he suffered equivalent to that merited by the world.

Taylor seemed unaware of his departures from Calvinistic verities and boldly attacked Hodge for having evolved beyond genuine Calvinism! Hodge, of course, owed little to the American Calvinistic tradition, for his roots were in the European Protestant scholastics, especially François Turretin. His reputation as a theologian was already established at the time of this debate by numerous essays that appeared in the *Biblical Repertory*. This debate merely sharpened his views, which were ultimately developed into a full-orbed *Systematic Theology* (1872-1873). His sense of history was never very clear, but his rebuttal of Taylor was lucid and decisive. If we are not "in" Adam, Hodge argued, then we cannot be "in" Christ, for the way we relate to the one is paralleled in scripture by the way we relate to the other. God appointed Adam as the federal head of those whom he represented. The new humanity is not numerically equivalent, however, to the whole of fallen humanity and therefore Christ in his death vicariously suffered in the place only of those whom he represented, which were the elect.

Complicating this debate was the problem of Charles Finney and his revivalistic "New Measures." New Schoolers were sympathetic to the revival even as Old Schoolers were cool to it. Taylor defended Finney; Hodge criticized him. Hodge found the ecclesiastical disruptions revivalists caused dangerous and their Arminian or even Pelagian theology abhorrent; Taylor and his colleagues were outraged that Old Schoolers would attack the work of God. This breach greatly weakened the church and paved the way for the emergence of the third of these remarkable theologians, Horace Bushnell.

Bushnell was a law student at Yale when he was deeply affected by the revival and went on to study under Taylor at the Divinity School. In 1833 he was appointed pastor of the Congregational North Church in Hartford, where he remained until his retirement in 1859. But his disaffection first with revivalism and then with Taylor's theological modifications became increasingly clear. In his *God in Christ* (1848) and its sequel *Christ in Theology* (1851), he argued that religious language has only a tangential connection to the realities it is describing and therefore, it is clear, debates such as those between Hodge and Taylor were asking language to bear more freight than was possible. Bushnell then went on to argue in *Nature and the Supernatural* (1858) for a vague and almost mystical relationship of the orders of reality that was closer to pantheism than anything contemplated in traditional thought. In *The Vicarious Sacrifice* (1866) he took some of Taylor's arguments one step further. At the cross Jesus was not acting as representative or substitute but as example. All suffering is in its own way atoning. Thus did Bushnell provide a theodicy for the Civil War: American was atoning for its national sins.

Nineteenth-century society changed dramatically in the closing decades of the century, and it was in this period that the influence of Christian orthodoxy declined sharply. These two developments were not unrelated to each other; but a further reason for the disintegration of traditional Christian faith was the failure to come to terms with itself of which these disagreements were the painful symptoms.

The Immigrant Church

America has always been a nation of immigrants, a welter of different ethnic, religious, and social groups. Yet at its inception the United States had a more cohesive culture than it would ever know again. At the time of the first census in 1790, British Protestantism was the common heritage of more than eighty-five percent of white Americans. When these Americans spoke of their nation becoming the vanguard of civil and religious liberty for the world, what they had in mind was a set of values that had grown out of Anglo-American soil. What few envisioned was that, before a century of national life had concluded, the United States would confront large-scale diversity. The boundaries of religious liberty would have to be expanded to encompass those who were strangers to republican and Protestant traditions.

By the time of the Civil War, some five million immigrants had made their way to America, a number greater than the entire population in 1790. The three million who made America their new home in the single decade after 1845 had landed in a country of about twenty million; they represented, in proportion to total population, the largest influx the United States has ever known. The difficulties of such a massive flow of immigrants were compounded by the simple fact

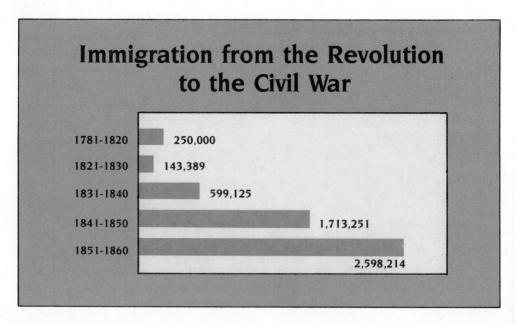

Immigration from the Revolution to the Civil War

1781-1820	250,000
1821-1830	143,389
1831-1840	599,125
1841-1850	1,713,251
1851-1860	2,598,214

Irish emigrants bound for America from Cahirciveen, County Kerry   LIBRARY OF CONGRESS

that the vast majority were Roman Catholic, almost four-fifths of them hailing from Ireland and Germany.

Cultural Conflicts

A virulent nativism was deeply entrenched in nineteenth-century America. It was seen, for example, in the blatant anti-Catholicism of Samuel F. B. Morse (1791-1872), the son of Jedediah Morse and inventor of the telegraph, who suggested in 1834 the formation of a political organization known as the "Anti-Popery Union"; in well-organized mobs of Protestants burning a Catholic convent in Charleston, Massachusetts in 1834, destroying two Roman Catholic churches in Philadelphia in 1844, and lynching several Irishmen indicted for crimes in San Francisco in 1856; and in a new political party, the "Know-Nothings," who, sworn to defend America from foreigners and Catholics,

showed sensational political strength in 1854 by sending seventy-five men to Congress and sweeping entire slates into state offices. What explains this kind of nativism in a land that took pride in its religious liberty and its role as a haven for the oppressed? Had some strange paranoia come to infect the body politic?

The simplest solution is to consider the vast cultural divide that separated native Protestants from immigrant Catholics. In several ways the latter were perceived as the exact antithesis of American ideals. Indeed, Roman Catholicism was viewed as the very symbol of Antichrist, that which the gospel would crush as it advanced. In the meantime, however, Roman Catholicism had become the largest single denomination in the country, expanding from 30,000 in 1790 to 3.5 million by 1860. Moreover, this Catholicism was decidedly foreign. Unlike earlier Catholics such

Lyman Beecher's Fear of Roman Catholicism

Lyman Beecher (1775–1863) NATIONAL PORTRAIT GALLERY, SMITHSONIAN INSTITUTION, WASHINGTON, D.C., GIFT OF MRS. FREDSON BOWERS

If they could read the Bible, and might and did, their darkened intellect would brighten, and their bowed down mind would rise. If they dared to think for themselves, the contrast of protestant independence with their thraldom, would awaken the desire of equal privileges, and put an end to an arbitrary clerical dominion over trembling superstitious minds. If the pope and potentates of Europe held no dominion over ecclesiastics here, we might trust to time and circumstances to mitigate their ascendence and produce assimilation. But for conscience sake and patronage, they are dependent on the powers that be across the deep, by whom they are sustained and nurtured; and receive and organize all who come, and retain all who are born, while by argument, and a Catholic education, they beguile the children of credulous unsuspecting protestants into their own communion.

Plea for the West, 1834

as John Carroll, the archbishop of Baltimore whose identification with American values was easily recognized, the Irish and Germans were cultural strangers. They frolicked on the sabbath which Americans "kept." With abandon they built the pub and the *Biergarten* at the exact moment that Protestants by the thousands were singing oaths of abstinence. They took little notice of cherished American institutions and values, opting instead for their own ethnic newspapers, mutual benefit societies, militia companies, and school systems. Rome did little to allay Protestant fears when it appointed primarily foreign-born archbishops: in 1852, the American hierarchy consisted of six foreign-born archbishops and seventeen of twenty-six foreign-born bishops. From top to bottom, the Catholic church at midcentury was unmistakably foreign.

Protestants were also troubled that foreigners, untutored in political democracy and religious freedom, would undermine republican institutions. Did not the Vatican and most European Catholic leaders take reactionary stands against democracy and the separation of church and state? Lyman Beecher's well-known work, *Plea for the West* (1834), carried on the century-old tradition that Catholics, untrained to think for themselves, were easy prey for tyrant or demagogue, not to mention the papacy to which they had sworn allegiance. These forebodings about politics seemed justified when political divisions came to take on an ethnic and religious cast, Catholic immigrants favoring the Democrats, native Protestants the Whigs. In St. Louis on the eve of the Civil War, it became difficult even to hold elections as political tensions spilled over into overt rioting between Germans and native-born Americans.

Such outbreaks of violence manifested yet another cultural tension: the felt differences in social status and economic position. The Irish, in particular, were forced into immi-

A Protestant nativist broadside imagining the threat of Roman Catholicism, 1855   LIBRARY OF CONGRESS

gration by ruinous potato famines during the mid-1840s that sent 2.5 million persons (twenty percent of the Irish population) in search of a new home. Crowded into eastern cities such as Boston, New York, and Philadelphia, many Irish were unskilled and were forced to take whatever forms of work were available. To the staid and prosperous Protestant middle class, buoyed by notions of self-help and individual achievement, the meager status of these strangers often was seen as evidence of sloth, instability, and lack of initiative.

A dramatic cultural divide, then, stood between Protestants and Catholics. This allowed misconceptions, half-truths, and speculation to stand in the face of reality. The rollicking irony was that Protestants, gripped by a fear of a monolithic Catholic conspiracy, never began to grasp how precarious the church was that Catholics were attempting to build on these shores.

Protestants and the Parochial School

ROCKNE McCARTHY

Education in early America was almost exclusively an activity of Protestant sects. From the outset, whether settlement was in the northern, middle, or southern colonies, sectarian education became one of the most important determinants of group life. Presbyterian, Episcopalian, Baptist, Methodist, Lutheran, and Quaker leaders recognized that education was a basic means by which a people internalize, defend, and propagate their deepest convictions about life. Denominational leaders, therefore, sought to carefully control education as they worked to perpetuate their group into future generations.

While almost every school in Revolutionary America was a Protestant school, not all of them were parochial or denominational schools. Private academies and community schools also played an important role in education. Academies were corporate entities with their own board of trustees who hired a schoolmaster and teachers and raised funds for the institution. Community schools were those maintained and supervised by elected authorities.

In the early republican period all three kinds of schools were considered public schools. This was the case because "public" implied the performance of a public function and service rather than ownership, control, and exclusive funding by government. Parochial schools and private academies were considered public schools even though they were managed by denominational groups or private individuals acting not as government officials but as trustees responsible for their institution's educational program and goals. These schools, moreover, often received money from local and state governments in the form of land grants and taxes.

"The modern conception of public education," writes Bernard Bailyn, "the very idea of a clean line of separation between 'private' and 'public,' was unknown before the end of the eighteenth century." The major force in shaping the modern meaning of public education was the sectarian rivalry between groups, particularly the Protestant and Catholic conflict that often erupted into violence in the early nineteenth century. As long as education was dominated by Protestants, the majority of citizens saw no reason why public funds should not support all schools. But once Catholics began to press the claim that their schools had a legitimate right to a proportional share of government funds, public opinion and policy underwent a dramatic reversal.

The Protestant and Catholic conflict in New York City in the 1830s was one of the important crucibles out of which there developed the modern conception of a "clean line of separation" between private and public schools. In 1831 a Protestant majority decided that the schools of the New York Public School Society were legitimately public schools and, therefore, could be publicly funded. This was done even though the schools were run by a private board of trustees and taught a Protestant world view complete with scripture readings from the King James Bible.

At the same time the Protestant majority decided that public funds could not go to Catholic schools. These schools, it was argued, were private schools because they were managed by a church and were sectarian in perspective. When Catholics responded that the schools of the New York Public School Society were also run by a nonpublic body and were just as sectarian as the Catholic schools because education could never be religiously neutral, their arguments fell on deaf ears. Protestants were in the majority and they took advantage of the fact to make policy by legally defining such terms as sectarian and nonsectarian education and public and private schools in a self-serving way. The result was the creation of a public school system where everyone's taxes were used to support schools which reinforced the world view of the majority.

By the middle of the nineteenth century a consensus of faith had come to so dominate the political culture that a majority assumed public education and Protestantism were allies. As a consequence Catholics, Jews, and a few Protestant groups, who either rejected the interdenominational consensus or simply wanted to maintain their ethnic identity, maintained and, in many cases, expanded their own schools, which have ever since been defined legally and politically as private and parochial.

Cartoon depicting "Popery Undermining Free Schools" — in literal terms   AMERICAN ANTIQUARIAN SOCIETY

The Perils and Promise of Ethnicity

Apart from the hostility of the Protestant majority, the chief difficulty facing immigrant Catholics was their own ethnic diversity. A New York priest, F. Jeremiah Cummings, described the situation in the following manner: "The Irish find it difficult to discard their affection for everything that concerns the Old Hybernia and thus would like to establish here an Irish Catholic Church. Germans stay on their own and do not want to have anything to do with the Irish. Frenchmen, in many instances, would like indeed a Roman, Apostolic Catholic church, but would like to dress her up *à la française*." Immigrant Catholics were not only strangers to American culture; they were also strangers to each other and worked diligently to preserve within Catholicism their own ethnic distinctives. Different patterns of immigration among the Irish and Germans partly resolved these tensions, the former remaining primarily in the East, the latter congregating in the upper Midwest, in cities such as Cincinnati, St. Louis, and Milwaukee. Where different ethnic groups were thrown together in the same neighborhood, as in New York City, the church's solution by the 1830s was to allow national parishes. By the end of the Civil War, for instance, forty to fifty thousand Germans in the city had eight parishes of their own as well as their own hospitals, orphanages, and secondary schools. Archbishop John Hughes finally drew the line when the Germans purchased land for a cemetery so that, even in death, they could avoid the Irish.

Such ethnic tensions also emerged among Americans who converted to Catholicism. Both Orestes A. Brownson (1803-1876) and Isaac Thomas Hecker (1819-1888), for instance, were notable for their efforts to show that Catholicism and American culture were not only compatible but even complementary. Brownson argued that the Irish-dominated church could best prosper if it made peace with American civilization. To the influential Archbishop Hughes of New York, this amounted to a betrayal of faith. Hughes publicly rebuked Brownson at a Fordham commencement in 1856.

At the same time, strong ethnic loyalties did reinforce Catholic faith in many ways. The experience of being wrenched out of familiar environments and of making one's way in a hostile culture threw many immigrants back upon traditional religious observance and custom. The urban parish became a center of ethnic community life, a primary means of conveying valued customs to a younger generation. Religious commitment, then, could blend with ethnic loyalty in positive ways to provide a measure of coherence amidst a world in flux.

The problem for the Catholic church as a whole was that by midcentury they could not hope to build and staff churches fast enough to accommodate the surge of immigrants. Even after building thirty-two churches in New York City before 1860, the Catholic hierarchy never could adequately encompass the increasing immigrant presence. As immigration became more complex after 1860, these organizational problems increased. What impressed Catholic leaders was how many of the faithful lost contact with the Church amidst the upheavals of immigration.

Orestes A. Brownson (1803–1876), Presbyterian turned Unitarian turned Roman Catholic, relentlessly pursued an Americanized Catholicism.
LIBRARY OF CONGRESS

German baptismal certificate, York County, Pennsylvania, 1836

German-American broadside depicting both a broad path and a sidetrack to hell with a single strait and narrow path to heaven BILLY GRAHAM CENTER

Strong ethnic loyalties also served to impede assimilation and thus ensure that certain traditions, Protestant and Catholic, would be preserved. The Missouri Synod Lutherans, established as a Lutheran "Zion on the Mississippi" in 1847, became the largest Lutheran Synod in America by World War I. This was partly a result of the shrewd leadership of men such as Carl F. W. Walther (1811-1887), partly of the vital blend of pietism and confessionalism offered to German immigrants, and partly of the pristine ethnic traditions which were preserved. The Missouri Synod, for instance, retained the German language in seminary education well into the twentieth century. The Christian Reformed church, founded in Zeeland, Michigan, in 1857, offered Dutch immigrants an equally powerful blend of confessional orthodoxy, vital piety, and uncompromising fidelity to Dutch traditions. For all the tensions ethnicity could generate, it did allow new religious traditions to take root in American soil. If more immigrants had immediately embraced the alluring ideals of America, the mosaic of Christianity in the United States would certainly have become far less rich than it is today.

Cincinnati's Religious Mosaic

JOSEPH M. WHITE

In the first half of the nineteenth century Cincinnati grew from a frontier outpost to the largest inland city in the United States and the capital of commerce and industry in the West. Attracted by the urban frontier's economic opportunities, immigrants from the eastern seaboard and Europe swelled Cincinnati's population to 116,000 by 1850. In that year, Germans, the largest foreign-born group, comprised a third of the city's population. They crowded into the area called "Over the Rhine" lying north of the Miami Canal that bisected the city. This neighborhood, as one German visitor observed, "swarms with German faces and one hears the dialects of Baden, Swabia, Austria, Frankfurt, Berlin, low German, and even Yiddish."

Diversity was the central fact of German-American life. Emigrating from several regions and adhering to opposing religious traditions, Germans were incapable of forming a unified community based on common values. Even language divided them. They ordinarily spoke the dialect of their native region rather than the correct but difficult *Schriftdeutsch* of the educated. The average German often had difficulty understanding someone from another German-speaking region. The community life in Over the Rhine institutionalized such differences from the homeland in a bewildering array of churches, militia companies, fraternal orders, social clubs, and mutual aid societies.

Religion also divided Cincinnati Germans. While most Germans professed to be either Protestant or Catholic, a significant minority were neither. German freethinkers stridently opposed all forms of organized Christianity. Local freethinkers started the first Turner society in the United States at Cincinnati in 1848 and a Free Men's Society to promote their world view upholding the superiority of reason over the superstitions of religion. Cincinnati, too, had a significant number of German Jews. In 1853 they called Isaac Mayer Wise to be rabbi of Temple Bene Yeshurun, where he promoted adaptations of traditional Jewish practices to modern life that became the national movement of Reform Judaism.

The Cincinnati waterfront in 1848, showing its skyline of church spires FROM THE COLLECTION OF THE PUBLIC LIBRARY OF CINCINNATI AND HAMILTON COUNTY

Most German Protestants adhered to six congregations that carried on the "union" or combined Lutheran and Reformed tradition as in the German state churches. Unassisted by any synod or denomination, Cincinnati Germans started the six congregations, which resolutely maintained their independence of each other and from any church body. These congregations subscribed to the rationalism that had held sway in German Protestantism since the eighteenth century. Belief and piety were antiorthodox, humanist, and stressed personal virtue. While not making exacting religious demands, the congregations commanded loyal support by providing religious services, preserving regional customs, and creating a basis for community life among like-minded people. Two small congregations that Germans established subscribed to Protestant orthodoxy and respectively joined Missouri Lutheran and Evangelical synods.

American Protestants launched efforts to convert Germans that resulted in the formation of several small German-speaking Baptist, Methodist, Presbyterian, and Reformed Congregations. Because of the exacting creedal and disciplinary demands that American Protestant churches made, relatively few Germans were willing to abandon their Protestant and Catholic heritage to join them.

Some three-fifths of the Cincinnati Germans who identified with a church were Catholics, constituting two-thirds of the local Catholic population. By the 1860s, every fourth Cincinnati resident was a German Catholic. With their numerical strength, German Catholics built an imposing religious subculture that appeared to many non-Catholic Germans as more Catholic than German and to the local Irish Catholics as more German than Catholic.

German Catholic life was centered in the ethnic parish where religion and German culture were integrated under the motto, "Language saves Faith." Between 1834 and 1860, Cincinnati Germans built eleven Catholic parishes, generally as the result of public meetings at which plans for constructing and financing parish building were openly determined. Once the parish was under way, the parishioners elected trustees to govern its operation. Lay leadership was also exercised in the operation of parish societies for men and women, married and unmarried, and mutual aid societies. Unlike German Protestants, German Catholics were deeply committed to supporting a school in each parish. In this undertaking, Germans were far in advance of their Irish coreligionists and the general policy of the American Catholic church. The German parish fulfilled several important functions for immigrants by providing the setting for worship in the familiar ways of the homeland, as a means of passing on faith and culture, and as a basis for a satisfying community life.

The spiritual leader of Cincinnati Catholics from 1833 to 1883, the Irish-born Archbishop John Baptist Purcell, happily allowed German Catholics to develop their own way of life. While the bishop established a newspaper, orphanage, and cemetery for the diocese, German Catholics incorporated and launched their own newspaper, orphanage, and cemetery with their bishop's blessing. Purcell sincerely admired German Catholics for their orthodoxy, piety, and eagerness to liquidate parish debts. From his perspective, there was ordinarily no need to intervene in local German Catholic affairs. Thus, unlike some urban Catholic communities, there were no serious ethnic conflicts to disturb the harmony of Catholic life in Cincinnati.

The non-German Catholic population was principally Irish. They were generally poorer than the Germans and, unlike Germans, came from a country where Catholic institutional life had long been rudimentary. Consequently, they had not developed a tradition of lay leadership in church affairs. The Irish attended religious services at the Cincinnati Cathedral where the bishop and the clergy of his household directed parish affairs or at the church attached to St. Francis Xavier College staffed by Jesuit priests. Later, the bishop established additional parishes for the Irish as needed.

Regardless of nationality, Cincinnati Catholics were powerfully affected by the revival of piety that was a major trend in nineteenth-century Catholicism. Renewed emphasis on devotional exercises ignited religious fervor in Europe and America, thus binding immigrant Catholics more closely to the church's rhythm of worship and sacramental life. In Cincinnati and elsewhere, the devotional and social elements of Catholicism reinforced each other in building secure communities standing between immigrants and the uncertain and occasionally hostile world surrounding them.

Trusteeism

PATRICK CAREY

Within American Catholicism during the national period (1785-1860), Trusteeism was the most persistent and widespread lay movement to adapt European Catholicism to American congregationalism and republicanism. The movement was a form of republican congregationalism emphasizing the centrality of lay participation in the church's life and exclusive lay control of ecclesiastical temporalities. Catholic bishops and many pastors vigorously resisted Trusteeism. Although they too perceived the necessity of accommodating European Catholicism to American experiences, they insisted upon preserving the centrality of pastoral and episcopal authority within the congregational and diocesan churches. The conflicting lay and clerical views of adaptation were one of the major causes of the prolonged and agitated lay-clerical dissensions that frequently arose in the Catholic community during this period.

The trustee system was a direct result of American legislation. Under American law, every congregation that owned property or contracted debts had to elect a board of trustees who would be legally responsible for ecclesiastical temporalities. The elected trustees were corporately responsible for church debts, pastors' salaries, and for hiring and firing those who worked for the church (e.g., sextons, organists, teachers, building contractors). From 1786 to 1855 in congregations from New York City to New Orleans, many lay trustees also asserted that they had the right and duty to select their pastors, establish a description of the pastoral role, and fire them when they proved incompetent or unacceptable in the congregation.

The Catholic trustees argued, as did members of other ecclesiastical traditions during the national period, that the church in the United States should be distinctively American in its manner of government. As elected representatives of the congregations, they believed they had the natural right to hire and fire their pastors. Their battle cry reflected the aspirations of many Americans at the time: the voice of the people is the voice of God — in church as in state.

The lay trustees' republican mentality created tremendous hostilities between themselves and their opponents. The antitrustee party, those who joined the bishops in opposition to the trustees' demands, rejected what they considered an attempt to identify Catholicism and republicanism. They believed that the separation of church and state provided a providential opportunity for the Catholic church to be freed from lay and governmental interference in ecclesiastical affairs and to develop episcopal authority without any lay restraints. Lay intervention in pastoral appointments represented the worst kind of tyranny, made pastors slaves of congregational whim, and imprisoned the preaching of the gospel. Under such circumstances not only would pastoral authority be completely eliminated, but the church's message itself would be utterly dependent upon the cultural and political condition of the congregation.

By 1855, the bishops — through individual efforts, conciliar legislation, and papal support — were able to crush the republican lay assertiveness behind Trusteeism and to gain for themselves the undisputed right to adapt Catholicism to the American experience. Trusteeism, however, had a significant effect upon the development of American Catholicism; the memories of the experience are almost indelibly etched upon the consciousness of contemporary Catholic leadership. The lay trustees' movement unwittingly aided the formation of a strong centralized episcopal authority in American Catholicism, made the subsequent episcopacy suspicious of lay participation in ecclesiastical government, and supported American nativists' charges that Catholicism and republicanism were ideologically and practically incompatible. Because the experience of republicanism was not appropriated in ecclesiastical government, American Catholicism after the Civil War was periodically disturbed by lay-clerical tensions, repeated calls for lay rights, and attempts to create a more effective constitutional balance of powers within the church.

Archbishop John Carroll

MICHAEL J. ROACH

Many argue that the most fortuitous event in the early years of Roman Catholicism in the United States was the appointment of John Carroll as first bishop of Baltimore. Born of Anglo-Irish stock in 1735, Carroll could claim kin with the most prominent families of colonial Maryland. A clandestine Jesuit school at Bohemia on Maryland's upper Eastern Shore provided his primary education. He continued his education at St. Omer in French Flanders, an establishment long favored by English Recusants and Catholic Colonials. Heeding the call of a Jesuit vocation, Carroll entered the novitiate of that order, studying philosophy and theology at Liege. He was ordained in 1769, a most disastrous time for the Society of Jesus. Following the lead of Portugal, virtually all the great Catholic powers of Europe turned on the influential Society and expelled them from their territories. Not satisfied with this, they pressured a harried papacy to suppress completely the Jesuit order. Yielding to these demands, Franciscan Pope Clement XIV issued the bull *Dominus ac Redemptor* in 1773. Carroll's beloved Society was to be no more.

Cut loose from the moorings of Jesuit life, Carroll returned to his mother's house at Rock Creek. He joined other former Jesuits in tending the spiritual needs of Catholic settlers in Maryland and Virginia. At this time the Catholic mission effort in the colonies was suffering from internal problems. With the Jesuits suppressed there was no immediate chain of authority or accountability for the colonial clerics. There was some minimal contact with Catholic authorities in London, but even this faded as the Revolution appeared on the horizon. As part of the war effort American colonials courted Canadian support in the battle against the British crown. Fr. John Carroll was asked to accompany a diplomatic mission to Montreal. It was hoped by John Adams and others that a priest's presence would assure the Canadians that toleration for Catholicism did exist in the new nation. By the Quebec Act the English government had already guaranteed freedom of worship to Canadian Catholics. They could not forget this, nor could they forget the howl of anti-Catholic sentiment it roused in the colonies to the south. From start to finish the mission was a failure. Perhaps the one lasting benefit for Carroll was the warm acquaintance forged between himself and Benjamin Franklin. Several years later when the question of a Catholic bishop for the United States came up, Dr. Franklin let it be known in European diplomatic circles that Carroll would be most acceptable. Meanwhile, in a singularly unusual move, Rome gave the clergy of the young nation permission to nominate a candidate for the episcopacy. Carroll was the overwhelming choice. In 1790 he travelled to England for his consecration as bishop of the first Catholic diocese in the United States, Baltimore. During Carroll's stay in England the French Seminary Priests of St. Sulpice approached him with an offer to found and staff a theological school in America. Carroll quickly accepted, and St. Mary's Seminary in Baltimore began in 1791. Carroll also founded a boy's academy on the Potomac, destined to grow into Georgetown University. Nor was women's education neglected. As early as 1799 a girl's school was begun adjacent to the Jesuit establishment at Georgetown. A decade later with Carroll's personal encouragement, Elizabeth Bayley Seton opened her girl's academy at Emmitsburg, Maryland.

John Carroll's record as a religious leader was outstanding. Even in the civic community he found wide acceptance. The influential position of the Carroll family certainly aided the bishop's success. His older brother Daniel signed the Constitution, while his younger cousin, Charles Carroll of Carrollton, signed the Declaration of Independence. In potentially acrimonious situations, John Carroll remained a gentleman. When his own cousin, Charles Wharton, renounced the

Archbishop John Carroll (1735–1815) NATIONAL PORTRAIT GALLERY, SMITHSONIAN INSTITUTION, WASHINGTON, D.C.

priesthood and the Catholic faith, the bishop answered Wharton's public accusations with restraint and objectivity. Carroll's mildness also was a factor in some of his failures. The young country had attracted any number of vagrant priests whom European bishops and superiors had been happy to release. These men often had long-established problems with authority and fought the new bishop's every prerogative. They exacerbated ethnic rivalries within the Catholic community and encouraged assertive church trustees. Carroll's greatest regret was not being able to eliminate this contention.

By 1808 the Catholic population of the United States had grown to such a degree that Baltimore was raised to metropolitan station with Carroll as archbishop, with suffragans at Boston, New York, Philadelphia, and Bardstown, Kentucky. At his death in the autumn of 1815, John Carroll left a well-established, well-respected Catholic community in the young Republic, quite a contrast to the struggling, scattered Catholic presence he had found upon his return to America on the eve of the Revolution. This transformation was due in large measure to his own tireless zeal and realistic leadership.

Edward Frederick Sorin and the Founding of Notre Dame

THOMAS J. SCHLERETH

When Edward Sorin and his fellow religious of the Congregation of Holy Cross, a French religious community begun in LeMans in 1839, set out for northern Indiana in November 1842 to found a college, they were doing a very American thing. They were part of what one contemporary noted as "the American mania for college funding," a building boom that prior to the Civil War produced more than seven hundred institutions, most of them begun under religious auspices and claiming to offer higher education.

Sorin, the first-born of a middleclass Brittany farming family and educated in the seminaries of Precigne and LeMans, was ordained in France in 1838. Four years later, he founded the *Université de Notre Dame du Lac* on a 525-acre tract outside of South Bend, Indiana. Over the next half century he served as its first president (1842-1865) and as first chairman of its

board of trustees (1865-1893). If ever Ralph Waldo Emerson's claim that an institution is the lengthened shadow of a man held true, Sorin assuredly could be said to personify nineteenth-century Norte Dame. He also typified nineteenth-century American Christianity in his exuberance, optimism, sense of mission, ambition, and in his immediate embrace of American political and economic democracy. His career calls to mind those of other nineteenth-century personalities such as Jean Baptiste Lamy of Santa Fe or James Gibbons of Baltimore, with whom Sorin's life shares several striking parallels.

Sorin's Notre Dame also shared many characteristics common to nineteenth-century denominational colleges: multiple student constituencies (e.g., he established a grade school, a prep school, a collegiate program, and a vocational school known as the Manual Labor Training School that continued until 1919), limited academic equipment (especially library materials), and a small, over-worked but dedicated faculty. Throughout his lifetime as an administrator, Sorin sought to rectify these deficiencies not only at Notre Dame but also at the other nine Catholic colleges and universities he either founded or administered (e.g., St. Mary of the Lake University, Chicago, Illinois; Sacred Heart College, Watertown, Wisconsin; St. Edward's University, Austin, Texas) during his five decades of work in American higher education.

Nothing tested Sorin's ingenuity like the perpetual financial insecurity of his religious institutions such as Notre Dame throughout the nineteenth century. To counter constant indebtedness, a cholera epidemic, over thirty campus fires (one, in 1879, destroying much of the physical plant at Notre Dame), mounting expenses, and demanding creditors, Sorin developed

ancillary incomes to supplement the university's meager tuition fees. Brick and plaster lime kilns produced building materials, and the apprentice trade school turned out shoes, cloth-ing, and even coffins for sale. Several campus farms (3,500 acres at their largest extent) yielded ample fare for the university dining halls as well as a surplus to be sold in the grain and livestock markets of Chicago. In 1850 Sorin even outfitted an expedition of religious brothers and laymen to dig for gold in the California Gold Rush. Although this adventuresome project did not strike it rich and instantly solve the numerous mone-tary woes of his assorted religious enterprises, it indicates his typical entrepreneurial audacity.

Sorin, like any perceptive nine-teenth-century American, recognized the value of land. A family's donation of a city lot in Detroit, Indianapolis, Milwaukee, or Chicago paid for many a young man's education at Notre Dame. For instance, a farmer in Key-

Father Sorin arriving at the site of the University of Notre Dame in 1842 THE UNIVERSITY OF NOTRE DAME ARCHIVES

stone, Iowa, in 1866 gave Sorin 1,200 acres in payment for the education of his four sons. Sorin, in turn, sent out four religious brothers and a priest to work the land and set up a parish for the community. Spiritual and real estate development often occurred simultaneously. Like Joseph Smith and other powerful American religious leaders who engaged in real estate promotion and town planning, Sorin dealt extensively in land speculation, platting and developing a part of South Bend, Indiana, in the 1850s and laying out an entire town (St. Edward's, Nebraska) named after his patron saint in the 1870s.

With eclectic resources, an indomitable will, and a loyal band of religious men, women, and laypeople, Sorin slowly moved Notre Dame from its obscure, post-Civil War status of a provincial local college to an institution that possessed an increasingly national identity by the time he died in 1893. By that date Sorin's French *lycee* had the hallmarks of a religious *universite*. Two hallmarks, in particular, characterized fin de siècle Notre Dame: an aspiration toward intellectual achievement in higher education (especially in science and engineering) and a commitment to do so with a religious perspective of the Catholic faith tradition.

Besides his fellow clerics, Sorin's friends and correspondents were principally lawyers, judges, politicians, engineers — men of action like himself. Understandably therefore he established at Notre Dame the first Catholic colleges of law (1869) and engineering (1873) in the United States. It was the University's science faculty, however, aptly represented by scholars such as John and Albert Zahm, that achieved the greatest international fame for Sorin's institution in the last two decades of the nineteenth century. John Zahm, a priest-protégé of Sorin, was a theologian of science who wrote *Evolution and Dogma* (1896), often touted as the most astute nineteenth-century attempt by an

American Catholic to reconcile the theory of scientific evolution and Christian belief. Zahm's younger brother Albert, a specialist in aerodynamics, designed the first successful helicopter, the first windtunnel, and explained for the first time in America the method of launching an aircraft. Sorin delighted in these tangible achievements of his faculty. He encouraged another faculty member, historian James Edwards, to establish the Bishop's Memorial Hall at Notre Dame. Within the museum hall was exhibited every conceivable type of artifact (life-size paintings, sculptural busts, photographs, engravings, vestments, daguerreotypes, and funerary memorials) of Catholic bishops, missionaries, and laypeople who had played a role in American religious history. Perhaps of greater importance from the perspective of modern scholarly research in American religious history was the extensive documentary collection of religious manuscripts and archival materials that the indefatigable Edwards amassed from all over North America and Europe. This amazing collection forms the basis for the University of Notre Dame Archives' Catholic manuscript collections.

Edward Sorin sent part of that collection for exhibition at the 1893 World's Columbian Exposition in Chicago. He also authorized Notre Dame faculty participation in the World Parliament of Religions held in conjunction with that international exposition. If, as historian Perry Miller once wrote, "a man is his decisions," these two actions indicate something of what manner of man Sorin was: outgoing, future-oriented, enterprising, ecumenical, anxious to engage the world rather than to withdraw from it.

While Sorin's dominant (and domineering) personality might be partially explained by genetic factors, the American environment of an immigrant church also conditioned his clerical career; in turn, the immigrant American church was affected by his

Father Edwin Sorin (1814–1893)
THE UNIVERSITY OF NOTRE DAME ARCHIVES

ministry. Nativism and anti-Catholic prejudice greeted him almost immediately upon his arrival in northern Indiana. The local Know-Nothing political party in the late 1840s harassed Notre Dame and, occasionally, churches were desecrated or robbed. Sorin offset this hostility by holding county-wide Fourth of July celebrations at the University, replete with free picnic lunches, patriotic band concerts, and solemn readings of the Declaration of Independence. He likewise demonstrated his Americanism by becoming a U. S. citizen as early as 1851, by being elected to public office, serving as a local postmaster, and by sending eight Holy Cross priests and eighty Holy Cross sisters to serve, respectively, as chaplains and nurses in the Union Army during the Civil War.

In addition to his assimilation into and advocacy of the American way of life, Sorin saw the United States as a future center of Catholicism in the Western world. By the 1860s, Sorin came to believe that European

Catholicism, beset as it was by political revolution, ideological factionalism, and timid clerical leadership, had become a sterile, ossified, moribund faith. Much like American Catholics Isaac Hecker and Orestes A. Brownson (whom Sorin sought for over twenty years to add to his Notre Dame faculty), he concluded that the future of Catholic Christianity lay not in the Old World but rather in the New World.

His international administration of the Congregation of Holy Cross as that religious community's Superior General (1868-1893) bolstered this belief. Upon his election to govern the C.S.C. priests and brothers around the world, Sorin immediately moved the community's international headquarters from France to America (specifically, to Notre Dame) from where he directed the religious congregation's educational and missionary activities in Canada, France, and Bengal, as well as in the United States. Twenty years later in 1888, the same year he celebrated the fiftieth anniversary of his priesthood, the French government conferred upon him the Insignia of an Officer of Public Instruction for his international service to education.

When Sorin died on October 31, 1893, a victim of Bright's disease, his friend and fellow ecclesiastical administrator, Cardinal John Ireland, said that "the Western Church had lost one of its 'grand old men.' " So it had. Sorin's mark, in terms of ideas and institutions, could be traced first on midwestern, then American, and, finally, on world Christianity.

Yet he remained a man, a priest, an administrator, a personality of amazing contradictions. In business transactions he could exhibit all the traits the French have in mind by the term *sangfroid*. Bishops and even his own religious superior knew his wrath and defiant disobedience. Shrewd, opinionated, versatile, the type of nineteenth-century American that historian Daniel Boorstin has labelled "the booster upstart," Edward Sorin by 1893 had parlayed 524 acres, $300, and a line of credit that he held in 1842 into an extensive portfolio of religious institutions so complex that it took eighteen years to settle his estate.

Yet there was another Sorin, a man of great heart and great hope that tempered the man of salt and savvy. A priest of almost childlike religious faith, he deeply loved children — especially the grade school students and orphans he brought to Notre Dame — with the extravagance of a doting grandfather. A cleric of unquestioning religious belief (he never appears to have experienced the slightest crisis of faith), he nonetheless greatly admired one of American Catholicism's leading social philosophers (O. A. Brownson) as well as one of its most controversial evolutionists (J. A. Zahm). A French emigré who never seems to have considered any vocation other than that of the ministry, Edward Frederick Sorin typified much that historians see in the nineteenth-century American character: mobility (e.g., he made fifty-two transatlantic voyages), ambitious innerdirected individualism (e.g., he was head of his first university at the age of twenty-eight), and an energetic, resourceful entrepreneurialism (e.g., in addition to being priest, missionary, college president, religious superior, and papal diplomat, he was also a land speculator, clarionetist, railroad investor, postmaster, public official,

historian, magazine publisher, avid marble player, playwright, farmer, and civic leader).

A pious yet ever pragmatic priest, part paterfamilias, part visionary, Sorin's career as an educational administrator and a religious superior spanned two major phases of American Catholic history. Recruited by the last of the French emigré episcopacy who had first nurtured Catholicism in the Midwest, his own fifty-year ministry paralleled the beginning and the middle years of the so-called immigrant period of American Catholicism under Irish hegemony.

Never a paragon of docility, Sorin's strong personality contained an impulsiveness which sometimes approached foolhardiness. His was a stubbornness which would make him implacable in his opposition when his emotions were aroused. Yet like every good sojourner to a newfound land, he was also flexible, self-confident, practical, eager to try, willing to change. Without a doubt, had Sorin not been a missionary priest but a simple French immigrant to nineteenth-century America, he would have sought (and, most likely, found) his fortune on or near the frontier line of settlement, engaged in speculation in land or minerals or livestock, running for Congress or state office, while also building an institution of some sort: an industry, a newspaper, a town — or perhaps even a university.

Mother Elizabeth Ann Seton
MICHAEL J. ROACH

Elizabeth Ann Seton is unique in the calendar of saints of the Roman Catholic church. No one else of that august rank provides such ease of identification with contemporary American women. Her salvation was worked out in her life as wife, mother, teacher,

administrator. Add to this that for more than half her life she was an Episcopalian. Her letters that survive reveal a woman emotional, educated, vivacious, full of strong resolve. How refreshing to hear a saint call herself "Wild Betsy."

Born in 1774 of English and French Huguenot stock, Elizabeth could call many of New York's best her relatives. She would never remember her mother who died when she was but three, but her father, Dr. Richard Bayley, would exert a very heavy influence. The doctor remained on the side of the crown during the American Revolution, but after the war he soon reestablished his reputation as a physician, professor, and pioneer in public health. He insisted on a thorough education for all his children, and Elizabeth acquired particular fluency in French.

At seventeen Elizabeth met William Magee Seton, and after a courtship of two years they were joined in marriage by Samuel Provoost, first Episcopal bishop of New York. The first years of their marriage were particularly happy, and five children blessed their union. With a diverse group of Quaker women and society matrons, the young Mrs. Seton joined an organization to aid destitute widows and orphans. Some time later the group was given the accolade of Protestant Sisters of Charity. Elizabeth's Christianity manifested itself not only in her work with the needy but also in Bible study and time allotted to prayer. Her spiritual guide was John Henry Hobart, then a young minister at her church.

Clouds appeared on the horizon for the Setons when William began to show signs of the old family nemesis, tuberculosis. At about the same time his importing business began to falter. In a futile attempt to recapture his health William Seton took Elizabeth and their daughter, Anna Maria, on a sea voyage to Italy. He also hoped to inject life into his failing business career by renewing some mercantile contacts. William's health declined during the trip, and a damp quarantine period sealed his fate. Elizabeth Seton became a widow in Pisa less than six weeks after her arrival in Italy.

The Filicchi family, old Seton business associates, came to their aid and

Mother Elizabeth Ann Seton (1774–1821) became the first American-born saint when she was canonized in 1975. MOUNT ST. VINCENT ARCHIVES

took Elizabeth and Anna Maria to their home at Leghorn. It was here that the widow Seton had her first serious contact with Catholicism. She was impressed both by the worship and the personal piety of Italian Catholics. In particular, she was taken by their belief in the doctrine of Christ's real presence in the Eucharist. Encouraged by the Filicchi family, she began reading a great deal about Catholicism.

After her return to New York her interest continued, in spite of John Henry Hobart's dire warning. After much prayer and struggle, Elizabeth Bayley Seton made her profession of faith in the Roman Catholic church in March 1805. Her family and friends were aghast. Some claimed she had gone mad. Most of them ostracized her socially and ceased any financial support. In fact, New York became such an unpleasant place for her and her children that she resolved to move somewhere less hostile to Catholics.

At first she considered Canada, but with the encouragement of Bishop John Carroll and the French Sulpician Fathers she decided on Baltimore. The Sulpicians conducted a school there that her two sons might attend and a little house on the property where she might open a school for girls. Though Elizabeth would only stay in Baltimore for a year, it was here that the first candidates for her religious community joined her, and it was here that they appeared for the first time in a common religious garb. Many good contacts were made in Baltimore, friends who would support Elizabeth for many years to come. The generosity of one of the seminarians, Samuel Cooper, made possible the purchase of land some fifty miles west of Baltimore near the village of Emmitsburg. In the summer of 1809 Elizabeth Seton with her family and community moved to this remote and hauntingly beautiful valley. Catholic settlers had lived in the valley between Frederick and Emmitsburg for almost a century when Elizabeth Seton arrived. A boy's school conducted by the French emigré priest John DuBois was two miles from the new foundation. Strong spiritual links would bind the two establishments, St. Mary's on the mountain, St. Joseph's in the valley.

At Emmitsburg Elizabeth Seton took on the title of Mother. She was mother now not only to her own children but also the orphans she took in from the surrounding farmland and her religious companions as well. She had made it very clear that while she intended establishing a religious sisterhood she was not going to surrender her rights over her own family. Her foundation knew tremendous poverty in those early years. Many young sisters died during the harsh winters. Mother Seton lost two of her own daughters. Her benefactors continued to remember her, particularly the French Sulpicians who sent her a spiritual director amazingly in tune with her, Simon Gabriel Brute. He understood this woman's profound spirituality perhaps more than anyone else in her life. Some of the clerics Mother Seton had had to deal with had been singularly high-handed, but she had never let this turn her away from the church. In fact, as she lay near death in the winter of 1821, among her last words was an admonition to her daughters: "Be children of the church."

From the meager beginnings in Baltimore her community had grown to several dozen members in Maryland and Pennyslvania at the time of her death. Today almost six thousand American Sisters of Charity in the United States and Canada trace their spiritual roots to this determined woman of God.

Catholic Revivalism

JAY P. DOLAN

When Charles G. Finney, one of the premier Protestant revivalists of the nineteenth century, was writing his memoirs, he included a brief passage about a convert at his 1842 revival in Rochester:

Several of the lawyers that were at this time converted in Rochester, gave up their profession and went into the ministry. Among these was one of Chancellor W — — 's sons, at that time a young lawyer in Rochester, and who appeared at the time to be soundly converted. For some reason, with which I am not acquainted, he went to Europe and to Rome, and finally became a Roman Catholic priest. He has been for years laboring zealously to promote revivals of religion among them, holding protracted meetings; and, as he told me himself, when I met him in England, trying to accomplish in the Roman Catholic church what I was endeavoring to accomplish in the Protestant church. ... When I was in England, he was there, and sought me out, and came very affectionately to see me; and we had just as pleasant an interview, so far as I know, as we should have had, if we had both been Protestants. He said nothing of his peculiar views, but only that he was laboring among the Roman Catholics to promote revivals of religion.

The person to whom Finney referred was Clarence Walworth, lawyer, convert, Roman Catholic priest, and one of the foremost parish mission preachers in nineteenth-century Catholic America.

As Finney acknowledged, Walworth and other Catholic preachers like him were promoting revival religion in the Roman Catholic church. These Catholic revivals, known as parish missions, fostered an evangelical spirit of religion throughout Catholic America in the second half of the nineteenth century and in the process shaped the piety of the people and strengthened the institutional church.

The Catholic revival first surfaced in the sixteenth century when the Roman Catholic church was seeking to revitalize the piety of the people. Preachers from religious orders such as the Jesuits traveled about Europe conducting revival meetings in both urban and rural areas. The movement expanded during the seventeenth century and reached its golden age during the early eighteenth century. After a brief period of decline, the parish mission once again skyrocketed to popularity in nineteenth-century Europe. When immigrant Catholics came to the United States, one piece of their cultural and religious baggage was the parish mission. By the 1860s it was becoming a common event in Catholic communities across the land, and before long revival religion became a central feature of Catholic piety. The parish mission remained in vogue well into the twentieth century, but with the mainstreaming of American Catholicism after World War II and the renewal ushered in by the Second Vatican Council the old-time parish mission disappeared. But the spirit of evangelical religion, fostered by that phenomenon, did not vanish from the Catholic community; it was revived in the Catholic charismatic movement, the modern-day version of Catholic revivalism.

The parish mission was, as one preacher put it, "a time when God calls with a more earnest voice than at other times all persons, but sinners especially, to work out their salvation with fear and trembling." The setting for the revival was the parish church;

the preachers were itinerant specialists, religious order priests trained
in the revival technique, and men who
could paint vivid scenes of hellfire
and damnation as well as moving
portraits of the crucified Jesus. Most
Catholic religious orders took part
in the parish mission movement, but
the most celebrated groups were
the Redemptorists, the Jesuits, and
the Paulists. Some of the more notable preachers in the nineteenth
century were Fr. Walter Elliot of the
Paulists, Fr. Francis X. Weninger of the
Jesuits, and Fr. Joseph Wissel of the
Redemptorists; both Wissel and
Weninger were German-speaking
priests and gave missions in German
Catholic communities. Other preachers
conducted foreign-language missions
among the Polish, the Italians, and
scores of other Catholic immigrant
groups.

Catholic revivals clearly attracted a
broad spectrum of people — lowerclass
as well as upperclass, church members and non-church members, men
as well as women, Protestants and
Catholics. Like a parish fair they
seemed to offer something for everyone — renewed commitment for the
zealot, momentary consolation for the
negligent, and a new religious adven-
ture for the seeker. They represented
the church's best effort in the evangelization of "the masses and the poor,"
of the large working-class population
that made up the bulk of American
Catholics. Yet, any community, regardless of its location or its social status,
was a potential candidate for the
revival. Rich and poor, professionals
and laborers, farmers and steelworkers
were all touched by the enthusiasm
of revival religion.

The goal of the Catholic revival was
the conversion of sinners, and the
preachers used elaborate rituals and
music as well as the spoken word
to gain heartfelt conversions. Such
personal conversion experiences are
the trademark of evangelical religion,
and they were commonplace at a
parish mission. But these revivals
were noticeably Roman Catholic. They
were marked by a heavy emphasis
on a sacramental ratification of conversion through participation in the
sacraments of penance and the Holy
Eucharist. Nor were the people at a
Catholic revival being converted for
the first time; they were baptized
Roman Catholics in need of saving
grace. Through the preacher's word
and the sacraments, Catholics
believed they received this saving
grace. Thus, Catholic revivalism
blended the gospel of evangelicalism
with the ritual of the sacraments; the
result was a sacramental evangelicalism. This gave Catholic piety a new
tone by placing the heart above the
head, feeling above reason. Personal
religious experience became an
important ingredient in the pursuit of
holiness. The sacraments ratified
this experience and nurtured the converted as they struggled to attain
"the perfection of the saints." Through
the revival meeting, evangelicalism
had become a trademark of Catholic
piety.

The Church
and the Impending Crisis

When the guns of Fort Sumter sounded, Leonidas Polk, the Episcopal bishop of Louisiana, put aside his episcopal duties and entered the Confederate Army as a major-general. Having already signed a call for an independent Protestant Episcopal church in the South, he confessed: "I believe most solemnly that it is for our constitutional liberty, which seems to have fled for us for refuge, for our hearth-stones, and our altars that we strike. I hope I shall be supported in the work and have gone to do my duty." Meanwhile, in Newport, Rhode Island, Thomas March Clark, the Episcopal bishop of Rhode Island, addressed a farewell service for state militia as they left for the war: "Your country has called for service and you are ready. It is a holy and righteous cause in which you enlist. ... God is with us; ... the Lord of hosts is on our side." With a flurry of such benedictions, the North and the South went to war equally convinced of the rightness of their cause and of the victory which divine providence would ensure.

It is no easy task to explain how a brutal war that claimed 600,000 lives and more than one million casualties could have been so routinely baptized in piety. Whatever else, it points to the intertwining of evangelical Protestantism and American culture. It also reveals the difficulty the church experienced in retaining an independent voice once northern and southern values grew apart. The Civil War represented a deeply religious event in American life. Its origins lay in the unresolved moral dilemma of slavery; and both sides approached martial endeavor with the zeal of a religious crusade. In the end, however, the stark disparity between ideals and actuality wrought its own evil work,

dashing hopes, nurturing cynicism, and swelling pride. Born of the golden age of democratic evangelicalism, the Civil War contributed to what would become the spiritual crisis of the Gilded Age.

Slavery and Southern Nationalism

It was no accident that the Constitution of the United States studiously avoided the word slavery. Among the threats confronting its framers, none was greater than the division over the issue of the South's "peculiar institution." The result was that the issue was postponed for a future generation, an expedient that by 1820 had come to haunt the aged Thomas Jefferson: "This momentous question," he announced, "like a firebell in the night, awakened and filled me with terror." The passing of time, unfortunately, had deepened the problem and left the nation less capable of resolving it.

The invention of the cotton gin in the 1790s allowed upland cotton to become profitable from the Carolinas to Texas. This shifted the South's center of gravity toward the Gulf states and left slavery the economic lynchpin

---

We hesitate not to affirm that it is the particular mission of the Southern Church to conserve the institution of slavery and to make it a blessing both to master and slave.

Formal Resolution,
Southern Presbyterian church, 1864

The Anti-Slavery Almanac was only one of a host of abolitionist publications.   BILLY GRAHAM CENTER

of an emerging "Cotton Kingdom." The number of slaves in the South grew from 700,000 in 1790 to 3.5 million by 1860. Accompanying this economic shift was a closing of ranks throughout the South. While Jefferson and southerners of his generation had seriously discussed the ills of slavery, even debating the possibility of abolition, the generation after 1830 came to defend it as a "positive good" and to stiffle any dissent on the issue. Ministers from a variety of denominations developed an elaborate "scripture argument" that recited biblical texts on Negro inferiority, patriarchal and Mosaic acceptance of servitude, and St. Paul's advice of obedience to masters. All of this was woven into an image of the South's humane paternalism contrasted with the alleged brutality of industrial "wage slavery" in the North.

Two other realities also set the teeth of southerners on edge. The nineteenth century witnessed a dramatic increase in the frequency and intensity of slave revolts both in the West Indies and in North America. The Denmark Vesey plot in Charleston, South Carolina, in 1822 and the Nat Turner rebellion in Southampton County, Virginia, nine years later served as symbolic reminders that even the most obedient and religious slave might become a fierce avenger. The parallel rise in militant abolitionism, which the South viewed as inciting such revolts, raised tensions yet another notch. If abolitionist literature could permeate the South through the U.S. mail, any reading slave became a potential incendiary.

Elijah Lovejoy (1802–1837), a Presbyterian minister and newspaper editor, was killed in Alton, Illinois, in 1837 for his abolitionist journalism.
LIBRARY OF CONGRESS

Frederick Douglass on the Religion of Slaveholders

I find, since reading over the foregoing Narrative, that I have, in several instances, spoken in such a tone and manner, respecting religion, as may possibly lead those unacquainted with my religious views to suppose me an opponent of all religion. To remove the liability of such misapprehension, I deem it proper to append the following brief explanation. What I have said respecting and against religion, I mean strictly to apply to the *slaveholding religion* of this land, and with no possible reference to Christianity proper; for, between the Christianity of the land, and the Christianity of Christ, I recognize the widest possible difference — so wide, that to receive the one as good, pure, and holy, is of necessity to reject the other as bad, corrupt, and wicked. To be the friend of the one, is of necessity to be the enemy of the other. I love the pure, peaceable, and impartial Christianity of Christ: I therefore hate the corrupt, slaveholding, women-whipping, cradle-plundering, partial and hypocritical Christianity of this land. Indeed, I can see no reason, but the most deceitful one, for calling the religion of this land Christianity. I look upon it as the climax of all misnomers, the boldest of all frauds, and the grossest of all libels. Never was there a clearer case of "stealing the livery of the court of heaven to serve the devil in." I am filled with unutterable loathing when I contemplate the religious pomp and show, together with the horrible inconsistencies, which every where surround me. We have men-stealers for ministers, women-whippers for missionaries, and cradle-plunderers for church members. The man who wields the blood-clotted cowskin during the week fills the pulpit on Sunday, and claims to be a minister of the meek and lowly Jesus. The man who robs me of my earnings at the end of each week meets me as a

Frederick Douglass (1817?–1895), the eloquent black abolitionist LIBRARY OF CONGRESS

class-leader on Sunday morning, to show me the way of life, and the path of salvation. He who sells my sister, for purposes of prostitution, stands forth as the pious advocate of purity. He who proclaims it a religious duty to read the Bible denies me the right of learning to read the name of the God who made me. He who is the religious advocate of marriage robs whole millions of its sacred influence, and leaves them to the ravages of wholesale pollution. The warm defender of the sacredness of the family relation is the same that scatters whole families, — sundering husbands and wives, parents and children, sisters and brothers, — leaving the hut vacant, and the hearth desolate. We see the thief preaching against theft, and the adulterer against adultery. We have men sold to build churches, women sold to support the gospel, and babes sold to purchase Bibles for the *poor heathen! all for the glory of God and good of souls!* The slave auctioneer's bell and the church-going bell chime in with each other, and the bitter cries of the heart-broken slave are drowned in the religious shouts of his pious master. Revivals of religion and revivals in the slave-trade go hand in hand together. The slave prison and the church stand near each other. The clanking of fetters and the rattling of chains in the prison, and the pious psalms and solemn prayer in the church, may be heard at the same time. The dealers in the bodies and souls of men erect their stand in the presence of the pulpit, and they mutually help each other. The dealer gives his blood-stained gold to support the pulpit, and the pulpit, in return, covers his infernal business with the garb of Christianity. Here we have religion and robbery the allies of each other — devils dressed in angels' robes, and hell presenting the semblance of paradise.

Narrative of the Life of Frederick Douglass,
1845

A *Georgia religious association proposed in 1856 that "missionaries" be sent to the slave population of the region.*

BILLY GRAHAM CENTER

LUMPKIN, NOVEMBER 30, 1856.

DEAR SIR : The religious destitution of the slave population of this portion of Georgia has for some years forced itself on the minds of conscientious Christians—and has from time to time been the subject of anxious consultation. This subject, at the late session of the Bethel Baptist Association, was brought prominently before that body, and it was felt that something must be done, and that speedily, to obviate this lamentable destitution. Accordingly the Association organized the undersigned into a board, or central committee, to hold correspondence, collect facts and devise means that might result in sending, by this body of Christians, a special missionary of the gospel, to the blacks within our bounds.

In taking the liberty of addressing you, we beg that you will be assured that we, as slaveholders, have a full community of interest with yourself, and that we design doing nothing that will, in any sense, make these people as servants, less obedient and faithful ; but on the contrary, by imparting to them from Sabbath to Sabbath, the duties which our holy religion enjoins upon all men, in all the relations of life, we expect and believe, that the obligations to faithful service to their owners, will be greatly enhanced, and the master's interest promoted.

No man will be sent to your plantation as a missionary, who is not known not only to be a deeply pious and conscientious man, but he must be a Southern man of discreet and prudent character, and deeply imbued with Southern principles. In short, believing as we do, that there is no incompatibility between the interest of the master and the religious instruction and wellfare of the slaves, it is our wish and desire, with your consent and co-operation, to send to your slaves, by the mouth of the living preacher, the saving influences of the gospel of peace. To this benign object, so intimately connected with your own interest and with the temporal and eternal wellfare of your people, we feel that you cannot but be friendly. Our plan is to employ a missionary to the blacks who shall itin-rate amongst the large plantations, have a fixed routine of labor, preaching on the Sabbath from time te time at such places as may suit the convenience of the owners of the slaves.

This measure will require two things—

1. The consent of the slaveholder, that his people shall be instructed.

2. That the slaveholder shall co-operate in raising funds to pay the salary of an approved missionary. In answer to this circular, you will be pleased to inform us whether this enterprise meets with your approbation ; and to what extent we can calculate on your pecuniary aid to carry it out. Let us hear from you at your earliest convenience, and believe us, dear sir,

Your obedient servants,

JAMES CLARKE,
CHARLES S. GAULDEN,
SIDNEY ROOT,
J. M. CLARKE,
JAMES WADE,
C. F. BEMAS,
C. IRVIN.

Harriet Beecher Stowe (1811–1896), author of Uncle Tom's Cabin (1852) BILLY GRAHAM CENTER

O, Church of Christ, read the signs of the times! Is not this power the spirit of HIM whose kingdom is yet to come, and whose will is to be done on earth as it is in heaven? But who may abide the day of his appearing? "For that day shall burn as an oven: and he shall appear as a swift witness against those that oppress the hireling in his wages, the widow and the fatherless, and that turn aside the stranger in his right *and he shall break in pieces the oppressor."*

HARRIET BEECHER STOWE,
Uncle Tom's Cabin, 1852

The Revolution in the North

The growth of abolitionism in the North—by 1838 the American Antislavery Society claimed 1,350 auxiliaries and 250,000 members—was part of the acceleration of thought in Western nations toward a larger understanding of freedom and equality. In America the attack upon slavery took on the force of a campaign for the conscience. It was a cause premised upon biblical argument and advocated with moral suasion. Although more radical abolitionists such as William Lloyd Garrison (1805-1879) sought to work outside of the church, perhaps the most effective reformers were those such as Theodore Dwight Weld (1803-1895), who had the explicit goal of converting people in much the same way as revivalists had done earlier. Weld's approach was to proclaim the sin of slavery. His most influential written work, *Slavery As It Is: The Testimony of a Thousand Witnesses* (1839), linked disclosures about slavery from southern newspapers to the biblical judgment, "Out of thine own mouth I condemn thee." The book in four months sold 22,000 copies.

An even greater sensation came in 1852 with the serial publication of Harriet Beecher Stowe's *Uncle Tom's Cabin*, a phenomenal best-seller that one scholar has called "perhaps the most influential novel ever published . . . a verbal earthquake, an ink-and-paper tidal wave." The daughter of Lyman Beecher, sister of Henry Ward Beecher, and wife of an Old Testament professor, Harriet was a shrewd theologian in her own right, and her ethical passion was perfectly in tune with the culture of northern evangelical Protestantism. Her powerful stories encouraged every reader who sympathized with the harrowed slaves to share the guilt of a nation that permitted one person to own another. Possibly her most telling argument was that a system of chattel slavery could not preserve the integrity of slave families despite the best intentions of upstanding Christian masters. By the 1850s, then, one finds Americans North and South who are equally honest, God-fearing, and pious, the one not about to condone slavery or rest while it exists, the other equally resolute in the conviction that they could not live without it.

The Splintering of Churches

American churches were even less capable of absorbing these tensions than were political institutions. The three largest Protestant denominations, buffeted by heated debate over

Military chaplain conducting services for a regiment of Ohio volunteers in Kentucky, November 1861
LIBRARY OF CONGRESS

slavery, suffered serious division. Although the Presbyterians did not divide into northern and southern denominations until after secession, the Old School–New School division of 1837 did reflect, along with a broad range of theological issues, the growing sectional tension. The New School generally sympathized with the abolitionists while the Old School maintained that the church should not meddle in politics. Not unexpectedly, the latter had considerable support below the Mason-Dixon line.

The issue of slavery was more central to the severing of Methodism in 1844 and the founding of the Methodist Episcopal Church, South. The southerners chose to withdraw after the delegates at the General Conference voted that Bishop James O. Andrew of Georgia, a slaveholder, desist from carrying out his ecclesiastical office. Northern Methodists were attempting to remain true to the firm conviction of the entire denomination before 1800 that slavery was "contrary to the laws of God, man, and nature." That twenty-five thousand Methodist laypeople and some twelve hundred clergy in the South held slaves in 1844 is testimony not only to changes within southern Methodism but also to how entrenched this labor system had become. Similar tensions among Baptists surfaced in the one strong cooperative agency that these churches shared, the General Convention for Foreign Missions. In 1844 this board refused to license missionaries who were slaveholders. This action led churches in the South, who a generation before had decried slavery, to bring into existence the Southern Baptist Convention.

American churches, thus, were unable to serve as instruments of compromise and moderation. In fact, they may have contributed to the hardening of attitudes, as churchmen played leading roles in the moral revolutions that swept North and South in opposite directions. For twenty years before the Civil War the churches shored up cultural positions with theological justifications. The resulting zeal for God and country gave both sides in the impending crisis great confidence that they belonged to a movement through which God's truth was marching on. "When the cannons roared in Charleston harbor," Sydney Ahlstrom has written, "two divinely authorized crusades were set in motion, each of them absolutizing a given social and political order. The pulpits resounded with a vehemence and absence of restraint never equaled in American history."

What a sermon! The preacher stirred my blood. . . . A red-hot glow of patriotism passed through me. . . . There was more exhortation to fight and die, a la Joshua, than meek Christianity.

MARY BOYKIN CHESTNUT,
after a sermon by the
Confederate Presbyterian
Benjamin Palmer

The American Tract Society provided Union soldiers with devotional reading material
BILLY GRAHAM CENTER

THE

Soldier's Text-Book:

OR,

CONFIDENCE IN TIME OF WAR.

BY THE REV. J. R. MACDUFF, D. D.

"Though a host should encamp against me, my heart shall not fear: though WAR should rise against me, IN THIS WILL I BE CONFIDENT." Psa. 27:3.

PUBLISHED BY THE
AMERICAN TRACT SOCIETY,
150 NASSAU-STREET, NEW YORK.

Turner, Brown, and Lincoln:

Christian Morality and Slavery

RONALD A. WELLS

If it be true that a religious perspective was the mode in which most nineteenth-century Americans did their thinking about human nature and destiny, there was no issue which more surely vexed the Christian mind than that of slavery. If the Bible was the major source of truth for nineteenth-century Americans, it was a not unambiguous source when its guidance was sought on the question of slavery. In vain could any agreement be found on whether or not slavery should continue to exist in the United States. When the North and South went to war in 1861, as Lincoln later noted, both sides went to war reading the same Bible and praying to the same God. The careers of Nat

Turner, John Brown, and Abraham Lincoln can illustrate and illumine the difficulties of developing a common "biblical" mind, even among those opposed to slavery. Turner and Brown reached to the Bible to bring judgment both upon the United States for allowing slavery and upon the slaveholders themselves. Lincoln appropriated the biblical heritage to evoke mercy; while opposing slavery

Both read the same Bible.

ABRAHAM LINCOLN,
Second Inaugural, 1865

Lincoln nevertheless remembered that only the merciful will obtain mercy.

A significant direction was set in Nat Turner's life by his birth on the Virginia plantation of Benjamin Turner in 1800. Benjamin Turner was a committed Christian, and he personified the "uneasy conscience" of southern Methodism about slavery. He was eager to have his slaves become Christians, so he insisted that they learn to read and write in order to understand the Christian message in the Bible. After his owner's death in 1809, however, Nat Turner was the successive property of four other owners before he was twenty-five. The early promise of Nat's precocity and the potential benevolence of Benjamin Turner were of no avail when Nat was put to work as an ordinary field hand. In the slave quarters, his congenital bumps and markings were taken as a sign of his great potential, and Nat sought a word from God about the riddle of his enslavement and about the "great purpose" for which his life was intended. He studied the Bible, fasted, and prayed regularly. He began preaching in the local "black praise" meeting which the owners allowed their slaves on Sunday afternoons. In 1825 Nat believed that God had given him a vision of the impending end of the world, in which the last would be first and the first last. He awaited a sign. On August 13, 1831, there was an atmospheric disturbance in which the sun appeared to change colors. As Nat watched, a black spot appeared to pass over the sun. To Nat it was the sign he awaited, and he told his lieutenants that "as the black spot passed over the sun, so shall blacks pass over the earth." The day of the rising would be Sunday, August 21, 1831. Without a clear plan, Nat and six others began the murder of whites in Southampton County. Apparently his goal was to smash his way into the county seat, with ironic significance named Jerusalem. All Nat's men were caught by the end of the first day, although Nat remained a fugitive for more than two months. When finally caught, he was tried, convicted, and executed quickly. The authorities boiled his carcass into grease, perhaps in an attempt to boil away the memory of that dark night. In the end, the rebellion cost the lives of sixty whites and more than two hundred blacks. The significance of Nat Turner's rebellion was that it shattered forever the myth of "happy darkies and affectionate masters" in the old South.

John Brown was given a proper Connecticut Calvinist upbringing by his father, Owen Brown. Dedicated to doing God's will, he became a determined foe of slavery as a young adult. In the development of his personal theology were two influences: the sermons of Jonathan Edwards and the Declaration of Independence. Asked to preach in several Ohio churches, he frequently read Edwards' "Sinners in the Hands of an Angry God." He and others around him trembled at the

John Brown (1800–1839)
BOSTON ATHENAEUM

prospect of God's justice and judgment, which would surely come. The Declaration reinforced his ideas about equality, and gave theoretical backing to his opposition to slavery.

Brown was heavily involved with the "underground railroad" and helped many escaped slaves to freedom in Canada. He went to Kansas to help "save" that territory for the free states, and in that salvation committed murder in cold blood. His favorite text for the abolitionist crusade was Hebrews 9:22: "All things are by the law purged with blood, and without shedding of blood is no remission." He was a charismatic leader, and the leading black abolitionist Frederick Douglass said after being with Brown that he had never been in the presence of a stronger religious influence. Abolitionist Thomas Wentworth Higginson remarked that Brown would pick up Calvinist attempts at social regeneration where Cromwell left off.

His plan to assault the federal arsenal at Harper's Ferry, Virginia, was fantastic, even by Brown's other-worldly standards. It never stood a chance of success. His dream of seizing the weapons, distributing them to slaves, and then leading the final uprising which would purge the guilty land of the sin of slavery was not planned with any attention to the important details. This did not bother Brown because he trusted God ("In all thy ways acknowledge him, and he shall direct thy paths"). On the evening of October 16, 1859, Brown and twenty-two other men set out for Harper's Ferry. Once the shooting began the whites in the countryside mobilized quickly and the slaves did not rise — in both cases the opposite of what Brown expected. Federal troops soon appeared, under the command of Col. Robert E. Lee. Tried, convicted, and executed, Brown became in death the symbol in the North of the struggle against slavery.

In penetrating the mythic shroud of "the Lincoln legend," it appears that Abraham Lincoln may well have been a representative American for the middle third of the nineteenth century, at least insofar as his opinions about slavery are concerned. Despite the compelling moral nature of slavery, most people in the North were slow to make up their minds about the South's "peculiar institution," and it is clear that nothing approaching a majority ever championed abolition. Thus, Lincoln may have been representative of Northern opinion because, while he opposed slavery, he could not conceive of an American society in which freed slaves could take their places alongside whites. In time, of course, he did become a determined foe of slavery, and with the Emancipation Proclamation in 1862 he set in process the eventual freeing of the slaves.

While one cannot claim that Lincoln opposed slavery on "religious" grounds, he nevertheless had a "religious sense" which informed his attitudes. He had an ability to empathize with the dilemma of the slaveholder whose way of life was threatened. Because he believed that the United States' very existence was crucial to the survival of liberty in the world, he sought to establish a policy which would end slavery but allow Southerners to reenter the Union amicably. For Lincoln, the Civil War was not a Northern crusade, but a punishment visited upon a guilty nation and people for the American accommodation to slavery. In Lincoln's view, the war would only be successful if it was not solely vindictive but reconciling as well.

Later Christian interpreters found it tempting to value Lincoln (the man of charity and mercy) more than Turner and Brown (the men of justice and judgment). Because as Christians they recalled that " 'tis not with the sword's loud clashing, nor roll of stirring drums, but with deeds of love and mercy, the heavenly kingdom comes." Yet, one must ask what deed of love and mercy would have ended the injustice of slavery, especially with the present knowledge of slavery's great profitability and the fact that it was not "dying out." Lincoln could offer a policy of graciousness and mercy once the war to end slavery was largely won. It was the violent men with prophetic voices like Turner and Brown who helped to focus the question which perhaps made that war inevitable. To a nation still haunted by questions of race, the

words of John Brown immediately before his hanging in 1859 still speak with power: "I wish to say that you had better ... prepare yourselves for a settlement of this question. ... The sooner you are prepared the better. You may dispose of me very easily – I am nearly disposed on now; but this question is still to be settled – this negro question I mean; the end of that is not yet. ...."

The Religion of Abraham Lincoln

RONALD D. RIETVELD

"The most truly religious of all our Presidents was Lincoln," declares historian Arthur Schlesinger, Jr. Abraham Lincoln's spiritual training began at his mother's knee. Nancy Hanks Lincoln died when her son was nine years old. But before Lincoln had learned to read as a boy, he had heard his mother saying over certain Bible verses day by day as she worked. Young Lincoln learned these verses by heart. In fact, as he read these verses from the Bible in the White House years he seemed to hear her voice speaking through them.

The crude emotionalism and denominational disputes exhibited in frontier religion encouraged a lack of interest in specified creeds and institutionalized Christianity. The Bible, apart from churches, remained his source of inspiration, however. Coming of age in 1830, Lincoln left his family and went off on his own. There was no church at New Salem, and very few of his neighbors cared greatly about ideas. Although the deep sense of reverence which developed in those Indiana years never left him, he began to speculate in ways which made some people think him to be verging on infidelity.

As early as 1843, Lincoln's religion or lack of religion had reportedly hurt his political aspirations. He admitted he was not a member of "any Christian Church," but that he did not deny the truth of the scriptures and had never spoken with intentional disrespect of religion in general, or of any denomination of Christians in particular. In fact, he declared he could not support a man for political office who would be "an open enemy of, or scoffer at, religion."

A series of crisis events in Lincoln's life further shaped his spiritual life. Lincoln's broken engagement to Mary Todd in 1841 caused him spiritual anguish. It was at this time that a dear friend gave him a new Oxford Bible as a gift, which Lincoln declared was "the best cure for the 'Blues' could one but take it according to the truth." He emerged a man of deep religious feeling out of this experience. Lincoln and Mary Todd were joined in marriage on November 4, 1842. This union brought him closer to the organized church because Mary attended the Episcopal church in Springfield.

When Lincoln's second son, Edward Baker, died in 1850, Mary's Episcopalian pastor was away, and the Rev.

Abraham Lincoln (1809–1865)
LIBRARY OF CONGRESS

James Smith of the First Presbyterian Church took charge. After that the Lincoln family worshipped in Smith's church. Describing Smith as "an intimate personal friend of mine," Lincoln and Smith remained close friends until the president's death.

Up to the time of Lincoln's presidency, a key to his religious development involved the moral issue of slavery. Lincoln's conception of morality was derived from his religion. He declared that without the revelation of the Bible man could not distinguish between right and wrong. "In regard to this Great Book," he would declare, "I have but to say, it is the best gift God has given to man. All the good the Saviour gave to the world was communicated through this book."

The occasion of Lincoln's election in 1860 and the disintegration of the national structure as one Southern state after another seceded from the Union had a deep and profound effect upon his personal spiritual life. The experience determined Lincoln in what he called "a process of crystallization" going on in his mind. An exact date cannot be given of "change" in his Christian life because Lincoln himself did not do so, but evidence supplied by Mrs. Lincoln, his Washington pastor, Dr. Phineas D. Gurley, and Noah Brooks, his friend, seems to note a "change" by the middle of 1862.

After the death of his son, William Wallace, on February 20, 1862, Lincoln said: "I will try to go to God with my sorrows. . . . I wish I had that childlike faith. . . , I trust He will give it to me. I had a good Christian mother, and her prayers have followed me thus far through life." Lincoln's views in relation to spiritual things did seem to deepen over time. Lincoln declared, "I think I can safely say that I know something of that CHANGE. . . ." From this time on he was seen often with the Bible in his hands, and he is known to have prayed often. His personal relation to God occupied his mind much.

The flowering of this richer faith and Lincoln's deep human sympathy are evidenced in both the private and public writings of the remaining presidential years. From the Gettysburg Address of 1863 to the Second Inaugural of 1865, Lincoln's growing faith led him to a profound understanding of God's will for the war-torn nation as well as himself. "The purposes of the Almighty are perfect, and must prevail, though we erring mortals may fail to accurately perceive them in advance," he averred.

Christian statesmanship clearly marks the final address of Lincoln's life in the closing days of Civil War. Declaring that "He, from whom all blessings flow, not be forgotten," he announced a proposed national day of thanksgiving. It was not to be so. Thanksgiving gave way to mourning when Abraham Lincoln was shot by an assassin's bullet on Good Friday, April 14, 1865.

Abraham Lincoln Interprets the War:
"The Almighty Has His Purposes"

Both parties deprecated war; but one of them would *make* war rather than let the nation survive; and the other would *accept* war rather than let it perish. And the war came.

One eighth of the whole population were colored slaves, not distributed generally over the Union, but localized in the Southern part of it. These slaves constituted a peculiar and powerful interest. All knew that this interest was, somehow, the cause of the war. To strengthen, perpetuate, and extend this interest was the object for which the insurgents would rend the Union, even by war; while the government claimed no right to do more than to restrict the territorial enlargement of it. Neither party expected for the war, the magnitude, or the duration, which it has already attained. Neither anticipated that the *cause* of the conflict might cease with, or even before, the conflict itself should cease. Each looked for an easier triumph, and a result less fundamental and astounding. Both read the same Bible, and pray to the same God; and each invokes His aid against the other. It may seem strange that any men should dare to ask a just God's assistance in wringing their bread from the sweat of other men's faces; but let us judge not that we be not judged. The prayers both could not be answered; that of neither has been answered fully. The Almighty has His own purposes. "Woe unto the world because of offenses! For it must needs be that offenses come; but woe to that man by whom the offense cometh!" If we shall suppose that American Slavery is one of those offenses which, in the providence of God, must needs come, but which, having continued through His appointed time, He now wills to remove, and that He gives to both North and South this terrible war, as the woe due to those by whom the offence came, shall we discern therein any departure from those divine attributes which the believers in a Living God always ascribe to Him? Fondly do we hope — fervently do we pray — that this mighty scourge of war may speedily pass away. Yet if God wills that it continue, until all the wealth piled by the bond-man's two hundred and fifty years of unrequited toil shall be sunk, and until every drop of blood drawn with the lash, shall be paid with another drawn with the sword, as was said three thousand years ago, so still it must be said "the judgments of the Lord are true and righteous altogether."

With malice toward none; with charity for all; with firmness in the right, as God gives us to see the right, let us strive on to finish the work we are in; to bind up the nation's wounds; to care for him who shall have borne the battle, and for his widow, and his orphan — to do all which may achieve and cherish a just, and a lasting peace, among ourselves, and with all nations.

Second Inaugural, 1865

For Further Reading

General works that deal suggestively with the Early National Period are Sydney E. Ahlstrom, *A Religious History of the American People* (1972); Winthrop S. Hudson, *Religion in America*, 3rd ed. (1981); and Martin E. Marty, *Righteous Empire: The Protestant Experience in America* (1970). Useful collections of primary materials are Edwin S. Gaustad, ed., *A Documentary History of Religion in America: To the Civil War* (1982); Hilrie Shelton Smith, Robert T. Handy, and Lefferts Loetscher, *American Christianity: An Historical Interpretation with Representative Documents*, 2 vols. (1960); and John Tracy Ellis, *Documents of American Catholic History* (1962). Nineteenth-century European observers of American Christianity include Robert Baird, *Religion in America* (1843; repr. 1970); Philip Schaff, *America: A Sketch of Its Political, Social, and Religious Character* (1855; repr. 1961); and the collection by Milton B. Powell, *The Voluntary Church: American Religious Life (1740-1865) Seen Through the Eyes of European Visitors* (1967).

The comprehensive study of the separation of church and state is Anson Phelps Stokes, *Church and State in the United States*, 3 vols. (1950), abridged into a single volume by Leo Pfeffer (1964). The role of evangelicals in this process is ably sketched in William B. McLoughlin's readable biography, *Isaac Backus and the American Pietist Tradition* (1967). For the influence of the Enlightenment, see Henry F. May, *The Enlightenment in America* (1976), and Donald H. Meyer, *The Democratic Enlightenment* (1976). Stephen A. Marini discusses popular religious ferment in *Radical Sects of Revolutionary New England* (1982).

Two classic works treat the ethos of revivalism in antebellum America: Perry Miller, *Life of the Mind in America: From the Revolution to the Civil War* (1965; repr. 1970), and Timothy L. Smith, *Revivalism and Social Reform in Mid-Nineteenth Century America* (1957; repr. 1980). Important local studies include Paul E. Johnson, *A Shopkeeper's Millennium: Society and Revivals in Rochester, New York, 1815-1837* (1979), and Don H. Doyle, *The Social Order of a Frontier Community: Jacksonville, Illinois, 1825-1870* (1978). The antebellum South is ably discussed in John B. Boles, *The Great Revival, 1787-1805: The Origins of the Southern Evangelical Mind* (1972), and Donald G. Mathews, *Religion in the Old South* (1977). In *Catholic Revivalism: The American Experience, 1830-1900* (1978), Jay P. Dolan argues that even Roman Catholicism was not immune from evangelical mores.

An excellent survey of reform impulses is Ronald G. Walters, *American Reformers, 1815-1860* (1978). For the advent of foreign missions, see Joan Jacob Brumberg, *Mission for Life: The Story of the Family of Adoniram Judson* (1980), John A. Andrew III, *Rebuilding the Christian Commonwealth: New England Congregationalists and Foreign Missions, 1800-1830* (1976), and Clifton J. Phillips, *Protestant America and the Pagan World: The First Half Century of the American Board of Commissioners for Foreign Missions, 1810-1860* (1969). Whitney R. Cross explores a full range of religious novelty in *The Burned-Over District: The Social and Intellectual History of Enthusiastic Religion in Western New York, 1800-1850* (1950). The best recent studies of Mormon beginnings are Leonard J. Arrington and Davis Bitton, *The Mormon Experience* (1979), and Klaus J. Hansen, *Mormonism and the American Experience* (1981). On Millerites and Adventists, consult the essays in Edwin S. Gaustad, ed., *The Rise of Adventism: Religion and Society in Mid-Nineteenth Century America* (1975). An excellent comparative study of the Mormons, the Shakers, and the Oneida community is Lawrence Foster, *Religion and Sexuality: Three American Communal Experiments of the Nineteenth Century* (1981). On the subject of abolition, see David B. Davis, *The Problem of Slavery in the Age of Revolution, 1770-1823* (1975), Bertram Wyatt-Brown, *Lewis Tappan and the Evangelical War Against Slavery* (1971), and Gerda Lerner, *The Grimke Sisters from South Carolina: Pioneers for Women's Rights and Abolition* (1967). Two other significant studies that discuss women and religion are Katherine K. Sklar, *Catharine Beecher: A Study in American Domesticity* (1973), and Ann Douglas, *The Feminization of American Culture* (1978).

A superb introduction to nineteenth-century theology is Sydney E. Ahlstrom, ed., *Theology in America: The Major Protestant*

Voices from Puritanism to Neo-Orthodoxy (1967). Other helpful studies include William R. Hutchison, *The Transcendentalist Ministers: Church Reform in the New England Renaissance* (1959; repr. 1972), James Hastings Nichols, *Romanticism in American Theology: Nevin and Schaff at Mercersberg* (1961), George M. Marsden, *The Evangelical Mind and the New School Presbyterian Experience* (1970), and Barbara M. Cross, *Horace Bushnell: Minister to a Changing America* (1958). Donald M. Scott discusses the changing role of the clergy in *From Office to Profession: The New England Ministry, 1750-1850* (1978).

Many themes in the complex story of Roman Catholic immigrants are suggested in Jay P. Dolan, *The Immigrant Church: New York's Irish and German Catholics, 1815-1865* (1975). A recent one-volume survey of Catholicism is James J. Hennessey, *American Catholics: A History of the Roman Catholic Community in the United States* (1982). John Carroll, the central figure in early American Catholicism, has been made much more accessible with the publication of Thomas O'Brien Hanley, ed., *The John Carroll Papers*, 3 vols. (1976).

Two outstanding treatments of black religion are Eugene Genovese, *Roll, Jordan, Roll: The World the Slaves Made* (1974), and Albert J. Raboteau, *Slave Religion: The "Invisible Institution" in the Antebellum South* (1978).

The theme of religion and the sectional crisis is ably presented in Donald G. Mathews, *Slavery and Methodism: A Chapter in American Morality, 1780-1845* (1965), Dwight L. Dumond, *The Antislavery Origins of the Civil War in the United States* (1959), William J. Wolf, *Lincoln's Religion* (1970), and James H. Moorhead, *American Apocalypse: Yankee Protestants and the Civil War, 1860-1869* (1978).

Separation of Church and State
ROBERT M. CALHOON

The eloquence, simplicity, and directness of the First Amendment's affirmation of religious liberty — "Congress shall make no law respecting an establishment of religion or restricting the free exercise thereof" — obscures the complexity and ambiguity of the American commitment to both freedom of belief and a Christian heritage of morality and righteousness. While religious liberty in the United States owes much to a libertarian tradition, it owes even more to circumstances which prevented any single philosophical or theological orientation from becoming incorporated within government and the political system as well as to a strong streak of antiauthoritarianism and antiinstitutionalism in American life.

The term "separation" must be used here with caution. The relationship between government and religion has been both adversarial and collaborative. Church and state have not so much confronted each other as each has arisen from, and has sought relationship with, the whole society. In a republican system of government, the whole people embody authority, legitimacy, and power. In a self-consciously Christian, even Protestant, religious culture, the whole populace is the potential seedbed of the kingdom of God and society the setting of struggle between the forces of darkness and of light. As church and state have dealt with the American social order, along evangelical and republican lines respectively, they have often come into contact with each other; those points of overlapping secular and spiritual activity and the constitutional and legal rules which have come to regulate the coexistence of religion and politics in

that common sphere are what is meant by separation of church and state.

In the colonial period religious toleration and governmental sanctions in support of religious practice were both ways in which colonial governments sought to attract settlers and create a viable society. In Massachusetts, Plymouth, and Connecticut, where charters placed power in the hands of covenanted Puritan leadership, taxation paid ministerial salaries, church attendance and observance of the sabbath were required by law; individuals defying the authority of civil magistrates in Massachusetts on religious grounds — Roger Williams in 1636, Anne Hutchinson in 1638 — faced banishment, and four defiant Quaker missionaries were executed in Boston in 1659-1661. In each of the southern colonies, the Church of England became established by law (Virginia after 1624; Maryland in 1702, following the overthrow of the Catholic proprietors, the Calvert family; South Carolina in 1704; North Carolina in 1741, though a dispute over enabling legislation creating local vestries delayed complete establishment until 1765; Georgia in 1758; and four New York counties in 1693). Only in Virginia, prior to the 1740s, however, was Anglican worship legally enforced. Throughout all the colonies, by midcentury religious dissent flourished. Even in the face of official harassment, Baptists and Presbyterians gained widespread followings in Virginia by the middle of the eighteenth century, as did Anglicans and Baptists in Connecticut and Massachusetts. In every other colony Protestants enjoyed toleration — a status extended to all Christians in Pennsylvania, Delaware, and Rhode Island and to Jews in Pennsylvania, the proprietary colony of west Jersey, Delaware, and Georgia.

More fundamentally, colonial churches and governments interacted functionally at several points. While the New England clergy stood aloof from politics, they served as informal, persuasive enforcers of social control and public interpreters of the reciprocal duties of subject and magistrate. In Virginia, the vestries performed a wide array of civil functions in law enforcement, poor relief, and land distribution. Particularly in New England and the middle colonies, Anglican clergy — often missionaries sent by the Society for the Propagation of the Gospel — presented themselves as defenders of royal authority in the colonies, and their clamorous demands for bishops resident in the colonies aroused genuine fears among dissenters of an Anglican plot to subvert religious liberty. In Pennsylvania, where Quakers dominated the Assembly until the emergence of rival political factions in the 1730s, benevolence and pacifism rooted in Quaker belief were hallmarks of public policy. Churchmen and assemblies shared responsibility in the creation of colonial colleges: Harvard and Yale (Congregationalist), King's and William and Mary (Anglican), and Brown (Baptist).

The American Revolution opened the way to a wholesale reordering of church-state relations and at the same time enhanced the public role of religion in America. The southern states and New York disestablished the Anglican church, although the Congregationalist establishment in Connecticut and Massachusetts remained intact. The creation of republican government seemed to require the promulgation of morality and virtue through tax support for all Christian ministers in South Carolina, Maryland, Massachusetts, New Hampshire, and Connecticut (individuals could contribute to churches of their own choice or to a general assessment fund for distribution to all approved clergy) and religious tests for officeholding (only Christians in Pennsylvania and Delaware and only Protestants in North Carolina, Maryland, Georgia, and New Jersey). South Carolina in 1778 went further by allowing Christian denominations to seek incorporation from the state and

thereby legal control of their property if they subscribed to a five-part definition of a "Christian" church (drawn loosely from John Locke's Fundamental Constitution of Carolina), which included a definition of the relationship of God and man and statements on worship, Christian truth, scripture, and discipleship. Virginia, however, rejected general assessment in 1786 after a fierce struggle between proassessment Episcopalians and tidewater Presbyterians and antiassessment evangelicals including Shenandoah Valley Presbyterians as well as Methodists, Baptists, and rationalists like James Madison, who successfully sponsored a bill on religious liberty which totally separated church and state. South Carolina followed suit in its 1790 constitution, but not until 1818 in Connecticut and 1833 in Massachusetts was the Congregationalist establishment finally abolished.

At work in these post-Revolutionary struggles, especially the adoption of the First Amendment, were two different motivations for separation of church and state. Rationalists like Madison and Jefferson believed that the sanctity of private judgment was the ultimate source of virtue in a republic and therefore "the opinions of men are not the object of civil government nor under its jurisdiction." Evangelicals, led in New England by the Baptist minister Isaac Backus, saw separation as a guarantee that the United States would be a Christian republic in which churches would be free from political influence and hence fully open to the leading of the Holy Spirit: "RELIGION," wrote Backus, "was prior to all states and kingdoms in the world and therefore could not in its nature be the subject of human laws."

Like other constitutional doctrines, separation of church and state has been a dynamic, troubled amalgam of contrasting values. Judicial rulings and legislation on the subject during the nineteenth and twentieth centuries have embodied both the rationalist ideal of a secular state and the evangelical vision of a righteous nation. In one category of cases, the courts have steadily and severely restricted the power of the state to compel pious behavior or foster religious observance by proscribing

Sunday "blue laws," ordinances against blasphemy, compulsory school prayer, voluntary released time for religious training in the public schools, and religious test oaths. The outlawing of religious discrimination in public life and the marketplace, demanded by Jewish organizations in the 1930s and 1940s, prepared the way for similar attacks on racial and sexual injustice in the 1950s, 1960s, and 1970s.

In another area, however, the courts have struck a pragmatic middle ground permitting functional cooperation between churches and government in the advancement of common social goals including federal and state aid to parochial schools and church colleges, conscientious objection to the draft, and military chaplaincy.

Potentially, the most delicate of all areas of church-state relations involves disputes over the control of church property carried into state and federal courts. In the landmark case, *Watson* v. *Jones* (1972), the Supreme Court held that while the courts may not enter into the theological disputes which almost always lie at the base of such schisms, they can and must enforce the ecclesiastical procedures governing control of church property in the churches and denominations involved. Thus, in hierarchical denominations property rights remain with the denomination, and in strictly congregational structures the decision-making process commonly used within the church — be it majority rule or delegation of authority to a governing board — must be upheld in the courts. In *Jones* v. *Wolf* (1979), however, the Supreme Court by a 5-4 verdict modified this rule by allowing "neutral principles" of property and ecclesiastical law to take precedence over a church judicatory's interpretation of its own denominational polity. This decision, which apparently will draw the courts more deeply into evaluating the extent of presumptive hierarchical control of parish property when schisms occur, illustrates anew the fragility of a constitutional principle compounded out of respect for both conscience and the rule of law.

Christianity and American Literature

THOMAS WERGE

In 1838, Ralph Waldo Emerson noted that "the Puritans in England and America found in the Christ of the Catholic Church and in the dogmas inherited from Rome, scope for their austere piety and their longings for civil freedom. But their creed is passing away, and none arises in its room." Images of Christ, conceptions of the church in both its visible and invisible forms, traditional Christian doctrines of sin and grace, free will and predestination, damnation and salvation, and the inevitable tensions between faith and doubt pervade the American literary imagination from its inception. The great American writers do not define "literary" in a narrow aesthetic way. For them, the imagination has a religious dimension. Literature matters because life does; its dramatic conflicts imitate American moral experience. As Flannery O'Connor states, "the greatest dramas naturally involve the salvation or loss of the soul. Where there is no belief in the soul, there is very little drama." The incessant struggle between God and the powers of evil over the individual soul and, indeed, over America's soul constitutes the essential drama of American literature.

The very forms of American literature are inseparable from their religious origins and purposes. The importance of the sermon continues not only through such figures as Jonathan Edwards, William Ellery Channing, and Theodore Parker, but finds expression in the structure and passionate tone of Thomas Paine's prophetic utterances, Emerson's intensely incantatory essays, Father Mapple's crucial sermon in *Moby Dick*, and the apocalyptic prose of James Baldwin and Norman Mailer. Emily Dickinson's starkly simple forms and metrics echo the *New England Primer*. For Calvinist, Catholic, and Quaker, meditation and self-scrutiny were indispensable parts of the habit of being, and the continual introspection of the diary, journal, and "spiritual autobiography" recurs in Edwards, John Woolman, the "ungodly Puritan" Benjamin Franklin, Thoreau, Hawthorne, Melville, Emerson, and Henry Adams. The spiritual power and simplicity of Woolman's *Journal*, a classic of Quaker piety, becomes a means of conversion for Dreiser's protagonist in *The Bulwark* some two centuries later. Even the naturalistic tradition in American literature draws on Christian doctrines and images.

Biblical sources and influences suffuse American literature. In new and startling ways, Whitman's *Leaves of Grass* and Steinbeck's *The Grapes of Wrath* use the form and rhythms of the Psalms. Genesis, Job, the Gospels, the Apocalypse affect through their images and deepest meaning all major American writers. The very titles of American classics are biblical phrases — James' *The Golden Bowl*, Steinbeck's *East of Eden* and *Grapes of Wrath*, Faulkner's *Absalom, Absalom!*, Hemingway's *The Sun Also Rises* — and the influence of the King James or Authorized Version of the Bible is omnipresent. The *Book of Common Prayer* was "seldom out of [Hemingway's] reach," writes Carlos Baker, and the deepest impulses of Faulkner's characters lead them to return to the scripture: "He didn't have His Book written to be read by what must elect and choose, but by the heart ... by the doomed and lowly of the earth who have nothing else to read with but the heart."

Our whole life, comments Thoreau, is "startlingly moral." The moral intensity of the Christian vision animates the preoccupations, ideas, and images of American literature. From the seventeenth century through Edwards and Emerson, who insists that "all things are moral" and asks, "What is a farm but a mute gospel?" Nature becomes a mode of revelation, a divine hieroglyphic the soul must seek to decipher. Yet despite the persistent vision of Adamic innocence in the natural and human order, sin provides an equally persistent fact of moral experience, as Melville makes clear when he acknowledges the importance of "that Calvinistic sense of Innate Depravity and Original Sin, from whose visitations, in some shape or other, no deeply thinking mind is always and wholly free." Whether the American writer views Nature as opaque and oppressive or as a sacramental sign of the divine presence, and whether original sin constitutes a doctrine to be rejected or accepted, the soul's drama is incessantly moral. Water (*Moby Dick*), the forest (*The Scarlet Letter*, "Young Goodman Brown"), the desert (*Grapes of Wrath*), or cities of chaos and torment (*The Wasteland*, *Native Son*) may locate the controlling images of evil and destruction—and also potential conversion, renewal, and salvation—but the soul's movement always comprises both a pilgrimage and a narrative. "To a Christian," writes G. K. Chesterton, "existence is a story."

The dramatic religious imagination in America is perennial and, given its biblical roots and historical traditions, inevitable. Images themselves, says William F. Lynch, are relentlessly theological: "Theology gets into the interior of our images and is not an exploiting appendage." The dramatization of the soul in American thought and literature owes much to the Bible, to medieval forms of Catholic literature and doctrine— Dante figures importantly here, the Puritans were steeped in scholasticism, and Cotton Mather greatly admired Thomas à Kempis— to Luther and Calvin, to Bunyan and other Dissenters, to Quakers and evangelicals, to the Methodist hymns of the Wesleys, and to the sermons of Bellamy and Hopkins. It is as important to understand Harriet Beecher Stowe's later Anglicanism as her earlier and formative Calvinism. Mark Twain's fascination with Catholic doctrine and ritual, like Hawthorne's and Melville's, demands as much interpretation as what he called his "trained Presbyterian conscience." Thomas Pynchon's apocalyptic visions, Mailer's belief in the reality of the devil and apparently Manichaean dualism, and Flannery O'Connor's profoundly orthodox Catholicism and continual portrayals of intensely believing fundamentalists cannot be easily categorized. But each is a seminal writer, and none can be understood without reference to the religious dimensions of their thought and writings.

In his insistence that America was in potential "the glory of the earth" and that "not a place upon earth might be so happy as America," Thomas Paine presupposed that America had it in its power to "begin the world again." As in John Winthrop's recurring image of New England as a "city upon a hill"—an image extended to America as an exemplary and "elect" nation— Paine's emphasis bound the world to America's purpose: "The cause of America is, in a great measure, the cause of all mankind." The deepest nature of this cause was not simply political and democratic, nor was it primarily material. Edwards, like others, envisioned America's ultimate meaning as a catalyst for universal redemption: "The changing of the course of trade and the supplying of the world with its treasures from America is a type and forerunner of what is approaching in spiritual things, when the world shall be supplied with spiritual treasures from America."

Given this "errand," it is understandable that one of the most intense preoccupations of American literature revolves around the gain or loss of our national soul and identity. The Russian literary tradition continually exalts for its visions and indicts for its lapses "Holy Mother Russia." The American literary tradition images the journey toward salvation and the consistent threat of apostasy and damnation not only as an individual but as a communal act. The cries for autonomy, individualism, and freedom, as D. H. Lawrence recognized, may be evasions unless they are complemented by a sense of place and commitment: "Men are free when they are in a living homeland, not when they are straying and breaking away. Men are free when they are obeying some deep, inward voice of religious belief ... and when they belong to a living, organic, *believing* community, active in fulfilling some unfulfilled, perhaps unrealized purpose."

In its communal as in its individual form, the goal is eschatological, and the most potent and exactly descriptive language for the pilgrimage and destination is Christian. The soul, afflicted by suffering, quests after love, forgiveness, and the kingdom of God. At the end of one such quest in *Armies of the Night*, Mailer hears and is moved by the prayers of several Quakers, prayers "as Catholic as they are Quaker." He is compelled to reflect that "if the end of the march took place in the isolation in which these last pacifists suffered naked in freezing cells, and gave up prayers for penance, then who was to say they were not saints? And who was to say that the sins of America were not by their witness a tithe remitted?" This vision of the saints bearing witness is inseparable from Mailer's conception of language as testament and witness. The imagination's most profound impulse is religious.

Just as American literature dramatizes the individual's search for community, the mind's search for a place of the spirit, and even the restless imagination's search for a literally sacramental order of being, so it extends and mirrors aspects of these searches in the very soul of America and in a metaphysical and ontological order. Exiles seek deliverance; the wounded seek resurrection; the anonymous soul or character seeks realization and identity; the life of the modern corporation, remembering even if unconsciously the image of the mystical body, cannot escape being measured according to a transcendent vision of the kingdom of God. Even when such writers as Mailer see Christ and American culture as antithetical — "the center of Christianity was a mystery, a son of God, and the center of the corporation was a detestation of mystery, a worship of technology" — they always speak to the hope of transformation and conversion. Even in an increasingly secular culture, the writer's compulsion to judge and, indeed, to condemn is so often part of

a Christian vision of man that it is not an end but a means — an admonition rather than a curse. Baldwin, like Mailer, Bellow, and so many keepers of the moral imagination, feels "the shape of the wrath to come." America, like the individual soul, requires and awaits judgment. Yet Baldwin addresses his readers, as does the American writer traditionally, "out of the most passionate love, hoping to make the kingdom new, to make it honorable and worthy of life." Despite the ravages of secularism, life continues to be a moral and even apocalyptic drama. The soul's hope for conversion, sanctification, and salvation — for the coming and renewal of the kingdom — remains as perennial as the doubt and even nihilism through which it seeks the way.

The Era of Crisis:
From Christendom
to Pluralism

BY GEORGE M. MARSDEN

The United States at midcentury;
several of what appear to be western states
were as yet territories. THE NEWBERRY LIBRARY

Colton's
UNITED STATES
OF AMERICA

An Era of Crisis

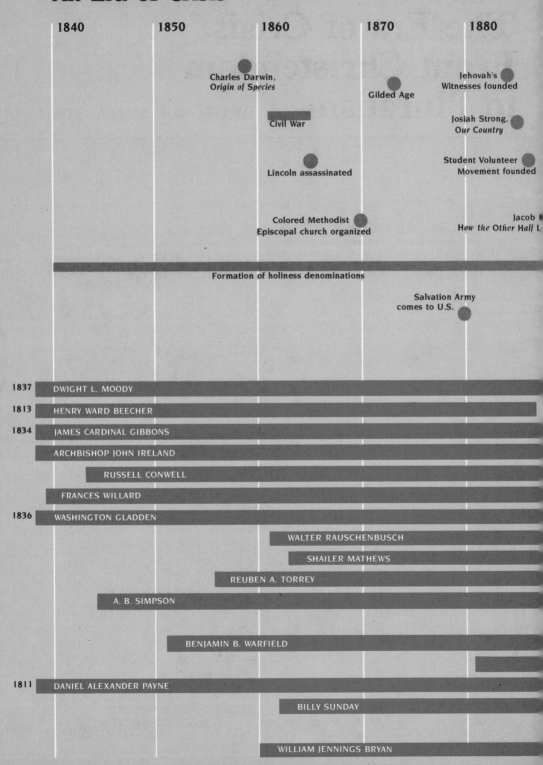

| 1840 | 1850 | 1860 | 1870 | 1880 |

Charles Darwin,
Origin of Species

Gilded Age

Jehovah's
Witnesses founded

Civil War

Josiah Strong,
Our Country

Student Volunteer
Movement founded

Lincoln assassinated

Colored Methodist
Episcopal church organized

Jacob ▶
How the Other Half L

Formation of holiness denominations

Salvation Army
comes to U.S.

1837	DWIGHT L. MOODY
1813	HENRY WARD BEECHER
1834	JAMES CARDINAL GIBBONS
	ARCHBISHOP JOHN IRELAND
	RUSSELL CONWELL
	FRANCES WILLARD
1836	WASHINGTON GLADDEN
	WALTER RAUSCHENBUSCH
	SHAILER MATHEWS
	REUBEN A. TORREY
	A. B. SIMPSON
	BENJAMIN B. WARFIELD
1811	DANIEL ALEXANDER PAYNE
	BILLY SUNDAY
	WILLIAM JENNINGS BRYAN

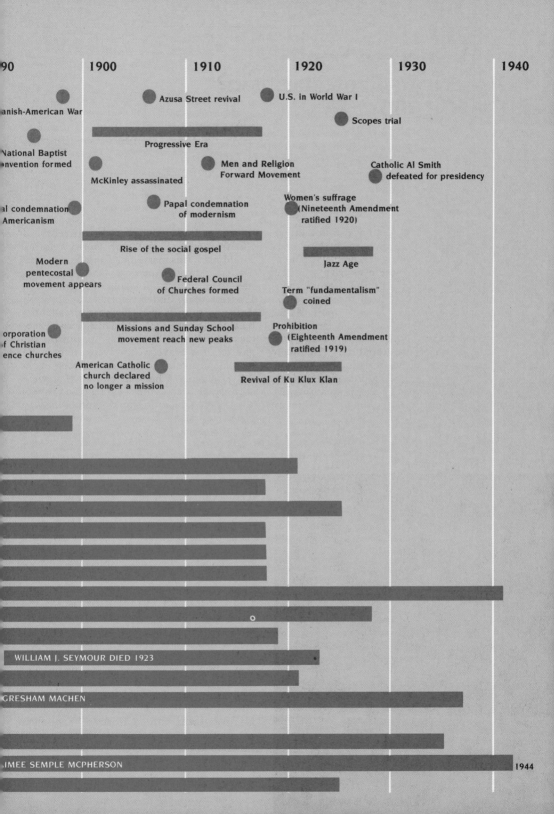

90　　　　　1900　　　　　1910　　　　　1920　　　　　1930　　　　　1940

Azusa Street revival　　　　U.S. in World War I

anish-American War

Scopes trial

National Baptist
nvention formed

Progressive Era

McKinley assassinated

Men and Religion
Forward Movement

Catholic Al Smith
defeated for presidency

al condemnation
Americanism

Papal condemnation
of modernism

Women's suffrage
(Nineteenth Amendment
ratified 1920)

Rise of the social gospel

Jazz Age

Modern
pentecostal
movement appears

Federal Council
of Churches formed

Term "fundamentalism"
coined

orporation
f Christian
ence churches

Missions and Sunday School
movement reach new peaks

Prohibition
(Eighteenth Amendment
ratified 1919)

American Catholic
church declared
no longer a mission

Revival of Ku Klux Klan

WILLIAM J. SEYMOUR DIED 1923

GRESHAM MACHEN

IMEE SEMPLE MCPHERSON　　　　　　　　　　　　　　　　1944

Did Success Spoil American Protestantism? (1865-1890)

At the height of the Civil War, Northerners often equated the advances of the Union armies with the advances of Christ's kingdom. When they sang, "Mine eyes have seen the glory of the coming of the Lord," their thoughts were not far from the victories of General Sherman or General Grant. While today such equations may seem far-fetched, they made sense to those who first sang "The Battle Hymn of the Republic." American Protestants at midcentury frequently had proclaimed that a Christian millennium was not far away. Theirs was an age of great revivals which, if continued, seemed capable of

Julia Ward Howe (1819–1910), author of "The Battle Hymn of the Republic" and ardent reformer
KEYSTONE-MAST COLLECTION, UNIVERSITY OF CALIFORNIA, RIVERSIDE

bringing the majority of the citizenry to Christ. National, and even world, reforms would mark this marvelous Christian millennial era. Already American Christianity was identified with the freedoms of democracy. Progress toward other reforms was apparent on numerous fronts. Drinking, sabbath-breaking, prostitution, Romanism, and Freemasonry all were opposed by formidable organizations. Slavery, however, seemed the leading obstacle to America's becoming a fully righteous Christian nation. If it were eliminated, even at the cost of a bloody apocalyptic struggle, little would stand in the way of the advancing kingdom. Surely a golden age was at hand.

The "Gilded Age"

What followed was in fact the "Gilded Age." The era marked by the assassination of two presidents and the impeachment of another, a stolen election, and a reign of rampant political and business corruption and greed, was well named by Mark Twain. A veneer of evangelical Sunday-school piety covered almost everything in the culture, but no longer did the rhetoric of idealism and virtue seem to touch the core of the materialism of the political and business interests. It was a dime-store millennium.

Outwardly Protestantism prospered. Few Protestants doubted that theirs was a "Christian nation." Though religion in America was voluntary, a Protestant version of the medieval ideal of "Christendom" still prevailed. American civilization, said Protestant leaders, was essentially "Christian." Christian principles held the nation together by providing a solid base of morality in the citizenry.

Much of the education in late nineteenth-century America was carried out in schools such as that above, using texts such as that below. STATE HISTORICAL SOCIETY OF WISCONSIN, CHARLES VAN SCHAICK COLLECTION

Without principles to govern individual and social responsibility, democracy would be impossible and the nation would fall into tyranny and ruin.

Such claims were plausible. American civilization, while never "Christian" in a strict sense, was held together in part by a shared set of values that had a large Protestant component. Children were taught from an early age to play by the rules, and virtually everyone knew of the Ten Commandments, the value of work, and the idea that virtue should be rewarded. During the Gilded Age these principles were still taught not only in the homes but also in the public schools. The most popular grade school textbooks of the era were *McGuffey's Eclectic Readers*. Between 1826 and 1920 an estimated 122 million of these readers were sold. From them generations of America's public school children learned lessons that included "Respect for the Sabbath Rewarded," "The Goodness of God," "Religion the only Basis of Society," "The Righteous never Forsaken," "The Hour of Prayer," "Work," "No Excellence without Labor," "The Character of a Happy Life," "Sowing and Reaping," "My Mother's Bible," and "The Bible the Best of Classics." In the all-important area of a culture where the ideals of one generation are passed to the next, American virtues were presented in an overwhelmingly Protestant framework.

ECLECTIC EDUCATIONAL SERIES.

M^cGUFFEY'S

SECOND

ECLECTIC READER.

REVISED EDITION.

NEW YORK ❖ CINCINNATI ❖ CHICAGO
AMERICAN BOOK COMPANY

The Corrupt Senator Dilsworthy Addresses a Sunday School

Now, my dear little friends, sit up straight and pretty — there, that's it — and give me your attention and let me tell you about a poor little Sunday-school scholar I once knew. . . .

Well, this poor little boy was always in his place when the bell rang, and he always knew his lesson; for his teachers wanted him to learn and he loved his teachers dearly. Always love your teachers, my children, for they love you more than you can know now. He would not let bad boys persuade him to go to play on Sunday.

There was one little bad boy who was always trying to persuade him, but he never could.

So this poor little boy grew up to be a man. . . . And by and by the people made him governor — and he said it was all owing to the Sunday-school.

After a while the people elected him a Representative to the Congress of the United States, and he grew very famous. Now temptations assailed him on every hand. People tried to get him to drink wine, to dance, to go to theaters; they even tried to buy his vote; but no, the memory of his Sunday-school saved him from all harm; he remembered the fate of the bad little boy who used to try to get him to play on Sunday, and who grew up and became a drunkard and was hanged. He remembered that, and was glad he never yielded and played on Sunday.

. . . *That man stands before you!* All that he is, he owes to the Sunday-school.

MARK TWAIN *and* CHARLES DUDLEY WARNER,
The Gilded Age, 1873

Senator Dilsworthy addressing the Sunday school in Mark Twain's The Gilded Age (1873)
SOUTHERN METHODIST UNIVERSITY PRESS

The Evangelical Empire

Protestants' apparent cultural dominance rested on a strong base of the wealthiest and the oldest American families and institutions. Protestants had been the first to settle almost everywhere in the American colonies and so naturally their heirs held most of the positions of power and influence. Leading Americans of the late nineteenth century almost all had Anglo-Saxon, Scottish, or Germanic names—Johnson, Grant, Hayes, Tilden, Garfield, Blaine, Arthur, Harrison, Cleveland, Gould, Fisk, Rockefeller, Morgan, Carnegie, Howells, Clemens, Moody, Beecher, Brooks—reflecting the continuing strength of these predominantly Protestant ethnic groups. It is hardly surprising, then, that the prevailing moral values of the civilization reflected this heritage.

Somewhat more remarkable is that the specifically Christian aspects of this heritage had not eroded more. In Europe during the same era the winds of frankly secular ideologies were blowing strongly, and one might have expected that America, the land of revolutionary liberal political ideals, might by now have adopted a genial democratic humanism, freed from explicitly Christian dogmas and institutions. The fact that America had not in the nineteenth century followed the course set in the eighteenth by leaders like Franklin and Jefferson was due largely to vigorous evangelical enterprise. The United States had not drifted religiously during the nineteenth century. It had been guided, even driven, by resourceful evangelical leaders who effectively channeled the powers of revivals and voluntary religious organizations to counter the forces of purely secular change.

At the heart of the evangelical empire were the great denominations, led by the Methodists, the Baptists, the Presbyterians, the Disciples of Christ, and the Congregationalists, all centers of energetic organization and respectability. Except for the unhealed denominational divisions between North and South, the evangelicalism of these and related groups still presented a united front. Numerous interdenominational organizations—for missions, evangelism, Sunday schools, Bible distribution, moral crusades, social work, and publications—sealed an essential evangelical unity within the context

In the 1880s the nation's best-known infidel, Robert Ingersoll, announced that "the churches are dying out all over the land." Charles McCabe of the Methodist Church Extension Society replied by telegram:

> *Dear Robert:*
> *All hail the power of Jesus' name—we are building more than one Methodist church for every day in the year, and propose to make it two a day!*

of friendly denominational rivalries. Moreover, steady growth, both in actual numbers and relative to the population, characterized evangelical and other American religious groups during the whole era into the early decades of the twentieth century. Major Protestant groups in fact tripled their membership from 1860 to 1900.

The evangelical establishment, as successful as it was in many respects, confronted an unusually severe set of problems. First of all, it faced unprecedented tests intellectually. Skeptics like Robert G. Ingersoll were brandishing with considerable skill a new set of weapons for their views. The publication of Charles Darwin's *Origin of Species* in 1859 had sparked an intellectual crisis for Christians that no educated person could ignore.

The Christian family's reliance upon and study of the Scriptures formed the cornerstone of the evangelical edifice. BILLY GRAHAM CENTER

The YMCA (above) was in the vanguard of the "evangelical empire" in an increasingly urban America (right).   BILLY GRAHAM CENTER

Darwinism focused the issue on the reliability of the first chapters of Genesis. But the wider issue was whether the Bible could be trusted at all. German higher criticism, questioning the historicity of many biblical accounts, had been developing for more than a generation, so that it was highly sophisticated by the time after the Civil War when it became widely known in America. It would be difficult to overstate the critical importance of the absolute integrity of the Bible to the nineteenth-century American evangelical's whole way of thinking. When this cornerstone began to be shaken, major adjustments in the evangelical edifice had to be made from top to bottom.

Urbanization and Secularization

The uniquely disconcerting feature of the post-Civil War era was that this staggering intellectual crisis coincided exactly with a social crisis for Protestantism of equally gigantic proportions. American Protestantism had grown up in an era of villages and towns, and so its institutions were adjusted to such settings. In a town, even if many of the people were not actually communicant members of a church, most had family and nominal ties with a denomination so that evangelical beliefs and moral standards enjoyed considerable support from an influential social consensus. In a city such support disappeared. Anonymity, lack of tight Protestant community, and hosts of other attractions eroded church loyalties. Americans, moreover, were moving to the cities in unprecedented numbers. By the beginning of the twentieth century the nation would be approaching the point where most people lived in the cities, whereas only a generation before it had been overwhelmingly rural. As the historian Henry Adams observed in 1905 of his own experience: "the American boy of 1854 stood nearer the year 1 than to the year 1900."

The church crisis associated with massive urbanization was all the more difficult for Protestants because the new industrial workers crowding the cities were not just moving in from the countryside, but were coming largely from abroad. Most of these, moreover, now were coming from Catholic, and increasingly from non-English-speaking countries. So while between 1860 and 1900 the major Protestant churches tripled in members (from five million to sixteen million) the Catholic membership quadrupled (from three million to twelve million). Many Protestants saw this steady rise of Catholicism as a major threat to the national welfare. Catholics did not keep the sabbath, they danced, being Europeans most of them drank, and since they were often poor, they were regarded as a threat to the stability and moral health of the nation generally. Nonetheless, there was little that Protestants could do but learn to live with Catholics, however mutually bitter the rivalries might be. The facts of the matter for Protestants were simple. In a nation with a large Catholic (and other non-Protestant) population, they could not simultaneously claim to believe in democracy and also claim that Protestant ideals and values should always rule. This logic, of course, did not prevent widespread anti-Catholic, anti-Jewish, and anti-"foreign" efforts. Nonetheless Protestants, especially in the cities, were faced with the fact that they would have to live with irreversible religious pluralism.

Further compounding the massiveness of the crisis was simply a basic secularization of American culture. The process was more difficult to see since church membership was rising, so this secularization was not taking the most obvious form of simple decline of interest in religious institutions. The opposite seemed true. Yet a steady decline in religious influences was just as certainly well under way. Gradually, various areas of American culture were drifting away from any real connections with religious influences.

Higher education and science reflected this trend most dramatically during the period after the Civil War. In 1850 the vast majority of American colleges had for their presidents evangelical clergymen who ensured a distinctly evangelical and moral flavor in key courses on "moral science," "political economy," or "evidences of Christianity." American science similarly was dominated by evangelical Christians. The chief reason to study nature had been to glory at the marvels of God's design. At midcentury evangelical scientists had confidently proclaimed the sci-

Many of the new churches in America's cities were established by immigrants.   BILLY GRAHAM CENTER

entific confirmations of the Bible. By the end of the century all this seemed almost as distant as the era of the dinosaurs. The best colleges were now "universities" or imitators of universities. Universities, in turn, were based on a German scientific model. Each area, whether it was economics, political science, sociology, psychology, or even history and literary criticism, had become a separate professional discipline. Professional standards no longer were influenced by the Bible, but rather were modeled after the standards of the natural sciences. In the natural sciences themselves, few self-respecting practitioners would publicly reflect on the relation of scientific work to scripture. Darwinism had seen to that. Instead of science supporting the argument that the design in the universe proved there was a designer, people now talked of "the warfare between science and religion." Within hardly a generation, vast areas of American thought and academic life had been removed from all reference to Protestant or biblical considerations.

In other areas of American life the process of their separation from religious concerns was less dramatic largely because it had been going on for much longer. This was true of economic life and politics, two activities near the heart of the culture. One would have to think back to the early days of the Puritans or the Quakers to appreciate the extent of the change. In any case, by the Gilded Age it was clear that these activities seldom came under real religious review. Moral considerations, with some genuinely Christian roots, could occasionally have an impact, as they did in the Progressive movement after the turn of the century. By and large, however, American politics operated by its own rules, effectively free from internalized moral restraints. So Henry Adams lamented in his novel, *Democracy* (1880). He characterized the nation's leading Washington politician as a person who "talked about virtue and vice as a man who is colour-blind talks about red and green." The business world operated with a similar relationship between Christian and ethical concerns and practical considerations. John D. Rockefeller, Sr., an active Baptist, might say "God gave me my money," even though he gained much of it by shrewd monopolistic practices that drove his competitors out of business. Andrew Carnegie

God gave me my money.

JOHN D. ROCKEFELLER

might preach a frankly more secular "Gospel of Wealth." In either case, the religious and moral concerns seemed directed toward justifying what the competitive demands for business success would have dictated anyway.

American Protestants in the late nineteenth century, then, faced a peculiar situation. Externally, they were successful. One could see that from the great stone edifices that were gracing the street corners of cities and towns. Internally, also, they could point to some real spiritual health. Millions of men, women, and young people were profitting from their ministry, growing spiritually, and dedicating their lives toward serving God and their fellows. Enthusiasm for foreign mis-

This Currier and Ives print held up "The Little Alms-giver" as an example to the Gilded Age.
BILLY GRAHAM CENTER

"Family Devotion — Morning," Currier and Ives

sions, for instance, had never been higher, and the motives for those who made arduous journeys to foreign lands were often self-sacrificial. Many others served their neighbors in quiet ways which were never recorded. And while in many public areas the impact of Protestant Christianity was receding, in countless private ways—especially in family life and the teaching of virtue and responsibility—the influences were strong and positive.

Nonetheless the success was deceptive. Behind it, as has been seen, lurked problems of immense magnitude: formidable intellectual challenges were eroding faith in the Bible, and massive migration to cities and immigration of non-Protestant people produced a secularism which removed much of the nation's life from effective religious influence. The problems were huge, perhaps in human terms insurmountable. Yet the success itself had a tendency to obscure the dimensions of the crises. It also sometimes had the effect of inviting superficial solutions, such as working to preserve Protestant respectability but at the expense of a prophetic Protestant message that would challenge, rather than simply confirm, the value systems that were coming to control American life.

The Stars

The careers of the most popular religious figures of the era probably are more revealing of the Protestantism of the era than are the histories of the major denominations. Denominations did indeed command loyalties, especially tied to one's ethnic heritage. But in America the popular belief was strong that the individual was the basic religious unit. Denominational affiliation was ultimately a matter of free choice. As a result, the denom-

inational structures were somewhat weak. If you did not like one church, you could simply leave and go to the one down the street. Accordingly, the strongest religious loyalties of many people were attractive preachers. This trait became particularly apparent after the Civil War when, as in the business world of the same time, this sort of free enterprise system produced great stars who rose to the top in the competition for public acclaim.

Puck cartoon satirizing the rivalry between popular preachers, in this case Henry Ward Beecher and T. DeWitt Talmadge, both of Brooklyn   BILLY GRAHAM CENTER

Henry Ward Beecher (1813–1887)
BILLY GRAHAM CENTER

These traits and the messages of these religious stars are quite revealing, therefore, of popular Protestant opinion.

Henry Ward Beecher

The most famous preacher of the era was Henry Ward Beecher (1813-1887). Beecher was from the first family of nineteenth-century Protestantism. His father, Lyman Beecher, was second in fame only to Charles Finney as a Congregationalist and Presbyterian leader. Several of Lyman's children were illustrious, including Harriet Beecher Stowe, known everywhere as the author of *Uncle Tom's Cabin*. Henry Ward Beecher was almost as well known and was widely regarded as representative of all that was forward-looking in American Protestantism.

For forty years (from 1847 to 1887) Henry was pastor of the Plymouth (Congregational) Church of Brooklyn, New York. Brooklyn in that day was a thriving middleclass suburb, a prototype of the suburban culture that would characterize twentieth-century America. Beecher's role was to smooth the way in making the religious transition from one era to another. The religious heritage of pious Americans of older Anglo-Saxon stock had been strongly Calvinistic. Henry's father, Lyman, had been known in Boston as "Brimstone Beecher." Now, however, the polite modern temper of suburbia seemed unsuited for the harsher Calvinist doctrines such as total depravity or God's eternal decrees to elect some to salvation and leave others to the endless flames of Hell. Modern thought, especially Darwinism, raised further questions about the basis for traditional beliefs. Beecher, the chief popularizer of the "new theology," reassured his audiences that Christianity progressed with the modern age. One need not worry about the literal accuracy of biblical doctrines. The oaks of civilization, he said, had evolved since biblical times. Should we then "go back and talk about acorns?" The religion of the modern age, moreover, was a matter of the heart rather than a question of strictly orthodox doctrine. Such sentiments appealed to the romantic sensibilities of the time. Christianity, Beecher assured his audiences, had evolved into the highest ethical principles.

The appeal of this message was immense. Side-stepping but not denying many traditional doctrines, Beecher identified Christianity with the highest ideals of respectable

Phillips Brooks (1835–1893)
RELIGIOUS NEWS SERVICE PHOTO

The Law of Growth

"For whosoever hath, to him shall be given; and whosoever hath not, from him shall be taken even that which he seemeth to have." — Luke viii. 18.

... Jesus went on frankly to declare that the truth of the parable was a truth everywhere; that everywhere there was a law of growth, a law of accumulation and of loss, which drew more blessing where blessing was already, and condemned to decay that which had no real vitality. It was a sort of "survival of the fittest" declared to be existing throughout the world.

... Believe me, my friends, there is something better for you to do than to accept the patent inequalities of life with forlorn resignation. There was never any champion of individuality like Jesus, and yet He recognized and found no fault with the law of privilege, the law by which wealth and culture and the patent forms of happiness flow together and collect in the rich lives of certain men. It is possible for you, though a poor man, to take so wide a view of the world, and of your race, that you shall be thoroughly glad that some other men are rich.

PHILLIPS BROOKS,
from a sermon preached March 11, 1877, Trinity Episcopal Church, Boston

middleclass culture. So great was his prestige that his reputation survived a scandal in which in 1874 he was accused of having seduced the wife of one of his parishioners. The jury was out eight days and after fifty-two ballots was unable to agree on a verdict. So Beecher was presumed innocent, perhaps exonerated, and quickly returned to his role as leading American saint. His prestige was demonstrated a few years later when members of the regional congregational association were taking steps to bring heresy charges against his theological doctrines. Beecher simply left the association. The individual had become more influential than the institution.

Phillips Brooks

Slightly less colorful, but nearly as much revered, was Beecher's counterpart in Boston, Phillips Brooks (1835-1893). Brooks, like Beecher, could point to Puritan lineage, and as rector of the Trinity Episcopal Church from 1869 to 1893 he helped ease his Boston congregation away from the remaining vestiges of the rigors of the Calvinist heritage. Brooks was an early representative of a line of positive thinkers in American pulpitry. "Believe in yourself," he advised, "and reverence your own human nature; it is the only salvation from brutal vice and every false belief...."

His views of human nature were, in fact, just the opposite of those of Calvinism. "The ultimate fact of human life," he said, "is goodness and not sin." Like every popular American preacher in the modern era, Brooks had a great faith in America itself. "I do not know how a man can be an American," he said in sentiments endlessly reflected by American preachers and their audiences, "... and not catch something with regard to God's purpose as to this great land." And, like Beecher, Brooks was a master at integrating modern thought and Christianity into an optimistic, though socially and politically conservative, "American" message.

Josiah Strong

Much as Brooks in "The Law of Growth" used Darwinism to explain a Christianity of self-help and individualism, Josiah Strong (1847-1916) applied Darwinism to suggest new dimensions of Christian American nationalism. Strong was a star of a different sort than Beecher or Brooks. He rose to fame from a book, *Our Country* (1885), which quickly became a best-seller. Strong was a secretary of the Congregational Home Mission Society, and his book was frankly a plea for more vigorous Christian missionary efforts throughout the nation. Perceptive in defining the social dimensions of the American

And our plea is not America for America's sake; but America for the world's sake. For, if this generation is faithful to its trust, America is to become God's right arm in his battle with the world's ignorance and oppression and sin. If I were a Christian African or Arab, I should look into the immediate future of the United States with intense and thrilling interest; for as Professor Hoppin of Yale has said: "America Christianized means the world Christianized." And "If America fail," says Professor Park, "the world will fail."

JOSIAH STRONG,

Our Country, 1885

crisis, Strong frankly urged Christianization. "Christianize the immigrant," he declared, "and he will be easily Americanized." The situation was becoming desperate. "Our cities, which are gathering together the most dangerous elements of our civilization, will, in due time, unless Christianized, prove the destruction of our free institutions." Strong's views reflected current social Darwinistic theories about race. He believed that the Anglo-Saxons were proving their superiority by their survival and growing dominance around the world. The superiority of the British and American peoples was seen in their Protestant and democratic principles. The white man, however, had a duty to strengthen other races by sharing with them these ideals, especially Christianity.

Views such as Strong's had a definite effect on American foreign policy. The most famous and striking instance is when during the Spanish-American War (1898) President William McKinley was faced with the question of what to do with the Philippines, recently won from the Spanish. Late one night after kneeling in prayer, he reached the solution: "There was nothing left for us to do but to take them all and to educate the Fili-

The American Dream

I say that you ought to get rich, and it is your duty to get rich. How many of my pious brethren say to me, "Do you, a Christian minister, spend your time going up and down the country, advising young people to get rich, to get money?" "Yes, of course I do." They say, "Isn't that awful! Why don't you preach the gospel instead of preaching about man's making money?" "Because to make money honestly is to preach the gospel."

... One of the best things in our life is when a young man has earned his own living, and when he becomes engaged to some lovely young woman, and makes up his mind to have a home of his own. Then with that same love comes also that divine inspiration toward better things, and he begins to save his money. He begins to leave off his bad habits and put money in the bank ... he goes out in the suburbs to look for a home ... and then goes for his wife, and when he takes his bride over the threshold of that door for the first time he says in words of eloquence my voice can never touch: "I have earned this home myself. It is all mine, and I divide it with thee." That is the grandest moment a human heart may ever know.

RUSSELL H. CONWELL,

"Acres of Diamonds," 1915 (*Used with permission of Harper and Row, Publishers*)

Revivalist Dwight L. Moody and musician Ira Sankey at the opening services of a revival in Brooklyn, New York
BILLY GRAHAM CENTER

pinos and uplift and civilize and Christianize them, and by God's grace do the very best we could by them, as our fellow men for whom Christ also died."

Baptist Russell H. Conwell (1843-1925), who in Philadelphia built America's largest church, responded to the missionary needs of the day with another version of the gospel of uplift. Conwell, like Josiah Strong, saw the cities as the critical area for home missionary efforts. Not as content as Beecher or Brooks to preach only to those who had arrived socially, the Baptist pastor worked strenuously to make his church responsive also to those who had not yet reached the Protestant middle class. Conwell accordingly made his Baptist Temple into an "institutional church," or a center for social service institutions to serve the neighborhood throughout the week. His complex of institutions offered gymnasiums, athletic programs, reading rooms, day nurseries, educational lectures and cultural activities, a college (eventually Temple University), and the Conwell School of Theology.

While Conwell was a social reformer and philanthropist who responded to the changing needs of the city, his message was that people should help themselves. Conwell was one of the most famous lecturers in America. He delivered his lecture, "Acres of Diamonds," an incredible six thousand times (which would mean an average of 150 repe-titions a year for forty years), perhaps the most well-worn discourse in history! Its message was one of success. Specifically, it was the duty of Christians to become rich: you can find acres of diamonds in your own backyard if you only look.

Dwight L. Moody

Dwight L. Moody (1837-1899), the leading professional evangelist of the day, illustrated the American dream of success in his own life. Moody was a Horatio Alger figure. Reared in a small town in New England, he developed a successful shoe business in Chicago but soon turned to evangelism. After some profitable years in local work, he and his singing partner, Ira Sankey, traveled to Great Britain for a modestly conceived preaching tour. The tour in fact became an immense success and lasted from 1873 to 1875. When they returned home Moody and Sankey were national heroes. Through the rest of his career Moody held massive evangelistic campaigns in cities throughout America.

Moody was not a sensationalist evangelist like Charles Finney before him or Billy Sunday in the next generation. Rather, he looked like one of the businessmen of the era and captivated his audiences with a homey and sentimental style of storytelling. His message

Moody preaching at the Hippodrome in London

was simple. It involved "Three R's": Ruin by Sin, Redemption by Christ, and Regeneration by the Holy Ghost. Saving souls was his preeminent goal. "I look upon this world as a wrecked vessel," he said in his most famous remark. "God has given me a lifeboat and said to me, 'Moody, save all you can.'"

This stress on saving souls out of a wrecked world reflected some change in emphasis in popular American evangelism. Many Protestants since the Civil War were losing confidence in social solutions to the world's

Ira V. Sankey, Moody's singing partner
LIBRARY OF CONGRESS

problems. One sign of this shift was the increasing popularity of premillennialism, which emphasized that the world would not be improved until Jesus personally came again and set up his kingdom on earth. Moody and all his closest associates preached such doctrines. Their premillennialism, however, did not lead to complacency. Rather, it impelled them to more vigorous missionary and evangelistic efforts ("save all you can"). Moody himself established centers out of which such work radiated. In Chicago he adopted in 1886 a Bible Institute (later called Moody Bible Institute) to train laymen for evangelistic efforts. More important at the time were his Northfield Conferences, held near his Massachusetts home. Out of these grew one of the largest missionary efforts of the era, the Student Volunteer Movement founded in 1886. Thousands of students during the subsequent years pledged themselves to lives of missionary work. The motto of SVM well summarized Moody's own goals: "The evangelization of the world in this generation."

The Student Volunteer Movement

DONALD TINDER

The Student Volunteer Movement for Foreign Missions arose in 1886 under Dwight Moody's inspiration at his conference grounds at Mt. Hermon, Massachusetts. Similar organizations soon were started in other countries, bringing college graduates into the missionary ranks as never before. Thousands signed the pledge to become a foreign missionary "if God permit," which he did in only a minority of the cases, but presumably most of those who didn't go helped to strengthen the supporting base. Even so, by 1920 some 8,140 former college students who had joined the SVM had actually sailed abroad as foreign missionaries. More than 2,500 had gone to China, while 1,500 went to India and Africa received about 900.

The SVM's watchword was "the evangelization of the world in this generation," and every four years giant student missionary conventions presented the challenge. The peak of the movement was reached at the Des Moines convention in 1920, with 6,900 delegates from 950 colleges. The next year 637 SVMers sailed abroad. But the thrust of the movement was changing. The watchword was dropped, and interest in social issues was attracting more concern than evangelism. By 1934 only thirty-eight SVMers sailed, and fewer than five hundred delegates attended the 1940 convention. The missionary church among collegians had passed to other hands.

The Era of Crusades
(1890-1917)

The motto of the Student Volunteer Movement summarized well the spirit of much of the American Protestantism of the day. Not only was it an era of great piety and enthusiasm; it was also an era of go-getters. To get something done, one had to approach it with enthusiasm and organization. The sky was the limit if one organized enthusiasm efficiently. The most efficient organizations were voluntary ones—people enlisted and dedicated to a specific cause. So the real cutting edges of American Protestantism were voluntary organizations and crusades. By these means vast networks of Protestants from all major denominations were mobilized for Christian missions and service.

Dwight Moody's career epitomized this trend. While remaining on the best of terms with denominations, Moody spurned denominational affiliations and built his own evangelistic empire, free from ecclesiastical control. Moody's evangelistic career itself had in fact begun in one of the most important of the earlier parachurch organizations—the Young Men's Christian Association. Imported from England, as were many such evangelical organizations, the YMCA and the YWCA were designed at midcentury as centers for evangelism to young persons moving to the cities. As such they were important components in the evangelical home missionary efforts.

Missions

Missions, whether as evangelism at home or in efforts abroad, were the central Protestant crusades. American Protestants had been active in missions abroad since early in the century, but their enthusiasm burgeoned after 1890. Together with their British counter-parts they were leading an advance of Christian missions so great that historian Kenneth Scott Latourette has called the period from 1815 to 1914 "the great century" of Christianity. Certainly in America the period from 1890 to World War I was the golden age of Protestant missions.

Efforts to mobilize at home were equally ambitious. Prior to the Civil War there had been an "empire" of evangelical agencies for home and foreign missions, Sunday schools, Bible and tract distribution, benevolence, and reform. In the postwar era these "voluntary societies," often cooperating with denominational agencies, continued to provide the leading edge in organizing spiritual impulses.

The growth of the Sunday-school movement is a good example. For a generation the American Sunday School Union, based on a British agency, had been evangelizing children throughout the nation. With the growth of the cities after the Civil War Sunday schools appeared as most important means for reaching the unchurched. Often families could be reached through their children. Enterprising leaders accordingly revitalized the Sunday-school movement by introducing new organizations and techniques. Under the leadership of the Baptist B. F. Jacobs, "decision days" and "rally days" were organized. Teachers were brought together in regular county conventions, and a "uniform lesson" plan was devised so that members of various denominations could meet together to prepare the next week's lesson. Young people and adults were also mobilized through Sunday-school classes so that the whole Protestant community might be turned into an agency for evangelism. "Each one win one" became the motto for many Baraca (for men)

Parade of Sunday school children through Brooklyn, 1868

and Philathea (for women) classes by the turn of the century, and by 1913 these nationally organized classes were involving a total of nearly one million members from thirty-two denominations and had spawned many imitators. Sunday schools sometimes even overshadowed the local congregation, and the Sunday-school superintendent might be nearly as important a figure as the minister.

A similar case is the growth of the Christian Endeavor Society. Francis E. Clark, a Congregationalist minister, founded this organization in Maine in 1881 "to promote earnest Christian life" and to provide training for Christian service. Typically, Christian Endeavor groups held weekly devotional meetings and monthly meetings for special consecration. "Trusting in the Lord Jesus Christ for strength," read the simple pledge, "I promise Him I will strive to do whatever He would have me do." Clark's organization grew so rapidly among young people that by 1885 he could found an international organization, claiming 3.5 million members by 1910, with perhaps two-thirds of these in the United States and Canada. Such enterprises had the important side effect of uniting Protestants from almost every denomination.

In this context the more famous crusades of the era should be viewed. Of these the most successful was the temperance movement, which attempted to ban the use of alcoholic beverages. This movement, as many others, had substantial roots from earlier in the nineteenth century but was effectively revived and efficiently organized during the new age of crusading Protestantism. Temperance was an issue on which liberals and conservatives could thoroughly agree, and one of the few issues on which Protestants could make common cause with some Catholic leaders.

Dwight Moody and J. V. Farwell with their first Chicago Sunday school class in the late 1860s

BILLY GRAHAM CENTER

Foreign Missions, 1865-1930

DONALD TINDER

As a base for foreign missions, America essentially followed the lead of Britain throughout the nineteenth century. But as the twentieth century approached, a new burst of enthusiasm and organizational ability began to make American influence more widely felt both in receiving lands and among the sending countries. By the time of the world-wide Great Depression, the initiative for Protestant foreign missions had passed from the Old World to the New.

In 1865 America was still looked upon as a mission field itself by Roman Catholics (remaining officially so until 1908) and many continentally based denominations. They were sending funds and personnel to help their American counterparts cope with the flood of immigrants, many of whom were poor both materially and spiritually. They feared, with good reason, that if the newcomers were not ministered to by their fellow Catholics, Lutherans, or Reformed, they would be easier prey for the aggressively evangelistic Baptists, Methodists, and other free spirits that flourished in the New World.

The first Catholic agency, the Catholic Foreign Mission Society of America, generally known as the Maryknollers after the name of their headquarters north of New York City, was launched in 1911 and soon began sending the first of several hundred priests and sisters overseas. Many other Americans went abroad as Jesuits, Dominicans, Franciscans, and the like. Nevertheless, in stark contrast to the pattern that emerged for Protestants, American Catholics remained proportionately behind several European countries in numbers of missionaries.

The large and historically English-speaking denominations — Baptists, Congregationalists, Disciples, Episcopalians, and Presbyterians — had generally launched their sending agencies early in the nineteenth century. The distractions of the Civil War, including bitter denominational divisions preceding it and numerous ministries to the freedmen in the aftermath, together with constant efforts to keep up with western settlements and to minister to floods of immigrants, helped to keep involvement in foreign missions at a low level. There were at most a few hundred Americans serving abroad in the 1870s.

White Americans, however, worked actively among the nonwhite population at home. Much of the black population, involuntarily brought over from Africa, was converted to Christianity, mostly by Baptists and Methodists. By 1915 there were as many black Protestants in the United States as there were Protestants in all of Africa and Asia. And since the days of the Puritans there were substantial missions to the American Indians, though with much less success than among the blacks.

Teddy Roosevelt visits the mission field BILLY GRAHAM CENTER

As late as 1890 only about nine hundred Americans were serving as missionaries overseas. But by 1900 the total had jumped to nearly five thousand. The northern Baptists, Methodists, Congregationalists, and Presbyterians had between 540 and 770 each, and Americans composed more than twenty-five percent of the world total of Protestant missionaries. By 1915 the number of American missionaries had nearly doubled since 1900, and by 1925 more than thirteen thousand were from America, nearly half of the global total.

What accounted for this dramatic rise more than any other one factor was the emergence of the Student Volunteer Movement for Foreign Missions in 1886. By 1936 a total of more than thirteen thousand missionaries had sailed for the foreign fields as a result, at least in part, of membership in the SVM.

The SVM was only one of many new organizations that were not themselves sending societies but existed alongside of them as recruiters and promoters and, to a lesser extent, coordinators of the Protestant missions movement. However, the enthusiasm of the Missionary Education Movement (founded 1902) and the Laymen's Missionary Movement (founded 1907) was spent by the 1920s. More long lasting was the Foreign Missions Conference of North

The Sunday School Times *portrayed modernism as a sinister threat to the foreign mission endeavor.* BILLY GRAHAM CENTER

America (founded 1893), which eventually included most of the older denominational societies. By 1925 some eighty percent of American missionaries were with member boards of the FMC.

In 1900, the FMC sponsored a ten-day missions convention in New York City that attracted four thousand persons daily, including many Europeans. It helped to pave the way for a global conference in 1910 in Edinburgh, Scotland, chaired by a prominent American missions administrator, John R. Mott. Edinburgh 1910 was the organizational launching pad for the ecumenical movement.

The tensions of the modernist-fundamentalist conflicts of the 1920s, however, led to a redirection of the missionary force away from the older mission societies. When the Laymen's Foreign Mission Inquiry, founded by John D. Rockefeller, Jr., in 1930, issued its controversial report *Re-Thinking Missions* two years later, the extent of liberalism's redefinition of the missionary message and task was evident. Though the denominations tried to distance themselves from the recommendations of the report, the fears of conservatives as to where things

Theological disputes within mission societies tended at times to distract from the ultimate goal. BILLY GRAHAM CENTER

were headed were shown to be well founded. The future of missions was to be largely outside of the older denominational boards.

In 1865 an Englishman, J. Hudson Taylor, launched the China Inland Mission, which became the pattern for interdenominational or "faith" missions. A North American council for the CIM was established in 1888. Other missions of this nature started in both Britain and America for different parts of the world. Among the earliest from America were the Woman's Union Missionary Society (1861), the Sudan Interior Mission (1893), Africa Inland Mission (1895), and the Inland South America Missionary Union (1914). These four plus the CIM and two others founded the Interdenominational Foreign Mission Association in 1917 to serve as a kind of accrediting agency and a forum for the expression of common concerns. The "inland" name in so many conveyed their going beyond the easily accessible port cities where the older societies had become institutionally entrenched. The Wycliffe Bible Translators (1934) and the World Radio Missionary Fellowship (1931) were later expressions of American initiative to reach specialized constituencies, such as linguistically isolated and illiterate tribes, and to utilize new technologies, such as radio.

A different pattern had as its largest representative the Christian and Missionary Alliance (1881), a group of congregations with a strong foreign missions commitment at its heart. Later, as theological tensions rose in such denominations as the Baptists, Disciples, and Presbyterians, new mission agencies were started that were independent of the denominational leadership.

Meanwhile the Wesleyan tradition, largely embodied in the Methodist denominations, had been undergoing its own theological controversies. First there emerged the Holiness movement in the mid-nineteenth cen-

An 1895 *cartoon criticizing the British and American military support of missionaries to China* BILLY GRAHAM CENTER

tury, from within which countless new denominations emerged, each eventually with its own mission board. Also a few interdenominational missions appealed to the Holiness tradition. Secondly, just as the twentieth century was dawning, the Pentecostal movement appeared. Soon its missionaries were going forth everywhere, not only to bring the message of salvation but to proclaim the subsequent filling of the Holy Spirit as evidence by speaking in unknown tongues. This message of Pentecost quickly spread

Graduating class of the China Bible School BILLY GRAHAM CENTER

to Europe and then to other mission fields around the world, often to the consternation not only of Catholics (for Pentecostals were to become by far the largest Protestant group in Latin America and in much of Latin Europe) but also of the older Protestant missions, both liberal and conservative.

By the 1930s, the comparatively unified missions thrust from America of the mid-nineteenth century had been greatly enlarged, but also greatly fractured. Modernism was one source of division, as was Pentecostalism. Roman Catholics were sending out missionaries in increasing numbers. Moreover, Seventh-day Adventists and the far more unorthodox Jehovah's Witnesses and Mormons were going forth in such numbers from these shores and with such success that a large proportion, when not a majority, of their constituencies would eventually be found in other lands. If it had ever been possible to speak of a missionary movement from America, it was now clear that there were instead large and diverse movements that reflected the enormous diversity of American Christianity.

John R. Mott
DONALD TINDER

John R. Mott (1865-1955) was the most widely travelled and influential mission and ecumenical administrator of his time. A lifelong Methodist layman, he was a student at Cornell when he committed his life to Christian service. Soon he was one of the first hundred volunteers at the 1886 conference that launched the Student Volunteer Movement. Two years later he was the SVM chairman. He was also active at the national level with the college chapters of the YMCA. In 1895 he was instrumental in founding the World Student Christian Federation, the pioneering organization of the ecumenical movement, and was one of its top leaders until 1929. In 1910 he chaired the Edinburgh missionary conference and then its Continuation Committee which became the International Missionary Council, which he served until retiring in 1942. Mott was typically American in wedding personal Christian commitment with superb organizational and administrative skills along with a desire to transcend historic confessional distinctives in the interests of truly international Christian cooperation.

John R. Mott (1865–1955)
GLOBE AND MAIL PHOTO

Women's Causes

Closely connected to the temperance movement was the women's movement. Missions and voluntary organizations of all sorts were among the few areas where women had opportunities for real public leadership, as is well illustrated in the life of Frances Willard. In fact, the majority of church members were women. This meant inevitably that women were assuming more significant roles, especially in new enterprises where voluntary service was at a premium. Similarly, in some of the newer denominations less bound by tradition the idea that this was a new age when "your daughters shall prophesy" brought public acknowledgment of women's leadership. Such leadership had been particularly prominent in some holiness groups since midcentury. In some of the newer groups to grow out of that movement women preached and were ordained.

The least successful of the major campaigns was the crusade for sabbath observance. The Puritan sabbath, in which the Lord's Day was strictly observed for worship rather than work or play, was one of the chief symbols of Protestant civilization in America. European immigrants, both from some Protestant groups who were not Sabbatarian and especially from Catholic countries, threatened this custom. Their "continental sabbath" was more like a holiday. Secularization favored the continental trend as well, as did some Protestant reaction to overly strict sabbath-keeping. Many Protestants fought staunchly, however, to enforce their sabbath customs by legislation, attempting to ban commercial enterprises, industries, and places of amusement from operating on the sabbath. Particularly notorious were efforts to close the Centennial Exposition of Philadelphia on Sundays in 1876 and the Columbian Exposition in Chicago in 1893. In the latter in-

Currier and Ives, "Remember the Sabbath Day, to Keep it Holy." The campaign for sabbath observance was among the least successful of the reform crusades.   BILLY GRAHAM CENTER

The temperance crusade was one of the most sustained of the reform efforts and generated some of the more imaginative analogies.

BILLY GRAHAM CENTER

stance, Sabbatarian efforts were thoroughly defeated. Throughout the era, however, businesses and industries in most areas remained closed on Sunday.

Both the temperance campaigns and Sabbatarianism were viewed among their proponents as not only questions of personal morality but also important social reforms. Alcoholic consumption was often viewed as a "drug" problem in the cities in much the same way as narcotic drugs have been more recently. Urban poverty often seemed related to squandering money, time, and energy on alcohol. Sabbatarianism was viewed in a similar light. Before effective labor unions, when industrialists often required their employees to work sixty-hour weeks or even more, enforced sabbath rest was an important piece of labor legislation. Paradoxically, Protestant zeal had not carried over to other labor reforms so that a Sabbatarianism that banned recreation as well as work on Sunday held only slim attractions for those who had to work almost every waking hour for six days a week.

Frances Willard
SUSAN B. HOEKEMA

Frances Willard (1839-1898) was a leader of church women and an example of what a woman with vision and determination could achieve. Her life and work were devoted to many of the causes for which women were active in the late nineteenth century, including social welfare reform, moral education, female education, and the women's suffrage campaign. She is best known as the leader of the Woman's Christian Temperance Union, having served as president of the WCTU from 1874 to 1898. Through this organization she inspired church women to work to impress their moral force on the society at large, extending their influence from their own families to those who owned and ran liquor-selling establishments, those who supplied them, and those who patronized them. The campaign against strong drink was not simple, narrow moralism, however. Alcohol stood condemned, not simply because it inebriated, but because it left women and children destitute, broke up homes, and engendered domestic violence. As Frances Willard's slogan — "Home Protection" — made clear, the rights and welfare of women and children were central to the temperance movement.

Frances Willard (1839–1898) BILLY GRAHAM CENTER

This Currier and Ives print projected the crusading spirit of the temperance reformers; Frances Willard, however, sought to channel women's energy in more directions. LIBRARY OF CONGRESS

Willard addressed these issues through other channels as well. She prompted the WCTU to institute kindergartens for young children and industrial schools to teach older girls skills with which they could support themselves. She supported labor organizations, allying herself with Terence V. Powderly and the Knights of Labor, in the conviction that the welfare of families depended on good working conditions and fair wages. In addition, she involved herself in electoral politics, trying to build a strong third party that supported temperance and women's rights.

A central concern of Willard's Home Protection campaign was women's suffrage. She believed that only with equal political rights would women effectively guard against social evils. In 1876 she publicly declared her support for women's suffrage, by 1880 she won a majority of the WCTU to her position, and for the rest of her life she worked to win the vote for women. Her support contributed to making the suffrage campaign respectable since she attracted and was seen to represent conservative, upright church women.

Willard did not think it enough that women influence the world through reform movements or with the ballot. She believed that society needed the talents of everyone and that women, like men, should be free to exercise their gifts fully. In her advice book, *How To Win: A Book for Girls*, she urged young women to examine their abilities and develop to the fullest their particular talents. Women, she thought, could serve society in the pulpit and office as well as in the home. Some of the members of the WCTU did not share Willard's expansive vision and focused their energies on combatting the evils of drink. She led other church women to broaden their outlook and their concern, however, and inspired them to work through a variety of means for a better society.

A *variety of aids were available to those willing to join the crusade.*

Roles of Women in the Church, 1860-1920

SUSAN B. HOEKEMA

In mid-nineteenth-century America the roles open to women were few. Convention ascribed to women the gifts of gentleness, patience, and sensitivity and decreed that the woman's sphere of action was the home. There she was expected to use her moral influence and nurturing ability to foster Christian families, the foundation for a Christian nation. Her role was important, but severely restricted. Society frowned on the woman who spoke publicly, pursued a career, or sought an education. Matters of general social welfare, as well as political and economic concerns, were considered the responsibility of men.

In the first half of the nineteenth century some church women had moved beyond the confines of the family. Some had joined societies to support missions and charities; a few, such as Sarah and Angelina Grimké, spoke out on reform issues, including abolition and care for the mentally ill. During the Civil War many more women became active outside their homes. They supported the war effort by creating and coordinating a complex relief program, organizing fairs to raise money for medical and devotional work among the soldiers, and forming societies to supervise the transportation of supplies and to care for women and children left behind in duress.

This war experience encouraged women to more direct action in missions and benevolence. Before the war, most of the women's foreign mission societies supported work directed by men; in the 1860s and 1870s women began organizing much larger societies that sent out and supported female missionaries and the schools and hospitals they founded in India, Burma, China, and elsewhere. These societies, which gave women a sense of involvement in important and exotic endeavors, developed a fervent and dedicated membership.

In their own cities women created institutions and programs in response to the needs of the destitute and displaced. In Chicago, for example, women had major responsibility for the Home for the Friendless, the Chicago Half-orphan Asylum, a home for wayward girls, and vocational training programs for young women. Their involvement extended far beyond throwing parties and organizing fairs to raise money. They administered funds, arranged facilities, set policies, and supervised operations.

In many ways these organizations built upon the conventional notion of the woman as nurturer and guardian of the family. Through the organizations women cared for other women and children. Primary goals of the benevolent associations were to aid those who were alone and to help the displaced rebuild their families. The women's missionary outreach was motivated by a desire to improve conditions for foreign women as well as to bring the gospel. Although the women involved did not throw over all convention, they did move beyond the restriction of their society, building formal organizations which addressed major social problems.

Reform movements provided another route by which church women could work for the general welfare of society. Women were involved in many causes in the late nineteenth century, including the pure food and drug campaign, political reform, women's suffrage, and labor issues such as the eight-hour day, protection for female workers, and regulation of child labor. The campaign that attracted the greatest number of church women, however, was the Prohibition movement. In 1874 women formed their own national, independent organization — the Woman's Christian Temperance Union — and from then until the enactment of the Eighteenth Amendment establishing prohibition in 1919 women carried the temperance banner in a crusade that extended their moral influence over the nation.

While the reform, benevolence, and missionary movements of the late nineteenth century expanded under the attention of church women, women also began to challenge their limited role in the institutional churches. The feminist movement, inaugurated at Seneca Falls in 1848, deplored the fact that Man allowed Woman "in Church as well as in State, but a subordinate position, claiming Apostolic authority for her exclusion from the ministry, and, with some exceptions, from any public participation in the affairs of the church." The women at the Seneca Falls Woman's Rights Convention vowed to fight for the equality of women in the church as well as in other areas of life. Some sectarian and evangelistic movements — including Quakers, Seventh-day Adventists, Universalists, the Salvation Army, Christian Science, and the Holiness movement — recognized women as equals with men and encouraged female participation. But the major denominations accorded women no official positions and resisted change.

By the 1880s laywomen were calling for more recognition and responsibility in the churches, but they met with strong opposition. The Methodist Episcopal church refused to allow a delegation of women, which included Frances Willard, president of the Woman's Christian Temperance

Many reform-minded church women were active in the women's suffrage movement.   LIBRARY OF CONGRESS

Union, to speak before the General Conference in 1880 and again in 1888. The 1880 General Conference also refused to open the offices of deacon and elder to women; in 1888 it created a special office of deaconess, primarily for women working as nurses. Women were permitted to be ordained as local preachers in 1924, but only in 1954 could women be ordained ministers in the Methodist Episcopal church. Other churches changed even more slowly. In the Presbyterian church, for example, all offices were closed to women until 1922, when the General Assembly agreed to allow them to be ordained deacons. In 1930 the office of ruling elder was opened to women, but they were excluded from the ministry until 1956. Some churches, including the Congregational and the Methodist Protestant church, allowed the ordination of women in the 1880s, but women who felt called to the ministry faced opposition from family and friends as well as church authorities, and few were ordained before the 1920s.

While women were engaged in the long and painful struggle for recognition of their gifts and talents in the institutional churches, their autonomy in the extrainstitutional benevolent and mission societies was being eroded. With little consultation with the women involved, the Methodist Episcopal church reorganized the women's missionary societies under the control of the denominational Board of Missions in 1906, and seventeen years later the Presbyterian church did the same, merging the women's societies into a male-run mission board. Other denominations followed suit in the 1910s and 1920s. Women were given positions on the predominantly male boards, but they lost autonomy over funds and projects and, with it, the strong support that a sense of involvement had fostered. Control of benevolent institutions also shifted out of the hands of church women during the early 1900s. Social services were becoming professionalized, and as volunteer organizers began to hire trained social workers, their own involvement diminished. The advancement made in opening church offices to women was thus counterbalanced by the loss of other roles. The gifts and talents of a few found expression in ordained offices, and many more served in Sunday school and other programs. But other women who might previously have helped run an orphanage or direct a missionary society found no outlet for their organizational skills in the church or in church-related programs.

Social Involvement and Retraction

The discovery of urban poverty was, however, one of the major causes for a crisis in conscience in this deeply moralistic Protestant community. During the latter decades of the nineteenth century the prevailing convictions about self-help and laissez faire economics, together with considerable distrust or dislike of the new American working classes and their unions, stood in the way of dealing with the problems at their roots. So when one reads from the prominent church paper *The Congregationalist* in 1886 that in response to labor riots in Chicago "a Gatling gun or two, swiftling brought into position and well served, offers, on the whole, the most merciful as well as effectual remedy," it might appear that the quality of Protestant mercy is a bit strained. *The Congregationalist*'s sentiments, however, were not unusual, given the assumptions and social position of most Protestants of the day. Nevertheless, the new problems of the poverty of the teeming cities were too intense, and the American Protestant conscience too tender, for such callous

solutions to prevail everywhere. Those Protestant leaders who knew most about the real conditions of the poor during this era often were the evangelists who sought to convert the urban poor. Such work led evangelists to slums and tenements and convinced many of them of the urgency of supplementing preaching with simple Christian charity, such as by providing the poor with ice in the summer and coal in the winter. Groups with strong evangelistic emphases, especially holiness groups such as the Salvation Army but including also some of the leading evangelistic associates of Dwight L. Moody, led in these efforts. The rescue mission movement, serving the down-and-out with food, lodging, and the gospel, provided one of the important new institutions of the era.

Gradually, other Protestants awakened to the enormity of the new social problems facing urban America and began to assume responsibility. In part this was due to work of effective reformers such as that of the Danish immigrant Jacob Riis, whose *How the Other Half Lives* (1890) shocked Victorian sensi-

The Cherry Street Mission gospel service, led by its Champion Slum Corps   BILLY GRAHAM CENTER

When the "Dens of Death" were in Baxter Street, big barracks crowded out the old shanties. More came every day, I remember the story of those shown in the picture. They had been built only a little while when complaints came to the Board of Health of smells in the houses. A sanitary inspector was sent to find the cause. He followed the smell down in the cellar, and digging there discovered that the water pipe was a blind. It had simply been run into the ground and was not connected with the sewer.

JACOB RIIS,
America's pioneer reform photo-journalist,
ca. 1890

bilities with its exposure of slum conditions in New York City. More importantly, the political mood of the nation was beginning to shift. During the Gilded Age, conservatism on social issues had prevailed. By 1890, however, winds of change were blowing. The Populist movement, primarily a farmers' movement in the South and the western Midwest, included radical proposals for national social reform. By 1896 Populism had become such a potent political force that it virtually captured the Democratic party with the nomination of the eloquent Christian spokesman for the people, William Jennings Bryan. Another ardent Christian, William McKinley, representing more conservative political assumptions, was elected, but the spirit of reform was in the air. After the death of McKinley in 1901 and the ascendency of Theodore Roosevelt, reformist "progressive" views came to prevail even in the middle classes. Through the election of 1916 every major presidential candidate considered himself "progressive."

This political setting fostered a new wave of social concern in the churches and new types of proposals for social reform. "Social

service," such as that promoted by the *Christian Herald*, increased, but new progressive suggestions from Christians for more comprehensively reforming the social and economic order became especially prominent. These progressive proposals came to be known collectively as "the social gospel." Social gospel proponents explicitly rejected the individualism and laissez faire economics that had prevailed in the Gilded Age and insisted rather that the government take an active part in alleviating the harshest effects of an unrestrained free enterprise system. Their reform proposals were essentially identical with those of the "progressive" politics of the same era. Social gospel advocates tended to make these social concerns central to their understanding of the gospel. While not necessarily denying the value of the traditional evangelical approach of starting with evangelism, social gospel spokesmen subordinated such themes, often suggesting that stress on evangelism had made American evangelicalism too otherworldly (concerned about getting people to heaven) and individualistic (concerned with personal purity more than with the welfare of one's neighbor). Such themes fit well with the emerging liberal theology of the day, which was optimistic about human nature, ethical in emphasis, and hopeful about establishing the principles of the kingdom in the twentieth century. So while some more traditional evangelistically minded evangelicals, such as William Jennings Bryan, might be progressive politically, the social gospel itself came generally to involve an association of progressive politics with liberal and nonevangelistic theology.

When I look upon that unhappy girl's face, I think that the Grace of God can reach that "lost woman" in her sins; but what about the man who made profit on the slum that gave her up to the street?

JACOB RIIS,
"Dens of Death," from *The Battle with the Slum,* 1902

This association of progressive politics with liberal theology came at the same time as a deep crisis was brewing over theological issues. The result of this conjunction of theological and social crises was that twentieth-century American Protestantism began to split into two major parties, not only between conservatives and liberals in theology but correspondingly between conservatives and progressives politically. Conservative theology began to be associated with conservative politics and liberal theology with progressive politics. This development, which was gradual, has sometimes been called "the great reversal" in American evangelicalism. Until this time in American history considerable numbers of revivalist evangelicals had always been in the forefront of social and political reform efforts (antislavery, for instance), even though many other evangelicals had been socially conservative. In the twentieth century, however, evangelical participation in progressive reforms, except in some of the older crusades such as for prohibition, dwindled sharply. As theological liberals spoke more and more about the social implications of the gospel, revivalist evangelicals spoke of them correspondingly less.

This division over both the theological and the social issues was only beginning to become apparent in the first two decades of the century. The crusading spirit and a zeal for Protestant unity based on action still prevailed. Despite the deep tensions, said one survivor of the era, "the ten or fifteen years before the war were, controversially, a kind of Truce of God." Nowhere was this more manifest than in the emergence in 1908 of the Federal Council of Churches. This organization for cooperative action among the Protestant denominations embodied many of the same impulses that were uniting Protestants in Christian Endeavor, the Sunday schools, and prohibition campaigns. At this point the social questions were not yet so clearly divisive as to prevent the new ecumenical agency from concentrating first on social issues. These, in fact, were first on its agenda when the new cooperative body met in 1908. Such vigorous social emphases brought criticism from conservatives who said that the ecumenical body was losing sight of the central goal of the gospel, of winning souls to Christ. In response, the Federal

William Jennings Bryan (1860–1925) combined conservative evangelicalism with progressive politics.
LIBRARY OF CONGRESS

Council in 1912 balanced its commission on social service by adding a commission on evangelism. The same year saw the culmination of one of the last great united crusades of the era, the Men and Religion Forward Movement. This huge effort (whose name and program revealed that the women's movement still had a way to go) attempted to mobilize men and boys for both social service and soul-winning. The effort seemed too much planned, and did not live up to expectations.

The final message is redemption, the redemption of the individual in the world, and through him of the world itself, and there is no redemption of either without redemption of the other.

Federal Council of Churches,
"The Church and Modern Industry," 1912

A deeper problem was developing, however. Evangelicals who emphasized revivalism and those who emphasized social reform were coming more and more to comprise two parties. This was apparent in another incident in 1912. Billy Sunday, who was just rising to fame as the latest of America's leading evangelists, conducted a revival campaign in Columbus, Ohio. After the campaign Washington Gladden, a Congregationalist pastor in Columbus and one of the leading spokesmen for the social gospel, bitterly criticized Sunday's sensationalist techniques and his gospel of soul-saving. A heated debate developed in the religious press. Sunday, while not condemning social service, charged that the recent emphases were "trying to make a religion out of social service with Jesus Christ left out." He claimed that this was the reason for the failure of the Men and Religion Forward Movement. "We've had enough," he said, "of this godless social service nonsense."

Beneath such accusations were more serious problems that could not be ignored

We've had enough of this godless social service nonsense.

BILLY SUNDAY

much longer. Activism and good will had kept a semblance of unity within the dominant Protestant community. Divisive theological and intellectual issues were considered best kept away from public attention, and indeed most of the church-going public was not aware of how deep the rift had become. Success and progress still seemed the dominant mood, underlined by much rhetoric about unity, together with activism, and by beating the drums for the latest crusade. Eventually, however, American Protestantism would have to pay the price of side-stepping the hard theological questions. In fact, there were controversies simmering that were too deep to ignore. To understand these requires a closer look at some of the new trends of the day.

The Social Creed of the Churches

We deem it the duty of all Christian people to concern themselves directly with certain practical industrial problems. To us it seems that the churches must stand—

For equal rights and complete justice for all men in all stations of life.

For the right of all men to the opportunity of self-maintenance, a right ever to be wisely and strongly safeguarded against encroachments of every kind. For the right of workers to some protection against the hardships often resulting from the swift crises of industrial change.

For the principle of conciliation and arbitration in industrial dissensions.

For the protection of the worker from dangerous machinery, occupational disease, injuries and mortality.

For the abolition of child labor.

For such regulation of the conditions of toil for women as shall

safeguard the physical and moral health of the community.

For the suppression of the "sweating system."

For the gradual and reasonable reduction of the hours of labor to the lowest practical point, and for that degree of leisure for all which is a condition of the highest human life.

For a release from employment one day in seven.

For a living wage as a minimum in every industry, and for the highest wage that industry can afford.

For the most equitable division of the products of industry that can ultimately be devised.

For suitable provision for the old age of the workers and for those incapacitated by injury.

For the abatement of poverty.

The Federal Council of Churches, 1908

Social Service and the Churches, 1865-1930

NORRIS MAGNUSON

The decades following the Civil War produced striking changes in American life, one of the most far-reaching of which was the rapid shift from a rural-agricultural to an urban-industrial social and economic order. The poverty and attendant miseries spawned by that transition were intensified by a growing tide of immigrants that by 1920 totalled nearly forty million people, many of whom settled in the already troubled cities. Only gradually and incompletely did the nation awaken to the new poverty and its causes.

Among those who responded early were an increasing number of Protestant and Catholic urban missionaries who entered the slums of virtually every American city with a spiritual witness that soon came to include generous practical assistance. Hundreds of individual congregations such as St. George's Episcopal Church of New York City, denominational agencies and organizations such as the Society of St. Vincent de Paul (Roman Catholic) and the Church Army (Episcopal), and institutions, programs, and organizations that crossed denominational lines, such as the King's Daughters and the Convention of Christian Workers, were among the multifaceted efforts that together came to fairly blanket the nation's slums as well as the wide-ranging needs of the poor.

Among the largest and most well-known of the organizations then operating in American cities, and one that in many ways typified the larger movement, was the Salvation Army. With its origins in the evangelistic efforts of William Booth in the slums of East London in the mid-1860s, and taking its familiar name in 1878, the Salvation Army by the latter date had multiplied to include eighty stations in London and other cities in the British Isles. In 1880, as part of what soon became world-wide expansion, the first official Salvation Army contingent arrived in the United States.

Entering the slums to evangelize, the Booths and their coworkers were driven by the needs of the poor into increasingly extensive efforts to help.

Evangeline Booth (1865–1950), daughter of the founder of the Salvation Army and the Army's commander in the United States BILLY GRAHAM CENTER

Salvation Army coal depot, providing inexpensive fuel for slum dwellers, from a 1902 *cover of the* War Cry,
the Army's official gazette   NEW YORK PUBLIC LIBRARY

Unstructured personal assitance and
simple programs mounted until, in
1890, the publication of William
Booth's In Darkest England and the Way
Out signalled the launching of the
Salvation Army's ambitious "social
scheme." In addition to meeting the
fundamental needs for food, shelter,
clothing, and medical assistance with
such means as shelters, soup kitchens,
and simple dispensaries, the Army
attempted to provide useful training
and employment through schools,
factories, farms, and "farm colonies."
Summer camps and excursions and
holiday "banquets" ministered, meanwhile, to psyche as well as to body.
"Antisuicide" bureaus, searches for
missing persons, legal aid, prison
ministries, and seasonal distribution
of low-cost ice and coal, further illustrate the diversified and wide-ranging
response of Salvationists and other
workers in the slums.

Salvation Army religious service
BILLY GRAHAM CENTER

Led on the North American continent beginning in 1886 by members of the Booth family (Ballington and his wife Maud, who resigned in 1896 to establish the similar Volunteers of America, Emma and her husband, Frederick Booth-Tucker, and the famous Evangeline), the Salvation Army attracted a growing number of adherents. From the tiny American beginnings in 1880 came expansion to nine hundred corps by 1904 and to more than 1,700 by the late 1920s, while on the world front the eighty British Isles' stations of 1878 had mounted to 3,500 two decades later, and to seven thousand by 1904. Some 4,600 new corps came into existence during the thirteen years after William Booth's death in 1912. The rapid growth after 1912 was due in part to popularity gained through Salvationist wartime service among American troops, and was evident, for example, in the dramatic postwar rise in circulation of the Army's paper, the *War Cry*, from a long-term plateau of about 70,000 to 200,000 by 1920.

Less than two years after the first contingent of Salvationists landed in New York in 1880, the Rev. Albert Benjamin Simpson, gifted pastor of the Thirteenth Street Presbyterian Church of that city, resigned to embark upon an independent ministry among the poor that before the turn of the century was to result in an organization — the Christian and Missionary Alliance — of hundreds of missions-oriented groups of Christians in the United States and Canada. With a fourfold gospel that included evangelism, sanctification, divine healing, and the second coming of the Lord, that "Alliance" of people from various Protestant denominations supported hundreds of missionaries and their spiritual and social ministries overseas, as well as a host of institutions and programs on the North American continent.

During the same years, through the efforts of such leaders as Jerry McAuley, S. H. Hadley, Emma and Sidney Whittemore, and Charles Nelson Crittenton, scores of missions and homes for outcast men and women were springing up in American cities. The Water Street and Bowery missions in New York, and the Pacific Garden Mission in Chicago, were among the most prominent of an increasing number of rescue institutions that banded together in what in 1913 became the International Union of Gospel Mis-

The rescue mission movement became an active force for good among the down and out. BILLY GRAHAM CENTER

sions. Prominent within the larger movement were the Door of Hope, Florence Crittenton, and Salvation Army groups of rescue homes for women. The Woman's Christian Temperance Union, King's Daughters, Convention of Christian Workers, Christian and Missionary Alliance, and many other organizations and individual churches supported similar missions and homes.

In addition to publishing their own papers, most organizations working in the slums received publicity and support in the pages of the *Christian Herald*, a magazine begun in England and circulated widely in the United States during the 1880s. The *Herald*, which by the early 1900s became the largest circulation American religious magazine, oriented itself increasingly to social ministries following its purchase in 1890 by Louis Klopsch, a New York businessman. A summer children's home on the Hudson River, the Bowery Mission in New York, and large-scale support of famine and medical relief overseas were among its many ventures.

Significant for these groups were their undergirding attitudes toward the poor and outcast. In an era when the vulnerable classes — whether for reason of race, economics, sex, or nationality — were often oppressed and brutalized, Salvationists and kindred workers were generally characterized not only by openness, acceptance, and appreciation of the worth of the dispossessed, but an identification with the poor that issued in vigorous support across a wide range of social questions. Contrasting sharply with the apathy and even hostility exhibited toward the lower classes by most Americans and churchmen of that and later eras, that kind of identification, assistance, and support places these missionaries and their organizations within the vital stream of those who across the Judeo-Christian centuries have responded caringly and effectively to human need.

The Social Gospel
GRANT WACKER

As the nineteenth century drew to a close, Americans awakened to the astonishing fact that ten percent of the families had somehow cornered ninety percent of the nation's wealth. Many middleclass Protestants believed that something had gone terribly wrong. Unregulated capitalism had become an excuse for unregulated greed. But they also believed that the gospel redeems sinful social structures as well as sinful lives. Through concerted moral effort, they insisted, the economic and political institutions of American society could be molded to fit biblical standards of ethical conduct.

When this powerful reform impulse first emerged in the 1870s and 1880s, it was known as social Christianity or Christian socialism, but by 1900, to underscore the difference from non-Christian socialist movements, it was more commonly called the social gospel.

Although the social gospel could be interpreted as a continuation of the reforming zeal unleashed by the Second Great Awakening early in the nineteenth century, it is probably more accurate to see it as a direct response to the strain created by rapid industrialization and urbanization in the later years of the century. Bloody confrontations between labor and capital, inhumane conditions in the factories, the wretchedness of the tenements, the widespread use of child labor, and a growing awareness that the largely middleclass churches of mainline Protestantism were hopelessly out of touch with the urban working class, combined to spark an eruption of sermons, newspapers, books, and interdenominational organizations calling for the Christianization of the social order.

The message was proclaimed in a variety of ways. Washington Gladden, often dubbed the father of the movement, was a hard-working pastor who somehow found time to write more than a score of books exposing the effects that an economic law of the jungle had had upon American life. Some, like Francis Greenwood Peabody, were seminary professors who sought to make social ethics a staple of theological education. Others, such as Richard T. Ely, were distinguished scholars who tried to infuse the newly developing social sciences with Christian moral principles. Still others took the message to ordinary people through imaginative literature. Most notable was Charles M. Sheldon's 1896 novel, In His Steps. This sentimental tale, which sold millions of copies, suggested that daily ethical decisions be governed by a single question, "What would Jesus do?"

The social gospel embraced a surprisingly broad range of economic and political ideas. Some proponents were safely conservative, prodding church members to become more aware of the suffering that surrounded them, but proposing little more than renewed commitment to the Golden Rule. None of the social gospel advocates was Marxist, but a few were quite radical, calling for complete economic socialism as described in the book of Acts. Most struck a moderate position. They urged reforms such as abolition of child labor, reduction of the twelve-hour day, and the need for one day of rest in seven. They believed that times had changed and that it had become necessary for government to protect the mass of citizens from economic abuse by a handful of "robber barons."

Eventually the concrete goals of the movement were formalized in 1908 in the Social Creed of the Federal Council of Churches. Reflecting the same buoyantly reforming spirit that animated Teddy Roosevelt's Square Deal and Woodrow Wilson's New Freedom, the Creed asserted Christ's regenerative power in all aspects of life, personal and social, economic and political. Indeed, the pervasive interweaving of Christian ethics and social reform at the turn of the century was nowhere better symbolized than in the Progressive party's 1912 campaign theme song: "Onward Christian Soldiers"!

The social gospel differed from evangelical reform movements like the Salvation Army in at least two respects. First, it tended to emphasize structural reforms — changes in law, government policy, and the formal and informal institutions of society. Second, it was firmly rooted in Protestant liberal theology. Although many liberals remained aloof from the social gospel, all or virtually all advocates of the latter presupposed the main notions of liberalism: the immanence of God, the evolutionary progress of civilization, the historical conditioning of the Bible, and the centrality of Jesus' ethical precepts (rather than miracles). Taken together these ideas provided a warrant and a motivation for radically broadening the older, individualistic interpretation of the gospel.

The most important theologian of the movement was Walter Rauschenbusch, a Baptist professor at Rochester Theological Seminary from 1897 until his death in 1918. In A Theology for the Social Gospel and other books he argued that the cozy alliance between the mainline churches and the business interests of the middle class had cut the heart from the gospel. Deeply pious, he nonetheless insisted that the gravest danger facing the church was not mutilation but complacency.

Yet Rauschenbusch was, as Winthrop S. Hudson has suggested, something of a "lonely prophet." His

Walter Rauschenbusch (1861–1918)
RELIGIOUS NEWS SERVICE PHOTO

enduring contribution was a grim conception of the kingdom of Evil and a strikingly evangelical conception of the kingdom of God. While never minimizing individual sin, he stressed the evil in unredeemed social structures — inherited customs and institutions that foster self-love so that "one generation corrupts the next." On the other hand, he insisted that the kingdom of Evil is transcended in the kingdom of God, which synthesizes personal and social salvation, abolishing "all forms of slavery in which human beings are treated as mere means to serve the ends of others." The kingdom of God is never confined to the limits of the Church. Rather it "embraces the whole of human life. It is the Christian transfiguration of the social order."

In retrospect, it is clear that the social gospel was the American expression of a growing concern on both sides of the Atlantic to translate Christian faith into socially meaningful terms. It was also part of a much broader reforming impulse in the United States that spurred Prohibition, women's suffrage, pacifism, world missions, the improvement of rural life, and to some small extent, the healing of race relations. Admittedly, the reforming spirit of the social gospel dissipated in the 1920s, and when it reemerged in the civil rights marches of the 1960s it was cloaked not so much with liberal theology as no theology at all. But for one brief moment the movement embodied an exhilarating conviction that the kingdom of God is, as Rauschenbusch phrased it, the "eternal in the midst of time," the "energy of God realizing itself in human life."

New Departures and Conservative Responses (1865-1917)

Beneath the surface unity within middleclass white Protestantism some extremely deep rifts were developing. Like the tremors that presage the eruptions of a volcano, the preliminary manifestations were not entirely indicative of the convulsions that were heating up beneath. So the prevailing mood of Protestants in the era from the Civil War to World War I was one of prosperity, progress, and confidence. The truth of the matter was, however, that vastly different understandings of the gospel were developing. Ultimately these differences were so great as to precipitate what historian Sydney Ahlstrom describes as "the most fundamental controversy to wrack the churches since the Reformation."

Liberalism and Modernism

Perhaps the most important point for understanding theological liberalism or modernism (the terms often are used interchangeably) is that it was a movement designed to save Protestantism. As has been seen, the generations of Protestants that came of age between 1865 and 1917 were faced with the most profound challenges to their faith. Darwinism and higher criticism were challenging the authority of the Bible and the new historical, sociological, and Freudian-psychological ways of thinking were revolutionizing thought at almost every level. Immense social changes plus rapid secularization, especially in science and higher education, were eroding Protestantism's practical dominance.

In personal terms, this meant that many people brought up to accept unquestioningly the complete authority of the Bible and the sure truths of evangelical teaching found themselves living in a world where such beliefs no longer were considered intellectually acceptable. Such was typical of the personal histories of the leaders of the liberal movement. Brought up in moderately well-to-do evangelical homes, they formed close attachments to the Christian faith, although usually they did not have a dramatic conversion experience. When they reached the universities, however, they were confronted with a most difficult choice. They could hang on to evangelicalism at the cost of sacrificing the current standards for intellectual respectabil-

---

Facing the Intellectual Challenge

False ideas are the greatest obstacles to the reception of the gospel. We may preach with all the fervor of a reformer and yet succeed only in winning a straggler here and there, if we permit the whole collective thought of the nation or of the world to be controlled by ideas which, by the resistless force of logic, prevent Christianity from being regarded as anything more than a harmless delusion. Under such circumstances, what God desires us to do is to destroy the obstacle at its root. . . . What is to-day matter of academic speculation begins tomorrow to move armies and pull down empires.

J. GRESHAM MACHEN,
Princeton Theological Seminary convocation,
September 20, 1912

ity. If they were going to retain such intellectual respectability, it seemed they must either abandon Christianity or modify it to meet the standards of the day. For many the latter choice seemed the only live option. Many church-going people must have shared these liberal sentiments. By the first decades of the century, liberalism, or modernism as it was coming to be called, was well entrenched in almost all of the leading theological seminaries. Probably more than half of Protestant publications leaned toward modernism, and liberals occupied perhaps one-third of the nation's pulpits.

A movement of this proportion and which stressed freedom from tradition (hence the term "liberalism") and adjustment to the modern world (hence "modernism") inevitably encompassed wide variety. Nonetheless, a good picture of the outlook can be gained by considering three of its most typical strategies for saving the faith in the face of the modern intellectual onslaught.

Deifying Historical Process

The first method of responding to the intellectual challenges was for liberals typically to deify historical process. Simply put, this meant that God revealed himself in history and was incarnate in the development of humanity. Christ, who stood at the center of liberal theology and at the center of history, embodied this close relationship between the divine and the historical. The kingdom of Christ was the continuing manifestation of the power of God to change human relationships. The Bible was a record of the religious experience of an ancient people. It was not an encyclopedia of dogma but rather an ancient model of religious experience. Today this model should not be followed slavishly, but its best principles developed as science and modern civilization advance the understanding of God's reconciling actions. The progress of humanity, then, especially in the moral sphere, is identified with the progress of Christ's kingdom.

One of the beauties of this reinterpretation of Christian tradition for the turn-of-the-century church member was that this version of Christianity was immune from the ravages of modern historical and scientific criticism. For that generation, Darwinism provided the standard for thinking about almost everything. Just as Darwin explained biological development through natural processes, so history and society were interpreted in much the same way. The social sciences and new scientific history claimed that human religions were products of social evolution. They were the natural developments in the efforts of the race to adjust to a threatening environment. The Bible, accordingly, was regarded just as any other religious book, the product of the experiences of the Hebrew people. The new Christian liberalism, however, had a striking answer to this challenge. The history of people's religious experiences is just God's way of working. The Bible need not be proven historically or scientifically accurate to be regarded as a faithful rendering of the religious perceptions of the Hebrew people. In their history, however much it might be mixed with human elements, one finds a people who understood God's working with humanity in a unique way. A person can benefit much from this example, even without following it slavishly. Scientific history and biblical criticism were not a threat to such a faith.

Stressing the Ethical

Closely related was a second emphasis of liberalism or modernism that kept it safe from attack. The key test of Christianity was life, not doctrine. Christianity could be saved by stressing the ethical. This, said the liberals, was the heart of Jesus' teaching. Calvinism and other traditional theologies had stressed too much the judicial elements of God's relationship to humanity. Jesus, by contrast, had emphasized the fatherhood of God and the brotherhood of mankind. Whatever else might fall before the withering blasts of criticism, the ethics of Jesus would survive.

In practical terms, such ethical emphases appeared in several varieties. Most liberals stressed Christian education, as in Sunday schools, where moral lessons predominated. This emphasis was consistent with the personal experiences of many liberals who had grown gradually to love the faith through Christian nurture, rather than through a radical conversion experience. Among some of the early liberals, such as Henry Ward Beecher or Phillips Brooks, the content of their ethics often reflected the individualism of the day.

The Fatherhood of God and the Brotherhood of Man

If God is the Father of all men, all men are brethren; and there can be but one law for home and school and shop and factory and market and court and legislative hall. One child of the common Father can not enslave another nor exploit another; the strong and the fortunate and the wise can not take advantage of the weak and the crippled and the ignorant, and enrich themselves by spoiling their neighbors; each must care for the welfare of all, and all must minister to the good of each. This is the law of brotherhood which directly follows from Christ's doctrine of Fatherhood, and which is beginning to be seriously considered, all over the world, as the only solution of the problems of society.

WASHINGTON GLADDEN,
1899

Washington Gladden (1836–1918), generally regarded as the father of the social gospel movement

In the progressive era, however, liberal leaders such as Washington Gladden and Walter Rauschenbusch rediscovered and developed the social message of the faith. At the popular level, such social concerns were well represented by Charles M. Sheldon's book, *In His Steps* (1896), a moving story of how a congregation was awakened by taking seriously the question, "What would Jesus do?" During the next decades Sheldon's book sold millions of copies, which was no small indication of the power of the Christian ethical challenge to Americans of that day.

The Centrality of Religious Feelings

The third element widespread in the liberal defense of Christianity was the conviction that religious feelings were central to Christianity. Following the German theologian Friedrich Schleiermacher (1768-1834), liberals held that the basis of religion is the sense of absolute dependence. As with the stress on ethics, religious feelings could readily be contrasted to the religion of reason, dogma, or the literal interpretations of the Bible. Science and historical criticism, moreover, could not touch the intuition of the heart "which reason does not know." Appealing to the romantic and idealistic sentiments of the day, liberal Christians could let science reign freely in its own domain, but insist on a realm of religious truth that science could not reach.

Though liberals and modernists were sheltering important aspects of their Christian heritage from the challenges of modern thought, they were simultaneously acquiring considerable opposition on their other flank from conservatives who saw their accommodations to modernity as a sell-out. At first, especially during the 1870s and 1880s, the controversies centered on Darwinism. Darwin's theory of evolution by natural selection hit particularly hard at evangelical Protestantism since it undermined the current defenses of the faith at two critical points. First,

Spiritual Truths Above (Not Against) Science

Our objection to evolution is not that it may not be true; but that if proved true, it is only a half-truth. We dare not put a part for the whole; we refuse to measure the possibilities of the universe by the diameter of the little circle of our knowledge. Besides the curve of the earth which we can measure, there is the immeasurable sweep of the sky above us. A philosophy worthy of the name must admit both sciences — the science of the natural and the science of the spiritual which transcends nature, — or its conclusions will be only half-truths. Physical evolution finds its complement only in a higher truth.

NEWMAN SMYTH,
Congregationalist theologian,
Old Faiths in New Light, 1879

WHEN I WAS A "COMMON ANCESTOR"

This spoof of Darwinism typified the level of much of the antievolutionary literature for nearly a century.

by implication it questioned the accuracy of the Bible, which had been the most important exhibit in demonstrations of "evidences" for Christianity. Second, Darwinism totally reversed the perceptions of the relation of science to the Christian faith. In the mid-nineteenth century American Christian apologists rested their case heavily on the argument from design. The scientific revolution of the past two centuries, they said, had uncovered some of the marvels of God's intricate and awesome design of the universe. It was inconsistent rationally to believe, they argued, that so complex and orderly a system could lack an intelligent designer. Darwinism, however, posited just the opposite. The apparent design in the universe was best explained by chance. With no prevision of the course of the universe, the species developed their intricate and marvelous structures simply because of the necessities of survival in a brutal universe. The order and apparent design, it seemed to many scientists, could be well explained with no reference to God.

Many conservative Protestants refused to accept this account entirely. Charles Hodge of Princeton Theological Seminary spoke well for them in *What Is Darwinism?* (1874). Focusing on natural selection, he argued that if one held consistently to this central Darwinist principle, Darwinism was simply a form of atheism. Rejection of Darwinism, accordingly, became for some a symbol of orthodoxy. This was especially true in the South, where Protestant leaders who spoke in favor of Darwinism risked their jobs, a fact clearly demonstrated by the highly publicized trial and dismissal of James Woodrow

What is Darwinism? It is atheism.
CHARLES HODGE

Lyman Abbot (1835–1922), Henry Ward Beecher's successor at Plymouth Church in Brooklyn, a proponent of theistic Darwinism, and the author of The Evolution of Christianity (1892)
KEYSTONE-MAST COLLECTION, UNIVERSITY OF CALIFORNIA, RIVERSIDE

(uncle of Woodrow Wilson) from the Presbyterian seminary in Columbia, South Carolina, in 1886.

In the North, on the other hand, defenders of Darwinism generally found acceptance in the mainline churches. Many pious evangelical scientists were among the first to endorse theistic versions of Darwin's views. God, they said, could work through natural selection and still be fully the creator. As popularizer John Fiske put it, "Evolution is God's way of doing things."

The more central issue that concerned conservatives was the place of the Bible. The

Evolution is God's way of doing things.
JOHN FISKE

authority for their whole belief system seemed to rest on this foundation. If the Bible were not true, then on what did Protestantism, the religion of *scriptura sola*, rest? And what if there were scientific and historical errors in scripture? Would not such flaws call into question other biblical claims? With both Darwinists and highly sophisticated higher critics suggesting that there were serious errors in scripture, many of the faithful of the turn-of-the-century generation had to be deeply disturbed.

As in the case of Darwinism, conservative Protestants themselves divided over these persistent questions. Some would make virtually no concessions to the new historical analysis of the Bible. Often these were the same people who would have nothing to do with Darwinism. On both issues, the most articulate of these conservative spokespersons were the theologians at the conservative Presbyterian theological seminary in Princeton. Carefully they defined what they took to be the church's traditional stance regarding the Bible. The text as originally inspired by the Holy Spirit, they insisted, was "absolutely errorless." This doctrine of "inerrancy," as it came to be known, was no invention of the late nineteenth century. Many Christians in the past had said or assumed much the same thing. But the fact that now some conservative Protestants were making biblical inerrancy a central doctrine, even sometimes virtually a test of the faith, signaled the degree to which the new scientific and historical threats to the Bible were forcing everyone to shore up whatever they considered the most critical line of defense.

The rise to prominence of the issues of inerrancy and the Bible's historical accuracy sparked considerable debate. The most spectacular case was that of Prof. Charles A. Briggs (1841-1913) of Union Theological Seminary in New York, a Presbyterian institution. In an inaugural address in 1891, Briggs directly attacked the doctrine of "inerrancy" as articulated by Princeton theologians Archibald Alexander Hodge (1823-1886) and Benjamin Breckinridge Warfield (1851-1921). Although Briggs was a traditionalist in most of his theology, he insisted that Christians ought to face up to the fact that the Bible contained numerous incidental errors not central to its teaching. For this

Briggs was brought to trial in the Presbyterian church and suspended from the ministry. The result, however, was that both he and his seminary left the Presbyterian church.

Between 1878 and 1906 almost every major Protestant denomination experienced at least one heresy trial, usually of a seminary professor. As in the Briggs case, however, the conservative efforts seemed to do little to retard the liberal trends. By the early 1900s the vast majority of Protestant seminaries in the North were controlled by liberals. The (Baptist) Divinity School of the University of Chicago, for instance, had been transformed by this time from an outpost for moderately conservative Baptist evangelicalism to one of the world's leading centers for liberal theology.

In the South, however, the story was different. The Civil War defense of the southern way of life helped seal the commitment of many white southerners to the evangelical Christianity that had prevailed before the war. With such social support and the continued dominance of the older white ethnic stock, theological conservatives could effectively hold the line against liberalism.

The contests between liberals and conservatives, however, did not directly touch those elements in American Protestantism which remained essentially conservative. In 1905 an astute Baptist observer estimated that this moderate conservative party constituted "still the vast majority" of Baptists throughout the nation. Probably ninety-five percent of Baptists, he thought, were not "conscious of any important change in theology or departure from the old Baptist orthodoxy." Even the leadership of Baptist conservatives often declined to take hard lines. President Augustus H. Strong (1836-1921) of Rochester Theological Seminary, for example, though unquestionably a conservative, explicitly repudiated in his widely used *Systematic The-*

ology the dogma of the inerrancy of scripture. The main lines of a conservative defense of Christianity, Strong maintained, should be personal religious experience and practical morality. President Edgar Young Mullins (1860-1928) of the Southern Baptist Theological Seminary in Louisville, though an opponent of liberalism, took his stand on this same experiential and practical line of defense. Probably for most American Protestants in the pews, especially in the two largest denominations, the Methodists and the Baptists, such assurances were sufficient against the rumors of intellectual assault.

This E. J. Pace cartoon called for a revival to drive out the evils of modernism. BILLY GRAHAM CENTER

What is the use of talking about two Isaiahs when most people don't know there's one?
DWIGHT L. MOODY

The Crisis in Authority of the Bible

In view of all the facts known to us, we affirm that a candid inspection of all the ascertained phenomena of the original text of Scripture will leave unmodified the ancient faith of the Church. In all their real affirmations these books are without error.

ARCHIBALD A. HODGE *and* BENJAMIN B. WARFIELD, *Presbyterian Review*, 1881

It is not a pleasant task to point out errors in the sacred Scriptures. Nevertheless Historical Criticism finds them, and we must meet the issue whether they destroy the authority of the Bible or not. . . . The Bible has maintained its authority with the best scholars of our time, who with open minds have been willing to recognize any error that might be pointed out by Historical Criticism.

CHARLES A. BRIGGS, *The Authority of Holy Scripture: An Inaugural Address*, 1891

Dispensationalism

C. NORMAN KRAUS

Dispensationalism is a system of scriptural interpretation which was first developed in Plymouth Brethren circles in England and Ireland in the 1830s and spread to North America beginning in the 1850s. John Nelson Darby (1800-1882) seems to have been the most seminal thinker in formulating the system. Almost all the distinctive doctrines of present-day Dispensationalism can be traced to his writings. In America the system appeared in its classic form in the notes of the Scofield Reference Bible (1909) which has had wide influence, especially among fundamentalists.

Distinctive Features

Dispensationalism shares much theological ground with conservative Protestant theology. However, it is a distinctive system and is unique in the way it divides and interprets sacred history. A dispensation is more than an era or epoch in history. Basic to the concept is the idea of covenant. A covenant is an agreement stipulated

by God for mankind, or some segment of mankind, which defines God's dispensational plan for them. It sets forth the required human response for salvation during the era. Such covenants mark the significant theological turning points of history. Most dispensationalist teachers enumerate seven dispensations, but the number varies from three to ten.

Dispensationalists strongly assert that their interpretation is a literal rendering of the biblical message. They insist on the most rigid definition of verbal and plenary inspiration. But more than this, they insist that their system is the Bible's own self-view, and that apart from the dispensational norm the Bible cannot be rightly understood.

Dispensationalists accept the premillennial teaching that this present age will end in judgment, and the historical kingdom of Christ on earth will be established in a future millennium. However, they have added many distinctive details. Especially important has been dispensationalists' new understanding of the role of the church.

According to dispensationalism the church age is a special dispensation of

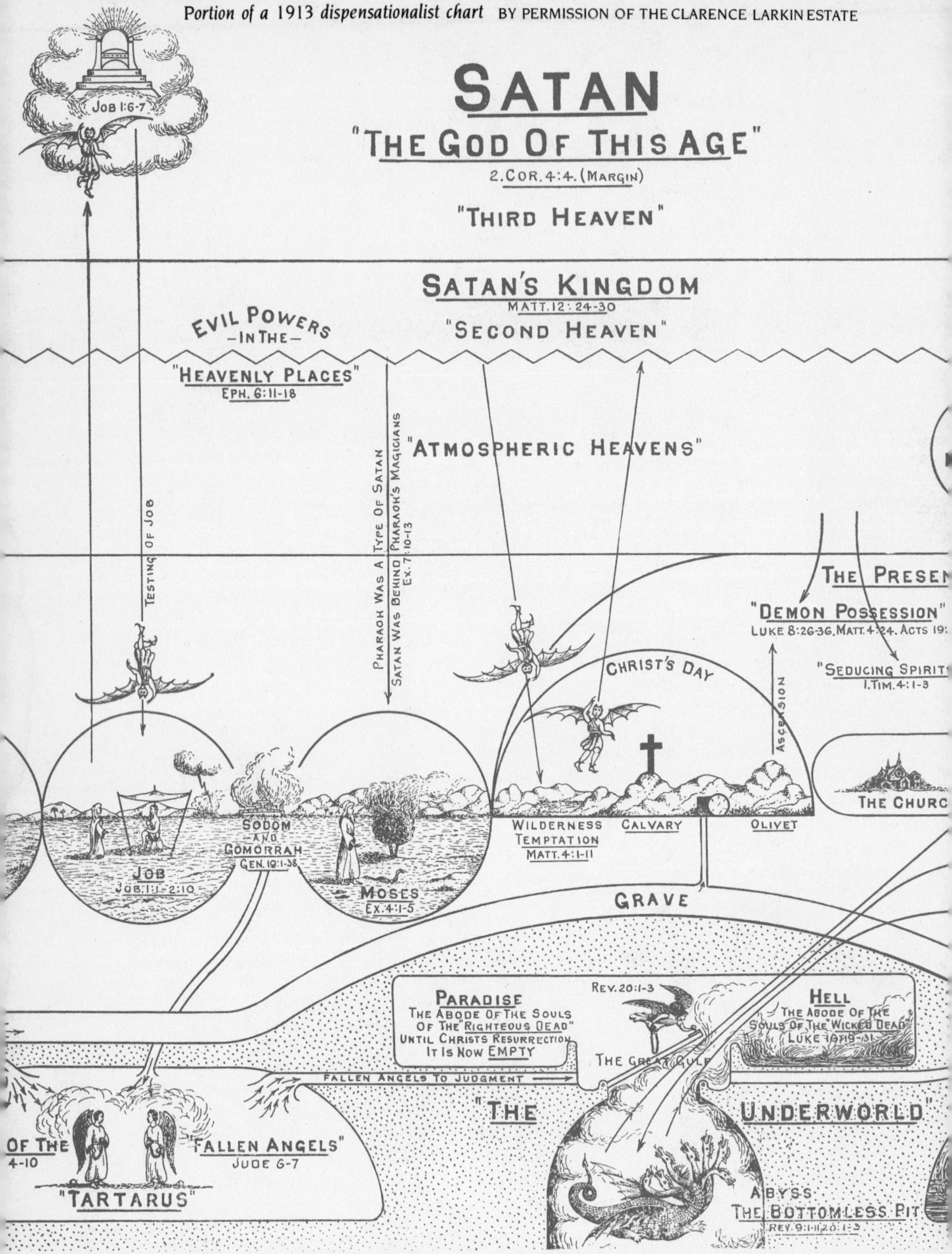

SATAN
"THE GOD OF THIS AGE"
2. COR. 4:4. (MARGIN)
"THIRD HEAVEN"
JOB 1:6-7
SATAN'S KINGDOM
MATT. 12:24-30
"SECOND HEAVEN"
EVIL POWERS
-IN THE-
"HEAVENLY PLACES"
EPH. 6:11-18
"ATMOSPHERIC HEAVENS"
TESTING OF JOB
PHARAOH WAS A TYPE OF SATAN
SATAN WAS BEHIND PHARAOH'S MAGICIANS
EX. 7:10-13
THE PRESEN
"DEMON POSSESSION"
LUKE 8:26-36, MATT. 4:24. ACTS 19:
"SEDUCING SPIRIT
I. TIM. 4:1-3
CHRIST'S DAY
ASCENSION
THE CHURC
JOB
JOB. 1:1-2:10
SODOM AND GOMORRAH
GEN. 19:1-38
MOSES
EX. 4:1-5
WILDERNESS TEMPTATION
MATT. 4:1-11
CALVARY
OLIVET
GRAVE
PARADISE
THE ABODE OF THE SOULS OF THE "RIGHTEOUS DEAD" UNTIL CHRISTS RESURRECTION
IT IS NOW EMPTY
REV. 20:1-3
HELL
THE ABODE OF THE SOULS OF THE "WICKED DEAD"
LUKE 16:19-31
THE GREAT GULF
FALLEN ANGELS TO JUDGMENT
"THE UNDERWORLD"
OF THE
4-10
"FALLEN ANGELS"
JUDE 6-7
"TARTARUS"
ABYSS
THE BOTTOMLESS PIT
REV. 9:1-11, 20:1-3

Portion of a 1913 *dispensationalist chart* BY PERMISSION OF THE CLARENCE LARKIN ESTATE

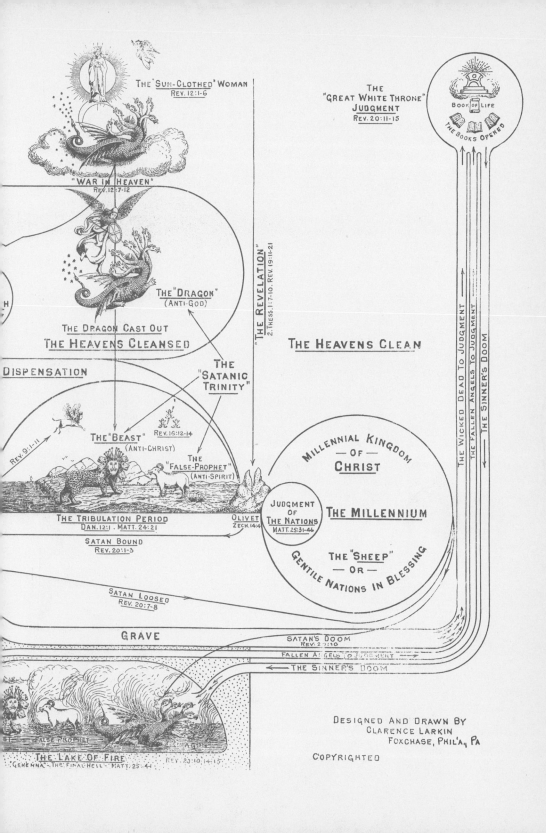

The "Sun-Clothed" Woman
Rev. 12:1-6

The
"Great White Throne"
Judgment
Rev. 20:11-15

Book of Life

The Books Opened

"War in Heaven"
Rev. 12:7-12

The "Revelation"
2. Thess. 1:7-10. Rev. 19:11-21

The "Dragon"
(Anti-God)

The Dragon Cast Out
The Heavens Cleansed

The Heavens Clean

DISPENSATION

The
"Satanic
Trinity"

The Wicked Dead To Judgment

The Fallen Angels To Judgment

The Sinner's Doom

Rev. 16:12-14

The "Beast"
(Anti-Christ)

The
"False-Prophet"
(Anti-Spirit)

Millennial Kingdom
— Of —
Christ

Rev. 9:1-11

The Millennium

The Tribulation Period
Dan. 12:1. Matt. 24:21

Olivet
Zech. 14:4

Judgment
Of
The Nations
Matt. 25:31-46

The "Sheep"
— Or —
Gentile Nations In Blessing

Satan Bound
Rev. 20:1-3

Satan Loosed
Rev. 20:7-8

GRAVE

Satan's Doom
Rev. 20:10

Fallen Angels To Judgment

The Sinner's Doom

Designed And Drawn By
Clarence Larkin
Foxchase, Phil'a, Pa

False Prophet

Dragon

The Lake Of Fire
"Gehenna" The Final Hell Matt. 25:41

Rev. 20:10, 14-15

Copyrighted

the Holy Spirit which began at Pentecost and ends at Christ's second coming. It will end, as have all the rest of the dispensations, in failure and catastrophic judgment. In the first phase of Christ's return, which is called "the rapture," the true saints will be "caught up into the air" to be with Christ. Then judgments of famine, cosmic disturbances, and wars will devastate the earth as the devil is let loose for a short time. Following this Christ will return with his raptured saints, restore the nation of Israel as his holy people, and set up an earthly kingdom in Jerusalem. Now that kingdom is being withheld from earthly fulfillment until the church dispensation is completed.

The "true church" is a strictly spiritual phenomenon which finds expression in nonclerical and nondenominational associations of true believers for worship and exhortation. Its work is purely spiritual, that is, calling out the elect of God to faith in Christ and a new birth. Christian social service can be justified only when it is an immediate means of evangelism.

The Spread of Dispensationalism

Dispensationalist teaching has been spread in North America through the Bible and Prophecy Conference movements, the Scofield Bible Correspondence Course published by Moody Bible Institute, many Bible schools, and a

few seminaries such as Dallas Theological Seminary. Beside this, many dispensationalist books have been immensely popular. Works by some of the early writers such as C. H. Macintosh, William Kelly, W. E. Blackstone, and Clarence Larkin are still in print. More recently popular authors such as Hal Lindsey and David Wilkerson have given these ideas a new boost among the Christian laity in books and films. But perhaps the Scofield Reference Bible remains the single most important purveyor of the system.

Lewis Sperry Chafer, a theologian at Dallas Theological Seminary, was the first to organize a full-orbed dispensationalist theology in his eight-volume Systematic Theology (1948). Theological and biblical scholars like Charles Ryrie, John Walvoord, and Alva McClain have continued to clarify and defend the system. In 1967 a revision of the Scofield Reference Bible was published which attempted to clarify some misunderstandings growing out of Scofield's work. In the 1960s and 1970s a large number of evangelical theological scholars abandoned the position. This defection was heralded by George E. Ladd's reexamination of the biblical issues in his Crucial Questions About the Kingdom of God (1952). Dispensationalism, however, remains popular in many evangelical, fundamentalist, and pentecostal circles.

Many dispensationalist leaders attracted large followings to their tabernacles, such as those of Scoville in Aurora, Missouri (left), and Bob Jones in Galveston, Texas (right).   BILLY GRAHAM CENTER

Conservative Innovations

Liberals and modernists were not the only Protestants of the era who met the challenges of the day with substantial innovations. Three other important movements, all essentially conservative on most points of theology and all active in revivalism, offered new directions for Protestant renewal.

Dispensational Premillennialism

Dispensationalism, or dispensational premillennialism, was the fruit of renewed interest in the detail of biblical prophecy which developed after the Civil War. Rejecting the prevailing postmillennialism which taught that Christ's kingdom would grow out of the spiritual and moral progress of this age, dispensational premillennialists said that the churches and the culture were declining and that Christians would see Christ's kingdom only after he personally returned to rule in Jerusalem. They thus offered a plausible explanation of the difficulties the church was facing. These failings had been predicted in biblical prophecy. "Christendom," or "Christian civilization," had always been an illusory ideal. Now that was being made apparent by the secularization of the culture and the apostasy (liberalism) within the churches themselves. Yet the Bible also provided firm hope for the coming of the kingdom.

This new form of premillennial teaching, imported from England, first spread in America through prophecy conferences where the Bible was studied intently. Summer conferences, a newly popular form of vacation in the age of trains, were particularly effective. Most importantly, Dwight L. Moody had sympathies with the broad outlines of dispensationalism and had as his closest lieutenants dispensationalist leaders such as Reuben A. Torrey (1856-1928), James M. Gray (1851-1925), C. I. Scofield (1843-1921), William J. Erdman (1833-1923), A. C. Dixon

(1854-1925), and A. J. Gordon (1836-1895). These men were activist evangelists who promoted a host of Bible conferences and other missionary and evangelistic efforts. They also gave the dispensationalist movement institutional permanence by assuming leadership of the new Bible institutes such as the Moody Bible Institute (1886), the Bible Institute of Los Angeles (1907), and the Philadelphia College of the Bible (1914). The network of related institutes that soon sprang up became the nucleus for much of the important fundamentalist movement of the twentieth century. Dispensationist leaders, in fact, actively organized this antimodernist effort. Notably, they oversaw the publication between 1910 and 1915 of the widely distributed twelve-volume paperback series, *The Fundamentals*. This conservative "Testimony to the Truth," financed by Lyman and Milton Stewart, included writings from a considerable variety of antimodernist spokespersons, including many nondispensationalists such as the Princeton theologians and moderates such as E. Y. Mullins.

Dispensationalism itself was strikingly antimodernist. In many respects it looked like the mirror image of modernism. Modernism was optimistic about modern culture; dispensationalism was pessimistic. Most importantly, each centered around an interpretation of the relation of the Bible to history. Modernism interpreted the Bible through the lens of human history. Dispensationalists interpreted history exclusively through the lens of scripture. Where modernism stressed the naturalistic, seeing social forces as being crucial to understanding religion, dispensationalists accentuated the supernatural, making divine intervention the direct solution to the modern problem of explaining historical change.

The Holiness Movement

A second major innovative evangelical movement—the holiness movement—may be understood as a mirror image of another modernist theme—the stress on morality. When liberals emphasized the ethical, they typically spoke of the natural tendencies to good in all people. Christianity could cultivate these tendencies and bring them to fruition. The parallel holiness movement also accentuated the ethical, but with the opposite

emphasis. The supernatural work of the Holy Spirit was essential to overcome natural tendencies. Moreover, whereas the liberals spoke of gradual cultivation or of Christian education, the advocates of holiness maintained that nothing less than a dramatic work of the Holy Spirit could cleanse the heart of sin. So holiness teachers were distinguished from most other revivalist evangelicals by insisting not only on a dramatic conversion experience but also a definite "second blessing" in which the work of the Spirit freed one from sin's power.

The holiness movement was actually a variety of movements growing out of the teachings of John Wesley. By the mid-nineteenth century holiness teachings were thriving in many different forms, and often went beyond the bounds of Methodism itself. By the second half of the century such teachings were leading to the formation of new denominations. Stressing ethical duty, holiness groups usually were concerned not only with personal purity but also with responsibilities toward the poor. In the latter half of the century, holiness organizations, of which the best known is the Salvation Army, were leaders in Protestant care for the poor and evangelism to the outcasts.

Holiness groups, often separating from the larger and more respectable denominations, and often winning converts from less established people in the immigrant and working classes, tended to have a more modest socioeconomic base than did older groups like Episcopalians, Congregationalists, Presbyterians, and even Baptists and Methodists. This correlation illustrates a general point in modern church life: the more well-to-do a group, the less demanding its requirements for sanctification. Liberal Protestants, as a group, were better off socially than any other body of Protestants. For them virtue was found in the best developments of modern civilization and in their own lives. Traditional denominationalists stood somewhere in the middle, having more ambivalent attitudes toward how much of the world had to be renounced in order properly to live the Christian life. Near the far end of the spectrum were the holiness groups, speaking of much radical separation from worldliness but having, in a material sense, less of the world to renounce.

The Holiness Movement

GRANT WACKER

John Wesley's theology of Christian perfection was the wellspring of a powerful reform impulse that permeated Methodism and much of mainstream Protestantism just after the Civil War. The euphoria did not last, however. By the end of the nineteenth century this holiness movement, as it was widely called, had been largely forced out of the established denominations. But the movement continued to thrive in a score of rapidly growing holiness sects that by 1980 reported more than 1.5 million regular members.

Wesley was a practical man, yet he never doubted that the biblical admonition, "Be ye perfect," was meant to be taken literally. As he saw it, moral growth, or sanctification, is both progressive and instantaneous. From the moment of conversion the will is progressively freed from the stranglehold of sin. Even so, he insisted, corrupt impulses persist until their root, "inbred sin," is eradicated in an instantaneous second moment of grace that perfects the will and brings about entire sanctification. The result is not sinless perfection, but the perfection of love, the ability to triumph over sinful desires and selfish motives. "Be of sin the double cure," it is phrased in a hymn long cherished by Methodists, "Save from wrath and make me pure."

These notions crossed the Atlantic early in the nineteenth century, but they underwent a partial sea change. At one level American Methodists never forgot that sanctification is a long-term process, shrouded in the mystery of God's dealings with his people. In practice, however, they often stripped away the subtleties, compressing spiritual growth into distinct stages: unconverted, converted, entirely sanctified. This was particularly true of Phoebe Palmer, the most influential proponent of the holiness message in the first half of the century. In her monthly publication, *Guide to Christian Perfection*, she insisted that entire sanctification is won not by spiritual struggle, but by trustfully claiming it as one of God's promises. Palmer, like many others, also departed from Wesley by identifying the second moment of grace — or the second blessing, as it had come to be called — with the baptism of the Holy Spirit.

A woman exhorter prays for the family of a convert at a late nineteenth-century holiness camp meeting. BILLY GRAHAM CENTER

By the time of the Civil War the Methodist Episcopal church was riven by interrelated controversies over slavery and holiness. In 1843 and 1860, respectively, the Wesleyan Methodist Connection and the Free Methodist church broke away, partly because they believed that the denomination had grown cold to the doctrine and the experience of entire sanctification as an instantaneous second work of grace. Yet the great majority of holiness Methodists determined to stay. In 1867 a group of ministers led by John S. Inskip established the National Camp Meeting Association for the Promotion of Christian Holiness. Within a decade the National Association had directly sponsored or indirectly fostered an extensive network of national, regional, and local holiness associations, periodicals, missions, schools, camps, conferences, and weekly prayer meetings. For a time, it appeared that holiness sentiment would sweep both the northern and southern wings of the church.

Serious opposition started to emerge, however, in the mid-1870s, leading to unofficial disavowal of the movement in the North in 1881 and official disavowal in the South in 1894. Theological and cultural differences were involved, but the critical issue was ecclesiastical authority. Methodist bishops had become convinced that the movement had turned into a church within a church — and a rather unruly one at that. Until the end of the century leaders of the National Association struggled to keep the movement within the boundaries of the denomination, but it had a momentum of its own. Between 1880 and 1905 some 100,000 spilled out of the church to form a bewildering profusion of sectarian organizations.

The largest of these were the Church of the Nazarene, founded by Phineas F. Bresee in Los Angeles in 1895, and the Pilgrim Holiness church, established in 1922 after a complicated series of mergers. (In 1968 the

The Salvation Army became one of the most visible of the holiness groups. BILLY GRAHAM CENTER

Pilgrim Holiness group joined the old Wesleyan Methodist Connection to form the Wesleyan church.) In addition, holiness ranks were swelled by non-Methodists who had adopted the Wesleyan view of sanctification. These included the Salvation Army, Church of God (Anderson, Indiana), Cumberland Presbyterian church, Mennonite Brethren in Christ, and numerous Quakers. Today many of these groups are informally linked in the Christian Holiness Association, the direct successor of the National Association of the nineteenth century.

Holiness will be forever associated with Methodism, but it is important to remember that many Presbyterians, Congregationalists, and Baptists were influenced by a distinctly Reformed, or non-Wesleyan, form of the impulse. Like the Wesleyans, these men and women believed that sanctification begins at conversion, but they differed from the Wesleyans in two respects. First, they were persuaded that "inbred sin" is a permanent part of the human condition. It is progressively subjugated, but this side of heaven's gate, it is never eradicated.

Second, they agreed that there is indeed a second moment of grace, and some of them called it the baptism of the Holy Spirit, but they insisted that its primary purpose is not to purify the heart but to empower the will to act — to witness, sacrifice, and serve.

The sources of this Reformed holiness tradition were diverse, but two stand out. The first, commonly — and often derisively — nicknamed Oberlin Perfectionism, was associated with Asa Mahan and Charles G. Finney, successive presidents of Oberlin College in the mid-nineteenth century. The second, known as the Keswick Higher Life movement, took its name from a conference held every summer (from 1875 to the present) at Keswick in northwest England. To a significant extent this movement was prompted by Hannah Whitall Smith, an American Quaker whose devotional classic, *The Christian's Secret of a Happy Life*, eventually sold three million copies. In the

An itinerant preacher and his holiness wagon, Mechanic Falls, Maine BILLY GRAHAM CENTER

1870s, 1880s, and 1890s Oberlin Perfectionism and Keswick Higher Life teachings crisscrossed the Atlantic, readily merging with dispensational premillennialism and the doctrine and practice of faith healing. All of these traditions blended in varying degrees in the ministries of A. J. Gordon, A. T. Pierson, A. B. Simpson, and Reuben A. Torrey. By the turn of the century these men, along with Dwight L. Moody (whose views are more difficult to categorize), had become a virtual Establishment on the Reformed side of the holiness movement. Ultimately their understanding of holiness was institutionalized in the Christian and Missionary Alliance, founded in 1881, and, in a modified form, in influential schools like Moody Bible Institute and Dallas Theological Seminary.

In retrospect, it is clear that despite sharp theological differences, the various components of the holiness movement were unified by a common cultural style. Unrestrained emotionalism, puritanical mores, sentimental music, and hostility to modern biblical scholarship were a persistent part of the story. Yet throughout the nineteenth century the movement exhibited a degree of humanitarian concern unsurpassed and, at the grass roots, rarely paralleled in other sectors of American Christianity. The movement also displayed a spiritual vitality and an equality of social classes and genders not seen since the early days of the Quakers. Its real contribution was, however, a lucid perception that the discipline of holiness is the essence of freedom.

Pentecostalism

Pentecostalism, which, after 1900, developed first in some holiness groups, was even more radical in its teachings and even more prone to attract the socially disinherited. It was for a time, in fact, the only portion of Protestantism to be integrated racially. Again, a contrast with liberalism is helpful. One of the liberal strategies was to emphasize religious experience as an unassailable authentication of Christianity. In a sense, the Pentecostals emphasized the same thing. As in the other cases, however, theirs was a mirror image of the liberal view. Pentecostals accentuated the supernatural just at the point where the liberals stressed the divine elements in the natural. So while modernists might speak of a gentle "religion of the heart," Pentecostals insisted that true heart religion be evidenced by unmistakable signs of the Spirit's radical transforming power, especially the pentecostal sign of speaking in tongues.

These three new evangelical movements—dispensationalism, holiness, and pentecostalism—were each innovative in its own way; yet they had in common a distinctly antiliberal stress on dramatic intervention of the

supernatural. The three, accordingly, had many similarities, and, in fact, there were many interconnections among them. Moody's lieutenant, Reuben A. Torrey, for instance, is revered in all three traditions, although he himself did not agree with the pentecostal demands for visible signs of the Holy Spirit's work. Inevitably, these connections led to controversies and many divisions, resulting in a wide variety of emphases within the three movements. The three, however, united at least in their common opposition to modernism, had much to do with shaping twentieth-century American evangelicalism.

All the movements considered in this section could be regarded as either conservative or innovative. Liberalism, despite its forward-looking posture, was an attempt to preserve the essentials of the Christian faith. Even denominational conservatives developed new emphases, such as in making inerrancy of scripture a test of orthodoxy, as part of their response to the challenges of the modern era. Dispensationalism, holiness movements, and pentecostalism also were conservative in most of their teaching yet clearly innovative in their distinctive themes. Regardless of one's stance, some adjustments had to be made to meet the challenges of the onset of modern secular and pluralistic culture.

Not surprisingly, these unsettled conditions brought the rise of some more radical religious movements. Of these, the two most successful of the era were Mary Baker Eddy's Christian Science and Charles Taze Russell's Jehovah's Witnesses. Each grew out of a deep dissatisfaction with traditional Christian teaching, although they stood at opposite ends of the religious spectrum. Christian Science, a New England movement, reflected some of the same impulses that spawned Protestant liberalism. It embodied

an idealism that was, in a sense, an extreme form of positive thinking. Closer to Transcendentalism than to Protestantism itself, it often appealed to the cultured and well-to-do.

The Jehovah's Witnesses, midwestern in origin, were in their basic impulses closer to the innovative Protestant movements that had grown out of conservative revivalism. Russellism was preeminently a premillennialist movement with strict ethical teachings. It also involved a number of dogmas that placed it beyond the bounds of traditional Christian orthodoxy. In contrast to Christian Science, the Witnesses' demanding doctrines appealed primarily to social outsiders.

The Pentecostal Movement

GRANT WACKER

Pentecostalism may be the largest mass religious movement of the twentieth century. No one knows how many millions of adherents are scattered around the world, but a Gallup poll published in 1980 revealed that in the United States alone nearly thirty million Protestants and Catholics identified with the movement, and five million claimed to have experienced its most distinctive trait, the ability to speak in "unknown" tongues, technically called glossolalia.

Born in the American lower Midwest at the turn of the twentieth century, pentecostalism appears to have grown from the confluence of five historically distinct traditions. The first was an emphasis upon a life-transforming experience, subsequent to conversion, that eradicates sinful desires. Commonly known as entire sanctification, this notion was rooted in the preaching of John Wesley and nurtured by the holiness wing of the Methodist Episcopal church. The second tradition also emphasized a life-transforming experience subsequent to conversion, but defined it, not as a

moment of purification, but as an enduement of power that equips the believer for witness and service. Often called the higher Christian life, this influence grew from the work of Charles G. Finney and other Presbyterian and Congregationalist writers. By the end of the nineteenth century, in both traditions, this second experience had widely come to be known as baptism in (or of) the Holy Spirit.

The third and fourth traditions that led to pentecostalism were dispensational premillennialism and a new theology of faith healing. The former entailed the idea of an imminent secret rapture of the saints, immediately followed by seven years of great tribulation, the second coming of the Lord, and the millennium. It stemmed from the teachings of the Plymouth Brethren and was articulated by well-known preachers such as Reuben A. Torrey. The new theology of faith healing departed from historic Christian doctrine (which had enjoined elders to anoint and pray for the sick) by insisting that Christ's atonement provides physical healing just as it

J. Wilbur Chapman (right) carried on the work of urban revivalism after Moody retired from the scene in 1892. He is pictured here with the famous revival singer Charlie Alexander.

provides spiritual healing. The idea was popularized especially by A. B. Simpson, founder of the Christian and Missionary Alliance, and by the first of the "big-time" faith healers, John Alexander Dowie.

The fifth tradition that influenced pentecostalism was a great longing for restoration of the power and miracles of the New Testament church. Many expected that the former rain, the signs and wonders described in the book of Acts, would soon be complemented by the latter rain, a final outpouring of the Holy Spirit's power at the close of history. The origins of this influence are difficult to pin down, but various forms of restorationism were pervasive throughout the region, strongly affecting groups such as the Churches of Christ and Landmark Baptists.

These forces interacted in different ways, but by 1900 many who sought holiness in one tradition or another were persuaded that the growing hunger for baptism in the Holy Spirit, leading to a life of purity and service, was a token of the Lord's imminent return. The availability of physical healing through faith stirred expectation that other New Testament miracles would soon be restored.

About this time an itinerant faith healer named Charles Fox Parham started to teach that in the book of Acts all instances of baptism in the Holy Spirit were accompanied by speaking in tongues. He also insisted that this pattern is normative for all Christians. There is considerable disagreement about when speaking in tongues became a regular practice.

Some scholars believe it is universal, while others suspect it is largely restricted to twentieth-century pentecostalism. In any event, the modern tradition is commonly traced to a revival led by Parham in Topeka, Kansas, in 1901.

After migrating to Texas, Parham passed the torch to William J. Seymour, a black hotel waiter associated with a holiness and restorationist band called the Evening Light Saints. Seymour, in turn, carried the message to Los Angeles, where his preaching sparked the legendary Azusa Street revival in the spring of 1906.

Between 1906 and 1911 several small but thriving Wesleyan sects were drawn into pentecostalism through the influence of persons who had visited the Azusa Mission. The largest of these included the predominantly black Church of God in Christ, centered in the rural South; the Church of God (Cleveland, Tennessee), based in the southern Appalachians; and the Pentecostal Holiness church, concentrated in the Carolinas and Georgia. All of these bodies eventually spread across the United States, but late in the century they are still noticeably regionalized in the South and Southeast.

After a slow start the pentecostal message also caught fire in the states of the lower Midwest. In 1914 many of Parham's followers joined with pentecostal converts in the Christian and Missionary Alliance to form the Assemblies of God, now the largest pentecostal denomination. A schism in 1916 over the nature of the Trinity led to the formation of several unitarian or "oneness" groups. The largest of these are the United Pentecostal church and the largely black Pentecostal Assemblies of the World. Aimee Semple McPherson also launched her ministry in the Assemblies of God, but soon established her own following in Los Angeles, incorporated in 1927 as the International Church of the Foursquare Gospel. None of these groups

Pentecostalism flourished and continued to thrive in many black communities (drawing by Prentice Taylor). BILLY GRAHAM CENTER

is as regionalized as the older Wesleyan denominations, but over the years they have grown most rapidly in the lower Midwest and Far West.

In the early days pentecostal churches were often called Full Gospel tabernacles. By this pentecostals meant to stress that the full gospel entails personal conversion, baptism in the Holy Spirit as evidenced by tongues, physical healing by faith, and promise of the Lord's imminent return. Third- and fourth-generation pentecostals still share these beliefs, but they are divided by deep internal differences. Unitarian pentecostals are separated from the trinitarian majority by numerous disagreements over doctrinal matters. Moreover, the older Wesleyan groups, unlike the Reformed or non-Wesleyan bodies, insist that baptism in the Holy Spirit must be preceded by a definable sanctification experience. Yet the most persistent differences are sociological rather than theological. Middleclass black and white pentecostals are largely segregated. Beyond this, since World War II, many rank and file pentecostals have shared their loyalties with independent evangelists such as A. A. Allen, who have stressed faith healing, and, more controversially, faith as an avenue to financial prosperity.

By 1980 the pentecostal movement had become extremely diverse.

John Stewart Curry drawing of a holiness-pentecostal meeting BILLY GRAHAM CENTER

Fiercely independent outposts of the sort that flourished in skid-row missions and Appalachian hollows contrasted with the magnificent suburban churches of the Assemblies of God and with the billion-dollar television ministry increasingly dominated by pentecostals. Speaking in tongues had deeply penetrated the Roman Catholic church and some of the liturgical Protestant groups, but major theological and cultural differences separated these neo-pentecostals from the classical denominations. Yet the movement as a whole was bonded by a common conviction that the gospel was still true. Not the old-fashioned gospel of the nineteenth century, but the miraculous, wonder-working gospel of the first century.

Christian Science
ANTHONY A. HOEKEMA

On August 23, 1879, the Church of Christ (Scientist), with headquarters in Boston, was incorporated and given a charter. The founder of the movement, Mary Baker (later to become Mary Baker Eddy), was born in Bow, New Hampshire, on July 16, 1821. Mary disagreed with her father, a stern Calvinist, on such points as the final day of judgment and the doctrine of endless punishment.

For years Mary was a semiinvalid. One of her main concerns, therefore, was recovering what she considered to be a lost emphasis in primitive Christianity: an emphasis on healing. It is not surprising that she was attracted by the ideas of Phineas P. Quimby from Portland, Maine, a person who was effecting remarkable cures without medicine, claiming to have rediscovered Jesus' healing methods. Though there is difference of opinion on this point, Mrs. Eddy must have been indebted to Quimby for at least some of her ideas.

In 1875 the first edition of Mary Baker Eddy's best-known book, *Science and Health According to the Scriptures*, appeared. The Christian Science church which she founded was more than a church; it involved a philosophy and a theology. As such, the movement had affinity with New England Transcendentalism as well as with the nineteenth-century interest in spiritualism and mesmerism.

Mary Baker Eddy (1821–1910) © 1930, RENEWED 1958, THE CHRISTIAN SCIENCE BOARD OF DIRECTORS USED BY PERMISSION

The First Church of Christ, Scientist, in Boston — the "Mother Church" THE CHRISTIAN SCIENCE BOARD OF DIRECTORS

The Christian Science church, now beginning its second century of existence, is apparently no longer growing. Whereas in 1962 there were 3,284 Christian Science churches, in 1980 there were, according to figures obtained from Christian Science headquarters, "just under three thousand." Only about one-fourth of these churches are found outside of the United States. Christian Science practitioners are persons who devote their full time to the practice of Christian Science healing methods. Whereas in 1962 there were about eight thousand Christian Science practitioners, in 1980 there were only about 4,500.

The Christian Science church claims to use the Bible as its source of authority. In actual practice, however, this group accepts the Bible only as interpreted by Eddy. Her *Science and Health* is for Christian Scientists the final court of appeal.

Christian Science denies the existence of matter, evil or sin, disease, and death. Since disease does not really exist, the cure for sickness is to come to the realization that the imag-ined disease is only the result of a false belief.

Christian Science teaches that all is God and that God is all. Whatever is not an aspect of God does not exist. One cannot say that the God of Christian Science is personal or rules the universe. Since matter is not real, God did not create the universe. The universe consists of the thoughts of God, which have always existed.

Man is only spirit or soul; he has no material body. Man has never fallen into sin. Man is said to be incapable of sin; he is actually a part of God.

Jesus was a certain man who lived in Palestine about two thousand years ago. Christ, however, is the ideal truth which heals sickness and sin. Jesus, then, was the man who most fully represented and demonstrated the idea which is Christ. That the person of Jesus is not really important for Christian Science is evidenced by Eddy's conviction that "If there had never existed such a person as the Galilean Prophet, it would make no difference to me."

Christian Science denies that Christ

atoned for human sin by shedding his blood. Jesus' work was rather to show people the truth and to set an example.

Salvation for Christian Science occurs either when one simply quits sinning or when one stops believing that sin is real. In either case, the death of Christ has nothing to do with salvation.

The Christian Science church admin-isters no sacraments: there is no rite of baptism, and neither bread nor wine is served at its semiannual "communion" services.

Christian Science does not have an eschatology in the usual sense of the word. Doctrines such as the return of Christ, the resurrection of the body, the final judgment, and the new earth are all denied. Heaven and hell are states of mind.

Jehovah's Witnesses

ANTHONY A. HOEKEMA

The official beginning of the movement now called Jehovah's Witnesses was on December 13, 1884, when Zion's Watch Tower Tract Society was given a legal charter. The first president of the organization was Charles Taze Russell (1852-1916). Russell started a Bible class in Pittsburgh in 1870 and wrote a seven-volume series of *Studies in the Scriptures*. In 1917 Joseph Franklin Rutherford became the second president. During his presidency the emphasis of the group changed from Bible study to making calls and placing literature, and the name Jehovah's Witnesses was adopted. Nathan Homer Knorr became president in 1942; during his term of office the society's training program was improved, many doctrinal books were published, and the New World Translation of the Bible was produced. After Knorr's death in 1977, Frederick Franz became president.

From its headquarters in Brooklyn, New York, the Watchtower Bible and Tract Society publishes two periodicals, *The Watchtower* and *Awake*; each claims a worldwide circulation of more than seven million. Books and periodicals are published in a number of languages. According to the January 1,

1980, issue of *The Watchtower* the average number of active Jehovah's Witnesses throughout the world (those who spend time regularly each month making calls for the organization) was 2,097,070. The total number of congregations at the end of 1979 was listed as 42,600. The extent of the foreign expansion of the movement is indicated by the fact that three out of every four active Witnesses are found outside the United States.

Jehovah's Witnesses oppose smoking and drinking, refuse to salute the flag, refuse to vote or hold office, object to all forms of military service, and forbid blood transfusions. The last-named prohibition rests on a literal interpretation of Old Testament passages which forbid the drinking of animal blood.

Jehovah's Witnesses claim that their source of authority is the Bible. However, their New World Translation incorporates some of their leaders' own peculiar teachings. Further, the Witnesses may only understand the scriptures as interpreted by the leaders of the Watchtower Society in their publications; any questioning of official doctrine is forbidden.

Jehovah's Witnesses are strict unitarians. The doctrine of the Trinity,

Charles Taze Russell (1852–1916)   LIBRARY OF CONGRESS

created archangel called Michael. In his human state he was a man, born of the virgin Mary. In his posthuman state he is once again a spirit, since his body was not raised. There is no real continuity between these three states; in none of them is Christ equal to Jehovah. The work of Christ was to rescue people from the annihilation in which they would otherwise have remained after death: in other words, to enable them to be raised from the dead.

Salvation, however, in the sense of continued happiness after death, was not earned by Christ but is a human achievement. All must earn their right to future blessedness by carrying out their dedication to Jehovah faithfully until death.

Jehovah's Witnesses claim that they alone are God's true people — all others, including not only non-Christian religions but Christian denominations as well, belong to the devil's organization. The Witnesses divide themselves into two groups. The "anointed class," numbering 144,000, are the privileged class who provide leadership for the organization; when they die they are "raised" as spirits; they will spend eternity not on earth but in heaven with Christ. The "other sheep" are the lower and larger class of adherents; after death they are raised with bodies and, if they pass the millennial tests, continue to live everlastingly on the renewed earth.

Not all individuals are raised after death, however. Those who will be killed in the forthcoming Battle of Armageddon will not be raised but will be annihilated. Those raised during the millennium who later disobey God will also be annihilated. The final destiny of the wicked, both humans and angels, is not hell but nonexistence.

it is said, originated with Satan. God exists in only one person, whose name is Jehovah. The Son was created by Jehovah, and the Holy Spirit is neither divine nor personal.

The first creature Jehovah made was the Son, who may be called "a god" but not God. With the help of this Son, Jehovah later created the realm of angels and the material universe.

Jehovah's Witnesses oppose the view that man consists of body and soul. Man, they say, does not possess a soul but is a soul. The immortality of the soul is denied. The Witnesses believe in a literal fall into sin; the penalty for Adam's sin, however, was not eternal torment but physical death followed by annihilation.

Christ in his prehuman state was a

Beyond the Walls
of Anglo-Saxon Zion

The story of American Christianity has many parts. One is the story of culturally central, largely evangelical, Protestantism. This semiofficial religious "establishment" was always numerically dominant, and its influence was disproportionate to its numbers. This group, whose status was built on the older migrations to North America, was largely "Anglo-Saxon," that is, British or at least northern European.

The rest of the story is really many other stories. It is of Christian groups outside the walls of this dominant "establishment." Some of these might be outside these walls clearly by choice, as was generally true of Christian Scientists, Jehovah's Witnesses, or of scattered converts to Catholicism. For the vast majority, however, an ethnic or racial factor played a critical role. Being Polish, or Italian, or Greek, or Afro-American meant almost automatically that one was a cultural outsider. It meant also that one would not participate in the mainstream of American religious life in quite the same way as would one's Anglo-Saxon neighbor.

One might be tempted to conclude, then, that religion was just a side-effect of one's race or national origin, that tastes in religions varied in much the same ways as tastes in foods might vary among Italians, Greeks, and Anglo-Saxons, and for much the same reasons. It might seem, in other words, that religion was just a "folkway" associated with one's cultural heritage. Sometimes, of course, this was the case. Many people wear their inherited religion only on special occasions, just as they might wear green for St. Patrick's Day or a new hat for Easter. The intimate relation of religion to cultural heritage, however, is far more illuminating if one looks at

the relationship the other way around, seeing the religion not as primarily a side-effect of a cultural heritage but rather as a key factor in shaping the heritage itself. This relationship was particularly crucial as a people entered American society. Almost invariably an ethnic or racial group would settle together in a community separated from the mainstream of American civilization. In such a setting, cut off from homeland and the securities of old cultural relationship, religion played a major role in shaping a community and defining for a people their own identity and the values of the heritage they were bringing to America.

Christianity Among Blacks

Afro-Americans were a unique case in America, seldom paralleled in the history of any civilization. Brought to America by capitalistic Christians who treated them as though they were simply property, they were robbed of most of what gives people a sense of identity. When they were brought from Africa they had been removed from almost all ethnic and family connections, and separated from the dignity of work. They were also separated from their traditional religions so that only vestiges of those ancient practices survived. In slavery only two major factors had been available for building a positive black subculture: kinship ties and evangelical Christianity. The latter they had appropriated with appreciation, enthusiasm, and imagination, seeing in evangelicalism not just a white person's religion but a true gospel of spiritually based liberation. At the root of evangelicalism, they had found, was the Bible, and the Bible was not about white people but about all peoples for whom God had cared. To the oppressed, God had brought redemption and hope even in the times of deepest trouble.

Liberation from slavery, although truly revolutionary, did not change the social standing of black people nearly as much as might have been hoped. Even with slavery removed the vast majority remained in the rural South. There black people had to contend with at least three other factors, any one of which was sufficient to ensure that they would remain at the lowest rung socially: lack of education, poverty, and racial prejudice. The first of these was attacked immediately after the Civil War, especially with the aid of some self-sacrificing New Englanders, and soon continued with some black leadership to provide at least modest beginnings of an educational system up to the college level. Such efforts were severely restricted by

the other two factors. After the war, black people in the South were very quickly forced into economic dependence, especially in the sharecropping system. That made a rise from sheer rural poverty extremely difficult and unlikely. Absolutely sealing the social fate of the Afro-Americans, however, was the issue of race. The central theme in the southern history of the time, as was later observed, was the absolute determination that the South remain a white person's country. For a brief time during the "Reconstruction" that followed the Civil War, blacks were guaranteed their civil rights and even participated substantially in political leadership. These roles, however, were guaranteed only by the presence of federal troops in the South. When these were finally removed in 1877 as part of a political compromise, blacks were soon put back "in their place" by a caste system that

Freedmen's school, Vicksburg, Mississippi, during Reconstruction

kept them apart from participation in the white-dominated society. "Jim Crow" laws demanded that they shop, eat, and travel separately from whites. Southern white church members, firmly convinced of the inferiority of the black race and reinforced in these views by growing racial prejudices in both North and South, often lent theological support to such separation and discrimination. In the southern culture at large, increasing racial hatred aggravated the plight of the black person. In the 1890s lynchings of blacks in the South took place at an average rate of three per week.

In this new, separate, and hostile setting, the black churches and Christianity played tremendously important roles. Two major contributions are distinguishable. Institutionally, the black churches were the most important agencies in providing structure and leadership to the newly separate black communities. Spiritually, the Christianity of the black people was incalculably important in their extreme circumstances in providing them with meaning, acceptance, hope, and a moral dignity that surpassed that of their evangelical white oppressors.

During slavery southern blacks had worshipped in white churches, albeit in separated areas. Freedom quickly brought accord that blacks should form their own congregations and denominations. For the whites separation was a means of institutionalizing their revulsion at dealing with the Negroes on any basis that resembled equality. For the blacks, separation was essential for establishing their ecclesiastical independence from white control.

These almost universally welcomed southern black churches were virtually the only black institutions to survive Reconstruction without being seriously crippled. The growth of these churches was remarkable. They included about forty-three percent of the black population by World War I. The sphere of influence in the community was much larger than the strict membership statistics. W. E. B. DuBois in 1903 observed that "In the South, at least, practically every American Negro is a church member." DuBois added a social explanation that is generally accepted. "A proscribed people," he said, "must have a social center, and that center for this people is the Negro church." Indeed, the influence of

the church in the black communities during this era seems difficult to overestimate. The ministry was virtually the only profession open to blacks, and, except for the brief period of Reconstruction, was almost the only avenue there ever had been in America for black male leadership. Moreover, the churches were the only institutions that belonged fully to the black people. They were often sources of pride, as some notable edifices in southern cities testify, and in the towns and countryside they were the primary social centers for black communities. Southern black peoplehood during this era was built largely on the church. The famous remark of a rural Alabama black about his neighboring town serves as an astute, if unintended, sociological commentary. "The nationality in there," he said, "is Methodist."

The character of the Christianity in the black churches was shaped by several factors. On the surface it was much like the white Baptist and Methodist traditions out of which it had grown. But there were several differences. First of all, coming from cultures that were far closer to biblical cultures than were European-Americans, Afro-Americans did not hear Christian teaching through the abstract categories of Greek thought and the theological controversies of the Western world. Their Christianity was more immediately biblical. "Bible-believer," rather than "evangelical," was the term used to describe their heritage. Their faith was also more spontaneous than that of their white counterparts and was marked especially by the responsive and antiphonal character of the worship services— a melodic and creative dialogue between preacher and congregation, anticipating patterns later found in jazz. Moreover, although blacks and whites had in slavery listened to the same preaching, the blacks heard in the gospel different meanings than had their white oppressors. In freedom, these characteristics of their theology were articulated. Particularly, they were sensitive to the mysteries of God's providential care. In stories such as the exodus or in the theme of the baby Jesus they saw that God cared for his people, both as a mighty warrior and as a tender friend who shared human frailties and infirmities. Hopes for heaven were prominent, as in some spirituals, yet such interests were not opposed to concern for the gospel's

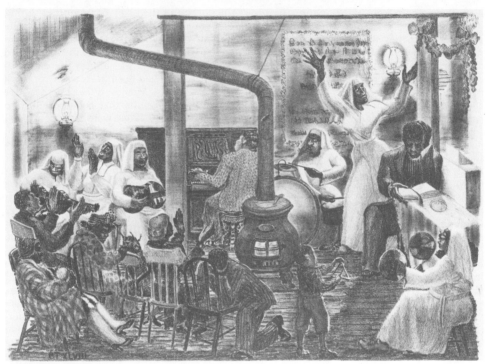

"Assembly Church" in a storefront, by Prentiss Taylor   NATIONAL MUSEUM OF AMERICAN ART, SMITHSONIAN
INSTITUTION

impact in this life. In fact, a striking factor of black Christian consciousness, contrasted with the white evangelical counterparts, is that from their vantage point of being the poor and the oppressed they heard more clearly the biblical themes of Christian responsibilities to brothers and sisters in need.

The strength of this black Christian community was tested by many of the same forces of secularization that were transforming all of America. These themes became especially prominent after the turn of the century when the great migration to the northern cities began. Francis J. Grimke, a black preacher in Washington, D. C., summarized the situation well in 1899. While demanding that the black person must be recognized as a "full-fledged citizen," and deploring the revival of "southern barbarism" manifested in recent lynch laws, Grimke maintained that the greatest dangers to his people were the social vices of materialism, drunkenness, and sexual license they faced in the cities.

Without the social supports of the close-knit rural communities, the black churches in the cities, though still predominantly traditional, were often being reshaped by the unsettled conditions and the competition of a free enterprise system. In this setting storefront churches flourished. Holiness and pentecostal groups of bewildering varieties provided channels of expression for depths of emotion among the migrants. Sects and cults flourished as well. The most famous of these was that of Father Divine (*ca.* 1879-1965) who claimed to be God incarnate and who rose to fame in Brooklyn and Harlem during the 1920s and 1930s. Such extravagances, though widely publicized, should not be exaggerated. Nearly two-thirds of black church membership was Baptist, and most of the other third was from the Methodist tradition. The center of black life was still the church, not only in the rural South, but even in the cities of the North to which the balance of the population was shifting. The churches, though battered during the jazz age, were still forces to be contended with.

The Black Church Grows

DAVID W. WILLS

The Civil War and Emancipation were for Afro-American Christians a vindication of their deeply cherished belief that a righteous God would one day punish their oppressors and set the captives free. These events and the ensuing period of Reconstruction also for the first time opened the entire South to the missionary efforts of the independent black churches. They were not slow to seize this new opportunity. In May 1863, the African Methodist Episcopal church, under the leadership of Bishop Daniel Alexander Payne, dispatched two of its clergymen to work among the freedmen

African Methodist Episcopal bishop Daniel Alexander Payne LIBRARY OF CONGRESS

behind Union lines in the sea islands of South Carolina. James Walker Hood of the AME Zion church began his denomination's southern missionary labors in January 1864 at New Bern, North Carolina, a Union military stronghold still subject to Confederate attacks. Northern Afro-American Baptists affiliated with the American Baptist Missionary Convention and the Northwestern and Southern Baptist Convention, both black, were also at work in Federally controlled areas of the South well before Appomattox.

With the end of the war, these pioneer missionaries were joined by many other black clergymen from the North. Together with the numerous and influential ex-slave preachers of the South, these black leaders organized hundreds of churches, established dozens of schools, and generally made the church the organizational center of the black community. During the period of Reconstruction, they also provided important political leadership for the newly enfranchised southern freedmen. Mississippi's Hiram Revels, the first Afro-American to serve in the United States Senate, was a Methodist clergyman. Richard Harvey Cain, who twice in the 1870s was elected to Congress from South Carolina, was an AME clergyman who had come into the state as a missionary in 1865. He later became an AME bishop. Many other influential black church leaders were politically active and held office at the state level.

The work of these black missionaries to the freedmen transformed the two leading black denominations of the antebellum period from relatively small, northern-based organizations to large nationwide institutions with a predominantly southern constituency. In 1856, the AME church had a total membership of only twenty thousand persons, half of whom lived in the Philadelphia or Baltimore areas. By 1880 the denomination reported a total membership of slightly over 400,000. The greatest concentration of members was now in South Carolina and Georgia. The AME Zion church, though somewhat smaller, underwent a similar transformation, with North Carolina becoming its major center of strength.

Active missionary work among the southern freedmen also allowed the predominantly white Methodist Episcopal church, North, greatly to increase its black membership. By the 1880s, this denomination counted more than 200,000 black communicants. The trend of the period, however, was away from black membership in white denominations, and no other predominantly white church retained a black constituency comparable to that of the Northern Methodists.

By mutual agreement, the black membership of several of the predominantly white southern Protestant churches withdrew to form separate denominations. The most important of the churches created in this way was the Colored Methodist Episcopal church (renamed in 1954 Christian Methodist Episcopal). Organized in 1870, it consisted initially of blacks who had formerly belonged to the Methodist Episcopal church, South. Since many of that church's black adherents had already defected to the AMEs, the AMEZs, or the Northern Methodists, the new denomination was smaller than the other black Methodist groups. Still, by the 1880s, it reported 100,000 members.

The largest number of black Christians were Baptists. By the 1880s, the nation's ten thousand black Baptist congregations, mostly in the South, counted a total membership of more than one million. As early as 1866, with the creation of the Consolidated American Baptist Missionary Convention, northern black Baptist leaders sought to organize their massive constituency of freedmen into an independent denomination. Baptist localism, regional rivalries, and disagreement over the degree of collaboration possible with whites thwarted this effort, and the convention collapsed in 1879. The effort at national organization was not abandoned, however, and in 1895 it finally reached a successful conclusion with the organization of the National Baptist Convention. In spite of a major schism in 1916 (in which the National Baptist Convention of America, unincorporated, split off from the very similarly named parent body, the National Baptist Convention, U.S.A., Incorporated), this has remained the largest of the black denominations.

By 1906, the various Baptist and Methodist denominations together accounted for more than ninety-five percent of the reported black church membership. But an important twentieth-century challenger emerged that year with the launching of pentecostalism. A black preacher, William J. Seymour, presided over the famous Azusa Street meetings where modern pentecostalism was born. Other blacks were also centrally involved in the movement from the outset. Together with the preceding and closely related holiness movement, pentecostalism gave rise to several additional independent black denominations. The most important of these was the Church of God in Christ. Organized initially as a holiness church in the mid-1890s, it was led into pentecostalism in 1907 by its widely influential founder, Charles H. Mason. It eventually became the largest of the black pentecostal denominations.

Education, Publication, and Foreign Missions in the Black Church

DAVID W. WILLS

The striking numerical growth of black Christianity and the multiplication of independent black church organizations was matched during this period by the rapid development of denominational programs in such areas as education, publishing, and overseas missions.

During the period of Reconstruction, the black churches had sponsored and housed many schools offering basic instruction in literacy to the freedmen. Programs in higher education, however, were almost entirely under the sponsorship of the well-financed northern white missionary associations. The exception was Wilberforce University, an Ohio school purchased by the AME church from the Northern Methodists in 1863. (Its president, Bishop Daniel Alexander Payne, was the first black president of a black-controlled college in the United States.) After 1880, however, the picture changed as black Christians founded and supported several additional colleges, such as Livingstone College, North Carolina (AME Zion), Lane College in Tennessee (CME), Morris Brown College in Atlanta (AME), and Virginia Theological Seminary and College (Baptist). By the end of the century, there were more than two dozen of these new black church colleges. They benefitted from the continuing growth of the black denominations and by the late 1920s were on the average better supported financially than were the many private black colleges which relied for their support on the charity of northern white churches.

These same years witnessed a major expansion in the publishing programs of the black churches. This came partly in relation to an increased effort to promote Sunday schools.

The AME church's Sunday School Union established a publishing house in 1887 and began to produce instructional literature for use in the denomination's Sunday schools. Other black churches soon developed comparable programs. Educational material was by no means, however, the sole or even the primary publication of the black churches. They also produced a number of newspapers (usually weeklies) that covered black affairs generally as well as events within the church. The best known of these was probably the AME church's *Christian Recorder*. Established in 1852, this paper was in the late nineteenth century — and remains today — the oldest continuously published black newspaper in the United States. The churches also pioneered in the publication of black periodical literature. The AME *Church Review* (established in 1884), the AME *Zion Quarterly Review*

Soil analysis laboratory of George Washington Carver at Tuskegee Institute, ca. 1900 THE GRANGER COLLECTION

(1890), and the *National Baptist Magazine* (1894) served as influential journals of opinion, not only for their denominations, but for the black cultural elite generally. Meanwhile, the black denominational publishing houses produced dozens of books by black authors on topics ranging from theology and church history to autobiography and strategies for racial advancement.

The overseas missionary activities of the black churches also took on a new level of significance during this period. As in the antebellum period, some of these missionary efforts were directed toward Caribbean nations, particularly Haiti. But especially after 1880, the major focus of black missionary attention was Africa. Black Christians viewed with mixed feelings the rapid European partition of the African continent occurring after that date. Most believed that Africa needed both the Christian gospel and the "uplifting" influences of "Christian civilization." But many also feared that white rule over blacks would be as cruel and oppressive in Africa as it had generally been in the United States. Only if black Americans themselves took the lead in "Christianizing and civilizing" Africa, some black church leaders argued, could Africa experience the blessing of the gospel without also suffering the curse of racist domination.

Among the black Baptists, a new level of interest in foreign missions was evidenced by the organization in 1880 of the Baptist Foreign Mission Convention. Working primarily in West Africa, this body developed a missionary program that was carried on after 1895 by the National Baptist Convention. The African work of the AME Zion church was begun in Liberia in the late 1870s and gradually extended into the British-controlled areas of West Africa. The AME church, under the energetic leadership of Bishop Henry McNeal Turner, developed the most extensive African missionary effort of any of the black churches. Making four trips to Africa during the 1890s, Turner organized annual conferences in Sierra Leone and Liberia and arranged for the separatist Ethiopian Church of South Africa to become part of the AME church.

The missionary societies of black church women played a crucial role in fostering and supporting these expanded overseas programs. AME women led the way, organizing the Women's Parent Mite Missionary Society in 1874. Though denied access to ordination, some black churchwomen themselves served abroad — either as missionary wives or church workers in their own right. One of the best known was Amanda Smith, a prominent "lady evangelist" active in the holiness movement, who made a missionary tour of India in 1880 and then worked for the remainder of the decade in Liberia.

Here as in other areas, the ability of the black churches to develop effective programs was severely hampered by a lack of financial resources. A further problem was the opposition of many white colonial administrators, who often suspected Afro-American missionaries of encouraging rebelliousness. Though blocked by these and other obstacles from becoming the primary agents for the Christianization of Africa, the black churches were nonetheless able to develop an important missionary program and to forge ties with Africa that have endured into the late twentieth century.

The Double Crisis of Black Christianity
DAVID W. WILLS

Black Christianity in the late nineteenth and early twentieth centuries experienced a crisis that was simultaneously both racial and religious.

Mounting racial injustice made these decades a severe time of trial for all black Americans. Violent intimidation had been part of black experience in the South (where ninety percent of the black population still lived) since Reconstruction. But it seemed to worsen in the late 1880s and early 1890s, when the number of lynchings sharply increased. Around the same time, the southern states passed a series of new laws enforcing an increasingly strict segregation in all public facilities, while hundreds of thousands of southern black voters were eliminated from the electorate by "reforms" in southern state constitutions. In a climate of increasing racism nationwide, this concentrated assault on the lives, dignity, and basic political rights of black Americans was accepted with little protest by most northern whites.

Black leaders were hard pressed to resist effectively this surging tide of racism. Booker T. Washington, the southern black educator (and Baptist) who emerged in 1895 as the race's dominant leader, counseled blacks to acquiesce temporarily to the harsh inequalities of the caste system. He hoped that a generation of black economic achievements would reopen the doors to full citizenship and greater social equality. Many black churchmen, having themselves long taught a "Protestant ethic" of hard work, thrift, and upward social mobility, supported Washington's approach. Others agreed with W. E. B. DuBois, Washington's most influential black critic, that it was a mistake, even in dangerous times, to mute the voice of protest. They criticized Washington and joined in the early 1900s in renewed demands for black rights and full equality. A few of these anti-Bookerites shared with some white social gospellers a strong sympathy for contemporary working class movements. Reverdy C. Ransom (an AME pastor in the urban north) and George Washington Woodbey (a California Baptist) saw racial injustice as part of capital's exploitation of labor and therefore called upon blacks to become socialists. Other black churchmen, even as they attacked American racism, saw it as incurable and called upon Afro-Americans to look to Africa for their deliverance. AME Bishop Henry McNeal Turner, the leading spokesman for such views, urged a vanguard of black Americans to migrate to Africa and help build there a great black Christian nation that would give blacks everywhere a new sense of pride and self-respect.

Difficult as it was, choosing an effective strategy for a renewed counterattack on white racism was not the only major challenge that confronted black church leaders during this period. They were also faced with the demanding task of making sense religiously of the world in which black Americans now found themselves.

Black Christians had seen in the Civil War and Emancipation a vindication of their trust in the righteousness and power of God. But when already impoverished southern blacks were being disfranchised, segregated, and lynched and Africa was falling completely under the yoke of European domination, the triumph of God's justice was harder to discern. Black church leaders were also well aware that the theological traditions of evangelical Protestantism, upon which Afro-American Christians had long relied for an interpretation of their experience, were themselves being challenged by Darwinians, biblical critics, and others.

In a flow of books and articles not matched until the black theology movement of the 1960s and 1970s, an emerging elite of theologically informed black churchmen struggled to meet these challenges to black faith. They did so with an increasing sense that black Christians needed to develop their own tradition of theological reflection. "The time has come," declared AME *Review* editor Benjamin Tucker Tanner in 1888, "for the Negro, and even all the colored races of the earth to construct a theology for themselves." Like most black theologians of his time, Tanner preferred to build on the old foundations. He vigorously defended the inerrancy of the Bible and repeatedly attacked Darwinism and the "higher" criticism — in part because he saw attacks on Genesis as being simultaneously assaults on black people. By rejecting the biblical theory of human origins, Tanner argued, whites sought to deny the common descent of all humanity from Adam and Eve. Other black theologians, also relying on the Bible, sought to renew black hope and restore confidence in the final triumph of God's justice by fresh readings of biblical prophecy. James Theodore Holly, a black American who had emigrated to Haiti and become bishop of the Episcopal church there, saw in scripture evidence that white predominance in the world would soon end in a bloody Armageddon. In the millennium to follow, black people would hold the place of honor among the reigning elect. In *The End of the World* (1888), AME theologian Theophilus Gould Steward presented a similar picture of an imminent millennial reversal of the situation of the white and "darker races."

Black theological creativity subsided in the early twentieth century. The growing secularization of black life turned the educated elite increasingly away from the study of theology. World War I also marked the beginning of the mass migration of black Americans to the urban North, a development that transformed black life and created many new and demanding challenges to the black churches. But the idea that Afro-Americans must reinterpret the Christian faith in light of the world-wide struggle of black people did not disappear. It was carried forward in the aftermath of World War I by the internationally influential Garvey movement, in which many black churchmen actively participated, and its influence continues to be felt today.

God is a Negro

African Methodist Episcopal Bishop Henry McNeal Turner was ridiculed in the religious paper, The Observer, for remarking "God is a Negro." The following is part of his defense.

Yet we are no stickler as to God's color, anyway, but if He has any we would prefer to believe that it is nearer symbolized in the blue sky above us and the blue water of the seas and oceans; but we certainly protest against God being a white man or against God being white *at all*; abstract as this theme must forever remain while we are in the flesh. This is one of the reasons we favor African emigration, or Negro nationalization, wherever we can find a domain, for as long as we remain among the whites, the Negro will believe that the devil is black and that he (the Negro) favors the devil, and that God is white and that he (the Negro) bears no resemblance to Him, and the effect of such a sentiment is contemptuous and degrading, and one-half of the Negro race will be trying to get white and the other half will spend their days trying to be white men's scullions in order to please the whites; and the time they should be giving to the study of such things as will dignify and make our race great will be devoted to studying about how unfortunate they are in not being white.

We conclude these remarks by repeating for the information of the *Observer* what it adjudged us demented for — *God is a Negro.*

The Voice of Missions,
February 1898

This 1897 Harper's *drawing of a black church in the Virginia pines may have been an accurate representation of the rural black experience, but its serenity belies the passion of black theologians in the 1890s.* BILLY GRAHAM CENTER

American Catholicism

The problems that the black migrants to the northern cities faced in the early twentieth century resembled, in some respects, those that had confronted huge numbers of Catholic immigrants to America since the mid-nineteenth century. Both groups were predominantly poor and were discriminated against by the white Protestants who held most of the nation's economic, political, and social power. For each, the antagonism toward them had been renewed especially during the 1890s. In the case of the Catholics, these machinations were led by the American Protective Association, founded in 1887 for the purpose of inflaming fears of a takeover by Rome and "foreigners."

The situation of the Catholics, however, differed in many ways from that of the blacks, most in ways that in the long run gave Catholics many advantages. Most importantly, Catholics in America had the support of one of the oldest continuously functioning institutions in the world. This meant that the Catholic church in America was the American institution least susceptible to be blown about by every wind of cultural change. Though the church proved adjustable to the American situation and was shaped by the American experience, it proved a solid haven for bringing much of the American population through the ordeals of adjustment to a new way of life.

In retrospect, this perception of the relative stability that the Catholic church proved to have may shield from vision the storms it did have to weather. The history of the Catholic church from 1865 until the severe immigration restrictions imposed in 1924 is, in large part, the history of one of the largest migrations of peoples in the history of the world. At the end of the Civil War the population of the United States had been slightly more than thirty million. By 1930 approximately the same number of new Americans had arrived by immigration. The majority of these were at least nominally Catholic, so that the size of the church grew from some three million in 1860 to nearly twenty million by 1930, representing by then about one-sixth of the total American population and one-third of the total church membership. This immense growth, largely from among the poor, meant tremendous challenges and problems for the Catholic church.

These problems were amplified by the very large ethnic diversities within the church itself. At the same time that Catholics faced antagonisms from Protestants, they had to deal with severe ethnic tensions within their own community. These rivalries were acutely practical. Control of the local churches was at stake. A German-speaking immigrant was not happy to find his or her parish wholly in the control of Irish clergy.

The conflicts between the Irish and the Germans were the most intense throughout much of the nineteenth century. The Irish were the first Catholic group to migrate to the United States in massive numbers. By midcentury they had taken over much of the leadership in the American church. By this time, however, German Catholic migrations were becoming comparable to the Irish, and many parishes and some dioceses came under German control. Even when conflicts were resolved on the local level, the problem remained that the Irish controlled the church hierarchy. A number of important policy matters were at stake. For instance, many of the Irish clergy had come to share with their Protestant counterparts the conviction that prohibition of alcoholic beverages was essential for urban social welfare. Germans loved their beer, and German monasteries even had breweries. More essential conflicts took place, however, over the schools. German Catholic immigrants were convinced that the Irish-dominated church was losing many German Catholics because in the church and its schools the language (other than liturgical Latin) was English. "Language saves the faith," was the German slogan. To preserve both the language and their faith, German Catholics (like many of their Lutheran counterparts) insisted on parochial schools. The Irish, somewhat more Americanized and not sympathizing on the language question, often were slower in moving toward building a complete Catholic school system. After 1884 the building of parish schools became official church policy, though in many areas progress in building the system continued to be slow until after the turn of the century.

In all such controversies the immigrant groups from various nations were divided not only among each other, but within them-

Approximate Church Membership and Affiliations 1855 and 1930

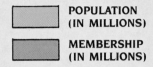

POPULATION (IN MILLIONS)

MEMBERSHIP (IN MILLIONS)

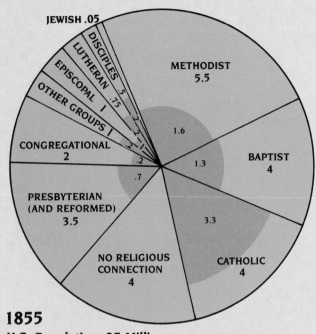

JEWISH .05
DISCIPLES .5
LUTHERAN .75
EPISCOPAL 1
OTHER GROUPS 1
CONGREGATIONAL 2
PRESBYTERIAN (AND REFORMED) 3.5
NO RELIGIOUS CONNECTION 4
METHODIST 5.5
BAPTIST 4
CATHOLIC 4
1.6
1.3
3.3
.7
.2
.2
.2
.75

1855
U.S. Population: 27 Million

U.S. Population: 122 Million

1930

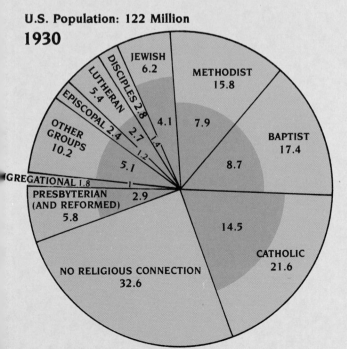

JEWISH 6.2
DISCIPLES 2.8
LUTHERAN 5.4
EPISCOPAL 2.4
OTHER GROUPS 10.2
CONGREGATIONAL 1.8
PRESBYTERIAN (AND REFORMED) 5.8
NO RELIGIOUS CONNECTION 32.6
METHODIST 15.8
BAPTIST 17.4
CATHOLIC 21.6
4.1
7.9
8.7
14.5
2.9
5.1
1.2
1.4
2.7
1

NOTE: Church membership figures are notoriously unreliable. Churches count members in different ways. In the earlier period many people were loosely connected with a church but not full members; in most Protestant denominations in the twentieth century occasional attenders and older children were much more often full members. The 1855 chart is adapted from Robert Baird, *Religion in America* (rev. ed., 1856). His "population" figures are broad estimates to include children and occasional church attenders; for the Catholics he makes no such distinction. The 1930 chart is based on reports of adult membership in the 1933 *Yearbook of American Churches*; these figures are doubled to determine "population," which would include children and persons loosely affiliated. Since Catholic and Jewish groups attempted to include all nominal members in their reports, their population figures more closely approximate their membership figures. In all cases the population figures are sheer estimates.

selves. In every group two parties inevitably developed. One would be the party of Americanization, seeking to lead the people into the mainstream of American life as much as was possible without sacrificing the essentials of the heritage. Another more conservative party would be convinced that any concession to American ways would compromise the faith itself. Retaining ideological ghetto walls of separateness was their solution to the threats of their new situation. So the lines of conflict were not strictly ethnic. Among the Irish, for instance, a conservative party resisted every trend to compromise with the American way of life.

These conflicts, perennial among immigrant groups, took a particularly dramatic form in the development of the Catholic church in America in the late nineteenth century. The factor that helped dramatize the issue was that the Catholic church in the last analysis was not essentially an American institution but an international body. Moreover, from the perspective of international Catholicism, "Americanism" was a controversial issue. America in the nineteenth century was identified with political liberalism. The papacy, in the meantime, was suffering from the combination of Italian political liberalism and nationalism that brought the unification of Italy and in 1870 the removal of the vestiges of the pope's temporal power. In 1864 Pius IX had issued his famous antiliberal *Syllabus of Errors*. In 1870 his declaration of papal infallibility further embarrassed those American Catholics who had more democratic leanings. The relation of the Catholic church to the United States was, moreover, not a normal one in terms of international Catholicism. Nowhere else did such a large Catholic body exist without support of the state. The question arose as to whether the American situation, where the church existed as one of many voluntary agencies in a pluralistic society, should be accepted as normal. Some conservative Catholics both in America and abroad let it be known that such an arrangement should not be accepted as normal, thus fanning the flames of Protestant fears that massive immigration would eventually lead to a Catholic political takeover.

Such issues stood in the way of the leading figures in the American church, such as Bal-

Archbishop John Ireland (1838–1918) of St. Paul stood for a full Americanization of Roman Catholicism. LIBRARY OF CONGRESS

Americanizing Sentiments

We should live in our age, know it, be in touch with it. . . . We should be in it and of it, if we would have its ear. . . . For the same reason, there is needed a thorough sympathy with the country. The Church of America must be, of course, as Catholic as even in Jerusalem or Rome; but as far as her garments assume color from the local atmosphere, she must be American. Let no one dare to paint her brow with a foreign taint or pin to her mantle foreign linings.

ARCHBISHOP JOHN IRELAND,
1889

timore's James Cardinal Gibbons (1834-1921) and John Ireland (1838-1918), archbishop of St. Paul, who wished to lead the church into full-fledged participation in American life. Their Americanization, in the sense of assimilation to the American way of life, was easily confused with the Americanism that in European Catholicism was raising intense opposition. While no serious doctrinal issues seem to have been involved, the pope's warning to the Americans in his encyclical letter *Longinqua Oceani* in 1895, his removal of some prominent Americanist leaders from key educational posts during the next year, and his condemnation of Americanism in 1899, placed real restraints on Catholic tendencies to embrace American culture too readily. The condemnation of modernism by Pius X in 1907 further sealed strong tendencies toward conservatism that were coming to dominate American Catholic intellectual life.

The Americanist controversy and its conservative outcome spared American Catholics some of the traumas of adjustment to the intellectual ideals and values of twentieth-century life. The recent immigrant status of most of the church ensured a basic isolation from many of the prevailing cultural and intellectual trends. The "new immigration" of important new ethnic groups, such as the Poles and the Italians, was bringing new internal concerns for the church and repetitions of the perennial tensions of adjustments to a new cultural setting. Substantial numbers of French, Portuguese, Belgians, Slovaks, Croatians, Hungarians, and Spanish-speaking Catholics added to the complexity. The growing educational system of the church, covering everything from the earliest school years through universities, further ensured the continuing separation and integrity of Catholic traditions. The importance of

Georgetown University, Washington, D.C., was founded as Georgetown College by John Carroll in 1789, became a Pontifical University in 1833, and flourished after introducing graduate professional schools in the 1870s. GEORGETOWN UNIVERSITY NEWS SERVICE

these institutions, especially at the higher levels, should not be overlooked, since they provide an important contrast to the Protestant model. While during the early twentieth century Protestants were rapidly dismantling the vestiges of their educational system in a desperate effort to remain "relevant" to modern trends, Catholics retained an aloofness, partially imposed from abroad, to such trends and concerns. The result was that even though Catholic universities contributed relatively little to American intellectual life in the early decades of the century, these institutions nonetheless were the only Christian universities to survive on the North American continent in the twentieth century.

In general during the early decades of the century the Catholic church in America was beginning to show signs of maturity. This status was, in fact, recognized by the international hierarchy in 1908 when Rome ended the official "mission" status of the American church and placed it on the same footing as Catholic churches in European countries. World War I accelerated the process of assimilation with American culture. During the war Catholics demonstrated their patriotism. The war also accentuated the belief among Americans in the superiority of America over other cultures. The melting-pot ideal was also

Far Eastern relief organized by the National Catholic Welfare Conference CATHOLIC RELIEF SERVICES

at its height. All these factors helped speed up the breakdown of some of the ethnic distinctiveness in Catholic ghettoes. National unity was also at a premium, manifesting itself among Catholics in the central organization of the American church in the National Catholic War Council, which after the war was made the permanent organization for coordinating American Catholic affairs under the new name of the National Catholic Welfare Conference. Included in the work of the NCWC was coordination of missions and social action. Foreign missions by American Catholics previously had been small, and its substantial increase after 1920 reflected the maturing of the church. As to social welfare, American Catholicism had always been largely working class and hence democratic politically and prounions. Its social work was confined primarily to work through charitable institutions—an area where the church had much experience and success. Only after World War I did the spokesmen for the church venture into progressive political pronouncements. Resurgent anti-Catholicism in the 1920s, however, manifested especially against the campaign of Catholic Al Smith as Democratic candidate for the Presidency in 1928, kept the church basically on the defensive.

Father John A. Ryan, Social Action Director of the NCWC and author of the 1919 "Bishops' Report" on social reconstruction LIBRARY OF CONGRESS

Polish-American Catholics

ANTHONY J. KUZNIEWSKI, S.J.

The religious life of Polish-American Christians has been shaped by strong allegiances to faith and fatherland. In partitioned Poland, cultural expression and hopes for the revival of the nation centered in Roman Catholicism. "Through the use of the Polish language we remain good Catholics," ran a popular line, "and through allegiance to the church we are good Poles." Such sentiments helped shape Polish experience in America.

About 2.2 million Poles emigrated to the United States between 1850 and 1924. The majority found homes in the industrial and mining centers of the Northeast. There, Catholic parishes formed the nucleus of their social life, providing places for belonging and recognition, outlets for traditional piety, and the means of transmitting cultural and religious values to younger generations through the schools.

Building churches was the first priority. Immigrants pooled scant resources and even mortgaged homes to build structures praised — and criticized — for their extravagance. The forty-five thousand members of Chicago's St. Stanislaus Kostka parish, for instance, held church properties worth $500,000 in 1899; and in Milwaukee a much smaller congregation, St. Josaphat's, erected a monumental basilica whose costs eventually overtaxed their financial resources.

The increasing number of Polish-American institutions emphasized the need for priests and religious sisters. At first these were sent from various communities in Poland, though by the early twentieth century Polish-Americans were training their own leadership. Religious sisters were especially prominent in the schools. By 1914, nearly 2,200 sisters were teaching more than 128,000 children. The Polish schools reached a peak enrollment of about 250,000 in 1932.

Laypeople, though restricted in leadership prerogatives, still played significant roles. Organists, particularly, held important positions; they had the right to collect certain fees and were often the first schoolmasters in the parishes. Religious societies of laypeople abounded at every parish. On solemn occasions proud officers with bright banners led the members in procession down streets and through churches.

At first Polish Catholics acquired a reputation for great devotion and periodic parish disputes. The disagreements usually resulted from the uprooted immigrant circumstances and the often conflicting feelings toward the parish and its personnel. In time, a characteristic Polish-American Catholicism stressed a somewhat ethnocentric view of church and society which some outsiders criticized as clannish. A good example of the resulting institutional solidarity was Sacred Heart parish in New Britain, where the Rev. Lucyan Bójnowski established a church and school, orphanage, old age home, newspaper, and cemetery, and founded a congregation of sisters to help staff the thriving enterprise.

For many, the most crucial issue was the desire for Polish-American bishops. This crusade grew in reaction to the growth of independent Polish sects and from a desire for recognition and "equality" within the larger church. Three Polish-American Congresses between 1896 and 1904 considered the matter, and the Rev. Wenceslaus Kruszka was sent to petition Pope Pius X for help. But Poles were locked out of the American hierarchy until the appointment of Paul Rhode as auxiliary bishop in Chicago in 1908 in an unusual process which implied that his responsibilities would be limited basically to the Polish Catholics.

St. Stanislaus Kostka church, Chicago. These buildings
served one of the largest Polish parishes in the world.
STATE HISTORICAL SOCIETY OF WISCONSIN

In the second and subsequent generations, the specifically Polish elements of the community have yielded to the forces of assimilation. But studies show a persistent loyalty to Roman Catholicism and a willingness to support its institutions long after the Polish language has been forgotten. Certainly, John Paul II's election as pope brought much recommitment to the religious dimension of the Polish heritage.

The Polish National Catholic church — a group which broke with Rome in 1897 — has been a unique development within immigrant Catholicism. Arising from misunderstandings between Irish and German-American bishops and Polish congregations over parish administration and pastoral assignments, separate movements in Chicago and Buffalo were incorporated into the group which originated in Scranton under the leadership of Francis Hodur. Hodur carefully maintained the principle of apostolic succession by accepting episcopal consecration from the Old Catholics in the Netherlands. His reforms included greater lay participation in parish administration and church government, restrictions on clerical salaries, translations of the Mass and other worship services into Polish, optional celibacy for the clergy, and the introduction of more specifically Polish feasts into the liturgical calendar. The church, now somewhat Americanized, is headed by a prime bishop, who acts in association with other bishops, priests, and laypeople. The PNCC was, until 1978, in communion with the Protestant Episcopal church and by 1980 claimed an American membership of 270,000.

Italian-American Catholics
JOHN BRIGGS

Italians have been actively involved in the religious life of America as priests, missionaries, and teachers from the earliest settlements. The mass migration of the late nineteenth and early twentieth centuries greatly widened the Italian place in American religious history. Seven hundred thousand Italians entered the U.S. in the 1890s, followed by more than two million in the first decade of the twentieth century. They joined other non-English-speaking immigrants in adding great diversity to the Roman Catholic church.

Though of rural peasant and artisan origins, they settled in industrial urban America. Early migrants were highly transient young men seeking employment wherever it was offered. Initially they considered their sojourn temporary, a search for capital to advance their positions in their home villages. They encountered an ecclesiastical leadership fearful of potential external and internal threats from pluralism, after earlier Irish and German struggles over the shape and character of the American church. With the bishops unsure of how to respond to the sudden appearance of new immigrant groups, initiatives to establish congregations came as often from the immigrants as from the American church.

As women and children arrived they provided more balanced populations, a greater sense of permanency, and new religious and social needs. Parishes serving a single national group provided a core around which communities grew. The "national parish" was, after the family, the most important institution in the immigrants' new homeland. No other reached into so many areas of Italian-American life. It provided religious services in familiar form and language, thus preventing traumatic disruption of the immigrants' religious life while blending many local traditions into a broader Italian-American religious culture. For the ever growing American-born generation, which knew America better than Italy, it provided American-style devotional, social, educational, and recreational activities. Separate parishes also offered immigrants wide participation in life and leadership of the parish which they would not have enjoyed had they been forced into existing territorial parishes.

National parishes, then, preserved the immigrants' religious heritage while supporting their gradual Americanization. Americanization was the goal of the missions Protestants opened in every sizable Italian community. Proselytizing produced few converts, but the popularity of their social, recreational, and educational programs prompted Catholics to similar efforts.

The Italian religious experience was not without strife. Italians differed from other contemporary immigrants in ways that engendered conflict with the American church. The unification of Italy was accomplished at the expense of the church's temporal authority and landholdings. In America a small, stridently anticlerical group of Italian intellectuals intensified a preexisting Irish distaste for Italian nationalists as usurpers of church property and imprisoners of the pope. Any manifestation of Italian patriotism, including religious involvement in celebration of Italian national holidays, met ecclesiastical condemnation. The American hierarchy also sought to ban or modify many religious practices and beliefs of southern Italian immigrants which it considered superstitious, irreligious, or heretical. Of particular concern were the ubiquitous carnivallike festivals venerating patron saints of the immigrants' home villages. To church leaders these events diverted scarce resources from the parish, created unnecessary competition between supporters of various saints, and subjected the Italians and the church to ridicule by Americans.

Italian immigrant family disembarking at Ellis Island
GEORGE EASTMAN HOUSE COLLECTION

Provision of competent priests for Italian communities was a persistent problem. Italian-speaking Americans seldom proved successful as mediators between church and immigrants. Suitable Italian priests were few. Northern Italians often alienated their southern Italian parishioners. Southern priests were viewed from most quarters as being of questionable character and poorly prepared for the difficult task of satisfying the immigrants, while helping them to learn to live in America and not alienating their American bishops in the process. Only a few priests, for example, those sent by Bishop Scalabrini, were especially trained for this difficult mission.

Italy, with a state-supported church, poorly prepared the immigrants for life in America where maintenance of religion was a voluntary activity. Contemporary observers expressed great concern for the "Italian problem" — usually defined as superstition, indifference to the church's welfare in America, anticlericalism, and a fear of widespread apostasy among immigrants. Yet, Italians retained their faith and fashioned places for themselves in America, as much by their own efforts as through the agency of others.

Cardinal Gibbons and Americanism

JOHN TRACY ELLIS

"Americanism," like many other terms, has various meanings. The most common connotation relates to an attachment or loyalty to the ideals and traditions of the United States. In the present context, however, the term relates rather to a movement that had its origins in the 1880s among a few articulate Catholic leaders who were sympathetic to the ideas of the convert priest, Isaac T. Hecker (1819-1888), founder of the Paulist Fathers. Faced with the thousands of Catholic immigrants of a wide variety of ethnic backgrounds and languages — their number approximated 9.5 million in the century, 1820-1920 — these churchmen were eager that this vast addition to the Catholic community be assimilated to American modes of life in a manner that would prepare them for permanent citizenship, and at the same time lessen the frequently heard charge from native Americans that the Catholic church represented a "foreign"

influence in the Republic. It was a delicate undertaking and led at times to severe internal strain among Catholics, e.g., the German resentment of Irish domination of the church in the 1890s.

In pursuit of Hecker's concept of Americanization, certain churchmen at times made statements that were open to misinterpretation by conservatives fearful that the efforts at accommodation to the nation's ideals would endanger traditional theological teaching, e.g., the need to stress the "active" over the "passive" virtues, the lessening of the value assigned to the vows of chastity, poverty, and obedience taken by members of religious orders, and in general the need for the church to adapt to the spirit of the age. These ideas were seized upon by French Catholic conservatives, especially after they read a French translation of a faulty biography of Hecker by the Paulist Walter Elliott. These Frenchmen, moreover,

James Cardinal Gibbons (1834–1921)
LIBRARY OF CONGRESS

America, and Denis J. O'Connell, rector of the North American College, Rome. Thus when O'Connell read a paper at a Catholic congress in Fribourg, Switzerland, in 1897 entitled "A New Idea in the Life of Father Hecker," Gibbons told him:

> I regard its appearance as most opportune, & the paper itself is clear, precise in terms, giving a defi-nition of "Americanism" to which every honest Catholic must sub-scribe ... & the relations of Church & State are admirably set forth especially for the eye of Rome. "If this be treason, let them make the most of it," to use the words of Patrick Henry.

The doctrinal overtones of the con-troversy frankly horrified James Gibbons as they came out of France and were taken up at the Holy See, seconded by a group of conservative Catholics in America, among whom were certain Jesuits, the German bish-ops, and a few non-German bishops such as Michael A. Corrigan, arch-bishop of New York. In spite of strenuous efforts by Gibbons, Ireland, and others to prevent official notice being taken by Rome of the matter, they failed. On January 22, 1899, Pope Leo XIII signed the letter, *Testem bene-volentiae*, which condemned the idea of active vs. passive virtues, of denigrat-ing religious vows, as well as efforts to have the church change its traditional teaching to accommodate to the mod-ern age. To his credit, the pope made it clear that he was not accusing American Catholics of holding these ideas, only that it was said by some that such concepts were circulating in the United States; he likewise clearly prescinded from the loyalty and attachment that Catholics felt for their country.

resented holding up the United States as a model for church-state relation-ships, since most of them were monarchists completely opposed to their own republican government. The result, in brief, was a veritable explo-sion in France in the late 1890s over the alleged heresy of "Americanism."

As the controversy grew more heated and threatened action from Rome, James Cardinal Gibbons became gravely concerned lest the basic teaching of Hecker and his fol-lowers should be distorted in a way to suggest doctrinal errancy among American Catholics. His sympathies were totally in favor of Americanism in the sense of bringing the immigrant Catholics to an acceptance of the nation's political and social customs, surely, but this was something else. Throughout the subsequent conflict he firmly supported the so-called Ameri-canists, such as John Ireland, arch-bishop of St. Paul, John J. Keane, rector of the Catholic University of

Testem benevolentiae was addressed to Cardinal Gibbons and reached him in mid-February 1899. On March 17 he signed his reply in which he first thanked Pope Leo for his concern, and then in terms rarely employed by the

Cardinal Gibbons was a highly visible presence in American life at the turn of the century; here he pronounces a benediction in 1899, flanked by President McKinley and Admiral Dewey. KEYSTONE-MAST COLLECTION, UNIVERSITY OF CALIFORNIA, RIVERSIDE

mild-mannered archbishop of Baltimore, he declared:

> This doctrine, which I deliberately call extravagant and absurd, this Americanism as it has been called, has nothing in common with the views, aspirations, doctrine and conduct of Americans. I do not think that there can be found in the entire country a bishop, a priest, or even a layman with a knowledge of his religion who has ever uttered such enormities. No, that is not — it never has been and never will be — our Americanism. I am deeply grateful to Your Holiness for having yourself made this distinction in your apostolic letter.

As for the aftermath of the Americanism question, the conservative opponents continued to assert it was a reality, and even pictured it as the forerunner to the later more serious doctrinal controversy known as modernism. The papal letter was a severe disappointment to Gibbons and his friends at a time when the progressive wing of the American hierarchy had sustained serious blows such as the forced resignations of Denis O'Connell in 1895 and that of John Keane the following year. Meanwhile, the overwhelming majority of American Catholics were only dimly aware, if they were aware at all, of the alleged threat to their doctrinal orthodoxy.

In many ways it was rightly described as a "phantom heresy," for it changed nothing basic in the beliefs or conduct of Catholics generally. It did, however, mark a reverse for the so-called Americanizers and their progressive program. If at the time of *Testem benevolentiae* Cardinal Gibbons and his associates felt disappointment, they were consoled three years later when Leo XIII acknowledged the happy contrast of the church in the United States to the treatment accorded it on other lands. The pontiff remarked to Gibbons on this occasion:

> . . . while the changes and tendencies of nearly all the nations which were Catholic for many centuries give cause for sorrow, the state of your churches, in this flourishing youthfulness, cheers Our heart and fills it with delight.

The Papal Condemnation of Modernism

... these latter days have witnessed a notable increase in the number of the enemies of the Cross of Christ, who, by arts entirely new and full of deceit, are striving to destroy the vital energy of the Church, and, as far as in them lies, utterly to subvert the very Kingdom of Christ. ...

... the partisans of error are to be sought not only among the Church's open enemies; but what is to be most dreaded and deplored, in her very bosom, and are the more mischievous the less they keep in the open. We allude, Venerable Brethren, to many who belong to the Catholic laity, and, what is much more sad, to the ranks of the priesthood itself, who, animated by a false zeal for the Church, lacking the solid safeguards of philosophy and theology, nay more, thoroughly imbued with the poisonous doctrines taught by the enemies of the Church, and lost to all sense of modesty, put themselves forward as reformers of the Church; and forming more boldly into line of attack, assail all that is most sacred in the work of Christ, not sparing even the Person of the Divine Redeemer, Whom with sacrilegious audacity, they degrade to the condition of a simple and ordinary man. ...

PIUS X,
Pascendi Dominici Gregis,
September 8, 1907

Protestant Immigration

Much of the immigration during this period was Protestant. Most of this immigration was northern European—German, Scandinavian, and Dutch. The story of the church life of these Protestants parallels that of the Catholics in the pivotal role that the churches played in helping immigrants meet the challenges of their new setting and the perennial conflicts within communities between those who strove to hold onto the old language and ways, and those who hoped to lead the communities into the mainstream of American life. The latter was a greater possibility for white northern European Protestants than for any other new group, so that in every such community many individuals might with little fanfare transfer into older American churches or adopt American ways. In general, however, the immigrant communities tended to be conservative, preserving the traits of the religious life of the homeland from the era when most of the immigrants had left. Such conservatism was reinforced by language barriers. Moreover, while the bulk of the Catholic immigrants tended to crowd into the cities, most of these northern European Protestants moved into the farmlands of the Midwest, a factor contributing further to their religious conservatism.

By far the largest grouping was the Lutheran. Numbering less than a half million in 1870, Lutheranism in America reached well over two million by 1910 and had become the fourth largest religious grouping, behind Catholics, Methodists, and Baptists. Lutheranism at this time, however, was more a grouping than a group. The number of separate Lutheran denominations was well into the dozens and constantly changing through divisions or mergers. Lutherans had almost as much diversity as Catholics, but none of the necessity of working together. They resolved their differences in the meantime largely by remaining apart. This diversity had a number of important sources—degrees of Americanization (some synods used English, for instance, while most did not), ethnic differences (as among Germans, Danes, Swedes, and Norwegians), and geographical separation. Despite these differences, most of the Lutherans manifested a deep commitment to the Augsburg Confession, and many

Immigration by Country

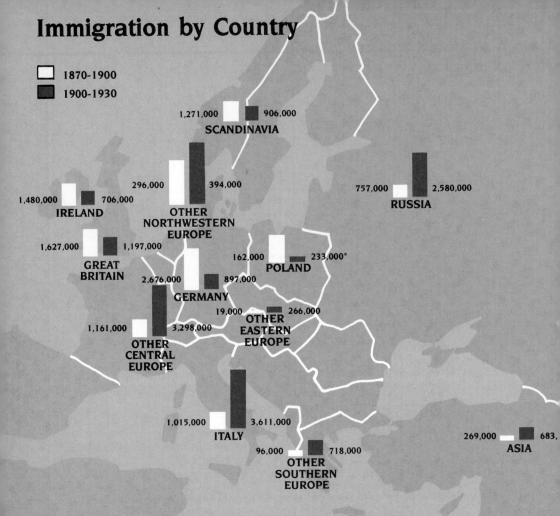

☐ 1870-1900
■ 1900-1930

SCANDINAVIA — 1,271,000 / 906,000

IRELAND — 1,480,000 / 706,000

OTHER NORTHWESTERN EUROPE — 296,000 / 394,000

RUSSIA — 757,000 / 2,580,000

GREAT BRITAIN — 1,627,000 / 1,197,000

POLAND — 162,000 / 233,000*

GERMANY — 2,676,000 / 897,000

OTHER EASTERN EUROPE — 19,000 / 266,000

OTHER CENTRAL EUROPE — 1,161,000 / 3,298,000

ITALY — 1,015,000 / 3,611,000

OTHER SOUTHERN EUROPE — 96,000 / 718,000

ASIA — 269,000 / 683,

*Most of the Polish immigration for this era was included in Austria-Hungary (Central Europe), Germany, and Russia.

Derived from 1971 *Annual Report, Immigration and Naturalization Service* (Washington, D.C.

preserved their identity through separate school systems. Notable in these respects was the conservative Missouri Synod. As in American churches generally, World War I brought a sense of unity. Accordingly, it brought a large number of Lutheran mergers. The war with Germany also put large pressures on the churches to Americanize and to abandon the German language.

Reformed churches with northern European heritages, such as the Dutch Reformed and the German Reformed, grew substantially in this era as well. Among the Dutch,

a series of schisms in Holland and America led to the Christian Reformed church (1857), a separatist and conservative body, much like the Missouri Synod Lutheran, strictly confessional and built on a substantial ethnic subculture and educational system. Many other northern European groups, such as some varieties of Mennonites, the (Methodistic) Evangelical Association and the United Brethren in Christ, the Evangelical Free church, the Swedish Evangelical Mission Covenant, and the Swedish Baptists grew in America from the immigration of this era.

The Eastern Orthodox Churches

Of the major Christian traditions, that which has had least representation in American life has been the Eastern Orthodox. Originating out of the split between the Eastern and the Western Roman Empire, the Orthodox church finally separated officially from the Roman in 1054. Vigorous missionary efforts spread Eastern Christianity to the Slavic countries of eastern Europe and to Russia. In 1453 the Eastern Roman Empire in Constantinople finally fell to the Turks, but in 1452 Russia under Ivan the Great had assumed effective leadership in the Eastern church, proclaiming Moscow the "Third Rome."

During this long separate history the Eastern churches developed a heritage distinct from their Roman Catholic counterparts. While the creeds and the liturgies bore some similarities, Greek practices were more thoroughly ritualistic and mystical. These non-Western modes of Christian expression were seldom understood by the non-Orthodox in America and fit into the American setting only with difficulty.

The history of the Eastern churches in America falls largely in the twentieth century. The acquisition of Alaska from Russia in 1867 brought the beginnings of an Eastern church, but by 1900 the total of Orthodox in the nation was only some 100,000. When, however, immigration in the next decades shifted considerably toward eastern Europe, the Orthodox population grew rapidly. This influx included large numbers of Russians, Greeks, and Ukrainians, as well as Albanians, Bulgarians, Rumanians, Serbians, Syrians, and other eastern Europeans. Until World War I these were united under one jurisdiction of the Russian church. Whereas World War I tended to bring unity to other religious groups, it marked a crisis for these recent arrivals, due to the communist takeover in Russia in 1917. This, plus the growth of the various ethnic communities, fostered separations during the next decades. These ethnic divisions were complicated by fac-

Orthodox church in Sitka, Alaska, ca. 1900
KEYSTONE-MAST COLLECTION, UNIVERSITY OF CALIFORNIA, RIVERSIDE

tional struggles within the Orthodox ethnic groups, leaving the Orthodox churches in America somewhat in disarray. Moreover, these churches, which often had been dependent on very close state support, tended to have more difficulty than most immigrant groups in retaining the loyalties of those whose ethnic identities made them nominally Orthodox. Nonetheless, the churches in America eventually gained stability and have successfully preserved their venerable Christian heritage for millions of Americans in the twentieth century. Their reconciliation to the American religious situation was signaled by their participation in the National Council of Churches after midcentury, thus also ending the Protestant monopoly in America's largest ecumenical organization.

End of an Era:
World War I and the 1920s

Wars are the catalysts of history. They precipitate and accelerate trends already present in a culture. World War I had an especially momentous impact on American life. Until this time the United States had stayed off the center stage of world affairs. Prewar America, despite its problems of assimilating so many diverse peoples, had been remarkably optimistic. No challenge was too great to be mastered by American idealism and know-how. Americans threw all their confidence and moral fervor into the war effort, and they succeeded. Yet the success was confined very largely to the battlefield. Despite some expectations to the contrary, war was not a sanctifying experience. Abroad, the crusade

to "make America safe for democracy" was soon left in a shambles. At home the war unleashed the forces of secularization that brought the jazz age. It also sparked an era of bitterness and reaction. American idealism was overwhelmed by dissension. Although rearguard actions were fought to keep America Protestant, the fact of the matter was that the age was over when the United States was in any significant sense a bastion of "Christendom."

While, as has just been seen, every major Christian group in America was significantly changed by the war, the impact on the culturally dominant white Protestant community probably was the most intense. The cultural changes associated with the war and its aftermath sent this community reeling for two decades, and, when it recovered to some extent after World War II, it was not the same.

A Liberal's Disillusion

. . . during the last three light-hearted decades, we have been smoking the opium pipe of evolution, telling the world how far it has risen, chiefly by its own force, from the depths in which it began, describing the speed by which it has mounted under our sage and dreamy eyes, and prophesying of its complete ascension in the near and sweet bye and bye. Recent events have broken the opium pipe and dispelled the delusion.
GEORGE A. GORDON, 1915

Responses to the War

When war broke out in Europe in August 1914 Americans had little reason to think that they would be involved. In this age of idealism opinions among churchmen were widely divided over questions of war and peace. As international tensions had built up, so had various peace movements. The most recent was the Church Peace Union, endowed by Andrew Carnegie, and founded in February 1914. Immediately the European conflict brought some deep disillusionment among liberals who had hoped for the steady progress of humanity. Theological liberals and conservatives alike were divided on war and peace. Two of the leading peace advocates, for instance, were liberal New York pastor Henry Sloane Coffin and the theologically conservative William Jennings Bryan. Bryan,

Evangelical enterprise helped to provide such facilities as this YMCA recreation hall at Camp MacArthur, Waco, Texas, in 1917. LIBRARY OF CONGRESS

in fact, resigned as Woodrow Wilson's secretary of state in 1915 rather than take steps that he feared would lead to war.

As war for America neared by early 1917, sentiment for American militancy grew stronger among church leaders. Once U.S. participation was declared in April 1917, enthusiasm for the war in the churches, Catholic as well as Protestant, was overwhelming. Only the historic peace churches such as the Quakers and the Mennonites and the new Jehovah's Witnesses were sizable bodies of Christians who refused to give in to the nation's prowar hysteria.

Those who held out for peace were subject to abuse and harassment; the nation was caught up in an extraordinary enthusiasm for the war. The Sedition Act passed by Congress in 1918 forbade any remark that in any way suggested less than reverence for the U.S. flag, uniform, its form of government, or the war effort. This law reflected public opinion. America and its international crusade had unquestionably been deified. As had long been true of American civil religion—the religion of American patriotism—the language of Christianity was applied directly to the nation so that it was virtually impossible to tell where the Christian religion stopped and the national religion began.

For most of the American clergy there was no distinction between the two. "Christianity and Patriotism are synonymous terms," said evangelist Billy Sunday directly, "and hell and traitors are synonymous." Sunday was just at the height of his fame when the war broke out, and he incorporated the war in his message with extravagant enthusiasm. Of all

George M. Cohan Versus Billy Sunday

George Cohan has neither the punch nor the pace of Billy Sunday. . . . It is true that Cohan waved the flag first, but Billy Sunday has waved it harder. . . . It is in language that the superiority of Sunday is most evident. . . . All in all we believe that Sunday has more of the dramatic instinct than Cohan.

HEYWOOD BROUN,
drama critic, *The New York Tribune*, 1915

the major American evangelists such as Finney, Moody, Sunday, and Graham, Billy Sunday was the greatest showman. An ex-baseball player, his sermons were filled with acrobatics, jumping, falling, whirling, and sliding. When flushed with patriotism, he would end his sermon by jumping on top of the pulpit and waving the American flag! Although he was a gospel preacher, his unrestrained style and nationalism were comparable to that of vaudeville actor, George M. Cohan, author of the wartime hit "Over There."

Except for style, theological liberals had nothing to concede to conservatives on the patriotic front. Whereas evangelists such as Sunday mixed a patriotic folk religion with their Christianity, liberals had a deeper theological stake in the war to "make the world safe for democracy." The most modernistic versions of their gospel saw God as working through the progress of civilization, especially democratic civilization as found in America. The war was then for them quite explicitly a sacred cause. So said Shailer Mathews, dean of the University of Chicago Divinity School, in a characteristic statement: "For an American to refuse to share in the present war . . . is not Christian."

Billy Sunday at a "Hang the Kaiser" rally in 1918   BILLY GRAHAM CENTER

Among both conservative and liberal Christians, moderates on the war issue wrestled with the moral dilemmas involved. The pressures of public opinion, however, forced most nonenthusiasts into a discreet silence. Many, including preachers and theologians, were ready to cast the first stone at a suspected slacker. At the University of Chicago Divinity School, for instance, dispensational premillennialism (which rejected the equation of the progress of the kingdom and the progress of democratic society) was considered subversive to the war effort and subjected to scathing attacks.

Such pressures soon brought almost everyone into line with extravagant avowals of their patriotism. By 1918 such sentiments were aided by widely circulated and accepted atrocity stories about Germany, convincing many that the war was a matter of Christian civilization versus bloodthirsty and barbaric huns. A leader in creating this belief was the Rev. Newell Dwight Hillis, pastor of Henry Ward Beecher's old church, Plymouth Congregational in Brooklyn. During 1917 Hillis lectured some four hundred times on German atrocities, enflaming his audiences with stories of how German soldiers typically raped and then mutilated innocent women. He claimed that the Kaiser had given every soldier explicit license to "commit any crime he may desire." (One of the worst consequences of this hysteria only became apparent much later, when journalists who reported Hitler's atrocities were ignored and their accounts discredited as nothing more than wartime propaganda.)

The main effect at the time, however, was to create American hatred of anything German. The teaching of the German language was forbidden in some public schools, and in many places church services in any language other than English were regarded as evidence of insufficient patriotism. Public opinion against the use of foreign languages in religious services during the war together with pressures to demonstrate total Americanism were important factors in hastening the Americanization of many Catholics, Protestants, and Orthodox who had recently immigrated.

Billy Sunday

JOEL CARPENTER

William A. Sunday (1862-1935) was the nation's most successful revivalist in an era when urban mass revivalism flourished. Like other popular success symbols of the early twentieth century such as Henry Ford and Thomas Edison, he was born and reared in the rural Midwest (Iowa) and made good in the city despite early poverty and little education.

Billy first succeeded at baseball. While he played with major league clubs from 1883 to 1891, he came to know the city theaters, saloons, and street slang. Later as an evangelist he charmed the crowds with his baseball stories, saloon impersonations, and vaudeville antics. Though many imitated him, no evangelist captured the era's mood like Billy Sunday.

Billy Sunday striking characteristic poses (above, below, and overleaf)
BILLY GRAHAM CENTER

His conversion came in 1886, in Chicago, and shunted his success drive into more sanctified and bourgeois channels. Billy had been drinking when he heard evangelistic singers from the Pacific Garden Mission. Soon after he visited the mission and "got saved." He attended a preparatory school in the 1887-1888 winter term and soon after married a proper Presbyterian girl, Helen Thompson.

While still playing ball, he gave inspirational talks at local YMCA chapters. After he resigned from baseball he joined the YMCA staff to teach self-improvement and Christian manhood to others.

In 1893 he joined J. Wilbur Chapman's evangelistic team and as his "advance man" learned the revival business thoroughly. When Chapman accepted a parish ministry in 1895, Sunday struck out on his own, preaching revival services in the small towns of Iowa. By the early 1900s he had graduated to larger midwestern towns, and traded Chapman's refined preaching for his own sensational style. He built a businesslike evangelistic staff of advance men, secretaries, a man-

promised to revive churches, close saloons, and end labor unrest — all for two dollars a soul.

Thousands in each crusade shook Billy's hand, signifying their "getting right" with God. Billy appealed to mothers' prayers, to patriotism, to manhood, to ethnic, fraternal, and union loyalty, and to decency. What decent American would refuse this invitation? Some critics doubted the lasting impact of Sunday's conversions, though. Relatively few converts became new church members, and many were vague about their conversion's meaning. But in a nation that worshipped winners, Sunday's success was his strongest argument. Even the liberal spokesman Lyman Abbott guardedly praised him.

Sunday's success did not survive the cultural upheaval of the 1920s. The united Protestant support mass revivalists needed ended in the modernist-fundamentalist controversy. As the Model T, the radio, and the movies surpassed Sunday's vaudeville appeal and postwar disillusion made reform crusading unfashionable, Sunday's audience dwindled. But mass revivalism did not die in 1935 when he did. Radio preachers were already developing a media-oriented vehicle that Billy Graham would ride to national fame.

ager, a building supervisor, a chorister, and scores of local volunteers.

After 1910, Billy Sunday crusaded in the major cities of the nation. In an era of big business domination and Progressive reform, Sunday billed himself as both an efficient soul-winner and an urban reformer. He

Tabernacles such as this one, built for Sunday in Syracuse, New York, were intended to be dismantled and sold for scrap when the crusade moved on.   BILLY GRAHAM CENTER

"The Premillennial Menace" to the War Effort

The American nation is engaged in a gigantic effort to make the world safe for democracy. . . .

Under ordinary circumstances one might excusably pass over premillenarianism as a wild and relatively harmless fancy. But in the present time of testing it would be almost traitorous negligence to ignore the detrimental character of the premillennial propaganda. By proclaiming that wars cannot be eliminated until Christ returns and that in the meantime the world must grow constantly worse, this type of teaching strikes at the very root of our present national endeavor to bring about a new day for humanity, when this old earth shall be made a better place in which to live, and a new democracy of nations shall arise to render wars impossible. . . .

Premillennialists resent the suggestion that enemy gold is behind their activities, and one group of them has publicly affirmed that the federal authorities' inspection of their books failed to justify this suspicion. However that may be, we have in the premillennial propaganda as a whole an instance of serious economic waste by which large sums of money are being diverted from projects that might contribute directly toward the success of the war.

SHIRLEY JACKSON CASE,
Professor of Church History, University of Chicago, 1918

While the charge that the money for premillennial propaganda "emanates from German sources" is ridiculous, the charge that the destructive criticism that rules in Chicago University "emanates from German sources" is undeniable.

Editorial, The King's Business, 1918

The Aftermath

When the war ended in November 1918 the crusading zeal of the nation had not yet reached its crest. The extreme patriotism built up by the wartime propaganda was reinforced by the decisive successes of the American armies. But then as enthusiasm was still building, the sudden peace left the nation at an extreme psychological pitch but no longer with a clearly defined enemy. During the next years, the high-pitched enthusiasm was mixed with the dregs of bitterness, suspicion, and hatred. As usual, the churches played a central role.

At first the overwhelming mood in most of the churches was a sense of unity and idealism. The most dramatic manifestation of this mood was the final victory of prohibition. During 1917 this movement, which had been steadily growing for decades, suddenly emerged victorious in the midst of the wartime enthusiasm. Many Protestants, Catholics, and progressives united in this remarkable effort to clean up the home front. Several laws banning the manufacture or sale of alcoholic beverages were quickly passed, soon followed by the Eighteenth Amendment, which only reaffirmed the accomplished fact when it finally went into effect in 1919. The apparent triumph of this social experiment was largely a tribute to the Christian idealism of the age.

The war at first had a unifying effect. This has already been seen with regard to American Catholicism, which established a national coordinating agency, the National Catholic War Council, later the National Catholic Welfare Conference. Among Protestants zeal for Christian unity and worldwide reform ran especially high. The most important effort to organize this zeal was the massive interdenominational Interchurch World Movement, launched immediately after the war. This movement, reflecting the same enthusiasm that earlier had inspired the Men and Religion Forward Movement, was designed to unite Christian benevolent, missionary, and spiritual efforts throughout the world. Amid talk of actual church union, the leaders of the movement shared a "vision of a united church uniting a divided world."

By the summer of 1920 the Interchurch World Movement was in a shambles. Conservative opposition brought about a fate much like that of the League of Nations, which President Woodrow Wilson had proposed with such high hopes, only to have the United States itself in 1920 refuse to join.

In the churches, as in the nation generally, the idealism of World War I was very quickly overshadowed by a growing mood of bitter reaction. When the war ended abruptly it seemed as though a considerable element of the American people needed to find new enemies on whom to vent their superheated emotions. The Marxist revolution in Russia

A *Klan march in St. Petersburg, Florida,* ca. 1926
KEYSTONE-MAST COLLECTION, UNIVERSITY OF CALIFORNIA, RIVERSIDE

in 1917 together with labor unrest and a series of frightening terrorist bombings fueled the "Red Scare" during 1919 in which much of the nation was gripped with fears of communist infiltration and uprising. More directly involved with the churches was the revival of the Ku Klux Klan. Reorganized in 1915, this antiblack organization extended its range of hatreds to include Catholics, Jews, and non-Nordic people generally. If the war had accelerated the assimilation of these non-Nordic groups into the mainstream of American life, its aftermath accelerated the reactions and prejudices against them among many northern European Americans. By 1923 the Klan had reached a peak membership of nearly three million. While not identified directly with any one denomination or Protestant movement, and disclaimed by liberals and conservatives alike, the Klan claimed explicitly to be Protestant. It appropriated Christian teaching, hymns, and symbols, and represented a notable segment of the professing Protestant community. The symbol of the flaming cross perhaps best captures the way in which this movement, like the Nazi movement in Germany between the wars, represented an amalgamation of Christian tradition with nationalistic folk religion, self-interest, and hatred.

The Klan, of course, did not represent the vast majority of American Protestants either in the South or the North. It was, however, an extreme manifestation of tendencies that in milder forms were more pervasive within the dominant American community. Specifically, sentiments were strong against "foreigners." Economically they seemed to be a threat and socially they were at the center of urban problems. Moreover, religiously and culturally their continued influx would spell the end of Protestant Anglo-Saxon dominance. Together, such sentiments led to immigration restrictions after the war, culminating in the Johnson-Reed Act of 1924, which placed severe quotas on immigration and based the quotas on the proportions of the U.S. population as it had been in 1890. Such efforts struck directly at the growth of the Jewish, southern and eastern European Catholic, and Orthodox communities.

All American religious communities faced serious and disconcerting challenges on another front during the 1920s. The war had

The Bare Knee Instead of the Bended Knee

... "a mild sensation has been created by the bare knees of some of the Methodist choir young ladies who are taking part in a big religious spectacle entitled 'The Wayfarer' now running at Madison Square Garden."

The old-fashioned method of the Methodists was the bended knee, and the bended knee brought blessing to the hearts of many people, but the new-fangled method by which the world is to be made better every day evidently is a less solemn but more spectacular method, and more to the taste of the choir girls. ...

Who is responsible for this change of custom from the bended to the brazen, bared knee? Is this performance, authorized by the church officials, supposed to be to the glory of God and the getting of gold? How can such officials preach separation from the world?

Dancing used to be an abomination to the Methodist Church and contrary to its doctrines. Is there need of some new kind of doctors to treat this new disease?

Editorial, The King's Business, March 1920

accelerated and brought out into the open the secularization that had been growing in American life. Whereas in 1900 one might have talked about religion in polite company but never would have dared mention sex, by the 1920s the opposite was often the case. This "revolution in morals" was especially apparent in the cities and in the eastern and educated culture that dominated the America media. The modern tabloid newspaper, headlined with sensational and suggestive stories, began in 1919. The movies made the most of sex stars. Semiserious popular literature was filled with discussions of Freud, Freudianism, and the importance of freedom of expression. Modern advertising exploited the new freedom, selling soap, as it was remarked, as though it were an aphrodisiac. Along with this change in the popular culture came the virtual collapse of communal enforcement of standards of personal behavior that had been among the mainstays of the churches. Women smoked in public, did not always cover their knees (even in church), and refused to follow the domestic examples of their mothers. Dancing, which had long been a taboo for many Protestants, now was an integral part of social acceptability in the age of the flapper. While some church leaders simply conceded the issue and even brought dancing into church youth group meetings, others were horrified. The new dances, one conservative

John Roach Straton in the pulpit of Calvary Baptist Church, New York, where he broadcast one of the first church radio programs in 1923
RELIGIOUS NEWS SERVICE

Southern Methodist bishop complained, brought "the bodies of men and women in unusual relations to each other." The rumble seats of the new automobiles did the same. Despite the passage of prohibition, then, the battle to enforce traditional Victorian and Methodistic mores was a losing one.

Such a climate of crisis brought extreme conflict of opinion in many Protestant churches. Many liberals remained optimistic and saw the breakdown of traditions as opportunity for building a new liberal Christian consensus. Conservatives, on the other hand, reacted strongly. So the same diverse postwar forces that produced both the Interchurch World Movement and the revival of the Klan, the legal triumph of prohibition and the actual triumph of a general revolution against traditional Protestant mores, brought deep division over serious theological and ecclesiastical issues. These differences had long been developing. Both liberalism and sizable conservative countermovements had been building for a generation; but before the war the activism of the era had overshadowed theological debates and relative peace had been preserved. The war and postwar crisis, however, forced each party to confront the others and to see how widely they actually differed in their visions for the churches and for American culture.

The Prohibition Movement

MARK A. NOLL

American consumption of alcoholic beverages has never been a joke, and — in spite of many attempts to treat it that way — neither was the effort to control it. Behind the Eighteenth Amendment to the Constitution (ratified 1919), which prohibited "the manufacture, sale, or transportation of intoxicating liquors," lay more than a century of organized effort to stem the flow of alcohol. It may come as a surprise that the temperance movement, which — confusingly — has usually meant total abstinence, had nothing to do with the Puritans; Cotton Mather proclaimed wine "of God," while consigning drunkenness to the devil. The movement arose, rather, out of complex developments at the beginning of the nineteenth century. Overproduction of corn (salable more easily as whiskey than as grain) and social anxieties stemming from the westward movement and the swift democratization of American life combined to produce a liquor problem which was, in every respect, staggering. In some regions annual consumption of absolute alcohol exceeded ten gallons for each adult white male. Thomas Jefferson, Andrew Jackson, and Abraham Lincoln were only a few of the public figures who spoke out against this national excess. But evangelical leaders, with revivalist Lyman Beecher in the vanguard, rapidly became the chief opponents of drink. To them the progress of the gospel and the moral perfection of the nation depended upon the control of alcohol. Neal Dow, who spearheaded the drive for the first state prohibition law (Maine, 1846), called the effort "Christ's work" for which "every true soldier of the Cross" should fight.

After the Civil War temperance efforts shifted from the states to the nation. Americans were, in fact, drinking less, but the hazards of overindulgence seemed greater in the new cities and in its effects upon industrial production. The tavern, once a place of community conviviality, had become the saloon. And the saloon business — the "whore-making, criminal-making, madman-making business" as prohibitionists saw it — loomed every bit as threatening to America as Communism would in the 1950s.

The campaign for national prohibition enlisted many members. Methodist Frances Willard, a sometime associate of Dwight L. Moody, was the driving force behind the Woman's Christian Temperance Union. Willard's public activity, which included support for female suffrage, marked a new prominence in America for women's evangelical reform. The Anti-Saloon League, founded in 1893 and turned by Methodist minister Alpha J. Kynett into a national movement two years later, was the most effective lobbying agent for prohibition in the states and in Congress. The Methodist church, with its traditional perfectionist theology, led most of the Anglo-American Protestant denominations in the fight. Some Catholics, preeminently the archbishop of St. Paul, John Ireland, also joined the crusade against liquor. They saw prohibition as a way both to remedy a desperate social ill and to prove the "Americanness" of their denomination, whose Irish and German members Protestants regularly slandered as drunkards. Businessmen, social scientists, and proponents of the social gospel also added their strength to this effort to remake American life. World War I, which linked the crimes of the Kaiser to the beverages of the brewers, set the stage for passing the Prohibition Amendment.

Carry Nation (1846–1911), *made famous for what she termed the "hatchetation" of "joints" in her native Kansas, received little support from the national temperance organizations.* BROWN BROTHERS

The "great social and economic experiment, noble in motive and far-reaching in purpose," as Herbert Hoover called prohibition, failed. It did not, as evangelist Billy Sunday predicted, "turn our prisons into factories and our jails into . . . corncribs." Although prohibition probably did improve public health and morals generally in the country, it also led to public mockery of the law, to the stimulation of organized crime, and to widespread disillusionment with efforts at enshrining the ideals of nineteenth-century reform into national legislation. The Prohibition Amendment was repealed in 1933, but the issues which the Prohibition movement raised still remain for Christians.

Fundamentalists Versus Modernists

The outstanding manifestation of this mutual discovery was the fundamentalist-modernist controversy that dominated much of the religious news of the 1920s. It would be difficult to say who fired the first shot in this conflict since by the end of World War I major salvos were being issued from both sides. Liberals were more aggressive than previously in organizing for unity and action and in specifically attacking their conservative opponents. Conservatives, likewise, were organizing, most notably in the founding in 1919 of the World's Christian Fundamentals Association, a dispensationalist-premillennialist group organized to combat modernism. The next year conservatives in the Northern Baptist Convention instituted a "Fundamentals" conference to muster opposition to liberalism in that denomination. The term "fundamentalist," originated on this occasion, soon spread to refer to antimodernist Protestants generally.

In the early 1920s the conflict mushroomed in Protestant churches as well as in the culture generally. In major denominations and their mission fields conservatives attempted to forestall the advances of modernism by various types of legislation designed to require adherence to fundamental doctrines of traditional supernaturalistic Christianity. On foreign mission fields, where evangelicals considered the very salvation of souls to be at stake, conservative versus liberal rivalries were especially intense, and these conflicts were reflected in the crisis at home. Such conflicts were especially severe in denominations where fundamentalism and liberalism were represented by parties of almost equal strength. The Northern Baptist Convention and the (northern) Presbyterian Church in the U.S.A. were the centers of denominational controversy. Among the Disciples of Christ a parallel conflict was waged between liberals and Disciples traditionalists, leading to a virtual separation of the two parties by the mid-1920s. The Protestant Episcopal church and the Northern Methodists experienced minor fundamentalist furors during this same era, but in these denominations liberalism and moderation were so far advanced that fundamentalists had little chance of success. The same was true of

The threat to fundamentalist orthodoxy is very clear in this E. J. Pace cartoon. BILLY GRAHAM CENTER

Congregationalists, among whom there was no real controversy. In the South, by contrast, conservatives were so dominant that little controversy was necessary to bring endorsements from such denominations as the Southern Baptist Convention and the (southern) Presbyterian Church in the U.S.

Christianity and Liberalism: Two Religions

But one thing is perfectly plain — whether or not liberals are Christians, it is at any rate perfectly clear that liberalism is not Christianity. And that being the case, it is highly undesirable that liberalism and Christianity should continue to be propagated within the bounds of the same organization. A separation between the two parties in the Church is the crying need of the hour.

J. GRESHAM MACHEN,
Christianity and Liberalism, 1923

of their northern "fundamentalist" counterparts. Ever since the Civil War most southerners had been against liberalism and modernism, which they associated with Yankee culture.

In the battle for the denominations the leading spokesperson for the fundamentalist-conservative coalition was Presbyterian J. Gresham Machen, professor of New Testament at Princeton Theological Seminary. In *Christianity and Liberalism* (1923), Machen argued that since the new liberalism denied that human salvation was dependent on the historical fact that Christ had died to atone for human sins, such liberalism was not Christianity at all, but a new religion. It was essentially a faith in humanity even though it used Christian language and symbolism. In honesty, he said, liberals should withdraw from churches that had been founded on a very different basis of biblical Christianity. Liberals responded in kind, arguing that they were preserving the essence of Christianity and that conservatives were endorsing only "theories" about what the Bible taught. Most importantly, liberals took their stand on the question of tolerance. Since even within the denominations such as the Northern Baptist and northern Presbyterian, where the contests were most heated, most American Protestants were neither modernists nor militant fundamentalists, overtures

"*Higher criticism,*" *with its origins in nineteenth-century Germany, is shown sinking biblical Christianity*   BILLY GRAHAM CENTER

for peace and tolerance often could command substantial support. So while in these denominations fundamentalists won some token victories, by 1926 it became clear that policies of inclusiveness and tolerance would prevail.

Modernism as Evangelical Christianity

In brief, then, *the use of scientific, historical, social method in understanding and applying evangelical Christianity to the needs of living persons, is Modernism.* Its interests are not those of theological controversy or appeal to authority. They do not involve the rejection of the supernatural when rightly defined. Modernists believe that they can discover the ideals and directions needed for Christians living by the application of critical and historical methods to the study of the Bible; that they can discover by similar methods the permanent attitudes and convictions of Christians constituting a continuous and developing group; and that these permanent elements will help and inspire the intelligent and sympathetic organization of life under modern conditions. Modernists are thus evangelical Christians who use modern methods to meet modern needs.

SHAILER MATHEWS,
The Faith of Modernism, 1924

The fundamentalists despaired of those denominations willing to tolerate "modernism" and "rationalism."
BILLY GRAHAM CENTER

This candidate in the 1926 North Carolina election campaign made it clear that he was against the teaching of evolution.   FROM COPY IN NORTH CAROLINA COLLECTION, UNC LIBRARY, CHAPEL HILL

In the meantime, the fundamentalist controversy had gained additional attention on the cultural front as fundamentalists organized to save the whole of American society from "infidelity." World War I had produced among many conservative evangelicals both a sense of crisis over the revolution in morals and a renewed concern for the welfare of civilization. For one thing, the war had coincided with the Marxist revolution of 1917 which brought widespread fear of the spread of a frankly atheistic political system. Even more to the point, so far as American culture was concerned, was the model of Germany. German civilization during the war was portrayed as the essence of barbarism, despite its strongly Christian heritage. Could the same thing happen here? The strong winds of change suggested that it could.

The central symbol organizing fears over the demise of American culture became biological evolution. German culture, antievolutionists loudly proclaimed, had been ruined by the evolutionary "might-makes-right" philosophy of Friedrich Nietzsche. Darwinism, moreover, was essentially atheistic, and hence its spread would contribute to the erosion of American morality. Accordingly, soon after the war fundamentalists began organizing vigorous campaigns against the teaching of biological evolution in America's public schools. This effort was greatly aided when in 1920 William Jennings Bryan, three times Democratic candidate for presi-

dent and one of the nation's greatest orators, entered the fray against Darwinism. Fundamentalist antievolution efforts were essentially political and so attracted a wider constituency than the nucleus of theologically conservative evangelical Protestants. By the middle of the decade laws banning the teachings of evolution in public schools had been passed in a number of southern states, and legislation was pending in numbers of others. These efforts led to the famous Scopes Trial testing the Tennessee antievolution law in 1925, an event that both thrust fundamentalism into world-wide attention and brought about its decline as an effective national force. The event was comparable to Lindbergh's transatlantic flight in the amount of press coverage and ballyhoo.

The rural setting of the trial and the caricature of fundamentalists as rubes and hicks fostered by the eastern press discredited fundamentalism and made it difficult to pursue further the serious aspects of the movement. After 1925 fundamentalists had difficulty gaining national attention except when some of their movement were involved in extreme or bizarre efforts. For instance, one of the most highly publicized religious figures of the era was evangelist Aimee Semple McPherson. She was not strictly a fundamen-

Aimee Semple McPherson, the flamboyant evangelist, with her touring car (below) and at the microphone BILLY GRAHAM CENTER

talist in the sense of being involved in the antimodernist campaigns, but was essentially a Pentecostalist, emphasizing healing and the gift of tongues. In 1926, in a widely publicized and sensational event, she disappeared for a month, claiming to have been kidnapped. Others accused her of scandal, but she survived the episode more popular than ever, founding in Los Angeles in 1927 her own denomination, the International Church of the Foursquare Gospel.

Such sensations recurred many times over in both the white and the black revivalist Protestant communities. Among the blacks this was the era of large-scale transition to cities, of storefront churches, and also of charlatans such as Father Divine. Such extremes, however, shielded the degree to which legitimate revivalist Protestantism of all sorts was growing outside the mainstreams of Protestant church life. In the meantime, the mainstream denominations themselves had been hurt by the lengthy fundamentalist controversies and by their own lack of clear direction.

While the fundamentalist-modernist controversy dominated Protestantism and most of the religious news of the decade, various non-Protestant and nonwhite Protestant

Al Smith, first Roman Catholic candidate for president, campaigning in 1928 MUSEUM OF THE CITY OF NEW YORK

Billy Sunday campaigning for Herbert Hoover in 1928 BILLY GRAHAM CENTER

groups were establishing stronger footholds as permanent parts of American culture and religion. The most dramatic manifestation of these gains was the nomination of Al Smith, a Catholic, as Democratic candidate for president in 1928. Smith's campaign, however, elicited from conservative Protestants a barrage of polemics against Catholicism. "Tomorrow we might have Smith," they reasoned, "the next day the Pope." Such accusations turned votes, but not the election, which almost certainly would have gone to Herbert Hoover in any case. This episode, however, as was also true of the support of immigration restriction earlier in the decade, indicated that many Protestants were not yet willing to give up the idea that America was a Protestant land.

Protestant Modernism

WILLIAM R. HUTCHISON

In popular or casual usage, the term modernism has been applied vaguely to almost any form of extreme religious liberalism, just as fundamentalism has been used for most kinds of conservatism. But Protestant modernism at the time of its rise to prominence (about 1910) embodied a quite distinctive set of liberal ideas, all of which had been fermenting for at least a generation. The main components — cultural adaptation, immanentism, and progressivism — had been brought together in the thinking of some religious liberals as early as the 1880s.

Most obviously, modernists urged the revision of religious forms in response to the intellectual and other demands of a changing culture. Unlike many other kinds of liberal (unlike most Transcendentalists, for example), they found much to praise in contemporary science and a technological civilization; and they advocated a self-conscious, principled adjustment of religious language and institutions to these and other developments. But in addition, unlike many rationalists and "free religionists," they sought to ground their adaptationism in a biblically supported conception of the immanence — or indwelling — of God. Religious forms, they argued, are comparable to other cultural expressions because both derive from religious experience — from the innate and irreducible sense of dependence that Schleiermacher's generation had called "the religious sentiment." For that reason, they said, and because the Holy Spirit is operative throughout both nature and culture, sharp distinctions between sacred and secular are not valid. Such distinctions, Theodore Munger contended, ignore "the very process by which the kingdoms of this world are becoming the kingdom of our Lord Jesus Christ."

As Munger's remarks suggest, a progressive and generally optimistic view of human history was important to modernism, and in fact held the system together. Though the opposition sometimes claimed otherwise, modernists were not proposing to conform religion indiscriminately to whatever might call itself modern. They could champion closer bonds with culture, instead of distance or alienation from it, because they were sure the essential movement of history is upward, and that with the aid of the Holy Spirit one can distinguish what is essential from what is not. Later, when this type of progressive confidence declined, so did the other modernist tenets. By the 1930s, the entire synthesis was in serious disrepair, even though many of its elements persisted or were destined for revival in the 1960s.

The modernist impulse in its heyday affected most of the "mainline" Protestant denominations. Having appeared first among Unitarian liberals of the mid-nineteenth century, it had then spread to the older denominations by way of the mainly Congregationalist "New Theology" of the 1880s. Between 1890 and 1910, the impulse affected the Episcopal, Presbyterian, and Methodist bodies and strongly influenced Baptists and Disciples in the North and West. Well before the term itself (borrowed from the Catholics) came into common usage, modernist ideas had achieved expression in widely used systematic theologies like those of William Newton Clarke (Baptist) and William Adams Brown (Presbyterian), and had been applied distinctively to such concerns as missions, religious education, and the theory of Christian social action. By the 1920s, modernists filled enough pulpits and professorships, and controlled so many publications and mission boards, that opponents bitterly characterized modernism as having "taken over."

But in becoming widespread and respectable, the movement had also become increasingly vulnerable. On one side, the opposition involved a blunt popular fundamentalism, in league with a sophisticated biblicism stemming from the theology of Princeton and other conservative centers. On its other flank, modernism was assailed by secularists and scientific humanists. And by the 1930s, long-standing criticisms from within the movement had blossomed into a "neo-orthodoxy" that had little in common with any of the earlier forms of opposition. Neo-orthodoxy shared most modernist attitudes toward scriptural and creedal interpretation, and it exceeded modernism in active social concern; yet its adherents protested vehemently against the adaptationism of the modernists and against their stress on the immanence of God.

Despite that powerful rebuke, and despite the long-range importance of modernist contentions concerning the Bible, the movement made its most lasting and pervasive impression through its candid acceptance of cultural adaptation as an inevitability in the operations of any religious system. More affirmatively, this amounted to an insistence that theology must make every attempt, within human powers of discernment, to discover where the divine is revealing itself in the processes of culture; and to accept the guidance of this variety of revelation along with more traditional forms.

Fundamentalism

GEORGE M. MARSDEN

"Fundamentalism" in America is best defined as militantly antimodernist evangelical Protestantism. The term was not invented until 1920 when Curtis Lee Laws, conservative editor of the Baptist paper, The Watchman-Examiner, coined it to describe those ready "to do battle royal for the Fundamentals." Soon the term caught on to describe all sorts of American Protestants who were willing to wage ecclesiastical and theological war against modernism in theology and the cultural changes that modernists celebrated.

The fundamentalist forces of the 1920s were formidable because they represented a coalition of conservative Protestants that had been growing for some time. At the center of this coalition were dispensationalist pre-millennialists who had been promoting dispensationalist teachings for nearly half a century through prophecy conferences, Bible institutes, evangelistic campaigns, and the Scofield Reference Bible (1909). These same leaders had promoted a wider coalition with the publication and wide free distribution of The Fundamentals, twelve paperback volumes containing defenses of fundamental doctrines by a variety of American and British conservative writers.

Also prominent in the emerging coalition were denominational conservatives, particularly Presbyterians and Baptists in the northern United States, who were battling theological modernism in their denominations. In general such conservatives united in defense of several "fundamental" doctrines including the inerrancy of scripture, the virgin birth of Christ, his substitutionary atonement, his bodily resurrection, the authenticity of the biblical miracles, and sometimes premillennialism. During the 1920s some combinations of these doctrines became known informally as "the five points of fundamentalism."

Fundamentalism built to a peak in the two-pronged controversies in the 1920s against modernism in some major denominations and against the teaching of biological evolution in the public schools. After 1925 these efforts collapsed and the movement appeared to be in some disarray. In fact, however, fundamentalism was entering an era of relocation and rebuilding — growing substantially in the South as well as the North, and building up a formidable set of institutions outside the traditional mainstream of American denominations. During the 1930s, in fact, separation from such denominations became for some fundamentalists a test of purity.

During the middle decades of the century the fundamentalist coalition of the 1920s split into two major parts. One part, while remaining doctrinally conservative, moderated fundamental- ist militancy and began to call themselves evangelicals or neo- evangelicals. Billy Graham was the archetypical representative of this side of the fundamentalist heritage. Others, however, including leaders such as Carl McIntire, Bob Jones, and John R. Rice, continued to call themselves fundamentalists and were more mili- tant than ever. For them strict adherence to inerrancy, separatism, and usually dispensationalism were necessary conditions for being a true fundamentalist. In fact, the narrowness of these groups suggests that they might best be designated hyper- fundamentalists.

In the early 1980s fundamentalism reemerged on the American scene as a wide coalition reminiscent of the 1920s. Often associated with the con- servative "moral majority" in politics, this renewed fundamentalism remained more militant (attacking now "secular humanism" rather than mod- ernism) than the conservative "evangelicals" of the same era. They were also more totally identified with American nationalism, nineteenth- century economic theories, and a gospel of personal success than had been their predecessors of the 1920s.

The Scopes Trial

JOEL CARPENTER

John Thomas Scopes, a first-year high- school science teacher in the small town of Dayton, Tennessee, stood trial in 1925 to test the state's new law forbidding the teaching of evolution. His highly publicized trial became a symbol of the cultural upheaval of the 1920s which pitted a secular, mod- ernistic mentality against the evangelical ethos of the nineteenth century.

The defendant found himself shoved aside very quickly as groups representing these competing forces took over. The American Civil Liber- ties Union had solicited Scopes in the first place to contest the constitution- ality of antievolution laws. The World's Christian Fundamentals Association, however, fought cultural modernism with an antievolution campaign. Soon after Scopes' arrest, the WCFA offered

Clarence Darrow and William Jennings Bryan at Dayton, Tennessee, July 1925 BROWN BROTHERS

the prosecution William Jennings Bryan as counsel.

Bryan was a populist Democrat, three-time candidate for president, former secretary of state, and perennial champion of reform. He had been crusading for the fundamentalist cause, especially against evolution, and coveted the national publicity this trial would give. He saw evolution as a threat to the nation's faith and hence its ethical foundation. Evolution allegedly caused the militarism of Germany, and in the wake of the Great War Bryan feared that evolutionism would also erode American national character. He believed it was the right of voting parents to exclude the subject from the schools.

Against the better judgment of some ACLU officials, Clarence Darrow led

their defense team for Scopes. Darrow was a reformer, too, but of a different sort than Bryan. As a flamboyant and successful trial lawyer he had defended radicals, labor leaders, and murderers. An outspoken agnostic, he had once challenged Bryan to debate his religion. To Darrow, Bryan and fundamentalism represented a meddlesome bigotry that violated American minorities' rights. He agreed with critic H. L. Mencken that " 'Doing Good' is in bad taste."

Mencken led a horde of journalists to Dayton in July 1925. The town's citizens were as enlightened as any other Americans, and had been tolerant of Scopes' teaching. But the reporters made sport of the trial's carnival atmosphere, the hawkers selling stuffed monkeys, and the snake-handling hillbilly sects. Mencken gleefully described the "peasants and ignoramuses" to his eastern readers and helped form a lingering stereotype of fundamentalism as bigoted, ignorant, and rural.

Scopes' guilt was almost assumed, so the climax of the trial came as Bryan testified as an expert on the Bible. In two hours of questioning, Darrow made him look narrow-minded and foolish. And Bryan could not strike back as the defense waived the summary statements. To many, fundamentalism seemed discredited.

Bryan died five days later, not of chagrin, but of diabetic-induced exhaustion. He thought he had done well, and his admirers agreed. The fundamentalists' public crusade suffered defeat at Dayton, but the movement was far from dead. The old-time religion sheltered millions in a stormy era and outlived many of its modern surrogates.

For Further Reading

Robert H. Wiebe, *The Search for Order, 1877-1920* (1966), is a valuable general history of the era. William E. Leutenburg, *The Perils of Prosperity, 1914-1932* (1958), is an entertaining overview of that later era.

Paul A. Carter, *The Spiritual Crisis of the Gilded Age* (1971), provides interesting, though unsystematic, interpretation. Two biographies give a good picture of the era: Clifford E. Clark, *Henry Ward Beecher: Spokesman for a Middle Class America* (1978), and James F. Findlay, Jr., *Dwight L. Moody, American Evangelist: 1837-1899* (1969), a truly outstanding work. Samuel S. Hill, Jr., *The South and the North in American Religion* (1980), includes an essay on 1885-1900 that helpfully explores the distinctiveness of southern religion and culture.

One can gain a picture of American Protestant missions efforts from C. Howard Hopkins, *John R. Mott, 1865-1955* (1979), a very detailed biography of a leading figure from the time of Moody to World War II. On social issues, Henry F. May, *Protestant Churches and Industrial America* (1963), is very valuable for the nineteenth century. C. Howard Hopkins, *The Rise of the Social Gospel in American Protestantism, 1865-1915* (1940), is comprehensive, but dated.

Jacob Henry Dorn, *Washington Gladden: Prophet of the Social Gospel* (1968), is a fine biography. Paul A. Carter, *The Decline and Revival of the Social Gospel: Social and Political Liberalism in American Protestant Churches, 1920-1940*, 2nd ed. (1956; repr. 1971), provides a good impression of the degree to which religious groups follow the general political trends. Aaron Abell, *American Catholicism and Social Action: A Search for Social Justice, 1865-1950* (1960), is a very valuable work.

William R. Hutchison, *The Modernist Impulse in American Protestantism* (1976), is the outstanding work on this subject. Lefferts A. Loetscher, *The Broadening Church: A Study of Theological Issues in the Presbyterian Church Since 1869* (1957), is, despite its denominational focus, an excellent account of the major theological issues of the era. Ernest R. Sandeen, *The Roots of Fundamentalism: British and American Millenarianism 1800-1930* (1970; repr. 1978), is very valuable on the origins of dispensationalism. For the holiness movement, Charles Edwin Jones, *A Guide to the Study of the Holiness Movement* (1974), is the place to begin. Vinson Synan, ed., *Aspects of Pentecostal-Charismatic Origins* (1975), is a collection of essays that leads one into most aspects of the origins of both the holiness and the pentecostal movements. Robert Mapes Anderson, *Vision of the Disinherited: The Making of American Pentecostalism* (1979), is a fine scholarly treatment, but overemphasizes sociological explanations.

On black Protestantism since the Civil War, despite its great potential as a field for historical investigation, one must rely on general texts or rather specialized studies. E. Franklin Frazier, *The Negro Church in America*, rev. ed. published together with C. Eric Lincoln, *The Black Church Since Frazier* (1973), is the place to begin. Thomas T. McAvoy, *The Great Crisis in American Catholic History, 1895-1900* (1957), is the standard work on the Americanist controversy. Jay P. Dolan, *Catholic Revivalism: The American Experience, 1830-1900* (1978), portrays an evangelical side to Catholic popular religion. Various denominational histories deal with other distinctive groups.

On the fundamentalist-modernist controversies of the 1920s, Hutchison, *Modernist Impulse*, and Sandeen, *Roots of Fundamentalism*, are important. George M. Marsden, *Fundamentalism and American Culture: The Shaping of Twentieth-Century Evangelicalism 1870-1925* (1980), traces the rise of militant evangelical Protestantism through World War I and the controversies of the 1920s. Lawrence W. Levine, *Defender of the Faith: William Jennings Bryan, The Last Decade, 1915-1925* (1965), is a good biography relating the religious and cultural outlook of a controversial fundamentalist spokesman.

Christianity and American Higher Education

MARK A. NOLL

From the founding of Harvard in 1636 to the creation of fundamentalist Bible colleges in the 1980s, American higher education has never lacked a Christian presence. Harvard, the only college in the colonies for nearly sixty years, arose from self-conscious Christian purposes. New England's First Fruits (1643) stated it plainly: "After God had carried us safe to New England, and wee had builded our houses, provided necessaries for our livelihood, rear'd convenient places for Gods worship, and setled the Civill Government: One of the next things we longed for, and looked after was to advance Learning, and perpetuate it to Posterity, dreading to leave an illiterate Ministry to the Churches, when our present Ministers shall lie in the Dust. And as wee were thinking and consulting how to effect this great Work; it pleased God to stir up the heart of one Mr. Harvard ... to give the one halfe of his Estate ... towards the erecting of a Colledge, and all his Library."

Harvard and the few other early American colleges served a colonial elite. Students, who were a few years younger than their modern counterparts, studied Latin and Greek, with some math, science, and philosophy. They made numerous public recitations and speeches. They were supposed to be well behaved, studious, and respectful, but frequently were not. And they left college to enter places of respect, or even eminence, in colonial society.

The Great Awakening of the 1740s led to the creation of several more colleges, established both to increase the number of ministers and to spread the stabilizing virtues of education. During this early period, however, the college graduate who wished to become a minister normally spent a postgraduate period with a more experienced clergyman before seeking a church for himself. Not until the founding of Andover Theological Seminary, established in 1807 as a protest against Harvard's drift into Unitarianism, did seminary education as it is now known begin in America.

After the Revolution, collegiate education expanded with the contours of the growing country. The nearly five hundred colleges that existed at the time of the Civil War were overwhelmingly patriotic, moralistic, and Protestant. Many, like coeducational Oberlin (Ohio) which shared Charles Finney's twin commitment to evangelism and social righteousness, were also centers for reform. Although institutions of higher learning never enrolled more than one percent of the college-age population before the Civil War, they were found in nearly every corner of the land. In the Midwest and South, a combination of eastern influence (especially from Yale and Princeton) and local energy, funds, and denominational ties greatly increased the number of colleges. Methodists and Baptists led in this effort, but they were joined by most of the other Protestant denominations and by Roman Catholics. In fact, an 1847 broadside from the University of Notre Dame sounded very much like publicity from a typical Protestant college: "The disciplinary government is mild, yet sufficiently energetic, to preserve that good order, so essential to the well-being of the Institution. The morals and general deportment of the pupils are watched over with the greatest assiduity and solicitude; their personal comfort receives the most paternal attention, and no pains are spared to prepare them for fulfilling their respective duties in society." Antebellum college presidents normally addressed the relationship

THE COLONIAL COLLEGES OF BRITISH NORTH AMERICA WITH FOUNDING DATES AND CLOSEST DENOMINATIONAL TIES

1636	Harvard (Congregational)	1754	King's, later Columbia (Anglican)
1693	William and Mary (Anglican)	1764	Brown (Baptist)
1701	Yale (Congregational)	1766	Queens, later Rutgers (Dutch Reformed)
1746	College of New Jersey, later Princeton (Presbyterian)	1769	Dartmouth (New Light Congregational)
1751	Philadelphia Academy, later the University of Pennsylvania (unaffiliated)	1775	Hampden-Sydney (Presbyterian)

between faith and learning in the senior "Moral Philosophy" course which showed how the truths of science and the demands of good citizenship fit together with the Christian faith.

Between the Civil War and the Great Depression the Christian character of much higher education passed away with the birth of the modern American university. The most important intellectual factor behind this change was the great prestige of Charles Darwin's biology, a new and exciting approach to science that rapidly became the model for many other disciplines. The popular view of evolution did not need God to explain the material world and did not place much value in "primitive" religious authorities like the Bible.

Beyond the impact of evolution, the "revolution" in American higher education had social causes as well. While the country's population rose threefold from 1870 to 1930, its number of college students multiplied more than twenty-one times. The rapidly growing number of students along with the growing demands from industry for technical expertise required quantum increases in libraries, facilities, and endowments. The era's great entrepreneurs, who had scant concern for traditional orthodoxy, provided much of the needed money. Under the pressure of new learning, new students, and new funds, colleges rapidly dropped their Christian distinctives. Universities named professional academics rather than ministers as presidents. Businessmen replaced clergy as trustees. In the hiring of faculty, specialization (represented best by the new Ph.D. degree) became more important than Victorian morality or Christian beliefs.

After World War I, Christian concerns no longer dominated American higher education, but they had certainly not vanished

entirely. The fundamentalist era generated a host of Bible colleges and institutes, among which Chicago's Moody Bible Institute was the most effective and most widely imitated. A number of Christian colleges continued to resist secularization even as they sought the goals of liberal arts education. Older denominational schools often retained at least general acknowledgment of their founders' Christian purposes. Large Bible colleges have recently arisen in association with the great churches of fundamentalist leaders. Black colleges still bear the marks of earlier Christian influence. Seminaries reflect the same range of belief found in the church at large, although theologically conservative schools have grown dramatically since World War II. Even state institutions long retained a nineteenth-century casualness about the separation of church and state — as late as 1945, in fact, eleven percent of the country's state-supported colleges still had compulsory chapel. Catholic institutions of higher learning also reflect the full spectrum of faith and practice now found in that communion. Unlike the Protestants, however, differences among Catholics are more likely to show up on the same campus rather than in separate and antagonistic institutions. And Christian scholars also continue to ply their trades in secular institutions where they sometimes assume leadership in their disciplines.

No longer do Christians rule the colleges, nor Christian colleges the marketplace of ideas, as was the case 150 years ago. Yet Christians in higher education continue to work in a vast range of institutions and still retain the capacity to spark renewal in the churches, even if they are now only rarely in a position to shape the thinking of an entire culture.

American Worship: Contrasting Styles

THOMAS WERGE

In American public worship, observed Alexis de Tocqueville in the nineteenth century, the idea of equality made believers resist the "subjection" of their minds to external forms and images. Since Americans were "unmoved by ceremonial observances," he continued, it was necessary for churches to separate their creeds and articles of faith from the "accessories connected with them." American religious institutions, including the Roman Catholic church, had done so: "I have seen no country in which Christianity is clothed with fewer forms, figures, and observances ... or where it presents more distinct, simple, and general notions to the mind." Tocqueville's generalizations, while sweeping, implicitly define three means by which one might differentiate the many forms and liturgies of American worship: the value attached to an historically apostolic and sacerdotal idea of ceremony; the emphasis placed on the altar, Eucharist, and sense of sight, as opposed to the scripture, preaching, and sense of hearing, as focal points; and the place given to the individual's direct and personal "felt experience" of redemption and salvation in the larger action of corporate worship and devotion.

Calvin's complaint that "every little ceremony" in the Roman Catholic liturgy was defined as "apostolic" points up the central role of history and tradition in Roman Catholicism. Eastern Orthodoxy, through its many national churches in America; the Episcopal church – one of eighteen churches in the global Anglican communion; and the Lutheran churches, most especially the Lutheran Church–Missouri Synod, accentuate the importance of liturgical ceremony. The Roman, Orthodox, and Episcopal rites reflect the views expressed by the second Synod of Nicea and the Council of Trent that

images of Christ, Mary, and the saints are to be venerated. Kneeling, genuflecting, making the sign of the cross, the presence of holy water, candles, and icons are vital to these ceremonies and are seen as bound up with ancient creeds and church doctrines. Although Lutheran doctrine views only baptism and the Eucharist as sacraments, these others hold to the seven sacraments by including confirmation, penance, holy orders, marriage, and extreme unction. Orthodox rites are highly elaborate, often lasting for three hours, and their sense of the significance of the apostolic order and priesthood, hierarchical, corporate, and historical, is pronounced – as it is in the Roman and Episcopal rites as well.

With the exception of the Episcopal church, "apostolic authority" in Protestantism has little to do with the historical institution of the church and the laying on of hands. All professing believers are "apostolic" when they adhere to the true Word and sacrament. The Reformed and Presbyterian churches in America, while structured in their ecclesiology and liturgy, moved toward the more "distinct" and "simple" order of worship Tocqueville had noted. The Methodist church moved into the American frontier while the Episcopal church remained largely in the East. In the process, Methodism's circuit-riding ministers, frontier settings, and revivals intensified the flexibility of its hymn-singing and "democratic" style of worship. The Baptists, America's largest Protestant body, moved even further in this direction. Interpreting baptism as a testimony of faith rather than a sacrament in the traditional sense, they emphasized the believer's "decision for Christ" and the rite of total immersion. The order of worship of such non-Trinitarian denominations as the Unitarian church is equally free from historic confessions of faith, rituals, and external ceremonies — a practice which culminates in the Quakers, for whom Christ speaks as the voice and light within every believer. Traditional rites, hierarchies, and images — with the possible exception of the Cross — have little place in these forms of worship. To varying degrees, they assent to the Second Helvetic Confession of 1566, which approvingly quotes Lactantius: "Undoubtedly no religion exists where there is an image."

For many forms of Protestantism, mistrust of images and external ritual stems from an exaltation of the Word of God as the only norm of faith and practice. The Council of Trent's conviction (1564) that sacred images should be "set before the eyes of the faithful" for gratitude, piety, and imitation conflicts with a Protestant fear of idolatry, suspicion of the imagination, and the view, here expressed by John Donne, that "the eye is the devils doore ... but the eare is the Holy Ghosts first doore." The importance of preaching in Protestant worship is rooted in St. Paul's statement that "faith cometh by hearing, and hearing by the word of God" (Romans 10:17, AV). The Eucharist, of course, is also central to traditional Protestant worship. But it serves as a sign and "seal" of grace already conferred rather than as a "means of grace." Its "symbolic" and "commemorative" nature — only the Episcopal and Lutheran communions profess the "real presence" of Christ in the bread and wine — differs sharply from the Orthodox and Roman Catholic conception. Whether scripture is viewed as "literally inspired" and inerrant, the proclamation of the Word through scripture and sermon constitutes the center of the Protestant liturgy.

In the Catholic, Orthodox, and Episcopal conceptions of liturgy and Eucharist, the altar becomes as central a focal point as the Word. The three faiths differ over the doctrine of transubstantiation. But they share a view of the "real presence" as literal and tangible rather than incorporeal, as well as a sense of the Mass as an imitation, repetition, and renewal of Christ's crucifixion, death, and resurrection. Ritual becomes mimetic and redemptive. As part of this corporate event, the faithful are to share in the mystical body of Christ through a conse-

cration of sensory experience and particular images. In the Orthodox liturgy, the priest's ritual preparation of the offering of the bread involves the cutting of a square particle (the Lamb of God), a triangular particle (the Virgin Mary), and nine smaller particles in imitation and memory of the nine ranks of "Archangels and angels, Prophets, Holy Fathers, Prelates, Martyrs, devout God-Fearing Fathers, wonder-working unmercenaries, the righteous Ancestors of Jesus and Saints of the day." Scripture remains vital to this liturgy. Yet the proclamation of the Word through the Eucharist — which, for Catholicism and Orthodoxy, was part of a tradition existing prior to the appearance of canonical scripture — constitutes the center of these sacramental forms of worship.

John Wesley's conversion came about as he listened to someone reading from Luther's works. When he experienced this saving faith, said Wesley, "I felt my heart strangely warmed." In much of Protestantism, salvation is based in an individual and "experiential" conversion of the heart, and a theology of personal redemption seems to dominate. In the Orthodox and Catholic traditions, salvation is often more corporate and communal — the church, not only the individual soul, is the object of divine judgment and grace. A theology of church history and even the order of creation prevails. Yet the Orthodox and Catholic liturgies, through their forms of intercession and mediation, also address the inner life, while the more direct and unmediated liturgies of Protestantism have an undeniably corporate dimension. Further, Roman Catholicism has placed renewed emphasis on the place of scripture in worship, while the post-World War II "liturgical movement" in American Protestantism reflected a strong interest in traditions, rituals, and forms. In discussing the role of external forms in worship, Pascal implicitly acknowledges that these several traditions of worship are complementary rather than mutually exclusive in their means, emphasis, and ultimate purpose: "The Christian religion is adapted to all, being composed of externals and internals. It raises the common people to the internal, and humbles the proud to the external; it is not perfect without the two, for the people must understand the spirit of the letter, and the learned must submit their spirit to the letter."

A 1942 *map depicting the projects undertaken by the*
Public Works Administration, one of the New Deal programs
NATIONAL ARCHIVES

Christianity in a Secular Age: From the Depression to the Present

BY DAVID F. WELLS AND
JOHN D. WOODBRIDGE

From the Depression to the Present

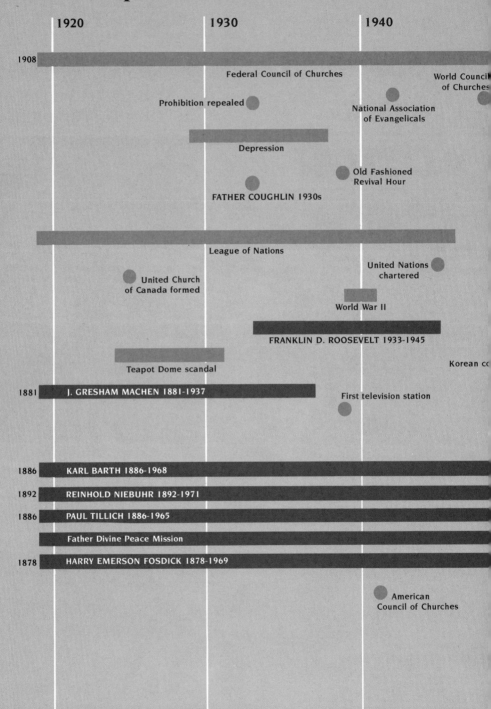

1920   1930   1940

1908

Federal Council of Churches

World Council
of Churches

Prohibition repealed

National Association
of Evangelicals

Depression

Old Fashioned
Revival Hour

FATHER COUGHLIN 1930s

League of Nations

United Nations
chartered

United Church
of Canada formed

World War II

FRANKLIN D. ROOSEVELT 1933-1945

Teapot Dome scandal

Korean co

1881   J. GRESHAM MACHEN 1881-1937

First television station

1886   KARL BARTH 1886-1968

1892   REINHOLD NIEBUHR 1892-1971

1886   PAUL TILLICH 1886-1965

Father Divine Peace Mission

1878   HARRY EMERSON FOSDICK 1878-1969

American
Council of Churches

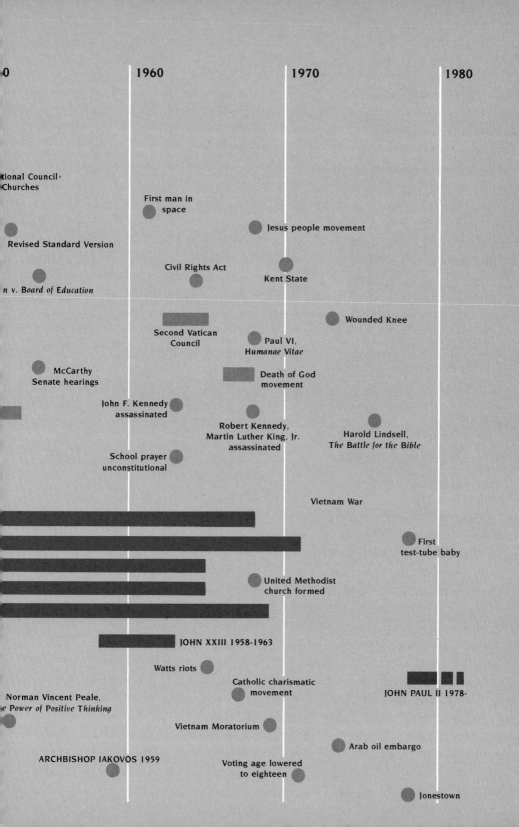

1960   **1970**   **1980**

...tional Council, Churches

Revised Standard Version

First man in space

Jesus people movement

Civil Rights Act

Kent State

...n v. *Board of Education*

Second Vatican Council

Wounded Knee

Paul VI, *Humanae Vitae*

McCarthy Senate hearings

Death of God movement

John F. Kennedy assassinated

Robert Kennedy, Martin Luther King, Jr. assassinated

Harold Lindsell, *The Battle for the Bible*

School prayer unconstitutional

Vietnam War

First test-tube baby

United Methodist church formed

JOHN XXIII 1958-1963

Watts riots

Catholic charismatic movement

JOHN PAUL II 1978-

Norman Vincent Peale, *The Power of Positive Thinking*

Vietnam Moratorium

Arab oil embargo

ARCHBISHOP IAKOVOS 1959

Voting age lowered to eighteen

Jonestown

Looking Back on Fifty Years (1930-1980)

As the history of Christianity in America begins to overlap living memory, it loses much of its clarity. We experience it as a mixture of events in which it is difficult to discriminate the important from the trivial. Time usually renders this service. But before that happens we often find ourselves blinking in confusion at what William James called "the bloomin', buzzin' confusion" of our lives. This incomprehension is evident in many ways but not least in the question as to whether or not the United States has moved into a "post-Christian" era.

It is not difficult to find textbooks which write the story of the United States since 1930 as if religion had more or less disappeared. By so doing, they reflect an obvious secularization in American life. The most influential purveyors of twentieth-century popular culture no longer concentrate on religious themes as did Currier and Ives in the nineteenth century. The periodicals of the elite seldom feature extended reporting on missionary and evangelistic work as, say, *Harper's Weekly* did throughout the previous century. Public school children no longer start the day with prayer, and the Bible fares badly in many colleges and universities. From one perspective, it seems clear that the nation is building self-consciously and deliberately without religious foundations.

We are tired of religious revivals as we have known them in the last half century.

WILLIAM SPERRY,
Dean of Harvard Divinity School, 1946

From another perspective, however, it is plain that Americans are at least as religious today as they have ever been. Pollsters have never found more than a tiny fraction of the people which disbelieves in the existence of God. Historians who look in the right places discover vast numbers of Americans who have always attended church and who have continued to provide significant financial support for religious causes. A population which, in 1980, was more than one-fifth Roman Catholic (nearly fifty million people, including baptized children) and more than one-tenth Baptist (more than twenty-five million)—to name only the two largest denominations—and in which one-third of the nation's adults claimed to have had a "born-again" experience and to believe that the Bible is God's written revelation, is hardly one that is in a "post-Christian" era.

Historians are tempted to interpret the last fifty years from one or the other of these angles of vision. To do so, however, means not only to disregard half the story but also to miss the real key to understanding these years. For this period is frequently enigmatic until one sees that its real shaping forces have lain in this nexus between Christ and culture. What must be understood, then, is how so much religion has coexisted with so much secularization.

At the beginning of this period, the interpenetration of religious belief and cultural assumptions was most evident in the liberal theology which dominated many divinity schools, such as those at Harvard, Yale, and Chicago, as well as the mainline denominations into which they fed their graduates. An inbred affinity bound together a self-confident culture and a theology convinced of hu-

Church in Washington, D.C., 1939

man nature's goodness and life's progressive betterment. But liberal theology in the United States was as unprepared for the catastrophe of the Depression as its parent movement in Europe had been for the First World War. Both were crushed by cultures that suddenly revealed, within their calamitous suffering, a hardness that liberals had never dreamed was there.

The situation, of course, was quite different for the liberals' fundamentalistic opponents. Painful ecclesiastical trials and denominational upheavals, lost battles, and lost influence had shattered any illusions which fundamentalists might have retained about the friendliness of the environment. For fundamentalists in the 1930s and 1940s, America was a dangerous place. The Depression, with its bread lines and wandering waifs, its human scavengers working the city dumps, its tarpaper huts, its sharecropper shacks, its pain and disillusionment, did not shatter the fundamentalists. Their world view had not lost its understanding of human depravity.

The separation between Christ and culture which fundamentalists had been forced to accept and liberals regarded as so wrong-headed eventually paid its dividend. Fundamentalists passed through the Depression unscarred cognitively; liberal Protestantism was fatally wounded by it.

In this period, then, fundamentalism is seen as withdrawn into tight, self-contained enclaves surrounded by a menacing and unfriendly world. Fundamentalism assumed the psychology of a minority. Like other minorities, it also felt threatened and feared that it would be absorbed into the larger, godless whole. But this fear was intensified in fundamentalism in a way that does not occur in ethnic minorities. It is not possible to change one's status as a member of an ethnic minority; a black will always be a black, and a Pole will always be a Pole. In cognitive minorities, however, it is very simple to change one's status. One merely jettisons those beliefs which are not broadly held in the culture. It is the ease with which this can be done that explains the "citadel mentality" of the fundamentalists. The cognitive boundaries of Christian faith had to be marked clearly and defended fiercely; those who lived within these boundaries needed to be given the therapy of close fellowship and protected against the insidious pressures which the world exerted against them.

One Nation. . . ?

The world outside, however, was itself in danger. The threat did not come from abroad, despite deep-rooted fears about the global ambitions of communism, but from within. And once again it was a war which both crystalized and accelerated the changes that were to come.

The Vietnam War revealed a nation at cross-purposes with itself, and the turmoil which it created took its toll on national unity. More than that, it left many people feeling disillusioned about the nation's most fundamental institutions. It was a disillusionment that was slow to heal. In 1980, for example, half the nation (fifty-one percent) still refused to believe that the government had the capacity to solve national problems such as energy shortages, inflation, and crime. Half the population (forty-eight percent) remained convinced that serious problems such as these should not be left in the hands of the nation's leaders.

If confidence in the nation's institutions and structures has been shaken, so, too, has the sense of what it means to be American. It was fashionable once to think of America as a melting pot in which ethnic distinctives were softened and its immigrant peoples absorbed into the larger whole of the nation. It is now clear that if anything has been melting, it has only been the pot of sociological theory. Ethnic minorities have, to a surprising extent, preserved their uniqueness of language, culture, and social organization. Indeed, the histories of many of North America's largest cities, such as Boston and Chicago, coincide in large measure with the story of immigrant groups and the changes which their arrival made in the city. These minorities often preserved their religious ways, and their religion sustained their cultural identity. In many instances, such as among the

Irish, Polish, and Italian immigrants, being part of an ethnic minority has implied being part of a cognitive minority, being Catholic. These enclaves of ethnicity have preserved that faith which to many is inextricably a part of being Irish or Polish. "Through the use of the Polish language," the saying goes, "we remain good Catholics, and through allegiance to the church we are all good Poles."

This factor is particularly significant in terms of black Christianity. Although most black Christians have believed the cardinal tenets of fundamentalist-evangelical faith, few have ever been part of the fundamentalist-evangelical movement. In part, this is the legacy of slavery. Whites may have forgotten this episode in their past, but blacks have not. But what is equally important is that for blacks, Christianity has fashioned their identity, not only as Christians, but also as blacks.

The Amish have preserved a largely traditional culture within a technological society. © FRED J. WILSON 1973

Under God?

If the 1960s and 1970s at times left the impression of several nations dwelling simultaneously within the territorial limits of the United States, they also presented the option of a variety of gods whose worship and service were for selection. Cultural fragmentation and religious pluralism went hand in hand.

This development was, of course, most obvious in the arrival from the Orient of religions and cults that had formerly never flourished on American soil, but it was nowhere more important than in the astonishing changes which it wrought in Catholicism. By the end of the 1970s, only a small minority believed in papal infallibility (thirty-three percent), an overwhelming majority (ninety percent) was disobeying Pope Paul VI's teaching on contraception, and a substantial number (between thirty and ninety percent, depending on the issue) believed that faith should be defined, not by what the church teaches, but by what the individual thinks.

Yet it is not hard to find commentators who glibly ignore this pluralism. Some speak of Americans as being Protestant, Catholic, or Jewish, as if there were only three categories. And even these categories have only very limited usefulness. A liberal Presbyterian probably shares more with a progressive Catholic and a Reformed Jew than he does with an evangelical in his own denomination. Even to divide Protestants into liberals and conservatives, or Catholics into progressives and traditionalists is a precarious undertaking. And where do the Mennonites fit, who take the Bible literally but reject the American military? Or fundamentalist Bob Jones University, which stands for stringent social conservatism and yet boasts one of the best collegiate art collections in the country and supports a sophisticated program of drama? Or Dorothy Day and the *Catholic Worker*, who affirm high orthodoxy and attack the structures of capitalism with the language of the far left? The effort to establish neat historical categories is always chancy but never more so than when one tries to sort out the immediate past.

The interplay between faith and culture has many facets and has wrought not a few ironies in the immediate past. Its existence both complicates and clarifies current perception as to what has happened. It complicates analysis because so often this interplay has been unconscious; but to recognize its presence provides a way of looking at the last fifty years without which they would be inexplicable. This is immediately apparent upon viewing the Thirties, a period both socially destructive and richly religious.

The Church and Minorities
DONALD TINDER

In America the ethnic or racial minorities have always tended to have their own churches. And it is well to remember that the sum of all active churchgoers has always been only a minority of the total population. Many whole denominations can be identified with a particular minority, while others are noted for the low numbers of minorities in their ranks. Even in the denominations that comprise both majority and minority members, the local congregations are usually composed of one or the other.

In no other way are the multiple origins of the American people more persistently demonstrated than in the distinguishable ethnic composition of their churches. Neighborhoods, schools, sports, and occupations that were once noted for the dominance or absence of various minorities are generally becoming more integrated or are shifting from one minority to another. But for denominations, only cosmetic changes, such as the dropping of ethnic designations as part of the official name, have been common.

Church buildings may change hands but often this is because the old congregation chooses to move on rather than absorb the newcomers.

Originally the numerical majority of the United States population consisted of whites of British Protestant background. This has continued to be the culturally dominant "mainstream" even though numerical predominance was lost in the nineteenth century. Germans and Scandinavians were generally admitted to majority status as their descendants came to be English-speaking. More recently, Irish Catholics and descendants of immigrants from the European continent, whether Protestant, Catholic, Orthodox, or Jewish in background, have tended to be admitted to the mainstream unless they cling to distinctive subcultural traits.

The churches of the original majority are chiefly the Baptist, Christian (Campbellite), Congregational, Episcopal, Methodist, Presbyterian, and Quaker. All were rooted in Britain, the first two tenuously so. The Adventist, holiness, and pentecostal denominations and the Bible churches have been later developments within the mainstream; the Mormons are a distinctive doctrinal break from it. It is noteworthy that the non-European minorities in America have usually

Blackfoot Indian Father Ksistaki-Poka, the first western Indian ordained a Roman Catholic priest, blesses a delegation of Blackfoot, Flathead, and Coeur D'Alene Indians. RELIGIOUS NEWS SERVICE PHOTO

expressed their Christianity through allegiance to one of these mainstream traditions. The convoluted course of American religious history has been largely shaped by developments and conflicts within this mainstream, but that does not excuse talking about the church as if minorities were not part of it.

The continental traditions — Catholic, Lutheran, Orthodox, Reformed, plus some smaller groups — had their independent histories mainly before becoming part of the cultural mainstream. But much of their history has been shaped by their contacts, and conflicts, with majority Protestantism. As Protestant minorities have passed into the mainstream culturally, many of their church members have switched their denominational allegiance to one of the original majority groups. In addition, some once clearly ethnic bodies, such as the Scandinavian free churches, are increasingly attracting members from other backgrounds. In other cases, such as the Lutherans, bodies from neighboring ethnic groups have merged.

But what of the Hispanic and non-European minorities that are still outside the mainstream? Together they number nearly one-fourth of the American population. While each has tended to have its own congregations if not whole denominations, it is also true that there is no major example of a denominationally distinctive Christian movement among the non-European peoples of America. This is in contrast to many countries in Africa and Asia where adherents of nonmissionary-related forms of Christianity are numerous. However, the relationships to the churches of the four largest minorities — American Indians, blacks, Asian-Americans, and Hispanics — vary widely. Population estimates for minorities are unavoidably vague. According to the 1980 census blacks are nearly 12 percent of the total population, Hispanics are approaching 7 percent (though some claim 10 percent is more accurate), while Asian-Americans are 1.5 percent and American Indians are 0.6 percent.

Blacks are the only minority to have the great majority of their congregations in their own denominations, chiefly within the Baptist, Methodist, and pentecostal families. The black role in the origins of pentecostalism was crucial. Historically, leadership in the black community is far more likely to have come from the churches than is the case with the other minorities. Through its music, the black church has contributed to mainstream culture. And, of course, the blacks in their slavery were the occasion for the only American civil war and for long-lasting divisions in major denominations.

Though blacks had their religions stripped from them, they have been more receptive to evangelism than others. American Indians and Asian-American churches must compete with traditional religions as well as with secularism. Most churches of both groups are affiliated with one of a variety of largely white denominations. Asian-Americans are proportionately more church-going than in Asia, though less so than the general population. Especially with the recent influx from southeast Asia there may be 1,000 or so Asian congregations, almost all of them led by Asian ministers. However, the more than 2,000 Native American congregations are served by fewer than six hundred ordained Indian ministers. Indeed, only about a dozen Indian priests are to be found in the Native American Catholic community of about 180,000, which is more than half the total Native American Christian population.

Hispanics are almost all of Roman Catholic background. However, Latin American, in contrast with Iberian, Catholicism has never been particularly vigorous. Hispanic participation in American Catholic life and leadership is proportionately below that of most other groups. Correspondingly, there has been a greater proportion of Protestants, chiefly pentecostals and Baptists, among the Hispanics that are religiously active than among the other Catholic ethnic groups. In the large Hispanic center of Los Angeles, for example, some fifteen percent of the Hispanic population is Protestant.

Over the decades, numerous ethnic minorities have been more or less assimilated into the majority. Presumably this process will continue, though at a slower rate since non-Europeans are involved, along with Hispanics in sufficient concentrations to keep linguistically distinct. Moreover, there is a reassertion of ethnic and racial pride and a well-justified questioning of the value of surrendering to Anglo-Saxon cultural distinctives. The counterpart is an unwillingness on the part of at least some in the mainstream to welcome new additions, but such "nativism" has greeted every minority and, so far, eventually been overcome.

There are those, therefore, who oppose assimilation or integration on quite diverse grounds. There are others who think that the churches in America are much further than they should be from expressing what Paul intended when he wrote, "Here there cannot be Greek and Jew, circumcised and uncircumcised, barbarian, Scythian, slave, free man, but Christ is all, and in all" (Colossians 3:11).

Annual Fiesta of Santiago, Chimayo, New Mexico
COURTESY OF MARYNOLL MISSIONERS, M. SANDOVAL PHOTO

American Christianity and the New Pluralism

J. GORDON MELTON

The 1970s saw a dramatic increase in religious affiliation in America, but this affiliation with few exceptions was not among the larger mainline churches. Growth did occur among some of the older evangelical, conservative churches, among newer charismatic groups, and, most importantly, a new set of alternative religions.

No simplistic scheme adequately characterizes the new alternative faiths that are even now restructuring the American religious scene and creating the new, radically pluralistic religious environment. They follow widely divergent lifestyles and hold very different perspectives. Their divergence from traditional Christianity is the only characteristic they share in common.

Maharishi Mahesh Yogi, one of the most effective popularizers of eastern religion RELIGIOUS NEWS SERVICE PHOTO

Eastern religions, among the most important of the alternative faiths, came into their own in the 1970s. Seeing America as a fertile mission field after the 1893 World Parliament of Religions in Chicago, Hindu and Buddhist leaders began indigenous works. Their efforts, however, were sharply curtailed by the strict immigration restrictions imposed before World War I.

A new growth began after World War II when members of the U.S. occupation forces in Japan brought 'Buddhism home with them. In the mid-1960s President Johnson lifted the old immigration restrictions and set the stage for the arrival of missionaries from Tibet, Hong Kong, Japan, and India. They established new work that spread rapidly.

Some of the more successful new groups grew up around the teaching of an independent teacher or prophet. These include such groups as the Church of Scientology of L. Ron Hubbard and the Unification Church of Sun Myung Moon, which have, like the Latter Day Saints of Joseph Smith, held some degree of popular appeal.

A growing but almost invisible set of new religious communities has even attempted to recover the pre-Christian pagan myths. These groups, going under the names of paganism and witchcraft, worship the Great Mother Goddess and her consort, the Horned God, frequently pictured as the old Greek deities, Diana and Pan.

The emergence of the new churches and alternative faiths has created a new image of America which is no longer that of a dominant Protestant majority and a lesser number of Catholics and Jews. America is now home to more than eight hundred denominations offering a multitude of variations on Christian belief, and every urban area offers the full range

Pentecostal snake handlers are one of the more unusual sects fostered on American soil.
BILLY GRAHAM CENTER

of the world's religious teachings and worship in some six hundred alternative religions.

The new pluralism that the 1970s created confronted the church at various levels. The building down the street, for example, is now as likely to be a Buddhist or Hindu or Sikh temple as a Baptist or Methodist church. Families have found themselves split when one member decided to join a different church or religion. Most denominations have been entangled in the struggles of the newer faiths to find recognition in the free religious environment of America.

The response to the new pluralism has varied. The more traditional response, that of the churches offering refutations of what they considered heresies and non-Christian teachings, has continued. Pastors and religious leaders have warned their followers not to become involved with the new groups.

But some people have gone beyond polemics to coerce forcefully members of both the newer evangelical churches and the alternative faiths to renounce their allegiance to their beliefs. This practice, called "deprogramming," has stirred controversy as members of conservative evangelical bodies and even mainline denominations have become targets.

Deprogramming groups have also tried to get legislative bodies to hold hearings and pass laws against the new religions.

Most church leaders and churches have opposed the activities of the deprogrammers. As early as 1974, the National Council of Churches denounced religious kidnapping and, along with most of the major denominations, objected to legislative hearings aimed at curtailing the new religions.

The presence of the new pluralistic situation in America and the controversy caused by those attempting to inhibit new religions through deprogramming and legislation set a new context for the churches in the immediate future. Religious pluralism is a worldwide phenomenon wherever religious freedom is allowed. Possibly, the new pluralism offers the opportunity to discover new ways to share Christ with the non-Christian world by moving away from an emphasis on the differences between Christianity and the alternative faiths (which have often been exaggerated to the extreme) and seizing the chance to discover their commonalities.

Hare Krishna devotees chant and distribute literature on a city street. RELIGIOUS NEWS SERVICE PHOTO

From the Great Depression to the War

The Great Crash of the stock market in October 1929 brought an abrupt end to America's Roaring Twenties. Looking back from the present, this traumatic event can also serve as a convenient break in America's religious history. The 1920s had been the decade of highly publicized controversy between fundamentalists and modernists among the northern Baptists and Presbyterians. It was the decade of the Scopes trial. Most importantly, it was the decade that severely shook the long-held conviction that America belonged in a special sense to white, Anglo-Saxon, and Protestant culture.

In the years between the start of the Depression and the beginning of World War II, other concerns became more important than the fundamentalist-modernist controversy for American Christians. As institutions, the churches passed through a diverse mixture of experiences. In theology, American believers hardened some positions, modified others, and took on still others from European influences. Only in their response to public events did the churches show much similarity, for—with a few notable exceptions—Christians during the 1930s exerted little obvious influence on the national scene. This alone sets the Depression era off from the religious history that had gone before and much of which was to follow.

The Torn Social Fabric

Franklin Delano Roosevelt was elected to a staggering task. Economic life was in chaos. Between July 1, 1929, and July 1, 1931, 2,193 banks closed, unemployment rose to 16.1 percent, and the gross national product tum-

bled precipitously. During the Thirties, more than 300,000 southern blacks moved to northern cities only to find that jobs were scarce and white discrimination was often as blatant as in the South. In the North, moreover, blacks lost the supportive family structure they had known previously. The deprivations they suffered were enormous, and the effects were destructive. But blacks were not alone in their suffering. Between 1931 and 1936, more immigrants returned to lands from which they had come than arrived on American shores.

President Roosevelt, sensing a failure of nerve, a collapse of morale, in the country,

With the failure of material security in the Great Depression (below and right), many believed that only a sturdy faith could see them through the economic crisis. BILLY GRAHAM CENTER

instituted his famous fireside chats on the radio. He sought to rally public opinion in support of a remarkable array of legislation, much of which was sent to Congress in his first one hundred days in office. There can be no question that the public life of the nation entered a new phase with FDR's New Deal. Government began to take unprecedented responsibility for the well-being of American citizens and for the preservation of the social structure. As it did so, church people mostly stood on the sidelines—some to cheer, some to harass, but most without much to say, despite the fact that the government was assuming many of the responsibilities which the churches had traditionally shouldered.

To be sure, some of the country's more liberal denominations urged the government to take vigorous economic and social action even before Roosevelt became president. And when the New Deal began, it was applauded by the Protestants' Federal Council of Churches as being a political fulfillment of the social gospel. Reinhold Niebuhr, in fact, wanted the president to go further. As a spokesman for the Fellowship of Socialist Christians (founded in 1930), he called for a far more radical restructuring of society, charging that the New Deal was piecemeal and ineffective.

The New Deal received a different kind of

Neither the individual nor the race is improved by alms-giving.

ANDREW CARNEGIE,
June 1889

attention from the other side of the political spectrum. Premillennialist evangelist Gerald B. Winrod saw a plot behind Roosevelt's "Jewish New Deal" and rallied fundamentalists in opposition to it. In fact, in the election of 1936, the majority of Protestants voted for Roosevelt's opponent, Republican Alf Landon. They saw the New Deal as the brain child of political radicals who were really intent upon destroying capitalism and "traditional American values." They also viewed Roosevelt as subservient to big-city interests and unduly receptive to Roman Catholic concerns.

The New Deal excited all of the worst fears and prejudices among the more politically conservative Protestants, but the furor it provoked was not productive. Roosevelt was reelected in 1936 in a political landslide. Although he had jeopardized much Protestant support, he was endorsed three to one by blacks and, additionally, carried the Roman Catholic and Jewish vote.

Probably the most important religious voice during this time belonged to a Detroit Catholic priest, Fr. Charles Coughlin. Coughlin had been a successful radio preacher before the Crash, but this event had led him to comment increasingly on national affairs. He first supported FDR, but then turned against him for the president's failure to cure the nation's ills. His proposals called for greater national regulation, but his appeal was to the old, the poor, and the powerless for whom all had gone wrong in the 1930s. And he appealed to the prejudiced. Heard by ten million people a day, he fanned the flames of anti-Semitism. Significantly, Coughlin enjoyed little support from official Catholic sources, even for those views which were responsible. But the same could be said about religious support for most of the era's politically involved figures. They spoke not for the mass of Christians, who evidenced little stomach for public affairs, but mostly for themselves.

Father Charles Coughlin (1891–1979), popular radio demogogue of the 1930s, shown during one of his broadcasts and shortly before his death (inset) RELIGIOUS NEWS SERVICE PHOTO

Seattle brewers demonstrate in favor of the repeal of prohibition in a 1932 "beer parade." THE SEATTLE TIMES

This is not to say that Christians remained on the sidelines altogether during this period. Protestant fears about the pope had played some role in defeating the presidential bid of Catholic Al Smith in 1928. And many churchmen were involved in efforts to forestall further widespread warfare. The effort, of course, failed as did the crusade against the repeal of Prohibition.

In 1931, Herbert Hoover's attorney general George Wickersham had reported that Prohibition was unenforceable. In December 1933 the Twenty-first Amendment was ratified, ending the "noble experiment." The defeat of Prohibition not only signalled a triumph of urban over rural values, but it also frustrated those who had striven to have their moral principles accepted as the nation's law. Coupled with the failure to oust Roosevelt from office in 1936, the defeat of Prohibition put a considerable damper on those conservative Christians who had sought to remake national life in their own image. But it is also true that for most Christians, the 1930s became a breathing space in religious involvement in American public life.

The Depression may have had an impact on the churches in one other area. The intense patriotism of World War I and the end

to free immigration in the 1920s had begun to push the "immigrant churches" closer to the American center. With fresh migration cut off and with consciousness heightened about being American, these groups had begun to set aside some of their distinctiveness. This process may have been retarded by the Depression. To be sure, immigrant churches did reach out further to their fellow Americans during the decade. The Missouri Synod's "Lutheran Hour," for example, was

"Now will you be good?" Sunday closing laws remained in effect in much of the nation at a time when religion had less and less impact on public affairs. LIBRARY OF CONGRESS

one of the pioneering radio ministries in the country as the scholarly Walter Maier preached his message of Law and Gospel over hundreds of radio stations—in English. Yet the Depression also encouraged immigrant groups to remain on their own. Why race to join a society that was not working? Why reach out to strangers when economic uncertainties demanded the faithful support of tight-knit communities? World War II and the passing of foreign-speaking older generations would hasten Americanization for these groups. But for the decade of economic crisis that process moved more slowly than before, and, in retrospect, did not move as far as it even appeared at the time.

How the Churches Survived

For mainline Protestant denominations, the 1930s proved to be a difficult decade. This was so in spite of the fact that they enjoyed a good measure of internal unity. For Baptists and Presbyterians in the North, the boiling controversies of the 1920s had been reduced to a simmer that would not heat up again for a generation. The Congregationalists, Methodists, and Episcopalians had become liberal denominations with only small minorities of active theological conservatives. Southern Methodists (who rejoined the northern body in 1939) and Presbyterians continued to be united around more conservative convictions than their northern counterparts, in theology and social values alike. But in spite of unity, these older denominations suffered greatly from the difficulties of the era, especially its economic collapse and the resulting ideological uncertainty.

It was these less conservative and dominantly northern denominations which passed through a "religious depression," the counterpart to the economic disaster affecting the whole country. Northern Baptists, Methodists, and Presbyterians lost two percent of their membership between 1930 and 1935, their financial support evaporated, and many of their pastors left the ministry.

Other less well-connected groups, however, knew better how to redeem the times. The fundamentalists may have been vanquished in the denominations, but this did not stop them from sustaining a thriving variety of evangelistic, educational, and mis-

sionary activity. Entire bodies of theological conservatives were also alive and well. Such groups excelled on at least two accounts that mattered dearly in the 1930s—they knew how to provide a religious home for ordinary people and how to proclaim a convincing Christian interpretation of daily life. To cite just two kinds of churches, the Southern Baptists grew from slightly less than 3.8 million members in 1929 to over 5.2 million in 1941, while Seventh-day Adventists increased even more rapidly, from 112,000 to 181,000, during the same period. The urban black churches of the North, the older holiness bodies, as well as the newer pentecostal groups both black and white also belied the accepted picture of religious stagnation by making rapid strides during the decade.

But this was also a time of institutional retrenchment and reshaping within fundamentalism. The cause of theological conservatives in the mainline denominations was not always a happy one. In the nineteenth century, conservatives had been able to flex

J. Gresham Machen (1881–1937), intellectual leader of the conservative evangelical cause

Religious Memberships and Affiliations
The Five Largest Groups in 1935

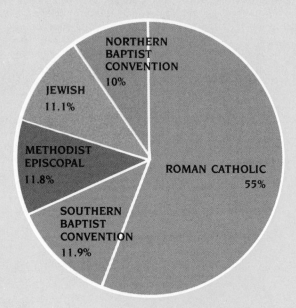

NORTHERN BAPTIST CONVENTION 10%

JEWISH 11.1%

METHODIST EPISCOPAL 11.8%

SOUTHERN BAPTIST CONVENTION 11.9%

ROMAN CATHOLIC 55%

NOTE: Membership statistics should be regarded with caution. Groups employ different methods of numbering members as well as varying theological considerations in determining what constitutes membership. These figures, then, should be viewed only as providing a general picture.

their muscles theologically. Thinkers who were viewed as too liberal, like Preserved Smith, Albert Barnes, and Charles Briggs, were tried. By the Thirties, the tide had changed. Gresham Machen, who had provided theological leadership for the conservatives in the Presbyterian Church, U.S.A., provides an example. He was expelled from his denomination for refusing to disband the Independent Missions Board which supported conservative missionaries. Out of this expulsion was born the Orthodox Presbyterian church. Already the conservatives in the Northern Baptist Convention had been forced by theological pressure to break off from their

parent denomination. In 1933 the General Association of Regular Baptists had been formed. These developments were indicative of much broader trends. Not all conservatives left their older denominations, but there was a strong move in this direction.

At least from the point of the media, it was the liberals' Federal Council of Churches which spoke for Protestant Christendom. The fundamentalists, by retreating from the established denominations and throwing over any further desire to shape the fabric of social life through political involvement, had forfeited a public presence. The virulent anti-intellectualism which often emanated from fundamentalist enclaves only encouraged the press in thinking that this was not a movement to be taken seriously.

In point of fact, fundamentalists were thriving in their isolation. Through a network of educational institutions, such as their Bible schools, their barrage of the airwaves through revered preachers such as Charles Fuller of "The Old Fashioned Revival Hour," and a cascade of books, pamphlets, and journals, they sustained their beliefs and enlarged their numbers. They were ignored as a political force, and most of them had long since ceased to influence the direction of the older denominations, but it was foolish to discount their presence.

It is perhaps surprising that Roman Catholicism flourished institutionally during the 1930s as well. But then it must be remembered that its support was to be found mainly in the immigrant settlements in the large cities. These were the people who were affected first and most by the Depression. They turned to the church for help and they found it. In 1932, when the nation's school-age population was 20 million, no fewer than 2,605,500 young people were enrolled in Catholic parochial schools. The National Catholic Welfare Conference effectively coordinated relief work among those hardest hit by the Depression. And during the Thirties Catholics emerged as a significant political force. Al Smith was defeated in 1928, despite Catholic support, but Roosevelt sensed the political power which Catholics represented. After he was elected president, he appointed fifty-one Catholics as Federal judges out of a total of 196 appointments. By contrast, the previous three presidents had appointed a total of only eight Catholics. And it was Catholic support that accounted in part for Roosevelt's reelections.

The Aftermath of Protestant Controversy

JOEL CARPENTER

The problem of recovery which gripped the American people during the 1930s profoundly shaped the Protestant churches. In this age of social uprootedness, economic collapse, and political insecurity, what was the "American Way of Life"? What was worth remembering and preserving? The Protestant churches had been torn by controversies both within their ranks and in the culture at large, and now their major problem was recovering a sense of purpose. With increased competition from secular concerns and amusements, how could people be convinced that church was worth their time?

As Robert T. Handy has shown, most of the old-line denominations entered the Depression in an already depressed state. Ministers and denominational leaders sensed a demise in status and authority. Church attendance and membership declined, missions and social agencies slashed budgets, ministers' salaries averaged the same as garbage collectors', and people turned for leadership and counsel from the clergy to businessmen, scientists, and psychologists.

During the 1930s many liberal churchmen blamed themselves for this crisis. Their failure to educate laity and preachers in modern religion, they thought, caused the fundamentalist-modernist controversy. Harry Emerson Fosdick admitted another failure: liberals had abdicated their prophetic role by embracing modern culture. "We have been all things to all men long enough. We have adapted and adjusted ... long enough. We have at times ... talked as though the highest compliment that could be paid to Almighty God was that a few scientists believed in Him."

To recover a prophetic stance, leading theologians such as Reinhold Niebuhr, H. Richard Niebuhr, and Edwin Lewis moved to the right theologically and to the left politically, toward biblical theology and preaching, a renewed appreciation of the church, and a critique of capitalistic civilization. Yet the neo-orthodox movement was resisted by many liberals and was not easily understood by the laity. Most Protestants had only a depressed liberalism or a vigorous yet discredited evangelicalism from which to choose.

Meanwhile, fundamentalists and other evangelicals had become alienated toward much of urban America, prone to conspiratorial thinking, and encased in their own subcultures. In the wake of the battles over religious and cultural modernism they were stereotyped as ignorant, contentious reactionaries and argued among themselves over strategies of separation from the world. Fundamentalists contributed to Protestant fragmentation as some of them stayed within the older denominations while others formed new sects such as the Regular Baptists and Bible Presbyterians, and still others became entirely independent.

Evangelicals did not become totally isolated, however. Their vigorous evangelism made them leaders in the national religious recovery of the 1940s and 1950s. In stark contrast to the old-line denominations, evangelicals thrived during the Depression. Pentecostal denominations, black and white, and holiness Wesleyans such as the Church of the Nazarene were doubling and tripling in size. Southern-based conservatives such as the Southern Baptists and ethnic Protestants including the Lutheran Church –Missouri Synod grew steadily. But the fundamentalists – millenarian evangelicals of Baptist, Presbyterian, and independent churches – most visibly and vocally represented the evangelicals.

Fundamentalists led in adopting such culturally responsive evangelistic techniques as radio programs and youth rallies to capture popular interests. Charles E. Fuller's "Old Fashioned Revival Hour," for instance, played on more stations than any other single-release prime-time broadcast in 1939. Their agencies such as the Sudan Interior Mission and Moody Bible Institute expanded their activity and support while old-line denominational programs contracted.

By the early 1940s, under fundamentalist leadership, the evangelical party consolidated its strength by forming a National Association of Evangelicals and by laying foundations for a revival. Religious recovery came, but from fragmented churches in a fragmented culture where no one establishment could speak for all Americans.

New Churches of the 1920s and 1930s

J. GORDON MELTON

Two factors provided the dynamic in the continually changing scene in American religion during the 1920s and 1930s. First, after World War I, mobility increased dramatically. Many young adults took advantage of the new rail tracks and highways spanning the nation to find new homes and new lives. Second, when they moved, they found their way into the cities. In 1920 for the first time, more Americans were urban dwellers than residents of small towns and the countryside. Within the city people could always be found to share new beliefs, and neighbors did not care what church one attended. Thousands of black people, who were among the most mobile of this new displaced generation, deserted the rural South and created the northern urban ghettos.

To meet the new world they encountered, this generation created almost two hundred new churches and religious bodies to replace the older churches they left behind. Thus they considerably widened the religious options open to individuals. They also turned in large numbers to smaller church bodies formed in earlier decades and made them significant denominations. Benefiting most from this shift of church membership were the holiness and pentecostal churches, which became national forces.

Holiness churches grew out of the post-Civil War revivals. They taught the possibility of individual sanctification given to the believer as a second definite act of grace. The gift of sanctification was made visible in a life of love and holiness. Members of holiness churches placed great stress upon personal discipline and morality.

Pentecostalism, which emerged within the holiness movement, grew out of a search for the "sign" of sanctification and assurance of the indwelling of the Holy Spirit. It found that sign in the gift of speaking in tongues, glossolalia, and in the presence of the gifts of the Spirit — healing, prophecy, and miracles. For pentecostals, a definite shift of emphasis toward a stress upon religious experience (without giving up the stress on holy living) became the distinguishing feature of their life.

Both holiness and pentecostal churches became known for their free, emotionally expressive worship style, a factor that led to condemnation from both ministers and scholars of the more staid denominations and from social scientists. In fact, these churches represented the Methodist alternative to the fundamentalist movement of the previous generation which was Calvinist in theology. In returning to their fundamentals, Methodists found their roots more in piety and religious experience than doctrine.

The phenomenal growth of pentecostal and holiness churches can be seen by comparing the membership figures (as reported to the U.S. Census) of several major bodies:

HOLINESS CHURCHES	1926	1936
Church of God (Anderson, Indiana)	38,249	56,911
Church of the Nazarene	63,558	136,227
Christian and Missionary Alliance	25,930	43,536

PENTECOSTAL CHURCHES		
Church of God (Cleveland, Tennessee)	21,377	52,206
Pentecostal Holiness church	8,096	12,955
Assemblies of God	47,950	148,043

Spiritualism also experienced one of its sporadic growth periods following World War I. It was built around mediums who claimed the ability to contact psychically the spirits of the dead, and has flourished after each major war as bereaved families sought contact with deceased loved ones. The modern era of spiritualism really began in 1893 with the formation of the National Spiritualist Association. Other associations soon followed, but more than ten were formed in the period after the war.

Spiritualist activities centered on the seance in which "spirits" talked through the medium, bringing information about loved ones or discourses on the nature of the spirit world. While continually plagued with outside accusations of fraud, spiritualists fought over the different teachings of various mediums. New associations disagreed over reincarnation, the compatibility of spiritualism and Christianity, and the emphasis within some associations of mediumistic

Father Divine (George Baker, 1878–1965), the flamboyant founder of the enormously popular Peace Mission   BILLY GRAHAM CENTER

phenomena such as materialization, floating trumpets, and apports.

Finally, groups arose which served black people as a means to declare their new freedom as well as their increased aspiration to participate fully in American culture. One major focus of the new spirit of liberation, Marcus Garvey, a West Indian black, formed the International Negro Improvement Association and from his New York City headquarters called for black people to unite around a sense of racial consciousness and pride.

This new militancy found expression in a variety of urban black religious groups. George McGuire, an Episcopal priest and member of Garvey's ITIA, received Old Catholic orders and founded the African Orthodox church as a black alternative to both Episcopalianism and Roman Catholicism. Islam offered blacks a dignity denied by many American churches. Still other black people found their own story in reading the biblical account of the Exodus and declared themselves Jews. One black Jewish group, the Church of God and Saints of Christ, jumped from 6,741 members in 1926 to 37,084 a decade later.

Capturing the imagination and attention of the ghettos of the depression era, Father Divine and his Peace Mission symbolized most clearly the plight and hope of black people. The Peace Mission, beginning as an offshoot of the New Thought Movement, called members to demonstrate in the midst of poverty the prosperity and abundance of God's presence. Increasingly seeing Father Divine as the embodiment of that presence, the Mission offered both black and white victims of the Depression a new start.

These many new groups of the 1920s and 1930s did not die after their period of success. Rather they settled down to a stable life, became a permanent part of the American landscape, and prepared to find new surges of life when time once more favored them.

Catholics and the American Nation

DAVID J. O'BRIEN

When Maryland's John Carroll was appointed first bishop for the Catholic church in the new nation of the United States, his flock numbered only some 25,000 persons scattered from Indian villages in Maine through French trading centers in the Ohio Valley to the more settled plantations of Carroll's family and friends. In 1960, when Pope John XXIII announced the Second Vatican Council, American Catholics numbered over 40 million, and they were the richest, best organized, and most diligent practicing Catholics in the world and the largest Christian community in the United States. The years that followed the Council were to be marked by controversy, division, and a marked decline of church attendance. Nevertheless, anyone familiar with the Catholic church's creative adjustment to the "strange new world" of America over two centuries might have had a justified confidence that Catholics would overcome even the turmoil occasioned by the most profound challenges to its traditional way of life.

The story of American Catholicism is entwined with the history of European immigration. John Carroll's tiny church, enriched by a succession of notable converts, grew slowly until, in the 1840s, it was overwhelmed by masses of Irish and German refugees, so that by the time of the American Civil War the much-feared Catholic church was the nation's largest. After the war, they continued to come, from Ireland, Germany, Quebec, and, after 1890, from Italy and the polyglot lands of eastern Europe. Immigrants and working people, Catholics provided the manual labor for an industrializing America, and they were the urban poor. Without landed endowments or wealthy families, they were forced to build churches for themselves; in a country without organized public services, they had to provide hospi-

tals and orphanages, homes for the aged and protectories of young men and women. Even more remarkably, they built schools, academies, colleges, and local parish elementary schools, staffed heavily by religious men and women, paid for by the sacrificial offerings of the people themselves. Catholicism was a people's church, its worship and community life linking each group to old world traditions and the historic faith, but always with a part of itself invested in the American future. Immigrant Catholic communities may have appeared to be ghettos to outsiders, but inside they were filled with celebration of new freedoms enjoyed and marked by eager anticipation of a better life, freer and more secure, where men and women could and would be loyal both to the faith of their forebears and the land of their new opportunity.

Catholicism was a mosaic church, each parish and institution marked by the character of its constituency. United under pastoral bishops and a vigorous and increasingly disciplined clergy, the church contained a bewildering variety of devotions and rituals, languages and organizations reflecting the differing cultures and historical experiences of its many nationalities. Its apparent foreignness, in both faith and culture, along with its evident unity and the poverty and occasional anger of its people, regularly excited the fears and anxieties of natives. Recurrent waves of anti-Catholicism served to unite the church, for Catholics knew they were outsiders, both because they were immigrants and because they were Catholics. Cultural conflicts over Prohibition, birth control, education, and politics reinforced minority consciousness in each generation, climaxing with the presidential campaign of Catholic Alfred E. Smith in 1928. Yet these conflicts helped unify the church and provide Catholics

THE

KU KLUX
KLAN

HOLDS

That Any Man Who

KNEELS

Before His Fellow-Man

KISSING

Hand or Ring

Will Do The

BIDDING

of That Fellow-Man

The Klan relied on nativist bigotry, asserting that Roman Catholics, in their devotion to Rome, were not true Americans. BILLY GRAHAM CENTER

with a distinctive identity, a distinctiveness reinforced by the cultural and organizational separatism fostered by the hierarchy in the twentieth century.

In a series of events at the end of the nineteenth century, the nation's bishops brought greater organizational coherence to a Catholic culture previously centered on the parish. In 1899 Rome condemned practices aimed at too rapid an assimilation of Catholics to the American mainstream, while the condemnation of modernism by Pope Pius X put a blanket on critical scholarship for two generations. The commitment to parochial schools, formalized at that time, was designed in part to instill a sense of loyalty and religious unity among the laity. The appointment of a permanent Apostolic Delegate from Rome in 1893 tightened ties between bishops and the Vatican and inhibited the definition of a distinctive role and mission for the church in the United States. Church leaders never challenged America's separation of church and state, and they actively encouraged the political independence of their people. In addition, they placed no barriers in the way of trade union organization, and they actively encouraged the economic advancement of their people. Bishops were champions of American nationalism in war and of moderate liberal reforms in peacetime. Yet, this very Americanization might jeopardize the unity and coherence of the church, so the boundaries of the Catholic subculture were clearly defined. Religious separatism, even self-righteousness, characterized Catholic relations with other Christians. Catholics were warned of the evils of public school education, mixed marriages, and religious indifference. They were encouraged to socialize with one another, to attend church-related schools, to read Catholic magazines and newspapers, to identify with Catholics in other nations suffering persecution at the hands of Communists.

In its fascination with material success, its organizational genius, its powerful and symbolic concrete structures which marked the skyline of every urban neighborhood, the Catholic church showed its Americanness. In a different way, its rigid clerical structure, its insistence upon dogmatic uniformity and a moral orthodoxy rooted in natural law, not pragmatism, and its pattern of distinctive behavior, Friday abstinence from meat, rejection of birth control, and demand for weekly church attendance all showed an equally American need to specify the boundaries of identity, to fix and root persons within a distinctive subculture in a self-conscious strategy for survival arising out of America's incredible diversity and mobility.

In the years of the great depression, American Catholicism was a church of working-class people, who welcomed the New Deal's efforts to reduce unemployment and relieve the plight of those in need. The bishops endorsed New Deal reforms, and Catholics became a solid component of the Roosevelt coalition in the Democratic party. Thousands of Catholics joined the new CIO unions, and the church backed their cause, supporting the National Labor Relations Act and assigning priests to work with the unions. Liberal on domestic policy, Catholics and their bishops tended toward isolationism in foreign policy and clashed openly with American liberals over the Spanish Civil War. In a decade of social unrest, Catholics shared with other Americans the sense of crisis. Dorothy Day and Peter Maurin founded the Catholic Worker movement to practice the works of mercy and contribute to renewing the entire social order. Msgr. John A. Ryan, director of the bishops' own social action office, championed New Deal reforms and called for greater governmental intervention to assure that private capitalism resulted in justice for all Americans. While the 1930s were a decade of social activism, the church remained religiously conservative, and many Catholics remained preoccupied with preserving the faith, attacking supposed threats to Christian morality in secular society, and achieving a greater degree of respectability and success. Toward the end of the decade anticommunism began to provide a means of blending patriotism, loyalty to the church, and distinctive identity, and it would exert a powerful influence on American Catholicism in the years following World War II.

The success of Catholicism's pastoral strategy, and evidence of how closely it was related to the needs and hopes of masses of Catholics, was seen in the years 1945 to 1960. The Catholic population doubled in less than a generation, and the numbers of priests and religious increased even more rapidly. Aided by the GI Bill and the postwar prosperity, masses of Catholics left urban neighborhoods for the automobile suburbs, there to build churches and schools that were not Irish or French or Italian, but Catholic and American. Colleges and universities thrived in those years, and the Catholic press boomed. By the time Pope John made his momentous decision, American Catholicism had arrived. The historic goals of retaining the faith of millions of immigrants while achieving acceptance and respectability in American society had been fulfilled.

Success, however, always exacts a price. For Catholics acceptance and respectability, now taken for granted, have loosened the ties of the old subculture. A new kind of Americanization has taken place. Ecumenical understanding with other Christians, more democratic forms of participation in church life, the independence of an educated laity, and a renewed emphasis upon the mission of the church to redeem, and thus free, all men and women, has opened new horizons of Catholic consciousness. In the process, however, individual Catholics have become more aware of their ability to choose their own religious identity and to define for themselves the terms of their affiliation with their church. Pluralism, once the environment to which Catholicism had to adapt, has now become a precondition for life and work within the church itself. To affirm the value and the faith of each person, and at the same time to set boundaries which can define a distinctive Catholic identity and purpose, these are the new challenges confronting Catholicism in the United States. Catholics once faced the American nation as outsiders, hoping to become part of the national community. Now that they are inside, they will, whatever they do, help shape the future of their church and of the nation.

Patterns of Belief

The numerical strength of theological conservatives was not, however, matched by a comparable vigor in conservative theology itself. Fundamentalists continued to affirm the propositions for which they had done battle in the 1920s. These propositions combined historic Christian orthodoxy, the distinctive forms of nineteenth-century Protestant evangelicalism, and the newer emphases of dispensationalism. While a great deal of fundamentalist writing appeared during the 1930s, it was mostly popular in style, directed more toward the faithful than toward the public marketplace of ideas. Fundamentalist publications illustrated again how the movement had become a cognitive minority which sought to define itself over against the world at large. In the area of thought, this definition involved the rejection of everything that smacked of biblical criticism, evolution, or social radicalism. Critics of fundamentalism now regularly labeled it an antiintellectual movement. Surprisingly, the fundamentalists did not protest. In so doing, however, they obscured their own debt to the carefully developed theologies of the nineteenth century on which fundamentalism still rested. In short, if there was a religious depression for the fundamentalists in the 1930s, it was in the world of thought.

The only conservatives who made long-lasting theological contributions during this period were the ethnic confessionalists. Groups such as the Lutheran church–Missouri Synod and the Christian Reformed church retained the vigor of a strong European heritage, but did so only by minimizing contacts with the wider world of American theology. The *Christian Dogmatics* (1917-1924) of the Missouri Synod's Franz August Otto Pieper was a forceful statement of conservative Lutheranism which served his denomination and other Lutherans well during the 1930s. But it was published in German. The *Reformed Dogmatics* (1932) of Louis Berkhof provided a similar reservoir of theological insight for the Christian Reformed church. Yet although Berkhof published this work in English, it had little immediate impact beyond the Dutch immigrant community in which he moved.

The story of the liberal branches of Protestantism was quite different. Liberals were caught within a relentless vise. On the one side was a romantic theology which heralded a benign deity and encouraged confidence in human nature; on the other were the country's economic collapse and the rise of European nazism, two events which exposed the romanticism on which liberalism was predicated.

Protestant modernists, like their Catholic counterparts in England and Europe a generation before, argued that cultural assumptions and Christian presuppositions were not opposed to one another. The essence of faith, it was felt, was to achieve a synthesis between them. Harry Emerson Fosdick argued typically that Christianity took "the intellectual culture of a particular period as its criterion and thus adjusted Christian teaching to that standard." As late as 1928, when the writing was already on the wall for those who had eyes, the Federal Council of Churches seriously argued that, with the help of science, a new industrial order would evolve characterized by righteousness and peace.

The collapse of liberal ideas was as rapid as the social order on which they had rested. In 1933 ethicist John Bennett declared that "the most important fact about contemporary theology is the disintegration of liberalism." And by 1935 a chastened Fosdick was arguing that the time had come to go "beyond" modernism. Now he was critical of its confidence in inevitable social progress and its absorption of the reality of God into purely subjective feelings and the natural order.

This shifting of mood coincided with the visit to North America of the Swiss neo-orthodox theologian Emil Brunner in 1928 and the emigration of Paul Tillich in 1933, hounded from his German homeland by the Nazis. And the massive theological reconstruction entitled *Church Dogmatics* by Swiss theologian Karl Barth began to be published in its revised edition in 1932, albeit in German. They all heralded a radically different mood.

Brunner and Barth were not fundamentalists. Neither believed in the doctrine of inspiration maintained by fundamentalists nor affirmed Jesus' resurrection as they did, and neither had any interest in fundamentalist schemes of prophecy. They had both been reared as Protestant liberals, but for both the First World War had shattered their optimism about social progress. Moreover, both began an offensive against liberal ideas. In *The Mediator* (first published in German, 1927), Brunner demolished liberal christology, showing that the liberals' Christ was merely a profoundly religious person and not God incarnate, and that Jesus had died merely as an example rather than a substitute for sinful humanity before a God who was really angry about sin. Together Brunner and Barth reasserted the forgotten doctrine of fallen human nature. Barth was especially ferocious in arguing not only that all the capacities and facets of human nature are perverted by sin but even that the "image of God" itself has been destroyed. There is, therefore, no means by which we are able to find God in ourselves or in the world. He is not there. And he cer-

Emil Brunner (1899–1966) and Karl Barth (1886–1968) together in 1960   KARL BARTH ARCHIVES

tainly is not to be confused with human religious feelings as the liberals were prone to do. God cannot be "found" by human effort; it is God who finds mankind as he breaks through in revelatory insight. The inbreaking occurs in conjunction with reading or hearing the written Word of God, but this knowledge can never be the result of simply learning about God in the Bible. It is a directly God-given knowledge to which the Bible is but a witness. Liberals in Europe complained loudly that Barth's thought was simply an expression of a "wartime mentality" and a reversion to the Dark Ages; but it also happened to provide the tools for understanding the inhumanity of the First World War. Barth's famous commentary on Romans (1919), in which most of these ideas were first broached, itself marked the demise of European liberalism.

With the onslaught of the Depression in the 1930s, Americans experienced at a psychological level something comparable to what had happened in Europe. H. Richard Niebuhr roundly castigated the liberals for teaching that "a God without wrath brought men without sin into a kingdom without judgment through the ministration of a Christ without a cross." Both he and his brother Reinhold had themselves been shaken by the Depression and had become skeptical about the vaunted values of Western civilization. They were not fundamentalists either, but their ethical vision keyed into many of the older Protestant concerns about a supernatural order and the fallenness of all human nature.

Like the Niebuhrs, Paul Tillich shared many of the concerns of the European neoorthodox such as Barth and Brunner, but he was also greatly enamored of Heideggerian existentialism. So, on the one hand, Tillich could argue against the liberals that God is not identical with religious feeling; he is so transcendentally removed that mankind can know nothing about him as he is in himself. Humans can speak of him only in symbols. But at the same time, while not being personal, he is the "ground" of all being. And, as a matter of fact, he is revealed in world history in general and in the Christ in particular. This Christ, however, is not identical with the historical Jesus about whom virtually nothing is known. The important thing

Paul Tillich (1886–1965)
RELIGIOUS NEWS SERVICE PHOTO

is how Jesus surrendered himself to the "ground" of his being. Mankind should do likewise. In so doing people are healed of those inner divisions, those psychological fractures, which is what Tillich considered sin. For Tillich the incarnation, atonement, and resurrection are events which are endlessly repeated in the life of those who seek the healed and authentic existence; they are not unique to Jesus himself. Tillich had less use for traditional theology than Barth, Brunner, or the Niebuhrs. But he still represented a more subdued vision of human possibilities than had prevailed before 1930 among American liberals.

While Protestants adjusted various forms of nineteenth- and twentieth-century thought to the 1930s, American Catholics were looking further back into the past for theological foundations. During this period a neo-scholastic synthesis, rooted in the thought of Thomas Aquinas, became the dominant influence among Catholic thinkers. The vague modernism that had enjoyed a brief moment in the sun at the turn of the century was no longer visible. Now American Catholics were exerting their greatest efforts at providing intellectual, ecclesiastical, educational unity to the church. Neo-Thomism—which stressed the authoritative teachings of the church, the value of disciplined reasoning, and the unifying spirituality of the sacraments—offered a welcome ballast for the burgeoning, but still largely immigrant Catholic community. Summarizing its comprehensive aspirations for Catholic thought, the Catholic Educational Association said in 1933 that "because a materialistic attitude and philosophy have dominated secular education, giving it a divided and distorted view of life, from which God and morality have been excluded, the Catholic colleges emphatically assert that their function is to give a totality of view regarding life, in which God and the things of God have their proper place." During this era Catholic theologians sought no rapprochement with modern thought. They saw their duty, rather, in preserving the best of the past, and providing their community the stability of a consistent picture of the world.

In this, they bore a striking formal resemblance to the fundamentalists. Catholics and fundamentalists differed markedly on specific Christian doctrines, but both had—at least for a time—resolved to practice the life of the mind on their own, without presuming to talk to or for America as a whole.

Ethnic and cognitive enclaves, however, have been assaulted by a variety of influences which have made the preservation of the old ways difficult. The mobility brought by the automobile provided a new freedom in going to church. The parish church lost its monopoly on the neighborhood. Whereas in 1916 only three million owned cars, by 1929 this had swelled to twenty-three million. On the Catholic side in particular, social mobility had a special impact. In the early decades of the twentieth century Catholics were objects of suspicion to many Protestants and, beyond question, suffered discrimination in business and politics. That began to change in the 1930s.

The Church Must Go Beyond Modernism

If we are successfully to maintain the thesis that the church must go beyond modernism, we must start by seeing that the church had to go as far as modernism. . . .

In the intellectual culture to which modernistic Christianity adapted itself, such lush optimism was a powerful factor, and the consequences are everywhere present in the natural predispositions of our thought today. . . .

For example, modernistic Christianity largely eliminated from its faith the God of moral judgment. To be sure, in the old theology, the God of moral judgment had been terribly presented so that little children did cry themselves to sleep at night for fear of him and of his hell. Modernism, however, not content with eliminating the

excrescences of a harsh theology, became softer yet and created the general impression that there is nothing here to fear at all . . .

. . . Because I know that I am speaking here to many minds powerfully affected by modernism, I say to you as to myself: Come out of these intellectual cubicles and sentimental retreats which we built by adapting Christian faith to an optimistic era. Underline this: Sin is real. Personal and social sin is as terribly real as our forefathers said it was, no matter how we change their way of saying so. And it leads men and nations to damnation as they said it did, no matter how we change their way of picturing it. . . . And because I have been and am a modernist it is proper that I should confess that often the modernistic movement, adjusting itself to a man-centered culture, has encouraged this mood, watered down the thought of the Divine, and, may we be forgiven for this, left souls standing, like the ancient Athenians, before an altar to an Unknown God!

On that point the church must go beyond modernism. We have been all things to all men long enough. We have adapted and adjusted and accommodated and conceded long enough. We have at times gotten so low down that we talked as though the highest compliment that could be paid Almighty God was that a few scientists believed in him.

... Fundamentalism is still with us but mostly in the backwaters. The future of the churches, if we will have it so, is in the hands of modernism. Therefore let all modernists lift a new battle cry: We must go beyond modernism! And in that new enterprise the watchword will be not, Accommodate yourself to the prevailing culture! but, Stand out from it and challenge it!

HARRY EMERSON FOSDICK,
1935

Karl Barth Speaks

Human Nature

But the trouble in which we find ourselves lies still deeper and extends still further. The true, the real trouble we are in, my dear friends, consists quite simply in the fact that man is as he is and cannot make himself any different. He is the cause of his own trouble. He suffers from himself. "O man, bewail thy great sin," an old hymn says. Man is a fallen, perverted being. It is not a matter of the sins which we have committed and are committing, but of the sin from which all sins come and so of the particular trouble in which all our troubles, the personal and general ones, have their source, just as weeds cannot help growing again and again from a weed root. Man himself is the true, the real trouble. Anyone who does not know about that does not really know what trouble is: even if he sighs ever so loudly and touchingly and complains about what is causing trouble to him personally, even if he is ever so angry and despairing about what he reads in the paper.

The Bible

It is not the right human thoughts about God which form the content of the Bible, but the right divine thoughts about men. The Bible tells us not how we should talk with God but what He says to us; not how we find the way to Him, but how He has sought and found the way to us; not the right relation in which we must place ourselves to Him, but the covenant which He has made with all who are Abraham's spiritual children and which He has sealed once and for all in Jesus Christ. It is this which is within the Bible. The Word of God is within the Bible.

Jesus Christ

The Christian message about Him — and without this it is not the Christian message — is established on the certainty that He is responsible for it, that He as the truth speaks through it and is received in it, that as it serves Him He Himself is present as actuality, as His own witness. He Himself by

His Spirit is its guarantor. He Himself is the One who establishes and maintains and directs the community which has received it and upon which it is laid. He Himself is the strength of its defence and its offensive. He Himself is the hope of freedom and enlightenment for the many who have not yet received and accepted it. He Himself above all is the comfort, and the restlessness, and yet also the uplifting power in the weakness of its service. In a word: the Christian message lives as such by and to the One who at its heart bears the name of Jesus Christ. It becomes weak and obscure to the extent that it thinks it ought to live on other resources. And it becomes strong and clear when it is established solely in confidence in His controlling work exercised by His Spirit; to the extent that it abandons every other conceivable support or impulse, and is content to rest on His command and commission as its strength and pledge. ... But, again, it is He Himself who bears this name that has called and led and drawn them [His community], and it is as that happens that it is given to them, too, to pass on to others their report of actuality as such. Therefore the One who shows and persuades and convinces and reveals and communicates from man to man that it is so, "God with us," is the One who bears this name, Jesus Christ, no other, and nothing else. That is what the message of the Christian community intends when at its heart it declares this name.

The Niebuhrs

MALCOLM A. REID

Reinhold (1892-1971) and H. Richard (1894-1962) Niebuhr were born in Missouri and educated in the college and seminary of the German Evangelical church and then later at Yale. Following service in their denomination — Reinhold as a pastor in Detroit, Richard as a professor and college president — each began distinguished careers as moral theologians at Union Theological Seminary in New York and Yale Divinity School respectively.

The two brothers shared a deep common concern to illuminate the continuously problematic relationship between faith and history, church and world, Christ and culture. They were both self-conscious and loyal Protestant moralists, yet in numerous books and articles they produced the most sustained and penetrating critique of American Protestantism in twentieth-century theological litera-ture. The younger Niebuhr concentrated his attention primarily on the problem of "Culture Protestantism" and the consequent need for the church clearly to confess its faith in the sovereign presence, power, and goodness of God in all natural and human events. Reinhold, on the other hand, spoke more often and more directly to fundamental sociopolitical problems in contemporary Western societies. Constructively, each worked on, even if they did not to their own satisfaction fully work out, a comprehensive Christian ethic.

Reinhold Niebuhr's social and political thinking was rooted in the following fundamental theological and ethical convictions. Man is finite yet free; his understanding and actions are historically conditioned, yet he is a self-transcending creature; he is full of an inordinate self-love that corrupts all his relations, yet in his person he images the full personhood of God and remains the object of God's covenant love. The salvation of man lies in his repentant acceptance of the grace of God perfectly demonstrated in the self-sacrificial love of Jesus Christ. This love at once fully defines the sinfulness of man and provides the ultimate norm for judging the quality of his individual and social behavior. But precisely because all people deny, ignore, or compromise this ideal it is not by itself a sufficient principle for ordering the moral life. Justice, defined as impartiality between persons and groups, is required to mediate between the

Reinhold Niebuhr (1842–1971)
RELIGIOUS NEWS SERVICE PHOTO

absolute ideal of love and the self-interested power struggles of social groups. The principle of justice by itself, too, is insufficient. Love is required both as the goal toward which justice must move and as the motive for establishing a proximate justice between men. The direct relevance of an ethic of love for effectively ordering political behavior is denied.

Theologically, Richard Niebuhr's basic convictions were three: the being and value of God are ontologically prior to, and transcendent over, all other beings and values; man is a sinner insofar as he denies the sovereignty of God and idolatrously regards some other being(s) as a "center of value" and ultimate object of trust (all selves live by faith in some "center of value" that functions to give existential meaning to their lives); to live by faith in the ultimate trustworthiness of that "God" who is the ground of all being, value, and personhood is a miraculous gift mediated effectively, if not exclusively, through the ministry of Jesus Christ. The question of a person's ultimate trust was also the central ethical issue for Richard Niebuhr. Beyond all the rules, virtues, and vices that may form or deform a person's character is the fundamental ethical question about that "center of value" in relation to which good and evil, right and wrong are defined. Those who "incarnate" this radical faith in all their roles and relations, in all their motives and actions, live as truly "responsible selves" and experience the freedom and the joy of living a fully human life.

World War II and Postwar Revival

From Pearl Harbor to Hiroshima

World War II brought immediate changes to the United States. It finally succeeded, where so many peaceful measures had failed, in bringing the country out of the Depression. It changed permanently the lives of sixteen million citizens who served under arms, nearly twelve million of whom were sent overseas, including some of the 200,000 women who had volunteered for service. The families of the 405,000 who died would never be the same again, and many of the 670,000 who were wounded never fully recovered.

America entered the war only with the greatest reluctance. In August 1928 representatives of fifteen nations had signed the Kellogg-Briand Pact vowing to settle all future disputes by "pacific means" rather than by war. The pact was approved overwhelmingly by the U.S. Senate in January 1929. This was followed by the congressional Neutrality Acts of 1935, 1936, and 1937. Repeatedly in the 1930s church bodies condemned war-mongering. Anyone could see that the First World War had not made the world safe for democracy, the ideal for which the war had been fought. But all of these good intentions were wrecked by the unexpected bombing of Pearl Harbor on December 7, 1941. The following day Congress declared war against Japan, and against Germany on December 11. The one lone dissenter to those votes in Congress was Jeanette Rankin. "Who can say that her vote was wrong?" the *Christian Century* asked. "Only those," it replied, "who know nothing of the anguish with which the Christian conscience of our time is wrenched and burdened by the paradox into which it is thrown by the fact of war."

This paradox of mind, however, seemed to resolve itself quickly as the country threw itself into the war effort. It is true that the overzealous enthusiasm of the First World War was usually not evident during this conflict. But the war had the approval of the overwhelming majority. Even the devastation of Hiroshima and Nagasaki by atomic bombs was supported by eighty-five percent and opposed only by ten percent. Dissent was rare against the war. The civilian Public Service gathered about 12,000 conscientious objectors, and of the 6,500 who went to prison for refusing military service, 4,665 came from the Mennonites alone. Most Christians, however, concluded that the horrors of war were an evil necessarily to be endured if the

---

We are convinced that war has become the supreme enemy of mankind. Its continuance is the suicide of civilization.

Methodist Episcopal church statement, 1928

May we seek always, not that God may be on our side, but that we may be on His side, so that the victory may in the end be His.

Living Church, journal of the Episcopal church, December 17, 1941

greater evil of Nazi domination was to be avoided. So the churches provided chaplains and relief supplies. In a typical response to mobilization, the National Catholic Welfare Conference placed its "institutions and their consecrated personnel" at the service of the country.

If the war's greatest significance abroad was to defeat German fascism and Japanese militarism, its greatest significance at home was to hasten social change. As in World War I, the great migrations of soldiers and their families loosened traditional ties of family, place, and occupation. Sons of agriculture joined sons of industry in the democracy of the barracks. They underwent breakneck training in the technology of destruction, and they traveled much further from home than most would ever have gone on their own. Soldiers who had marched across Europe and sailors who had traversed the Pacific were not always willing to return to the status quo antebellum. When a grateful government made it easier through the GI Bill for veterans to attend college, it only increased the social mobility of the young men and women who had fought the nation's battles.

The war also accelerated the movement of hitherto neglected social groups into the mainstreams of American life. Women, who were called upon to staff the factories and to organize previously masculine domains, were often as reluctant as their husbands and sons to return to traditional forms of life. Blacks, who served in the armed forces to preserve the freedom of the West, were increasingly reluctant to tolerate the frustration which the West's "freedom" brought them. Even during the war, in 1941 and 1942, blacks under the leadership of A. Philip Randolph had made known their grievances, but to little avail.

The social changes which the war hastened had a profound impact on American religion. At home, churches were forced to adjust to the dislocations caused by the war; familiar patterns and habits were shaken, preparing people for the startling changes to come.

On the conservative side, Harold John Ockenga led evangelicals in forming the National Association of Evangelicals in 1942. The year before, Carl McIntire had forged the American Council of Christian Churches to harness fundamentalist energies. The NAE,

Peter Marshall of New York Avenue Presbyterian Church in Washington, D.C., was among the most popular of the World War II era preachers. He is shown at left preaching at an Easter sunrise service in 1942; at right is the line outside his church later that same Easter morning. LIBRARY OF CONGRESS

Chaplaincy at war, hot and cold: prayer service for the dead of an airborne unit in France, 1944 (above); mass in Korea (below, left); church service at a California missile base, 1956 (below, right)   U.S. ARMY PHOTOGRAPHS

Executive Committee of the National Association of Evangelicals meeting in 1942 BILLY GRAHAM CENTER

which included Protestant conservatives unwelcome in strict fundamentalist circles, was not so much a reaction to McIntire's group as a new effort to express an awakening social conscience and to end the scandal of needless division.

The ecumenical movement gathered strength as well. The World Council of Churches was formed in 1948, and as a part of this worldwide movement, the National Council of Churches of Christ was formed in the United States in 1950, succeeding the Federal Council of Churches. The National Council represented 143,000 congregations whose collective membership numbered thirty-three million.

Even the most prescient, however, could not have predicted the course of postwar events. Most obvious was an unprecedented economic boom. The American standard of living had improved only gradually from the founding of the country in 1776 to the outbreak of World War II in 1939. But due to the crash programs of the war and the United States' dominant position worldwide after its closing, the country experienced an economic upturn that brought genuine prosperity to more Americans than ever before. Among other results, it created the suburb and the two-car family. But it also raised expectations for the up-and-coming generation, increased the prestige of education, created vast markets for leisure activities, and made women an important factor in the marketplace. It also had much to do with the postwar religious revival.

The Churches and War
KEVIN CRAGG

American church leaders on the eve of World War II overwhelmingly inclined toward a pacifist position. The embarrassment from the churches' close identification with Wilson's "War to End Wars" still rankled. Only a few voices suggested that the evils of fascism then engulfing Europe might demand more of the church than moral denunciation. On the whole, American churchpeople supported a neutralist, isolationist perspective, many denouncing President Roosevelt's efforts to aid hard-pressed Britain.

Pearl Harbor changed those attitudes virtually overnight. A defensive (therefore just) war allowed most clergy to lend their support to the war effort. There were fewer illusions about this war radically altering the state of the world; rather, it was seen as a grim but necessary undertaking. Clergy participated in various ways; a vastly expanded chaplain corps required cooperation among religious bodies, as well as sufficient clergy to serve the spiritual needs of the armed forces (8,000 served as chaplains). Local churches at embarkation centers and transfer points offered coffee and counsel as well as worship. Many who experienced combat found themselves severely dependent on God, giving rise to such slogans as "God is My Co-Pilot," "There are no atheists in foxholes," and "Praise the Lord and pass the ammunition." Many in the stress of battle dedicated themselves to Christian service, and after the war there was a significant increase of interest in missions, fueled by the experiences of men who had "been there."

The Cold War with the Soviet Union brought renewed fear and loathing by Christians of the godless materialism espoused by the dominant Communist party. The search for domestic subversives, characterized as the McCarthy era, tended to cast suspicions on anyone, including Christians, concerned for social justice and economic reform, and in some circles the term "liberal" was used in opprobrium not for theological positions, but for attitudes on the application of the gospel. Nuclear weapons brought a ghastly new dimension to war, and so efforts to preserve peace became important for numerous Christians. Many hoped that the U.N. might offer a forum to solve disputes without war; and, indeed, the limitation of the Korean conflict to conventional warfare and its negotiated ending served partially to justify that hope. The Korean action itself was treated by most Christians as just war, and there appears to have been little dissent or discussion of its implications for Christians.

The U.S. involvement in Vietnam (1960-1974), on the other hand, provoked a major conflict of conscience among American Christians of all persuasions. The moral ambiguity of the war was further clouded by questions of its legality under both the U.S. Constitution and international law. Attitudes among Christians were not simply polarized between prowar "hawks" and propeace "doves," but were graduated finely along a spectrum, differentiated by questions of methods or goals of the conflict. And attitudes changed. According to polls, in 1965 a sixty-percent majority of Americans essentially supported the war effort. By 1970, a similar percentage thought the war was a mistake. Evidence suggests that church members followed a similar, though more hawkish pattern. A vocal segment of Christian clergy, morally disquieted by the war, actively engaged in peaceful protest and dissent, coordinated by the organization, Clergy and Laymen Concerned about Vietnam. Fewer clergy vocally supported U.S. policy, and they grew fewer as the war went on. The largest portion of American Christians — both clergy and laity — were not outspoken on this issue. There was substantial criticism of clergy who were socially active (not just in antiwar protests, but also in civil rights agitation). Although most Christians active against the war were theologically liberal, the leading evangelical political figure of the day, Sen. Mark Hatfield of Oregon, was an early and persistent critic of administration policy.

The general turmoil over this war forced many Christians who previously had assumed that the U.S. would only pursue just wars to reexamine that trust. Some denominations had to face the issue of selective conscientious objection to wars, with all the complexities that entails (the United Church of Christ favored such selectivity). Historic peace churches, such as the Mennonites, received considerable attention for the consistency of their positions. As the U.S. entered the 1980s, with the likelihood of a reinstitution of the military draft, a renewed discussion of the church's relationship to war was to be expected.

The Ecumenical Movement

ROBERT G. TORBET

The ecumenical movement is aimed at achieving unity and cooperation among all Christians. In a sense, it is an effort to reverse the trend of separation that occurred during and since the Reformation of the sixteenth century. For many, the World Missionary Conference at Edinburgh in 1910 marked the beginning of the movement in its modern form.

In the century prior to 1910, instruments developed for efforts in this direction included: (1) interdenominational societies for mission and social action; (2) an Evangelical Alliance in England (1846) and an American branch (1867); (3) worldwide confessional bodies: Lambeth Conference (1867), Alliance of Reformed Churches (1875), World Methodist Council (1891), Baptist World Alliance (1905); (4) ecumenical organizations to serve youth: YMCA (1844), World Alliance of YMCAs (1855), Christian Endeavor Society (1881), YWCA (1884), World Alliance of YWCAs (1894), World Student Christian Federation (1895).

In the United States, the Federal Council of Churches of Christ was organized in 1908 to provide a Protestant witness on religious and social questions. Following World War I, the Interchurch World Movement of North America (1919-1920), established to raise $376 million for postwar relief and reconstruction, failed in reaching its goal, but led to increased support for the Federal Council of Churches.

Following the Edinburgh conference of 1910, the ecumenical movement developed internationally along three lines. First was the organization of the International Missionary Council in 1921 to facilitate cooperation between sending and receiving churches. Second was the Life and Work movement, inspired by Swedish Archbishop Nathan Söderblom (1866-1931) to engage the churches in a stronger witness in the secular order through world conferences at Stockholm (1925) and Oxford (1937). Third was the Faith and Order movement, initiated by the American Episcopalian bishop Charles Harold Brent (1862-1929) to enable frank discussion of doctrinal issues in world conferences at Lausanne (1927) and Edinburgh (1937).

Participants in the Oxford and Edinburgh conferences of 1937 laid plans to unite their respective emphases in a World Council of Churches strong enough to resist the growing threat of totalitarian ideologies and secularism. Their plans led in 1938 to formation of a provisional structure which functioned on an interim basis throughout the war years (1939-1945) and until the World Council of Churches was formally constituted in Amsterdam in 1948. In 1961 the International Missionary Council was merged with it, bringing together unity and mission, the two major concerns of the ecumenical movement.

The World Council of Churches not only provided an instrument of ser-

Speaker's rostrum at the WCC Assembly in Evanston, Illinois, in 1954. The Greek word "oikoumene" means "the whole inhabited earth" and refers to the universality of the church. RELIGIOUS NEWS SERVICE PHOTO

vice to meet postwar needs, but inspired formation of continental and national councils where such did not yet exist. In the United States, the number of state and city councils of churches multiplied from a combined total of 58 in 1940 to 328 in 1960. In 1950, organization of the National Council of Churches of Christ in the U.S.A. brought together twelve interdenominational agencies. It became a center of cooperation for twenty-nine denominations in evangelism, education, pastoral work, home and overseas mission, social service, and social action.

American support of the World Council of Churches came mainly from a coalition of churches that were also members of the National Council of Churches. It took the form of financial aid for refugees and war-stricken churches, participation in theological studies conducted by the Council's Commission on Faith and Order, cooperation in the international missionary channels afforded by the Council, and engagement in a constructive political witness in relation to the United Nations and human rights.

The decade of the sixties, troubled by racial conflict and an unpopular war in Vietnam, was a testing time for the churches. The National Council responded to the social unrest by aligning itself with the Civil Rights movement, by helping to establish an antiwar protest, and by supporting migrant farm workers in their struggle for economic justice. The World Council's Fourth Assembly at Uppsala in

WCC officials at Soldiers Field, Chicago, in 1954. Left to right, they are Dr. W. A. Visser't Hooft, Dr. Marc Boegner, Bishop G. Bromley Oxnam, Archbishop Athenagoras, Bishop B. K. A. Bell, and Bishop Eivind Berggrav. RELIGIOUS NEWS SERVICE PHOTO

1968 adopted a Program to Combat Racism, which proved to be as controversial in some Western churches as it was reassuring to Third World churches. At the same time, both World and National Councils sought within their respective structures to develop an open system with adequate representation of minorities, and to balance biblical and theological positions with a continuing commitment to social justice.

Meanwhile, conservative evangelicals opposed membership in these Councils out of fear that it would result in compromise of doctrinal convictions, a loss of ecclesiastical freedom, and sacrifice of evangelism to social action. Many sought ecumenical relationships in the National Association of Evangelicals (1942), the American Council of Christian Churches (1941), or the World Evangelical Fellowship (1951). A significant group of younger evangelicals, dismayed by moral decadence in national life, were calling in the 1970s for faithfulness both in evangelism and in fulfilling the social implications of the gospel.

Roman Catholic participation in the ecumenical movement was enabled by the Vatican's formal recognition of it when Pope John XXIII, in 1960, established the Secretariat for Promoting Christian Unity that in turn prepared the Decree on Ecumenism adopted by Vatican Council II in 1964. This led in 1965 to the forming of a Joint Working Group Between the Roman Catholic church and the World Council of Churches, and in 1966 to the creation by the American bishops of a Commission for Ecumenical and Interreligious Affairs.

The ecumenical movement has also been expressed in a number of denominational mergers, including the United Church of Canada (1925), the Church of South India (1947), and twenty-six mergers in the United States between 1906 and 1968. A still unconsummated effort to unite nine churches is the Consultation on Church Union begun in 1962.

Revival and Civil Religion

The foundation of the religious resurgence after the war was the "Baby Boom," a fifty-percent increase in the birth rate between 1948 and 1953. This was followed by a surge in Sunday-school attendance: 24.6 million (1945), to 30 million (1950), to 38.6 million (1956). And church membership as a proportion of total population went up correspondingly: forty-nine percent (1940), to fifty-seven percent (1950), to sixty-one percent (1955), to a peak of sixty-two percent (1956). What this signified, however, is not entirely clear.

Sociologist Will Herberg contended that this increase in religious interest had less to do with religious commitment than it did with being American. Religion had become a part of the American way of life. It was indulged as one might a harmless habit. "The typical American," he charged, "has developed a remarkable capacity for being serious about religion without taking religion seriously."

Being serious about religion frequently went hand in hand with being serious about three other matters. First among these was affluence. Contrary to expectations, the country emerged from the war with astonish-

... with the rapid spread of content-less religiousness, the very meaning of religion in its authentic sense may be lost for increasing numbers.

WILL HERBERG,
1960

The official emblem adopted by the National Council of Churches in 1955 NATIONAL COUNCIL OF CHURCHES

ing economic strength. In 1939 the gross national product was a mere $91 billion; by 1948 it had climbed to $226 billion. After the deprivations of the war years, the new affluence seemed like pennies from heaven. Americans went on a spending binge. In 1950 alone, they purchased no fewer than eight million automobiles. The possibility for ordinary Americans to own homes replete with washing machines and gadgets had become a reality. And it began to affect the way people looked at life. This abundance of goods and services created materialistic appetites and the values to justify them. And those values coexisted peacefully with a benign religiosity.

The second important factor was a renewed pride in being American. It was a pride that expressed itself abroad and at home. In 1947, when the Soviet Union was intimidating West Berlin, the United States spearheaded the Allied airlift to the beleaguered city. And in 1950, in another effort to contain communism, American soldiers once again went to war. Although the conflict between North and South Korea was relatively contained, it still cost 33,629 American lives. Being American meant that one was anti-Soviet; it also meant that one was religious. The phrase "In God We Trust" became the country's motto and in 1954 the words "under

God" were added to the Pledge of Allegiance. "Our government makes no sense," President Eisenhower declared, "unless it is founded on a deeply felt religious faith—and I don't care what it is."

Being American, moreover, also meant supporting traditional values. Nowhere did these seem more threatened than by covert Communists allegedly plotting the overthrow of the country. Roman Catholic Senator Joseph McCarthy made it his special mission to ferret out subversives, claiming, in the late 1940s, that he had a list of Communists working in government. As it turned out, there was even less to McCarthy than met the eye. His lists were phony. But by the time his popularity had crested in 1954, security checks had been run on no fewer than 6.6 million people. His bullying tactics on the House Committee on Un-American Activities ruined reputations and harassed thousands of people. McCarthy, however, did not lack the tribute of imitation. Less important figures also engaged in similar accusations. Fundamentalist Cart McIntire, for one, labeled Bishop G. Bromley Oxnam and the

Methodist Bishop G. Bromley Oxnam (1891–1963), head of the NCC during the 1950s
METHODIST INFORMATION SERIVCES

National Council of Churches as Communists. Thus did McIntire fuse together an antipathy toward liberalism, a loathing of communism, and a prejudice for things American.

The third factor in this resurgence of religion was the increasing mobility of American society. In the affluence of the postwar era, a large number of people were able to buy automobiles and move to the suburbs which housed twenty-seven percent of the population in 1950 but grew to thirty-seven percent by 1970. Suburbanites looked for an antiseptic environment where neither poverty nor congestion corrupted and thieves did not break in and steal. They did not bargain for detachment, sterility, or loneliness. But in spite of shared backyard fences, suburbs only offered a little sense of community. For better or for worse, the cultivation of affluent privacy also affected the style of suburban Christianity.

The resurgence in religion, then, had a strong core of civil piety to it. Blended together indiscriminately were religious attitudes, American patriotism, affluence—which came to be viewed as a "right"—and that kind of privacy which sheltered suburbanites from many of the harsher facts of life.

It was not difficult, consequently, to be ignorant of what was happening in the cities. It was an ignorance whose price was extracted later, in the 1960s and 1970s. For beginning in the 1940s, there had been a steady migration from the countryside toward the cities. Each year brought in upward of one million people. In the 1950s, 800,000 left the farms each year and headed for urban areas. Here the poor congregated, often in ethnically defined areas, frequently out of work, and commonly powerless to change their circumstances. Small towns have had their frustrations, as chronicled, for example, by Sinclair Lewis in his *Main Street* (1920) or Sherwood Anderson in *Winesburg, Ohio* (1919); these frustrations, however, cannot be compared to the sense of desperation which the urban poor have felt in recent decades. The "good life" of the suburbs, with its decent religiosity, has been closed to them. And religion has fared poorly in the cities.

New York, if not a model of other cities, has nevertheless exemplified some common trends. Between 1960 and 1980 it lost eleven percent of its population. But among Protestants, church membership dropped by fifty-three percent. Episcopalians, heavily hit by the city's eroding financial status, lost fifty-

By the 1960s, comfortable suburban piety had lost touch with the increasing despair of the urban poor.
BRUCE DAVIDSON/MAGNUM

seven percent. Some churches made gains but not those tied into the white establishment. Among New York Protestants, eighty percent now are black, ten percent hispanic, and only ten percent are white.

Few phrases have been used in so many different ways as "civil religion." Whatever it means—whether a basic Christianity overloaded with patriotism or a basic nationalism garnished with Christian concepts—it was flourishing in the 1950s. But it flourished most among those who had something to lose. It was not unrelated, then, to the broader political situation—the Cold War, Mao Tse Tung's conquest of China, the United Nations "police action" in Korea, the Russian invasion of Hungary, and the launching of Sputnik. The international crises compounded the insecurities of postwar America. Public faith, it seemed, had to reassure citizens not only that peace was possible from God but also that the American way of life could be saved.

A different aspect of this resurgence can be seen upon observing its dominant religious figures. They were, inevitably, people of the media. They knew how to exploit radio, television, movies, and the printed word to bring their message to the people. Foremost in this group was Billy Graham, who continued a revival tradition stretching back into colonial days even as he cultivated it to fit the postwar world. Graham had many rivals among the traveling evangelists, but his real peers were media figures who did not fit into traditional categories of either parish minister or itinerant revivalist. Of these a New York pastor and a Catholic scholar were most important. Norman Vincent Peale was a Methodist until, in 1938, he became minister of New York City's Marble Collegiate Church, a congregation of the Reformed Church in America. From there he issued a series of best-selling books, including *The Power of Positive Thinking* (1952), which guided millions of Americans in their search for inner peace. Msgr. Fulton J. Sheen, longtime speaker on radio ("The Catholic Hour") and eventually an effective television orator, performed with similar success from a Catholic perspective. Bishop Sheen held a theological doctorate and was on the faculty of the Catholic University of America, but these distinctions did not prevent his speaking

forcefully and persuasively to the public at large. These public figures enjoyed widespread visibility, access to high places, and respect from the humble and the exalted. Their eminence spoke eloquently of a new place for religion in American life.

If one sees in these men the continuation of the older revival tradition, then its adaptations to contemporary culture were very large indeed. Only in Billy Graham could one catch a faint echo of Jonathan Edwards' unabashed Calvinism—that God alone can save the sinner, for the sinner cannot turn to God on his own. Only in pronouncements of the National Council of Churches such as those against segregation in 1952 could one hear an echo of Finney's call for public righteousness. And none of the new leaders was as brash as Billy Sunday or as rhetorically innovative as George Whitefield.

The postwar revival flourished as much as a response to psychological and national crises as to religious and moral ones. Norman Vincent Peale led the others in offering rest, hope, and—above all—peace amidst the changes and stresses of modern life. This need produced a parade of successful "peace" books which began with Rabbi Joshua Loth Liebman's *Peace of Mind* (1946), but soon went on to include Peale's *Guide to Confident Living* (1948) and *The Power of Positive Thinking* (1952), Sheen's *Peace of Soul* (1949), and Graham's *Peace with God* (1953). A great deal of Protestant orthodoxy remained in Graham's message, as did traditional Catholicism in Sheen's. Yet these succeeded where other, more strident voices did not, in part because they could adapt their message to a society which warfare and affluence were turning upside down.

These leaders also adapted their message to a sense of international crisis. Billy Graham's first radio broadcast of "The Hour of Decision" in 1950, for example, featured a traditional appeal for prayer, repentance, and moral reform. But it also included a rendition of the "The Battle Hymn of the Republic," a reading of nationalistic texts (including Proverbs 14:34 and 2 Chronicles 7:14), and stern warnings from Graham about "the tragic end of America" and the "hour of tragic crisis all across the world." Other religious leaders were just as insistent that the only way to save America was to return to God.

Civil Religion

SYDNEY E. AHLSTROM

The term "civil religion" is usually attributed to Jean Jacques Rousseau, who asserted in *The Social Contract* (1762) that an essentially religious commitment of the people was necessary to the maintenance of public order. The concept, however, has been defined in countless ways, especially in the United States where an enormous literature on the subject has arisen.

Most elementally, civil religion is an affection for place and the related manifestations of commitment, reverence, duty, love, and nostalgia that constitute a collective religious syndrome. It can arise in many times, places, and contexts: a locality, a region, political jurisdiction, or an ethnic group. It will be more deeply felt if nourished by a rich culture and a long tradition, and still more deeply if threatened by enemies, in which case a resort to violence or war may ensue. On the other hand, it may be a benign and beautiful sense of obligation such as that expressed by the Roman poet Horace: *Dulce et decorum est pro patria mori* (to die for the fatherland is sweet and becoming).

In Western civilization the most distinctive and powerful source of civil religion is the absolute claims of the Hebrew scriptures that God had chosen the Jews as an elect nation for whom a holy land had been set apart. Almost as fateful was the claim of the early Christian church to be God's New Israel. Due to the universalism of Rome and the Roman Catholic church, however, the full force of these claims did not emerge until the Protestant Reformation precipitated the rise of religio-political territorialism. In this new context the Calvinistic, Reformed, and English Puritan traditions revived many Judaic beliefs and practices.

With the accession of Queen Elizabeth in 1558, John Foxe, the Marian exiles, and other radical Protestants assigned the role of an elect nation to the English church and people, but under King James I the stricter and more militant Puritans concluded that God's New Israel should be established only in America. To that end they founded several Bible commonwealths and gradually shaped a new and revolutionary civilization in America. Midst the millennial fervor of the Great Awakening, Jonathan Edwards and many others would proclaim that the kingdom of God was coming first to America. Thus, to a degree the ultimate American hope is akin to those of Israel and some Moslem states. In 1763 the Treaty of Paris

The bicentennial provided the occasion for this and similar declarations that America was a chosen land.
BILLY GRAHAM CENTER

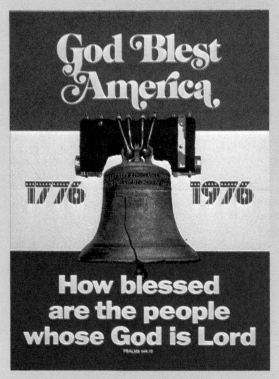

God Blest America.

1776 1976

How blessed are the people whose God is Lord

PSALMS 144:15

enlivened this hope by returning to Protestant hands the vast Catholic empires of France and Spain in North America. Because the Treaty had the further effect of estranging the colonies from British rule, it also ushered in the Revolutionary era. Most remarkable in the long course of events that finally led to the inauguration of George Washington in 1789 was the way in which the Founding Fathers often justified their deeds in the rhetoric of elect nationhood and the principles of the Puritan Revolution.

The new nation was the providential kingdom; its destiny was manifest. On this basis the civil religion became a potent force in the unification of an increasingly pluralistic nation, whether celebrated in a formal religious manner or in a thoroughly secular way. For nearly all Americans this civil religion provided the substance of the country's patriotic tradition, and it flourished all through the nineteenth century and beyond.

By the time of the war with Spain even the South, hitherto a land of the Gentiles, returned ideologically to the Union. Not until the 1960s and 1970s would stresses of governmental scandal, racism, imperialism, and mounting inequality drain it of its former power. If it is to regain its former status, America must recognize that justice is the first virtue of government. The loyalty and national affection of a people are chiefly sustained by fairness, equality, and social compassion.

Billy Graham

DAVID EDWIN HARRELL

Organized revivalism in America, delineated in its modern forms in the 1830s by Charles G. Finney, reached its culmination in the career of Billy Graham. In his hundreds of crusades Billy Graham has been beheld personally by more people than any other human in history, over 50 million. He has traveled nearly everywhere, made the acquaintance of nearly everyone of importance, and become the personal friend — and sometimes the advisor — of every American president since Harry Truman. He has received countless honors, and in a poll conducted by *Christian Century* to determine the number of religious leaders known to American Christians, Billy Graham was first, sixty-two percentage points ahead of his next colleague.

Born in 1918 on a farm near Charlotte, North Carolina, William Franklin Graham was reared in a pious home in a God-fearing community. Trained in a series of evangelical schools, by 1946 the committed young evangelist had joined a new evangelistic movement called Youth for Christ. In

Billy Graham (1918–   )   BILLY GRAHAM CENTER

1949, Graham conducted a tent revival in Los Angeles which caught the attention of William Randolph Hearst. Hearst, purportedly because Graham was obsessed with fighting communism, issued an order to "puff Graham," and the national publicity that followed launched the evangelist's national career. By 1980, Graham still conducted several campaigns a year; he also reached millions of people through a nine hundred-station radio network, several special telecasts a year aired on more than three hundred stations, *Decision* magazine which had a circulation of over four million, a syndicated column which appeared in more than two hundred newspapers, and a number of other ministries including books written by Graham and the production of motion picture films.

Graham's remarkable success, as that of earlier revivalists, seemed to have rested upon his clear and simple evangelistic message, an efficient organization, and the evangelist's attractive and charismatic personality. First gaining national publicity during the orderly conservatism of the 1950s, Graham's message and his character seemed to fit the mood of the times. But, remarkably, Graham remained through three radically different decades an immensely popular figure, surviving a damaging friendship with Richard Nixon and a charge in the 1970s that his organization had unethically shielded a large fund.

Through all of this, Billy Graham changed very little. His message remained remarkably the same, though he became sufficiently less literal in his biblical interpretations to alienate some conservatives. But the center of Billy's message remained the sinfulness of man, the necessity of conversion, and the anticipated splendor of heaven. Nor, apparently, did Billy Graham the man change much, a

Graham, pictured here with television host Johnny Carson, has become a familiar presence in American culture, perhaps the most well known religious figure of this age. BILLY GRAHAM CENTER

fact that more than any other explains his continued hold on the affection of the people. Clearly not a man with exceptional intellectual gifts, Graham won over many potential critics with his apparent humility and transparent sincerity. In the minds of many of the common people, Billy represents not only a preacher, but a model Christian, a man who could do what others wish they could do. "To me," said Graham's mother to his biographer Marshall Frady, "he lives almost a divine life."

Graham has been a major force in evangelical Christianity throughout the world through the work of the Billy Graham Evangelistic Association and through his support of such evangelical institutions as *Christianity Today* and Wheaton College. Entering the 1980s Graham seemed as committed as ever to preach the gospel throughout the world, his popularity undiminished, his audiences still large and enthusiastic. Some talented newcomer lurking in the wings might take American revivalism to new heights in the future, but for the moment no other religious figure in American history could come close to rivaling the popularity and prestige of Billy Graham.

Have You HEARD
The Young Man With A Burning Message?

Evangelist
Billy
Graham

Student Evangelist of the FLORIDA BIBLE INSTITUTE
Temple Terrace, Tampa, Florida

BILLY GRAHAM

Beginning SUNDAY, AUG. 14
AT THE
Capitola Baptist Church
REV. A. V. PICKERN, Jr., Pastor

Services **EVERY NIGHT AT 8:00**
Dynamic Preaching = Good Music

Your Neighbors Will Be There
—Why Not **YOU?**

A flyer from early in Graham's career; his message has changed remarkably little.   BILLY GRAHAM CENTER

The Psychology of a Frustrated Soul

During the war the Holy Father said that the postwar man would be more changed than the map of postwar Europe. It is this postwar, frustrated man, or what we will call the modern soul, which interests us in these broadcasts. This interest is heightened by the fact that the modern soul presents a new problem in technique to the Christian theologian for two reasons: (1) It no longer is interested in going to God through nature, and (2) it is imprisoned inside itself with its anxieties, fears, and worries. Let me explain. In other generations, man went to God through nature. Looking out on the vastness of creation, the beauty of the skies, and the order of the planets, man concluded to the power, the beauty, and wisdom of God who created and sustained the world. The modern man is unfortunately not using the approach for several reasons: (1) He is impressed less with the order of nature than he is with the disorder of his own mind; (2) the atomic bomb has made him realize that man can use nature to destroy man and even to commit cosmic suicide; (3) finally, science of nature is too impersonal. Not only does it make man a spectator of reality instead of

Monsignor Fulton J. Sheen, popular radio and television preacher of the 1940s and 1950s, at high school dedication; Francis Cardinal Spelman of New York is at left. RELIGIOUS NEWS SERVICE PHOTO

man now thinks of himself as limited to the surface of the earth — a plane whereon he moves not up to God nor down to Satan, but only to the right and left. The theological division of men into those who are in the state of grace and those who are not, has given way to the political one of whether man is a rightist or a leftist. The modern soul has definitely limited its horizons; having negated the eternal destinies, it has even lost its trust in nature, for nature without God is traitorous. Where can modern man go now that a roadblock has been thrown up against every external outlet? Obviously, like a city in war which has had all its outer ramparts seized, man must retreat inside himself. As a body of water that is blocked turns back upon itself, collecting scum, refuse, and silt, so the modern soul which has none of the outside securities of the Christian man, backs up upon itself, and in that choked condition collects all subrational, instinctive, dark, unconscious forces which would never have existed had there been the normal exits of more normal times. Man finds he is locked up within himself as his own prisoner, and he himself is the jailer. Imprisoned within himself, he now attempts to compensate for the loss of the three-dimensional universe of faith by finding three new dimensions with his own mind. Above his conscious level, in place of heaven he substitutes his own ideals, totems and taboos which he calls a superego. Below his consciousness, in place of hell he substitutes unconscious biological sexual instincts which he calls the id, although there are some who would call this hell their heaven.

its creator; it also demands that the personality never intrude itself in investigation. But it is now personality, not nature, which is the problem.

This does not mean that the modern soul has given up God but only that it has abandoned the more rational and even more normal way of finding Him. Not the order in the cosmos, but the disorder in himself, not the visible things of the world, but the invisible frustrations, complexes, and anxieties of his own personality, is the modern man's starting point of religion. In more happy days philosophers discussed the problem of man; now they discuss man as a problem. Formerly, man lived in a three-dimensional universe, where from earth he looked to heaven above and to hell below. With the modern forgetfulness of God this vision has been corrupted to a single dimension;

RT. REV. MSGR. FULTON SHEEN

Americanization

It is significant that Sen. McCarthy was a Catholic. His visibility in defense of the nation signaled how far Catholics had come into the mainstream of American life. For Catholics, the postwar years brought many of the same aspirations, fears, and innovations that their fellow citizens experienced. Historian Philip Gleason has described two important tendencies of these postwar years for Catholics: "mobilization" and "anti-ghettoism." As Protestants organized themselves into new configurations, like the National Association of Evangelicals and the National Council of Churches, so too did Catholics intensify efforts "to redeem all things in Christ," as Pope Pius X had phrased it much earlier in the century. This mobilization led to an enviable record in forming Catholic schools, colleges, service organizations, publications, and learned societies. The stability of these organizations, combined with the effectiveness of public spokesmen like Bishop Sheen, gave Catholics a whole new respectability. Yet this very success led some Catholics to criticize their coreligionists for insulating themselves from American life. These critics espoused a more complete pluralism and called on Catholics to move beyond the religious ghetto. In the late 1950s

Pope John XXIII meeting Brooks Hays (right), former president of the Southern Baptist Convention, in 1961 — the first such formal meeting between a Roman Catholic pontiff and a Southern Baptist leader. BAPTIST JOINT COMMITTEE ON PUBLIC AFFAIRS

and early 1960s, momentum seemed to shift to those who criticized Catholic insularity. At home, John Fitzgerald Kennedy showed how influential a Catholic could become by winning the presidency; abroad, Pope John XXIII seemed to be calling the entire church to the openness which these critics had asked for in America. In short, by 1960 only a few Americans still regarded the Catholics as alien outsiders in the nation's life.

Other Christian bodies that had kept mostly to themselves made a similar movement toward fuller participation in America during this same period. Forced mixing with the broader population during the war, movement from inner-city enclaves to more affluent suburbs, and a gradual loss of European languages led more and more Christians closer and closer to American patterns. This trend was unmistakable among Lutherans, who set aside ethnic differences to form large unified denominations in 1960 (American Lutheran church) and 1962 (Lutheran Church in America). It was also present among the surprisingly large Eastern Orthodox churches which ventured sufficiently far toward the ecclesiastical mainstream as nominally to join the National Council of Churches in the early 1950s.

The experience of these immigrant churches during the 1950s was one other index of important changes in American church life. The social basis of these churches had also felt the strain of World War II and postwar economic growth. They, too, had benefited from the Baby Boom. They, too, came to value the American way of life ever more dearly. They even ventured some contact with the major postwar religious figures. And they were also participating in the redefinition of what it meant to belong to a religious community in the modern United States.

Changes in American society that were altering the older churches of English heritage seemed more dramatic when experienced by the immigrant bodies. In 1850, for example, Irish and German Catholics knew very well the boundaries of their religious communities. They were fortified from the inside by their own leaders and from the outside by suspicious "native" Protestants. The same could be said for Swedish Lutherans in 1890, or for Greek Orthodox in 1925. By 1960, however, the boundaries were somewhat less distinct. Television and radio had done their part to break them down, as had public education, the patriotism of the war, and even the English language. Much that was distinct remained, a fact that the ethnic revival of the 1970s forcefully illustrated. But to be a Catholic, or a Lutheran, or an Orthodox Christian in 1960 was usually to be somewhat less a member of a distinct culture and somewhat more of an American than a generation or two before.

The most important exception to this pattern was the blacks. They remained part of their own culture and that culture remained shut off from the blessings of the new affluence. Ralph Ellison, a black, put it succinctly: "I am invisible, understand, simply because people refuse to see me."

The lot of black people was, in small ways, improved. In May 1954 the Supreme Court struck down the "separate but equal" doctrine on which much public school desegregation was based. President Eisenhower showed his determination to uproot old injustices when he sent federal troops to enforce integration in Little Rock, Arkansas, over the protests of Gov. Orval Faubus. But, a decade later, Martin Luther King, Jr., noted that only nine percent of blacks attended integrated schools.

Education is the key to more skilled and responsible jobs. Because of the comparatively poor education blacks received, they did not have open access to better paying jobs. In 1950 whites on the average earned 2.5 times as much as blacks. It is no surprise that the contrast between black poverty and white affluence should produce frustration and spill out in urban violence in the 1960s.

These eruptions might well have occurred much earlier except for the extraordinary role played by Martin Luther King, Jr. Pastor of Dexter Avenue Baptist Church in Montgomery, Alabama, King had come to prominence as the leader in the bus boycott designed to break the habits of white racism. In 1957 he became the first president of the Southern Christian Leadership Conference, and he was the most prominent figure in the Civil Rights movement (1954-1966). As such, he urged a peaceful resolution to the conflict that was building between the races, one

Troops armed with bayonets escort nine black students to classes at Little Rock's Central High School in 1957.
RELIGIOUS NEWS SERVICE PHOTO

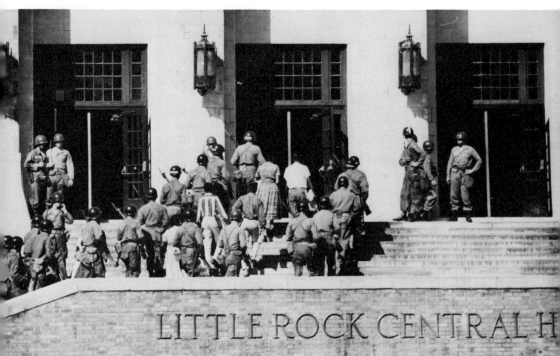

LITTLE ROCK CENTRAL H

Separate facilities such as these in Birmingham, Alabama, represented the racial discrimination that prompted the civil rights activism of the 1950s and 1960s. RELIGIOUS NEWS SERVICE PHOTO

based on equity and justice.

The races, however, barely understood one another. In 1963, ninety-one percent of blacks believed that the "race revolt" was supported by the rank and file of blacks, whereas only thirty-four percent of whites believed this. Whites largely (forty-five percent) blamed the troubles on outside agitators, but few (ten percent) blacks saw it this way. In fact, seventy-eight percent of whites thought that Communists had infiltrated the Civil Rights movement, and only sixteen percent believed that the black unrest was the result of white prejudice. The Kerner Commission, charged with investigating the urban riots of 1965-1967, concluded in 1968, however, that America was heading toward a racially divided society, and it laid the blame squarely on white racism.

The pacific dreams of King were, in time, passed up by more radical blacks. Black Panthers Huey Newton and Eldridge Cleaver as well as Malcolm X, who was assassinated on February 21, 1965, preached a black nationalism which employed violence. In one

In the summer of 1963, the knife of violence was just that close to the nation's aorta.
MARTIN LUTHER KING, JR.

respect this was not new. Blacks had never been able to compartmentalize their faith from their status in society. It was entirely natural and fitting that King and Ralph Abernathy should lead the bus boycott in Alabama. They boycotted as Christians, and they boycotted as blacks. Being black and being Christian defined themselves in terms of each other and sowed the seeds from which "black theology" would later grow. What was new was that black self-interest was being advanced as an end in itself, without regard for ethical concerns and with calculated hatred for white society. This radicalism probably made the leaders of the Civil Rights movement appear far more acceptable to whites, but the possibility of understanding between the races became more remote. Indeed, one of the staple charges later brought against President Reagan's economic policies by blacks was that he sought to bring about economic recovery on the backs of the poor. The fact of the matter is that blacks are still largely shut off from the nation's affluence, and despite the Civil Rights Act (1964) which Congress passed they are still deprived of their rights in many instances.

The presence of religious groups was vividly evident in the 1963 march on Washington for jobs and freedom. RELIGIOUS NEWS SERVICE PHOTO

The Orthodox Churches

STANLEY S. HARAKAS

The Eastern Orthodox church considers itself to be the "mother church" of Christianity. It traces its episcopal, doctrinal, and liturgical life through the centuries to the primitive Christian experience, and it counts Jesus Christ and his apostles as its historical foundation. Its continuity with the past is highlighted by its recognition as binding of the first seven ecumenical councils, the last of which was held in 787. The ninth century was the beginning of the Great Schism which separated Eastern and Western Christianity. Following the Fourth Crusade (1204), the split became definitive and permanent.

It had been the tradition of Eastern Christianity to maintain close bonds with the cultural and ethnic values of its peoples. Thus, in missionary work the Orthodox church used the vernacular in worship, adapted ecclesial practices to local traditions, and fostered the rapid indigenization of mission clergy, including the hierarchy. During the eighteenth and nineteenth centuries, the various local Orthodox churches gave firm support to nationalist movements in eastern Europe.

Eastern Orthodoxy came to the United States primarily through immigration from the traditionally old world eastern European countries. Though it is true that Russian missionaries brought Orthodoxy to the Aleuts in Alaska in 1867, even before it became a U.S. possession, the vast majority of Orthodox in the U.S. are of immigrant stock, who came in large numbers to the U.S. from the last decades of the 1800s through the beginning of World War I.

The decade 1930-1940 found Orthodoxy in the U.S. organized in numerous jurisdictions, based primarily on ethnic lines. Each tended to reflect not only the spiritual tradition of the Orthodox faith as exemplified in its particular land of origin, but also the current political and social upheavals taking place there.

Thus, the Greek Orthodox in the U.S. reflected in their parish and community life the Royalist-Venizelist (Republican) controversies in Greece. During the 1930s the Ecumenical Patriarchate of Constantinople assumed full responsibility in seeking to heal the divisions caused by the controversy. In 1931, Athenagoras Sperou was elected archbishop, bringing into existence the Greek Orthodox Archdiocese of North and South America. He successfully united the Greek-speaking Orthodox into the largest of the Orthodox jurisdictions on the American continent. The leadership of Greek Orthodoxy in the U.S.A. was enhanced upon Athenagoras' election as ecumenical patriarch in 1948, and with the subsequent election of Michael Constantinidies as archbishop of the Greek Orthodox Archdiocese — the first Orthodox hierarch to offer an invocation at a presidential inauguration. Archbishop Iakovos assumed

Orthodox Archbishop Iakovos delivers the benediction at the inauguration of President Johnson, 1965.
RELIGIOUS NEWS SERVICE PHOTO

the leadership of the church in 1959, becoming in practice the spokesman for Orthodox Christianity in the U.S.A. for more than twenty years. The new flood of Greek immigration in the 1960s helped the Greek Orthodox church maintain a bilingual policy for worship and church life.

The Russian Revolution of 1917 also had its consequences on the ecclesial life of the Russian Orthodox in the United States. At least three groups vied for recognition. One group remained loyal to the Patriarchate of Moscow. A second, strongly anti-communist, ethnic, and politically reactionary, is known outside Russia as the Russian Orthodox church. The third and largest of the groups, the Russian Orthodox Greek Catholic Church in America (commonly known as the Metropolia), had achieved de facto recognition from the ecumenical patriarchate. After many years of uncertainty, in a unilateral action not recognized by most of the mother churches, the Moscow patriarchate granted independence (autocephaly) to the Metropolia in 1970. Now known as the Orthodox Church in America, it is actively pursuing a policy of Americanization under the newly elected Metropolitan Theodosius. However, the division of the churches of Russian origin continues.

The Arabic-speaking Orthodox church is also present in significant numbers in the U.S. This was the first of the Orthodox churches to emphasize the use of English under the leadership of Archbishop Anthony Bashir. A schism had developed between the bishops of the Patriarchate of Antioch and the Metropolitan of Toledo, but this ended in 1976. Presently, metropolitan of the Antiochian Orthodox Christian Archdiocese is Philip Saliba. Other canonical Orthodox jurisdictions existing in the U.S. today are the Albanian Orthodox Diocese of America, the American Carpatho-Russian Greek Catholic Diocese, the Bulgarian Eastern Orthodox

church, the Romanian Orthodox Missionary Archdiocese, the Serbian Orthodox Church in the U.S.A. and Canada, the Ukrainian Orthodox Church of America, and the Ukrainian Autocephalic Orthodox Church in Exile.

In varying ways and at varying speeds, all of the Orthodox have taken their place on the American scene. Each jurisdiction agrees to the need for Orthodox unity, though the visions of the nature of that unity vary. In the meantime, the canonical Orthodox churches in North America cooperate through the Standing Conference of Canonical Orthodox Bishops in the Americas under the chairmanship of Archbishop Iakovos. SCOBA encourages Orthodox cooperation, particularly in the areas of campus ministry, education, and youth work. On the agreed agenda of the proposed Great and Holy Council of the Orthodox church, one of the major topics for discussion and resolution is the issue of the future of the Orthodox diaspora, chief of which is Orthodoxy in America.

Iconography executed by American artist in St. Nicholas Greek Orthodox Church, Flushing, New York
RELIGIOUS NEWS SERVICE PHOTO

Prodigals, Come Home!

I have a feeling that somebody ought to join the church tonight. Somebody that's not attached ought to join.
> Yes. *Amen.*

Somebody that never has been a member of a church ought to join.
> *Yes, yes.*

Or somebody ought to deem it necessary to choose First Calvary as his church home. Is there anybody—
> *Yes.*

That has ever been in trouble? Is there anybody here
> *Yes.*

That has a burden on your shoulders?
> *Yes.*

Is there anybody here
> *Yes.*

That has been mistreated?
> *Yes.*

Is there anybody here
> *Yes, yes.*

That has ever been out at night
> *Yes, yes.*

In the cold alone?
> *Yes, yes.*

I don't have any weapons, but I can open a door for you.
> *Yes.*

He can open a door for you.
> *Yes, yes.*

Is there anybody here
> *Yes, yes.*

That's ever gotten lonesome?
> *Yes, yes.*

I want to search them out tonight.
> *Yes.*

If you're out of the church
> *Yes.*

You ought to come home.
> *Yes.*

While the wind
> *Yes.*

Is still blowing,
> *Yes.*

You ought to come home.
> *Yes.*

While the sun is still shining on everything,
> *Yes.*

You ought to come home.
> *Yes.*

While God is still on his throne, you ought to come home.
> *Yes.*

You come on and join us. I'm going to sing for you tonight. You needn't help unless you want to.
> *Yes!*

Excerpt from transcript of a revival led by J. M. Kimball at First Calvary Baptist Church, Knoxville, Tennessee; Eleanor Dickinson and Barbara Benzinger, Revival! (New York: Harper & Row, 1974)

Many black congregations in urban areas meet in storefronts such as these.
PHYLLIS MOUW

Martin Luther King, Jr.

WESLEY A. ROBERTS

Martin Luther King, Jr. (1929-1968), Civil Rights leader, churchman, and Nobel Peace Prize recipient, was born in Atlanta, Georgia, into a prominent ministerial family. His father, Martin, Sr., was pastor of Ebenezer, one of the largest and most prestigious black Baptist churches in Atlanta. By the end of his first year at Morehouse College in Atlanta, Martin decided that he would follow his father and grandfather into the Baptist ministry. He continued his studies at Crozer Theological Seminary (B.D.) and Boston University (Ph.D.). At these two institutions he came under the influence of philosophies that would later shape the direction of his ministry.

King was propelled into prominence in 1955 when, as a pastor of the prestigious Dexter Avenue Baptist Church in Montgomery, Alabama, he led the Montgomery bus boycott against racial segregation. The success of the boycott pushed him into the leadership of what came to be known as the "Black Revolution." Combining the nonviolent methodology of Gandhi and the love ethic of Jesus' Sermon on the Mount, King developed a philosophy and strategy for social change that had world-wide appeal. Taking the position that violence was immoral and self-defeating and could best be counteracted by love, King and his followers submitted themselves to physical abuse and imprisonment in order to dramatize the racial oppression of the black people in America.

King's leadership in the heroic struggle for social justice made a significant impact on American society. Public consciousness was raised with regard to racism, discrimination, and exploitation of blacks. Among some of the achievements of blacks during

Civil rights demonstrators marching in Selma, Alabama, in 1965 WIDE WORLD PHOTO

I have a dream that one day,
on the red hills of Georgia,
sons of former slaves
and the sons of former slaveowners
will be able to sit down together
at the table of brotherhood.
I have a dream that one day
even the state of Mississippi,
a state sweltering with the heat of injustice,
sweltering with the heat of oppression,
will be transformed into an oasis
of freedom and justice.
I have a dream that my little children
will one day live in a nation
where they will not be judged
by the color of their skin
but by the content of their character. . . .
MARTIN LUTHER KING, JR., 1963

his thirteen years of leadership in the Civil Rights movement were desegregation of public facilities, more employment for blacks, access to better housing and better education, and Congress' passing of the Civil Rights Act (1964) and the Voting Rights Act (1965). King received international acclaim in 1964 when he was awarded the Nobel Peace Prize for his civil rights leadership.

The key to King's success as an outstanding black leader was his strong faith commitment to the God of the Judeo-Christian tradition. He possessed the ability to translate faith into action, and to show that social justice was a necessary demand of the gospel of Christ. This won for him the admiration and support of both Christians and non-Christians. Moreover, he was an excellent preacher who could keep his audiences spellbound with his oratorical ability.

When an assassin's bullet ended his life in 1968, America and the world lost one of the few great prophetic voices of the twentieth century.

Martin Luther King, Jr. (1929–1968)   RELIGIOUS NEWS SERVICE PHOTO

The Black Revolution and the Churches

WESLEY A. ROBERTS

The Montgomery, Alabama, bus boycott, led by Dr. Martin Luther King, Jr., in 1955, signaled the beginning of what came to be known as the Black Revolution. This freedom struggle received world-wide publicity as blacks throughout the southern United States organized themselves and waged war against racial segregation and racial discrimination.

Student-led sit-in demonstrations against public accommodation facilities, freedom riders' attacks on segregated interstate transportation, marchers' willingness to face physical abuse, imprisonment, and death to achieve their goals, violent eruptions in several urban centers, and widespread civil disobedience forced Americans to recognize that a social revolution was in progress. Some of the immediate visible results were the passing of civil rights laws, desegregation of public facilities, and opportunities created for blacks in education, employment, housing, and other vital areas.

Although in the latter stages of the revolution violent confrontation replaced nonviolent direct action as a weapon, it is important to recognize the churches' role in this struggle for social justice. The revolution began in the black church under the leadership of a black Baptist clergyman. It received its inspiration from the hymns, sermons, and charismatic leadership of the church, which became the meetingplace for the marchers. Opponents of the freedom movement recognized the important role of the church and directed much of their hostility against it. Many churches were burned to the ground and others bombed. The bombing of the Sixteenth Street Baptist Church in Birmingham, Alabama, caused the death of four little girls and injured scores of others. This cowardly act of violence galvanized the support of the black church community behind the civil rights struggle. Also significant is the role of the Southern Christian Leadership Conference, the primary base of Martin Luther King's operations. It was founded in 1957 at a meeting of some sixty churchpeople, most of them ministers. This organization gave the Civil Rights movement its direction and strategy during its early years, and until his death in 1968 its president was the most powerful voice among black Americans.

One result of the black churches' involvement in the nonviolent struggle

A bomb blast at a Baptist church in Birmingham, Alabama, during Sunday school classes killed four children in September 1963. UNITED PRESS INTERNATIONAL PHOTO

was that many white clergy realized how immoral it was to stand on the sidelines as passive observers or critics. Many of them were shamed into taking direct action. They joined their fellow black clergy in their marches and suffered at least one casualty — the Rev. James Reeb, a Unitarian from Boston. The involvement of various churches, denominations, and the National Council of Churches was demonstrated in the concentrated effort to pass the Civil Rights Bill. Protestants, Orthodox, Catholics, and Jews united in presenting testimony to Congress in support of legislation. Thousands of calls were also made to congressmen and senators by white Christians. It is estimated that more than 40,000 white churchpeople participated in the March on Washington in 1963. The churches were also involved through the volunteers they sent to places such as Mississippi and through direct aid given to the Civil Rights organizations. The white churches' involvement made a significant difference in focusing attention and concern on the black struggle in several places.

In June 1966 the freedom movement changed radically with the defiant cry for "Black Power" by Stokely Carmichael of the militant Student Nonviolent Coordinating Committee. This cry signaled the shift from nonviolent direct action to black power by any means necessary. King and church leaders such as Dr. Joseph H. Jackson, president of the National Baptist Convention, deplored this new trend. Liberal whites in the National Council of Churches were equally dismayed. The black church, however, had to deal with the issue of Black Power. The National Committee of Black Churchmen was organized in New York in July 1966 for this purpose. Its first public statement, entitled "Black Power," was published in The New York Times, July 31, 1966, in order to put the issue in historical and theological perspective. It was a carefully reasoned statement signed by some

Martin Luther King and Malcolm X, although they often disagreed on policies and tactics, met on friendly terms in 1964. RELIGIOUS NEWS SERVICE PHOTO

of the best-known black preachers in America.

Between 1967 and 1969 a number of articles by black scholars sympathetic to the goals of Black Power heralded the beginning of a new era of black theological reflection. Among the more important articles were those by Vincent Harding of Spellman College, Atlanta, entitled "Black Power and the American Christ" and "The Religion of Black Power." However, it was the publication of Black Theology and Black Power in 1969 by James H. Cone of Union Theological Seminary, New York, that inaugurated what is known today as black theology. As the child of the black revolution, black theology provides both a critique and a corrective to white American theological reflection as well as an explication of the ongoing task of liberation for an oppressed minority. The black revolution lasted approximately fifteen years, 1955-1970, but the questions it raised will never die as long as racism and oppression are facts of life for black people.

An Unruly Time
(1960-1980)

Within a generation of its introduction, television had become America's window to the world. This revolutionary medium transformed ordinary citizens into eyewitnesses of the myth-making events of the age. It brought unprecedented marvels (astronauts walking on the surface of the moon), exalted pageantry (Charles, the future king of England, taking his bride Diana), tragic pathos (young John-John Kennedy saluting his father's casket), and angry dismay (wounded soldiers whisked away in helicopters from "pacified" villages in Vietnam). Its extraordinary power allowed it to shape general perceptions of reality. TV excelled at broadcasting the Olympics and national political conventions. It had much more difficulty explaining the importance of sports in America or showing how political slogans sometimes became everyday reality. Its genius for instant analysis—which decreed, for example, that the 1950s were "complacent," the 1960s "turbulent," and the 1970s "nostalgic"—usually opened more questions than it answered. And it had a distressing ability to confound image and reality. The very real horror of Jonestown—slicked up for a month on the nightly news—probably penetrated no more deeply into the national psyche than the celluloid fables of crooks and robbers available every day of each year. Perhaps above all, the television mentality—the penchant to abridge consideration of every issue into the simplified format of the evening news—had difficulty communicating the complex nature of American religion.

Popular coverage of religion during the 1960s and 1970s did fasten upon slogans that spoke of genuinely significant developments.

Yet television, joined by the news weeklies and the impressarios of radio talk shows, could usually do no more than wave these slogans at unexpectedly arresting events. Frequently, in fact, the slogans represented realities which had existed for some time, but only later caught the attention of New York, Chicago, or Los Angeles. So it was that phrases like "New Morality," "Death of God," "Jesus People," and "Born Again" had their brief moment in the media sun before passing back into provincial oblivion. Other catchwords such as "the Age of Aquarius," "the Silent Majority," or that combative pair, "Right to Life" and "Freedom of Choice," also paraded through the vocabularies of the anchorpersons with only the slightest awareness that they, too, reflected a religious dimension. By 1980 the major media had improved their ability to discuss religion, but much of that discussion still went on without careful definition, without meaningful content, and without historical context. Nevertheless, the media had, for many people, become the main source of information on American religion.

The blood we shed in Vietnam makes a mockery of all our proclamations, dedications, celebrations. . . . There are many wild beasts in the human heart, but the beastliest of all is the brutality of arms.
ABRAHAM HESCHEL,
1967

Public Turmoil and Its Aftermath

A combination of events made the church's relationship to society a crucial concern during the 1960s. First in time, and probably in importance, was the Civil Rights movement. Black Americans, after two world wars fought for oppressed people overseas and after nearly two centuries of rhetoric about freedom that never seemed to mean much for themselves, began, as has been seen, to pursue the dream deferred. The Civil Rights movement, which was the most visible aspect of an entire black revolution, greatly altered the consciousness of many Americans. It also posed a challenge to churches, white and black, to rethink their acceptance of traditional American practices (like segregation) and accepted American values (like the assumption of white cultural superiority).

Another shock to the American social system was public violence. During the 1960s historians who recalled the brutality of Indian removal and the mistreatment accom-

Silent protest in Iowa City, Iowa, 1972

panying early industrialization tried to remind the public that violence was as American as apple pie. But their efforts did little to ease concern. The assassination of President Kennedy in 1963 and those of his brother, Robert, and of Martin Luther King, Jr., in 1968 not only changed the political alignments but—for a moment—also the American psyche.

Massive urban violence broke out in Watts, Los Angeles, in 1965. This was rapidly followed by the unleashing of black rage on Detroit, Newark, and Chicago. The social fabric seemed to be unravelling.

But the most sustained violence came from exposure to the Vietnam War. This was the first time in living memory that the civilian population had witnessed warfare, albeit through the television camera, for neither of the two world wars was fought on American soil. What it saw were some of the 50,000 soldiers who died in that faraway land. There was initially some support for the war, but there was little outright enthusiasm. The killing began to provoke a growing outrage at home, with violent social upheaval resulting. Sociologists and historians will ponder the effects of this violence for a long time to come. Whatever they may eventually decide, it certainly is true that it did not leave the country's churches untouched.

Arson, looting, and rioting broke out in cities across the nation following the assassination of Martin Luther King in 1968.
RELIGIOUS NEWS SERVICE PHOTO

We believe that sexual expression, in whatever form agreed upon between consenting persons of either sex, should be considered as an inalienable human right.
JEFFERSON POLAND,
founder of the Sexual Freedom League,
1966

The opposition to the war, however, was as much as anything a search for new values. In the 1960s this search was largely restricted to younger people, but by 1980 it had become a broad cultural phenomenon. Across the entire spectrum of issues, Americans were changing their minds. Symptoms appeared in the flowering of environmental issues, in the challenge to traditional roles which the women's movement posed, in the relaxation of sexual standards and the tolerance of eroticism, in the massive preoccupation with the body beautiful, and, above all, in the search for self and its fulfillment.

Looking Out for No. 1, How To Be Your Own Best Friend, and *Pulling Your Own Strings* were the best-sellers that gave shape to this last search. What these books and their devotees assumed was, as Daniel Yankelovich put it, that the self was simply "an endless series of gratifiable needs and desires." It merely had to be "found" and then to be gratified. What gratified it most was not work-centered orderliness, but freedom from restraint, abundant leisure, unrestricted creativity, and loose spontaneity. All of this assumed that affluence was a "right" which the government was obliged to honor. The postwar inflation showed this psychology of affluence to be at cross-purposes with economic realities. It should also have hammered home the lesson that inner feelings are not sacred, that they cannot fashion an ethical code, and that unremitting dedication to their caprices is self-destructive. Some churches, nevertheless, took up the chorus of selfism. Sanctification became reduced to a matter of adjusting one's self-image, and faith was offered as the best route to self-fulfill-

ment. Christians became one's "support group." Much of this had been pioneered by Harry Emerson Fosdick's *On Being a Real Person,* but in the 1970s it seemed strikingly innovative.

The Civil Rights movement and the Vietnam War, then, were among the most important events leading the country at large to reexamine basic values and to find a moral dimension in public life. But these developments coincided with, or perhaps induced, a widespread rethinking of traditional mores. The plight of the world's starving millions gradually gained greater visibility. The logic of nuclear warfare became increasingly a subject for public debate. Frustration with the national government led to radical proposals for its reconstitution. A new sensibility to public morality eventually drove President Nixon from office for crimes connected with the Watergate burglary and other misdeeds that earlier periods might have passed over as venial mistakes. The same sensitivity was probably a factor in frustrating the presidential aspirations of other would-be candidates, given their dubious social behavior and political involvements. And it may have contributed in other ways to presidential politics. Whatever their actual success or failure in office, presidents Ford, Carter, and Reagan earned considerable respect for the probity of their personal lives. This heightened concern for public morality—which arose during the 1960s and continues to the present—also called for responses from the churches. And rarely did anyone succeed in shielding him- or herself from the deceptions and seductions of television; rarely did even the most cloistered fail to see the deep wounds which the age's traumas had inflicted. The churches were buffeted by social change, but they also sought to guide and counteract it.

. . . this in a nation once notorious for its impatience with inwardness.
DANIEL YANKELOVICH,
April 1980

The Urban Church

RAYMOND J. BAKKE

More people moved north to cities in the twentieth century than moved west to farms in the nineteenth, but the consequences of this massive domestic migration were not experienced by the nation as a whole until the northern cities erupted beginning with Detroit in 1967. Southern blacks, victims of industrial mechanization and structured racism, and Appalachian whites, locked out of deep coal mines as a nation shifted fuel sources, were joined by Hispanics and native American Indians in cities throughout the nation, but especially in the cities of the North.

American cities, built by cheap European labor in a rapidly expanding national economy fueled by two great wars, had by the 1960s filled up with the drop-outs of rural America. Simultaneously, for numerous reasons, the traditional role of the cities as job centers changed. Typically, Chicago lost more than 600,000 jobs in the 1960s, either to the suburbs, the sunbelt, or to overseas nations with cheaper labor supplies. Increasingly cities became "throw-away" places for an upwardly and outwardly migrating middle class and caldrons of unfulfilled expectations and frustrations for the new, usually unskilled minorities.

Initially influenced by the British industrial experiences, mainline denominations developed a socio-religious analysis of urban industrial society and enacted programs of industrial chaplaincies and settlement houses after World War II; but the basic assumptions of this industrial society were not examined seriously until the turbulent sixties. Then, influenced by models such as East Harlem Protestant Parish, Protestant ministries began the shift from strategies of relief to reform and sought to identify with inner-city issues — housing, jobs, gangs, corrupt politics, the rise of ghettos, poverty, and racism. Two common patterns resulted. Many white congregations sold their buildings and followed their cultures up and out of the cities, or they set up experimental ministries run by white clergy in non-white communities. Simultaneously, the largest black Baptist denomination, largely controlled by southern-style leadership, split as the Progressive National Baptist Convention was formed to cope with the contemporary urban North. Pentecostals and sects picked up increased numbers of the poor, who remained largely unaffected by mainline churches, black or white.

The proliferation of urban action training programs for clergy and laity in most major cities was another phenomenon of the 1960s, as national mission boards and local judicatories turned away from the traditional seminaries to create and promote models influenced by the community organization resources of Saul Alinsky and the Industrial Areas Foundation, the Ecumenical Institute, and methodologies developed by Kurt Lewin and others in the National Training Laboratories. Techniques of power analysis, problem-solving, group self-direction, and change theory became the curriculum for the consciousness-raising, training, and mobilizing of mainline Protestants for inner-city advocacy. Nationwide, the Action Training Coalition included many training sites, but the two most significant were the Urban Training Center for Christians (UTC) in Chicago and the Metropolitan Urban Service Training Center (MUST) in New York. Thousands participated and millions of dollars were spent by foundations and denominations in these ecumenical mission efforts. They operated out of a kerygmatic or neo-orthodox theological perspective developed by Hans

Hoekendijk and others who affirmed God's love for the world (not the church), and, therefore, the church's secular involvement. The result was a very pragmatic Christianity in which faithfulness to the gospel was measured by actions and programs. For numerous reasons, nearly all these training centers and the coalition itself ceased operations in the 1970s.

Beyond the poor, the urban high-rise buildings also presented a challenge to the church. Multiplex housing represented the normalizing of the urban individual who was perceived as broken, rootless, and unrelated to society in meaningful ways. On the contrary, contemporary research has shown high-rise dwellers to have unique personalities. They have a wide range of interests. Multiple dwelling living is a chosen lifestyle, offering a full existence and easy mobility within the human-made environment of the city, wherein homes are expendable in the pursuit of happiness and where commitments to vocation and an experimentalist's outlook on life represent the norm. These perceptions were seldom recognized in the 1960s when numerous models of high-rise ministry were

developed, usually on the premise that the "cliff-dwellers" needed to be integrated into a larger community, usually implying a family context.

The impact of mainline urban Christianity in the 1960s upon evangelicals during that same period is difficult to assess precisely. Some evangelical participation in the training centers has been documented, and some conservative churches and denominations did experiment with transition churches, start new minority ministries, and issue pleas to save the cities. More often than not, however, cities were places for evangelistic crusades or parachurch ministries, and most of the minority evangelical work was unrelated to the needs of the poor. A coalition of evangelical seminaries did develop a summer urban training program in Chicago (UMPS), drawing upon UTC resources and experiences in the late sixties and early seventies. As late as 1980, it was difficult to find a significant evangelical urban ministry that had not been shaped or influenced either consciously or unconsciously by the experiences of urban mainline Protestantism in the significant 1960s.

Church and Society

The 1960s and 1970s witnessed much more religious involvement in public issues than had been the case since the nineteenth and early twentieth centuries. But these years also witnessed less unity among the churches as a whole—and even within individual communions—as they set their face to the world.

During the years of strife in Vietnam, the point of entrance into the public arena was over the merits of warfare. Martin Luther King, Jr., the Catholics Daniel and Philip

Martin Luther King addressing a meeting of Clergy and Laymen Concerned About Vietnam in Washington's New York Avenue Presbyterian Church JOHN GOODWIN

Berrigan, and a host of organized groups such as Clergy and Laymen Concerned orchestrated the opposition. In the 1960s the most vocal and visible were disenchanted young people; those who organized and inspired them were the shakers of the status quo.

By the mid-1970s a dramatic shift occurred. The most intensely religious, who, as often as not, had sat out the war years, now emerged as the most vocal. And many of them were not young at all. By 1980, there was a direct correlation between the level of religious commitment, which was high among conservatives, and the desire to be politically active. Religious conservatives, on the average, were also far more likely to be involved in community affairs than those who considered themselves religiously liberal. The result was that moral questions vaulted to the forefront of political discussion.

The specific catalyst for this change was almost certainly the Supreme Court's ruling on abortion (*Rowe* v. *Wade*, 1973) which overrode the laws of all fifty states in permitting abortion on demand. This decision angered many Catholics, whose theology of natural law had long predisposed them against any artificial tampering with the birth process. It also galvanized into action a significant number of evangelicals and fundamentalists. These groups, which had been accustomed to equate the status quo with Christian values, now became alarmed

Abortion foes in a 1978 "March for Life" in Washington, D.C. RELIGIOUS NEWS SERVICE PHOTO

because abortion symbolized a set of values completely at odds with their inherited traditions. It stood for the pursuit of happiness, even of hedonism, without regard for moral restraint. And it coincided with a rising apprehension, amidst the conjunction between economic decline and political turmoil, that everything stable and right in life was slipping away.

The expression of this concern, which began to take political form in the late 1970s, was far more varied than the media realized. What is newsworthy may be only part of a larger story. In this case, it was a mistake to imagine that the New Right, which undoubtedly had a strong contingent of theological conservatives, or Jerry Falwell's Moral Majority, were the sole expressions of this new Christian engagement with society. Nevertheless, media pundits often treated them this way, especially following the presidential contest between Jimmy Carter and Ronald Reagan in 1980.

The New Right represented something old and something new in America. Its emergence signaled a return into public life of traditional moral forces that had gone underground after the public defeat of the fundamentalists in the 1920s. From this point of view, their campaign to save America was only one more example of moral effort to preserve the Republic that also included earlier assaults on slavery and drink. The new element in the New Right was its unequivocal alignment of Christian zeal with political conservatism. Earlier moral crusades contained, in the context of their times, a decidedly progressive, or even radical element. This time, however, the New Right was struggling almost entirely to preserve its treasured values—whether for America in the world or for personal morality at home.

For all its super-patriotism, the religious New Right displayed an oddly ambiguous attitude toward America itself. The conservative evangelical theology held by many in the New Right featured a strong eschatological element. This predisposed its adherents to regard moral decay as a telltale sign of the second coming of Christ, and to view America, a sink of such decay, as akin to the Great Whore of Babylon. On the other hand, the New Right also resuscitated a theme from earlier eras by looking upon America as God's

New Israel, providentially designated for moral leadership in the world.

The emergence of the New Right provided a fitting counterpoise to religious political activity earlier in the period. In general, theologically liberal church leaders had supported much of the socially liberal legislation and judicial decisions of the 1950s and 1960s. Among Catholics also, liberal social action such as the support of Cesar Chavez's efforts to organize California agricultural workers, tended to have strongest support from the more theologically liberal arm of the church. As in previous periods, however, it was never safe to assume that theological and political liberalism always went hand in hand. *The Catholic Worker*, founded by Dorothy Day in 1933, mounted a strong attack on the American industrial system. But it also maintained fidelity to papal pronouncements and a devotion to liturgical renewal. Similarly, several evangelical groups emerged in the 1960s and 1970s, such as the Sojourner's community in Washington, D.C., which based a radical critique of American industry, militarism, and political traditions on a theologically conservative belief in biblical authority.

The cluster of volatile family and sexual controversies drove a deep wedge between American church people. While some denominations offered formal judgments on one side of the abortion issue or the other, many were split down the middle, if not on the issue itself, then on tactics to fight it. Members of churches, and synagogues as well, were generally agreed on the undesirability of abortion. However, the more liberal theologically generally thought it was a lesser evil than the social cost and infringement of personal freedom which restrictions on abortion entailed. Others, generally the more conservative theologically, saw it as an affront to moral law. But advocates of the latter view differed among themselves on tactics to halt abortion. Constitutional amendments, normal legislative and judicial processes, and civil disobedience were all called into play. One of the longer lasting results of this debate was to yoke together members of different religious groups whose manifest theological differences had long kept them apart. Not too long ago, for example, it had been customary for fundamentalists to look on the pope as Antichrist and on Mormons

Demonstrations both for and against feminist causes become increasingly frequent in the 1970s.
LEONARD FREED/MAGNUM

as pernicious cultists. Now at least some of these same fundamentalists were making common cause with Catholics and Mormons in public testimony against abortion.

A related social issue which the world thrust at the church concerned the religious roles of women. Most denominations reeled in confusion when confronting this issue. Socially progressive bodies—following, as it happens, the long-time practice of the theologically conservative Salvation Army—rapidly opened their leadership ranks to women when feminist points of view were raised. Yet these groups often found local churches unprepared for the admission of women to roles of traditional leadership. The Catholic church, with its dependence upon a sacramental system administered by male priests, was most reluctant to change. Yet it, too, experienced a lively debate and strong internal pressure to reform on this issue. The very resilience of Catholic male traditions led to an especially important debate on this issue in that communion with influential voices

Three Episcopal women ordained in 1974 celebrate the Eucharist in Riverside Church, New York City.
RELIGIOUS NEWS SERVICE PHOTO

who asked for the liberation of Catholic women (Rosemary Ruether, Mary Daly) against those who contended for the church's traditional position (Stephen Clark). Evangelicals advocated a series of positions ranging from the most conservative to the most liberal.

Education was yet another public issue engaging the attention of Christians in the 1960s and 1970s. Decline in the number of Catholic nuns and the dispersal of Catholics from the cities undercut what had been the country's most active program of private education for over a century. Other well-established parochial systems, as that of the Missouri Synod Lutherans or the Christian Reformed church, generally fared much better in their more limited spheres of activity. The greatest boom in parochial education came from independent fundamentalists who started an impressive number of new schools. Critics claimed that these were escapist or racist bastions. Their supporters countered that they were erected to protect traditional American values and to save children from the religion of "secular humanism." Christian issues also impinged upon the public schools. In many

areas of the country, worried parents questioned sex education programs or complained about dirty books. In California and a few other states, the public schools were also scenes of battle over the teaching of evolution as a fact and the legitimacy of equal time for "biblical creationism."

One of the specific problems arising out of the churches' recent involvement in the world—whether at the point of party politics, war and peace, sexuality, the family, or education—was the question of church and state. As late as 1931 the Supreme Court declared that "We are a Christian people according to one another the equal right of religious freedom, and acknowledging with reverence the duty of obedience to the will of God" (*U.S. v. Macintosh*). In 1952 the Court modified its attitude. "We are," it said, "a religious people whose institutions presuppose a Supreme Being" (*Zorach* v. *Clausen*). But in the 1960s the Court allowed some young men to claim exemption from military service despite the fact that their belief in a "Supreme Being" was vague and unconventional (*U.S.* v. *Seeger*, 1965; *Welsh* v. *U.S.*, 1970). "The law," the Court said, upholding an earlier ruling, "knows no religious heresy" (*Watson* v. *Jones*, 1972), and all religious beliefs are entitled to First Amendment protection. This conclusion may be most consistent with cultural and religious pluralism, but it is far removed

Public school students receiving "released time" religious education in a mobile classroom parked just off school grounds in Fort Wayne, Indiana
RELIGIOUS NEWS SERVICE PHOTO

from the earlier affirmation that "we are a Christian people." Congress, likewise, has successfully removed religious affiliation as a consideration in employment and housing. Paradoxically, however, as the wall between church and state has been built up, supposedly ensuring that mutual contamination will be avoided, the impact of religion on the affairs of state has not been greater in many decades.

The question of values, as a result, remained a fundamental consideration. Values are not merely the product of religious convictions but are also the basis of public order. Much nonsense and much nastiness result when values fundamental to different religious systems collide in public. The convictions which give rise to these collisions show no signs of going away.

The atheistic crusader, Madalyn Murray O'Hair, for example, has sought to take "In God We Trust" off the coins and "Under God" out of the Pledge, since these words do not speak for her or like-minded citizens. Others respond that society degenerates into anarchy without transcendent moral values. Some Jewish citizens ask for an end to the use of Christian symbols and music in the public schools at Easter and Christmas. Theological conservatives contend that a de facto religion, "secular humanism," rules the schools. "Freedom of Choice" proponents

Stamp celebrating the protest of the inhabitants of Flushing, Long Island, against the religiously restrictive policies of Peter Stuyvesant in 1657
RELIGIOUS NEWS SERVICE PHOTO

Frederik A. Schiotz (left), president of the American Lutheran Church, testified in 1964 against a constitutional amendment to allow prayer and Bible reading in the public schools, citing the principle of separation of church and state.
RELIGIOUS NEWS SERVICE PHOTO

accuse the Catholic church of illegitimate governmental entanglement when its bishops promote "the right to life." But commentators like Andrew Greeley see in such accusations a remnant of traditional anti-popery which would deny Catholics, simply because they are Catholics, the right to speak out on public issues.

Clearly, the moral consensus which prevailed in the United States throughout the nineteenth century and which maintained a hold on much of the population into the twentieth, is no more. Legal traditions originally based on that consensus have recently sought foundations free from all religious admixtures. Controversy and confusion are the result.

In the last third of the twentieth century American Christians are finally learning the significance of the great changes of the century's first third. Very few public values can any longer be taken for granted. There is doubt as to whether, or in what ways, the United States is a Christian nation. The memory (usually much more forceful than the reality) of America's Christian past drives some to recapture a fading Christian culture. It leads others to explore how the church should fend for itself in an alien society. In between are a host of religious people who love both God and their country very much, but who—perhaps for the very first time on a large scale in America—are beginning to recognize that the two are not the same thing.

Theology at Bay

The social turmoil of the 1960s and 1970s worked havoc with Christian belief. In particular, it made it extremely difficult to maintain any unchanging "system" of belief, for systems by their very nature are slow to build and cannot rapidly adjust to a shifting culture. The problem is that American culture refused to stand still for theologians trying to catch their breath.

Karl Barth's theology was at its height in America in the 1940s and 1950s, but the termites were already at work on its foundations. In fact, Barth's thought had only one foundation, Jesus Christ. God, Barth argued, has not revealed himself in the natural order or in human nature; he has revealed himself only in Jesus. God does not speak to mankind through history or natural experience. He does not even speak through the words of scripture apart from the direct use of those words by Christ. It is in Christ that God alone has broken into this world, in Christ that he alone has revealed himself, and in Christ that he alone speaks to mankind.

This, of course, assumed that the event in which these divine activities are concentrated—the incarnation—can be known. But can it? Barth was caught in a dilemma on this matter. On the one hand, this event had to be knowable or humans could know nothing about God whatsoever; on the other hand, it could not be knowable as other events are known because then people would be in a position of thinking that knowing God was the same as knowing about the incarnation.

One could construct a knowledge of God by the same means as constructing a knowledge of Roman civilization. To permit this would be to tolerate a "works righteousness." It was a fatal weakness in Barth's system, and it was ruthlessly exploited by the Bultmannians. Rudolf Bultmann, in fact, had participated with Barth in the earlier overthrow of Protestant liberalism, but he was determined, as against Barth, that Christian faith should not be tied into the historical plane at all. About Jesus' personality and teachings, he said, virtually nothing is known; all that is known is that Jesus was born, saw himself as a prophet, and was crucified. The earliest believers, however, in writing of his significance to them, employed mythological language which should not be read literally now. What is important is not knowing what Jesus said and did but how Christ comes to people now in existential encounter, repeating in them the pattern of incarnation, death, and resurrection which the earliest believers ascribed to Jesus.

In sum, Barth had placed all his theological eggs in the christological basket; but radical biblical criticism, following Bultmann's approach, rapidly dissolved the basket. God, Barth had said, could not be known apart from Jesus; but Jesus, Bultmann said, could not be known at all. So what was left? The answer, for many borne along by these systems, was nothing.

The most highly publicized expression of that "nothing" was the Death of God theology. It was born in 1966 and died abruptly in 1968. In between, however, it received national attention in *Time* magazine as well as an odd form of modern publicity—opposition expressed in automobile bumper stickers: "If your God is dead, try mine"; "God is not dead, I talked to him this morning"; and "My God is alive; I don't know about yours." No one, apparently, produced bumper stickers in favor of the theology.

The proponents of this theology—Thomas Altizer, Gabriel Vahanian, William Hamilton, and Paul van Buren—were mostly disenchanted Barthians who had found themselves with empty hands. What they meant by God's "death" varied a great deal. The meanings ranged from the actual demise of God (Altizer) to the collapse in the meaning of religious words (van Buren). This

TIME

THE WEEKLY NEWSMAGAZINE

Is
God
Dead?

In 1966 Time *put the latest theological debate in its simplest terms before the public.* COPYRIGHT 1966 TIME
INC. ALL RIGHTS RESERVED. REPRINTED BY PERMISSION FROM TIME

movement, however, signaled much broader changes, and therein lies its significance. It marked the end of the dominance of the large theological systems spawned by giants like Barth and Tillich; it echoed the rapidly changing culture by severing theology from fixed points like an unchanging God and a finished divine revelation; it freed theology to explore "truth" in terms of inner experience alone, which is what many purely secular people were also doing; and in the "death of God" it projected the sense of apprehension and the foreboding that enveloped many cultural institutions.

It takes either a melancholy disposition or a hardy constitution to embrace pessimism as a way of life. The Death of God theology unashamedly gloried in its bankruptcy, but that was hardly the stuff of which disciples are made. As a matter of fact, the pessimism of the 1960s which this movement reflected gave way to more mellow feelings as the Vietnam War ground to a halt and society began to lick its wounds in the early 1970s.

These more mellow feelings undoubtedly created the atmosphere in which the Theology of Hope found acceptance and succeeded the Death of God theology. Jürgen Moltmann, its author, argued that human nature is not the fixed essence it has always been thought to be; rather, it is fluid, malleable, open to change. Thus, the future will not be limited to reproducing the same set of flaws and evils of which the whole of human history is a sad chronicle. On the contrary, radical disjunctures can be expected. The future will be qualitatively different from the present. Human society will be remade by God to reflect that classlessness and economic parity which are the essence of justice. So Moltmann argued in *The Theology of Hope* (1967); but he put a slight chill on his proposal by proposing in his next book, *Religion, Revolution and the Future* (1969), that the means of bringing society into this utopia will be violence predicated on Marxist assumptions.

The adoption of Marxist categories did not, however, offend everyone. Those who felt that they were the victims of capitalism found in Moltmann's thought the conceptual tools for forging an ideology that opposed the United States while founding that opposition on religious convictions. It was for this reason that

Women are an oppressed class. Our oppression is total, affecting every facet of our lives. . . . We identify the agents of our oppression as men.

The Redstockings Manifesto, July 1969

Third World delegates, who dominated the deliberations of the World Council of Churches in the 1970s, were enthusiastic about Moltmann; so, too, were the South American liberation theologians, who also resented North American economic domination and could state that resentment in eschatological terms. And, within the United States itself, those disaffected with "the system" or bypassed in the distribution of affluence or victimized by the exercise of power in a society dominated by white males, quickly adopted Moltmannian themes. The hope for a society remade was fashioned from the particular grievance at hand. Feminist theologians such as Rosemary Ruether looked for that new day in which women would, by divine action, find liberation from oppression; black theologians such as James Cone looked for the new day in which the structures of power subservient to white interests would be overthrown and black people enter into the long-awaited promised land. It was a motif that lent itself to any group that could identify oppressors in the society. It was one which gave a divine sanction for exacting a penalty on those seen as responsible for bruised and wounded feelings. But it was also a motif that could extract from its heralds the price of a later disillusionment, for, beyond the worst exaggerations of the most brazen politicians, Moltmann promised more than will ever be delivered in a society always sinful.

The mellower mood of the 1970s also encouraged other lines of thought. Harvey Cox, for example, became fashionable by arguing a distinction between secularism and secularity. The city, with its loneliness and seeming "godlessness," is actually only an expression of secularity, not of secularism; here, within a secular dimension and within

ALL
POWER POWER
TO TO
THE THE
PEOPLE NBEDO
AND
SUPPORT THE BLACK
MANIFESTO

In 1969, Black Manifesto spokesman James Foreman forced a confrontation with the churches by occupying National Council of Churches offices in New York. RELIGIOUS NEWS SERVICE PHOTO

secular forms, God really does meet mankind, but he does so incognito. This was an adaptation to American culture of some of Bonhoeffer's more radical ideas; it was also an adaptation of Christianity to culture. And it was not clear what this kind of faith had to offer which could not be had under purely secular auspices without the obligation of having to appear religious.

In a different vein, the 1970s also saw the emergence of process theology, but this, unlike the political, ethnic, and secular theologies, defied all attempts at popularization. The problem lay in the extraordinarily complex nature of the philosophy which spawned it. At its center, however, it was concerned with a problem with which most of philosophy has wrestled. The question is whether the individual has reality, and if so, what that is. For it is clear that the temporal process is one of constant shifting, changing, and movement. Humans reflect this reality, for they are not only the product of their circumstances but an accumulation of diverse experience, experience which is never repeated in precisely the same way twice. Is there in

the world outside of oneself or in the world of the inner consciousness a unity which underlies this changing diversity? It is the search for this unity that both Hinduism and Buddhism have formalized, as has process theology.

In his books *Modes of Thought* (1968) and *Process and Reality* (1969), A. N. Whitehead argued that there is an interplay between the emerging world and the nature of God. It is that kind of interplay which brings the nature of God into fuller consciousness and greater reality. The world has the power to reject the "lures" which God inserts within it, in which case an inner devolution occurs, resulting in death, disease, and entropy; the world also has the capacity to accept these lures, and in accepting them it is not only impelled toward different and higher life forms but it also brings the nature of God into concrete being. As developed by Charles Hartshorne, this means that God is both absolute and relative, both realized and unrealized, both creative and created; in some ways he is eternal, and in other ways he is temporal.

Although process thought is a serious attempt to understand the nature of things, and whether there is a reality in which every aspect of the temporal process subsists, it also is a system of thought made for times of massive cultural transition. It gives full recognition to change; it credits change with reality. It holds out a way of looking at a mobile society which neither shrinks from the rapid movement nor becomes intoxicated with it. At the same time, however, it also extracts a price. God is recast in the image of the changing society. Since his being is still emerging and is always changing, the possibility of enduring moral norms is lost, the possibility of transcendent truth is abandoned, and human autonomy is justified since there is no fixed revelation to which one anchors his thought.

Liberation

Black Theology

It would seem that Black Power and Christianity have this in common: the liberation of man! If the work of Christ is that of liberating men from alien loyalties, and if racism is, as George Kelsey says, an alien faith, then there must be some correlation between Black Power and Christianity. For the gospel proclaims that God is with us now, actively fighting the forces which would make man captive. And it is the task of theology and the Church to know where God is at work so that we can join him in this fight against evil. In America we know where the evil is. We know that men are shot and lynched. We know that men are crammed into ghettos ... eschatology comes to mean joining the world and making it what it ought to be. It means that the Christian man looks to the future not for a reward or possible punishment of evildoers, but as a means of making him dissatisfied with the present. His only purpose for looking to a distant past or an unrealized future is that both disclose the ungodliness of the present. Looking to the future he sees that present injustice cannot be tolerated. Black Theology asserts an eschatology that confronts a world of racism with Black Power.

JAMES CONE,
1969

Feminist Theology

Sexual alienation and the depersonalizing of women define the Fall. But salvation cannot be found in these terms, since the solutions derived from them only recapitulate the problem. Salvation cannot appear save as the resurrection of woman; that is, in woman's self-definition as an autonomous person. Rather than being co-opted into male projections that make her the image of male ideals and phobias, she must establish herself as an autonomous person in any encounter. Her resurrection begins as an inner psychic revolution that gives her the transcending power to disaffiliate herself from male objectifications and to make her exodus from incorporations of her as an extension of male demands and alienation. ... Anger and pride are the power for Exodus, for disaffiliation from the Egypt of male definition and use.

ROSEMARY RADFORD RUETHER,
1973

The Relevance of Denominations?

Comparatively little of the most important religious "news" of the 1960s and 1970s involved the denominations, even though these structures continued to loom large in many discussions of American faith. In fact, a number of considerations could lead to the conclusion that they have become nearly irrelevant in American life. Vast changes have altered the social structures that once supported the denominations. Language, ethnic, and in some cases economic and social distinctions no longer line up with denominations as neatly as they once did. Divisive conflicts within traditional groups have strained old ties. This is true for both Protestants and Catholics as well as those who live under additional labels like evangelical, fundamental, neo-orthodox, or liberal. In addition, a wide range of responses to the crises of modern life have created strange ecclesiastical bedfellows as well as promoted bitter ecclesiastical divorce.

Denominations have felt the corrosions of modernity, the impact of individualistic empire builders, the effects of the antiinstitutionalism of television, and the competition of the freewheeling paradenominational organizations. If there are forces that fray denominational edges, there are also those that unite members across denominational barriers. The question of abortion is a case in point. It has brought together Catholics and evangelical Protestants in common cause whereas, had they been playing the game by the old rules, they would have kept each other at arm's length. The charismatic movement has leaped denominational bounds and forged links across the no man's land between the various structures and churches. So, too, has the flow of books. Writers of Catholic spirituality such as Thomas Merton and Henri Nouwen have gained a Protestant audience. Evangelical authors such as Donald Bloesch and Richard Lovelace mine a wide range of sources in search of a spirituality both Catholic and Reformed. The Lutheran Richard

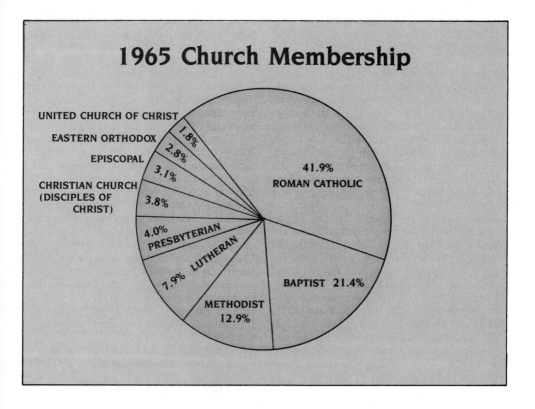

1965 Church Membership

- UNITED CHURCH OF CHRIST — 1.8%
- EASTERN ORTHODOX — 2.8%
- EPISCOPAL — 3.1%
- CHRISTIAN CHURCH (DISCIPLES OF CHRIST) — 3.8%
- PRESBYTERIAN — 4.0%
- LUTHERAN — 7.9%
- METHODIST — 12.9%
- BAPTIST — 21.4%
- ROMAN CATHOLIC — 41.9%

Neuhaus and the Episcopal William String-fellow find an audience with Protestants and Catholics, evangelicals and liberals, when they speak out on public issues. And most college graduates in American church life have read at least some of the works of the British Anglican C. S. Lewis and his Catholic friend, J. R. R. Tolkien.

Denominations do protect processes that nourish the lifeblood of local churches and thereby continue to retain some importance. They do provide placement services for church workers, publish educational materials for Sunday school, give ministers and lay leaders opportunities to share problems and successes at regional and national meetings, and they do monitor accreditation of seminaries. Nevertheless, the story of American religion can no longer be equated with that of the denominations, if it ever could. Denominations have a part to play in American religion, but that religion is finding many channels of expression outside denominational structures.

Protestantism

This development has affected both Protestantism and Catholicism, but in different ways. In Protestantism it has favored the resurgent evangelicalism which, since the 1930s at least, has been deeply suspicious about denominational structures. Indeed, spiritual authenticity has often appeared in such groups as the antithesis of denominational loyalties. In Catholicism this mood has favored those groups out of harmony with the magisterial consensus, from charismatics on the one side to radical theologians on the other. Each, in its different way, has been able to sit loose of the functioning of the church.

Protestantism has been declining in the United States. Those identified as Protestant slipped from 70 percent of the population (1962), to 67 percent (1967), to 63 percent (1972). This seepage, however, did not affect all denominational cisterns in the same way; religious declines do not always respect egalitarian principles! Between 1965 and 1975, the United Presbyterian Church, U.S.A., lost 12.4 percent of its membership, the United Church of Christ 12.2 percent, the Episcopal church 16.7 percent, Lutheran Church of America 5 percent, and the Presbyterian, U.S.,

7.6 percent. The Methodist church merged with the Evangelical United Brethren in 1968 to form the United Methodist church but also continued to lose members and missionaries; Methodist missionaries overseas numbered 1,453 in 1958 and only 1,175 in 1971. By contrast, during this time, Southern Baptists doubled their missionary strength from 1,186 to 2,494, and in 1967 overtook the Methodists to become the largest Protestant denomination. Other conservative groups, not known for their ecumenism or religious liberalism, also grew. The Seventh-day Adventists increased their membership by 3.2 percent per year, the Church of the Nazarene 2.6 percent per year, the Salvation Army 2.9 percent per year, the Christian Reformed 2.2 percent per year, the Free Methodists 1.6 percent per year, and the Assemblies of God 2.1 percent per year.

Was there a discernible pattern in all of this? Dean Kelley, an official of the National Council of Churches, thought there was. In his book, *Why Conservative Churches are Growing* (1972), he argued that the churches which had grown had done so by making serious demands on their members, by refusing to be indulgent about moral and religious relapses, and by maintaining Christian distinctives in the pluralistic culture. They offered a choice to, and not merely an echo of, the culture, and the world-weary found this attractive. But Kelley only knew half of the story. Somehow he managed to overlook the most rapidly growing groups of Protestants, the independent fundamentalist churches. These fiercely congregational bodies sometimes reached great size, attracting as many as 20,000 for Sunday-school instruction. They fellowshipped in loosely knit organizations like the Baptist Bible Fellowship, the Independent Fundamental Churches of America, and the Baptist Mission Association. From them has come much of the impetus for the Christian school movement and not a few of the troops of the New Right. And they have continued to exhibit an ambiguous relationship to the culture. In their gospel of salvation is offered a clear choice to secular humanism; in their patriotism is heard an echo of that nationalism which is resonant with civil piety. The reason for the growth of conservatives was more complex than Kelley realized.

Foundations of the Evangelical Resurgence

THOMAS A. ASKEW

By the end of the Second World War it became evident that new currents were emerging within the variegated movement known between the wars as fundamentalism. Finding primary support in the Midwest and on both coasts, these tides of self-assessment gathered momentum until in the 1950s they were dubbed the "new evangelicalism" or "neo-evangelicalism."

Understanding the coalescing of neo-evangelicalism in the postwar decade is essential for developing perspective on the renascence of evangelical religion during the 1960s and 1970s, a topic much explored by the popular and religious press. For it was during the formative period following the war that the base was laid for future gains.

Breaking with the stricter fundamentalists of the 1930s, those who would adopt the term neo-evangelical were outspokenly orthodox in doctrine but rejected what they considered to be the cultural and theological excesses in the fundamentalist mentality — sectarianism, testiness, antiintellectualism, cultural isolation, and lack of social ethic. During the 1940s and 1950s the neo-evangelical thrust was spearheaded by an interlocking group of prominent pastors, professors, writers, organizations, and institutions. This pacesetting cluster created a religious mood that provoked criticism from many fundamentalists even as it provided a new vitality for evangelical Protestantism.

There were several components in this revitalization. First was the National Association of Evangelicals, founded in 1942 as a corporate alternative to the Federal Council of Churches on the left and Carl McIntire's American Council of Churches on the right. Second was a

fresh engagement with society at a cultural and intellectual level, illustrated most strikingly by Carl F. H. Henry's *The Uneasy Conscience and Modern Fundamentalism* (1947). Third was a broad movement by educational institutions striving for full academic credentials. The founding of Fuller Theological Seminary in 1947 illustrates this, but the movement also involved many colleges which upgraded and expanded programs as well as Bible colleges which assumed collegiate status. Third was a dramatic growth in publishing houses and in the production of Christian reading material. Above all, *Christianity Today*, founded in 1956 and supported by most of the respected evangelical leaders, gave direction to the new movement. Fourth was the emergence of new missionary agencies and numerous ministries designed to disciple young people. Youth for Christ and Young Life were founded to evangelize teenagers, and InterVarsity Christian Fellowship and Campus Crusade for Christ serviced the needs of college students. These vast ministries provided national visibility for

Youth for Christ rally in the 1950s BILLY GRAHAM CENTER

several evangelical leaders. This was especially true for Youth for Christ evangelist Billy Graham, who created new acceptance for popular revivalism at the same time that he distressed older fundamentalists with a policy of cooperative evangelism. He has remained evangelicalism's most admired figure since 1950.

Keen observers of the American religious scene have long recognized that neo-evangelicalism owed more to parachurch enterprises than to resurgent denominational life. Leadership, influence, and ideas emanated from a network of seminary and college trustees and presidents, and from editors, authors, and key preachers, many of whom had radio or television ministries. It is not difficult to explain why parachurch corporations eclipsed ecclesiastical structures for the new evangelicals. These organizations offered efficiency and centralized decision-making. They were directed to specific goals rather than to the traditional parishioner. The parachurch cultivated a far-flung clientele with little obligation for full disclosure or open board meetings. The parachurch also could mobilize across denominations, use laypeople well, and produce specialized services for disparate interest groups.

Despite all the noteworthy accomplishments, the entrepreneurial spirit

President Eisenhower and United Presbyterian Church moderator Dr. T. M. Taylor following a prayer and communion service marking the opening of Congress in 1959
RELIGIOUS NEWS SERVICE PHOTO

of some parachurch agencies made them vulnerable to empire-building and factional politics. In addition, theoretical and practical questions remained in defining the parachurch relationship to the church itself. Parachurch groups, with their employees and hierarchical management structure, resemble the business corporation. The church is largely comprised of volunteer fellowships whose accountability and whose application of biblical values often move in a much different direction. Such tensions over definitions continue to blur distinctions in the broader evangelical movement.

In retrospect, it is also clear that the postwar American religious climate hastened the rise of neo-evangelicalism. Along with the drive for family financial security came a search for personal peace. While thousands were attracted to Billy Graham's meetings, others looked to Bishop Fulton Sheen or Pastor Norman Vincent Peale for inspiration. Church membership reached an all-time American high; a host of new sanctuaries were constructed. President Dwight D. Eisenhower's confidence in "faith," his exemplary church attendance, and his friendliness toward conservative religion helped set a national tone. The Cold War against atheistic communism encouraged the fusion between religion and politics and made it easier to identify the "American Way" with conservative Protestantism. Religious mottos were added to coins and the Pledge of Allegiance. In this context, neo-evangelicals figured prominently in the prayer breakfast movement at both state and national levels. By the end of the Eisenhower years these churchmen had reached a visibility and achieved an access to governmental and professional circles not known since the days of Woodrow Wilson.

One frequently overlooked ingredient in the emergence of the new evangelical movement is its reflection

Billy Graham has won the ear of several presidents. Pictured here are Lyndon Johnson's autograph to his "dear friend" (above, left); a prayer breakfast with John Kennedy (above, right); and the appearance of then candidate Richard Nixon at a Graham crusade (below).   ABOVE, LEFT AND RIGHT: BILLY GRAHAM CENTER
BELOW: RELIGIOUS NEWS SERVICE PHOTO

of economic prosperity. Anglo-American evangelical piety has for generations tended to resemble middleclass values; the values of neo-evangelicals seem quite close to professional and upper-middleclass tastes and viewpoints. Two decades of material abundance inevitably shaped the perception of Christian discipleship. Little imagination is required to see what the relationships were between escalating personal incomes and the suburbanization of Protestantism in the 1950s, the purchase of summer cottages at Bible conference grounds, the growing numbers journeying to the Holy Land, the purchase of books and recordings, or the vast resources demanded to support nationwide parachurch ministries in addition to local congregations.

On further scrutiny, however, the impact of prosperity more subtly impinged on basic religious values. Too easily personal success and upward mobility in an expanding economy came to be equated with God's normative blessing for the church. Thousands of evangelical collegians struggled to find "God's will" for their professional futures, enjoying a dilemma of opportunities never experienced by their grandfathers, working-class peers, or most believers in the history of the church.

As the stabilized 1950s gave way to youthful dissent in the 1960s and the implications of economic scarcity in the 1970s, critical voices would be raised, challenging the affluent Christian life. Many new evangelicals began to be troubled about following the path of Christian stewardship in a prosperous age.

The perspective of twenty years suggests that neo-evangelical accomplishments were substantial. While Christian influences on the nation's intellectual and cultural life did not amount to much, there were some gains. New structures for interdenominational cooperation were in place. In the strengthened colleges and seminaries a more professional professoriate trained thousands of youth for a broad range of services to church and society. A coterie of evangelical scholars authored creditable, and in some cases noteworthy, publications. Millions were evangelized at home and abroad. A few neo-evangelicals tried to show laypeople the connections between a personal faith and Christian perspectives on contemporary problems. And an institutional foundation was erected which directly contributed to the vigor of the larger evangelical wave that some observers claim swept through the church life of America by the mid-1970s.

Bible conference grounds have served as summer vacation spots for swelling numbers of evangelicals since the 1950s. BILLY GRAHAM CENTER

The Christian Counterculture

RONALD M. ENROTH

Historians and sociologists of religion have observed that new forms of religious expression which emerge in a particular historical period tend to reflect that period's special concerns. The decade of the 1960s represented a time of cultural dislocation and sociopolitical upheaval. For the first time, Americans expressed mass disaffection with the common understandings of their culture. Many young adults protested against "the system" — the established social institutions whose legitimacy they saw eroding. These protests assumed the form of a new social movement — the "counterculture."

The new religious consciousness that emerged was unconventional if not alien to the American scene. Eastern mysticism, new forms of self-awareness, and spiritual narcissism became popular. At the apex of the counterculture movement, many young people became disillusioned with the "new spirituality" and its psychedelic trappings. A significant segment of the youth culture was ripe for a return to old-time religion.

The late 1960s was the time frame for the emergence of one of the most colorful and widely publicized religious phenomena of recent decades — the Jesus people movement. From the cradle of the counterculture in San Francisco's Haight-Ashbury to the sun-tanned set of southern California's beach scene, thousands of young people were "turning on to Jesus."

These counterculture Christians, with little or no background exposure to organized Christianity, were brought into the fold through the fervent evangelism of hitherto unknown street preachers, ex-drug addicts, and middle-aged ministers with only marginal ties to the institutional church. The Jesus people — and their successor movements — were characterized by a kind of grass-roots diversity manifested in widely scattered subgroups which lacked a single leadership structure and clear-cut goals and objectives.

The persistent diversity of the Jesus movement and its rapid decline since the mid-1970s resulted in increased polarization between its various elements. On the one hand, the more moderate surviving "core" of the movement drifted in the direction of a more enlightened, balanced maturation. This shift toward established evangelicalism and a culture-affirming orientation is exemplified by churches such as Calvary Chapel in southern California. The evolution of mainstream evangelical forms out of this "high on Jesus hip church" is a dramatic example of what Max Weber called "the routinization of charisma." On the other hand, organizations like the Children of God represent the more clearly cultic, isolationist, culture-rejecting extremist groups with roots in the turmoil of the 1960s.

The secular counterculture as described by Theodore Roszak and others signaled a distrust of science and rationalism. It represented a cultural disjuncture of massive proportions, a disenchantment with technocracy and materialism, and a turning toward the mystical and the spiritual. The more extreme cultural forms of the movement eventually disappeared, but certain influences and focal values have endured. For example, the experience orientation of the youth counterculture was infused into the Jesus movement (religion became the "ultimate trip") and continues to impact segments of evangelicalism.

One of the characteristics of the secular counterculture was its widespread experimentation with alternatives. A wide range of alternatives to traditional institutions, values, and lifestyles emerged. A residual effect of this emphasis on experimentation can be seen in today's Christian counterculture, with its continuing interest in communal living arrangements, diverse modes of worship, and its emphasis on simplicity and naturalness.

The external trappings of the counterculture were especially visible in the youth-oriented Jesus movement: dress, length and style of hair, distinctive jargon, and a bumper-sticker mentality evidenced by such slogans as: "You're in the Rapture Generation," and "The Bible is Soul Food."

Some of the motifs of the psychedelic culture of the sixties have been retained by countercultural Christians and have filtered down to the larger evangelical subculture. The suffusive effects of informal worship styles and Jesus music is one example. Maranatha-style music has caught on in mainline evangelical circles far removed from the Jesus freaks of California.

Despite a lack of clear-cut definition and demarcation, the Christian counterculture of today serves the function of assisting in the creation of new forms of witness for new times. Its impact is perhaps greatest in that segment of Christianity which Richard Quebedeaux has called "The Young Evangelicals." Publications such as *Radix* magazine (formerly *Right On*) and *Sojourners* (formerly the *Post American*) chronicle a "radical" countercultural faith certain to remain a major force in American evangelicalism for the remainder of the century.

"Jesus freak" baptism on a California beach   COURTESY KQED-TV, SAN FRANCISCO

The growth of conservative churches, which looked all the more extraordinary when contrasted with the declining fortunes of the older mainline denominations, was actually part of a broad resurgence in evidence as much outside the evangelical denominations as in them. The Jesus movement first brought this resurgence to the attention of the media. An "old-time, foot-stomping, hand-clapping revival," the movement was called, with "California" written all over it. Before the "Jesus freaks" reached the Midwest, however, they had settled into countercultural communities in which they pursued a simple evangelical spirituality. Yet they were symptomatic of a wider flowering of Christian faith among younger people. Campus organizations, in particular, benefited from this. Tangible expression was given to this in Campus Crusade for Christ's Explo '72 which drew 80,000 students to Dallas, Texas, and InterVarsity Fellowship's Urbana conventions in the 1960s and 1970s which attracted thousands of serious-minded students, many of whom expressed a willingness to serve as missionaries.

But was this merely a youth revival? A chastened press, prodded by Gallup polls, began to realize that the phenomenon of evangelical renewal was actually nationwide. "The most significant—and overlooked—religious phenomenon of the 1970s," said Kenneth Woodward, religion editor of *Newsweek*, is "the emergence of evangelical Christianity into a position of respect and power." The year Jimmy Carter was elected as president, 1976, was quickly declared by the press to be "the Year of the Evangelical." In part this was because Carter, who was unabashed about his spiritual rebirth, was so heavily

Jerry Falwell in the pulpit of his giant Thomas Road Baptist Church, Lynchburg, Virginia BILLY GRAHAM CENTER

supported by white evangelicals who were delighted about having a born-again president. In 1976 his support came largely from the fifty-one percent of Protestants and eighteen percent of Roman Catholics who claimed to have experienced spiritual rebirth; in 1978, thirty-four percent of the adult population claimed this as well as believing the Bible to be "the actual word of God."

What was lost in the excitement of this new discovery was that many of those caught in Gallup's net were uncomfortable with being classified under the loose rubric of "evangelical." Some Southern Baptists thought that the term was more Yankee than anything else. They disliked being linked with "northern" organizations such as the National Association of Evangelicals. Fundamentalists looked on evangelicals as compromisers and denied them fellowship. Radicals distinguished between genuine evangelicals who opposed the political status

---

An old-time footstomping hand-clapping religious revival is happening, and it's got California stamped all over it. Look out, you other forty-nine states. Jesus is coming.

BRIAN VACHON,
February 1971

We are not evangelicals with a capital "E". That's a Yankee word. They want to claim us because we are big and successful and growing every year.

FOY VALENTINE,
Southern Baptist, 1976

quo and "establishment evangelicals" who went along with it. Blacks, by Gallup's reckoning largely evangelical in spirituality, felt that the designation was artificial since black and white evangelicals have had little to do with each other. Whether this was really a "movement" and who precisely was on the move was far less clear than the Gallup polls suggested.

Nevertheless, there was a rekindling of evangelical spirituality which, if it was not always deep, was certainly broad. Perhaps as many as 14 million of those in the National Council of Churches, whose membership totals 42 million, are evangelical; denominations such as the Southern Baptist Convention are dominated by evangelical interests; and a multitude of missions and evangelistic and service organizations now exist to serve the Evangel. This Evangel is God's good news of salvation. It arises from the sovereign kindness of God, is established through the substitutionary death of Jesus, is made known and interpreted only in the Bible, and is received only by faith.

The long-term impact of evangelical faith on American affairs will probably be determined by two considerations. First, will evangelicalism retain enough of its otherworldly character? Second, will it be able to control its penchant for rampant individualism?

The French philosopher Alexis de Tocqueville argued that the one thing which could destroy a religion was its involvement in the shifting tides of politics. That was why—observing America in the 1830s—he felt that Christianity would enjoy a long life there. The danger of self-destruction had been removed by the separation of church and state. What he did not see clearly enough was that

Christian faith can be involved in culture even where the separation of church and state is legally entrenched. And it can destroy itself, despite all legal safeguards.

In the early decades of the twentieth century, the fundamentalists were acutely aware of this threat. They created institutional bulwarks against the culture which they viewed as so alien to their religious interests. The price they paid for their cognitive survival was a forfeiture of influence in shaping that culture. Evangelicals, by contrast, have been acutely sensitive to the price paid by the fundamentalists' separation, but they seldom seem to be as aware of the danger of cultural involvement. At stake is cognitive integrity. The fact that a "born again" spirituality was, in the 1970s, frequently grafted onto a set of values which owed little to Christianity and much to secularism showed how extraordinarily difficult it was to be involved in the worldly process on terms other than those dictated by that worldly process. Such a marriage between culture and faith produced glimmerings of the "cultural Protestantism" that fundamentalists assailed in the liberals of an earlier generation; in being "relevant" to the culture these liberals lost their relevance to the essence of Christian faith. The lasting effect the vast numbers of evangelicals have had would seem to depend, then, on their ability to avoid the mistake made by liberalism.

The latent antiinstitutional mood of evangelicalism surfaced and united with an antiinstitutional mood in the country at the end

Sun Myung Moon, whose Unification Church members strive to emulate evangelical respectability
RELIGIOUS NEWS SERVICE PHOTO

Moses David's Children of God in mealtime prayer and praise   RELIGIOUS NEWS SERVICE PHOTO

of the 1970s. Ronald Reagan tapped this mood in his presidential campaign. Confidence that bureaucratic structures and government programs could solve the country's most pressing problems had plummeted; Reagan promised, therefore, to get this impotent and wasteful government off the people's back. In its place would come private business interest and individual resourcefulness. Individualism may be the key to economic recovery, but its presence in evangelical faith has not always been an unmixed blessing.

Few cults have been born on American soil that were not born in the cradle of evangelical piety. More recent examples of this are Sun Myung Moon, father of the "Moonies," who was raised in an evangelical Presbyterian home; Jim Jones, founder of People's Temple, who was "born again" in a Nazarene church; Moses David, leader of the Children of God, who was raised in the Missionary Alliance; Victor Wierville, founder of The Way, who was an evangelical Reformed pastor.

These and similar cults began in the same way. First emerged an individual with a new "insight." The insight was then developed in opposition to the local church or the prevailing orthodoxy. Once entrenched as a cognitive minority, devices to protect that minority rapidly emerged: a subcultural language to explain and protect the insight; a tight organization that repelled outsiders and cemented together insiders; a blind loyalty to the leader who, in his hermetically sealed world, was placed beyond reproach, criticism, or discipline.

This rampant individualism could be found in cultic accretions on the fringes of evangelicalism but, in more benign forms, was not unknown closer to the center. It could be seen, for example, in some of the pastors dominating huge churches in the Bible Belt; they, too, created personal kingdoms in which the "king" was beyond discipline. It could be seen in some of the renowned radio preachers and television personalities. The normal channels of accountability in these cases were circumvented, and the individual gained access to the power which millions of dollars could bestow. Radio audiences were estimated at 115 million per week and television at 14 million. Whereas most older, established denominations might take in $20 million to $30 million per year, effective evangelists in the late 1970s were each netting between $60 million and $80 million. This new form of "church," centered on powerful and talented individuals, appealed to what was best and worst in evangelicalism. It appealed to the sense that faith must be personal. That appeal, however, rode on the back of a suspicion about church structures, a toleration of authoritarian leaders, and an indulgence of most forms of individualism. The inability to discern between faith which is personal and that which is individualistic could check the solid advances made by evangelicals in finding a place to serve in the affairs of the nation.

The Bible Belt

DAVID EDWIN HARRELL

It was entirely fitting that Jimmy Carter, the first president from the Deep South since Zachary Taylor, should be a daily Bible reader, a Sunday-school teacher, and an unabashed Christian "witness" before visiting dignitaries. The president reflected many of the stereotypes long associated with southern religion.

The distinctiveness of southern religion is documented by denominational statistics. Baptists and Methodists have dominated the religious life of the section since the mid-nineteenth century and still comprise about seventy-five percent of southern church membership. Along with Mormon Utah, the southern states are the most homogeneous religious areas of the country. The intellectual leadership of Episcopalians, Presbyterians, and Roman Catholics has been important in the South, particularly in some subregions, but these churches have often supported the same evangelical values associated with the Baptist and Methodist establishment. Beneath this solid evangelical front, the South was also the nation's most fertile breeding ground for fast-growing new sects in the early twentieth century. The two most successful new American religious movements in the first half of that century were the Churches of Christ, which was almost entirely southern, and the pentecostal movement, which had its strongest bases of support in the South.

But the observers of southern religion in the early twentieth century who labeled the section the Bible Belt were not struck so much by the denominational forms they found — although many were taken aback by the more bizarre varieties of "holy rollers" — but by the content of southern religion. Southern theology was not unique, but by the post-Civil War period it had become uniformly con-servative; southern churches were almost untouched by the great social and intellectual challenges that shaped northern religion in the late nineteenth century. Church leaders in both North and South were conscious of the South's increasing religious isolation, and southerners wore this alienation as a badge of honor. "The bulk of the Democracy of the United States," wrote an Arkansas preacher in 1919, was made up of "the Baptist South and the riff-raff Roman Catholic elements of the North." In the frantic confrontation of the 1920s which centered on the teaching of evolution in the public schools, the organized fundamentalist movement spread throughout the country, but only in the South was the Bible still central enough to the culture to lead to the passage of antievolution laws. When the Scopes trial in 1925 centered the nation's attention on Dayton, Tennessee, many southerners viewed the trial as a showcase for southern piety, "one of the South's supremest advertisements." "There are millions of people in other parts of the United States," one southern editor wrote, "who do not want to raise their children in an atmosphere of agnosticism and atheism so prevalent throughout the North and West, where the alien foreign element is so dominant, and who, having learned as a result of this trial that there is a section in this country where religion pure and undefiled still holds sway, will turn their eyes longingly to the Land of Promise, hoping that in the South they may be able to have their children raised in an atmosphere of Christianity."

While the fight against evolution and other forms of modernism did most to gain the South its Bible Belt label, southern religion was, at least quantitatively, distinctive in other ways. In the aftermath of the Civil War, southerners embraced an elaborate doctrine of separation of church and state which divorced religion from some forms of social reform but allowed the churches to push for legislation enforcing personal morality. While strongly Bible-oriented and often literalistic, southern religion also gave new force to the personal experience of being "born again." This personal conversion experience was the doctrinal base for an ardent evangelistic spirit in most southern churches. While much of the evangelical fervor of southern churches was spent in local revivals and campaigns to convert the sinners of the region, southern churches were also fervent supporters of foreign missions.

The Bible Belt was the product of the unique historical experience of the South. Early southern history contributed to the section's distinctive tradition. The homogeneity of southern religion stems from the slight impact that immigration had on the region in the nineteenth century. The section's unique experience in race relations and the self-conscious racism of white southerners contributed to

Electronic church host Jim Bakker of the PTL Club interviewing his wife Tammy
RELIGIOUS NEWS SERVICE PHOTO

the development of legalistic biblical attitudes. Early nineteenth-century revivalism left behind an emphasis on enthusiasm and personal conversion.

But the Bible Belt remains primarily a post-Civil War development. Through much of the antebellum period the South had appeared to be the most liberal religious section of the country. The defeat of the Confederacy spawned what one recent scholar has called a "southern civil religion," a religion "less optimistic, less liberal, less democratic, less tolerant, and more homogeneously Protestant." Conservative religion became the core of a southern culture obsessed with understanding defeat and honoring the memory of the lost cause. Perhaps more important in shaping the religion of the late nineteenth-century South was the postwar dislocation of society and the grinding poverty which burdened the region for a century. Under these social stresses southerners turned to the reassertion of old values, to making themselves right with God, and to a righteous disdain for the optimistic liberal Christianity being embraced by their former enemies in the North.

The post-World War II South has outgrown much of the old Bible Belt image. The section is more heterogeneous today; it is no longer so defensively self-conscious; and increasingly the South has entered the mainstream of the American economy. And yet, the heritage of the Bible Belt is still visible. The southern connections with the electric church are impressive and more than coincidental — Billy Graham, Oral Roberts, Pat Robertson, James Bakker, Jimmy Swaggart, Kenneth Copeland, and a host of other southerners have become the millionaire superstars of the religious mass media. Their audiences are the world, not the South, and in varying degrees they have lost their southernness, but they all have roots that reach deep into the fertile religious soil of the Bible Belt.

Renewal Movements in the Mainline Denominations

RICHARD LOVELACE

The fundamentalist-modernist controversy of the 1920s was resolved in many denominations by the entrance of a new stream of theology critical of both confessional orthodoxies and liberalism. For several decades the neo-orthodox mediating theology controlled the center of many large denominations, satisfying with varying degrees of success the hungers of those on the right for nurture and evangelism, and the concerns for social action on the left. In the 1960s, however, tension began to develop between "secular theologies," new and more extreme forms of liberalism, a resurgent evangelicalism nourished by new currents of scholarship, and by the parachurch ministries emerging in the 1940s and 1950s. The entrance of neo-pentecostal theology in the Charismatic Renewal, affecting both mainline Protestantism and the Roman Catholic church, increased this tension.

Beginning in the 1960s and continuing into the next decade, evangelical and charismatic leaders organized themselves into movements of renewal and protest, representing a sector of the church which was growing vigorously, in contrast to the overall decline in mainline denominations. It was a sector, however, that was usually inadequately represented in church organizations and media. The United Presbyterian church, moving toward a new confession expressing a neo-orthodox consensus, found itself confronted and influenced by three different "conservative" movements: Presbyterians United for Biblical Confession, the Presbyterian Lay Committee, and the Presbyterian Charismatic Communion (the latter being an ecumenical renewal movement embracing many Reformed denominations). About the same time, in the mid-1960s, the Good News Movement appeared in the United

Methodist church, and the Fellowship of Witness in the Protestant Episcopal church. By the 1970s, many different renewal movements were working together in an Episcopal coalition called PEWSACTION, in conjunction with a Division of Evangelism and Renewal vigorously funded and supported by the church's administrative center. Controversy over homosexual and heterosexual ethics originated the youngest of the renewal groups. United Church People for Biblical Witness emerged in the United Church of Christ. Other mainline renewal organizations include ALMS (the Affiliation of Lutheran Movements), ministering in the American Lutheran and Missouri Synod Lutheran churches; the American Baptist Fellowship; the Covenant Fellowship of Presbyterians (PCUS); the Mennonite Renewal Service; and the Brethren Revival Fellowship in the Church of the Brethren.

These renewal groups have motivated or at least superintended a general movement in the mainline churches toward the recovery of their spiritual and theological roots. Part of this movement has resulted from new currents of entering leadership. Since the late 1960s vocations for the ministry in mainline churches have averaged thirty percent above the norm. A large percentage of these new leaders come out of parachurch ministries. Many of them are trained at evangelical college seminaries; those who are not have helped move mainline schools back toward traditional theology and more balanced understanding of mission. Since 1977 leaders from these organizations have been meeting together informally at least annually, comparing notes on shared problems, tools, and strategies, and they anticipate adding Roman Catholic charismatics to this mixture.

Issues confronting the various

The charismatic renewal is the most visible mainline renewal movement; thousands of Lutheran charismatics gather annually at one of the largest mainline charismatic conferences. RELIGIOUS NEWS SERVICE PHOTO

renewal movements are remarkably similar. These include the need for a resurgence of prayer and spiritual renewal; need for strengthening of the personal evangelism component in home and foreign missions; responses to liberation and process theologies; orientation toward the ministry of women; sex ethics; theological balance and biblical orthodoxy in media, Christian education literature, and denominational seminaries; church union and COCU; the tension between pluralism and proper church discipline; and the handling of candidates from nondenominational seminaries.

Instruments commonly used by the movements include newsletters and magazines; conferences; lay renewal ministries; chapter networks; support ministries for evangelical seminarians; and informal diplomacy with the churches' administrative centers. Episcopal conservatives have secured the acceptance of an evangel-

ical seminary, and Methodists in the Good News Movement have gained approval for an alternate Sunday-school curriculum.

Relations between the renewal groups, local judicatories, and administrative centers in the mainline denominations range from extreme polarization in some instances to high levels of trust in others. As evangelicals have been reawakening to the social dimension of mission, mainline leaders have become interested in prayer and spiritual formation, and this movement of convergence may lead to a shared theological consensus. Conservative leaders formerly aligned with neo-orthodoxy are increasingly joining the evangelicals on theological and ethical issues, and there is at least the possibility that in many denominations the future theological center will be controlled by these coalitions or by evangelical and charismatic leadership.

The Electronic Church

MARTIN E. MARTY

The development of printing with movable type coincided with the Protestant Reformation. It made possible the spread of religious ideas with new efficiency and power. The invention of radio and television in the twentieth century was an even more dramatic revolution in communications. This electronic revolution was a threat to Christianity, because it provided means for competing value systems to invade homes. But it was also a possibility for enlargement of Christian work.

In 1921, only a year or so after radio broadcasting began, radio station KDKA in Pittsburgh began to carry programs from Calvary Episcopal Church. Several years later a Lutheran pioneer, Walter A. Maier, became the voice of the international "Lutheran Hour," which typically worked to serve a denomination in its testimony to the message of Jesus Christ. In 1923

Robert Schuller's "Hour of Power" commanded the largest religious television audience in the early 1980s.

Dr. Charles E. Fuller, an evangelist, began to move radio preaching into nondenominational channels with "The Old Fashioned Revival Hour." Through the Depression, the use of radio spread, while numbers of denominations entered the field. Individual enterprisers in the 1930s ran the spectrum from people who broadcast their own church services or devotional programs to shut-ins, across to men like Fr. Charles Coughlin, a Roman Catholic anti-Communist whose church eventually silenced him for anti-Semitism and support of right-wing totalitarianisms.

After the Second World War the use of electronic media was greatly enlarged, thanks chiefly to television. With secular broadcasting distracting people from regular worship and offering jostling values, religious forces entered the field. Mainline Protestant and Catholic churches used the medium chiefly as a forum or a means of dramatizing the life of the church. But soon it became clear that television empires demanded the appearance of attractive personalities if they were to hold a following. The first master of the intimate use of television was Roman Catholic bishop Fulton J. Sheen, while his contemporary, evangelist Billy Graham, was especially successful with a public style. Graham used television to spread the sense of participation in his crusades.

By the 1970s a number of other celebrities had begun to win followings. Superimposed on a network of literally thousands of local radio broadcasters, a few surviving denominational ventures, and some low-budget television reproductions of church services, there developed almost independently of the organized church a network of operations that came to be called "The Electronic Church." This new cluster was marked by at least three characteristics. Almost all its leadership was of an evangelistic sort; television was to be

Pat Robertson, host of the interview and variety program "The 700 Club"
BILLY GRAHAM CENTER

the broadcasters had to adapt to their market research and reach for sensation. Others criticized the strident appeals for funds as debasements of Christian stewardship. Most of all, some argued that the electronic church was converting people only to a private form of religion alongside the real church that was made up of congregations; it was becoming a competitor to the latter. Surveys were inconclusive and probably never could give definitive guidance to Christian leaders, because of the diversity of broadcasting ventures and clienteles. What was clear was that the electronic church had established itself as a permanent agency only fifty years after it was born at KDKA in Pittsburgh.

a means of bringing new people to Christ. Second, after the example of Oral Roberts and Kathryn Kuhlmann, the act of healing became a regular feature. Finally, many of the leaders in the electronic church, knowing that they were competing in a world of bold advertising claims, offered success to those who would follow their interpretations of the gospel.

As the electronic church gained in power, it also acquired critics. Some questioned the integrity of the form of the gospel in what was fundamentally an entertainment medium, wherein

Oral Roberts has built a large following with his radio and television healing ministry. BILLY GRAHAM CENTER

Roman Catholicism

Statistics can conceal as much as they reveal. Roman Catholic church membership is a case in point. In 1957, 25.7 percent of the population over fourteen was Catholic; in 1962, this dropped to 23 percent; by 1972, it had climbed back up to 26 percent; by 1980, the figure for those over nineteen was up to 28 percent. What these figures do not reveal is that the recovery in membership was the result of recent Hispanic influxes and that relatively steady membership counts went hand in hand with revolutionary changes in the belief and practice of Catholic faith.

The Second Vatican Council (1962-1965) fulfilled Pope John XXIII's desire to open the windows of the church. The Council's concern for collegiality, for the laity, and for modern developments in scholarship and society led to particularly visible results in America. Since the Council, American Catholics have found it much more acceptable to "dialogue" with Protestants and members of other faiths or to look for religious "encounters." The liberal approach to church-state relations, for which John Courtney Murray had run afoul of the hierarchy during the 1950s, now prevailed. This point of view held that Catholics should participate in the free-for-all of American public life, not begrudging the loss of European privilege, but glorying in the abundant liberty. It received its greatest encouragement in the election of John Kennedy to the presidency in 1960.

Pope John XXIII, the innovative leader who summoned the Second Vatican Council
RELIGIOUS NEWS SERVICE PHOTO

John Kennedy was the first Roman Catholic to be elected president. RELIGIOUS NEWS SERVICE PHOTO

The Second Vatican Council on Religious Freedom

This Vatican Synod declares that the human person has a right to religious freedom. This freedom means that all men are to be immune from coercion on the part of individuals or of social groups and of any human power, in such wise that in matters religious no one is to be forced to act in a manner contrary to his own beliefs. Nor is anyone to be restrained from acting in accordance with his own beliefs, whether privately or publicly, whether alone or in association with others, within due limits.

The Synod further declares that the right to religious freedom has its foundation in the very dignity of the human person, as this dignity is known through the revealed Word of God and by reason itself. This right of the human person to religious freedom is to be recognized in the constitutional law whereby society is governed. Thus it is to become a civil right.

Although only thirty-eight percent of Protestants gave him their vote, the support of eighty-one percent of Catholics, together with that of Jews and blacks, carried the day. For the first time in American history, Roman Catholics in the Eighty-ninth Congress, which convened in January 1965, were the largest religious group.

The Council's attitude toward the Bible spawned an opposing pair of developments in America. Moderate encouragement given to biblical criticism by the Council dissolved the older cautions Catholic scholars had felt; in an astonishingly short time, Catholic scholarship became indistinguishable from Protestant work, operating with the same assumptions and often reaching the same radical conclusions. By contrast, the Council's benign attitude toward Protestantism—even allowing, for the first time, that Protestants have legitimate churches—encouraged some groups of lay Catholics to draw closer to Protestant evangelicals by adopting their methods of informal Bible study. The charismatic movement, no respecter of the formal differences between Catholics and Protestants, was important in this development.

Since it burst upon the Catholic church in 1967, the charismatic movement has created perplexity and sparked misunderstanding. Initially, the Catholic hierarchy, fearing that the movement would be antiinstitutional in temper, was sharply opposed to it; instead, charismatics proved to be among the most loyal in the church. Protestant conservatives rushed to embrace these Catholics, imagining they saw an imminent exodus from the church; instead, Catholic charismatics have remained Catholic. Protestant charismatics reasoned that it was only a matter of time before their Catholic brothers and sisters would shuck off the Catholic sacramental system; instead, Catholic charismatics have domesticated their glossolalia and integrated their experience of the Spirit into the structure of church teaching. While only six percent of Catholics have attended a charismatic meeting, the movement has exerted an influence out of all proportion to its number. "Both it and its ecumenical significance," says Catholic Kilian McDonnell, "are permanent elements in the life of the Roman Catholic church."

It was, however, something firmly ensconced in the Catholic past that was to have an even greater effect on the Catholic church than the charismatics. Vatican II quietly affirmed the traditional prohibition against tampering with the birth process; Paul VI, not so quietly, reaffirmed the church's opposition to artificial means of contraception after the Council had completed its work. His encyclical, *Humanae Vitae* (1968), was the "single decision," sociologist Andrew Greeley has said, which accounts for "the disaster of American Catholicism."

The "disaster" was recorded by the statisticians. Attendance at weekly mass fell from seventy-one percent in 1963 to fifty percent in 1974; monthly confession in these years dipped from thirty-eight to seventeen percent; the church's income declined $1.7 billion in that decade, which was also one of staggering inflation; enrollment in parochial schools tumbled from 5.6 million in 1965 to 3.5 million in 1975; in 1964, there were 49,000 seminarians but by 1975 only 17,000; between 1965 and 1975 the number of nuns declined twenty-five percent; defections from the priesthood became common. And Catholic belief was in turmoil. Whereas in 1964 seventy-percent of Catholics believed that Christ had founded the church and appointed Peter its first bishop, by 1974 this figure had fallen to forty-two percent. In that same year, 1974, only thirty-two percent believed in papal infallibility; in previous years no one had thought to gauge this sentiment, since it was always assumed that papal infallibility would at least be maintained by Roman Catholics.

What had happened? Apparently profound but subterranean changes had been taking place. What had been changing in particular was the attitude toward sexual values and practices. A rebellion against the church's teaching was afoot. The resistance to premarital sex was declining, the tolerance toward homosexuality increasing, the desire for artificial means of contraception was gaining ground, and the opposition to abortion was weakening. Catholic mores, in other words, were beginning to resemble those of the culture. Pope Paul VI's encyclical precipitated this rebellion. And what thousands of Catholics discovered was that the church could be disobeyed and the heavens would not fall.

It was—all at the same time—an exhilarating but troubling discovery.

Catholicism, with a doctrine of development not paralleled in the various Protestant bodies, has always managed to preserve its identity in the midst of change. Many Catholics felt that their commitment as Catholics had survived the crisis unscathed; many others, however, were shaken loose of the church either to be absorbed into the secular culture or to be attracted, more often than not, as satellites around various evangelical Protestant groups.

Fundamentalism and Catholicism have lived entirely independent of one another, but their histories have unfolded in parallel lines. In the 1930s both groups represented cognitive minorities in an unfriendly culture. Each was a world in itself. Neither fundamentalists nor Catholics spoke to or for the nation. For different reasons and by different routes, each group has been absorbed into the mainstream of American life. In the process each changed. Fundamentalism, to its regret, gave birth to an evangelicalism less angular, less rigid, and more sensitive to the need for cultural involvement; traditional Catholicism, to its regret, witnessed the birth of a "New Catholicism" which refused to keep either Protestants or the secular culture at arm's length. New Catholics and evangelicals were confronted with the dilemma of how to preserve their Christian identity in the midst of cultural involvement and con-

This annual harvest festival near Santa Fe, New Mexico preserves the ethnicity of Southwest Roman Catholicism.   COURTESY EDWIN S. GAUSTAD

tamination; traditional Catholics and fundamentalists were left pondering how to establish a meaningful presence in the nation while protecting their cognitive purity.

The Charismatic Movement

JOHN THOMAS NICHOL

The charismatic movement is an international interfaith spiritual revival which derives its name from the fact that its adherents claim to have received one or more of the spiritual gifts (Greek *charismata*) which are described in I Corinthians 12–14; for example, speaking in tongues (*glossolalia*), the ability to interpret tongues, to prophesy, to heal, or to expel evil spirits. Charismatic Christians declare that they receive one or more of these spiritual gifts after they have been "baptized in the Holy Spirit." Spirit baptism is a postconversion religious experience that corresponds to the initial outpouring of the Holy Spirit upon the disciples on the day of Pentecost as well as to the other instances of Spirit baptism that are reported in the book of Acts (1:12–2:4; 10:46; 19:1-7).

Although the penetration of the charismatic movement has been worldwide, its major expansion has occurred in the United States. Results

Charismatic prayer in a traditional pentecostal congregation

RELIGIOUS NEWS SERVICE PHOTO

of a February 1980 poll conducted by *Christianity Today* show that approximately 29 million Americans consider themselves to be charismatic Christians. Clearly members of traditional pentecostal groups (e.g., Church of God in Christ, Assemblies of God) constitute the most substantial bloc; however, the poll also reveals that practicing charismatics in the Roman Catholic church and in several major Protestant denominations make up additional sizable minorities — perhaps as many as 6 and 11 million members, respectively.

It is generally acknowledged that the contemporary charismatic movement, now encompassing nearly every major Protestant denomination — as well as Roman Catholics and Eastern Orthodox Christians — started in 1960. It emerged in the aftermath of widely circulated reports in the secular and religious media that Dennis Bennett, rector of St. Mark's Episcopal Church in Van Nuys, California, together with a goodly number of his communicants, had experienced a Spirit baptism, and was openly advocating speaking in tongues and related charismatic practices. *Time* and *Newsweek* carried the news of this outburst of charismatic activity, especially the uproar that

ensued: Father Bennett's resignation; the ban which the diocesan bishop of Los Angeles placed on speaking in tongues in churches under his jurisdiction; and Bennett's eventual success in transforming St. Luke's Episcopal Church in Seattle from a moribund parish into a thriving 2,000-member charismatic church. In the months that followed, innumerable clergy and laity from many denominations came forward to testify that they too had been "filled with the Holy Spirit" and endowed with at least one spiritual gift. Included among this group were several clergy who became articulate advocates for charismatic renewal not only within their respective churches but also at national and international religious conclaves: Larry Christenson (Lutheran), Harald Bredesen (Reformed church), Howard Ervin (Baptist), J. Rodman Williams (Presbyterian). Understandably, it was simply a matter of time until charismatic behavior began to manifest itself among Catholics too.

The Catholic branch of the charismatic movement started rather inauspiciously in the winter of 1967, when four members of the Duquesne University faculty attended a Protestant charismatic prayer meeting in Pittsburgh in hopes of satisfying their longings for personal spiritual renewal. According to their personal testimonies, they were not disappointed; they received spiritual blessings, including the gift of tongues and other charisms, that had life-transforming aftereffects. What happened at Duquesne reoccurred on several other Catholic campuses, with the result that by June ninety participants attended the first charismatic conference at Notre Dame. (Seven years later, 35,000 gathered for the eighth international meeting!) Unquestionably the Catholic Charismatic Renewal has developed into an influential, pervasive movement. A recent poll suggests that 4 million American Catholics actually attended a charismatic renewal meeting within the month they were surveyed.

The current charismatic movement is, admittedly, the offspring of a pentecostal revival that sprang up at the turn of the twentieth century; nevertheless, it is markedly different from its spiritual ancestor in several distinct ways: (1) The charismatic movement is neither a church nor a denomination. (2) It is inclined toward ecumenism rather than sectarianism.

(3) It stresses the diversity of spiritual gifts instead of emphasizing the uniqueness of one gift — speaking in tongues. (4) It attracts followers from all classes of society rather than appealing principally to those from the lower socioeconomic stratum.

To conclude, in the relatively short span of two decades charismatics have established themselves in almost every major denomination; nevertheless, reactions to them and to the movement they form remain mixed. On one hand, the charismatic movement has been accused of being divisive, antiintellectual; its followers self-righteous, and reluctant to assume responsibility for social and institutional reform. On the other hand, the movement has been praised for having enlivened and renewed institutional Christianity, and for having transformed routine worship into a joyful, spontaneous celebration that encourages participation, fellowship, sharing, and caring.

Participants at a Catholic Charismatic Renewal conference in 1976
RELIGIOUS NEWS SERVICE PHOTO

Change in American Catholicism

JOSEPH H. FICHTER

There was a time when one could tell the difference between a Catholic and a Protestant because the Catholic ate fish on Friday and attended Mass on Sunday, and such obligations were binding under "pain of sin." Catholics also had a higher birth rate than Protestants, and a lower rate of divorce. Catholic children went to the parochial schools, Protestant children to the public schools.

The winds of change began to blow over American Catholics with the pontificate of John XXIII, who instituted the Second Vatican Council and "opened the windows" for renewal. The implications of Vatican II were analyzed by the newly founded, lay-edited, and irreverent *National Catholic Reporter*, which introduced a refreshing open type of religious journalism to the American church. Publicity was widely given to the establishment of the National Federation of Priests' Council and to the National Assembly of Women Religious. The first black American bishop was consecrated, and the National Office of Black Catholics was opened. The laity was inspired to start the Catholic Charismatic Renewal, which has since spread to other countries.

The everyday life of the typical American Catholic has been changed in different ways. Some innovations seem to move in the direction of leniency, a relaxation of old rules that makes life easier. Others move in the direction of heavier obligations that put more conscience burdens on the faithful.

Liturgical changes, to which both

Mass is celebrated in a parish home in Philadelphia as part of an effort at spiritual renewal in the parish.
RELIGIOUS NEWS SERVICE PHOTO

clergy and laity had to become accustomed, suggest less rigidity and more informality. The Mass is now celebrated in English with the priest facing the congregation. Scripture is now read by lay lectors, even women; and the Eucharist may be distributed by laymen and -women who are called "extraordinary ministers of the sacrament." The laity may receive the Eucharist "in the hand," and are no longer required to abstain from food and drink from midnight. There has been a notable increase in the proportion of the congregation who receive Communion frequently.

On the other hand, the number of people who confess their sins sacramentally has decreased drastically. In place of long lines of people waiting their turn at the confessional on Saturday afternoons and evenings, the formula has been shifted to the so-called "rite of reconciliation," which requires more time than a quick confession and is a more personal and informal relationship with the priest. Confessions may be heard at any time, and the schedule of Masses, which used to be restricted to Sunday morning, now allows for Mass attendance on Saturday evenings as well as at any hour during the day on Sunday.

These changes may be recognized as a relaxation of previously rigid obligations and also as a greater convenience for the laity. The duty to fast (i.e., eat no more than one meal a day) during the Lenten season has been relaxed, and there appears to be little inclination toward "keeping Lent" by various pious practices of self-denial and mortification. Popular interest has waned in many of the special devotions, like honoring the Sacred Heart on first Fridays and the Blessed Mother on first Saturdays, Vespers, Benediction, Way of the Cross, and Novenas in honor of various saints.

A certain strictness, however, has been introduced in the area of knowledge and preparation for the sacraments. Parents of a newborn infant are required to come to the church for religious instructions and spiritual counsel before the baptism of their child. Couples who anticipate marriage must consult with their pastor several months in advance, submit to detailed interrogation, and attend pre-Cana conferences. American bishops are concerned about the growing divorce rate and the breakup of families, and insist that more careful attention be given to the seriousness of the marriage vocation. The so-called Marriage Encounter movement attracts large numbers of Catholic couples to renew the spirituality of their mutual commitment.

A significant change has occurred also away from the over-dependence on the clergy for moral guidance. Vatican II reemphasized the personal accountability of each individual before God. Catholics are now expected to consult their own conscience in moral areas where they once depended completely on the counsel of the clergy. The obligation of making up their own minds about the morality of behavior may have led some of them astray on matters of premarital sex and contraception. It appears that the sense of sin has been dulled, which may explain the decline in the frequency of sacramental confession.

The relationship between the clergy and the laity is changing in another way at the operational level of the parish. The organizational principles of

Some Catholics resisted the changes in Vatican II, including the vernacular mass; they continued to celebrate the traditional Latin liturgy (below and opposite).
RELIGIOUS NEWS SERVICE PHOTO

AVE MARIA CHAPEL
HOLY MASSES AND SERVICES
IN THE TRADITIONAL LATIN

ROMAN CATHOLIC
LITURGY
Under the sponsorship of the
CATHOLIC TRADITIONALIST MOVEMENT, INC.
FOUNDED 1964

And the protection of the
SOVEREIGN ORDER of ST. JOHN of JERUSALEM
KNIGHTS of MALTA
FOUNDED 1048

collegiality and coresponsibility, with which the pope and the bishops cooperate, are now being adapted to the diocesan and the parochial structures. Parish councils have been formed all over the country to which laypeople are elected by the congregation and in which they have a voice in the many decisions that were previously the exclusive activity of the pastor.

The participation of the laity in the church does not go as far as the kind of democracy one finds in some Protestant congregations. Just as the priests have no vote in the selection of bishops, parishioners have no vote in the selection of their pastors, and even the decisions in which they do participate can be vetoed by the pastor. The bishop invites laypeople to help him in running the diocese and appoints laypeople to various committees and councils, but as in the case of the parish the advice of the laity need not be heeded by the bishop.

In spite of these several restrictions, the laypeople are forming closer ties with the clergy and are engaging more than ever in the ministries of the church. A partial explanation of this change of role and status is the fact that the numbers of religious professionals have drastically declined since the mid-sixties. The annual ordination class is shrinking because fewer young men enter Catholic seminaries and novitiates. More remarkable, however, is the relatively large number of men who have resigned the priesthood, most of them to marry. This was an almost unheard-of phenomenon prior to Vatican II, when it was practically impossible to obtain a dispensation from the priestly vows. In those days the ex-priest was pitied as a kind of renegade or defector.

The participation of the laity and the expanding roles of women religious are helping to take up the slack of the gradually diminishing priesthood. There are still more than 120,000 nuns in the American Catholic church, which is a remarkable number when compared to other organized religions, but this is a serious decline from earlier figures. This means that many parochial elementary schools have either closed or have turned to the employment of lay teachers. The lack of religious sisters has also affected the available personnel in Catholic hospitals and other social welfare apostolates.

A novel proposal for the Catholic church has been the push for the ordination of women to the priesthood. Laymen have been accepted for training to the diaconate, but no room has been made for deaconesses. Nevertheless, the professional roles of women religious have tended to expand even as the number of sisters contracted. They are entering new ministries as associates in parishes, administrators in social work agencies, and trained chaplains in pastoral care departments of hospitals. As more of them earn graduate degrees, they are being employed on faculties and research institutes of colleges and universities.

As in all large voluntary associations, there tend to be disagreements between traditionalists and progressivists in the American Catholic church. Some feel that the time of experimentation should come to an end, that the church should settle down on a stable level. Others feel that many more changes are needed and that the spirit of renewal should be kept alive in the church.

Dr. Samuel Cavert, General Secretary of the
National Council of Churches, examines proof sheets
for the Revised Standard Version, 1952.
NATIONAL COUNCIL OF CHURCHES

The Bible Boom

In one aspect of the Christian faith, recent American activity may represent an all-time high. That is in the distribution, and perhaps the use, of the Bible. The postwar religious revival brought with it an upsurge in the publishing of the Bible. It also coincided with the publication of the complete text of the Revised Standard Version in 1952. Although some conservatives roundly denounced this modernization of the Authorized or King James Version, a modernization that used current biblical scholarship to establish the underlying Greek and Hebrew texts, it set the pace for an energetic period of Bible translation.

Monsignor Patrick Skehan of Catholic University of
America studies notes for the New American Bible,
1970. BAPTIST JOINT COMMITTEE ON PUBLIC AFFAIRS

The modern American appetite for the Bible is, in fact, insatiable. The RSV averaged one million copies a year during its first decade, and had risen to a total of 50 million copies in print by 1981. The RSV has been adopted for use by Catholics, who also sponsored the New American Bible (1970) and the critically praised Jerusalem Bible (1966). The Jewish Publication Society completed a new translation of the Hebrew scriptures in 1982. Still, the bulk of Bible production has proceeded under Protestant auspices. As of 1981, American sales of Kenneth Taylor's Living Bible paraphrase stood at 25 million; the New American Standard Bible, a conservative revision of the Authorized Version, at 14 million; the American Bible Society's Good News Bible (Today's English Version) and the British New English Bible at 12 million each; and the evangelically sponsored New International Version at 3 million. Bible sales amounted to $150 million in 1980. But these figures were only a fraction of the volume generated for biblically related literature published by a flourishing host of religious publishing houses. The American Bible Society stands by itself in the distribution of scripture at home and abroad. In 1979 alone it distributed nearly 110 million Bibles, testaments, portions, and selections in just the United States.

Public polling indicates that at least many who buy the Bible believe in it deeply. In 1952, eight out of ten adult Americans responded to a Gallup poll that they believed the Bible was the "revealed word of God." In 1978 George Gallup found forty-two percent of the population agreeing with an even more precise statement that "the Bible is the word of God and is not mistaken in its statements and teachings." To be sure, knowledge of scripture seems a bit skimpy among a populace which thinks of it so highly. The 1952 poll found that only thirty-five percent could name all four gospels. And in 1978, while eighty-six percent believed in the continuing validity of the Ten Commandments, only forty-nine percent of the Catholics and forty percent of the Protestants could name even five of them.

However well American churchpeople actually know the Bible, they are usually ready to fight about it. In the 1970s the Lutheran church–Missouri Synod and the Southern

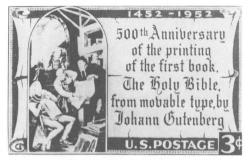

Stamp commemorating the five hundredth anniversary of the Gutenberg Bible, coinciding with the publicaton of the RSV in 1952
RELIGIOUS NEWS SERVICE PHOTO

Baptist Convention both experienced bitter debates over the nature of the Bible and its authority. In the case of the Missouri Synod, this debate led to an actual schism. It was perhaps a sign of the times, however, that more conservative forces held the denomination, while the more liberal felt constrained to depart. Southern Baptist Harold Lindsell, while editor of *Christianity Today*, sparked a sharp controversy with his book, *The Battle for the Bible* (1976). In it he argued that many evangelical institutions and individuals were abandoning the view of biblical inerrancy for which the opponents of modernism had done battle so faithfully earlier in the century. This "battle" soon spread to the Southern Baptist Convention, where that body's traditional congregationalism and the independence of its seminaries worked against a conclusive resolution of the difficulty. Many other denominations and parachurch groups also entertained sharp struggles over this same issue during the late 1970s.

The intense evangelical debate over the inerrancy of the Bible is, in fact, symptomatic of widespread turbulence in the churches. Denominations have continued to take their corporate lives very seriously and to protect their perceived interests tenaciously despite their shrinking importance. Besides the evangelicals' "battle for the Bible," for example, one could cite also the Catholic controversy over birth control, bitter debate among Episcopalians over the ordination of women to the priesthood, extended contro-

versy among Presbyterians on a number of doctrinal and ecclesiastical issues such as the divinity of Christ and the status of homosexuals, or acrimonious struggles in the National Council of Churches over positions toward Israel. These debates deserve to be treated with the utmost seriousness. Unless the issues are resolved wisely, however, they could become the means of further bitter division and internal distraction. At a time of great upheaval and danger in the world, the churches could become wholly absorbed with the drama of their inner lives. Who, then, will address the needs of the times? There is need, for example, for relief and spiritual nurture among Cuban, Haitian, and southeast Asian refugees; for churches to return to urban areas stripped, in recent decades, of many places of worship; or for effective Christian ministry to the burgeoning number of abandoned children, the divorced, and the elderly. Momentous questions involving the future of the world itself remain without answers— such as the nuclear arms race, the needs of the world's hungry, or the question of Third World development. In the country's great universities and among its most important media establishments a Christian witness, of whatever sort, is rare. The nature of much debate in American religion—not least the various questions relating to the Bible—has sometimes been determined not so much by the ecclesiastical importance of the questions under discussion as by the disengagement of the debaters from the modern world.

Harold Lindsell, defender of strict biblical inerrancy and author of The Battle for the Bible
BILLY GRAHAM CENTER

On the Brink
of the Future

The moment when this chronicling of American affairs and beliefs must end is most inconvenient. Although 1980 is the beginning of a decade, it marks no logical stopping point in the narrative. On the contrary, it comes at a time when both American culture and Christian faith are rushing headlong into a future wracked by uncertainty. To interrupt this narrative at this time is to cut off the story before some of its most significant developments happen.

Few people, however, are foolish enough to pretend they can see anything more than a few dim shapes looming up ahead. Visibility at the best of times is limited in such matters; it seems especially poor at present. For whether we interpret the present cultural chaos as the final death throes of Western culture itself or as the growing pains of a new order—or, even, as both of these things—there can be no doubt that it has left us confused and perceptually dulled.

The anomalies of this time are legion, and who can tell how they will resolve themselves? Who can know whether they will resolve themselves? Society teeters on the brink of chaos in which the factors which should provide stability—the institutions of government, law, and education—have lost their legitimacy. The shared meanings of American culture—what it means to be a man, a woman, to be successful, to drive a Cadillac, to be free—are the common possession of fewer and fewer people. Inherited values are breaking down.

Every day people find themselves face to face with an adolescent world torn by contrary forces that defy resolution. Mankind can split the atom but cannot heal fractured psyches. People want world peace but prepare for world war. They want intimacy but find isolation. People have shrunken the world by electronic wizardry, but their omniscience is so unbearable that they expand their minds by drugs to escape it. They are conversant with the whole world but unknown to their next door neighbors. Americans constitute the wealthiest nation on earth but forget their own poor. They claim to be one nation under God, but are many nations under many gods. They say that they believe in the rule of law, but why then are they the most unruly, the most violent, nation in the Western world? They want freedom, but find themselves paralyzed by the endless possibilities that confront them. Freedom is defined as not choosing, as dropping out of the rat race. The rich die from too much weight, and the poor from too little nourishment.

How will mankind shape its future in this world, a world marked by brilliance without wisdom, power without conscience? The key to the secrets of life and death is at hand, but can humans be trusted with such knowledge? Is mankind not, at one and the same time, adrift on the seas of high technology and shipwrecked on the reefs of low morality?

As the third millennium *anno Domini* approaches, it is with these cultural anomalies—and myriads of others like them—that Christian faith must wrestle. The result of this engagement could change the shape and morphology of Christianity more radically in the next two decades than has occurred in the last two centuries. And then 1980 will seem an even more curious moment to end a chronicle of American Christianity than it does now.

For Further Reading

Good general surveys of the course of recent American Christianity are offered by Sydney E. Ahlstrom, *A Religious History of the American People* (1972), Winthrop S. Hudson, *Religion in America*, 3rd ed. (1981), and Robert T. Handy, *A History of the Churches in the United States and Canada* (1977). Two solid narratives which flesh out, respectively, the more active and the more reflective sides of American Christianity for the early part of this period are Paul A. Carter, *The Decline and Revival of the Social Gospel: Social and Political Liberalism in American Protestant Churches, 1920-1940*, 2nd ed. (1956; repr. 1971), and Donald B. Meyer, *The Protestant Search for Political Realism, 1919-1941* (1960; repr. 1973). The twentieth century is an age of numbers, charts, graphs, and maps. Several careful books have used these devices to describe the state of American religion: Rodney Stark and Charles Y. Glock, *American Piety: The Nature of Religious Commitment* (1968), Edwin S. Gaustad, *Historical Atlas of Religion in America*, rev. ed. (1976), Albert J. Menendez, *Religion at the Polls* (1977), Jackson W. Carroll, Douglas W. Johnson, and Martin E. Marty, *Religion in America: 1950 to the Present* (1978), and George Gallup, Jr., and David Poling, *The Search for America's Faith* (1980). Also useful as a roadmap to American religious life is the monumental study of American denominations by Arthur C. Piepkorn, *Profiles in Belief: The Religious Bodies of North America*, 4 vols. (1977-1979). A singularly valuable study of American hymns which has provided fresh insights into the nature of American Christianity is Albert Christ-Janer, Charles W. Hughes, and Carleton Sprague Smith, *American Hymns: Old and New*, 2 vols. (1980).

In a class by himself as an analyst of modern American belief is Martin E. Marty of the University of Chicago. His many contributions to an understanding of contemporary religion include such studies as *The New Shape of American Religion* (1959), *Righteous Empire: The Protestant Experience in America* (1970), *A Nation of Behavers* (1980), and *The Public Church: Mainline–Evangelical–Catholic* (1981), as well as books which

he has edited, including *The Religious Press in America* (1963; repr. 1973) and *Where the Spirit Leads: Seventeen American Denominations Today* (1980). If Marty has a peer as a contemporary observer, it is the Roman Catholic sociologist Andrew M. Greeley, who has written very widely on his own communion, and beyond. Among his books are *The Catholic Experience: An Interpretation of the History of American Catholicism* (1967), *The Denominational Society* (1973), and a comprehensive study, *The American Catholic: A Social Portrait* (1977).

A number of works stand out among those which have attempted more reflectively to take the measure of recent religion in the United States. Will Herberg's *Protestant–Catholic–Jew*, rev. ed. (1955), was a pathbreaking volume which can still be read with much profit. Sociologist Peter L. Berger has written several profound depictions of American religiosity that are as sensitive in their understanding as they are sharp in their criticism, including *The Noise of Solemn Assemblies: Christian Commitment and the Religious Establishment in America* (1961) and *The Heretical Imperative: Contemporary Possibilities of Religious Affirmation* (1979). The modern discussion of "civil religion" received its classic treatment from Robert N. Bellah in *Religion in America*, ed. with William G. McLoughlin (1968), and *The Broken Covenant: American Civil Religion in Time of Trial* (1976). John F. Wilson, *Public Religion in American Culture* (1979), is the most perceptive analysis of the civil religion discussions begun by Bellah. The rise of theologically conservative forms of belief receives careful attention from the ecclesiastical official Dean Kelley, *Why Conservative Churches are Growing* (1972), and from the cultural savant Jeremy Rifkin (with Ted Howard), *The Emerging Order: God in the Age of Scarcity* (1979).

Students of American theology should read the major theologians themselves, for the works of Richard and Reinhold Niebuhr, Schubert Ogden, Carl Henry, and other major twentieth-century voices are widely and readily available. Good introductions to the theological landscape for the beginning and end of the period 1930-1980 come from Vergilius T. Ferm, ed., *Contemporary American Theology* (1933), and Deane William Ferm,

Contemporary American Theologies (1981). William E. Hordern, *A Layman's Guide to Protestant Theology*, rev. ed. (1968), is also a helpful resource. William R. Miller, ed., *Contemporary American Protestant Thought, 1900-1970* (1973), offers an anthology of more liberal Protestant theology and Carl F. H. Henry, *Contemporary Evangelical Thought* (1957), of more conservative. Consideration of more specialized developments may be found in Richard J. Coleman, *Issues of Theological Conflict: Evangelicals and Liberals*, rev. ed. (1980), Jackson Lee Ice and John J. Carey, eds., *The Death of God Debate* (1967), and C. Norman Kraus, *Dispensationalism in America* (1958).

Modern American church history has witnessed several strikingly new developments and others which seem new but are actually a renewal of historical themes and practices. Among these are the reemergence of preachers as leading cultural communicators, treated in Ben Armstrong, *The Electric Church* (1979), and Jeffrey K. Hadden and Charles E. Swann, *Prime Time Preachers: The Rising Power of Televangelism* (1981); the emergence of an active conservative politics joined to a conservative Protestant theology, covered by Richard V. Pierard, *The Unequal Yoke: Evangelical Christianity and Political Conservatism* (1970), Erling Jorstad, *The Politics of Moralism: The New Christian Right in American Life* (1981), and Robert Webber, *The Moral Majority: Right or Wrong?* (1981); and dramatic gains for the pentecostal and charismatic expressions of Christian faith, the subject of Vinson Synan, *The Holiness-Pentecostal Movement in the United States* (1971), David Edwin Harrell, *All Things Are Possible: The Healing and Charismatic Revivals in Modern America* (1976), Robert Mapes Anderson, *Vision of the Disinherited: The Making of American Pentecostalism* (1979), and Michael Pollock Hamilton, ed., *The Charismatic Movement* (1976).

Denominational historians have continued to make their mark, with especially important work being done on recent developments in the Roman Catholic church during the period following the Second Vatican Council. The following may be singled out as especially perceptive chronicles of these developments: Philip Gleason, ed., *Contemporary Catholicism in the United States* (1969),

David J. O'Brien, *The Renewal of American Catholicism* (1972), and Garry Wills, *Bare Ruined Choirs: Doubt, Prophecy, and Radical Religion* (1972). Other historians have probed more restricted chapters involving the recent history of American Catholics, including Myron A. Marty, *Lutherans and Roman Catholicism: The Changing Conflict, 1917-1963* (1968), Donald F. Crosby, *God, Church, and Flag: Senator Joseph R. McCarthy and the Catholic Church, 1950-1957* (1978), and Patricia F. McNeal, *The American Catholic Peace Movement, 1928-1972* (1978). And all who are interested in history, not just Catholics, should welcome the appearance of a full history which carries the story of American Catholics well past Vatican II, James J. Hennessey, *American Catholics: A History of the Roman Catholic Community in the United States* (1982).

Increased public visibility for theologically conservative Protestants has been reflected in book-length treatments of "evangelicals," including Ronald H. Nash, *The New Evangelicalism* (1963), David F. Wells and John D. Woodbridge, eds., *The Evangelicals* (1975), John D. Woodbridge, Mark A. Noll, and Nathan O. Hatch, *The Gospel in America: Themes in the Story of America's Evangelicals* (1979), Richard Quebedeaux, *The Young Evangelicals* (1974) and *The Worldly Evangelicals* (1978), and Robert Webber and Donald Bloesch, *The Orthodox Evangelicals* (1978). The Jesus Movement of the 1960s, which drew upon evangelical and countercultural motifs, was the subject of solid treatment in Ronald M. Enroth, Edward E. Ericson, Jr., and C. Breckenridge Peters, *The Jesus People: Old-Time Religion in the Age of Aquarius* (1972).

Good specialized studies of distinct denominational and other groupings in recent history include Timothy L. Smith, *Called Unto Holiness* (1962), a history of the Nazarenes, Leonard J. Arrington and Davis Bitton, *The Mormon Experience* (1979), and Hart M. Nelsen and Anne K. Nelsen, *The Black Church in the Sixties* (1975). Samuel McCrea Cavert, *Church Cooperation and Unity in America: A Historical Review, 1900-1970* (1970), treats efforts to draw different Christian groups together.

A series of books also have looked at expressions of religion that fall beyond the pale of traditional faith. Some of these studies are sophisticated accounts, such as Charles Y. Glock and Robert Bellah, eds., *The New Religious Consciousness* (1976), Margot Adler, *Drawing Down the Moon: Witches, Druids, Goddess-Worshippers, and Other Pagans in America Today* (1979), and Robert S. Ellwood, *Alternative Altars: Unconventional and Eastern Spirituality in America* (1979).

Finally, biographers have also been active in the recent past to chart the lifecourse of the movers and shakers of the religious world. Among some of the twentieth-century figures who have already received serious biographical attention are civil rights leader Martin Luther King, Jr. (David L. Lewis, 2nd ed., 1978; C. Eric Lincoln, ed., 1969), evangelist Billy Graham (Marshall Frady, 1979; John Pollock, 1966, 1979), theologian Reinhold Niebuhr (June Bingham, 1961; Charles W. Kegley and Robert W. Bretall, eds., 1956), Catholic social activist Dorothy Day (William D. Miller, 1981), Catholic theologian and social theorist John Courtney Murray (Donald E. Pelotte, 1976), missionary statesman John R. Mott (C. Howard Hopkins, 1979), and radio pioneers Walter A. Maier, a Lutheran (Paul L. Maier, 1963), and Charles E. Fuller, a fundamentalist/evangelical (Daniel P. Fuller, 1972).

Index

PEOPLE

Entries and page numbers in bold type
indicate an article or document featuring the entry.

ABERNATHY, RALPH 441
ADAMS, BROOKS 32
ADAMS, CHARLES FRANCIS
32
ADAMS, HENRY 287
ADAMS, JOHN 164, 221, 247
AHLSTROM, SYDNEY E. 221,
230
AITKEN, ROBERT 64, 154
ALCOTT, WILLIAM A. 198
ALEXANDER VI (Pope) 9
ALINSKY, SAUL 452
ALISON, FRANCIS 133
ALLEN, ETHAN 164
ALLEN, RICHARD **219-220**
ALLOUEZ, CLAUDE 16
ALTHAM, JOHN 53
ALTIZER, THOMAS 458
AMES, WILLIAM 22, 37
ANDREAE, JOHANN
VALENTIN 205
ANDREW, JAMES O. 262
ANNE (of England) 95
APTHORP, EAST 133
ASBURY, FRANCIS 166, 185,
216, 219
AUSTIN, ANNE 56

BABCOCK, WILLIAM SMYTH
167
BACH, JOHANN CHRISTIAN 83
BACH, JOHANN SEBASTIAN
83
BACKUS, ISAAC 75, **117-118**,
145, 272
BAILYN, BERNARD 238
BAIRD, ROBERT 180, 209
BAKKER, JAMES 475
BALDWIN, JAMES 274, 276
BALTIMORE, see LORD
BALTIMORE
BANCROFT, GEORGE 31
BARNES, ROBERT 20
BARTH, KARL 417, 418,
420-421, 458, 460
BAXTER, RICHARD 100

BEECHER, HENRY WARD 176,
290-291, 322
BEECHER, LYMAN 165, 171,
173, 176, 191, 208, 236, 290;
Plea for the West 236, 289, 376
BEISSEL, CONRAD 97
BENNETT, DENNIS 483
BENNETT, JOHN C. 417
BERGER, PETER 41
BERKELEY, GEORGE 52
BERKHOF, LOUIS 416
BERRIGAN, DANIEL 453-454
BERRIGAN, PHILIP 453-454
BILLINGS, WILLIAM 81, 82
BLAIR, JAMES 5, **51-52**
BLISS, P. P. 186
BLOESCH, DONALD 463
BOEHME, JAKOB 205
BOLEYN, ANNE 19
BOOTH, WILLIAM 315-317
BOUDINOT, ELIAS 195
BRADFORD, WILLIAM 5,
27-28, 33; *Of Plymouth
Plantation* 27
BRADSHAW, WILLIAM 37, 61
BRADSTREET, ANNE 66
BRAINERD, DAVID 90
BRAY, THOMAS 52
BRÉBEUF, JEAN DE 5, 13
BREDESEN, HARALD 483
BREEN, T. H. 49
BRESEE, PHINEAS F. 333
BRETT, PLINY 211
BREWSTER, WILLIAM 27, 28
BRIGGS, CHARLES A. 325
BROOKS, PHILLIPS 291, 322
BROWN, JOHN 263-266
BROWN, WILLIAM A. 383
BROWNE, ROBERT 22
BROWNSON, ORESTES A. 240,
251, 252
BRUNNER, EMIL 417, 418
BRYAN, WILLIAM JENNINGS
312, 368-369, 381, 386
BRYANT, WILLIAM CULLEN
229

BUCER, MARTIN 8
BULTMANN, RUDOLPH 458
BUSHMAN, RICHARD 101
BUSHNELL, HORACE **232-233**
BUTLER, ELIZUR 195
BYRD, WILLIAM, II 61

CAIN, RICHARD HARVEY 347
CALDWELL, JAMES 144
CALEF, ROBERT 71
CALVIN, JOHN 5, 8, 21, 22, 223
CALVERT, CECILIUS (Second
Lord Baltimore) 53, 54
CALVERT, GEORGE (First
Lord Baltimore) 53
CAMPBELL, ALEXANDER 170,
184, 211
CAREY, WILLIAM 192
CARLYLE, THOMAS 188
CARMICHAEL, STOKELY 448
CARNEGIE, ANDREW 287, 368
CARR, PETER 136
CARROLL, JOHN 236, 246-248,
254, 413
CARTER, JIMMY 451, 454, 471
CARTIER, JACQUES 5
CARTWRIGHT, PETER 178,
185, 223
CARTWRIGHT, THOMAS 21
CATHERINE OF ARAGON 19
CHAFER, LEWIS 330
CHAMPLAIN, SAMUEL DE 13
CHAPMAN, J. WILBUR 371
CHILD, LYDIA MARIA 192
CHRISTENSON, LARRY 483
CHURCHMAN, JOHN 95
CLARK, FRANCIS E. 298
CLARK, THOMAS M. 257
CLARKE, JOHN 45
CLARKE, WILLIAM N. 383
CLEAVELAND, REV. JOHN 184
CLEMENT XIV 246
CLYFTON, RICHARD 27
COFFIN, ELIJAH 214
COFFIN, LEVI 214
COLE, NATHAN 112, 113, 184

COLET, JOHN 19
COLTON, CALVIN 172, 178
COMMAGER, HENRY STEELE
221
COMSTOCK, ANDREW 154
CONANT, HANNAH 192
CONE, JAMES 448, 460, 462
CONSTANTINIDIES, MICHAEL
442
CONWELL, RUSSELL H. 293
CORNBURY, see LORD
CORNBURY
CORONADO, VASQUEZ 12
CORTEZ 10
COUGHLIN, CHARLES 405,
478
COX, HARVEY 460
CRANMER, THOMAS 8, 20, 21
CROMWELL, OLIVER 22, 29,
30, 54, 56
CROMWELL, THOMAS 20
CROSBY, FANNY 186
CROSS, WHITNEY 177
CUMMINGS, F. JEREMIAH 240
CUTLER, TIMOTHY 52

DARBY, JOHN NELSON 327
DARWIN, CHARLES 389; see
DARWINISM; Origin of Species
283
DAVENPORT, JAMES 108, 129
DAVENPORT, JOHN 34, 43
DAVIES, SAMUEL 90, 108, 215
DAVIS, DAVID B. 190
DAY, DOROTHY 415, 455
DE BRÉBEUF, JEAN 5, 13
DE CHAMPLAIN, SAMUEL 13
DE LA SALLE, RENÉ-
ROBERT 13
DE LA WARR, LORD 23
DE LAMBERVILLE, JACQUES
13
DE PADILLA, JUAN 12
DE PORTOLÁ, GASPAR 15
DE SOTO, HERNANDO 5
DICKINSON, JONATHAN 102
DIVINE, FATHER 346, 382, 412
DONNE, JOHN 67
DOUGLASS, FREDERICK
259-260
DUKE OF YORK 55
DUNSTER, HENRY 45
DU BOIS, W. E. B. 345, 351
DRAKE, SIR FRANCIS 19
DRUILLETTES, GABRIEL 16
DRYDEN, JOHN 67
DWIGHT, LOUIS 189
DWIGHT, TIMOTHY 162, 169,
171, 173, 174
DYER, MARY 57

EATON, THEOPHILUS 34
EDDY, MARY BAKER 336, 339
EDWARD VI (of England) 19,
20
EDWARDS, JONATHAN 42, 90,
99, 101, 102, **103-106**, 108,
113, 115, 116, 146, 171, 178,
190, 231, 232, 264, 274, 275,
434; The Distinguishing Marks
of a Work of the Spirit of God
105; A Faithful Narrative of the
Surprising Work of God 102,
104; Personal Narrative 104;
"SINNERS IN THE HANDS
OF AN ANGRY GOD" 104
EDWARDS, JUSTIN 189
EDWARDS, MORGAN 119
EISENHOWER, DWIGHT 440,
466
ELIADE, MIRCEA 39
ELIOT, JOHN 5, 9, 64, 87, 88,
89, 154
ELIZABETH I (of England) 7,
19, 21, 29
ELLIOT, WALTER 256
EMERSON, RALPH WALDO
188, 221, 229, **230-231**,
274-275
ERDMAN, WILLIAM J. 331

FALWELL, JERRY 454, 478
FERDINAND (of Spain) 5
FINNEY, CHARLES G.
174-177, 178, 186, 190, 210,
223, 224, 233, 255, 334, 336,
388, 433
FISHER, JOHN 19
FISHER, MARY 56
FISKE, JOHN 325
FORD, GERALD 451
FOSDICK, HARRY E. 409, 416,
417, 419-420, 451
FOWLER, ORSON 196
FOX, GEORGE 56, 57
FRANCIS OF ASSISSI 15
FRANCKE, AUGUST
HERMANN 75, 100
FRANKLIN, BENJAMIN 108,
110, 113, 135, 151, 247
FRELINGHUYSEN,
THEODORE J. 75, 101, 102,
116
FROBISHER, MARTIN 19
FULLER, CHARLES 409, 410,
478

GALE, GEORGE W. 175
GARRISON, WILLIAM LLOYD
261
GARVEY, MARCUS, 412

GAUSTAD, EDWIN SCOTT 101
GEORGE I (of England) 95
GEORGE, LYDIA 99
GIBBES, THOMAS (family —
John, Samuel) 65, 66
GIBBONS, JAMES CARDINAL
357, **362-364**
GILBERT, HUMPHREY 19
GLADDEN, WASHINGTON
314, 319, 323
GOEN, G. C. 116
GOOD, SARAH 68
GORDON, A. J. 331, 335
GRAHAM, BILLY 177, 372, 385,
433, **435-437**, 466, 478
GRAHAM, SYLVESTER 196,
197
GREBEL, CONRAD 8
GREELEY, ANDREW 457, 481
GREEN, JACOB 146
GREVEN, PHILIP 61, 86
GRIMKE, ANGELINA 308
GRIMKE, FRANCIS 346
GRIMKE, SARAH 308
GRINDAL, EDMUND 22
GURNEY, JOSEPH JOHN 214

HAMMETT, WILLIAM 211
HANDEL, GEORG FRIEDRICH
83
HANSON, J. W. 155
HARDING, VINCENT 448
HARVARD, JOHN 35
HATFIELD, MARK 427
HAWTHORNE, NATHANIEL
150
HECKER, ISAAC T. 240, 362
HENNEPIN, LOUIS 4, 13
HENRIETTA MARIA OF
FRANCE 29
HENRY, CARL F. H. 465
HENRY VII (of England) 19
HENRY VIII (of England) 7, 19,
20
HERBERG, WILL 430
HERBERT, GEORGE 67
HERDER, JOHANN 205
HICKS, ELIAS 214
HILLIS, NEWELL D. 370
HIMES, JOSHUA V. 179
HODGE, CHARLES 229,
232-233; Biblical Repertory,
Systematic Theology 232; What
is Darwinism 324
HODUR, FRANCIS 360
HOOKER, RICHARD 22
HOOKER, THOMAS 22, 34, 43
HOLLY, ISRAEL 145
HOLMES, OBADIAH **49**

HOPKINS, SAMUEL 91, 146;
Dialogue Concerning the
Slavery of Africans 146
HUBBARD, ELIZABETH 99
HUDSON, HENRY 54
HUGHES, JOHN 240
HUNT, ROBERT 23
HUS, JOHN 82
HUTCHINSON, ANNE 33, 37,
43, 45-47, 63, 64, 128, 271
HUTCHINSON, THOMAS 31

ISABELLA (of Spain) 5
INGERSOLL, ROBERT G. 283
IRELAND, JOHN 327, 363, 377

JACKSON, ANDREW 195, 221
JACOB, HENRY 37
JACOBS, B. F. 297
JAMES I (of England) 24, 27,
29, 53
JAMES II (of England) 43, 55,
58
JEFFERSON, THOMAS 135,
136, 137, 145, 151, 164, 169,
221
JOHN XXIII 413, 439, 480, 485
JOHNSON, EDWARD 65
JOHNSON, SAMUEL 52
JOLLIET, LOUIS 13, 16
Jones v. Wolf (1979) 273
JONES, ABNER 166
JONES, ABSOLOM 219
JONES, C. C. 217
JONES, BOB 385
JOSIAH (of England) 21
JUDSON, ADONIRAM 189, 192
JUDSON, ANN HASSELTINE
192

KEITH, GEORGE 58
KELLOGG, JOHN HARVEY 198
KELLOGG, W. K. 198
KELLY, DEAN 464
KENNEDY, JOHN F. 439, 450,
480-481
KING, MARTIN LUTHER, JR.
440, 445-446, 450, 453
KING PHILIP (Chief) 43
KINGSBURY, CYRUS 194
KNOX, JOHN 21
KUHLMANN, KATHRYN 479
KUNG, HANS 4
KYNETT, ALPHA 377

LA SALLE, RENÉ-ROBERT
DE 13
LAMBERVILLE, JACQUES DE
13
LATIMER, HUGH 20, 21

LATOURETTE, KENNETH
SCOTT 221
LAUD, WILLIAM 29, 34, 36
LAVAL, FRANCIS XAVIER DE
MONTMORENCY 14
LAWSON, DEODAT 71
LAWS, CURTIS LEE 384
LAY, BENJAMIN 95
LEDDRA, WILLIAM 57
LEO XIII 363
LEWIS, C. S. 4
LEWIS, EDWIN 410
LIEBMAN, JOSHUA L. 433
LINCOLN, ABRAHAM 185, 263,
265, 266-268, 376
LINDSELL, HAROLD 489
LOCKE, JOHN 104
LONGFELLOW, HENRY
WADSWORTH 229
LORD BALTIMORE 53, 54
LORD CORNBURY 56
LOVELACE, RICHARD 61, 463
LOYOLA, IGNATIUS 5, 8
LUTHER, MARTIN 5, 7, 8, 19,
20, 22, 64

McCARTHY, JOSEPH 431, 439
McGREADY, JAMES 173, 182
McGUIRE, GEORGE 412
McINTIRE, CARL 385, 424, 426,
431-432, 465
McKINLEY, WILLIAM 292, 312
McLOUGHLIN, WILLIAM 175
McPHERSON, AIMEE SEMPLE
338, 381
MacDONALD, A. J. 204
MacLURE, WILLIAM 207
MACHEN, J. GRESHAM 379,
408; Christianity and
Liberalism 379
MADISON, JAMES 145, 221
MAHAN, ASA 224, 434
MAIER, WALTER 407, 478
MAILER, NORMAN 274, 276
MAKEMIE, FRANCIS 56
MALCOLM X 441
MANN, HORACE 196
MARQUETTE, JACQUES 13,
16-17
MARSHALL, DANIEL 119
MARSHALL, JOHN (Chief
Justice) 195
MARTINEAU, HARRIET 213
MARY (of England) 19, 21, 63
MASON, CHARLES H. 348
MATHER, COTTON 5, 39, 56,
71, 74, 88, 98, 99-100, 102,
126
MATHER, INCREASE 32, 56,
71, 99, 125, 128

MATHER, RICHARD 99
MATHEWS, SHALLER 370
MAURIN, PETER 415
MAYHEW, JONATHAN 132,
133, 228; Discourse Concerning
Unlimited Submission 132
MAYHEW, THOMAS JR. 87, 88,
89
MAYHEW, THOMAS SR. 88, 89
MEAD, SIDNEY 137, 208
MELVILLE, HERMAN 170
MENCKEN, H. L. 31, 386
MERTON, THOMAS 463
METACOM (King Philip) 89
MICHELANGELO 7
MILLER, PERRY 32, 41, 172,
231
MILLER, SAMUEL 229
MILLER, WILLIAM 178, 179,
223
MILLS, SAMUEL J. 189
MOLTMANN, JÜRGEN 460
MOODY, DWIGHT L. 177, 186,
293-295, 296, 311, 331, 335,
377
MOON, SUN MYUNG 473
MORE, SIR THOMAS 19
MORGAN, EDMUND S. 32
MORISON, SAMUEL ELIOT 32
MORRIS, GOVERNOR 95
MORSE, JEDIDIAH 166, 168,
169, 235
MORSE, SAMUEL F. B. 235
MORTON, THOMAS 43, 150
MOTT, JOHN R. 300, 302
MUHLENBERG, HENRY
MELCHIOR 75, 143
MUHLENBERG, JOHN PETER
GABRIEL 143
MUHLENBERG, PETER 143
MULLINS, EDGAR YOUNG
326, 331
MURDOCK, KENNETH 32

NETTLETON, ASAHEL 173,
176
NEUHAUS, RICHARD 463-464
NEVIN, JOHN W. 208, 230; The
Anxious Bench 230
NICHOLS, THOMAS AND
MARY 196
NIEBUHR, H. RICHARD 410,
418, 421-422
NIEBUHR, REINHOLD 405,
410, 418, 421-422
NIXON, RICHARD 436, 451
NOYES, JOHN HUMPHREY
177, 196, 203-204

OCKENGA, HAROLD JOHN
424
O'HAIR, MADALYN MURRAY
457
O'KELLEY, JAMES 211
OSBURN, SARAH 68
OTTERBEIN, PHILIP WILLIAM
75
OWEN, ROBERT 207

PAINE, THOMAS 164, 274-275
PADILLA, JUAN DE 12
PALMER, THOMAS 274-275
PARHAM, CHARLES FOX
337-338
PARRINGTON, V. L. 32
PARRIS, SAMUEL 68, 71
PASTORIUS 95
PAUL III 10
PAUL VI 399, 481
PAYNE, DANIEL ALEXANDER
349
PEALE, NORMAN VINCENT
433, 465
PENN, ADMIRAL WILLIAM 57
PENN, WILLIAM 5, **57-58**; No
Cross, No Crown 57
PERKINS, WILLIAM 22
PETER, JOHANN FRIEDRICH
83
PETRARCH 7
PHILIPS, ABIGAIL 99
PIEPER, FRANZ OTTO, 416
PIERREPONT, SARAH 103
PIUS IX, 356
PIUS X, 357, 414, 439
PIZARRO 10
POCAHONTAS 24
POLK, LEONIDAS 257
PORTOLÁ, GASPAR DE 15
PROVOST, SAMUEL 165
PURCELL, JOHN B. 196, 244
PUTNAM, THOMAS 68

QUIMBY, PHINEAS 339

RALEIGH, SIR WALTER 19
RANDOLPH, A. PHILIP 424
RANKIN, JEANETTE 423
RAPP, JOHANN GEORG 205,
207
RAUCH, CHRISTIAN HENRY
89
RAUSCHENBUSCH, WALTER
319-320
REAGAN, RONALD 451, 454,
473
REEB, JAMES 448

REUTHER, ROSEMARY 460,
462
RHODE, PAUL 359
RICE, DAVID 174
RICE, JOHN R. 385
RICE, LUTHER 192
RIDLEY, NICHOLAS 20, 21
RIIS, JACOB 311-312
ROBERTS, ORAL 475, 479
ROBERTSON, PAT 475, 479
ROBINSON, JOHN 27
ROBINSON, WILLIAM 8
ROCKEFELLER, JOHN D. 287
ROLFE, JOHN 24
ROMAN, ROBERT AND PHILIP
74
ROOSEVELT, FRANKLIN D.
404-405
ROOSEVELT, THEODORE 312,
319
ROUSSEAU, JEAN JACQUES
434
Rowe v. Wade (1973) 454
RUSK, RALPH L. 231
RUSSELL, CHARLES TAZE
336, 341

SANKEY, IRA D. 186, 293
SAUER, CHRISTOPHER 64
SCHAFF, PHILIP 230
SCHLATTER, MICHAEL 75
SCHLEIERMACHER,
FRIEDRICH 323, 383
SCOFIELD, C. I. 331
SCOPES, JOHN T. 385-386
SCOTT, WALTER 184
SEABURY, SAMUEL 165
SERRA, JUNÍPERO 5, 12, **15**
SETON, ELIZABETH ANN
BAYLEY 247, **252-254**
SEWALL, JUDGE SAMUEL 65
SEYMOUR, WILLIAM J.
337-338, 348
SHAKESPEARE, WILLIAM 19
SHEEN, FULTON J. 433,
437-438, 466, 478
SHELDEN, CHARLES M. 319,
323
SHEPARD, THOMAS 65, 66
SIMPSON, A. B. 335, 337
SMITH, AL 358, 382, 406, 413
SMITH, ELIAS 169, 179
SMITH, HANNAH WHITALL
334
SMITH, CAPTAIN JOHN 23
SMITH, JOSEPH 178, **200-202**,
209
SMYTH, JOHN 45
SÖDERBLOM, NATHAN 428

SORIN, EDWARD FREDERICK
248-252
SPENER, PHILIP JACOB 74
STANDISH, CAPTAIN MILES
28
STEARNS, MARTHA 119
STEARNS, SHUBAL **119**
STEPHENSON, MARMADUKE
57
STEWART, LYMAN 331
STEWART, MILTON 331
STILES, EZRA 120, 133, 146,
171; Discourse on the Christian
Union 133
STODDARD, SOLOMON 42,
71, 102, 103
STOKES, ANSON PHELPS 118
STONE, BARTON W. 167, 173,
178, 184, 211, 223
STOUGHTON, WILLIAM 69
STOWE, HARRIET BEECHER
261, 290
STRONG, AUGUSTUS 326
STRONG, JOSIAH 291-293; Our
Country 291
STRONG, NATHAN 169
STUYVESANT, PETER 55
SUNDAY, BILLY 177, 314,
369-370, **371-372**, 377

TANNER, BENJAMIN TUCKER
352
TAPPAN, ARTHUR 190, 191
TAPPAN, LEWIS 190, 191
TAYLOR, EDWARD 66, **67-68**
TAYLOR, J. HUDSON 301
TAYLOR, NATHANIEL 171, 191,
221, 223, 224, **232-233**
TEGAHKOUITA, CATHARINE
13
TENNENT, GILBERT 102, 108,
121, 129
TENNENT, WILLIAM JR. AND
SR. 102
THOMPSON, CHARLES 154
THOMPSON, SAMUEL 196
TILLICH, PAUL 417, 418, 460
TITUBA 68, 69
TOCQUEVILLE, ALEXIS DE
172, 179, 390
TORREY, REUBEN A. 331, 335,
336
TUDOR, HENRY 7
TUFTS, ROBERT 81
TURNER, NAT 258, 263-264
TURRETIN, FRANÇOIS 229,
232
TYLER, BENNET 173

VAIL, REV. JOSEPH 168
VAN BUREN, PAUL 458
VESEY, DENMARK 258
VON ZINZENDORF, COUNT
    NIKOLAUS LUDWIG 75, 82,
    89, 100

WALTHER, CARL F. W. 242
WALWORTH, CLARENCE 255
WARE, HENRY 232
WARFIELD, BENJAMIN
    BRECKINRIDGE 325
WASHINGTON, BOOKER T.
    351
WASHINGTON, GEORGE 76,
    109, 135, 144, 164
Watson v. Jones (1972) 273
WATTS, ISAAC 144, 186
WAYLAND, FRANCIS 192
WEBSTER, NOAH 154
WELD, THEODORE DWIGHT
    176, 261
WENINGER, FRANCIS X 256
WESLEY, JOHN AND
    CHARLES 52, 75, 106, 115,
    166, 185, 224, 332, 336
WHEELOCK, ELEAZER 90,
    116, 129

WHITAKER, ALEXANDER 24
WHITE, ANDREW 53
WHITE, ELLEN G. **197-199**
WHITE, WILLIAM 165
WHITEHEAD, A. N. 461
WHITEFIELD, GEORGE 52,
    101, 102, 104, **106-113**, 115,
    119, 126, 127, 128, 184
WIGGLESWORTH, MICHAEL
    66
WILBERFORCE, WILLIAM 189
WILLARD, FRANCES **305-306**,
    309-310, 376-377
WILLARD, SAMUEL 128
WILLIAM AND MARY (of
    England) 43
WILLIAM III (of England) 95
WILLIAMS, ROGER 5, 33, 37,
    43, 45, **47-48**, 56, 57, 64,
    128, 145, 151, 271
WINEBRENNER, JOHN 211
WINROD, GERALD 405
WINSLOW, OLA 80
WINTHROP, JOHN 5, 22, 30,
    33, 34, **36-37**, 40, 43, 74, 83;
    "A MODELL OF CHRISTIAN
    CHARITY" 33, 37, **38-39**
WINTHROP, MARGARET 83

WISE, ISAAC MAYER 243
WISSEL, JOSEPH 256
WOJTYLA, CAROL (John Paul
    II) 4
WOODMASON, CHARLES 72,
    73
WOODROW, JAMES 324
WOOLMAN, JOHN 91, **94-95**;
    Considerations on the Keeping of
    Negroes 95
WORCESTER, SAMUEL 194,
    195
Worcester v. Georgia 195
WRIGHT, FRANCES 207
WRIGHT, HENRY CLARK 196
WYATT-BROWN, BERTRAM
    191
WYCLIFFE, JOHN 19

YANKELOVICH, DANIEL 451
YOUNG, BRIGHAM 202

ZAHM, ALBERT 250
ZAHM, JOHN 250, 252
ZINZENDORF, COUNT
    NIKOLAUS LUDWIG, see
    VON ZINZENDORF
ZWINGLI, ULRICH 8

EVENTS, MOVEMENTS, AND GROUPS

ABOLITIONISM 190, 260, 265
ABORTION 454, 455, 463
ACT OF SUPREMACY
  (England) 19
ADVENTISM 178, 179, 197-199,
  302, 407, 464
AFRICAN METHODIST
  EPISCOPAL CHURCH 219,
  220, 347, 349-350
AFRICAN METHODIST
  EPISCOPAL ZION CHURCH
  347-348, 349
AFRO-AMERICANS see
  BLACKS
AGE OF DISCOVERY 7
Age of Reason 164
ALGONQUIN (Indians) 16;
  BIBLE TRANSLATION 64, 87
AMERICAN BIBLE SOCIETY
  154, 155, 190, 488
AMERICAN BIBLE UNION 154
AMERICAN BOARD OF
  COMMISSIONERS FOR
  FOREIGN MISSIONS 191,
  192, 194
AMERICAN CIVIL LIBERTIES
  UNION 385-386
AMERICAN COUNCIL OF
  CHRISTIAN CHURCHES 424,
  430, 465
AMERICAN EDUCATION
  SOCIETY 190
AMERICAN LITERATURE AND
  CHRISTIANITY 274-276
AMERICAN LUTHERAN
  CHURCH 439
AMERICAN PHYSIOLOGICAL
  ASSOCIATION 198
AMERICAN PROTECTIVE
  ASSOCIATION 354
AMERICAN REVOLUTION see
  REVOLUTIONARY WAR
AMERICAN SISTERS OF
  CHARITY, 254
AMERICAN SUNDAY SCHOOL
  UNION 190, 296
AMERICANISM 356-358,
  362-364

AMERICANIZATION 439
AMISH 91
ANABAPTISM 49
ANDOVER THEOLOGICAL
  SEMINARY 189, 191, 192,
  195, 203, 388
ANGLICANISM 4, 21-24, 27,
  33, 36, 37, 39, 47, 49-52, 54,
  56, 57, 79-82, 91, 97, 133,
  272; LATITUDINARIANISM
  72
ANTICOMMUNISM 415, 427,
  431, 432
ANTI-INTELLECTUALISM 222,
  223
ANTI-POPERY UNION 235
ANTIOCH COLLEGE 196
ANTI-SALOON LEAGUE 377
ANTI-SEMITISM 405
The Anxious Bench 230
ARMINIANISM 29, 102, 105,
  115, 233
Arbella 37
ASSEMBLIES OF GOD 338,
  464, 483

BAPTIST BIBLE FELLOWSHIP
  464
BAPTIST MISSION
  ASSOCIATION 464
BAPTISTS 4, 33, 43-45, 49, 71,
  72, 75, 91, 97, 145, 326, 345,
  346, 348, 388, 391, 396, 400,
  407, 448, 474
Battle for the Bible 489
BAVARIAN ILLUMINATI 168
Bay Psalm Book 36, 80
BIBLE 8, 20, 22, 61-64, 74, 84,
  154-157, 186, 263, 266-267,
  274, 281, 288, 321, 325, 327,
  340, 342-343, 384, 418,
  474-475, 481, 488-489
BIBLE BELT 474-475
BIBLE COLLEGES AND
  INSTITUTES 331, 389-390,
  465
BIBLE COMMONWEALTH 35,
  43, 52, 66

BIBLE TRANSLATIONS
  154-157
"BIBLICAL CREATIONISM"
  456
Biblical Repertory 232
BIBLICAL INERRANCY AND
  INFALLIBILITY 325-326, 352,
  385, 488-489
BIRTH CONTROL 481
BLACK PANTHERS 441
BLACK PROTESTANTS 299,
  382, 398, 407, 433, 472
BLACK REVOLUTION 445,
  447-448
BLACKS (African Immigrants)
  61, 108 (Slavery) 86, 91-93,
  94, 95, 215-220 (general)
  343, 345, 352, 412, 424,
  440-441, 452
BOHEMIAN BRETHREN 82
Book of Common Prayer 20, 21,
  79, 80
BOOK OF MORMON 200, 201
Bonifacius 100
BOSTON TEA PARTY 131, 145
BRETHREN 71, 97 (United) 75
BROWN UNIVERSITY 116, 192
BUNKER HILL (Battle) 131,
  143

CALVINISM 22, 31, 55, 63, 100,
  101, 115, 120, 121, 146,
  166-167, 171, 190, 223, 224,
  232, 233
CAMBRIDGE, ENGLAND (and
  university) 20, 21, 22, 36, 47
CAMBRIDGE,
  MASSACHUSETTS 36, 64
CAMBRIDGE PLATFORM 35
CAMPUS CRUSADE FOR
  CHRIST 465, 471
CANE RIDGE, KENTUCKY
  (Revival) 182, 183, 185, 211
CATHOLIC FOREIGN MISSION
  SOCIETY OF AMERICA
  (Maryknollers) 299
CATHOLICISM, see ROMAN
  CATHOLICISM

CHARISMATICS, 464, 476, 481, **482-484**
CHEROKEE (Indians) 194, 195
Cherokee Phoenix 195
CHICKASAW (Indians) 195
CHILDREN OF GOD 473
CHOCTAW (Indians) 194, 195
Christ in Theology 233
CHRISTIAN (Campbellite) 400
CHRISTIAN AND MISSIONARY ALLIANCE 301, 317, 335, 337
CHRISTIAN COUNTERCULTURE **469-470**
CHRISTIAN ENDEAVOR SOCIETY 298, 313
Christian Herald 318
Christian Recorder 349
CHRISTIAN REFORMED CHURCH 242, 366, 416, 456, 464
CHRISTIAN SCIENCE 336, **339-341**
Christianity Today 437, 465
CHRISTIANOPOLIS 205
CHUMASH (Indians) 15
CHURCH MEMBERSHIP 283, 430, 480
CHURCH OF CHRIST 337
CHURCH OF ENGLAND *see* ANGLICANISM
CHURCH OF GOD 211
CHURCH OF GOD (Cleveland, Tennessee) 338
CHURCH OF JESUS CHRIST OF LATTER-DAY SAINTS *see* MORMONS
CHURCH OF THE BRETHREN 64
CHURCH OF THE NAZARENE 333, 410, 464
CIVIL RELIGION 369, 430-432, 433, **434-435**
CIVIL RIGHTS MOVEMENT 429, 440-441, 450
CIVIL WAR, 257, 265, 308
CIVIL WARS (England, 1640s) 20, 35
COLD WAR 427
COLLEGE OF NEW JERSEY *see* PRINCETON UNIVERSITY
COLLEGE OF WILLIAM AND MARY 51, 115, 165
COLLEGES 35, **225-227, 388-389**, 424
COMMUNAL SOCIETIES 203, 204
COMMUNISM 397

COMMUNITY OF EQUALITY 207
CONESTOGA (Indians) 90
CONGREGATION OF THE HOLY CROSS 248, 251
CONGREGATIONALISM 4, 22, 27, 32, 34, 37, 49, 56, 75, 91, 97, 99, 378, 400, 407
(Nonseparating) 34, 35
Connecticut Evangelical Magazine 173
CONSERVATIVE THEOLOGY 313, 376
Considerations of the Keeping of Negroes 95
CONTINENTAL CONGRESS 64, 117, 144
COSTANOANS (Indians) 15
COVENANTISM 33, 34, 38, 41, 63, 83, 134
Creeds of Christendom 230
CREEK (Indians) 194, 195
CREOLES 215, 216
CUMBERLAND PRESBYTERIAN CHURCH 211

DALLAS THEOLOGICAL SEMINARY 335
DARTMOUTH COLLEGE 116, 203
DARWINISM 285, 290, 321, 322, 323-325, 352, 381, 389
"DEATH OF GOD" THEOLOGY 458
DECLARATION OF INDEPENDENCE 91, 131
DEISM 164
DELAWARE (Indians) 95
DENOMINATIONS 288, 463-464, 476-477
DEPRESSION, GREAT 404-406, 409, 415, 418, 423
Dialogue Concerning the Slavery of the Africans 146
DISCIPLES OF CHRIST 221, 223, 378
Discourse, Concerning Unlimited Submission and Non-Resistance to the Higher Powers 132
Discourse on the Christian Union 133
DISPENSATIONALISM **327-330**, 331
The Distinguishing Marks of a Work of the Spirit of God 105
DOCTRINE AND COVENANTS 201

DOMINION OF NEW ENGLAND 43
DUQUESNE UNIVERSITY 483
DUTCH REFORMED 4, 54, 55, 97, 116
DUTCH WEST INDIA COMPANY *see* WEST INDIA COMPANY

EAST INDIA COMPANY 131
EASTERN ORTHODOX CHURCHES 367, 391-392, 400, 439, **442-443**
ECUMENICAL MOVEMENT 426, **428-430**, 452
EDUCATION 248-252, 349, **388-389**, 468
"ELECTRONIC CHURCH" **478-479**
ELIZABETHAN AGE 19
The Emancipation of Massachusetts 32
ENLIGHTENMENT 68, 73, 99, 100, 135, 151, 164, 228
ENTHUSIASM 47, 105, 128
EPHRATA COMMUNITY 97
EPISCOPACY 24
EPISCOPALIANISM 4, 22, 75, 80
ETHICS 322, 421-422
ETHNICITY 240-242, 343, 358, 397, 398
EVANGELICAL FREE CHURCH 366
EVANGELICAL FRIENDS ALLIANCE 215
EVANGELICALISM 223-224, 256, 343, 464, 465-468, 471-473
EVANGELICALS 410, 453, 472, 476-477
EVOLUTION 250; *see* DARWINISM, JOHN SCOPES

A Faithful Narrative of the Surprising Work of God 102, 104
FEDERAL COUNCIL OF CHURCHES 313-314, 319, 405, 408, 417, 426, 428
FIRST AMENDMENT TO THE CONSTITUTION 271-272
FOREIGN MISSION ASSOCIATION 301
FOREIGN MISSIONS 299-302, 350
FOREIGN MISSIONS CONFERENCE OF NORTH AMERICA 300
FRANCISCANS 9, 12, 13, 15, 54

FREE AFRICAN SOCIETY 219
FREE MEN'S SOCIETY 243
FREE METHODIST CHURCH
	333, 464
FREE THINKERS 243
FRENCH AND INDIAN WAR
	59, 89, 131, 133
FRIENDS (Quakers) 56, 57, 91,
	94, 95
FULLER THEOLOGICAL
	SEMINARY 465
FUNDAMENTALISM 383,
	384-385, 386, 397, 482
FUNDAMENTALIST-
	MODERNIST
	CONTROVERSY, 378-382,
	404
FUNDAMENTALISTS 397, 407,
	408, 409, 410, 411, 416, 419,
	465, 472
Fundamentals, The 331, 384

GABRIEL'S REBELLION 217
GENEVA BIBLE 63, 64, 154
GENERAL ASSOCIATION OF
	REGULAR BAPTISTS 408
GERMAN CATHOLICS 244,
	354, 439
GERMAN REFORMED 55, 75,
	97, 211
"GILDED AGE" 281-282, 312
GLORIOUS REVOLUTION 43
God in Christ 233
GREAT AWAKENING 52, 73,
	90, 92, **96-130**, 145, 173, 388
"GREAT REVERSAL," THE 313
GREAT REVIVAL 216
GREEK ORTHODOX 439, 442
GUILFORD COURTHOUSE
	(Battle) 144
GURNEYITES (Quakers) 214,
	215
GUY FAWKES DAY 144

HALF-WAY COVENANT 41, 42,
	43, 115, 130
HARMONIE, PENNSYLVANIA
	207
HARMONISTS 205
HARVARD COLLEGE 32, 35,
	45, 67, 81, 89, 99, 100, 108,
	109, 115, 128, 189, 225, 228,
	388, 396
HERESY TRIALS 326
HERRNHUT 100
HICKSITES (Quakers) 214, 215
HIGHER CRITICISM 325, 352,
	481
HISPANICS 400, 433, 452

HISTORICAL CRITICISM 322,
	326
History of the Christian Church
	230
HOLINESS MOVEMENT 301,
	331-332, **333-335**, 411
HOLY EXPERIMENT 58
HOUSE OF BURGESSES
	(Virginia) 51
HURON (Indians) 13, 16

ILLINOIS (Indians) 16, 17
ILLUMINATI *see* BAVARIAN
	ILLUMINATI
IMMACULATE CONCEPTION
	MISSION 17
IMMIGRATION 235-237, 354,
	357, 359, 360-361, 362,
	365-366, 374, 413
INDEPENDENT FUNDA-
	MENTAL CHURCHES OF
	AMERICA 464
INDIAN REMOVAL BILL 195
INDIANS (Native Americans)
	4, 5, 7, 9-18, 24, 28, 41, 43,
	47, 48, 52, 53, 58, 61, 66, 68,
	72, 108, 150, 155, 299
	(Missions) **86-90**, 95,
	193-195, 401, 452
INDIVIDUALISM 473
INQUISITION (Roman
	Catholic) 68
Institutes of the Christian Religion
	5
INTERCHURCH WORLD
	MOVEMENT 374
INTERNATIONAL CHURCH OF
	THE FOURSQUARE
	GOSPEL 338, 382
INTERNATIONAL UNION OF
	GOSPEL MISSIONS 318-319
INTERVARSITY CHRISTIAN
	FELLOWSHIP 465, 471
An Introduction to the Singing of
	Psalm Tunes 81
IRISH CATHOLICS 354, 439
IROQUOIS (Indians) 13
ITALIAN-AMERICAN
	CATHOLICS **360-362**

JAMESTOWN 8, 23
JEHOVAH'S WITNESSES 302,
	336, **341-342**
JESUITS 5, 8, 9, 13, 14, 15-18,
	53, 54
JEWS 4, 33, 97, 243, 399, 434,
	457
JONESTOWN MASSACRE 449
JESUS MOVEMENT 469-471

KASKASKIA (Indians) 17
KESWICK HIGHER LIFE
	MOVEMENT 334-335
KING JAMES VERSION
	(AUTHORIZED VERSION)
	64, 154, 488
KING PHILIP'S WAR 88, 89
KING'S COLLEGE (Columbia)
	52
KISKAKON (Indians) 16
KNOW-NOTHING PARTY 235
KOREAN WAR 427, 431
KU KLUX KLAN 374

LAMANITES 200
LANDMARK BAPTISTS 211,
	337
LATITUDINARIANISM 72
Laws of Ecclesiastical Polity 22
LIBERAL THEOLOGY 319,
	321-323, 397
LIBERATION THEOLOGY 460
LIBERALISM 321-323, 335, 376,
	409, 416-418
LITURGY 390-391, 485-486
LOLLARDY 19
LOYALISTS 135, 140, 144, 165
LUTHERAN CHURCH IN
	AMERICA 439, 464
LUTHERAN CHURCH—
	MISSOURI SYNOD 242, 366,
	390, 410, 416, 456, 488
LUTHERANISM 365, 391
LUTHERANS 21, 71, 74, 75, 82,
	91, 97, 242, 439, 476
	(Swedish) 4

MAINLINE DENOMINATIONS
	476-477
MANIFEST DESTINY 435
MARCH ON WASHINGTON
	(1963) 448
MARYLAND TOLERATION
	ACT OF 1649 54
MASSACHUSETTS BAY
	COLONY 22, 27, 30, 33, 35,
	36, 37, 47, 64, 87
MASSACHUSETTS GENERAL
	COURT 35, 36
MAYFLOWER 28
Mayflower Compact 28
McCARTHY ERA 427, 431
McGuffey's Eclectic Readers 281
MEN AND RELIGION
	FORWARD MOVEMENT 313
MENNONITES 4, 45, 57, 71,
	75, 91, 94, 144, 366, 369,
	423, 427
MERCERSBURG SEMINARY
	230

METHODIST EPISCOPAL
    CHURCH 333, 336
METHODIST EPISCOPAL
    CHURCH, SOUTH 262
METHODIST PROTESTANT
    CHURCH 211
METHODISTS 72, 75, 91, 166,
    327, 332-333, 345, 346, 377,
    388, 391, 407, 411, 464, 474
MILLENIALISM 167-170
MILLERITES 196, 198
MINORITIES 399-401
MISSIONS 296, 464
MODERNISM (Protestant)
    321-322, 335, 378-379,
    383-384, 416, 419
MOHICAN (Indians) 89
MOODY BIBLE INSTITUTE
    295, 331, 335, 389, 410
"MORAL MAJORITY" 385, 454
MORALITY 275
MORAVIANS 71, 82, 83, 87, 89,
    90, 97, 144 (Renewed) 75
MORMANS 196, 200-202, 302,
    400
MUSLIMS 7

NATIONAL ASSOCIATION OF
    EVANGELICALS 410, 424,
    426, 430, 465, 472
NATIONAL BAPTIST
    CONVENTION 348, 448
NATIONAL CAMP MEETING
    ASSOCIATION FOR THE
    PROMOTION OF
    CHRISTIAN HOLINESS 332
NATIONAL CATHOLIC WAR
    COUNCIL 358, 373
NATIONAL CATHOLIC
    WELFARE CONFERENCE
    424
NATIONAL COUNCIL OF
    CHURCHES 426, 429, 433,
    439, 448, 472
NATIVISM 251
Nature and the Supernatural 233
NEO-ORTHODOXY 384,
    417-418, 458, 476
NEO-THOMISM 418-419
NEPHITES 200
NEW DEAL, THE 405, 415
NEW ENGLAND COMPANY 30
The New England Psalm Singer
    81, 82
NEW ENGLAND WAY 35, 41,
    66
NEW EVANGELICALISM 465
NEW HARMONY 205-207
NEW LANARCK, SCOTLAND
    207

NEW LIGHTS (New Side) 116,
    119, 120, 146, 186
NEW MEASURES 174-177
NEW RIGHT 454-455, 464
NEW SCHOOL
    PRESBYTERIANS 262
NEW YORK STILLWELLITES
    211
No Cross, No Crown 57
NOTRE DAME UNIVERSITY
    248-252, 388, 483
NONCONFORMISTS 49
NORTHERN BAPTIST
    CONVENTION 378
NORTHERN METHODISTS
    378

OBERLIN COLLEGE 176, 190,
    224
OBERLIN PERFECTIONISM
    334
Of Plymouth Plantation 27, 28
OLD LIGHTS (Old Side) 116,
    119, 120
OLD NORTH CHURCH 52, 99
OLD SCHOOL
    PRESBYTERIANS 262
ONEIDA COMMUNITY 175,
    177, 188, 203-204
ORTHODOX CHURCHES
    442-443
OTTAWA (Indians) 16
OWENITES 205

PACIFIC GARDEN MISSION
    (Chicago) 317
PACIFISTS 135, 141-143, 144,
    149
PAMES (Indians) 15
PARACHURCH GROUPS 466
PARISH MISSION 255
PARLIAMENT 21, 24, 29, 35, 52
PATRIOTISM 135, 138, 139,
    144, 369-370, 454
PAXTON BOYS 90
PEARL OF GREAT PRICE 201
PELAGIANISM 233
PENTECOSTAL HOLINESS
    CHURCH 338
PENTECOSTALISM 301-302,
    335, 336-339, 410, 411, 482
PEQUOT (Indians) 66, 87
PERFECTIONISM 177, 188,
    189-191, 196, 203, 204, 205,
    207, 224, 228, 334
Personal Narrative 104
PIETISM 64, 71, 72, 74-75, 82,
    97, 121
PILGRIM HOLINESS CHURCH
    333

PILGRIMS 27, 28
PISCATAWAY (Indians) 53
Plea for the West 236
PLURALISM (Religious) 147,
    190, 416, 477
PLYMOUTH BRETHREN 327,
    336
PLYMOUTH COLONY 23,
    27-29, 33, 34, 35, 43, 45, 56
POLISH-AMERICAN
    CATHOLICS 359-360, 398
POLYGLOT BIBLE 154
PONTIAC'S WAR 95
POPULISM 312
PRAGMATISM 210
PREMILLENNALISM 294-295,
    327, 331, 336, 373, 384
PRESBYTERIAN CHURCH IN
    THE U.S.A. 378, 408
PRESBYTERIANISM 4, 22, 33,
    34, 49, 55-56, 72, 75, 91, 97,
    116
PRESBYTERY OF
    PHILADELPHIA 56
PRIMITIVE METHODISTS 211
PRIMITIVISM 210, 211
PRINCETON SEMINARY 229,
    232, 233, 325
PRINCETON UNIVERSITY
    (College of New Jersey) 103,
    116
Principle of Protestantism 230
PROCESS THOUGHT 461-462
PROGRESSIVE ERA 31, 32,
    312
PROHIBITION 309, 313, 373,
    376-377, 406
PROTESTANT EPISCOPAL
    CHURCH 165, 378
PURITANS, ENGLISH 4, 21-23,
    29, 30, 63; COLONIAL 5,
    23-29, 31-49, 52, 56, 57, 61,
    64, 65, 66-72, 75, 78-80, 82,
    83, 84, 86, 150, 151

QUAKERS (See also Friends)
    4, 33, 43, 56-59, 64, 91, 93,
    94, 95, 97, 144, 213,
    214-215, 335, 369, 400
QUEBEC ACT OF 1774 133
QUEEN'S COLLEGE see
    RUTGERS UNIVERSITY

RACIAL PREJUDICE 345, 351,
    374, 441, 445-446, 447, 448;
    see SLAVERY
RADIO 405, 473, 478
Reason the Only Oracle of Man
    164
RECONSTRUCTION 344-345

REFORMATION **5-8**, 22, 29, 104, 124, 135; ENGLISH **19-21**
Reformation Without Tarrying for Anie 22
REFORMED JUDAISM 243
REFORMED METHODISTS 211
REFORMED THEOLOGY 21, 22, 33, 34, 39, 41, 54, 55, 74
REFORMING SYNOD *see* SYNOD, REFORMING
Religion in America 209
RENAISSANCE 7, 151
REPUBLICAN METHODISTS 211
RESCUE MISSION MOVEMENT 311
Re-Thinking Missions (1930) 300
REVISED STANDARD VERSION 488
REVIVALISM **172-187**, 382, 430, 433, 435-437, 444, 475; CATHOLIC 255-256
REVOLUTIONARY WAR 31, 51, 64, 76, 78, 80, 96, 97, 128, 130, **131-151**, **163-171**
RHODE ISLAND COLLEGE *see* BROWN UNIVERSITY
RIMUCUAN 9
ROMAN CATHOLICISM 4, **8-17**, 19-22, 29, 33, 39, **53-54**, 81, 83, 89, 91, 97, 240, 243-256, 286, 339, 354-358, 390-391, 396, 398, 399, 400, 409, **413-416**, 418-419, 430, 439, 455, 456, 476, 480-482, 483, **485-487**
RUTGERS UNIVERSITY 116

ST. STEPHEN'S CHURCH (London) 34
SABBATH OBSERVANCE 303-305
SALEM (Massachusetts) WITCH TRIALS 64, 65, 68-71, 73, 100
SALVATION ARMY 311, 315-317, 332, 455, 464
SAN FERNANDO COLLEGE 15
SCHWENKFELDERS 71
SCOTCH-IRISH 55, 56, 59, 72, 89, 95, 116, 148
SCROOBY, NOTTINGHAMSHIRE, ENGLAND (Pilgrim Colony) 27, 34, 45
SECOND GREAT AWAKENING 167, 173, 174, 177, 210

SECOND VATICAN COUNCIL 413, 480, 481, 485, 487
SECULARISM 460, 472
SECULARIZATION 285-288, 346, 396
"SECULAR HUMANISM" 456, 457, 464
SELF-FULFILLMENT 451
SEMINOLE (Indians) 195
SENECA FALLS WOMAN'S RIGHTS CONVENTION 309
SEPARATION OF CHURCH AND STATE **271-273**
SEPARATE CHURCHES (of Great Awakening) 115, 116, 117, 118, 119, 145
SEPARATISTS 27, 37, 45
SEVENTH-DAY ADVENTISM *see* ADVENTISM
Siblimus Deus (Papal Bull) 12, 13
"SINNERS IN THE HANDS OF AN ANGRY GOD" 104
SIOUX (Indians) 16
SIX NATIONS (Indians) 89
SLAVERY **91-92**, 93, 94, 95, 96, 145, 146, 189, **215-218**, 257-266
SOCIAL DARWINISM 291
SOCIAL GOSPEL 312, **318-320**
SOCIAL SERVICE 315-318
SOCIALISM 318-319
SOCIETY FOR PROMOTING CHRISTIAN KNOWLEDGE 52
SOCIETY FOR THE PROPAGATION OF THE GOSPEL IN FOREIGN PARTS 52, 72, 91
SOCIETY OF JESUS *see* JESUITS
SOJOURNER'S COMMUNITY 455
SOUTHERN BAPTIST CONVENTION 262, 378, 407, 410, 464, 472, 488-489
SOUTHERN CHRISTIAN LEADERSHIP CONFERENCE 440, 447
SOUTHERN METHODISTS 407
SPANISH-AMERICAN WAR 292
SPANISH ARMADA 19
SPEAKING IN TONGUES 336, 339, 482, 483
SPIRITUALISM 196, 412
STAMP ACT 131, 133
STUDENT VOLUNTEER MOVEMENT **295**, 300
SUDAN INTERIOR MISSION 410

SUNDAY SCHOOLS 282, 296, 298, 313, 430
SUPREME COURT 456
SWEDENBORGIANISM 196
SWEDISH BAPTISTS 366
SWEDISH EVANGELICAL MISSION COVENANT 366
SWEDISH LUTHERANS 439
SYNODS 41; REFORMING 43, 64

TATE AND BRADY'S 1696 PSALTER 80
TELEVISION 440, 449, 451, 473, 478-479
TEMPERANCE MOVEMENT 298, 305, 376
THEOCRACY 34
THEOLOGY OF HOPE 460
THIRD GREAT AWAKENING 174
THIRTY-NINE ARTICLES 21
TOLERATION ACT OF 1689 (English) 56
TORIES *see* LOYALISTS
TRAIL OF TEARS 195
TRANSCENDENTALISM 177, 231
A Treatise Concerning Religious Affections 105
TREATY OF NEW ECHOTA 195
TRUSTEEISM (Catholic) 245-246
TUDORS (England) 19, 22
TURNER'S REBELLION 217

UNION THEOLOGICAL SEMINARY (New York City) 421, 448
UNITARIANISM 120, 176, 189, 190, 228, 229, 230, 231, 392
UNITED BIBLE SOCIETY 155
UNITED BRETHREN *see* BRETHREN, UNITED
UNITED CHURCH OF CHRIST 464
UNITED METHODIST CHURCH 464, 476
UNITED PRESBYTERIAN CHURCH, U.S.A. 464, 476
UNIVERSALISM 176, 228
UNIVERSITY OF NOTRE DAME 196
URBAN CHURCHES **452-453**
URBANIZATION 285, 311, 319, 432
URBAN MISSIONARIES 315
UTOPIANISM 203-207

The Varieties of Religious Experience 105
The Vicarious Sacrifice 233
VIETNAM WAR 397, 427, 429, 449, 450
VIRGINIA COMPANY 23, 24, 49, 53
"VOLUNTARY SOCIETIES" 296

WAMPANOAG (Indians) 28, 43
WAR OF 1812 90, 193
WAR OF THE ROSES 7
WARS OF RELIGION (1562-1594) 9
Watchtower, The 341
WATER STREET AND BOWERY MISSIONS 317
WESLEYAN CHURCH 334
WESLEYANISM 223

WESLEYAN METHODIST CONNECTION 333
WEST INDIA COMPANY 54
WESTMINSTER CONFESSION 35, 56, 116, 175, 210, 229
WILLIAMS COLLEGE 191
WOMAN'S CHRISTIAN TEMPERANCE UNION 305, 309, 372
WOMEN IN THE CHURCH 308-310
WOMEN'S MOVEMENT 303, 305
WOMEN'S ROLES 424, 426, 455, 462
WOMEN'S SUFFRAGE 306
WORKINGMAN'S INSTITUTE 207
WORLD COUNCIL OF

CHURCHES 426, 428-430, 460
WORLD STUDENT CHRISTIAN FEDERATION 302
WORLD WAR I 31, 368, 381
WORLD WAR II 423-424, **426-427**
WORLD'S CHRISTIAN FUNDAMENTALS ASSOCIATION 378, 385
WYCLIFFE BIBLE TRANSLATORS 156, 301

YALE COLLEGE 67, 103, 108, 109, 115, 120, 165, 171
YALE DIVINITY SCHOOL 203, 223, 224, 232, 233, 396, 421
YMCA 174, 296
YOUNG LIFE 465
YOUTH FOR CHRIST 435, 465

Acknowledgments

The illustrations in this book have been reproduced by permission of the person, institution, or agency credited in the legend accompanying each illustration. We are grateful to all these sources for their permission to reproduce their materials. We especially wish to extend our appreciation to the Billy Graham Center of Wheaton College, Wheaton, Illinois for providing a substantial amount of the illustrative material used in this volume. The staffs of the museum, archives, and library of the Center proved their collections to be a remarkable resource and themselves to be graciously accommodating. We also wish to thank Edwin S. Gaustad, who generously made available to us his extensive file of photographs pertaining to American religious history.

The photographs in "The Many Faces of the Church" (pp. xvii–xxxiii) are reproduced by permission of the following: American Baptist Assembly: p. xix (inset); Robert Barr: p. xxxiii; East Congregational Church, Grand Rapids, Michigan: p. xxii, p. xxxiii (inset); Billy Graham Center: p. xx (top inset), p. xxiv (lower right), p. xxix (both insets); Jackson *Citizen Patriot*, Jackson, Michigan: p. xxiii (lower left); Library of Congress: p. xviii (inset), p. xxi (inset), p. xxvii (both insets), p. xxviii (inset), p. xxxi (top inset); George Marsden: p. xxv; Phyllis Mouw: color photos on pp. xvii, xviii, xix, xx–xxi, xxiii, xxiv, xxvi–xxvii, xxviii, xxix, xxx–xxxi, xxxii; National Council of Churches: p. xxiv (lower left), p. xxxi (bottom inset); *Newsweek*: p. xxx (inset); Religious News Service: p. xx (bottom inset), p. xxvi (inset); U.S. Army: p. xxii (inset). The woodcut on p. xxxii (inset) is courtesy of Fritz Eichenberg from *The Green Revolution: Easy Essays on Catholic Radicalism* by Peter Maurin (1961).

Project Editor: Allen Myers
Photo Editor: Charles Van Hof
Design and Production Manager: Joel Beversluis
Layout and Keylining: Willem Mineur
Maps and Charts: Louise Bauer
Typesetting: Acraforms, Inc., in phototype Plantin (text),
Novarese Medium (articles and documents),
and Vladimir italic (quotations)
Lithography, Printing, Binding: R. R. Donnelley and Sons